I0031965

JANUARY 2019

Global
Economic
Prospects

Darkening Skies

WORLD BANK GROUP

ISSN: 1014-8906
ISBN (paper): 978-1-4648-1343-6
ISBN (electronic): 978-1-4648-1386-3
DOI: 10.1596/978-1-4648-1343-6

Cover design: Bill Pragluski (Critical Stages).

The cutoff date for the data used in this report was December 19, 2018.

Summary of Contents

Table of Contents

Foreword

Achieving the Sustainable Development Goals, the World Bank's twin goals—or any other development goal for that matter—hinges on sustained economic growth in emerging market and developing economies (EMDEs). This growth in turn depends on macroeconomic stability. The semi-annual *Global Economic Prospects* (GEP) report assesses the global outlook for growth and stability in these countries.

The January 2019 edition, *Darkening Skies*, highlights how precarious the current economic juncture is. In a nutshell, growth has weakened, trade tensions remain high, several developing economies have experienced financial stress, and risks to the outlook have increased. As the report points out, EMDEs face some of the greatest risks. If a trade war between the United States and China contributes to a global slowdown, the spillover effects on EMDEs could be profound. Similarly, a sharp increase in global interest rates would severely affect highly indebted EMDEs, as Turkey and Argentina painfully discovered last summer.

Since the global outlook depends heavily on advanced economies, the GEP also flags the implications of advanced-economy policies for EMDEs. In January 2018, when there was a celebratory mood about the synchronized recovery among advanced economies and EMDEs, the GEP questioned its duration, even in its title: *Broad-Based Upturn, but for How Long?* That skepticism came from a close study of potential growth—the amount by which the economy would grow if all factors were fully employed—which found this to be wanting in many economies because of the previous years' slowdown in productivity and investment growth.

The GEP does not just analyze short-run growth forecasts; it embeds these forecasts in a longer-run view of the economy.

This edition of the GEP continues that tradition with a comprehensive study of the informal economy, something which could in the short-run be a shock absorber, but in the long-run is associated with low productivity. The analysis suggests that the informal sector's role in absorbing labor during downturns is limited. However, the potential long-term gains from increasing productivity in the informal sector are substantial. This edition also presents evidence that debt in low-income countries is on the rise, an issue that is being discussed extensively in policy circles.

The GEP tries to hit the sweet spot between discussing topical policy issues and undertaking rigorous analytical work. On the one hand, analysts, especially those in international organizations, are sometimes cautious about speaking out on the global economy—especially when the prospects are not good—lest they exacerbate the pessimism. On the other hand, the public is subject to so much half-baked analysis, half-truths, and fake news that an analytically rigorous report such as the GEP is critical to an informed debate.

Public policy is not made by "whispering in the finance minister's ear." Rather, it is made by arriving at a political consensus. That consensus is more likely to improve people's lives if the public is informed with evidence. Like its predecessors, this edition of the GEP is a contribution to that evidence.

Shantayanan Devarajan
Senior Director
Development Economics Vice Presidency
The World Bank Group

Acknowledgments

This World Bank Group Flagship Report is a product of the Prospects Group in the Development Economics Vice Presidency. The project was managed by M. Ayhan Kose and Franziska Ohnsorge, under the general guidance of Shantayanan Devarajan.

Global and regional surveillance work was coordinated by Carlos Arteta. Chapter 1 was prepared by Carlos Arteta and Marc Stocker, with contributions from Patrick Kirby, Ekaterine Vashakmadze, and Collette M. Wheeler. Additional inputs were provided by John Baffes, Alain Kabundi, Eung Ju Kim, Csilla Lakatos, Peter Nagle, Rudi Steinbach, and Shu Yu.

Chapter 2 was coordinated by Marc Stocker and Patrick Kirby. The authors are Ekaterine Vashakmadze (East Asia and Pacific), Yoki Okawa (Europe and Central Asia), Dana Vorisek (Latin America and the Caribbean), Lei Sandy Ye (Middle East and North Africa), Temel Taskin (South Asia), and Gerard Kambou and Rudi Steinbach (Sub-Saharan Africa).

Chapter 3, Chapter 4, and the boxes in Chapters 1 and 2 were prepared by Sinem Kilic Celik, Jongrim Ha, Patrick Kirby, Wee Chian Koh, M. Ayhan Kose, David Laborde, Csilla Lakatos, Will Martin, Franziska Ohnsorge, Yoki Okawa, Rudi Steinbach, Temel Taskin, Ekaterine Vashakmadze, Dana Vorisek, Jinxin Wu, Lei Sandy Ye, and Shu Yu, with contributions from Mohammad Amin, Sinem Kilic Celik, Sebastian Essl, Ergys Islamaj, Sergiy Kasyanenko, Gene Kindberg-Hanlon, Cedric Okou, Andre Proite, Naotaka Sugawara, and Collette M. Wheeler.

Research assistance was provided by Miyoko Asai, Zhuo Chen, Liu Cui, Ishita Dugar, Brent Harrison, Mengyi Li, Maria Hazel Macadangdang, Claudia Marchini, Julia Roseman, Xinyue Wang, Jinxin Wu, and Heqing Zhao. Modeling and data work were provided by Rajesh Kumar Danda and Julia Roseman.

The online publication was produced by Graeme Littler and Mikael Reventar. Mark Felsenthal managed media relations and dissemination. Mark Felsenthal and Graeme Littler provided editorial support, with contributions from Adriana Maximiliano.

The print publication was produced by Maria Hazel Macadangdang, Adriana Maximiliano, and Quinn Sutton, in collaboration with Luiz H. Almeida, Andrew Charles Berghauser, Adam Broadfoot, Aziz Gökdemir, Michael Harrup, and Jewel McFadden.

Many reviewers offered extensive advice and comments. These included: Kishan Abeygunawardana, Issam Abousleiman, Abebe Adugna, Azamat Agaidarov, Junaid Kamal Ahmad, Anna Carlotta Allen Massingue, Sara Alnashar, Gallina Andronova Vincelette, Paloma Anos Casero, Jorge Araujo, Rabah Arezki, Kiatipong Ariyapruchya, Cindy Audiguier, Rajul Awasthi, Dilek Aykut, Marina Bakanova, Daniel Barco, Kevin Barnes, Rafael Barroso, Davaadalai Batsuuri, Hans Anand Beck, John Beghin, Robert Carl Michael Beyer, Mesfin Bezawagaw, Andrew Blackman, Enrique Blanco Armas, Fernando Blanco, Monika Blaszkiewicz-Schwartzman, Daniel Kwabena Boakye, Zeljko Bogetic, Elena Bondarenko, Denis Boskovski, Anne Brockmeyer, James Brumby, Cesar Calderon, Salvatore Capasso, Kevin Carey, Bledi Celiku, Derek Chen, Massarongo Chivulele, Yew Keat Chong, Ajai Chopra, Ibrahim Chowdhury, Tamoya Christie, Kevin Chua, Kevin Clinton, Fabiano Colbano, Andrea Coppola, Barbara Cunha, Stefano Curto, Anna Custers, Andrew Dabalen, Somneuk Davading, Simon Davies, Annette De Kleine Feige, Gabriel Demombynes, Agim Demukaj, Allen Dennis, Sebastien Dessus, Mame Fatou Diagne, Caroline Diaz-Bonilla, Tatiana Didier, Nora Carina Dihel, Viet Tuan Dinh, Makhtar Diop, Ndiame Diop, Annette Dixon, Mariam Dolidze, Jozef Draaisma, Bakyt Dubashov, Victor Duggan, Mark Andrew Dutz, Etaki Wa Dzon, Sebastian Eckardt, Kim Alan Edwards, Khalid El Massnaoui, David Elmaleh, Olga Emelyanova, Wilfried Engelke, Jorge Familiar Calderon, Yuting Fan, Marianne Fay, Manuela Ferro, Cornelius Fleischhaker, Manuela Francisco, Chisako Fukuda, Josip Funda, Kevin Thomas Garcia Cruz, Pedro Miguel Gaspar Martins, Michael Geiger, Rangeet Ghosh, Adnan Ashraf Ghumman, Frederico Gil Sander, Fernando Giuliano, Anastasia Golovach, Maria De los Angeles Cuqui Gonzalez Miranda, Errol George Graham, Margaret Grosh, Poonam Gupta, Gohar Gyulumyan, Kiryl Haiduk, Fiseha Haile Gebregziabher, Michael Hamaide, Birgit Hansl, Marek Hanusch, Wissam Harake, Zeina Hasra, Faya Hayati, Johannes Herderschee, Sandra Hlivnjak, Bert Hofman, Bingjie Hu, Sahar Sajjad Hussain, Elena Ianchovichina, Stella Ilieva, Fernando Gabriel Im,

Amina Iraqi, Yoichiro Ishihara, Ergys Islamaj, Ivailo V. Izvorski, Evans Jadotte, Saroj Jha, Gloria Aitalohi Joseph-Raji, Gerard Kambou, Bertine Kamphuis, Soukeyna Kane, Lanre Kassim, Atsushi Kawamoto, Majid Kazemi, Vera Kehayova, Zerihun Getachew Kelbore, Nazmus Khan, Tehmina S. Khan, Ewa Korczyc, Christos Kostopoulos, Megumi Kubota, Chandana Kularatne, Aurelien Kruse, Jean Pierre Lacombe, Emmanuel Lartey, Daniel Lederman, Ran Li, John Litwack, Sodeth Ly, Julio Ricardo Loayza, Norman Loayza, Julie Saty Lohi, J. Humberto Lopez, José Roberto López-Cálix, Cal MacWilliam, Sanja Madzarevic-Sujster, Sandeep Mahajan, Shireen Mahdi, William Maloney, Shiva Makki, Pierre Jean-Claude Mandon, Kemoh Mansaray, Marie Francoise Marie-Nelly, Daniela Marotta, Ashwaq Natiq Maseeh, Andrew D. Mason, Hideki Matsunaga, Elitza Mileva, Deepak K. Mishra, Aghassi Mkrtchyan, Lalita Moorty, Lili Mottaghi, Rafael Munoz Moreno, Rinku Murgai, Arvind Nair, Nur Nasser Eddin, Jean-Pascal Nganou, Ha Nguyen, Francesca de Nicola, Eduardo Olaberria, Harun Onder, Abdoulaye Ouedraogo, John Panzer, Jim Parks, Catalin Pauna, Ceyla Pazarbasioglu, Fernanda Ailina Pedro, Keomanivone Phimmahasay, Samuel Jaime Pienknagura, Emmanuel Pinto Moreira, Ruslan Pionkivsky, Abha Prasad, Mona Prasad, Rong Qian, Habib Rab, Erick Rabemananoro, Wojciech Pawel Rabiega, Martin Rama, Nadir Ramazanov, Martin Raiser, Richard Record, Saadia Refaqat, Julio E. Revilla, Alief Aulia Rezza, Daniel Riera-Crichton, David Robinson, Alberto Rodriguez, Pedro Rodriguez, Donato de Rosa, David Rosenblatt, Irina Rostovtseva, Pablo Saavedra, James Sampi Bravo, Miguel Eduardo Sanchez Martin, Apurva Sanghi, Ilyas Sarsenov, Cristina Savescu, Tahseen Sayed, Kinnon Scott, Asli Senkal, Claudia Paz Sepúlveda, Lazar Sestovic, Natasha Sharma, Dhruv Sharma, Sudhir Shetty, Alta Shiilegmaa, Emily Sinnott, Sophie Sirtaine, Karlis Smits, Abdoulaye Sy, Fulbert Tchana Tchana, Shakira Binti Teh Sharifuddin, Hans Timmer, Emilija Timmis, Aby Toure, Christopher Towe, Robert Townsend, Melanie Simone Trost, Eskender Trushin, Michal Tulwin, Angélique Umutesi, Cevdet Cagdas Unal, Zainab Usman, Robert Utz, Ralph Van Doorn, Axel van Trotsenburg, Sona Varma, Carlos Végh, Julio Velasco, Marijn Verhoeven, Ekaterina Vostroknutova, Muhammed Waheed, Georgia A. Wallen, Marina Wes, Siti Budi Wardhani, Maria Monica Wihardja, Christina Wood, Pinar Yasar, Pui Shen Yoong, Hoda Youssef, Gabriel Zaourak, Albert Zeufack, Yan Michelle Zhang, Luan Zhao, and Bakhrom Ziyaev.

Regional projections and write-ups were produced in coordination with country teams, country directors, and the offices of the regional chief economists.

Executive Summary

The outlook for the global economy has darkened. Global financing conditions have tightened, industrial production has moderated, trade tensions remain elevated, and some large emerging market and developing economies have experienced significant financial market stress. Faced with these headwinds, the recovery in emerging market and developing economies has lost momentum. Downside risks have become more acute and include the possibility of disorderly financial market movements and an escalation of trade disputes. Debt vulnerabilities in emerging market and developing economies, particularly low-income countries, have increased. More frequent severe weather events would raise the possibility of large swings in international food prices, which could deepen poverty. In this difficult environment, it is of paramount importance for emerging market and developing economies to rebuild policy buffers while laying a stronger foundation for future growth by boosting human capital, promoting trade integration, and addressing the challenges associated with informality.

Global Outlook. Moderating activity and heightened risks are clouding global economic prospects. International trade and investment have softened, trade tensions remain elevated, and some large emerging market and developing economies (EMDEs) have experienced substantial financial market pressures. Against this less favorable backdrop, EMDE growth has lost momentum, with a weaker-than-expected recovery in commodity exporters accompanied by a deceleration in commodity importers. Downside risks have become more acute. Disorderly financial market developments could disrupt activity in the affected economies and lead to contagion effects. Trade disputes could escalate or become more widespread, denting activity in the involved economies and leading to negative global spillovers. To confront this increasingly challenging environment, an immediate priority for EMDE policymakers is to brace for possible bouts of financial market stress, rebuild macroeconomic policy buffers as appropriate, and tackle adverse debt dynamics, all while sustaining historically low inflation. In the longer run, the need to foster more robust potential growth by boosting human capital, removing barriers to investment, and promoting trade integration remains.

Regional Perspectives. The rebound in EMDE activity has stalled. The cyclical upswing in regions with many commodity exporters has lost momentum, partly reflecting a substantial slowdown in some large economies, and is projected to plateau over the next couple of years. Growth in regions with large numbers of commodity importers was solid but has decelerated and is expected to stabilize around potential. For all regions, risks to the outlook are increasingly tilted to the downside.

This edition of *Global Economic Prospects* also includes a chapter on the challenges associated with the presence of large informal sectors in EMDEs and policy options to address informality; a box on the prospects for continued low inflation in EMDEs; and essays on rising debt vulnerabilities in low-income countries and the implications of large food price spikes for poverty.

Growing in the Shadow: Challenges of Informality. Informal sector output on average accounts for about one-third of GDP and informal employment constitutes about 70 percent of employment in EMDEs (of which self-employment accounts for more than a half). Informality is more widespread in less developed economies with large agricultural sectors and higher shares of unskilled workers. While sometimes providing the short-run advantage of flexibility and employment, a larger informal sector is associated with lower productivity, reduced tax revenues, and greater poverty and inequality. Overcoming the adverse implications of informality will require a balanced mixture of policies that carefully take into account country-specific drivers of informality. A well-designed policy framework should include measures aimed at reducing regulatory and tax burdens, expanding access to finance, improving education and other public services, and strengthening public revenue frameworks.

The Great Disinflation. Emerging market and developing economies (EMDEs) have achieved a remarkable decline in inflation, from 17.3 percent in 1974 to about 3.5 percent in 2018. This achievement has coincided with an even sharper decline in inflation in advanced economies. The great disinflation in EMDEs has also been accompanied by growing inflation synchro-nization as evidenced by the emergence of a global inflation cycle. It has been supported by long-term trends such as the widespread adoption of robust monetary policy frameworks and strengthening of global trade and financial integration. More recently, the disruptions caused by the global financial crisis also contributed to the decline in inflation. However, a continuation of low and stable EMDE inflation is by no means guaranteed. If the wave of structural and policy-related factors that have driven disinflation since the 1970s loses momentum or is rolled back, elevated inflation could re-emerge. If the global inflation cycle turns up, policymakers may find that maintaining low inflation can be as great a challenge as achieving it.

Debt in Low-Income Countries: Evolution, Implications, and Remedies. Debt vulnerabilities in low-income countries (LICs) have increased substantially in recent years. Since 2013, median government debt has risen by about 20 percentage points of GDP and increasingly comes from non-concessional and private sources. As a result, in most LICs, interest payments are absorbing an increasing proportion of government revenues. The majority of LICs would be hard hit by a sudden weakening in trade or global financial conditions given their high levels of external debt, lack of fiscal space, low foreign currency reserves, and undiversified exports. Efforts to reduce debt-related vulnerabilities are a policy priority for many LICs, and a key focus needs to be improving debt management and developing domestic financial systems.

Poverty Impact of Food Price Shocks and Policies. In the event of large swings in world food prices, governments sometimes intervene to soften the impact on domestic prices and to lessen the burden of adjustment for vulnerable groups. While individual countries can succeed at insulating their domestic markets from short-term fluctuations in global food prices, the collective intervention of many countries may exacerbate the volatility of world prices. Policies introduced during the 2010-11 food price spike may have accounted for 40 percent of the increase in the world price of wheat and one-quarter of the increase in the world price of maize. Combined with government policy responses, the 2010-11 food price spike tipped 8.3 million people (almost 1 percent of the world's poor) into poverty.

Abbreviations

ADB	Asian Development Bank
AE	advanced economies
CEMAC	Central African Economic and Monetary Community
CES	constant elasticity of substitution
CET	constant elasticity of transformation
CGE	computable general equilibrium model
CPI	consumer price index
DB	Doing Business
DGE	dynamic general equilibrium
DTF	Distance to Frontier score
EAP	East Asia and Pacific
ECA	Europe and Central Asia
ECM	error correction model
EMDE	emerging market and developing economies
EU	European Union
FAO	Food and Agriculture Organization of the United Nations
FAOSTAT	FAO Statistical Databases
FCV	fragility, conflict, and violence-affected economies
FICCI	Federation of Indian Chambers of Commerce
Fewsnet	Famine Early Warning Systems Network
G4	Euro Area, Japan, the United Kingdom, and the United States
GCC	Gulf Cooperation Council
GDP	gross domestic product
GEP	Global Economic Prospects
GIEWS	Global Information and Early Warning System
GNFS	goods and nonfactor services
GTAP	Global Trade Analysis Project
HRW	hard red wheat
ICSE	International Classification of Status in Employment
ICT	information and communication technology
IEG	Independent Evaluation Group
ILO	International Labour Organization
IMF	International Monetary Fund
ISS	International Sector Survey
LAC	Latin America and the Caribbean
LES–CES	linear expenditure system–constant elasticity of substitution
LIC	low-income country

MIC	middle-income country
MIMIC	Multiple Indicators Multiple Causes model
MMDA	Metro Manila Developments Authority
MENA	Middle East and North Africa
MSEs	micro and small enterprises
NBER	National Bureau of Economic Research
NEET	not in employment, education, or training
NPAs	non-performing assets
NRP	nominal rate of protection
OECD	Organisation for Economic Co-operation and Development
OLS	ordinary least squares
PPP	purchasing power parity
RHS	right-hand side (in figures)
SAR	South Asia Region
SDGs	Sustainable Development Goals
SEMP	self-employment rate
SMEs	small and medium-sized enterprises
SSA	Sub-Saharan Africa
SSRN	Social Science Research Network
UNCTAD	United Nations Conference on Trade and Development
UNDP	United Nations Development Programme
UNICEF	United Nations International Children's Emergency Fund
USDA	United States Department of Agriculture
VAT	Value-added taxation
WDI	World Development Indicators
WEF	World Economic Forum
WGI	World Governance Indicators
WVS	World Value Survey
WHO	World Health Organization
WTO	World Trade Organization

CHAPTER 1

GLOBAL OUTLOOK

Darkening Skies

Moderating activity and heightened risks are clouding global economic prospects. International trade and investment have softened, trade tensions remain elevated, and some large emerging market and developing economies (EMDEs) have experienced substantial financial market pressures. Against this challenging backdrop, EMDE growth has stalled, with a sharply weaker-than-expected recovery in commodity exporters accompanied by a deceleration in commodity importers. Downside risks have become more acute. Disorderly financial market developments could disrupt activity in the affected economies and lead to contagion effects. Trade disputes could escalate or become more widespread, denting activity in the economies involved and leading to negative global spillovers. To confront this increasingly difficult environment, the most urgent priority is for EMDE policymakers to prepare for possible bouts of financial market stress and rebuild macroeconomic policy buffers as appropriate. Equally critically, policymakers need to foster stronger potential growth by boosting human capital, removing barriers to investments, and promoting trade integration within a rules-based multilateral system. Such efforts would also help address the challenges associated with informality.

Summary

Global growth is moderating as the recovery in trade and manufacturing activity loses steam (Figure 1.1). Despite ongoing negotiations, trade tensions among major economies remain elevated. These tensions, combined with concerns about softening global growth prospects, have weighed on investor sentiment and contributed to declines in global equity prices. Borrowing costs for emerging market and developing economies (EMDEs) have increased, in part as major advanced-economy central banks continue to withdraw policy accommodation in varying degrees. A strengthening U.S. dollar, heightened financial market volatility, and rising risk premiums have intensified capital outflow and currency pressures in some large EMDEs, with some vulnerable countries experiencing substantial financial stress. Energy prices have fluctuated markedly, mainly due to supply factors, with sharp falls toward the end of 2018. Other commodity prices—particularly metals—have also weakened, posing renewed headwinds for commodity exporters.

Economic activity in advanced economies has been diverging of late. Growth in the United States has remained solid, bolstered by fiscal

stimulus. In contrast, activity in the Euro Area has been somewhat weaker than previously expected, owing to slowing net exports. While growth in advanced economies is estimated to have slightly decelerated to 2.2 percent last year, it is still above potential and in line with previous forecasts.

EMDE growth edged down to an estimated 4.2 percent in 2018—0.3 percentage point slower than previously projected—as a number of countries with elevated current account deficits experienced substantial financial market pressures and appreciable slowdowns in activity. More generally, as suggested by recent high-frequency indicators, the recovery among commodity exporters has lost momentum significantly, largely owing to country-specific challenges within this group. Activity in commodity importers, while still robust, has slowed somewhat, reflecting capacity constraints and decelerating export growth. In low-income countries (LICs), growth is firming as infrastructure investment continues and easing drought conditions support a rebound in agricultural output. However, LIC metals exporters are struggling partly reflecting softer metals prices. Central banks in many EMDEs have tightened policy to varying degrees to confront currency and inflation pressures.

In all, global growth is projected to moderate from a downwardly revised 3 percent in 2018 to 2.9 percent in 2019 and 2.8 percent in 2020-21, as economic slack dissipates, monetary policy accommodation in advanced economies is removed, and global trade gradually slows. Growth in the United States will continue to be supported by fiscal stimulus in the near term,

_____

Note: This chapter was prepared by Carlos Arteta and Marc Stocker, with contributions from Patrick Kirby, Ekaterine Vashakmadze, and Collette M. Wheeler. Additional inputs were provided by John Baffes, Alain Kabundi, Eung Ju Kim, Csilla Lakatos, Peter Nagle, Rudi Steinbach, and Shu Yu. Research assistance was provided by Liu Cui, Ishita Dugar, Brent Harrison, Mengyi Li, Claudia Marchini, Julia Roseman, and Jinxin Wu.

TABLE 1.1 Real GDP[1]

(Percent change from previous year)

Percentage point differences from June 2018 projections

	2016	2017	2018e	2019f	2020f	2021f	2018e	2019f	2020f
World	**2.4**	**3.1**	**3.0**	**2.9**	**2.8**	**2.8**	**-0.1**	**-0.1**	**-0.1**
Advanced economies	**1.7**	**2.3**	**2.2**	**2.0**	**1.6**	**1.5**	**0.0**	**0.0**	**-0.1**
United States	1.6	2.2	2.9	2.5	1.7	1.6	0.2	0.0	-0.3
Euro Area	1.9	2.4	1.9	1.6	1.5	1.3	-0.2	-0.1	0.0
Japan	0.6	1.9	0.8	0.9	0.7	0.6	-0.2	0.1	0.2
Emerging market and developing economies (EMDEs)	**3.7**	**4.3**	**4.2**	**4.2**	**4.5**	**4.6**	**-0.3**	**-0.5**	**-0.2**
Commodity-exporting EMDEs	0.8	1.7	1.7	2.3	2.9	2.9	-0.8	-0.7	-0.1
Other EMDEs	5.9	6.1	5.8	5.5	5.6	5.6	0.0	-0.3	-0.1
Other EMDEs excluding China	4.9	5.2	5.0	4.7	4.9	5.1	-0.1	-0.4	-0.2
East Asia and Pacific	6.3	6.6	6.3	6.0	6.0	5.8	0.0	-0.1	0.0
China	6.7	6.9	6.5	6.2	6.2	6.0	0.0	-0.1	0.0
Indonesia	5.0	5.1	5.2	5.2	5.3	5.3	0.0	-0.1	-0.1
Thailand	3.3	3.9	4.1	3.8	3.9	3.9	0.0	0.0	0.1
Europe and Central Asia	1.7	4.0	3.1	2.3	2.7	2.9	-0.1	-0.8	-0.3
Russia	-0.2	1.5	1.6	1.5	1.8	1.8	0.1	-0.3	0.0
Turkey	3.2	7.4	3.5	1.6	3.0	4.2	-1.0	-2.4	-1.0
Poland	3.1	4.8	5.0	4.0	3.6	3.3	0.8	0.3	0.1
Latin America and the Caribbean	-1.5	0.8	0.6	1.7	2.4	2.5	-1.1	-0.6	-0.1
Brazil	-3.3	1.1	1.2	2.2	2.4	2.4	-1.2	-0.3	0.0
Mexico	2.9	2.1	2.1	2.0	2.4	2.4	-0.2	-0.5	-0.3
Argentina	-1.8	2.9	-2.8	-1.7	2.7	3.1	-4.5	-3.5	-0.1
Middle East and North Africa	5.1	1.2	1.7	1.9	2.7	2.7	-1.3	-1.4	-0.5
Saudi Arabia	1.7	-0.9	2.0	2.1	2.2	2.2	0.2	0.0	-0.1
Iran	13.4	3.8	-1.5	-3.6	1.1	1.1	-5.6	-7.7	-3.1
Egypt[2]	4.3	4.2	5.3	5.6	5.8	6.0	0.3	0.1	0.0
South Asia	7.5	6.2	6.9	7.1	7.1	7.1	0.0	0.0	-0.1
India[3]	7.1	6.7	7.3	7.5	7.5	7.5	0.0	0.0	0.0
Pakistan[2]	4.6	5.4	5.8	3.7	4.2	4.8	0.0	-1.3	-1.2
Bangladesh[2]	7.1	7.3	7.9	7.0	6.8	6.8	1.4	0.3	-0.2
Sub-Saharan Africa	1.3	2.6	2.7	3.4	3.6	3.7	-0.4	-0.1	-0.1
Nigeria	-1.6	0.8	1.9	2.2	2.4	2.4	-0.2	0.0	0.0
South Africa	0.6	1.3	0.9	1.3	1.7	1.8	-0.5	-0.5	-0.2
Angola	-2.6	-0.1	-1.8	2.9	2.6	2.8	-3.5	0.7	0.2
Memorandum items:									
Real GDP[1]									
High-income countries	1.7	2.3	2.2	2.0	1.7	1.6	0.0	0.0	-0.1
Developing countries	4.0	4.6	4.4	4.4	4.7	4.7	-0.3	-0.4	-0.1
Low-income countries	4.8	5.5	5.6	5.9	6.2	6.3	-0.1	0.0	0.0
BRICS	4.4	5.2	5.3	5.2	5.3	5.3	-0.1	-0.2	-0.1
World (2010 PPP weights)	3.2	3.7	3.6	3.5	3.6	3.6	-0.2	-0.3	-0.1
World trade volume[4]	2.6	5.4	3.8	3.6	3.5	3.4	-0.5	-0.6	-0.5
Commodity prices[5]									
Oil price	-15.6	23.3	30.7	-2.9	0.0	0.0	-1.9	-1.5	-0.1
Non-energy commodity price index	-2.8	5.3	1.7	1.0	1.2	1.2	-3.4	0.8	0.7

Source: World Bank.

Note: PPP = purchasing power parity; e = estimate; f = forecast. World Bank forecasts are frequently updated based on new information. Consequently, projections presented here may differ from those contained in other World Bank documents, even if basic assessments of countries' prospects do not differ at any given moment in time. Country classifications and lists of emerging market and developing economies (EMDEs) are presented in Table 1.2. BRICS include: Brazil, Russia, India, China, and South Africa.

1. Aggregate growth rates calculated using constant 2010 U.S. dollar GDP weights.
2. GDP growth values are on a fiscal year basis. Aggregates that include these countries are calculated using data compiled on a calendar year basis. Pakistan's growth rates are based on GDP at factor cost. The column labeled 2017 refers to FY2016/17.
3. The column labeled 2016 refers to FY2016/17.
4. World trade volume of goods and non-factor services.
5. Oil is the simple average of Brent, Dubai, and West Texas Intermediate. The non-energy index is comprised of the weighted average of 39 commodities (7 metals, 5 fertilizers, 27 agricultural commodities). For additional details, please see http://www.worldbank.org/en/research/commodity-markets.
To download this data, please visit www.worldbank.org/gep.

which will likely lead to larger and more persistent fiscal deficits. Advanced-economy growth will gradually decelerate toward potential, falling to 1.5 percent by the end of the forecast horizon, as monetary policy is normalized and capacity constraints become increasingly binding.

Softening global trade and tighter financing conditions will result in a more challenging external environment for EMDE economic activity. EMDE growth is expected to stall at 4.2 percent in 2019—0.5 percentage point below previous forecasts, partly reflecting the lingering effects of recent financial stress in some large economies (e.g., Argentina, Turkey), with a sharply weaker-than-expected pickup in commodity exporters accompanied by a deceleration in commodity importers. EMDE growth is projected to plateau at an average of 4.6 percent in 2020-21, as the recovery in commodity exporters levels off. Per capita growth will remain anemic in several EMDE regions—most notably, in those with a large number of commodity exporters—likely impeding further poverty alleviation.

The projected gradual deceleration of global economic activity over the forecast horizon could be more severe than currently expected given the predominance of substantial downside risks (Figure 1.2). A sharper-than-expected tightening of global financing conditions, or a renewed rapid appreciation of the U.S. dollar, could exert further downward pressure on activity in EMDEs, including in those with large current account deficits financed by portfolio and bank flows. Government and/or private sector debt has also risen in a majority of EMDEs over the last few years, including in many LICs, reducing the fiscal room to respond to shocks and heightening the exposure to shifts in market sentiment and rising borrowing costs.

Escalating trade tensions are another major downside risk to the global outlook. If all tariffs currently under consideration were implemented, they would affect about 5 percent of global trade flows and could dampen growth in the economies involved, leading to negative global spillovers. While some countries could benefit from trade

FIGURE 1.1 Summary – Global prospects

Global growth is moderating, as industrial activity and trade decelerate, negatively impacting investor sentiment and equity prices. The recovery in EMDEs has stalled, owing to softening external demand, tighter external financing conditions, and heightened policy uncertainties. Many EMDE central banks have raised interest rates to fend off currency pressures. Per capita growth will remain anemic in several EMDE regions—most notably in those with a large number of commodity exporters.

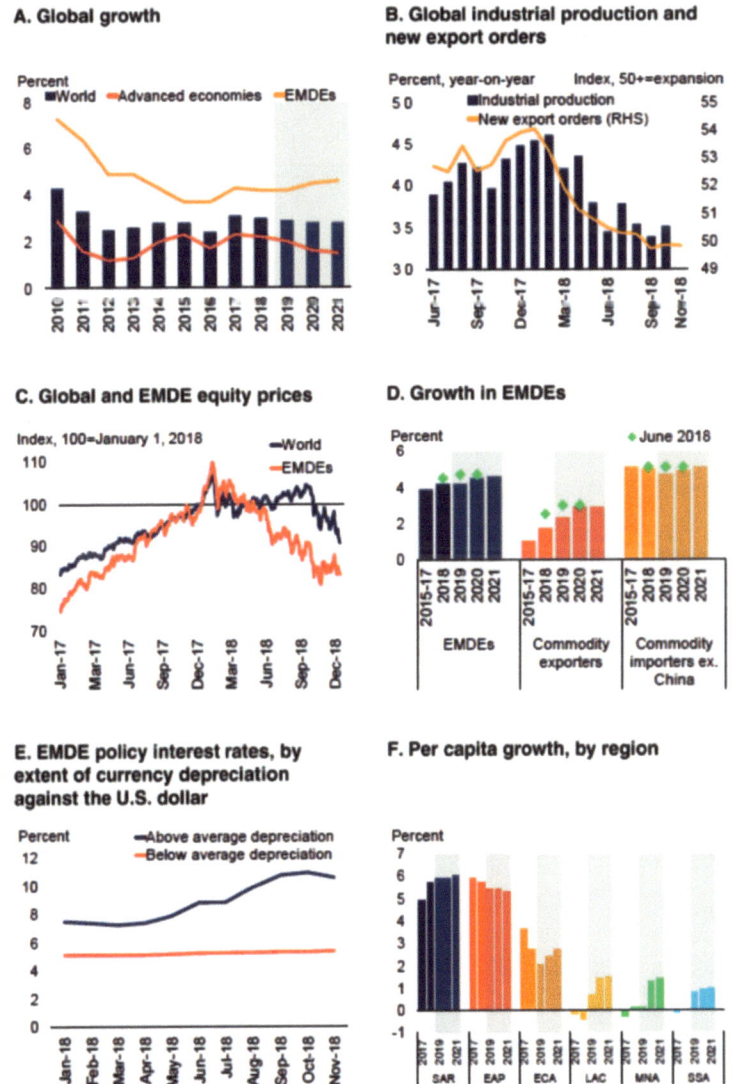

Source: Bloomberg, Haver Analytics, World Bank.
Note: EMDEs = emerging market and developing economies.
A.D.F. Shaded areas indicate forecasts. Data for 2018 are estimates. Aggregate growth rates calculated using constant 2010 U.S. dollar GDP weights.
B. New export orders measured by Purchasing Managers' Index (PMI). PMI readings above 50 indicate expansion in economic activity; readings below 50 indicate contraction. Last observation is November 2018 for new export orders and October 2018 for industrial production.
C. Figure shows MSCI Global and Emerging Markets Indexes. Last observation is December 19, 2018.
D. Data for 2015-17 are simple averages. Green diamonds denote forecasts in the June 2018 edition of the *Global Economic Prospects* report.
E. The aggregate policy interest rates are calculated using constant 2010 U.S. dollar GDP weights. The above average and below average currency depreciation groups are defined by countries above or below the sample average of the year-to-date percent change in the bilateral exchange rate against the U.S. dollar. The sample average is -9.3 percent and includes 27 EMDEs, of which 12 are above and 15 are below average. Last observation is November 2018.
F. EAP = East Asia and Pacific, ECA = Europe and Central Asia, LAC = Latin America and the Caribbean, MNA = Middle East and North Africa, SAR = South Asia, and SSA = Sub-Saharan Africa.

FIGURE 1.2 Global risks and policy challenges

Downside risks predominate, with the possibility of financial stress leading to further deterioration in activity in EMDEs. Escalating trade tensions involving major economies could spread globally. A simultaneous sharp slowdown in both the United States and China could have severe effects on the global outlook. Fiscal space is particularly limited in countries with high foreign-currency-denominated debt. Informality remains widespread in EMDEs and is associated with large productivity gaps between formal and informal firms.

A. Probability of 2020 global growth being 1-percentage-point below/above baseline

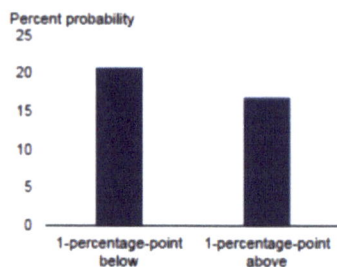

B. Growth forecast revisions and current account position, 2019

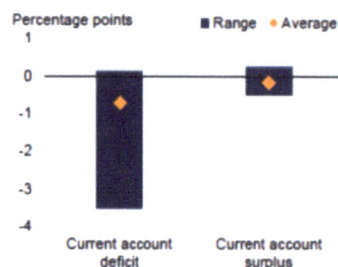

C. Imports affected by new tariffs

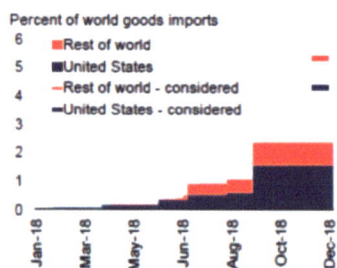

D. Impact on global growth of 1-percentage-point growth slowdowns in the United States and China

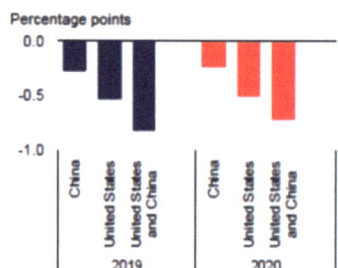

E. Fiscal sustainability gaps in EMDEs, by extent of reliance on foreign-currency-denominated debt

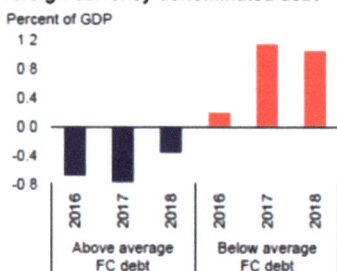

F. Average productivity in formal and informal firms

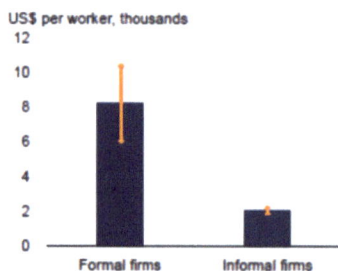

Source: Bloomberg; International Monetary Fund; Kose, Kurlat et al. (2017); Peterson Institute for International Economics; U.S. Census Bureau; World Bank.

A. Probabilities are computed from the distribution of 24-month-ahead oil price futures, S&P 500 equity price futures, and term spread forecasts. Each of the risk factor weights are derived from the model described in Ohnsorge, Stocker, and Some (2016). Last observation is December 18, 2018.

B. Forecast revisions for GDP growth in 2019 relative to June 2018. Sample includes 23 EMDEs. Current account position net of foreign direct investment in 2018.

C. Import tariffs implemented in the United States and the rest of the world in 2018, as well as those under consideration, as a percent of global goods imports.

D. Blue and red bars show scenarios assuming a 1-percentage-point growth shock in China, the United States, and the combination of the two. Shocks are applied in the second half of 2019. Based on the vector autoregression model presented in World Bank (2016). Deviations from baseline are all significantly different from zero.

E. FC debt = foreign-currency-denominated debt. A negative sustainability gap indicates government debt is rising along an accelerated trajectory. The sample includes 27 EMDEs. The above (below) average foreign-currency-denominated debt groups are defined by countries above (below) the sample average of external debt in foreign currency as a share of total external debt in 2017.

F. Blue bars represent estimates and orange vertical lines indicate two standard deviation error bands. World Bank's Enterprise Survey data for 135 countries (2008-18).

diversion in the short run, rising trade protectionism would stifle investment and severely disrupt global value chains, contributing to higher prices and lower productivity. Other downside risks—such as heightened political uncertainty, escalating geopolitical tensions, and conflict—further cloud the outlook.

Even though the probability of a recession in the United States is still low, and the slowdown in China is projected to be gradual, markedly weaker-than-expected activity in the world's two largest economies could have a severe impact on global economic prospects. Stimulus measures have bolstered the near-term outlook in these two countries but could contribute to a more abrupt slowdown later on. A simultaneous occurrence of a severe U.S. downturn and a sharper-than-expected deceleration in China would significantly increase the probability of an abrupt global slowdown and thus negatively impact the outlook of other EMDEs through trade, financial, and commodity market channels. A global downturn would be particularly detrimental for those EMDEs with reduced policy space to respond to shocks.

The softening outlook and heightened downside risks exacerbate various challenges faced by policymakers around the world. Advanced economies should use this period of above-potential growth to rebuild macroeconomic policy buffers and lay the foundation for stronger growth with reforms that bolster potential output. Care should be taken to avoid shifts in trade and immigration policies that could negatively affect longer-term growth prospects, both domestically and abroad. A renewed commitment to a rules-based international trading system would also help bolster confidence, investment, and trade.

In a context of limited policy buffers, EMDE policymakers need to bolster the capacity to cope with possible bouts of financial market volatility, including sharp exchange rate movements—while undertaking measures to sustain the ongoing period of historically stable inflation (Box 1.1). This immediate priority will require a credible commitment to price stability from central banks, underpinned by strong institutional independence, as well as efforts by regulators and prudential authorities to reduce persistent financial fragilities. EMDEs also face substantial fiscal challenges and the risk of worsening debt dynamics as global financing conditions tighten. For many EMDEs, it will be imperative to restore fiscal space given cyclical conditions, as well as address the vulnerabilities associated with elevated foreign-currency-denominated debt.

Equally critically, amid a projected deceleration in potential growth, EMDEs face the pressing challenge of ensuring sustained improvements in living standards. This will require investments in human capital and skills development to raise productivity and take full advantage of technological changes. In the current environment of limited fiscal resources, the urgency of these investments highlights the critical need to prioritize effective public spending and increase public sector efficiency.

Moreover, facilitating the expansion of small- and medium-sized enterprises, including by improving their access to international markets and finance, would also spur productivity and stimulate growth-enhancing investments. For many EMDEs, there is scope to further liberalize trade and improve the extent to which they are integrated into global value chains, which would foster a more efficient allocation of resources, job creation, and export diversification. Policies that help improve outcomes in these areas would also contribute to address the challenges associated with informality, thus reinforcing the basis for future productivity growth.

Major economies: Recent developments and outlook

Growth has moderated in most advanced economies, with the notable exception of the United States, where fiscal stimulus is boosting activity. Over the forecast horizon, growth in all major advanced economies is projected to slow toward potential as capacity constraints become increasingly binding and monetary accommodation is withdrawn. In China, activity remains robust, but headwinds are increasing in a context of heightened trade tensions.

FIGURE 1.3 Advanced economies

Activity has softened but still points to above-potential growth in major advanced economies. Growth is expected to continue to moderate over the forecast period. Fiscal policy will boost U.S. activity in 2019 but will become a drag thereafter.

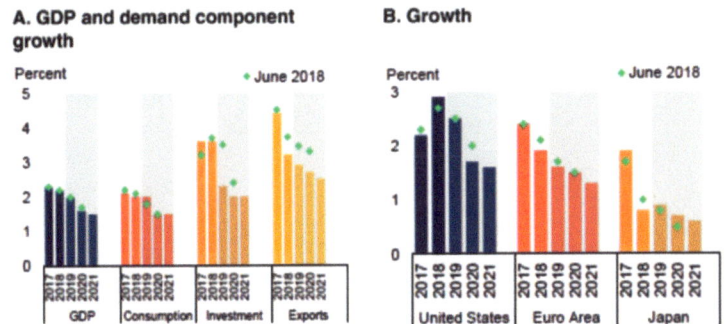

Source: World Bank.
A.B Green diamonds correspond with the June 2018 edition of the *Global Economic Prospects* report. Shaded areas indicate forecasts. Data for 2018 are estimates.
A. Aggregate growth rates and components calculated using constant 2010 U.S. dollar GDP weights.

Incoming data in advanced economies have softened but still point to above-potential growth. Unemployment rates have continued to decline, and for many countries are below levels seen prior to the global financial crisis. After slightly decelerating from 2.3 percent in 2017 to an estimated 2.2 percent last year, advanced-economy growth is expected to continue slowing over the forecast period, with a notable slowdown in investment and the eventual shift of U.S. fiscal policy from stimulative to contractionary (Figure 1.3).

United States

U.S. growth in 2018 is estimated to have picked up to 2.9 percent, up 0.2 percentage point from previous projections, mostly reflecting stronger-than-expected domestic demand (Figure 1.4). Activity is being bolstered by procyclical fiscal stimulus and still-accommodative monetary policy.

The labor market remains robust, bolstering consumption. The unemployment rate has fallen to an almost 50-year low, despite an influx of new workers—about three-quarters of the approximately 200,000 jobs being added every month are being filled by new entrants. Labor productivity is showing signs of picking up.

BOX 1.1 The great disinflation

"The greatest threat to today's low inflation, of course, would be a reversal of the modern trend towards enhanced central bank independence, particularly if trend economic growth were to slow, owing, say, to a retreat in globalization and economic liberalization." Kenneth Rogoff (2003)

Emerging market and developing economies (EMDEs) have achieved a remarkable decline in inflation, from 17.3 percent in 1974 to about 3.5 percent in 2018. This achievement has coincided with an even sharper decline in inflation in advanced economies. The great disinflation in EMDEs has also been accompanied by growing inflation synchronization as evidenced by the emergence of a global inflation cycle. It has been supported by long-term trends such as the widespread adoption of robust monetary policy frameworks and strengthening of global trade and financial integration. More recently, the disruptions caused by the global financial crisis also contributed to the decline in inflation. However, a continuation of low and stable EMDE inflation is by no means guaranteed. If the wave of structural and policy-related factors that have driven disinflation since the 1970s loses momentum or is rolled back, elevated inflation could re-emerge. If the global inflation cycle turns up, policymakers may find that maintaining low inflation can be as great a challenge as achieving it.

Emerging market and developing economies (EMDEs) have achieved a remarkable decline in inflation since the mid-1970s (Ha, Kose, and Ohnsorge 2019).[1] Median annual national consumer price inflation in EMDEs fell from stubbornly persistent double-digits during the 1970s to about 3.5 percent in 2018 (Figure 1.1.1). By 2017, inflation was within or below central bank target ranges in three-quarters of the EMDEs that had adopted inflation targeting. Inflation has also fallen around the world, from a peak of nearly 17 percent in 1974 to less than 2.5 percent in 2018. The decline in inflation began in the mid-1980s in advanced economies and in the mid-1990s in EMDEs. By 2000, global inflation had stabilized at historically low levels.

Low and stable inflation has historically been associated with greater output stability, higher growth and better development outcomes. EMDEs can continue enjoying the benefits of low inflation, but only if the confluence of structural and policy related factors that have fostered global disinflation over the past decades is sustained.

Against this backdrop, this box addresses the following questions:

- How has EMDE inflation evolved?

- How important is global inflation in explaining national inflation in EMDEs?

- Can EMDEs sustain the era of low inflation?

Evolution of EMDE inflation: A remarkable conquest

Disinflation. EMDEs have witnessed a significant decline in inflation since the mid-1970s, with median annual national consumer price inflation down from a peak of 17.3 percent in 1974 to about 3.5 percent in 2018. Disinflation over recent decades has been broad-based across regions and country groups.[2] For example, disinflation occurred across all EMDE regions, including those with a history of persistently high inflation, such as Latin America and Sub-Saharan Africa (Figure 1.1.2).[3] Even among low-income countries (LICs), inflation fell by two-thirds between the mid-1970s and 2017, to 5 percent.

EMDE disinflation was set against the backdrop of sharper disinflation among advanced economies, where median inflation dropped from its highest (15 percent in 1974) to its lowest level (0.3 percent in 2015) in more than 60 years. Since then, it has risen somewhat to just over 1.5 percent in 2018 but remains below the median inflation target of advanced-economy central banks. After 2008, below-target inflation and, in some cases, deflation became pervasive across advanced economies: for example, in 2015, inflation was negative in more than half of advanced economies. Some advanced-economy central banks have struggled to lift inflation back to their inflation targets over the past decade.

Drivers of low inflation. While the global financial crisis played a major role in pushing inflation down around the

Note: This box was prepared by Jongrim Ha, M. Ayhan Kose, and Franziska Ohnsorge.

[1] The "near-universal" character of the decline in inflation since the mid-1970s was recognized at an early stage by Rogoff (2003).

[2] Disinflation is a decline in inflation rates, regardless of inflation being negative (deflation) or positive.

[3] However, inflation remains in double-digits in some relatively large EMDEs, in part reflecting currency depreciations.

BOX 1.1 The great disinflation (continued)

world over the past decade, the longer-term trend of disinflation has been supported by a wide range of structural changes. The most significant of these have been the wide-spread adoption of more effective and more transparent monetary, exchange rate, and fiscal policy frameworks as well as globalization (Figure 1.1.2).[4]

- *Macroeconomic policies.* In the second half of the 1980s and during the 1990s, many EMDEs implemented macroeconomic stabilization programs and structural reforms, and gave their central banks clear mandates to control inflation. The adoption of resilient policy frameworks has facilitated more effective control of inflation (Taylor 2014; Fischer 2015). Twenty-four EMDEs have introduced inflation targeting monetary policy frameworks since the late 1990s and, in the median EMDE, the index of central bank independence and transparency rose more than one-and-a-half-fold between 1990 and 2014. Inflation tends to be lower in countries that employ an inflation targeting framework and that have more independent and transparent central banks. Changes in fiscal policy frameworks have also contributed: fiscal rules have been adopted in 88 countries, including 49 EMDEs. Other reforms, including labor market and product market liberalization, and the removal or easing of foreign exchange market controls, also assisted the disinflation process.

- *Trade and financial integration.* Trade integration has contributed to lower prices, as higher shares of imports in consumption and production result in competitive pressures from foreign producers (Figure 1.1.4). Financial integration has helped discipline macroeconomic policies since more financially integrated economies are more likely to implement monetary policies targeting low and stable inflation (Kose et al. 2010). In the median EMDE, as in the median advanced economy, the ratio of trade to GDP increased by half between 1970 and 2017, to 75 percent of GDP, and international assets and liabilities tripled (although they remain only half the level of advanced economies). Inflation tends to be lower in economies that are more open to trade and financial flows.

FIGURE 1.1.1 Global inflation

EMDE inflation remains near historic lows despite a recent normalization of inflation in advanced economies. Inflation is now within target ranges in the majority of EMDEs.

A. Median CPI inflation, by country group

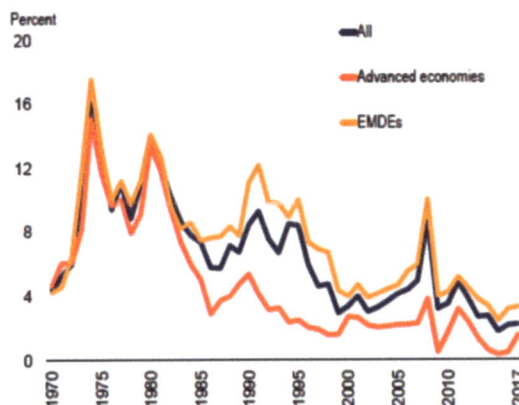

B. Share of advanced economies and EMDEs with inflation below or within target range

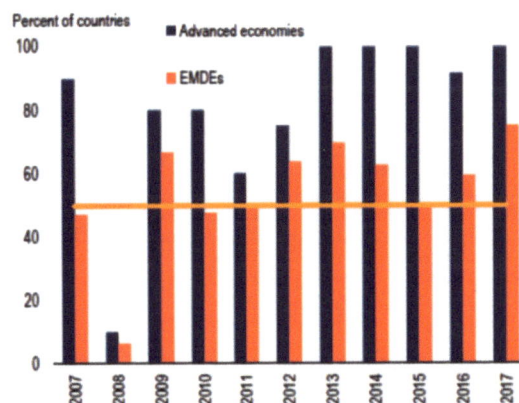

Source: Bloomberg, Consensus Economics, Haver Analytics, World Bank.
A. Median year-on-year consumer price inflation for 29 advanced economies and 123 EMDEs (including 28 LICs).
B. All inflation rates refer to year-on-year inflation. Share of 11 advanced economies and 24 EMDEs with consumer price inflation below-target or within target range. Horizontal line indicates 50 percent.

Global inflation cycle: Getting stronger

A critical feature of the international inflation experience of the past five decades has been the emergence of a "global inflation cycle" (Ciccarelli and Mojon 2010). This is reflected in a growing contribution of a common global factor to the variation in country-level inflation rates. To

---

[4] Other structural changes have also been important (Ha, Ivanova et al. 2019). For example, technological advances, including the digitalization of services and automation of manufacturing have also transformed production processes, attenuating inflation pressures. Population aging may also have contributed.

BOX 1.1 The great disinflation *(continued)*

FIGURE 1.1.2 Disinflation and factors associated with disinflation

EMDE inflation has declined in all EMDE regions and low-income countries. In most EMDEs, inflation is now below 5 percent. Lower inflation is associated with greater trade and financial openness. Inflation also tends to be lower in countries that employ an inflation targeting framework and that have more independent and transparent central banks.

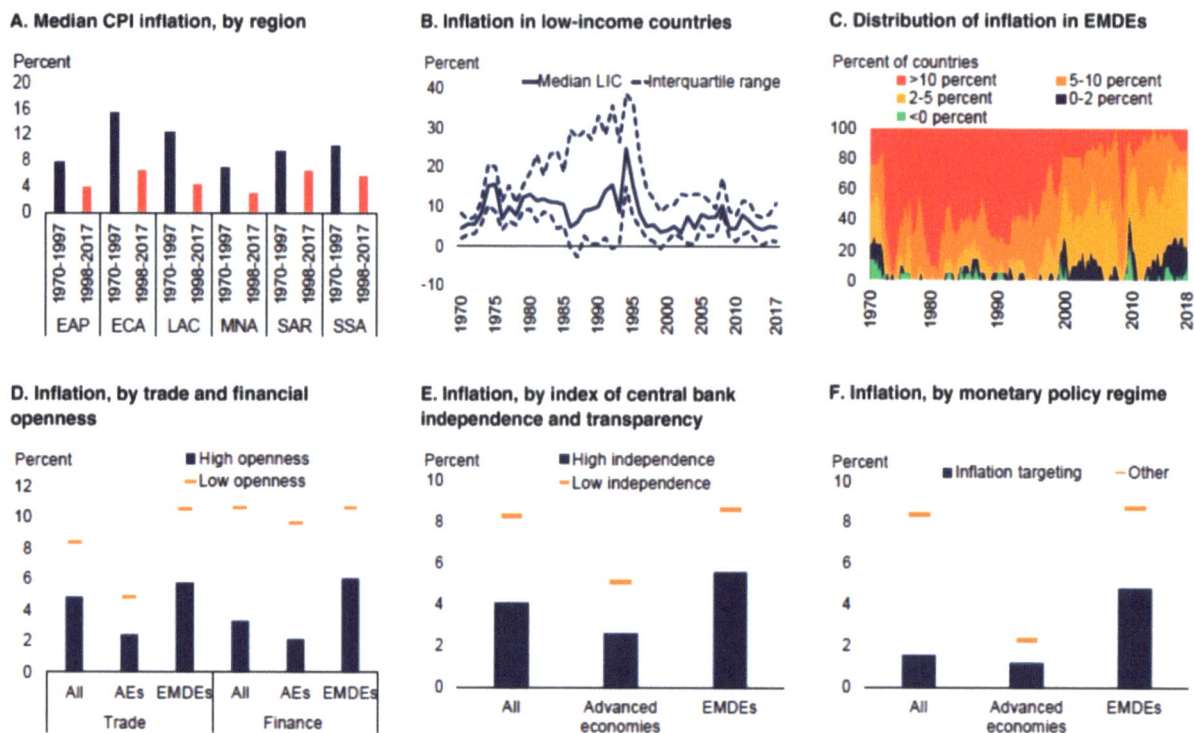

A. Median CPI inflation, by region

B. Inflation in low-income countries

C. Distribution of inflation in EMDEs

D. Inflation, by trade and financial openness

E. Inflation, by index of central bank independence and transparency

F. Inflation, by monetary policy regime

Source: Ha, Kose, and Ohnsorge (2019); Haver Analytics; IMF International Financial Statistics and World Economic Outlook databases; OECDstat; World Bank.
Note: Median headline CPI (consumer price index) inflation of 29 advanced economies and 123 EMDEs.
A. All inflation rates refer to year-on-year inflation. EAP = East Asia and the Pacific, ECA = Eastern Europe and Central Asia, LAC = Latin America and the Caribbean, MNA = Middle East and North Africa, SAR = South Asia, and SSA = Sub-Saharan Africa.
B. Solid line shows median year-on-year headline inflation and dotted lines refer to interquartile range, based on 28 LICs.
C. Inflation refers to quarter-on-quarter annualized inflation. Sample includes 50 EMDEs.
D. Columns indicate median inflation in countries high trade-to-GDP ratios ("Trade") or financial assets and liabilities relative to GDP ("Finance") in the top quartile ("high openness") of 175 economies during 1970-2017. Horizontal bars indicate countries in the bottom quartile ("low openness"). Differences are statistically significant at the 5 percent level.
E.F. Columns indicate median inflation in country-year pairs with a central bank independence and transparency index in the top quartile of the sample (E) or with inflation targeting monetary policy regimes (C). Horizontal bars denote medians in the bottom quartile (B) or with monetary policy regimes that are not inflation targeting (F). Differences are statistically significant at the 5 percent level.

analyze its importance, a dynamic factor model is estimated for annual consumer price inflation rates in 25 advanced economies and 74 EMDEs during 1970-2017 (Ha, Kose et al. 2019). The model includes a common global factor as well as group factors specific to advanced economies and EMDEs. The presence of group factors allows the model to account for the large differences in country characteristics between advanced economies and EMDEs.

Global inflation factor. Inflation has become increasingly globally synchronized (Figure 1.1.3). The contribution of the global factor to inflation variation has grown over

time: since 2001, it has almost doubled, and now accounts for 22 percent of inflation variation (Ha, Kose et al. 2019). It has explained about one-fifth and one-quarter of EMDE and advanced economy inflation variation, respectively, since 2001. Over the past four decades, an EMDE-specific factor has also become more prominent. The rising importance of these global and group-specific factors indicates that inflation synchronization has become more broad-based over time.

Global inflation versus global business cycle. Inflation synchronization is sizable by comparison with global business cycle synchronization. The international business

BOX 1.1 The great disinflation *(continued)*

cycle literature has established the presence of a well-defined global business cycle (Kose, Otrok, and Prasad 2012). In the sample used here, the global business cycle, as captured by a common global factor in output growth, has accounted for 5 percent of national output growth fluctuations since 1970—less than half the degree of inflation synchronization.

Tradables versus non-tradables. The role of the global factor has been more prominent in price baskets with a larger tradables content. The global factor's contribution to inflation variation was largest for import prices (54 percent in the median country) and smallest for core CPI inflation (5 percent). Between these two extremes, the global factor's contribution to variation in PPI inflation was 42 percent and that for GDP deflator growth was 13 percent and comparable to that for headline CPI inflation.

Maintaining low inflation: A greater challenge

The achievement of low inflation cannot be taken for granted (Rogoff 2014; Draghi 2016; Carstens 2018). If cyclical and structural forces become less disinflationary over the next decade than they have been over the past five decades, inflation could rise globally. Through the strengthening global inflation cycle, this may put upward pressure on EMDE inflation. More importantly, structural and policy related factors that have helped lower inflation over the past several decades may lose momentum or be rolled back amid mounting populist sentiment.

- *Slowing globalization.* The rising protectionist sentiment of recent years may slow or even reverse the pace of globalization. New tariffs and import restrictions have been put in place in advanced economies and EMDEs since 2017. The possibility of further escalation in trade restrictions involving major economies remains elevated.

- *Weakening monetary policy frameworks.* A shift from a strong mandate of inflation control, to objectives related to the financing of government, would undermine the credibility of monetary policy frameworks and raise inflation expectations. Among EMDEs, a decline in central bank independence and transparency has been associated with significantly less well-anchored inflation expectations and greater pass-through of exchange rate movements to inflation.

- *Weakening fiscal policy frameworks.* Growing populist sentiment could lead to a move away from

rule-based fiscal policies. Fiscal rules can become ineffective once commitment to them falters (Wyplosz 2012). Mounting public and private debt in EMDEs could also weaken commitment to strong fiscal and monetary policy frameworks. Government and/or private sector debt has risen in more than half of EMDEs since 2012, including in many LICs (World Bank 2018a). EMDE sovereign credit ratings have continued to deteriorate, with some falling below investment grade, reflecting concerns about rising debt and deteriorating growth prospects.

If unwanted inflation makes a comeback, policy frameworks may be tested in EMDEs: their inflation expectations are less well-anchored, and the absence of strong monetary policy frameworks in many of these economies means that inflation is sensitive to exchange rate movements (Kose et al. 2019; Ha, Stocker and Yilmazkuday 2019). Growing inflation synchronization also increases the risk of policy errors when the appropriate response differs depending on the origin of the underlying inflation shock (IMF 2018a).[5] EMDE central banks may struggle to contain inflationary pressures and may not receive adequate support from fiscal policy in stabilizing the business cycle. For some EMDEs, a significant increase in inflation could set back poverty reduction efforts.

The demise of previous periods of sustained low inflation is a reminder that low EMDE inflation is by no means guaranteed. Inflation has been low and stable before: during the Bretton Woods fixed exchange rate system of the post-war period up to 1971 and during the Gold Standard of the early 1900s (Figure 1.1.4). Yet directly following the low inflation period that ended in the early 1970s, the sharp increase in oil prices in 1973-74 led to a rapid acceleration in global inflation and sharp declines in growth in many countries (Kose and Terrones 2015). Global inflationary pressures also led to a significant increase in domestic inflation in developing economies, including those that experienced relatively low and stable inflation in the late 1960s and early 1970s (Cline 1981). All three episodes of sustained low inflation are characterized by inflation below 5 percent for an extended period. It is notable, however, that the two earlier episodes were followed by sharply rising inflation. This illustrates

---

[5] Major advanced-economy central banks have also acknowledged the need to consider the global environment in setting monetary policy in light of the highly synchronized nature of global inflation (Bernanke 2007; Draghi 2015; Carney 2015).

BOX 1.1 The great disinflation *(continued)*

FIGURE 1.1.3 Inflation synchronization

Inflation has become increasingly globally synchronized. The global factor accounted for a greater share of the inflation variance in advanced economies than in EMDEs. The global factor was more important in explaining the variance of price indices with a greater tradable goods and services content. The synchronization of inflation has been stronger than the synchronization of output growth, especially in EMDEs.

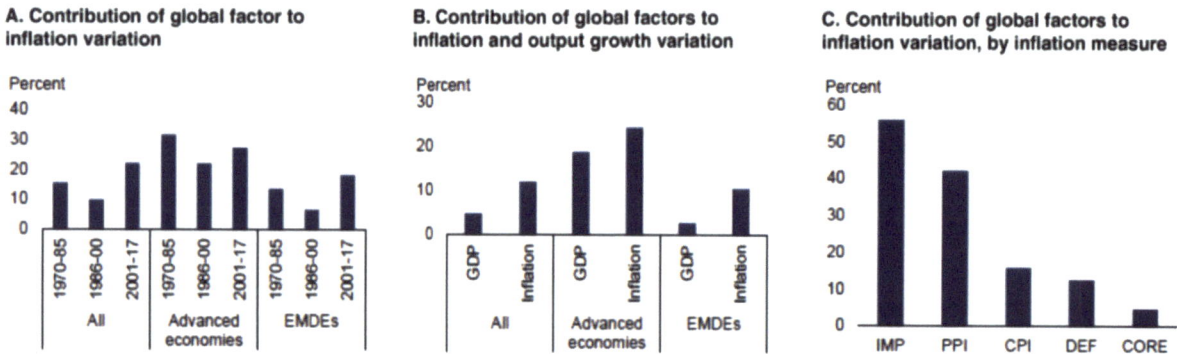

A. Contribution of global factor to inflation variation

B. Contribution of global factors to inflation and output growth variation

C. Contribution of global factors to inflation variation, by inflation measure

Source: World Bank; Ha, Kose, and Ohnsorge (2019).

A.B. The results are based on a two-factor dynamic factor model with inflation (A,B) or output growth (B) using a sample of 99 economies (25 advanced economies and 74 EMDEs) for 1970-2017. The model includes global and group inflation factors. All numbers refer to median variance shares of total inflation (A,B) or output growth (B) variance accounted for by the global factor.

C. The global inflation factors are estimated with two-factor dynamic factor models for annual inflation for each measure in 38 countries (25 advanced economies and 13 EMDEs) for the period 1970-2016, the size of the sample being constrained by data availability. "IMP" = import price index, "PPI" = producer price index, "CPI" = headline consumer price index, "DEF" = GDP deflator, and "CORE" = core consumer price index.

FIGURE 1.1.4 Low inflation episodes

Global inflation has been low and stable before: during the Bretton Woods fixed exchange rate system in the post-war period up to the early 1970s, and during the gold standard of the early 1900s.

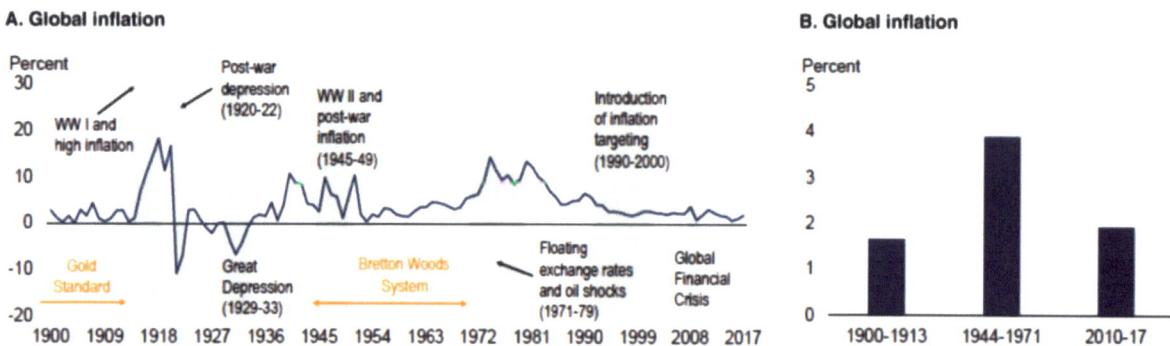

A. Global inflation

B. Global inflation

Source: World Bank; Ha, Kose, and Ohnsorge (2019).

A. Median of annual average inflation in a sample of 24 economies for which data are available across the full period.

B. Cross-country average of annual average inflation. 1900-13 spans the gold standard, and 1944-71 the Bretton Woods system.

that maintaining low inflation can be as great a challenge as achieving low inflation.

EMDE policymakers need to recognize the increasing role of the global inflation cycle in driving domestic inflation. Options to help insulate economies from the impact of global shocks include strengthening institutions, including central bank independence, and establishing fiscal frameworks that can both assure long-run debt sustainability and provide room for effective counter-cyclical policies. Low inflation in EMDEs in the past two decades is no guarantee of low inflation in the future.

Nominal wage gains have been outpacing inflation, resulting in modest real wage growth. Long-term inflation expectations have edged up but remain contained.

During 2018, the U.S. administration raised tariffs on about $300 billion worth of imports, mostly from China; other countries have retaliated with tariffs on about $150 billion worth of U.S. exports. In all, new tariffs have been imposed on about 12 percent of U.S. goods imports and may expand further, resulting in higher prices and elevated policy uncertainty (Kutlina-Dimitrova and Lakatos 2017; Lindé and Pescatori 2017).

During the forecast horizon, growth is expected to decelerate as monetary policy accommodation is removed, and as fiscal stimulus fades and subsequently begins to drag on growth. Higher trade tariffs are expected to further weigh on activity, especially exports and investment. In all, U.S. growth is projected to slow to 2.5 percent in 2019 and to an average of 1.7 in 2020-21—roughly consistent with potential.

Euro Area

Euro Area growth slowed notably in 2018 to an estimated 1.9 percent, 0.2 percentage point below previous projections. In particular, exports have softened, reflecting the earlier appreciation of the euro and slowing external demand (Figure 1.5).

While unemployment has declined, inflation remains stubbornly low. Headline inflation has risen to target, but largely due to a temporary acceleration in energy prices. Core inflation remains around 1 percent, while long-term inflation expectations continue to hover around 1.6 percent, as in the past three years. The European Central Bank has stopped adding to its balance sheet, although it is expected to maintain its negative interest rate policy until at least mid-2019. Financial system lending and profitability have continued to increase, though some European banks may be exposed to financial stress in some EMDEs.

Across the Euro Area, the stance of fiscal policy is expected to be mildly expansionary. Increased German expenditures are envisioned to lead to smaller surpluses, while deficits in France and Italy

FIGURE 1.4 United States

The U.S. economy is experiencing robust growth, with strength in domestic demand. There are signs that productivity and labor participation are increasing. Nominal wages have been outpacing inflation, resulting in modest real wage gains. Fiscal and monetary policies will stimulate activity in the near term but are likely to become a drag by 2020.

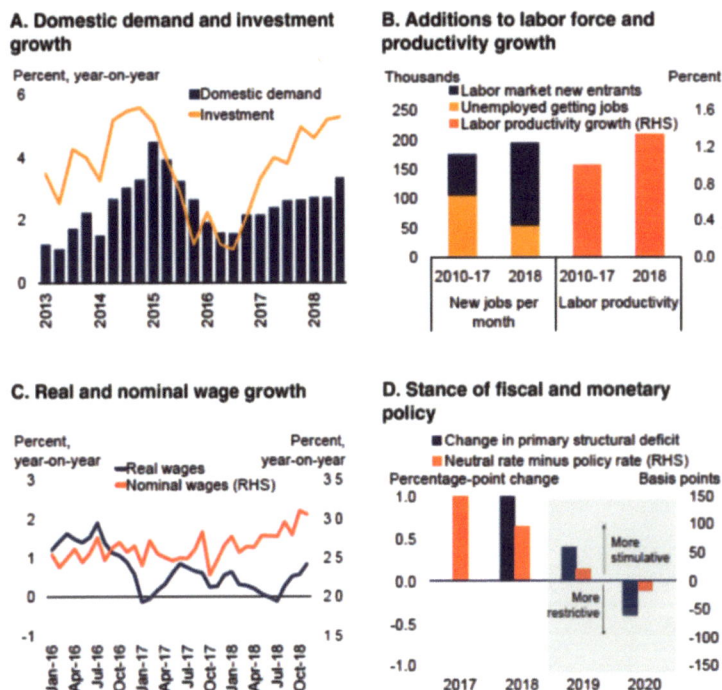

A. Domestic demand and investment growth

B. Additions to labor force and productivity growth

C. Real and nominal wage growth

D. Stance of fiscal and monetary policy

Source: Bureau of Economic Analysis; Bureau of Labor Statistics; Federal Reserve Bank of St. Louis; Haver Analytics; Holston, Laubach, and Williams (2016); International Monetary Fund; World Bank.
A. Investment is measured using gross fixed capital formation. Total domestic demand is GDP less net exports of goods and services. Last observation is 2018Q3.
B. Last observation is November 2018 for labor force data and 2018Q3 for productivity.
C. Wage growth is the average hourly earnings of private, non-farm production, and nonsupervisory employees. Last observation is November 2018.
D. Policy rate is the mid-range of the federal funds target rates. Forecast for the policy rate and inflation are market expectations. The neutral rate is the nominal short-term interest rate consistent with the economy operating at its full potential once transitory shocks have abated, and is estimated according to Holston, Laubach, and Williams (2016). The neutral rate is assumed to remain unchanged at its latest value (November 28, 2018) until 2020. Shaded area indicates forecasts.

are likely to rise amid public pressures for additional spending and tax relief. Italy's borrowing costs have increased and remain volatile, reflecting uncertainties about the outlook for the country's debt load.

In all, Euro Area growth is projected to further decelerate toward potential over the forecast horizon, to 1.6 percent in 2019 and an average of 1.4 percent in 2020-21, as monetary stimulus is withdrawn and global trade growth moderates.

Japan

Japanese growth slowed to an estimated 0.8 percent in 2018, reflecting contractions in the first

Source: Bloomberg, European Central Bank, Eurostat, Haver Analytics, World Bank.
A. Last observation is 2018Q3.
B. Inflation expectations are derived from 5-year over 5-year forward inflation-linked swap rates, averaged over the quarter. Horizontal line represents 1.9 percent, consistent with the ECB's inflation target of close to, but below, 2 percent. Last observation is November 2018.

FIGURE 1.5 Euro Area

A slowdown in exports has been the primary driver of cooling Euro Area activity. While headline inflation has risen to target, it is largely due to a temporary acceleration in energy prices.

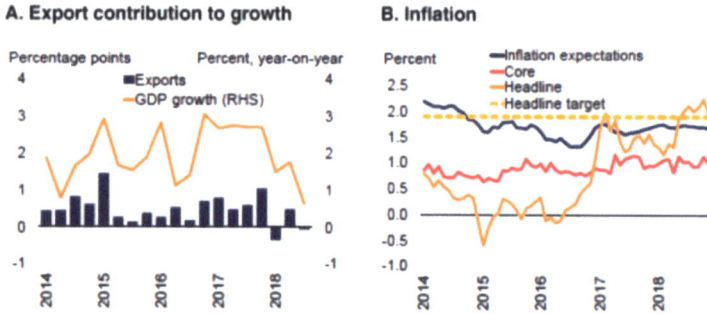

A. Export contribution to growth

B. Inflation

FIGURE 1.6 Japan

The economy is still growing above potential, as solid growth in employment offsets subdued productivity. The Bank of Japan is providing exceptionally supportive monetary policy by keeping long-term rates near zero and expanding its balance sheet, while the fiscal deficit is narrowing.

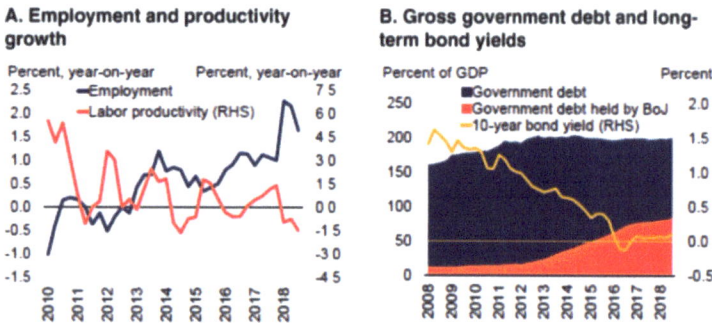

A. Employment and productivity growth

B. Gross government debt and long-term bond yields

Source: Bank of Japan; Cabinet Office of Japan; Haver Analytics; Japan Ministry of Finance; Japan Ministry of Health, Labor, and Welfare.
A. Last observation is 2018Q3.
B. BoJ = Bank of Japan. Bond yield is the quarterly average. Yellow horizontal line indicates the origin x-axis line corresponding to the right-hand scale (RHS). Last observation is 2018Q3.

and third quarters due to bad weather and natural disasters. Nevertheless, the labor market has been robust, with the unemployment rate at 2.4 percent, rising earnings, and the participation rate standing above 79 percent—up 1.5 percentage points since the beginning of last year. Rising labor force inputs, however, have been offset by weak productivity (Figure 1.6).

The Bank of Japan continues to provide stimulus by keeping long-term rates near zero and adding

to its balance sheet. It now holds about 40 percent of government debt. The government continues to run a primary deficit, and it has announced a temporary stimulus package to offset the short-term impact of a VAT hike in late 2019.

Growth is projected to pick up to 0.9 percent in 2019, reflecting a recovery from last year's temporary disruptions. As employment growth slows and fiscal policy tightens, growth is expected to moderate to 0.7 percent in 2020 and 0.6 percent in 2021.

China

Growth is estimated to have slowed to a still robust 6.5 percent in 2018, supported by resilient consumption (Figure 1.7). A rebound in private fixed investment helped offset a decline in public infrastructure and other state spending. However, industrial production and export growth have decelerated, reflecting easing global manufacturing activity. Import growth continued to outpace export growth, contributing to a shrinking current account surplus. Net capital outflows have resumed, and international reserves have been edging down. Stock prices and the renminbi have experienced continued downward pressures, and sovereign bond spreads have risen amid ongoing trade tensions and concerns about the growth outlook.

New regulations on commercial bank exposures to shadow financing, together with stricter provisions for off-budget borrowing by local governments, have slowed credit growth to the non-financial sector. However, in mid- and late 2018, the authorities reiterated their intention to pursue looser macroeconomic policies to counter the potential economic impact of trade disputes with the United States. Prices of newly constructed residential buildings have rebounded, including in Tier 1 cities, following several years of correction. Consumer price inflation has generally moved up since mid-2018, partly reflecting currency depreciation and higher energy and food prices in most of last year, but it remains below target.

Growth is projected to decelerate to 6.2 percent in 2019, slightly below previous projections as a result of weaker exports, and to further moderate to 6 percent by the end of the forecast horizon, broadly in line with its potential pace. Domestic demand is projected to remain robust aided by policies to boost consumption. Supportive fiscal and monetary policies undertaken or announced so far are expected to largely offset the negative impact of higher tariffs; however, additional stimulus may have the undesirable effect of slowing the deleveraging and de-risking process (World Bank 2018b).

Global trends

In 2018, global trade slowed more rapidly than expected, alongside softening industrial activity. Trade policy uncertainty remains elevated, dampening global investment and trade. Borrowing costs have generally tightened in EMDEs following a broad-based appreciation of the U.S. dollar, bouts of investor risk aversion, and increased focus on country-specific vulnerabilities. External financing conditions are expected to continue deteriorating in 2019, as monetary policy accommodation in advanced economies is unwound. Oil prices were markedly volatile in the second half of 2018, mainly due to supply factors, with sharp falls toward the end of the year. Most other commodity prices—particularly metals—also weakened, reflecting heightened trade tensions.

Global trade

Following strong momentum in 2017, growth in global goods trade markedly slowed during the first half of 2018 and has only partially recovered since then. The deceleration was more pronounced than previously expected, as reflected in decelerating export orders and global manufacturing activity (Figure 1.8).

In particular, global capital goods production, which is highly trade-intensive, has slowed notably in Europe and developing Asia, two tightly interconnected global manufacturing hubs (Raschen and Rehbock 2016). Nearly a third of European exports and more than half of German exports to developing Asia are of machinery and vehicles, while capital goods and electronics account for a third of exports from developing Asia to Europe.

FIGURE 1.7 China

Growth in China remains robust, in part reflecting resilient consumption. However, industrial production and new export orders have moderated, asset prices have experienced downward pressures, and sovereign bond spreads have risen amid trade tensions. Prices of newly constructed residential buildings have rebounded, including in Tier 1 cities following a period of correction.

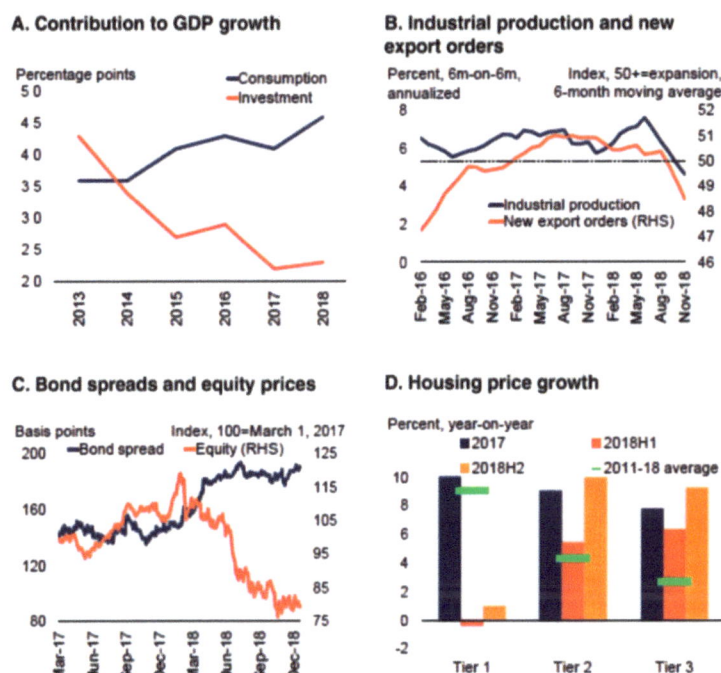

Source: National Bureau of Statistics of China, Haver Analytics, J.P. Morgan, World Bank.
A. Investment refers to gross capital formation, which includes the change in inventories. Consumption refers to total consumption, which includes public consumption and private consumption. Data for 2018 are estimates.
B. New export orders measured by Purchasing Managers' Index (PMI). PMI readings above 50 indicate expansion in economic activity; readings below 50 indicate contraction. Last observation is November 2018.
C. Bond spread measures the average spread of China's sovereign debt (as measured by J.P. Morgan's Emerging Market Bond Index) over its equivalent maturity U.S. Treasury bond. Equity index is the Shanghai Stock Exchange (SSE) Composite. Last observation is December 18, 2018.
D. Prices of newly constructed residential buildings. The National Bureau of Statistics of China surveys house prices in 70 cities and divides them into three tiers. The first tier includes Shanghai, Beijing, Guangzhou, and Shenzhen. The second tier includes 31 provincial capital and sub-provincial capital cities. The third tier includes 35 other cities. The green bars are the February 2011 to November 2018 averages. Data for 2017 reflect the average of monthly growth rates; 2018H2 covers data through November. Last observation is November 2018.

The softening of global goods trade comes against the backdrop of ongoing trade tensions involving major economies. New tariffs introduced since the beginning of last year have affected about 12 percent of U.S. goods imports, 6.5 percent of China's goods imports, and about 2.5 percent of global goods trade. In the United States, tariff increases were implemented citing national security concerns and unfair trade practices. Import restrictions and tariff increases were also put in place in some EMDEs, as retaliatory actions or as measures aimed at reducing current account vulnerabilities in the face of intensifying capital

FIGURE 1.8 **Global trade**

Global goods trade and industrial activity decelerated in 2018 amid trade tensions between major economies. A projected moderation of investment growth in China and major advanced economies is expected to lead to slower trade growth in coming years. Technological changes could continue to increase the share of services trade.

A. Global industrial production and new export orders

B. Capital goods production, G20

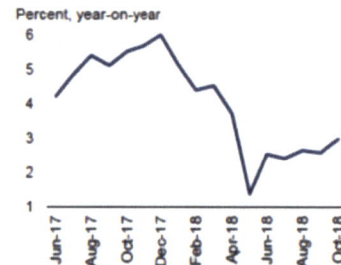

C. Share of goods imports affected by new tariffs, 2018

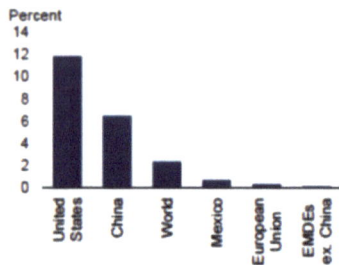

D. Global trade growth, volumes

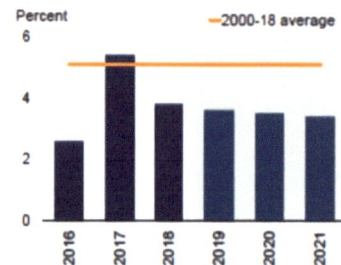

E. Import demand growth, volumes

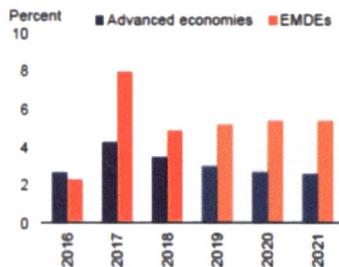

F. Global services trade, shares

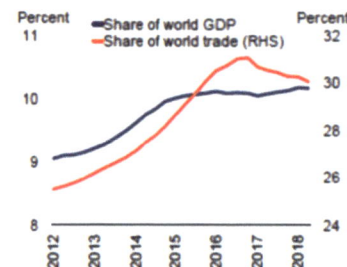

Source: Haver Analytics, World Bank, World Trade Organization.
A. New export orders measured by Purchasing Managers' Index (PMI). PMI readings above 50 indicate expansion in economic activity; readings below 50 indicate contraction. Last observation is November 2018 for new export orders and October 2018 for industrial production.
B. Industrial production indexes weighted by gross domestic product at constant 2010 U.S. dollars. Sample includes the G20 countries for which capital goods data are available. Last observation is October 2018.
C. Value of tariffs implemented as of December 19, 2018, as a share of total imports.
D.E. Shaded areas indicate forecasts. Aggregate growth rates calculated using constant 2010 U.S. dollar GDP weights. Trade measured as the average of export and import volumes.
F. Trade measured as the average of export and import values. Trade and GDP measured in current U.S. dollars. Data are 4-quarter moving averages. Last observation is 2018Q2.

outflow pressures (e.g., Arab Republic of Egypt, Indonesia, Islamic Republic of Iran, Pakistan, Sri Lanka, Turkey).

Combined with the rising prevalence of temporary trade barriers (such as anti-dumping and

countervailing duties and safeguards), recent protectionist measures have disproportionately affected trade in parts and components, with negative repercussions for international value chains (Baldwin 2018; Bown 2018; Johnson and Noguera 2017). Increased tariffs on certain goods, including on U.S. steel imports, is associated with an especially large negative effect on producers in poorer and smaller EMDEs (Bown, Jung, and Zhang 2018). In contrast, some EMDEs may be benefiting in the short term from trade diversion, as rising tariffs increase the cost of targeted goods in the United States and China.

The temporary pause in tariff hikes agreed by the United States and China during the G20 meeting in early December 2018 and the successful negotiations of the new United States-Mexico-Canada Agreement have somewhat tempered trade policy uncertainties. However, the possibility of escalating trade restrictions involving major economies remains elevated. This uncertainty is likely to weigh on firms' willingness to invest, export, and engage in international value chains, with negative effects on the global trade outlook (Feng, Li, and Swenson 2017; Handley and Limão 2015; Osnago, Piermartini, and Rocha 2018). In addition, rising interest rates in advanced economies and economic rebalancing in China is expected to contribute to slower global investment and trade growth, with the latter projected to decelerate from 3.8 percent in 2018 to 3.4 percent by the end of the forecast horizon (Ahuja and Nabar 2012; Kose, Ohnsorge et al. 2017). Global trade is still projected to grow somewhat faster than global GDP, but at a much weaker pace than previously envisaged, reflecting a deterioration in growth prospects in several large EMDEs and in the Euro Area, as well as trade policy uncertainties.

Structural factors continue to weigh on the medium-term outlook for global trade, including maturing international value chains (Constantinescu et al. 2018; ECB 2016; Hoekman 2015). However, technological change and progress in liberalization efforts under the Trade in Services Agreement (TiSA) should continue to increase the relative importance of services in global trade flows (Lodefalk 2014; Miroudot and Cadestin 2017).

Financial markets

Borrowing costs in advanced economies crept up during most of 2018, as inflation moved closer to central bank targets and monetary policy accommodation continued to be withdrawn. After notable fluctuations, U.S. long-term yields ended the year at 2.7 percent, up around 30 basis points from the start of 2018 (Figure 1.9). Notwithstanding a scaling back of central bank asset purchases in the Euro Area and Japan, negative interest rate policies in these economies have continued to keep a lid on global bond yields, with more than $7.5 trillion of outstanding debt still trading at negative interest rates (15 percent of all bonds). Investor concerns about softening growth prospects and a search for higher-yielding safe assets have led to a further compression of the U.S. yield curve, despite higher inflation and ballooning U.S. government deficits driven by fiscal stimulus measures. Global equity markets dropped in the final quarter of 2018, partly reflecting a deterioration in market sentiment regarding global activity and trade policy shifts.

Divergent monetary policy among major economies also contributed to a significant appreciation of the U.S. dollar in 2018. This, together with increased investor risk aversion and renewed attention to external vulnerabilities, contributed to significant capital outflows in many EMDEs. Since the U.S. dollar started strengthening in April 2018, EMDE currencies fell by an average of about 10 percent—the most significant episode of sustained depreciation since early 2016. Cumulative portfolio outflows from EMDEs also surpassed those seen after the 2013 Taper Tantrum, reflecting a broad-based sell-off in both equity and bond funds.

While financial market stress was most pronounced in Turkey and Argentina, many other EMDEs also suffered from deteriorating market sentiment. Countries with current account deficits financed by volatile capital flows, as well as countries with high short-term external debt, were most severely impacted, pointing to heightened investor focus on external vulnerabilities. Elevated domestic debt, above-target inflation, and idiosyncratic factors such as policy uncertainty

FIGURE 1.9 Global finance

Borrowing costs increased in the United States, as monetary policy accommodation continued to be withdrawn, while softening global growth prospects weighed on equity markets. Tighter external financing conditions contributed to significant capital outflows and more significant currency pressures in more vulnerable EMDEs. International bond issuances slowed markedly in some regions, with yields increasing at their fastest pace since 2013.

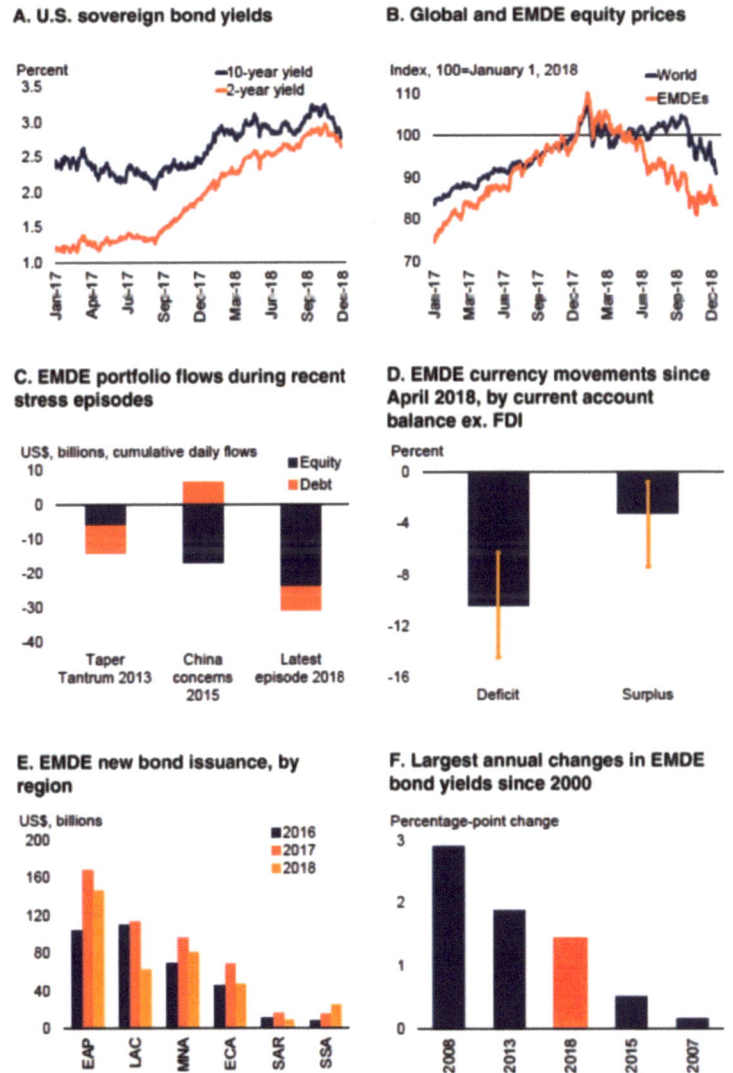

A. U.S. sovereign bond yields

B. Global and EMDE equity prices

C. EMDE portfolio flows during recent stress episodes

D. EMDE currency movements since April 2018, by current account balance ex. FDI

E. EMDE new bond issuance, by region

F. Largest annual changes in EMDE bond yields since 2000

Source: Bloomberg, Dealogic, Haver Analytics, Institute of International Finance, International Monetary Fund, J.P. Morgan, World Bank.
A. Sovereign yields reflect the yield on U.S. Treasury bonds. Last observation is December 19, 2018.
B. Figure shows MSCI Global and Emerging Markets Indexes. Last observation is December 19, 2018.
C. Cumulative flows to major EMDEs, excluding China, for the 250 days following the start of the stress episode. The start dates for the stress episodes are: Taper Tantrum: May 23, 2013; China concerns: June 12, 2015; Latest episode: April 15, 2018. Last observation is December 19, 2018.
D. FDI = foreign direct investment. Figure shows the median of cumulative changes in exchange rates since April 15, 2018. Orange lines indicate interquartile ranges. Last observation is December 19, 2018.
E. EAP = East Asia and Pacific, ECA = Europe and Central Asia, LAC = Latin America and the Caribbean, MNA = Middle East and North Africa, SAR = South Asia, and SSA = Sub-Saharan Africa. Figure shows the total new bond issuance from January to November for each year. Last observation is November 2018.
F. EMDE bond yields are calculated as the sum of the J.P. Morgan Emerging Market Bond Index (EMBI) spread and the 10-year U.S. Treasury yield. Last observation is December 19, 2018.

FIGURE 1.10 Commodity markets

Commodity prices are expected to generally stabilize in 2019, following sharp movements last year. Crude oil prices fluctuated markedly in the second half of 2018, mainly due to supply factors, with sharp declines toward the end of the year. Trade tensions between the United States and China, including the imposition of tariffs on a range of products, have had varying effects on metal and agricultural commodities. In particular, the impact has depended on whether tariffs were broad-based or commodity specific, such as in the case of steel and soybeans.

A. Commodity price forecasts, nominal

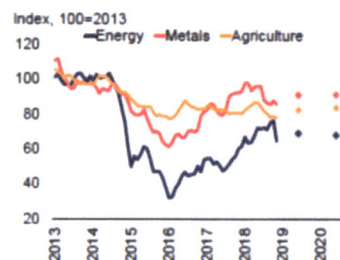

B. Crude oil prices, nominal

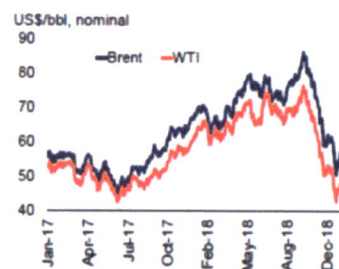

C. Change in oil supply in major oil-producing economies

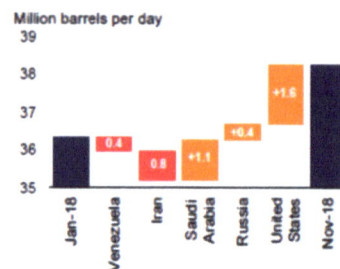

D. Metals price indexes, nominal

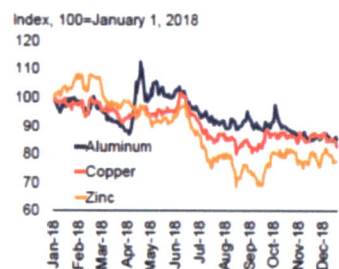

E. Benchmark steel price indexes, nominal

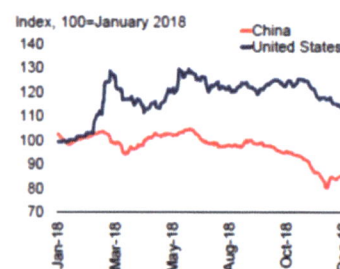

F. Soybean spot prices

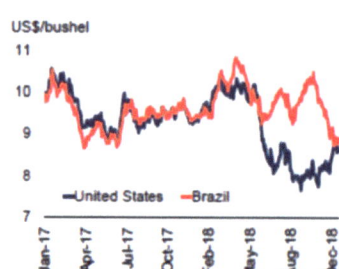

Source: Bloomberg, International Energy Agency, U.S. Department of Agriculture, World Bank.
A. Nominal price indexes. Shaded area indicates forecast.
B. WTI = West Texas Intermediate. Last observation is January 4, 2019.
C. Chart shows the change in oil production of five major oil-producing economies from January 2018 to November 2018. Blue bars indicate total oil production in January and November. Red bars indicate a decline in an economy's production over the period, and orange bars indicate an increase in production.
D. Last observation is December 18, 2018.
D.E. Indexes are based on nominal U.S. dollars.
E.F. Last observation is December 19, 2018.

played a role as well. As in previous episodes, EMDEs with more liquid currency and equity markets were particularly affected by shifting market sentiment and contagion effects (Ahmed,

Coulibaly, and Zlate 2015; Eichengreen and Gupta 2014).

Bond issuance has slowed markedly since mid-2018, particularly in Latin America and the Caribbean and Eastern Europe and Central Asia, amid worsening external financing conditions. EMDE sovereign credit ratings have continued to deteriorate, with some falling below investment grade, reflecting concerns about rising debt and deteriorating growth prospects. Yields on EMDE debt issued in international bond markets rose by 140 basis points in 2018—the third largest increase over the last two decades. Demand for cross-border bank loans has also weakened, with the appreciation of the U.S. dollar putting upward pressure on dollar funding costs. Various EMDE central banks have responded to currency and capital outflow pressures with interest rate hikes, leading to tighter domestic borrowing conditions and, in some cases, slower credit and domestic demand growth.

In contrast to the deceleration in portfolio and bank flows, foreign direct investment (FDI) into EMDE is estimated to have stabilized in 2018, while remittance flows continued to increase (World Bank 2018c). Outward FDI from China remained robust, boosted by the Belt and Road Initiative.

Looking forward, global interest rates are likely to rise at a slower pace than previously expected, reflecting increased headwinds to global growth. Nevertheless, external financing conditions are expected to tighten further in EMDEs, and capital flows to remain moderate, particularly among more vulnerable economies.

Commodities

Energy prices fluctuated markedly in the second half of 2018, mainly reflecting supply factors, with sharp falls toward the end of the year. Prices of most metals and, to a lesser extent, agricultural commodities also weakened, largely due to concerns about the effects of tariffs on global growth and trade. Prices of the three commodity groups are expected to generally stabilize in 2019 (Figure 1.10).

Oil prices averaged $68 per barrel (bbl) in 2018, a touch lower than June forecasts but about 30 percent higher than in 2017. While robust global oil consumption contributed to this increase, supply-side factors were the main drivers of price movements through the year. Continuing declines in production in Venezuela and market concern about the impact of U.S. sanctions on Iran contributed to rising Brent crude oil prices, which peaked at $86/bbl in early October. However, prices fell sharply in November after the United States announced temporary waivers to the sanctions on Iran for eight countries, including China and India. The decline in prices also reflected continued rapid growth in oil production in the United States, as well as a substantial increase in supply by the Organization of the Petroleum Exporting Countries (OPEC) and the Russian Federation.

Oil prices are expected to average $67/bbl in 2019 and 2020, $2/bbl lower than June projections; however, uncertainty around the forecast is high. While growth in oil demand is expected to remain robust in 2019, the expected loss in momentum across EMDEs could have a greater impact on oil demand than expected. The outlook for supply is uncertain and depends to a large extent on production decisions by OPEC and its non-OPEC partners. While these producers have agreed to cut output by 1.2mb/d for six months starting January 2019, few details have been forthcoming about the distribution of the cuts, and they may prove insufficient to reduce the oversupply of oil. Considerable uncertainty remains about the full impact of Iranian sanctions once the waivers end, as well as the outlook for Venezuelan production. Meanwhile, crude oil output in the United States is expected to rise by a further 1mb/d in 2019, with capacity constraints envisioned to ease in the second half of the year as new pipelines come onstream.

Metals prices rose 6 percent, on average, in 2018, less than previously expected. After increasing in the first half of last year, prices fell sharply in the second half following the imposition of broad-based tariffs by the United States on China's imports (World Bank 2018d). Heightened trade tensions involving these economies have raised market concerns about global trade and investment prospects; as a result, they have clouded the outlook for demand for commodities. Industrial metals have been particularly responsive to these concerns given their many uses in the manufacture of tradable goods, with some metals such as nickel falling more than 20 percent. In contrast, the price of steel and aluminum in the United States rose following the announcement of specific tariffs on imports of those metals from a wide range of countries. Metals prices are expected to stabilize in 2019 and 2020.

While agricultural prices were roughly flat in 2018 as a whole, they declined appreciably in the second half of the year, with developments varying by commodity. Soybean prices in the United States fell substantially following the announcement of tariffs by China on imports of U.S. soybeans, while prices were higher in other countries, particularly in Brazil. The imposition of tariffs has led to trade diversion, with China's imports of soybeans from the United States 25 percent lower in 2018 relative to 2017, while those from Brazil have risen 22 percent. More recently, the gap in prices has closed, as China has resumed purchases of U.S. soybeans. Wheat prices were slightly higher in 2018, as bad weather in Europe led to smaller harvests. Estimates for the 2018-19 crop forecast have been revised up for most commodities, and high stock-to-use ratios for rice and wheat reduce the likelihood of a food price spike. In all, agricultural prices are projected to remain broadly stable in 2019 and 2020.

Emerging market and developing economies: Recent developments and outlook

EMDE growth is expected to stall at 4.2 percent in 2019, markedly below previous expectations. The forecast reflects the lingering effects of recent financial market pressure in some large economies, with a substantially weaker-than-expected pickup in commodity exporters accompanied by a deceleration in commodity importers. Growth is projected to plateau at 4.6 percent toward the end of the forecast horizon, as the recovery in commodity exporters levels

FIGURE 1.11 Activity in EMDEs

EMDE activity has stalled, in part reflecting the effect of financial stress in some large economies with sizable current account deficits and high exposure to volatile capital flows. Domestic demand across EMDEs has generally moderated, and trade flows have softened. High-frequency indicators suggest that the weakness continues, particularly in more vulnerable economies.

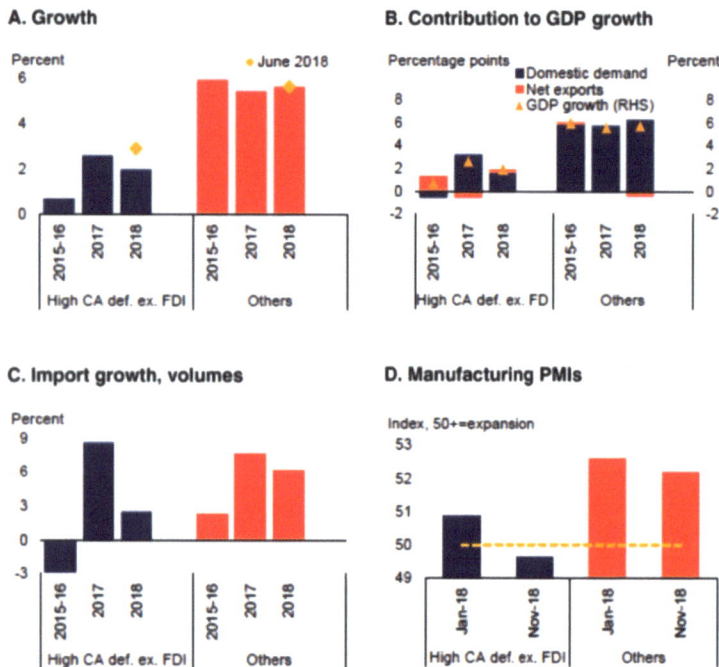

A. Growth

B. Contribution to GDP growth

C. Import growth, volumes

D. Manufacturing PMIs

Source: Haver Analytics, International Monetary Fund, World Bank.
A.-C. Aggregate growth rates calculated using constant 2010 U.S. dollar GDP weights. Data for 2018 are estimates. Data for 2015-16 are simple averages.
A.-D. High CA def. ex. FDI = high current account deficit excluding foreign direct investment, which refers to countries with zero or negative values of current account balances net of foreign direct investment. Others refers to countries with positive values of current account balances net of foreign direct investment.
A. Yellow diamonds correspond with the June 2018 edition of the *Global Economic Prospects* report.
B. Domestic demand includes government consumption, private consumption, and gross capital formation, which includes the change in inventories. Net exports are calculated as the volume of exports minus imports.
C. Figure shows imports of goods and services.
D. Figure shows average Purchasing Managers' Index (PMI) for manufacturing output for country groups. Readings above 50 indicate expansion in economic activity; readings below 50 indicate contraction.

off. In over 35 percent of EMDEs, per capita growth will be too low to avoid widening income gaps with advanced economies.

Recent developments

The recovery in EMDE activity has stagnated. Aggregate growth in EMDEs edged down to an estimated 4.2 percent in 2018—0.3 percentage point below previous projections—against the backdrop of a substantial strengthening of the U.S. dollar, weakening capital flows, heightened trade tensions, and moderating global manufacturing and trade. This more challenging international environment was accompanied by

renewed market attention to country-specific vulnerabilities and financial stress in some large economies with persistent macroeconomic fragilities—most notably, Argentina and Turkey. More generally, the weakness in activity was most pronounced in EMDEs that suffered financial market pressures in a context of elevated current account deficits and high exposure to portfolio and bank inflows (Figure 1.11). Many of these economies faced sizable currency depreciation, equity market declines, or foreign reserve losses (e.g., Angola, Argentina, Turkey, South Africa).

Domestic demand across EMDEs has generally moderated, reflecting tighter domestic borrowing conditions, softer confidence, and policy tightening in some large economies to ward off domestic price and capital outflow pressures. A rebound in EMDE gross capital formation that began in 2015 has slowed, and investor sentiment has deteriorated. On the external front, import growth has softened, partly due to sharp currency depreciations in some large economies, while export growth has also moderated, reflecting weaker external demand—notably, moderating global investment. Recent high-frequency indicators confirm the weaker momentum among EMDEs, particularly in those that have sizable current account deficits and rely heavily on portfolio and bank flows.

Commodity-exporting EMDEs

The pace of recovery in commodity exporters has weakened significantly, and activity across the group has become more heterogenous. Investor confidence has generally worsened, especially toward economies with external vulnerabilities and fragile domestic conditions (e.g., Angola, Argentina, Nigeria, South Africa). Recent declines in oil and other commodity prices have posited additional headwinds to activity.

Long-standing challenges in several large economies have resurfaced. In a number of countries, capital flows have softened, and asset prices and currencies have come under significant pressure amid weaker global trade, rising trade restrictions, and renewed investor attention to country-specific factors including sizable current account and fiscal deficits and elevated debt. As a consequence, the rebound in domestic demand has slowed and the recovery in investment has stalled (e.g., Argentina, Iran, South Africa). Private consumption growth has also cooled following several years of continued recovery, partly reflecting the dampening impact of higher inflation and tighter lending conditions.

Among the largest commodity exporters, growth in Argentina plummeted following acute financial market stress that resulted in sharp currency depreciation and monetary policy tightening. In South Africa, activity contracted in the first half of 2018 and, despite a recovery in the second half, it remains subdued, reflecting challenges in mining production, low business confidence, and policy uncertainty. Growth in Brazil was lackluster in 2018, reflecting a truckers' strike mid-year and heightened policy uncertainty. In Russia, growth has been resilient, supported by private consumption and exports; however, momentum has slowed, reflecting policy uncertainty, recent oil price declines, and renewed pressures on currency and asset prices. Output has contracted in a number of other commodity exporters that experienced declines in commodity production (e.g., Angola, Equatorial Guinea); social tensions (e.g., Nicaragua), or other idiosyncratic factors (e.g., sanctions in Iran).

In contrast, activity has firmed further in several oil-exporting economies where oil production rebounded in 2018 (e.g., Kuwait, United Arab Emirates). Recoveries have also continued, to varying degrees, in some large energy exporters where significant adjustments were introduced in response to the 2014-16 oil price plunge (e.g., Azerbaijan, Colombia, Saudi Arabia; World Bank 2018e, 2018f). Despite recent declines in industrial metals prices, growth among some large metals exporters has continued to show resilience (e.g., Chile, Mongolia, Peru). In addition, activity in a number of countries has been supported by infrastructure spending and foreign direct investment flows (e.g., Benin, Côte d'Ivoire, Ethiopia, Lao People's Democratic Republic, Morocco, Senegal, Uganda; World Bank 2018g).

Commodity-importing EMDEs

Growth in commodity importers has decelerated, reflecting capacity constraints, moderating export

growth, and deteriorated conditions in some large economies with elevated vulnerabilities and heightened policy uncertainty. Inflation has generally moved up, partly in response to higher energy prices in most of 2018 and closed or positive output gaps. Price pressures, widening fiscal and current account deficits, or in some cases currency and financial market volatility have prompted a shift to less accommodative monetary policy in some countries in this group (e.g., India, Mexico, Pakistan, the Philippines, Romania).

The moderation in activity is most evident among commodity importers with increasing capacity constraint, high current account deficits, or sizable public debt. The slowdown in Turkey—which faced a substantial deterioration in foreign investor confidence—has been especially severe. Activity is also slowing, and financial conditions have tightened, in a number of other commodity importers that have experienced financial market stress or continue to face widening fiscal and current account deficits (e.g., Pakistan, the Philippines, Romania).

Slowing Euro Area growth has diminished the positive trade and financial spillovers that had previously supported activity in several countries in Europe and Central Asia (e.g., Bulgaria, Croatia, Montenegro). However, in some economies, moderate inflation and low interest rates have supported a pickup in growth (e.g., Hungary, Poland, Serbia). Growth in Mexico remains moderate, partly owing to tighter financing conditions and domestic policy-related uncertainty.

Although activity continues to be generally more solid in Asia, external headwinds have increased. In India, growth has accelerated, driven by an upswing in consumption, and investment growth has firmed as the effects of temporary factors wane. However, rising interest rates and currency volatility are weighing on activity (World Bank 2018h). Other Asian economies (e.g., Bhutan, Cambodia, Vietnam) continue to benefit from pan-Asian infrastructure investment projects, including the China-led Belt and Road Initiative (World Bank 2018b).

BOX 1.2 Low-income countries: Recent developments and outlook

Growth in low-income countries increased only slightly in 2018, to 5.6 percent, but is expected to rise to 5.9 percent in 2019 and average about 6.3 in 2020-21. Oil producers are benefitting from higher oil prices and output, while softer metals prices are weighing on growth in the metals exporters. Higher agricultural production and continued infrastructure spending has supported growth in non-resource-intensive countries. However, progress on poverty reduction across all low-income countries will remain slow. Downside risks to the outlook include the possibility that commodity prices will soften as a result of trade disputes, global financing conditions will tighten abruptly, fiscal policies will slip, or extreme weather-related or health crises will emerge.

Recent developments

Economic growth is gradually improving in most low-income countries (LICs), even though the external environment is becoming less favorable (Figure 1.2.1). Robust growth in several non-resource-intensive countries has been supported by agricultural production (e.g., Rwanda, Uganda) and services (e.g., Nepal, Uganda) on the production side, and household consumption (e.g., Togo, Tajikistan) and public investment (e.g., Benin, The Gambia, Nepal, Tajikistan) on the demand side. However, in Ethiopia—the largest LIC—growth lost momentum as weaker activity in the construction and manufacturing sectors was aggravated by foreign exchange shortages. Among exporters of industrial commodities, Chad emerged from two years of recession partly due to the recovery in oil prices from their 2016 trough, as well as increased oil production. In contrast, the growth performance of metals exporters was more subdued, reflecting weaker metals prices and external demand, as well as mine closures (e.g., Sierra Leone), and heightened political uncertainty (e.g., Democratic Republic of Congo).

Progress on poverty reduction in LICs continues to be disappointing, with more than 40 per cent of the population in these countries living in extreme poverty—i.e., earning below $1.90 per day. And while this ratio has remained broadly unchanged in recent years, insufficient per capita GDP growth, especially in economies affected by fragility, conflict, and violence, means that the poverty headcount is rising.

Current account deficits are estimated to have widened in several countries in 2018. Among non-resource-intensive economies, as well as metals exporters, external balances have deteriorated as exports declined in response to weaker external demand and moderating metals prices and the effect of rising fuel prices on import bills. In contrast, oil

exporters, such as Chad, recorded smaller deficits, helped by higher oil export earnings.

The financing of current account deficits has become more challenging amid a less supportive external environment, as foreign direct investment (FDI) inflows slowed in almost 40 percent of countries (e.g., Mozambique, Tanzania, Zimbabwe; UNCTAD 2018). FDI inflows, in particular to LICs, are more vulnerable to fluctuations in international financial conditions (Burger and Ianchovichina 2017). However, in some countries, reduced political uncertainty and improved investor sentiment have supported stronger FDI inflows (e.g., Benin, The Gambia). In addition, remittance flows have recovered in several countries as growth in selected advanced economies improved in recent years (e.g., Benin, Guinea-Bissau, Haiti; World Bank 2018i). Nevertheless, for many LICs, the accumulation of sufficient international reserves remains difficult, leaving them below the three-months-of-imports benchmark and highly vulnerable to negative shocks.

Fiscal deficits generally widened among the LICs, with the median deficit increasing from 3.3 percent of GDP in 2017 to an estimated 3.5 percent in 2018. The deterioration reflected rising fiscal deficits among several industrial-commodity-exporting LICs as moderating metals prices dampened revenues. However, in oil-exporting countries (e.g., Chad), higher oil revenues combined with improved non-oil revenue collection yielded a fiscal surplus, and in some non-resource-intensive countries, fiscal consolidation delivered narrower fiscal deficits (e.g., Benin, The Gambia).

Debt levels remain elevated in many countries and continue to rise. In Liberia and Sierra Leone, the debt-to-GDP ratio has increased more than twofold over the last five years, driven by a significant slowdown in growth and continually weak revenue collection (Liberia) and a depreciating exchange rate coupled with new borrowings (Sierra Leone). In addition to the rise in debt ratios, changes in the composition of debt have made some countries more vulnerable to shifts in international financing conditions (Chapter 4). As countries have gained

---

Note: This box was prepared by Rudi Steinbach. Research assistance was provided by Hazel Macadangdang.

BOX 1.2 Low-income countries: Recent developments and outlook *(continued)*

FIGURE 1.2.1 Recent developments in low-income countries

Growth in LICs is gradually improving. Metals exporters are struggling owing to softer metals prices, while growth in non-resource-intensive countries is supported by higher agricultural production and infrastructure spending. However, the poverty headcount is rising, especially in economies affected by fragility, conflict, and violence. Current account and fiscal deficits have been widening, especially in metals exporters. Increased reliance on non-concessional debt is making LICs more vulnerable to global financial conditions, and the number of countries in debt distress has continued to rise.

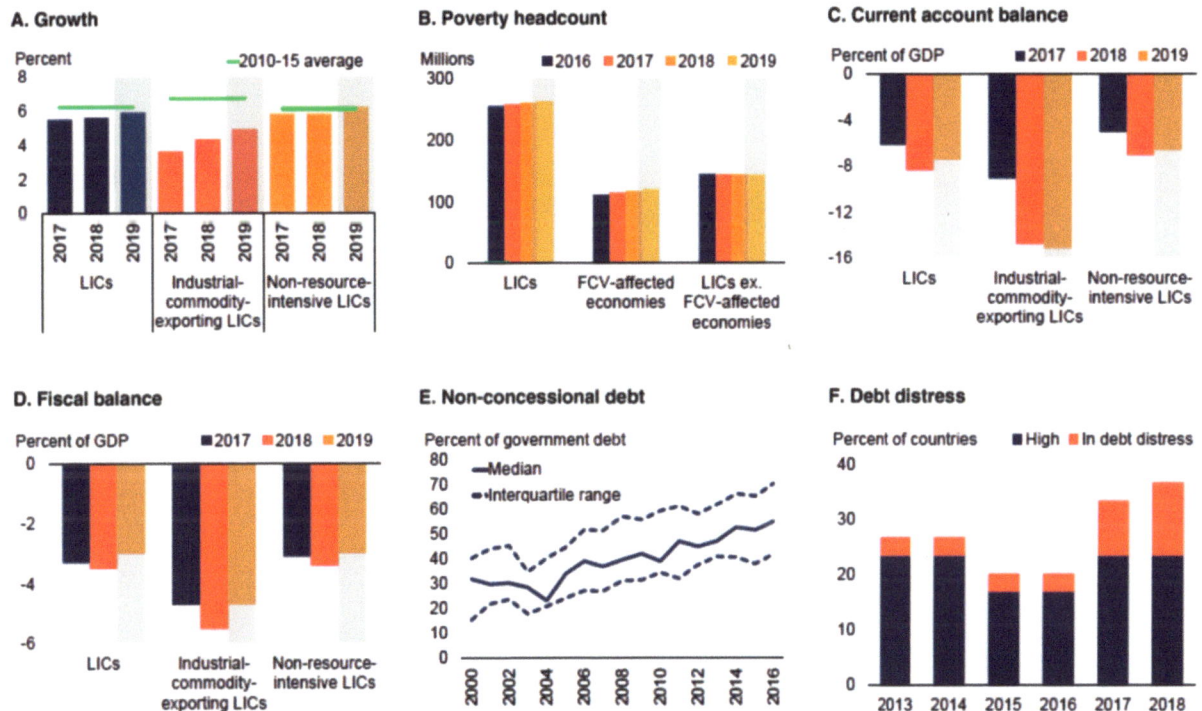

A. Growth

B. Poverty headcount

C. Current account balance

D. Fiscal balance

E. Non-concessional debt

F. Debt distress

Source: International Monetary Fund, World Bank.

Note: LICs = low-income countries. Industrial-commodity-exporting countries include energy- and metal- exporting economies, and the sample includes 8 countries. Non-resource-intensive countries include agricultural-exporting economies and commodity importers, and the sample includes 22 countries. Data for 2018 are estimates.

A. Aggregate growth rates calculated using constant 2010 U.S. dollar GDP weights.

B. The number of people living on or below the international poverty line of $1.90 per day. Data for 2016-18 are estimates and calculated using data from World Bank (2018h). FCV = fragility, conflict, and violence. Per capita GDP represents the average growth rate from 2016 to 2019.

C.D. Median of country groups.

E. Includes 30 low-income countries and excludes Somalia, South Sudan, and Syria due to data restrictions.

F. Percent of LICs eligible to access the IMF's concessional lending facilities that are either at high risk of, or in, debt distress. The sample includes 30 low-income countries.

access to international capital markets and non-resident participation in domestic debt markets expanded, non-concessional debt has increased, reaching more than 30 percent of total public debt in several LICs (e.g., Ethiopia, Mozambique, Senegal) and over half of total public debt in Zimbabwe.

As a result, debt sustainability has deteriorated in several LICs. By late 2018, The Gambia, Mozambique, South Sudan, and Zimbabwe were classified as in debt distress under the IMF-World Bank debt sustainability framework. In addition, Ethiopia was downgraded during the year from a moderate-risk to high-risk rating.

Outlook

Growth in LICs is expected to improve, rising to 5.9 percent in 2019 and an average of about 6.3 percent in 2020-21 (Figure 1.2.2). While the growth recovery among the metals exporters is expected to be sluggish, as lower revenues constrain fiscal spending, growth among oil exporters is expected to be spurred by higher oil

BOX 1.2 Low-income countries: Recent developments and outlook

FIGURE 1.2.2 Outlook

Growth among the LICs is expected to improve. In non-resource-intensive economies, growth will be supported by stronger agriculture production and continued infrastructure investment, while oil exporters should benefit from higher oil production. However, weaker metals prices and subdued external demand imply a sluggish recovery in metals exporters. Moreover, progress on poverty reduction in LICs is expected to be slow, as per capita income growth still remains modest, especially among fragility, conflict, and violence-affected economies.

A. GDP growth forecasts

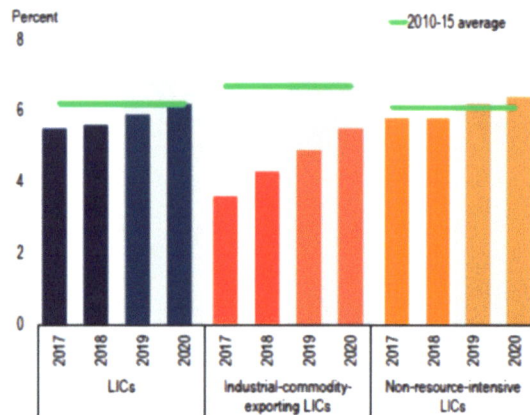

B. Per capita GDP growth

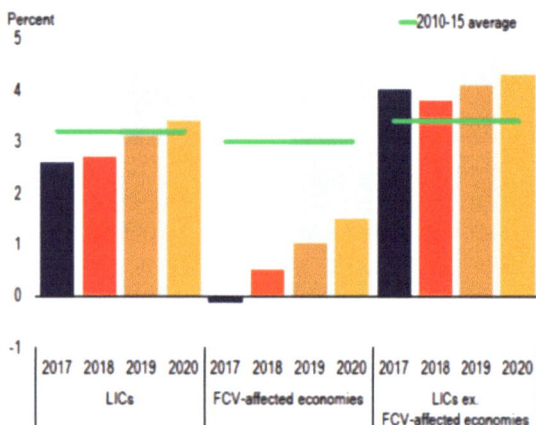

Source: World Bank.
Note: Shaded area indicates forecasts. Industrial commodity countries include energy- and metal- based economies, and the sample includes 8 countries. Non-resource intensive countries include agricultural exporters and commodity importers, and the sample includes 22 countries.
A. Aggregate growth rates calculated using constant 2010 U.S. dollar GDP weights.
B. FCV = fragility, conflict, and violence. Aggregate per capita growth rates calculated using the total GDP for each subgroup divided by its total population. Afghanistan, Liberia, and Tajikistan are excluded due to data limitations.

production and improving domestic demand. Economic activity is also expected to remain robust in non-resource-intensive LICs. In fast-growing countries, such as Rwanda and Tanzania, the expansion will be supported by public investment in infrastructure and strong agricultural growth. Similarly, infrastructure, agriculture, and energy investments related to structural reforms should sustain Senegal's growth recovery. While growth in Ethiopia is expected to remain strong, it will be weighed down by a tighter fiscal stance, as the government aims to stabilize public debt.

Per capita GDP growth in LICs is expected to increase only modestly from 2.7 percent in 2018 to 3.1 percent in 2019, and to an average of 3.5 percent in 2020-21. Moreover, among LICs affected by fragility, conflict, and violence, growth in per capita GDP is expected to be significantly lower—increasing from 0.5 percent in 2018 to an average of 1.6 per cent in 2020-21. In all, these rates are not sufficient to generate a marked reduction in poverty rates, and the number of people in LICs living below the international poverty line of $1.90 per day is expected to remain elevated.

Risks

The economic outlook is dominated by downside risks. On the external front, slower-than-projected growth in major world economies—such as the United States, Euro Area, or China—would adversely affect export demand and investment in several LICs, specifically countries that are heavily dependent on these large economies for trade and investment flows. Moreover, escalating trade tensions involving major economies (e.g., rising tariffs between the United States and China) would be detrimental to LICs that depend on extractive industries—specifically metals producers, as metals prices are likely to fall faster than other commodity prices in response (World Bank 2018j). Furthermore, an unexpected deterioration in international financial conditions could disrupt capital inflows (IMF 2018b), fuel disorderly exchange rate depreciations, and raise financing costs, especially in LICs with weaker macroeconomic fundamentals or higher political risks. Sharp increases in debt-servicing costs, specifically foreign-currency-denominated debt, would undermine much-needed fiscal consolidation efforts and crowd out poverty-reducing expenditures.

Risks to debt sustainability are high, as several countries are either already in debt distress or facing high risk thereof, according to the IMF-World Bank debt sustainability framework for LICs (Chapter 4). The recent increased reliance on foreign currency borrowing has

BOX 1.2 Low-income countries: Recent developments and outlook *(continued)*

TABLE 1.2.1 Low-income country forecasts[a]
(Real GDP growth at market prices in percent, unless indicated otherwise)

Percentage point differences from June 2018 projections[d]

	2016	2017	2018e	2019f	2020f	2021	2018e	2019f	2020f
Low Income Country, GDP[b]	**4.8**	**5.5**	**5.6**	**5.9**	**6.2**	**6.3**	**-0.1**	**0.0**	**0.0**
Afghanistan	2.4	2.7	2.4	2.7	3.2	3.2	0.2	0.2	-0.1
Benin	4.0	5.8	6.0	6.2	6.5	6.6	0.0	0.1	0.2
Burkina Faso	5.9	6.3	6.0	6.0	6.0	6.0	0.0	0.0	0.0
Burundi	-0.6	0.5	1.9	2.3	2.5	2.8	0.0	0.0	0.0
Chad	-6.3	-3.0	3.1	4.6	6.1	4.9	0.5	2.1	0.3
Comoros	2.2	2.7	2.7	3.1	3.1	3.1	-0.2	0.1	0.1
Congo, Dem. Rep.	2.4	3.4	4.1	4.6	5.5	5.9	0.3	0.5	1.1
Ethiopia[c]	8.0	10.1	7.7	8.8	8.9	8.9	-1.9	-0.9	-1.0
Gambia, The	0.4	4.6	5.3	5.4	5.2	5.2	-0.1	0.2	0.3
Guinea	10.5	8.2	5.8	5.9	6.0	6.0	-0.2	0.0	0.0
Guinea-Bissau	5.8	5.9	3.9	4.2	4.4	4.5	-1.2	-1.0	-1.0
Haiti[c]	1.5	1.2	1.6	2.3	2.4	2.5	-0.2	-0.1	0.0
Liberia	-1.6	2.5	3.0	4.5	4.8	4.8	-0.2	-0.2	0.0
Madagascar	4.2	4.2	5.2	5.4	5.3	5.3	0.1	-0.2	0.0
Malawi	2.5	4.0	3.5	4.3	5.3	5.5	-0.2	0.2	0.4
Mali	5.8	5.4	4.9	5.0	4.9	4.8	-0.1	0.3	0.2
Mozambique	3.8	3.7	3.3	3.5	4.1	4.1	0.0	0.1	0.5
Nepal[c]	0.6	7.9	6.3	5.9	6.0	6.0	0.0	1.4	1.8
Niger	4.9	4.9	5.2	6.5	6.0	5.6	-0.1	1.1	0.2
Rwanda	6.0	6.1	7.2	7.8	8.0	8.0	0.4	0.7	0.5
Senegal	6.2	7.2	6.6	6.6	6.8	6.9	-0.2	-0.2	-0.2
Sierra Leone	6.3	3.7	3.7	5.1	6.3	6.3	-1.4	-0.6	-0.2
Tajikistan	6.9	7.1	6.0	6.0	6.0	6.0	-0.1	0.0	0.0
Tanzania	7.0	7.1	6.6	6.8	7.0	7.0	0.0	0.0	0.0
Togo	5.1	4.4	4.5	4.8	5.1	5.1	-0.3	-0.2	0.1
Uganda[c]	4.8	3.9	6.1	6.0	6.4	6.5	0.6	0.0	-0.1
Zimbabwe	0.6	3.2	3.0	3.7	4.0	4.0	0.3	-0.1	0.0

Source: World Bank.
World Bank forecasts are frequently updated based on new information and changing (global) circumstances. Consequently, projections presented here may differ from those contained in other Bank documents, even if basic assessments of countries' prospects do not significantly differ at any given moment in time.
a. Central African Republic, Democratic People's Republic of Korea, Somalia, Syria, and Yemen are not forecast due to data limitations.
b. GDP at market prices and expenditure components are measured in constant 2010 U.S. dollars.
c. GDP growth based on fiscal year data. For Nepal, the year 2017 refers to FY2016/17.
d. Due to changes in the official list of countries classified as low income by the World Bank, the sample of LICs in this table is not comparable to June 2018. However, an identical sample is used for the comparison of the aggregate LIC GDP projection.
To download this data, please visit www.worldbank.org/gep.

increased the extent to which debt sustainability is vulnerable to sharp currency depreciations.

Weather-related shocks, such as flooding or severe and prolonged drought episodes remain an important risk for many LICs. A return of the drought conditions experienced in recent years would undermine the ongoing recovery in agricultural production. In addition, lower agricultural output, and the food price spikes that are likely to follow, could adversely affect poverty rates in many LICs, especially countries where agricultural activity accounts for a dominant share of domestic value added (e.g., Chad, Sierra Leone), or is the prevailing source of employment (e.g., Burkina Faso, Burundi; Chapter 4).

Health crises are a continuous concern. The recent Ebola outbreak in the Democratic Republic of Congo could have a detrimental impact on economic activity in the country and the sub-region should it spread to major urban centers and to neighboring countries.

BOX 1.3 Regional perspectives: Recent developments and outlook

The cyclical upswing in regions with many commodity exporters (such as Latin America and the Caribbean, and the Middle East and North Africa) is proceeding at a more moderate pace than previously anticipated, partly reflecting a substantial slowdown in some large economies, and is expected to plateau toward the end of the forecast horizon. Growth in regions with large numbers of commodity importers (such as South Asia and East Asia and the Pacific) is projected to remain solid at around 6-7 percent. For all regions, risks to the outlook are increasingly tilted to the downside.

East Asia and Pacific. Growth is projected to moderate to a still-robust pace of about 6 percent in 2019 and remain near that level over the forecast period, in line with earlier projections. In China, policies aimed at rebalancing the economy and countering the impact of higher U.S. tariffs will continue to tilt activity toward consumption and away from exports. Excluding China, regional growth is expected to remain steady at 5.2 percent over the forecast horizon. Risks to regional growth are to the downside and have intensified. They include a further escalation of trade restrictions and a faster-than-expected tightening of global financing conditions. Highly leveraged economies and countries with sizable external financing needs are particularly vulnerable to disruptions in real and financial activity.

Europe and Central Asia: Growth fell to an estimated 3.1 percent in 2018, driven by a slowdown in Turkey and in Central European economies. Turkish growth for this year has been revised sharply down due to substantial financial market stress and the associated economic effects, contributing to a deceleration in regional growth in 2019 to 2.3 percent. Growth in the region is expected to pick up to 2.7 percent in 2020, as a rebound in Turkey offsets a moderation in activity among other commodity importers. Risks are tilted to the downside and growing. They include the possibility of renewed stress in Turkey alongside larger-than-expected spillovers to the rest of the region, and unexpected shifts in policy.

Latin America and the Caribbean. Growth stalled at 0.6 percent in 2018, held back by a currency crisis and drought in Argentina, a truckers' strike in Brazil, and worsening conditions in Venezuela. Although regional growth is projected to strengthen over the forecast horizon, the improvement will be weaker than previously expected, partly owing to the effects of financial market tightening and trade policy uncertainty. However, firming momentum in Brazil and Colombia, together with gradual improvements in Argentina, will push regional growth to 1.7 percent in 2019 and 2.4 percent in 2020. Downside

risks dominate, including the possibility of an abrupt further tightening of external financial conditions, a further escalation of domestic or international trade policy uncertainty, adverse market responses to fiscal conditions, and disruptions from natural disasters.

Middle East and North Africa. Growth in the region is expected to pick up slightly to 1.9 percent in 2019, but prospects are uneven across countries. Accelerating activity in Saudi Arabia and Egypt is expected to be offset by a sharp contraction in Iran following the imposition of U.S. sanctions. Increased oil production and fiscal easing are supporting the recovery in some oil exporters, while oil importers continue to benefit from policy reforms. Regional growth is projected to rise to 2.7 percent in 2020-21, as domestic demand among both oil importers and exporters shows a broad-based pickup, supported by reforms and diversification policies. Key downside risks include the possibility of intensified geopolitical tensions, renewed volatility in oil prices, rising global trade restrictions, an abrupt tightening of global financing conditions, and delays in reform implementation.

South Asia. Growth is projected to accelerate to 7.1 percent in 2019. This mainly reflects strengthening domestic demand in India, as the benefits of structural reforms such as GST harmonization and bank recapitalization take effect. Elsewhere in the region, the forecast is for a moderation in activity, notably in Bangladesh and Pakistan. Over the medium term, growth is expected to remain at 7.1 percent, underpinned by robust domestic demand in the region. External vulnerabilities are rising, reflected in mounting external debt, widening current account deficits, and eroding foreign reserves. Risks to the outlook are to the downside. On the domestic front, vulnerabilities are being exacerbated by fiscal slippages and rising inflation, and there is a risk of delays in structural reforms to address balance sheet issues in the banking and non-financial corporate sectors. Key external risks include a further deterioration in current accounts and a faster-than-expected global financial tightening.

Sub-Saharan Africa. Regional growth reached an estimated 2.7 percent in 2018—a downward revision from previous projections, reflecting a sluggish expansion in the

---

Note: This box was prepared by Patrick Kirby, with contributions from Yoki Okawa, Rudi Steinbach, Temel Taskin, Ekaterine Vashakmadze, Dana Vorisek, and Lei Ye. Research assistance was provided by Hazel Macadangdang.

BOX 1.3 Regional perspectives: Recent developments and outlook *(continued)*

FIGURE 1.3.1 Regional growth

The cyclical upswing in regions with many commodity exporters is proceeding at a more moderate pace than previously anticipated. Growth in regions with large numbers of commodity importers is projected to remain solid.

A. Regional growth, weighted average

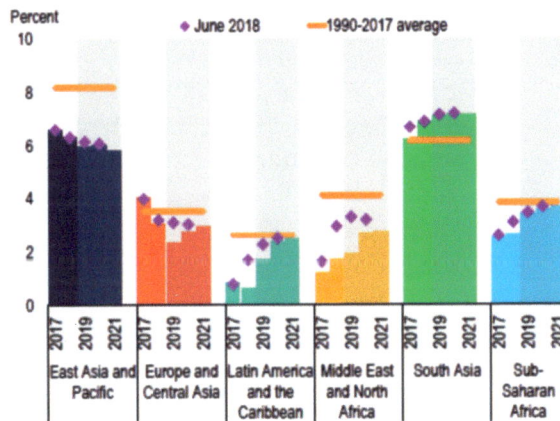

B. Regional growth, unweighted average

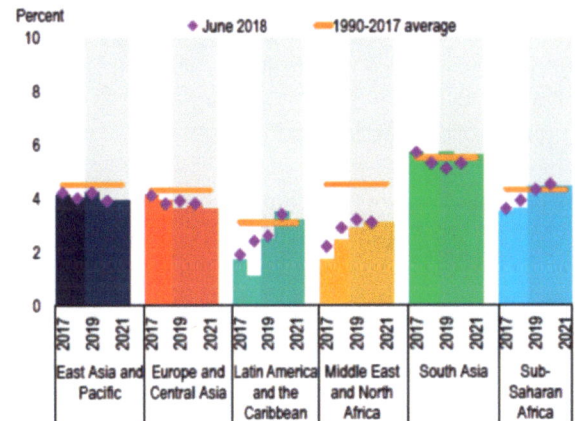

Source: World Bank.

A.B. Bars denote latest forecast; diamonds correspond to June 2018 forecasts in the *Global Economic Prospects* report. Average for 1990-2017 is constructed depending on data availability. For Europe and Central Asia, the long-term average uses data for 1995-2017 to exclude the immediate aftermath of the collapse of the Soviet Union.

A. Aggregate growth rates calculated using constant 2010 U.S. dollar GDP weights. Since largest economies account for about 50 percent of GDP in some regions, weighted averages predominantly reflect the developments in the largest economies in each region

B. Unweighted average regional growth is used to ensure broad reflection of regional trends across all countries in the region.

region's largest economies amid moderate trade growth, tightening financial conditions, and weak prices for key metals and agricultural commodities. Regional growth is expected to pick up, reaching 3.4 percent in 2019 and an average of 3.7 in 2020-21, predicated on diminished policy uncertainty and improved investment in large economies, together with continued robust growth in non-resource-intensive countries. Per capita income growth is predicted to remain well below its long-term average in many countries, yielding little progress in poverty reduction. Downside risks include the possibility of slower-than-projected growth in China and the Euro Area, further declines in commodity prices, a sharp tightening of global financing conditions, fiscal slippage, stalled structural reforms, and conflict.

Low-income countries

Economic activity has continued to strengthen in most low-income countries (LICs; Box 1.2). Increased agricultural production in the wake of easing drought conditions is supporting robust growth in several non-resource-intensive countries (e.g., Rwanda, Uganda), as well as infrastructure investment related to reforms (e.g., Benin, Senegal). However, in Ethiopia—the largest LIC—growth lost momentum as weaker activity in the construction and manufacturing sectors was aggravated by foreign exchange shortages. Among exporters of industrial commodities, growth performances have varied. Chad emerged from two years of recession partly due to the recovery in oil prices from their 2016 trough, as well as increased oil production. However, for metal exporters, growth was more subdued, reflecting weaker metals prices and external demand. Lower export growth, combined with higher fuel-related imports, has caused current account deficits to widen in many LICs. In addition, the less favorable external environment is making the financing of these deficits more challenging. Moreover, government debt has continued to rise,

FIGURE 1.12 EMDE growth prospects

EMDE growth is expected to remain at 4.2 percent in 2019, well below previous forecasts, partly reflecting the lingering effects of financial stress in some large economies. EMDE growth is subsequently projected to plateau at 4.6 percent, as the recovery in commodity exporters levels off. Growth is close to upper estimates of potential in commodity importers, while slack remains in commodity exporters. A decreasing share of EMDEs will see further acceleration in activity, in part reflecting a less favorable external environment. Drivers of long-term growth suggest softening potential over the next decade.

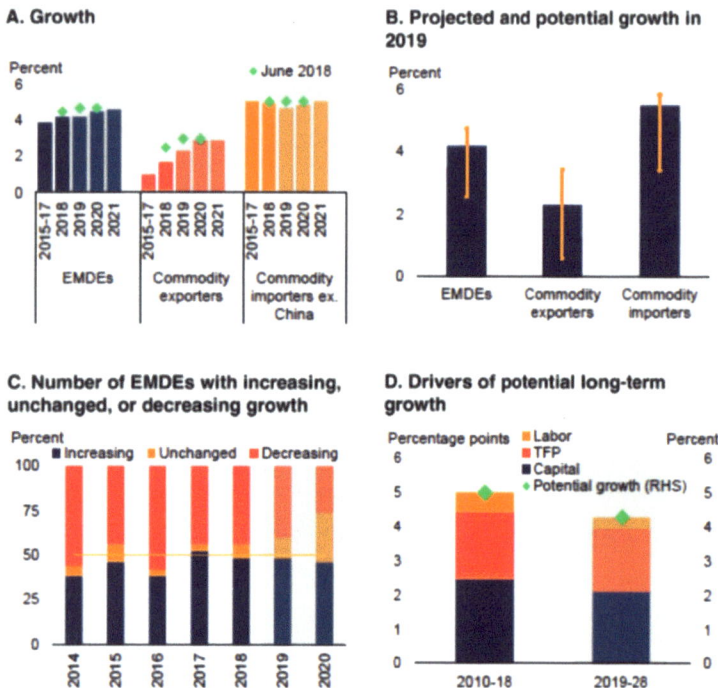

A. Growth

B. Projected and potential growth in 2019

C. Number of EMDEs with increasing, unchanged, or decreasing growth

D. Drivers of potential long-term growth

Source: International Monetary Fund, Organisation for Economic Co-operation and Development, World Bank.
A.-D. Aggregate growth rates are calculated using constant 2010 U.S. dollar GDP weights.
A.C.D. Shaded areas indicate forecasts. Data for 2018 are estimates.
B.D. Potential growth estimates based on eight different methodologies (production function approach; multivariate filter; three univariate filters, including Hodrick-Prescott filter, Christiano-Fitzgerald filter, and Butterworth filter; IMF *World Economic Outlook* estimates; and OECD *Economic Outlook* and *Long-Term Baseline Projections* estimates). For further details on potential growth estimates, refer to the January 2018 edition of the *Global Economic Prospects* report.
A. Data for 2015-17 are simple averages. Green diamonds correspond with the June 2018 edition of the *Global Economic Prospects* report.
B. Blue bars refer to average projected growth for 2019. Vertical orange lines show minimum-maximum range of potential growth.
C. Sample includes 50 largest EMDEs. Increasing/decreasing growth are changes of at least 0.1 percentage point from the previous year. Countries with a slower pace of contraction from one year to the next are included in the increasing growth category.
D. TFP = total factor productivity. The sample includes 23 EMDEs (11 EMDE commodity exporters and 12 EMDE commodity importers).

as fiscal deficits remain elevated due to commodity-related declines in revenue, as well as governance challenges in some countries (Chapter 4).

EMDE outlook

Growth outlook

EMDE growth is expected to stall at 4.2 percent in 2019—down 0.5 percentage point relative to

previous projections. This reflects the lingering effects of recent financial market stress on several large economies, a lackluster and notably softer-than-envisioned cyclical recovery in commodity exporters, and a further deceleration in commodity importers (Figure 1.12). Growth across EMDEs in 2019 is expected to be close to the upper bound of estimates of its potential pace—particularly among commodity importers, where slack has largely been exhausted.

Growth in EMDEs is foreseen to increase to 4.5 percent in 2020, with a large part of this acceleration reflecting the projected dissipation of severe headwinds in a few large economies (e.g., Argentina, Iran, Turkey). In 2021, EMDE growth is expected to plateau at 4.6 percent as the recovery in commodity exporters matures. Throughout the forecast horizon, the international context is expected to be increasingly less favorable, in light of a projected slowdown in advanced-economy growth, weakening trade and investment, tighter financing conditions, and trade policy uncertainty. These factors will impede further acceleration in EMDE activity.

Growth in commodity exporters is projected to pick up to 2.3 percent in 2019—sharply below previous expectations—and plateau at 2.9 percent in both 2020 and 2021. Some large economies that experienced sizable contractions in activity in 2018 are expected to gradually recover over the forecast horizon (e.g., Angola, Argentina, Iran). The outlook for commodity exporters is uneven, however, partly owing to renewed market attention to country-specific vulnerabilities.

Projections for about half of commodity exporters have been downgraded for 2019. Downward revisions reflect, to varying degrees, more adverse financial conditions and the resulting policy adjustment, softening confidence, lingering effects of strikes and political uncertainty, and weaker commodity prices and mining bottlenecks. These downward revisions are also reflected in forecasts for EMDE regions with a substantial number of commodity exporters (Box 1.3; Chapter 2).

Growth in commodity importers is expected to moderate to 5.5 percent in 2019 and remain steady at 5.6 percent in both 2020 and 2021—broadly in line with its potential rate. A structural slowdown in China is expected to be partly offset by a moderate pickup in other large economies in this group. In commodity importers excluding China, a downgrade to growth projections of 0.4 percentage point this year partly reflects the worsened outlook for Turkey as a result of the effects of recent financial market stress, and, to a lesser degree, in some other large economies (e.g., Pakistan, Romania).

Growth in LICs is expected to improve, rising to 5.9 percent in 2019 and 6.3 percent in 2020-21. However, for metals exporters, growth will be more sluggish than previously envisioned, with lower revenues constraining fiscal spending. In contrast, oil exporters should benefit from higher oil production and improving domestic demand. Economic activity is expected to remain robust in non-resource-intensive LICs. In fast-growing countries (e.g., Rwanda, Tanzania), the expansion will be supported by public investment in infrastructure and strong agricultural growth. Similarly, infrastructure investment related to structural reforms should sustain Senegal's growth recovery. While growth in Ethiopia is expected to remain strong, it will be weighed down by a tighter fiscal stance, as the government aims to stabilize public debt.

In the longer run, the underlying potential growth of EMDEs has fallen considerably over the past decade, reflecting softening productivity growth and, to a lesser degree, slowing capital accumulation and less favorable demographic trends (Vorisek et al. forthcoming; World Bank 2018k). Potential growth in EMDEs is expected to further decline, as its fundamental drivers continue to weaken. Moreover, tightening global financing conditions, higher borrowing costs, moderating capital flows, and lingering policy uncertainty are likely to hamper investment growth in coming years, further constraining potential growth.

Outlook for per capita income and poverty

Per capita income growth in EMDEs is expected to stabilize at 3 percent in 2019—insufficient to narrow income gaps with advanced economies in over 35 percent of countries (Figure 1.13). The share will be even greater among commodity

FIGURE 1.13 Poverty and per capita income growth

Per capita income growth in the near term will be insufficient to restart the catch-up with advanced economies in more than one-third of EMDEs. Poverty is increasingly concentrated in a few large lower-middle-income countries. Per capita GDP growth is expected to remain weak in EMDE regions with a large number of commodity exporters.

A. Share of EMDEs with widening income per capita gaps with advanced economies

B. Poverty in EMDEs, in 2015

C. Poverty projections for India and Nigeria

D. Per capita growth, by region

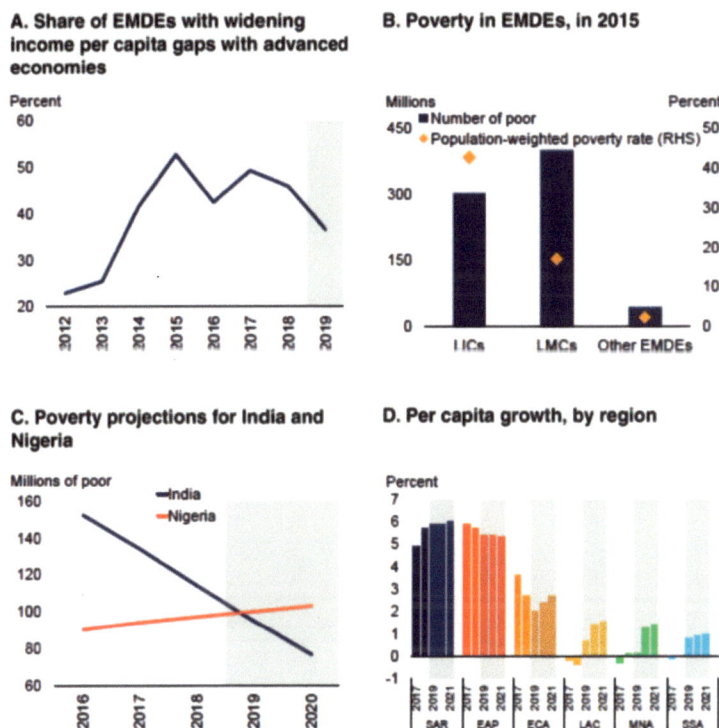

Source: United Nations, World Bank.
Note: EAP = East Asia and Pacific, ECA = Europe and Central Asia, LAC = Latin America and the Caribbean, MNA = Middle East and North Africa, SAR = South Asia, and SSA = Sub-Saharan Africa.
A.D. Shaded areas indicate forecasts. Data for 2018 are estimates.
A. EMDEs with per capita GDP growth of at least 0.1-percentage-point lower than advanced-economy per capita GDP growth are those counted as diverging. Advanced-economy growth rates calculated using constant 2010 U.S. dollar GDP weights. Sample includes 117 EMDEs.
B. LICs = low-income countries, LMCs = lower-middle-income countries, and Other EMDEs = EMDEs not classified in LICs or LMCs. Aggregate poverty rates are weighted by total population. Data as of 2015, the latest available observation.
C. The number of poor are people living on or below the international poverty line of $1.90 per day. Shaded area indicates forecasts. Data for 2016-18 are estimates and calculated using data from World Bank (2018l).
D. Aggregate growth rates calculated using constant 2010 U.S. dollar GDP weights.

exporters (41 percent) and in countries affected by fragility, conflict, and violence (nearly 60 percent).

Although the extreme poverty rate—defined at a threshold of $1.90 per day—has fallen below 3 percent in more than half of the world's economies in recent years, nearly one-fifth of countries faced rates above 30 percent in 2015, with the average for LICs standing above 40 percent. Poverty rates remain the highest among LICs, but the majority of extreme poor currently reside in large lower-middle-income countries, including India and Nigeria. Current growth

FIGURE 1.14 Risks: Tilted to the downside

Past global recessions often came unexpectedly following periods of highly synchronized growth. Risks to global growth are predominantly to the downside amid trade tensions, rising borrowing costs, and deteriorating financial market sentiment.

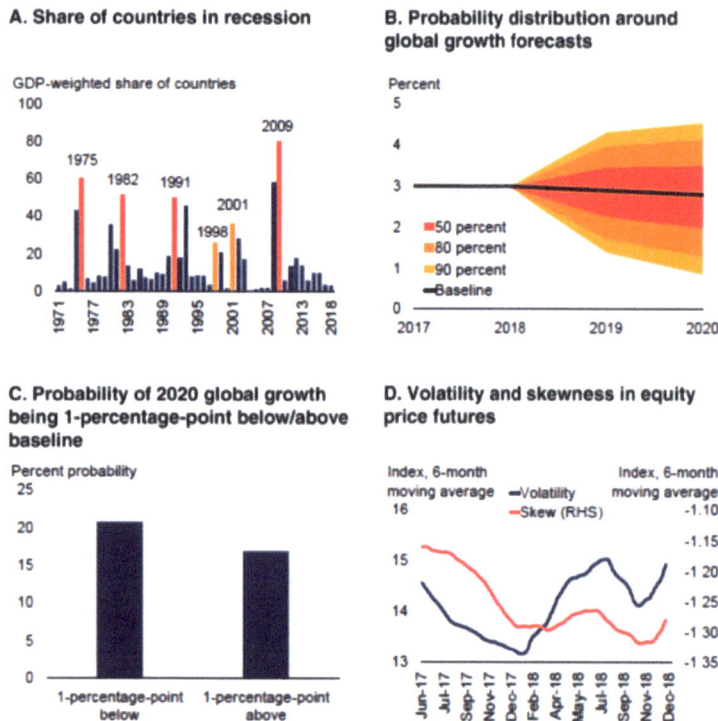

A. Share of countries in recession

B. Probability distribution around global growth forecasts

C. Probability of 2020 global growth being 1-percentage-point below/above baseline

D. Volatility and skewness in equity price futures

Source: Bloomberg, Kose and Terrones (2015), World Bank.
A. Recession is defined as a contraction in per capita GDP. Unbalanced sample includes 149 countries. Aggregate share is calculated using constant 2010 U.S. dollar GDP weights. Red bars show the four global recessions in 1975, 1982, 1991, and 2009, and orange bars show the two global slowdowns in 1998 and 2001.
B.C.D. The fan chart shows the forecast distribution of global growth using time-varying estimates of the standard deviation and skewness extracted from the forecast distribution of three underlying risk factors (oil price futures, the S&P 500 equity price futures, and term spread forecasts). Each of the risk factor's weight is derived from the model described in Ohnsorge, Stocker, and Some (2016). Values for 2019 are computed from the forecast distribution of 12-month-ahead oil price futures, S&P 500 equity price futures, and term spread forecasts. Values for 2020 are based on 24-month-ahead forecast distributions. Last observation is December 18, 2018.
C. Bars show the probability that global growth is 1 percentage point above or below baseline forecasts 24 months ahead.
D. The implied volatility and skewness are derived from 12-month S&P 500 equity price futures.

projections suggest that the number of extreme poor should continue to fall rapidly in India, but remain broadly unchanged in some other countries, including Nigeria. While extreme poverty has declined notably, progress in alleviating poverty at higher income levels has been slower, with nearly a quarter of the world's population still living with less than $3.20 per day.

Worryingly, per capita income growth in Sub-Saharan Africa is expected to average only 0.9 percent in 2019-21—insufficient to drive significant progress toward poverty alleviation. Indeed, if recent growth trends persist, the fraction

of the global poor residing in Sub-Saharan Africa could be as large as 87 percent by 2030 (World Bank 2018l).

Risks to the outlook

The balance of risks is more firmly on the downside. The risk of disorderly financial market developments has increased and could spread through EMDEs, amplified by elevated vulnerabilities in many countries. A marked intensification of trade restrictions remains possible, and its realization could be highly disruptive in the presence of complex value chains. Policy uncertainty and geopolitical risks remain elevated and could negatively impact confidence and investment both in the affected countries and globally. Although unlikely in the near term, the simultaneous occurrence of a severe U.S. downturn and a sharper-than-expected deceleration in China would trigger a marked slowdown in global activity.

Global growth is projected to gradually slow over the forecast horizon as economic slack dissipates, major central banks remove policy accommodation, and the recovery in commodity exporters matures. This moderation is somewhat more pronounced than previously expected, amid softer-than-expected global trade and industrial activity and heightened financial market pressures in some EMDEs. While an abrupt slowdown is only expected in countries that faced severe financial stress in 2018, the global outlook has become more uncertain, with downside risks becoming more predominant.

A faster-than-expected tightening of global financing conditions, or disorderly exchange rate movements, could have large adverse effects on activity, particularly among more vulnerable EMDEs. Escalating trade tensions represent another key risk to the global outlook, as they could significantly hamper cross-border trade and investment, with the impact amplified by complex regional and global value chains. Loss of confidence in international trading rules could inflict long-lasting damage, lowering opportunities for future growth in EMDEs. Rising political uncertainty and polarization, geopolitical risks, and conflict could also depress sentiment and investment in the affected countries and globally.

The materialization of one or several of these downside risks would result in a more abrupt slowdown in global growth than currently envisioned. In particular, a simultaneous occurrence of a severe U.S. downturn and a sharper-than-expected deceleration in China would significantly increase the likelihood of an abrupt global slowdown. Past experience illustrates that global slowdowns and recessions often come unexpectedly after spells of highly synchronized growth and rapid debt build-ups (Figure 1.14; Kose and Terrones 2015).

On the upside, a resolution of trade tensions between major economies could lift sentiment and support global investment and trade. Furthermore, the ongoing cyclical recovery in global productivity growth could prove more durable than expected, especially if the pickup in intangible investments in recent years leads to a broader diffusion of productivity-enhancing technologies. If so, this would help counter the dampening effect of population aging on potential growth in the longer term.

A quantification of possible global growth outcomes around the baseline provides additional evidence of elevated forecast uncertainty and the predominance of downside risks. At current market conditions, the probability of global growth being more than 1 percentage point below baseline in 2020 is estimated at 21 percent, while that of growth being more than 1 percentage point above baseline is 17 percent. This reflects uncertainty embedded in the distribution of key risk factors, including equity price futures.

Disorderly financial market developments

Risks of disorderly financial market developments have intensified substantially, reflecting the possibility of a faster-than-expected tightening of global financing conditions, sharp movements in major currencies, and contagion from financial stress in some EMDEs.

Despite bouts of volatility in bond and equity markets, as well as ongoing uncertainty about growth and inflation prospects, U.S. term premiums are still negative, raising the risks of sudden upward adjustments (Crump, Eusepi, and Moench 2018; Kopp and Williams 2018). While

investors appear to foresee an end to the tightening cycle in U.S. policy interest rates, the Federal Reserve continues to signal additional hikes, implying risks of disorderly market reassessments (FOMC 2018). In this context, a sharper-than-expected rise in U.S. borrowing costs remains possible. This could be triggered, for instance, by concerns about swelling fiscal deficits, intensifying wage pressures, or slowing foreign demand for U.S. government debt (Andolfatto and Spewak 2018; Kopp and Williams 2018). Following a decade of exceptionally low U.S. interest rates and growing debt levels, the effects of a sudden rise in borrowing costs could be amplified by increased investor risk aversion and sudden stops in capital flows to EMDEs (Arteta et al. 2015; Buttiglione et al. 2014; Dobbs et al. 2015; Mai 2018). The dampening effect could be particularly severe on cross-border bank loans to EMDEs (Bräuning and Ivashina 2018).

A further appreciation of the U.S. dollar, possibly triggered by diverging monetary policy and growth prospects among major economies, could also impact the outlook for EMDEs. Periods of dollar strength have been associated in the past with an increased frequency of disorderly currency depreciations in EMDEs. If currency crises were to materialize, they would be associated with slowing growth or outright contractions. In the past, a large proportion of crises were accompanied by a recession in the same year (Figure 1.15). When currency crises are accompanied by banking crises, as is sometimes the case, the likelihood of large output losses rises substantially (Laeven and Valencia 2018). These "twin" crises can occur in the presence of elevated foreign-currency-denominated debt or on the back of an abrupt end to capital inflows and credit booms leading to rising corporate defaults and large asset price corrections (Bordo and Meissner 2016; Caballero 2014).

Financial stress could spread through contagion effects. Excluding China and a few large regional economies (e.g., Brazil, Russia), direct trade and financial sector spillovers from most other EMDEs are limited (World Bank 2016). However, contagion across countries can result from heightened investor risk aversion and shifts in portfolio allocations between broad asset classes,

FIGURE 1.15 **Financial stress**

More than a third of currency crises in EMDEs are associated with negative growth in the same year. Currency crises are sometimes accompanied by banking crises, and their simultaneous occurrence can be particularly damaging. Financial stress can be amplified by persistent external vulnerabilities, potentially leading to further forecast downgrades for more exposed countries.

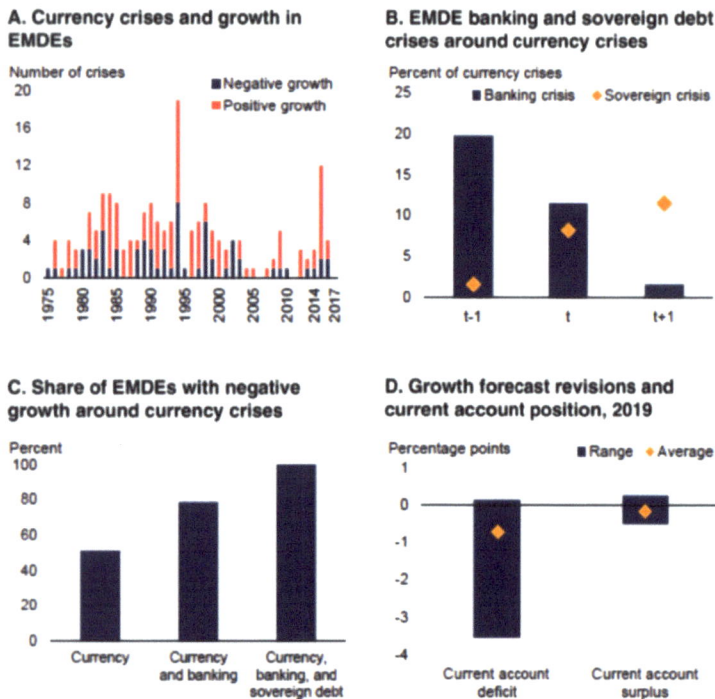

A. Currency crises and growth in EMDEs

B. EMDE banking and sovereign debt crises around currency crises

C. Share of EMDEs with negative growth around currency crises

D. Growth forecast revisions and current account position, 2019

Source: International Monetary Fund, Laeven and Valencia (2018), World Bank.
A. Currency crises with negative or positive GDP growth during the year of the crisis. Currency crises are defined as nominal depreciation of the currency vis-à-vis the U.S. dollar of at least 30 percent that is also at least 10-percentage-points higher than the rate of depreciation in the year before.
B. The percent of EMDE currency crisis episodes that were preceded by, coincided with, or followed by a banking or sovereign debt crisis, with t denoting the start of the currency crisis. Crises episodes are as defined in Laeven and Valencia (2018).
C. Share of countries that experienced negative growth in the current or next year following a currency crisis, a currency and banking crisis, or a currency, banking, and sovereign debt crisis between 1975-2017.
D. Forecast revisions for GDP growth in 2019 relative to June 2018. Sample includes 23 EMDEs. Current account position net of foreign direct investment in 2018.

amplifying the effects of shocks (Gelos 2012). Historically, the correlation across EMDE assets has been high and tends to increase during stress episodes (Eichengreen and Gupta 2016; Park and Mercado 2014).

These risks are particularly salient in the current context of persistent domestic and external vulnerabilities in EMDEs, as these can both amplify the impact of financial shocks and limit policy options in response to financial stress. On the domestic front, many countries have sizable government debt and primary fiscal deficits, elevated or rising private debt, and high non-performing loans. Corporate borrowers have

increasingly relied on bond markets to finance rising debt levels, and now face significant refinancing needs amid rising interest rates (Lund et al. 2018). This could result in sudden increases in corporate default rates and have a sustained negative effect on investment and financial stability (Borensztein and Ye 2018). On the external side, many EMDEs are faced with the challenge of financing large current account deficits and rely heavily on volatile capital inflows. Coupled with high levels of short-term external debt and low foreign currency reserves, this leaves them exposed to shifts in external financing conditions, which could exert further downward pressure on activity.

In low-income countries (LICs), public debt burdens and vulnerabilities associated with a greater reliance on non-concessional financing are rising (Chapter 4). About 40 percent of LICs are in debt distress or at high risk of debt distress—roughly twice the share in 2015 (IMF 2018c; World Bank 2018g). Most LICs also suffer from a lack of transparency in public sector accounts, further exacerbating vulnerabilities.

Escalating trade restrictions

The risk of rising trade protectionism remains high. New U.S. tariffs and the retaliatory response of trading partners now affect close to $430 billion of global imports—around 2.5 percent of global goods trade (Figure 1.16). Despite a temporary pause in tariff hikes agreed by the United States and China in early December, unsuccessful negotiations could lead to a renewed escalation in trade restrictions. These, along with previous measures, would affect close to all goods trade between the two countries. Additional tariffs on U.S. imports of motor vehicles and parts are also under consideration, which could cause serious adverse effects given tightly integrated global automotive value chains.

If all proposed tariffs increases were to be implemented, the average U.S. tariff rate would more than quadruple, rising to levels not seen since the late 1960s. These new tariffs, and the associated retaliatory actions, could substantially depress bilateral U.S.-China trade, increase demand for costlier substitutes, and lead to lower growth in both the United States and China. It is also likely to affect investment strategies by multinational companies and lead to changes in some value chains. While some countries could benefit from trade diversion in the short run, including those with comparative advantages in close substitutes to the goods subject to U.S. or China tariffs, adverse effects from weakening growth and rising policy uncertainty involving the world's two largest economies would have predominantly negative repercussions. In this context, a further escalation of trade frictions between the United States and China, coupled with possible negative effects on confidence, could reduce global exports by up to 3 percent and global income by 1.7 percent over the medium term (Freund et al. 2018).

More generally, a proliferation of trade barriers across both advanced economies and EMDEs could inflict lasting damage to the global economy. In particular, if all WTO members were to increase tariffs up to legally-allowed bound rates, this could translate into a decline in global trade flows of about 9 percent, similar to the drop seen during the global financial crisis in 2008-09 (Kutlina-Dimitrova and Lakatos 2017). In the presence of regional and global value chains, costs associated with increasing tariffs or other barriers to trade would cumulate through different stages of production (Koopman, Wang, and Wei 2014; World Bank et al. 2017). This amplification effect of vertical specialization would be particularly important for EMDEs, as the share of domestic value added in manufactured exports is usually lower and trade costs higher than in advanced economies. In the automotive sector, participation of EMDEs in global value chains has proliferated in the past decade, intensifying risks in the event of sudden pullbacks (Van Biesebroeck and Sturgeon 2011).

Intensifying trade disputes could eventually threaten the stability of the rules-based global trading system and undo the beneficial effects of trade liberalization and global integration achieved during decades of multilateral cooperation. Uncertainty about future trade rules could compound the negative effect of trade barriers on investment and activity (IMF 2018d; Kose, Ohnsorge et al. 2017).

FIGURE 1.16 Trade protectionism

If all new tariffs currently under consideration were to be implemented, more than 5 percent of global goods trade would be affected, and average U.S. tariff rates would increase to levels not seen since the late 1960s. The dampening impact of trade tensions involving major economies could be amplified by adverse confidence effects. The cost of protectionism can be multiplied through global value linkages, particularly in EMDEs.

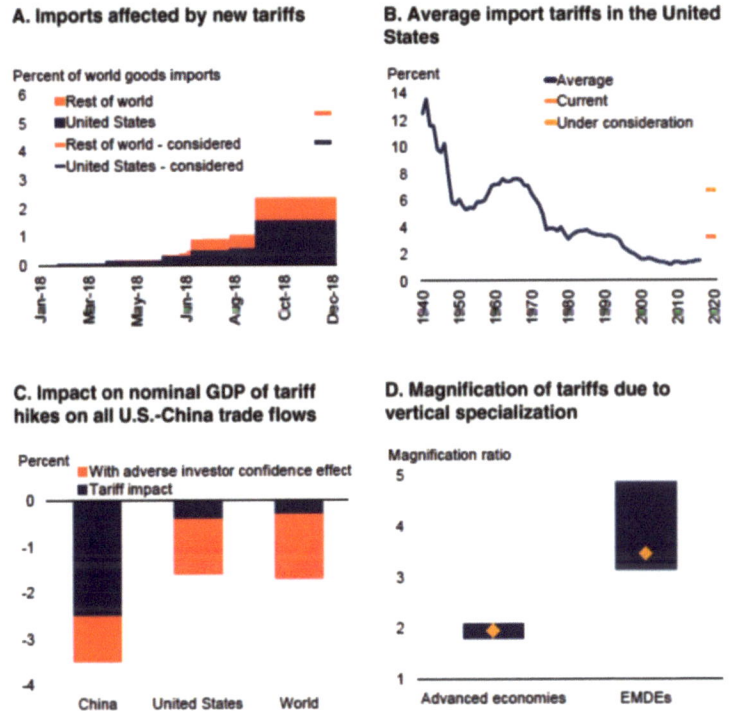

A. Imports affected by new tariffs

B. Average import tariffs in the United States

C. Impact on nominal GDP of tariff hikes on all U.S.-China trade flows

D. Magnification of tariffs due to vertical specialization

Source: Freund et al. (2018), Peterson Institute for International Economics, U.S. Census Bureau, U.S. International Trade Commission, World Bank.
A. Import tariffs implemented in the United States and the rest of the world in 2018, as well as those under consideration, as a percent of global goods imports.
B. Ratio of duties collected to the total value of imports. Data for 2018-20 are forecast from tariffs under consideration, excluding car imports from Canada and Mexico, as of December 19, 2018.
C. Blue bars depict the impact of a 25-percentage-point increase of the tariff surcharge on all bilateral U.S.-China trade flows. Red bars depict the additional impact from adverse investor confidence. The additional confidence shock assumes a decline of the investment-to-GDP ratio of 0.5 percentage point, similar to that observed during the global slowdown in 2001. The percent deviations from CGE simulations are applied to GDP in current U.S. dollars.
D. The magnification ratio of vertical specialization is estimated by comparing a country's standard tariff on exports and the gross effective tariff rate faced in export markets. A country's standard tariff on exports is defined as the trade-weighted tariff rate applied by a country's trading partners (in *ad-valorem* equivalent). The gross effective tariff rate is defined as the standard tariff rate divided by the domestic content share and weighted by trade. Higher magnification ratios in EMDEs are partly driven by their lower domestic value-added share.

Policy uncertainty and geopolitical tensions

Global policy uncertainty has increased since mid-2018, reflecting heightened trade tensions and geopolitical risks, as well as idiosyncratic developments in a number of large advanced economies and EMDEs. Elevated policy uncertainty tends to encourage investors to require higher risk premiums to hedge against negative outcomes. Financial market volatility remained exceptionally low in 2018, implying the risk of

FIGURE 1.17 Policy uncertainty and other downside risks

Policy and geopolitical uncertainties remain above historical norms, which could eventually lead to an increase in financial market volatility from current low levels. More frequent armed conflicts and extreme weather patterns can significantly dampen prospects in the affected countries and globally.

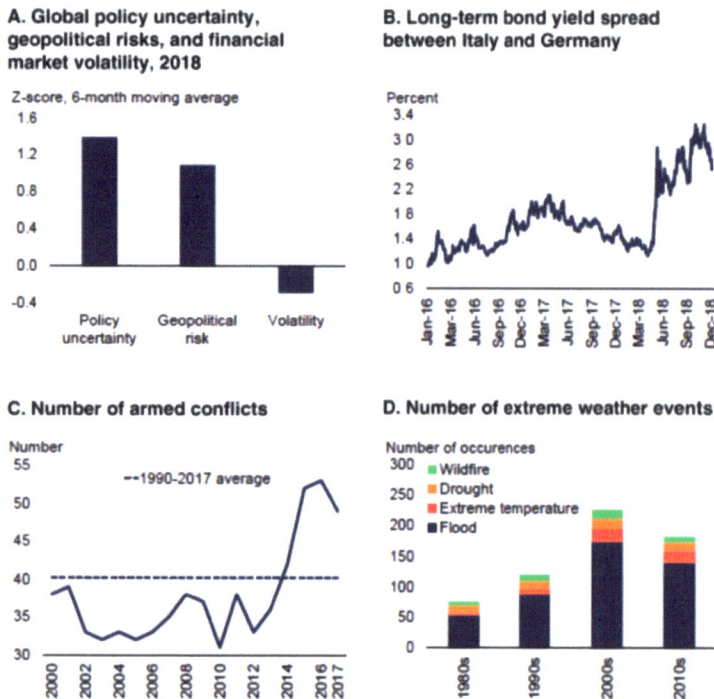

A. Global policy uncertainty, geopolitical risks, and financial market volatility, 2018

B. Long-term bond yield spread between Italy and Germany

C. Number of armed conflicts

D. Number of extreme weather events

Source: Baker, Bloom, and Davis (2016); Bloomberg; Caldara and Iacoviello (2017); Centre for the Study of Civil War at the Peace Research Institute Oslo (PRIO); EM-DAT, The CRED/OFDA International Disaster Database; Uppsala University; World Bank.

A. Z-scores computed as the index value minus the sample mean divided by the sample standard deviation. The global policy uncertainty index is computed by Baker, Bloom, and Davis (2016) and is based on the frequency of words in domestic newspapers mentioning economic policy uncertainty. The geopolitical risk index is computed by Caldara and Iacoviello (2017) and is based on the frequency of words in domestic newspapers mentioning geopolitical tensions, including military, nuclear, war, and terrorism. Financial market volatility is measured by the Chicago Board Options Exchange (CBOE) VIX implied volatility index of option prices on the U.S. S&P 500 index. Last observation is November 2018.

B. Bond yield spread is the difference between 10-year government bond yields in Italy and Germany. Last observation is December 19, 2018.

C. Conflicts are defined as when the use of armed force between two parties, of which at least one is the government of a state, results in at least 25 battle-related deaths in one calendar year.

D. Decadal simple averages.

disorderly repricing of policy-related risks (Figure 1.17). A further escalation of policy uncertainty could lead companies to delay or reconsider capital spending, contributing to a more rapid deceleration of global growth than currently projected.

Political uncertainty is generally associated with lower growth in both advanced economies and EMDEs (Aisen and Veiga 2013). It has increased

or remained elevated in a number of European countries—including in Italy where fiscal slippages have led to a market reassessment of country risk, and in the United Kingdom as it transitions out of the European Union (EU). In the absence of an approved withdrawal agreement, the exit of the United Kingdom from the EU could be accompanied by significant disruptions to activity in the short term and lasting economic losses over the medium term (Bank of England 2018; H.M. Treasury 2018). A sustained period of financial market stress and interruptions in cross-border financial flows associated with a disorderly exit process could cause significant adverse spillover effects and become a source of financial stability risks in systematically large economies (ECB 2018; FSOC 2018). Electoral outcomes in a number of EMDEs and advanced economies could result in further polarization and political fragmentation, making it harder to govern and formulate policies. A backlash against trade and immigration could also spur more inward-looking and populist policies (Aksoy, Guriev, and Treisman 2018; Moriconi, Peri, and Turati 2018).

Geopolitical risks intensified again in the Middle East, and persist in Central Asia, East Asia, and Africa. An intensification of these risks could impact growth in the affected regions, and their main trading partners. In the case of the Middle East, disruptions to global oil supplies could result in higher-than-expected oil prices, with negative impacts on aggregate demand and trade balances in major oil importers (Baffes et al. 2015; Stocker et al. 2018).

The number of armed conflicts also remains above historical averages. In particular, security conditions remain challenging in many countries in Sub-Sahara Africa, the Middle East, and North Africa. In the past, countries in conflict or in fragile situations suffered from below average growth in income per capita, delaying or derailing their catchup with advanced economy levels (UN and World Bank 2018). Beyond adverse short-term effects on growth, conflict can also substantially set back efforts to reduce poverty and child mortality, and can hamper access to education, implying longer lasting negative repercussions on development (Gates et al. 2012).

Region-specific downside risks

These global risks are compounded by multiple region-specific risks (Box 1.2; Chapter 2). Most regions are vulnerable to sudden shifts in policy, which could result in fiscal slippage, reduced investment due to policy uncertainty, and weaker potential growth resulting from insufficient structural reforms. Security-related risks remain present, in varying degrees, in Europe and Central Asia, the Middle East and North Africa, South Asia, and East Asia, and could rise in the face of renewed geopolitical tensions. A flare-up in violence would disrupt activity in various ways, weigh on potential output, and drive up refugee flows. A fall in the price of specific commodities could disrupt activity in large regional commodity exporters, with possible broader spillovers.

Severe weather events appear to be becoming more frequent, with particularly serious consequences for vulnerable countries, such as island nations in the Caribbean and East Asia and the Pacific. Adverse weather patterns are also problematic for countries with large agricultural sectors dependent on rainfall, including many in Sub-Saharan Africa and South Asia. In those countries, large food price increases could severely impact poverty (Chapter 4). For instance, the spike in food prices in 2010-11 is estimated to have increased extreme poverty by 8.3 million people. Other natural disasters, such as earthquakes and hurricanes, can inflict severe damage in the affected countries. These events are unpredictable and often force countries to overly rely on aid for reconstruction, even though recent progress in disaster risk finance has created opportunities for preventive actions (Végh et al. 2018).

Simultaneous slowdown in the two largest economies

Fiscal measures undertaken in the United States and China are supporting their near-term growth prospects; however, they could exacerbate imbalances and amplify risks of a more abrupt downturn later on. A sharper-than-expected and simultaneous slowdown in these two economies could have severe consequences for the global economy.

FIGURE 1.18 Simultaneous slowdown in the two largest economies

The U.S. expansion is on track to be the longest in more than a century. The probability of a U.S. recession in the short term is still low, but has increased, and corporate debt vulnerabilities are growing. Private debt in China exceeds levels that gave rise to significant adjustments in other EMDEs in the past. A simultaneous sharp slowdown in both the United States and China could bring the global economy closer to a global recession.

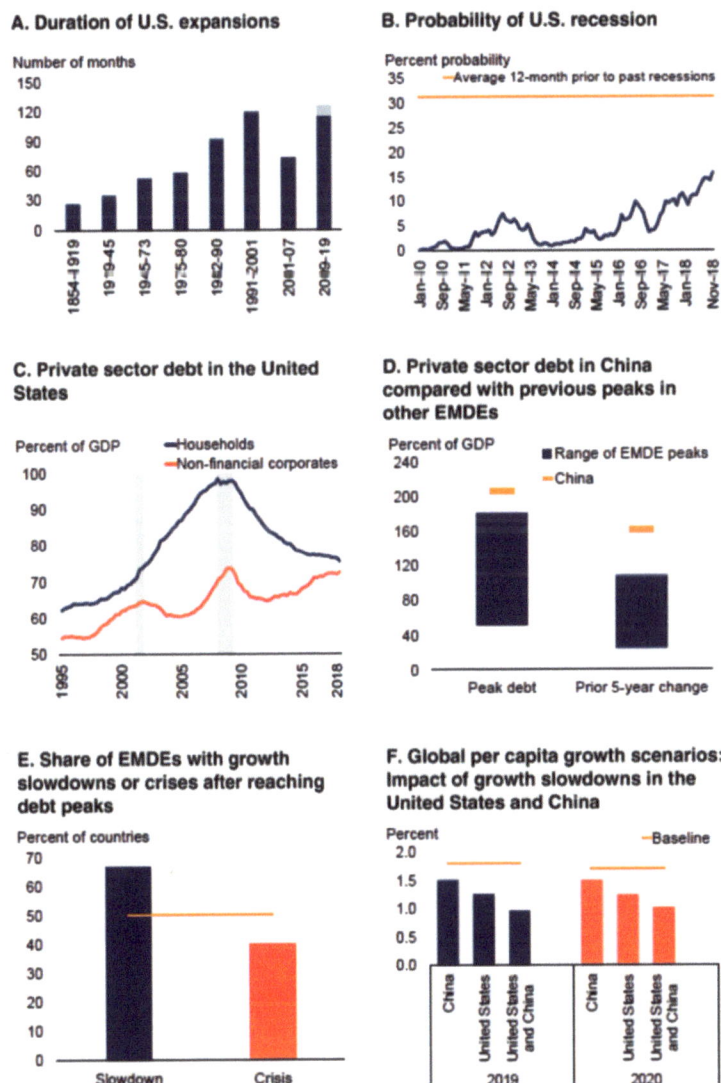

A. Duration of U.S. expansions

B. Probability of U.S. recession

C. Private sector debt in the United States

D. Private sector debt in China compared with previous peaks in other EMDEs

E. Share of EMDEs with growth slowdowns or crises after reaching debt peaks

F. Global per capita growth scenarios: Impact of growth slowdowns in the United States and China

Source: Bank for International Settlements, Federal Reserve Bank of New York, Haver Analytics, Institute of International Finance, Laeven and Valencia (2018), National Bureau of Economic Research, World Bank.
A. Shaded area indicates the number of months from January 2019 to December 2019.
B. Probability of a recession in 12 months derived from the U.S. yield curve model of the Federal Reserve Bank of New York. Last observation is November 2018.
C. Shaded areas indicate recessions, as identified by the National Bureau of Economic Research (NBER). Last observation is 2018Q2.
D. Debt peaks are defined as the highest value of the private non-financial credit to GDP ratio over the period 1960Q1 to 2018Q2. Sample includes 15 EMDEs. For China, values are the last observations in 2018Q2.
E. Countries must have experienced a currency, systemic banking, or sovereign debt crisis within two years after reaching the peak debt-to-GDP ratio. A slowdown is defined as a 1 percentage point or more drop in GDP growth between the two years before and the two years after peak debt-to-GDP ratio. Sample includes 15 EMDEs from 1960Q1 to 2018Q2.
F. Blue and red bars show scenarios assuming a 1-percentage-point growth shock in China, the United States, and the combination of the two. Shocks are applied in the second half of 2019. Based on the vector autoregression model presented in World Bank (2016). Deviations from baseline are all significantly different from zero.

The policy mix in the United States will shift from expansionary to contractionary during the forecast horizon, with monetary, fiscal, and trade policies all expected to become a drag on activity within the next couple of years. In this context, relatively small negative shocks have the potential to abruptly end the current expansion, which is on track to be the longest in more than century (Figure 1.18). Although the probability of a U.S. recession in the short term is still low, at about half its level prior to previous recessions, it has increased throughout 2018.

Economic expansions do not end and give way to recessions only because they have lasted long (Castro 2013; Diebold and Rudebusch 1999; Rudebusch 2016). Instead, they tend to end as a reflection of corrections from imbalances accumulated over the business cycle. In particular, recessions often follow periods of rapid increase in debt levels and excessive asset price valuations (Claessens, Kose, and Terrones 2012; Mendoza and Terrones 2012). These imbalances tend to suddenly unwind, often during or shortly after the end of a monetary policy tightening cycle (Bernanke and Gertler 1995; Sims and Tao 2006). In the United States, three of the last four tightening cycles were indeed followed by a recession within a year and a half, with the most severe contractions following unsustainable housing market booms (Berkovec, Chang, and McManus 2012; Gelain, Lansing, and Natvik 2018; Mian and Sufi 2009). The only exception was the productivity-driven growth revival around mid-1990, which continued uninterrupted despite interest rate hikes in 1994-95.

At the present juncture, the rise in U.S. private debt is smaller than prior to past recessions, mostly because of household and bank deleveraging since the global financial crisis. U.S. corporate debt is starting to accumulate, however, raising the risk that corporate bond defaults could amplify the next downturn (FSOC 2018). On balance, the U.S. economy has some of the characteristics that have preceded relatively mild recessions, but some corporate and non-bank financial sector risks are a source of concern (IMF 2018e).

In China, risks to the outlook are increasingly tilted to the downside. Fiscal and monetary policy stimulus measures could offset the adverse effect of trade tensions with the United States but may delay efforts to contain credit growth and limit the buildup of balance sheet vulnerabilities of corporates, local governments, and financial institutions (IMF 2017; World Bank 2018a, 2018k). Both the level and growth rate of private debt stocks are well above those observed during previous credit booms in other EMDEs—two thirds of which ended in significant growth slowdowns and more than a third in financial crises (Acharya et al. 2015; Alter and Elekdag 2016). In the case of China, risks are somewhat tempered by still low central government debt, extensive capital controls, large foreign reserves, and a low reliance on external financing. That said, if financial stress were to materialize, it would likely translate into a significantly sharper-than-expected slowdown in activity (Beltran, Garud, and Rosenblum 2017; Bernadini and Forni 2017; Maliszewski et al. 2016).

The simultaneous occurrence of a severe downturn in the United States and a sharper-than-expected deceleration in China, although still unlikely in the near term, would substantially increase the risk of an abrupt global slowdown. These two economies are, together with the Euro Area, the most important source of global spillovers, and can impact the outlook for EMDEs through trade, confidence, financial-market, and commodity-market channels (World Bank 2016).

In all, a 1-percentage-point decline in U.S. growth is estimated to translate after one year into a decline in other advanced economy and EMDE growth of 0.6 percentage point for both groups. The impact of slower growth in China is around half that of a U.S. slowdown for other advanced economies (-0.3 percentage point), but it is comparable for other EMDEs (-0.6 percentage point)—and, among them, significantly larger for commodity exporters (-1.2 percentage points). Slower growth in China tends to dampen commodity prices, as this country is a primary driver of global demand for industrial commodities, especially of metals (World Bank 2018d). Critically, a combined 1-percent negative growth shock in China and the United States would have severe consequences for global growth, reducing it by almost 1 percentage point after one year. Should such a risk materialize in the second half of 2019, global per capita growth would drop to around 1 percent in 2020, bringing the global economy somewhat closer to a global recession.[1]

The probability of a global recession tends to increase noticeably when one or several systemically large economies decelerate (Kose and Terrones 2015). For instance, a recession in the United States increases the probability of a global recession from 7 percent on an average year to 50 percent. The risk of a sharp global downturn could be magnified as policymakers' ability to respond is constrained by a lack of fiscal and monetary space and by a reduced appetite for coordinated policy responses among major economies. High levels of private and public debt also make EMDEs particularly vulnerable to adverse shocks (World Bank 2018k). The materialization of a global downturn could set back efforts to alleviate extreme poverty—including in Sub-Saharan Africa, where progress has been slow in recent years.

Possible productivity revival

Although global downside risks predominate, a sustained revival in productivity growth following cyclical improvements in 2017-18 could lead to stronger-than-expected global activity in coming years (Figure 1.19). An acceleration in patent applications and growing investments in intangible assets could be tentative signs of such a revival. Greater connectivity, falling computing costs, and open software architectures could also facilitate the adoption of digital technologies and enable less productive firms to catch up with the technological frontier (Andrews, Criscuolo, and Gal 2016; OECD 2018). Over the medium term, breakthroughs in data processing, artificial intelligence, and manufacturing could drive additional productivity-enhancing innovations (Brynjolfsson and McAfee 2014; Diamandis and Kotler 2012).

Economies experiencing faster productivity growth would benefit from additional policy

[1] Global recessions are defined as a decline in world real GDP per capita accompanied by a synchronized deceleration in multiple measures of global activity, including industrial production, trade, capital flows, employment, and energy consumption (Kose and Terrones 2015).

FIGURE 1.19 **Productivity revival**

A sustained revival in productivity growth following cyclical improvements in 2017-18 could lead to stronger-than-expected global activity. A significant productivity gap between leading and lagging firms suggests an untapped potential for existing technologies.

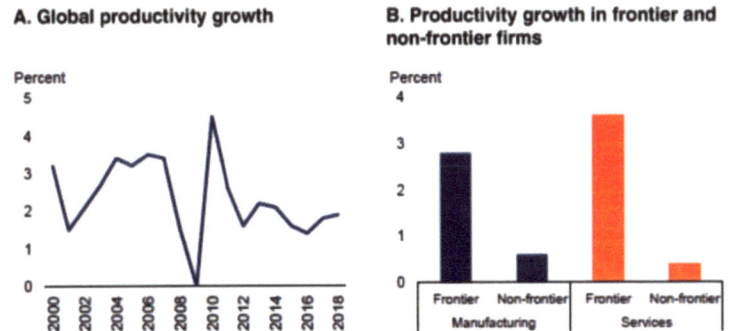

Source: Conference Board, Organisation for Economic Co-operation and Development, World Bank.
A. Labor productivity per person employed.
B. Productivity growth for frontier and non-frontier firms of the period 2001-13. The global frontier is defined as the top 5 percent of firms in terms of labor productivity levels within each two-digit industry at the start of the period, while non-frontier firms refer to all other firms. Aggregate productivity is calculated as the unweighted average of log labor productivity across firms, which the initial year, 2001, is indexed to 0 and separately for the manufacturing and services sectors.

room, as the recovery could continue without generating overheating pressures. This could allow for a more gradual pace of monetary policy tightening than currently envisioned and facilitate the necessary restoration of fiscal buffers given higher revenues. A sustained pickup in productivity could also spur additional investments and trigger a virtuous cycle between capital deepening and growth.

Policy challenges

Challenges in advanced economies

Advanced-economy monetary policy is expected to be less stimulative, especially in the United States, where tightening is proceeding more quickly than elsewhere partly in response to pro-cyclical fiscal easing. Advanced economies should use this period of above-potential growth to create the room to respond to future cyclical shocks. Longer-term prospects remain subdued and could be further eroded by major shifts in trade and immigration policies.

Monetary and financial policies

The U.S. Federal Reserve is gradually removing stimulus in response to low unemployment and near-target inflation amid pro-cyclical fiscal stimulus. In contrast, the European Central Bank

FIGURE 1.20 Monetary and fiscal policy in advanced economies

The U.S. policy rate is approaching the point where it may no longer be providing stimulus and is expected to peak at a lower level than in previous tightening cycles, with significantly less room to cut rates. Government debt has become the largest component of debt for advanced economies, which can lead to less effective fiscal stimulus during an economic slowdown.

A. U.S. federal funds rate

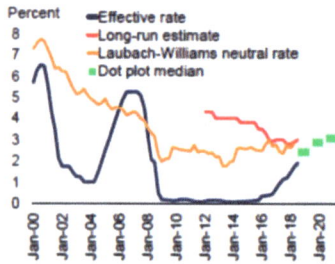

B. Peak and trough of Federal Reserve policy rates in previous cycles

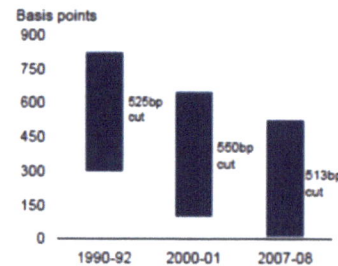

C. Debt in advanced economies

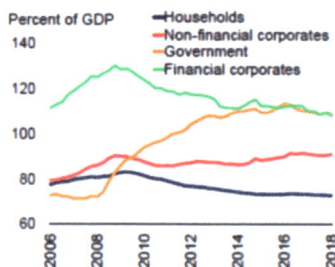

D. Fiscal multiplier, by level of fiscal space

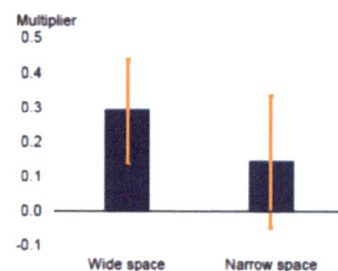

Source: Board of Governors of the Federal Reserve System; Federal Reserve Bank of St. Louis; Haver Analytics; Holston, Laubach, and Williams (2016); Huidrom et al. (2016); Institute of International Finance; National Bureau of Economic Research; World Bank.
A. The effective rate is the mid-range of the federal funds target rates. The long-run estimate is the federal funds rate that would be expected to prevail in the absence of shocks to the economy, as assessed by members of the Federal Open Market Committee. The neutral rate is the nominal short-term interest rate consistent with the economy operating at its full potential once transitory shocks have abated, and is estimated according to Holston, Laubach, and Williams (2016). Shaded area indicates forecasts. Last observation is 2018Q3 for the effective rate and long-run estimate, and 2018Q2 for the neutral rate.
B. Bars represent the peak policy rates in the four months prior the official recession dates of the National Bureau of Economic Research, and the trough policy rate in the subsequent expansion.
C. Aggregates calculated using current U.S. dollar GDP weights. Sample includes: Australia, Canada, Denmark, Finland, the Euro Area, Japan, New Zealand, Norway, Sweden, Switzerland, the United States, and the United Kingdom. Last observation is 2018Q2.
D. Figure shows fiscal multipliers 1 year on at different levels of fiscal space. These are based on estimates from the IPVAR model of Huidrom et al. (2016). A country is considered to have "wide" fiscal space if it is in the lowest quartile of advanced economies for government debt, and to have "narrow" fiscal space if it is in the highest quartile. Orange lines represent the 16-84 percent confidence bands.

and the Bank of Japan have signaled that they will be holding policy rates at current levels in the near term.

For the first time since the financial crisis, the main U.S. policy rate is approaching its neutral level (Figure 1.20). However, the policy rate is expected to peak at about 3 percent, which

suggests that the Federal Reserve has significantly less room to cut rates before reaching the zero lower bound should a new downturn occur—in the last three downturns, the Federal Reserve cut its policy rate by about 5 percentage points.

To varying degrees, central banks in other advanced economies currently have even less policy space. While unconventional monetary policies could again be deployed, their effectiveness in returning inflation to target and supporting growth is subject to debate (Bernanke 2017a; Engen, Laubach, and Reifschneider 2015; Greenlaw et al. 2018). This lack of monetary space highlights the importance of avoiding a policy-driven downturn in activity, combined with research into alternative methods of providing monetary policy stimulus (Bernanke 2017b; Williams 2017).

Fiscal policy

In many advanced economies, government debt-to-GDP ratios have reached unprecedented levels, with government debt becoming the largest component of total debt. This limits the capacity of countries to provide counter-cyclical fiscal stimulus in response to economic slowdowns (Huidrom et al. 2016).

The United States has enacted significant fiscal stimulus even though the economy is already at or above full employment. This stimulus is expected to result in persistent deficits equivalent to about 5 percent for most of the next decade (CBO 2018). In these circumstances, the consequence of pro-cyclical stimulus is likely to be inflation pressures, higher domestic interest rates, a crowding out of private sector activity, and a widening of the U.S. current account deficit.

Structural policies

Potential growth remains subdued in advanced economies and is likely to slow further in coming years, partly due to aging populations and declining birth rates (Figure 1.21; World Bank 2018k). An increasing number of countries are raising barriers to immigration, which might hasten this deceleration. Immigration is an important reason for rising labor forces in many advanced economies and may also contribute to productivity growth; immigrants skew younger than host populations, and younger populations have been associated with faster labor productivity growth for various industries and occupations (Maestas, Mullen, and Powell 2016; World Bank 2018m). Heightened restrictions on immigration could also worsen fiscal positions, by dampening growth and the net contribution that immigrants typically provide to the government budget (Clements et al. 2015).

Recent trade disputes represent a critical headwind to longer-term prospects. Rising tariffs may already be contributing to weaker productivity by increasing costs, disrupting global supply chains, stranding productive assets, and relocating activity away from the most efficient locations (Melitz 2003). Lack of policy clarity also risks causing firms to delay investment because of uncertainty over market access. This highlights the critical importance of a continued commitment to a rules-based international trading system.

Increasing restrictions to trade and immigration could therefore result in weaker growth and lower productivity. While international trade and immigration can impose costs on some sectors of the economy or vulnerable groups of workers, a better course is to adopt policies that mitigate these costs and redistribute more equitably the benefits of globalization.

Challenges in emerging market and developing economies

Recent financial market stress in some EMDEs highlights the pressing need to strengthen buffers against the risk of less favorable global financial conditions. Fiscal positions remain fragile, underscoring the urgency to improve domestic revenue mobilization and to commit to or deepen fiscal reforms aimed at controlling expenditures. In the longer term, steps to enhance human capital, encourage regional economic integration, and lower barriers to investment for small- and medium-sized enterprises would boost potential growth and help tackle challenges associated with high informality. China's key policy challenge is to foster the transition to more sustainable growth while dealing with trade-related headwinds without overstimulating the economy and delaying the deleveraging process.

FIGURE 1.21 Structural policies in advanced economies

Potential growth is expected to decelerate in advanced economies, partly due to demographic factors. This deceleration is likely to be more severe if government policies lead to heightened restrictions on immigration, as immigrants tend to be younger than the native population.

A. Potential growth in advanced economies

B. Immigrant versus native population age distribution to OECD destinations

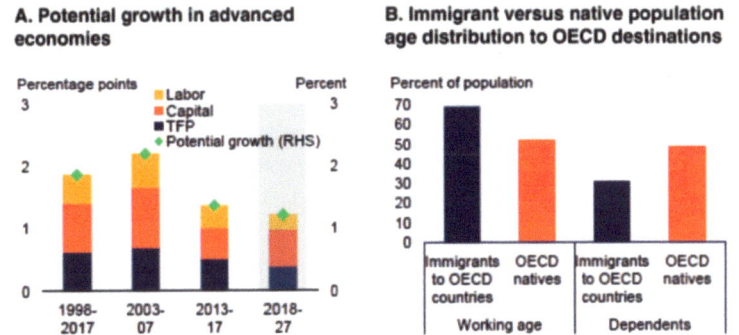

Source: Organisation for Economic Co-operation and Development, World Bank.
A. TFP = total factor productivity growth. Figure shows potential growth estimates based on the production function approach. For further details on potential growth estimates, refer to the January 2018 edition of the *Global Economic Prospects* report. Aggregates calculated using constant 2010 U.S. dollar GDP weights. Sample includes 30 advanced economies.
B. "Working age" includes population aged 25-64 years, "dependents" includes population aged 0-24 and above 65 years. Country-level age proportions are weighted by size of the immigrant population. Data are from the 2010-11 OECD Database on Immigrants in OECD and non-OECD Countries (DIOC-E).

Policy challenges in China

Authorities in China have shifted to looser monetary and fiscal policies in response to a more challenging external environment, including heightened trade tensions. They have cut reserve requirements, introduced new tax breaks for financial institutions lending to small firms, and encouraged banks to buy more local government bonds. They have also reduced taxes and fees, increased export tax rebates, and accelerated issuance of special purpose local government bonds to bolster infrastructure spending. In addition, the authorities have stepped up their structural reform efforts to improve the business environment, including for foreign firms, have strengthened intellectual property protection, and have lowered tariffs on imports—with the exception of some tariffs on U.S. imports in retaliation to U.S. tariffs on China's goods. The authorities' commitment to growth stability and structural reforms was reaffirmed in late December (CEWC 2018).

The trade disputes with the United States, as well as the ongoing moderation of global trade,

FIGURE 1.22 EMDE monetary policy

Monetary and financial policy challenges have been compounded by recent financial market pressures. Policy interest rates and inflation ticked up in EMDEs facing above-average currency depreciation against the U.S. dollar in 2018. The share of EMDEs hiking policy rates during U.S. tightening cycles is markedly higher than the share of EMDEs cutting rates during U.S. easing periods, suggesting that ongoing U.S. normalization may constrain the room of maneuvering for many EMDE central banks. Higher borrowing costs contributed to an increase in sovereign bond spreads, especially in EMDEs with large current account deficits.

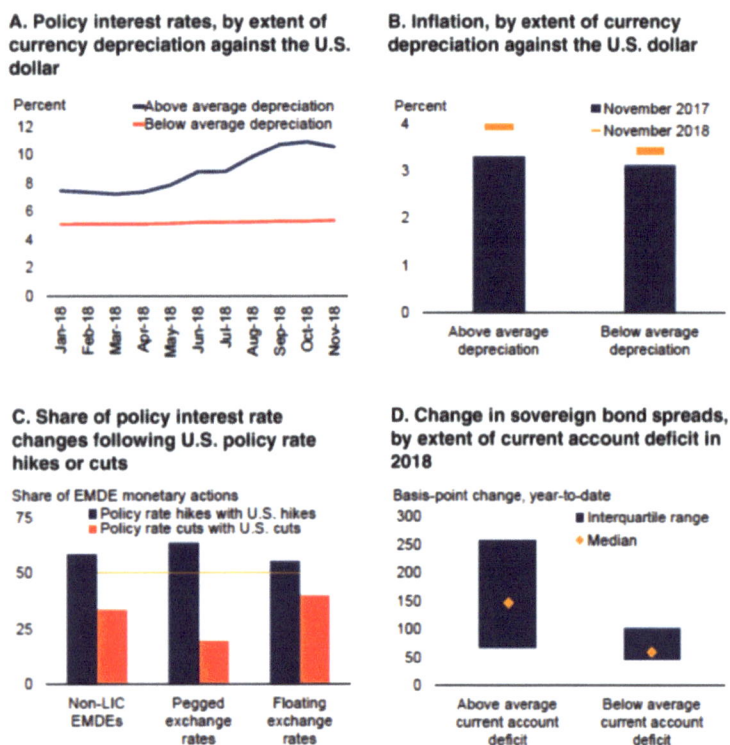

A. Policy interest rates, by extent of currency depreciation against the U.S. dollar

B. Inflation, by extent of currency depreciation against the U.S. dollar

C. Share of policy interest rate changes following U.S. policy rate hikes or cuts

D. Change in sovereign bond spreads, by extent of current account deficit in 2018

Source: Haver Analytics, International Monetary Fund, J.P. Morgan, Shambaugh (2004), World Bank.
A.B. The above average and below average currency depreciation groups are defined by countries above or below the sample average of the year-to-date percent change in the bilateral exchange rate against the U.S. dollar. The sample average is -9.3 percent and includes 27 EMDEs, of which 12 are above and 15 are below average. Last observation is November 2018.
A. The aggregate policy interest rates are calculated using constant 2010 U.S. dollar GDP weights.
B. Median consumer price inflation for each group.
C. Pegged exchange rates are defined, based on a de facto classification, as exchange rates fluctuating within a +/-2 percent band or, at most, a one-time devaluation over the preceding 11-month period relative to a country-specific reference currency. Refer to Shambaugh (2004) for details. Unbalanced sample includes 108 non-LIC EMDEs and considers policy rate actions from 1970 onwards. Last observation is November 2018.
D. The above average and below average current account deficit groups are defined by countries above or below the 2018 sample average of the current account balance. The sample average is -1.6 percent of GDP. The sovereign bond spread is measured by J.P. Morgan Emerging Market Bond Index (EMBI). Sample includes 38 EMDEs. Last observation is December 19, 2018.

highlight China's key policy challenge to foster the transition to more sustainable growth while dealing with trade-related headwinds without overstimulating the economy and delaying the deleveraging process (World Bank 2018b). This will require continued reforms to reduce financial vulnerabilities, including those associated with the accumulation of non-financial enterprise debt.

Additional efforts to enhance market competition, encourage a shift of capital and labor toward more productive firms and sectors, and bolster household consumption would also be needed (World Bank 2018n). Advancing reforms that boost innovation, including through stronger intellectual property rights, would also help alleviate trade frictions while enhancing China's competitiveness in the medium term. In addition, productivity-enhancing investments in health, education, and research and development would encourage a shift from growth that is dependent on physical capital and help offset the impact of adverse demographic trends.

EMDE monetary and financial policies

Policy challenges across many EMDEs have been compounded by recent financial market pressures that have been associated with sizable currency depreciations and capital outflows. Among some key EMDEs, currency and financial market pressures were substantial (e.g., Argentina, Turkey), leading to significant policy tightening and markedly clouding the near-term macroeconomic and financial outlook. More generally, monetary policy became less accommodative in EMDEs that faced above-average currency depreciation, or that used up reserves to stem it (Figure 1.22).

Weaker exchange rates have pushed up inflation across many EMDEs, particularly in some key commodity exporters, highlighting the role of the exchange rate pass-through to domestic prices (e.g., Argentina, Brazil, South Africa; World Bank 2018p). Among commodity importers, price pressures also reflect their cyclical positions, as suggested by their positive output gaps. Higher energy prices in most of 2018 also pushed up inflation in a number of net oil importers (e.g., Egypt, Kenya, Mexico).

The ongoing normalization of advanced-economy monetary policy will continue to pose challenges for EMDEs (Arteta et al. 2015; Obstfeld 2015; Sobrun and Turner 2015). In particular, U.S. tightening cycles spillover to EMDEs mainly through the availability of foreign credit, especially through portfolio bond flows (Bräuning and Ivashina 2018; Koepke 2018). Moreover, the share of EMDEs hiking policy rates during U.S. tightening cycles is markedly higher than the share of EMDEs cutting rates during U.S. easing periods, suggesting that ongoing U.S. normalization may constrain the room of maneuvering for many EMDE central banks. These challenges will be greater for those countries with large external vulnerabilities, such as sizable current account imbalances, weak foreign reserves, and high inflation or external debt (Iacoviello and Navarro 2018). In addition, higher borrowing costs may cause balance sheet, debt service, and rollover difficulties for some EMDE sovereigns and corporates, which could undermine financial stability (Borensztein and Ye 2018; World Bank 2018a). These may be particularly acute in economies facing currency mismatches on corporate and household balance sheets (Davies et al. 2014).

To confront these challenges, EMDE authorities need to urgently address persistent vulnerabilities that render their countries more susceptible to tighter financing conditions, capital flow reversals, and financial market shocks. This includes shoring up the financing of current account deficits to reduce the effects of net portfolio flow reversals, improving public and corporate balance sheet management, and implementing macroprudential frameworks that bolster banking and corporate sector resilience, such as countercyclical capital buffers and stricter reserve ratio or leverage ratio requirements (Cerutti, Claessens, and Laeven 2015; Forbes 2018). In addition, reducing exposures to foreign currency borrowing and currency mismatches, as appropriate, can help contain the financial system's vulnerability to dislocating exchange rate movements (Ahnert et al. 2018). For EMDEs that have made progress on macroprudential reforms, enhancing financial deepening and improving governance could further boost resilience to shocks (Sahay et al. 2015).

EMDE policymakers also need to uphold a credible commitment to medium-term price stability—one that is supported by macroeconomic frameworks that set attainable inflation targets where appropriate, as well as maintain strong institutional independence and transparency. This will be especially critical if the

FIGURE 1.23 EMDE fiscal policy

For the first time in several years, fiscal deficits are projected to be wider in commodity importers than in commodity exporters. Government debt is rising among EMDEs with high foreign-currency-denominated debt or persistent current account deficits. In low-income countries, the cost of servicing debt has risen as the composition has moved from concessionary to market financing. Greater government effectiveness is associated with stronger tax revenue collection.

A. Fiscal deficits

B. Fiscal sustainability gaps, by extent of reliance on foreign-currency-denominated debt

C. Interest rate payments on debt in LICs

D. Tax revenues, by extent of government effectiveness

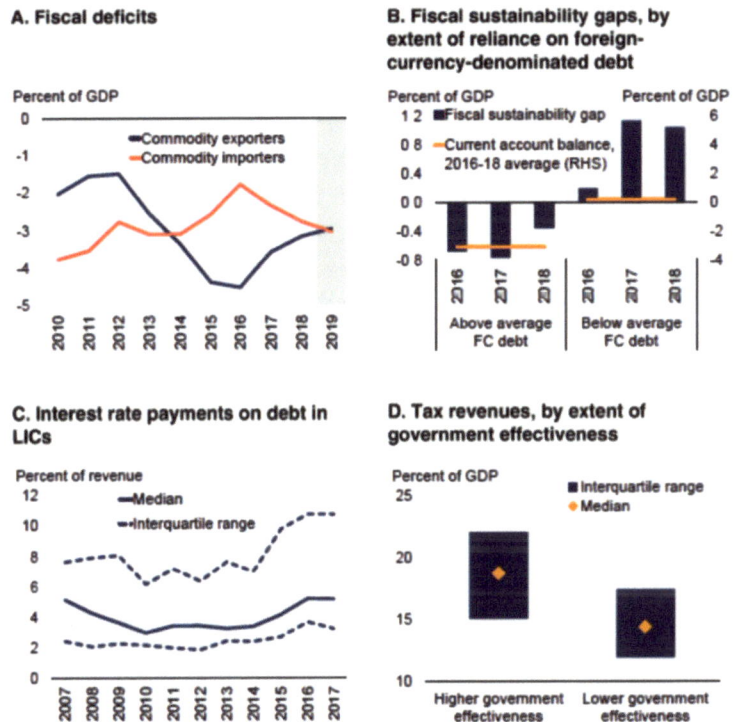

Source: Haver Analytics; International Monetary Fund; Kose, Kurlat et al. (2017); World Bank.
A.C.D. Figures show medians across groups.
A. Shaded area indicates forecasts. Sample includes 151 EMDEs.
B. FC debt = foreign-currency-denominated debt. The sustainability gap is measured as the difference between the primary balance and the debt-stabilizing primary balance, assuming historical median (1990-2016) interest rates and growth rates. A negative gap indicates government debt is rising along an accelerated trajectory. The aggregates are calculated using constant 2010 U.S. dollar GDP weights. The sample includes 27 EMDEs. The above (below) average foreign-currency-denominated debt groups are defined by countries above (below) the sample average of external debt in foreign currency as a share of total external debt in 2017. The sample average is 86.9 percent of GDP.
C. Interest rate payments include those made on government debt to domestic and foreign residents. Solid line represents median and area between the dashed lines represents the interquartile range. The sample includes 30 low-income countries and excludes Somalia, South Sudan, and Syria due to data restrictions.
D. Government effectiveness measured by the Worldwide Governance Indicators. Higher government effectiveness are EMDEs with 2000-17 averages above 0 (stronger governance); lower are EMDEs with 2000-17 average government effectiveness below 0 (weaker governance). Unbalanced sample includes 150 EMDEs.

ongoing period of low and stable global inflation comes to an end, perhaps driven by a slowdown or rollback of the structural factors that have held inflation at bay in recent decades—in particular, trade and financial integration—or an erosion of central bank independence. The reversals of these long-term trends could coincide with cyclical upward pressures on prices in some EMDEs, reigniting inflation (Box 1.1).

EMDE fiscal policy

Government finances in many EMDEs are in a fragile position, with deteriorating debt dynamics and limited fiscal space. In some cases, much needed reforms to improve fiscal space have either stalled or not been fully implemented, while funding new or increasing liabilities, such as public-sector wage bills, have put further strain on domestic revenues (e.g., Brazil, South Africa).

Oil exporters continue to face fiscal sustainability challenges, with recent oil price volatility highlighting the need for these countries to continue to reduce their reliance on oil revenues by deepening reforms that bolster the non-resource budget (e.g., Ecuador, Russia; IMF 2018f). In metals and agricultural producers, weaker-than-envisaged commodity prices could put further pressure on already fragile public finances (e.g., South Africa, Zambia). Among commodity importers, for the first time since the oil price collapse that began in 2014, fiscal deficits are projected to be larger as a share of GDP than those in commodity exporters, as waning revenue growth continues to be accompanied by strong expenditure growth (Figure 1.23).

Across EMDEs, rising global interest rates will make financing fiscal deficits through sovereign debt issuance more costly, underscoring the need to realign government spending with revenue and to manage the composition of debt, particularly in countries with elevated foreign-currency-denominated debt or persistent current account deficits (Du and Schreger 2016). In a rising global interest rate environment, employing expansionary fiscal policy with limited fiscal space can amplify vulnerabilities by increasing market perceptions of sovereign credit risk, which may lead to higher sovereign bond yields and borrowing costs (Bi, Shen, and Yang 2014; Corsetti et al. 2013). LICs are more vulnerable to rising global financial costs than in the past, as LIC debt has increasingly shifted from concessionary to market financing (Chapter 4; World Bank 2018a). More generally, EMDE governments with high private-sector debt are exposed to contingent liabilities if banking sector stress materializes in a rising interest rate environment (World Bank 2018k).

Regaining policy buffers is a key priority to be able to use countercyclical fiscal policy to stabilize growth (World Bank 2015). Efforts to build fiscal space could include implementing credible medium-term expenditure or deficit targets, better managing contingent liabilities to contain fiscal risks, stabilizing debt, and reforming the tax system to improve domestic resource mobilization and the investment climate—e.g., adjusting statutory rates, broadening bases, eliminating loopholes and exemptions, and improving tax administration and compliance. Managing the composition of debt can also help address public-sector balance sheet vulnerabilities. For EMDEs with elevated foreign-currency-denominated debt, bolstering domestic-currency bond markets, if feasible, could help stem rollover and currency risks.

To complement these efforts, improving government effectiveness and strengthening institutions would support tax revenue collection (Ajaz and Ahmad 2010; Prichard 2010). If fiscal adjustment remains necessary to ensure long-term fiscal sustainability, policymakers need to evaluate the efficacy of public expenditures, prioritizing spending on quality investment and safeguarding poverty-reducing social transfers, while reining in programs that are unproductive or inefficient (World Bank 2018k, 2018p). EMDE fiscal policymakers also need to confront the longer-term challenges posed by high informality, as its prevalence in some regions reduces government revenues through tax base erosion (Chapter 3).

EMDE structural policies

EMDEs also face substantial longer-term challenges to ensure sustained improvements in incomes and living standards amid rapid technological and demographic changes. Meeting these challenges will require, among other actions, effective investments in human capital, efforts to accelerate regional and global integration, and measures to free up a large untapped potential for growth and productivity gains among small- and medium-sized enterprises. Progress in these areas would also help bring people and companies out of informality.

Improving human capital

Under-investment in human capital has left large parts of the workforce in EMDEs unprepared for rapid technological changes and future skill requirements (Flabbi and Gatti 2018). This represents a significant bottleneck to growth in many countries. Moreover, continued divergences in the demand for high- and low-skilled labor could exacerbate income inequality over time. How education systems adapt to skills needs will be a key determinant of the productivity and distributional effects of technological change (Barro and Lee 2015).

Improving student learning is particularly important, starting with an effective measurement of the performance of education systems. Measures that capture both the quantity and quality of learning, such as learning-adjusted years of schooling, reflect relevant dimensions of success and are better predictors of subsequent growth across EMDEs (Figure 1.24; Filmer et al. 2018). A focus on both schooling participation and learning results can more properly inform policy actions and support effective investments in human capital (World Bank forthcoming).

Beyond a heightened focus on learning outcomes, a comprehensive approach to human capital improvements in EMDEs should also address other dimensions, including malnutrition and health throughout the life cycle. In this context, a human capital index has recently been developed to assess productivity gains that could be achieved by matching education and health outcomes to best practices (Kraay 2018). This benchmarking exercise helps to identify areas of intervention to improve public spending and governance in education and health systems—and to raise awareness of the costs of inaction (World Bank 2018q).

The urgency to bolster human capital comes in a period of constrained public-sector resources and elevated debt levels, creating a notable policy challenge. Accordingly, more effective spending in education and health will need to be accompanied by renewed efforts to prioritize government spending, improve efficiency of public administrations and revenue mobilization, and encourage private sector participation.

FIGURE 1.24 EMDE structural policies

Learning-adjusted years of schooling are a good predictor of growth performance in EMDEs. Greater trade integration, as well as lower barriers to investment in small- and medium-sized enterprises, could help boost productivity in EMDEs. Informality remains prevalent in EMDEs and is generally associated with large productivity gaps between formal and informal sectors.

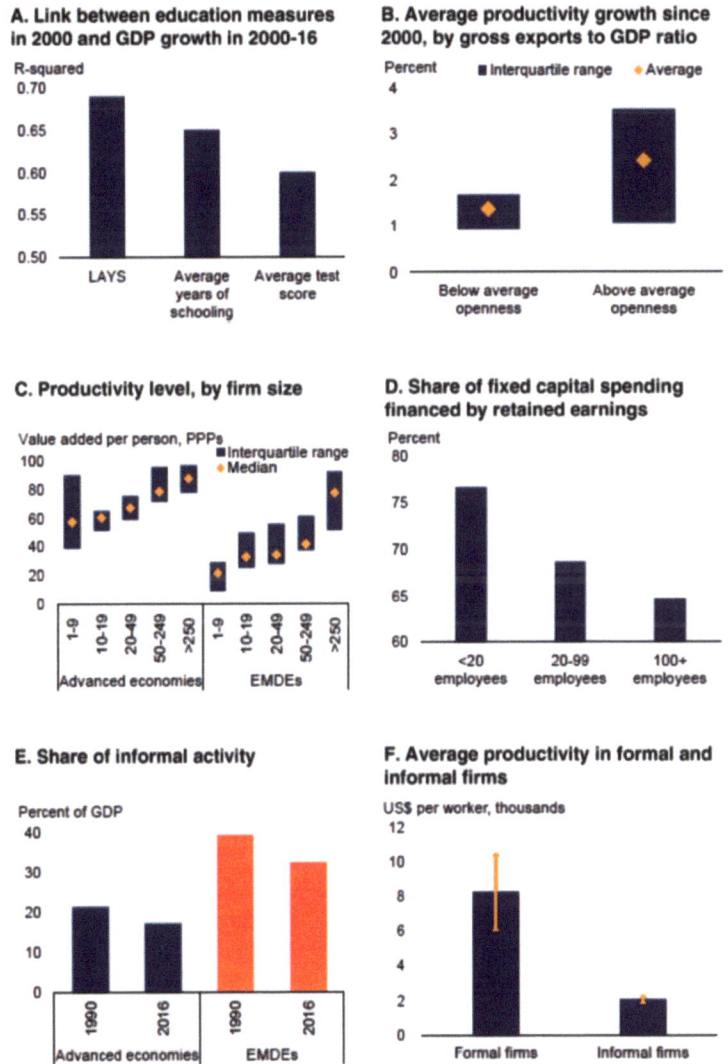

A. Link between education measures in 2000 and GDP growth in 2000-16

B. Average productivity growth since 2000, by gross exports to GDP ratio

C. Productivity level, by firm size

D. Share of fixed capital spending financed by retained earnings

E. Share of informal activity

F. Average productivity in formal and informal firms

Source: Ayyagari, Demirgüç-Kunt, and Maksimovic (2017); Borensztein and Ye (2018); Elgin et al. (forthcoming); Filmer et al. (2018); Organisation for Economic Co-operation and Development; World Bank.
A. LAYS = learning-adjusted years of schooling. Figure shows regression of three measures of education in 2000—LAYS, average years of schooling, and average test score—on average GDP growth over the period 2000-16 across EMDEs. Test scores are from the mathematics assessment of the 1999 Trends in International Mathematics and Science Study (TIMSS) and 2000 Program for International Student Assessment (PISA). Regression conditioned on original GDP per capita levels.
B. Above average and below average indicate above and below average changes in gross exports to GDP ratios over the period 2000-14.
C. Productivity is defined as the value added per person employed, measured in thousands of U.S. dollars in current PPP terms. Data as of 2015, or latest available year. Advanced economies include Austria, Denmark, Finland, France, Germany, Italy, Netherlands, Spain, Sweden, and the United Kingdom. EMDEs include Brazil, Hungary, Mexico, Poland, and Turkey.
D. Proportion of the purchase of fixed assets financed by internal funds or retained earnings.
E. Unweighted averages, in percent of official GDP. Estimates of informal output derived from a deterministic dynamic general equilibrium model, as described in Chapter 3.
F. Blue bars represent estimates and orange vertical lines indicate two standard deviation error bands. World Bank's Enterprise Survey data for 135 countries (2008-18). Labor productivity is proxied by annual sales per worker.

Boosting regional and international integration

If faced with growing protectionist measures, policymakers in EMDEs may be tempted to resort to retaliatory action or unilateral increases in barriers to trade. While such measures could help recapture some of their terms-of-trade losses, an increase in trade barriers would likely lead to significant distortionary effects and efficiency losses for EMDEs (Devarajan et al. 2018). Instead, continued commitment to regional and international integration through trade liberalization, properly designed free trade agreements, and participation in global value chains (GVCs) within an open and rules-based multilateral trading system could yield significant, previously untapped benefits for EMDEs. The call of G20 members to consider additional reform of the World Trade Organization could be a chance to maximize development opportunities for EMDEs.

International integration enables firms of all sizes to increase their participation in international trade. In particular, participation in GVCs helps companies specialize in tasks closely aligned with their comparative advantage and can contribute to a more efficient allocation of resources, job creation, and export diversification. In turn, increased trade openness and GVC integration boost productivity growth and helps the diffusion of technologies (Criscuolo and Timmis 2017; Elms and Low 2013).

Many EMDEs and LICs, however, still face important challenges in fostering an environment conducive to greater GVC integration. Although their participation has increased during the last two decades, LICs still have little presence in GVCs. Participation is hindered by domestic capacity constraints and restrictive trade and investment regimes. Tariffs and other barriers to trade increase costs for firms, reduce their ability to access foreign inputs, and can impede the development of downstream industries (Miroudot, Rouzet, and Spinelli 2013). Reducing these barriers remains a key priority to support GVC participation, and to increase trade gains for many EMDEs (Kowalski at al. 2015). Closer physical integration of transport networks and other

regional infrastructure can also help reduce the cost of trade and support increased openness (Donaldson 2018).

That said, increased international integration and participation in GVCs does not guarantee positive and sustainable development outcomes for EMDEs. Targeted policies that encourage the upgrading of domestic production are crucial in ensuring that the social and development impacts of GVC activities are optimized (Fessehaie and Morris 2018; Taglioni and Winkler 2016).

Untapping SME growth potential

Supported with appropriate frameworks, small- and medium-sized enterprises (SMEs) can be key drivers of growth and job creation in EMDEs (Ayyagari, Demirgüç-Kunt, and Maksimovic 2017). They can play a central role in industrial development and restructuring, support larger firms with inputs and services, and allow increased sectoral specialization. However, their growth potential continues to be hindered by many factors, including insufficient access to finance; tax and regulatory burdens; skills mismatch; limited access to infrastructure, particularly electricity; and corruption (Wang 2016). Alleviating those obstacles could lead to significant growth windfalls for EMDEs, given that SMEs have the largest untapped potential for productivity catch-up with advanced economies (Cusolito, Safadi, and Taglioni 2017). Supporting SME development could also help reduce high informality in some regions, which is most prevalent among micro-enterprises.

Limited access to finance is most often cited as a key obstacle to SME growth in EMDEs, forcing these companies to rely on retained earnings to fund investment. This leads to sub-optimal capital spending and an unrealized potential for expansion and job creation. Key obstacles include the lack of reliable credit information, the absence of suitable collateral, and weak legal institutions. Increasing SME access to finance could help boost their average size and support innovation and job creation (Ayyagari, Demirgüç-Kunt, and Maksimovic 2017; Ayyagari et al. 2016). Improved access to finance for women entrepreneurs could also lead to more investment, while access to savings account for female-headed households could result in additional spending on education (Demirgüç-Kunt et al. 2018; Sahay and Cihak 2018). Bankruptcy protection laws also lag international best practices in many EMDEs. Historical experience suggests that strengthening bankruptcy protection can boost investment activity and facilitate responsible corporate risk-taking, helping to relieve the costs of debt overhang (Gopalan, Mukherjee, and Singh 2016; World Bank 2014).

Beyond basic education, technological know-how, managerial capabilities, and tolerance for risk are also key factors underlying successful entrepreneurship and vibrant firm dynamics (Cusolito and Maloney 2018). Conditions that encourage experimentation and do not penalize failure are crucial to support the upgrading of firm capabilities and diffusion of technological progress. Tax, registration, and other administrative simplifications can also be successful tools to facilitate SME creation and expansion (Bruhn 2011). Finally, restrained access to infrastructure, particularly electricity, is often mentioned as a major barrier to the development of SMEs and start-up companies in many EMDEs, especially in Sub-Saharan Africa. Improvements in both traditional power line supplies and off-grid solutions such as solar energy and micro grids need to be achieved in tandem, supported by proper policy incentives and effective regulations (World Bank 2017).

Growing out of informality

Informality remains widespread in many EMDEs (Chapter 3). It is particularly prevalent in less developed regions, with South Asia and Sub-Saharan Africa accounting for nearly 60 percent of all informal workers in EMDEs. It is also elevated in regions with weak institutions and high levels of fiscal and regulatory burdens, such as Latin America and the Caribbean and Europe and Central Asia.

While the informal economy provides an important safety net to workers, particularly during downturns, it can dampen growth by weighing on physical and human capital formation (Docquier, Müller, and Naval 2017; Oviedo, Komas, and Karakurum-Ozdemir 2009). In particular, firms operating in the informal economy tend to limit their size to avoid detection and use less advanced production technologies (Dabla-Norris et al. 2018). Their lack of compliance with regulations and taxes may help them stay in business despite low productivity (La Porta and Shleifer 2014; Schneider and Enste 2000; Box 3.4).

High informality can also limit fiscal revenues and thus can constrain the ability of governments to provide public services, conduct countercyclical policies, and implement effective redistributive measures (Besley and Persson 2014; Ordóñez 2014). Both government revenues and expenditures are lower in EMDEs where informality is widespread. High informality is often associated with lack of development, limited access to finance, low human capital, poor governance, and heavy regulatory burdens. If properly designed, policies that help improve outcomes in those areas would bolster growth prospects and encourage workers to participate in the formal economy, thus helping reduce informality and its associated challenges.

Policies that are implemented with other purposes in mind also need to take into consideration the unintended consequences on informality. For example, changes in labor market regulation accompanying the decentralization of minimum-wage-setting responsibilities or the liberalization of trade have resulted in higher informality in some countries (Attanasio, Goldberg, and Pavcnik 2004; Goldberg and Pavcnik 2003; Chapter 3; Box 3.4). These experiences are a reminder of the need to design comprehensive reform packages that are calibrated to country circumstances.

TABLE 1.2 List of emerging market and developing economies[1]

Commodity exporters[2]		Commodity importers[3]	
Albania*	Madagascar	Afghanistan	Panama
Algeria*	Malawi	Antigua and Barbuda	Philippines
Angola*	Malaysia*	Bahamas, The	Poland
Argentina	Mali	Bangladesh	Romania
Armenia	Mauritania	Barbados	Samoa
Azerbaijan*	Mongolia	Belarus	Serbia
Bahrain*	Morocco	Bhutan	Seychelles
Belize	Mozambique	Bosnia and Herzegovina	Solomon Islands
Benin	Myanmar*	Bulgaria	Sri Lanka
Bolivia*	Namibia	Cabo Verde	St. Kitts and Nevis
Botswana	Nicaragua	Cambodia	St. Lucia
Brazil	Niger	China	St. Vincent and the Grenadines
Burkina Faso	Nigeria*	Comoros	Thailand
Burundi	Oman*	Croatia	Tunisia
Cameroon*	Papua New Guinea	Djibouti	Turkey
Chad*	Paraguay	Dominica	Tuvalu
Chile	Peru	Dominican Republic	Vanuatu
Colombia*	Qatar*	Egypt	Vietnam
Congo, Dem. Rep.	Russia*	El Salvador	
Congo, Rep.*	Rwanda	Eritrea	
Costa Rica	Saudi Arabia*	Eswatini	
Côte d'Ivoire	Senegal	Fiji	
Ecuador*	Sierra Leone	Georgia	
Equatorial Guinea*	South Africa	Grenada	
Ethiopia	Sudan*	Haiti	
Gabon*	Suriname	Hungary	
Gambia, The	Tajikistan	India	
Ghana*	Tanzania	Jamaica	
Guatemala	Timor-Leste*	Jordan	
Guinea	Togo	Kiribati	
Guinea-Bissau	Tonga	Lebanon	
Guyana	Trinidad and Tobago*	Lesotho	
Honduras	Turkmenistan*	Macedonia, FYR	
Indonesia*	Uganda	Maldives	
Iran*	Ukraine	Marshall Islands	
Iraq*	United Arab Emirates*	Mauritius	
Kazakhstan*	Uruguay	Mexico	
Kenya	Uzbekistan	Micronesia, Fed. Sts.	
Kosovo	Venezuela*	Moldova, Rep.	
Kuwait*	West Bank and Gaza	Montenegro	
Kyrgyz Republic	Zambia	Nepal	
Lao PDR	Zimbabwe	Pakistan	
Liberia		Palau	

* Energy exporters.
[1] Emerging market and developing economies (EMDEs) include all those that are not classified as advanced economies. Dependent territories are excluded. Advanced economies include Australia; Austria; Belgium; Canada; Cyprus; the Czech Republic; Denmark; Estonia; Finland; France; Germany; Greece; Hong Kong SAR, China; Iceland; Ireland; Israel; Italy; Japan; the Republic of Korea; Latvia; Lithuania; Luxembourg; Malta; Netherlands; New Zealand; Norway; Portugal; Singapore; the Slovak Republic; Slovenia; Spain; Sweden; Switzerland; the United Kingdom; and the United States.
[2] An economy is defined as commodity exporter when, on average in 2012-14, either (i) total commodities exports accounted for 30 percent or more of total goods exports or (ii) exports of any single commodity accounted for 20 percent or more of total goods exports. Economies for which these thresholds were met as a result of re-exports were excluded. When data were not available, judgment was used. This taxonomy results in the classification of some well-diversified economies as importers, even if they are exporters of certain commodities (e.g., Mexico).
[3] Commodity importers are all EMDEs that are not classified as commodity exporters.

References

Acharya, V., S. Cecchetti, J. Gregorio, Ş. Kalemli-Özcan, P. Lane, and U. Panizza. 2015. "Corporate Debt in Emerging Economies: A Threat to Financial Stability?" Brookings Institution Report, Washington, DC.

Ahmed, S., B. Coulibaly, and A. Zlate. 2015. "International Financial Spillovers to Emerging Market Economies: How Important Are Economic Fundamentals?" International Finance Discussion Papers 1135, Board of Governors of the Federal Reserve System, Washington, DC.

Ahnert, T., K. Forbes, C. Friedrich, and D. Reinhardt. 2018. "Macroprudential FX Regulations: Shifting the Snowbanks of FX Vulnerability?" NBER Working Paper 25083, National Bureau of Economic Research, Cambridge, MA.

Ahuja, M. A., and M. M. Nabar. 2012. "Investment-Led Growth in China: Global Spillovers." IMF Working Paper 12/267, International Monetary Fund, Washington, DC.

Aisen, A., and F. J. Veiga. 2013. "How Does Political Instability Affect Economic Growth?" European Journal of Political Economy 29 (March): 151-67.

Ajaz, T., and E. Ahmad. 2010. "The Effect of Corruption and Governance on Tax Revenues." Pakistan Development Review 49 (4): 405-417

Aksoy, C., S. Guriev, and D. Treisman. 2018. "Globalization, Government Popularity, and the Great Skill Divide." NBER Working Paper 25062, National Bureau of Economic Research, Cambridge, MA.

Alter, A., and S. Elekdag. 2016. "Emerging Market Corporate Leverage and Global Financial Conditions." IMF Working Paper 16/243, International Monetary Fund, Washington, DC.

Andolfatto, D., and A. Spewak. 2018. "On the Supply of, and Demand for, U.S. Treasury Debt." Economic Synopses, Federal Reserve Bank of St. Louis.

Andrews, D., C. Criscuolo, and P. Gal. 2016. "The Best Versus the Rest: The Global Productivity Slowdown, Divergence Across Firms and the Role of Public Policy." OECD Productivity Working Paper 5, Organisation for Economic Co-operation and Development, Paris.

Arteta, C., M. A. Kose, F. Ohnsorge, and M. Stocker. 2015. "The Coming U.S. Interest Rate Tightening Cycle: Smooth Sailing or Stormy Waters?" Policy Research Note 2, World Bank, Washington, DC.

Attanasio, O., P. Goldberg, and N. Pavcnik. 2004. "Trade Reforms and Wage Inequality in Colombia." Journal of Development Economics 74 (2): 331-366.

Ayyagari, M., A. Demirguc-Kunt, and V. Maksimovic. 2017. "SME Finance." Policy Research Working Paper 8241, World Bank, Washington, DC.

Ayyagari, M., P. F. Juarros, M.S. Martinez Peria, and S. Singh. 2016. "Access to Finance and Job Growth: Firm-level Evidence Across Developing Countries." Policy Research Working Paper 7604, World Bank, Washington, DC.

Baffes, J., M. A. Kose, F. L. Ohnsorge, and M. Stocker. 2015. "The Great Plunge in Oil Prices: Causes, Consequences, and Policy Responses." Policy Research Note 1, World Bank, Washington, DC.

Baker, S. R., N. Bloom, and S. J. Davis. 2016. "Measuring Economic Policy Uncertainty." The Quarterly Journal of Economics 131 (4): 1593-1636.

Baldwin, R. 2018. "Trump Can't Fix a 21st Century Problem with 20th Century Thinking", VoxEU.org, CEPR Policy Portal, 27 September 2018. https://voxeu.org/content/trump-can-t-fix-21st-century-problem-20th-century-thinking.

Bank of England. 2018. EU Withdrawal Scenarios and Monetary and Financial Stability: A Response to the House of Commons Treasury Committee. November. London: Bank of England.

Barro, R., and J. Lee. 2015. Education Matters: Global Schooling Gains from the 19th to the 21st Century. New York, NY: Oxford University Press.

Beltran, D., K. Garud, and A. Rosenblum. 2017. "Emerging Market Nonfinancial Corporate Debt: How Concerned Should We Be?" International Finance Discussion Paper Notes, June, Board of Governors of the Federal Reserve System, Washington, DC.

Berkovec, J., Y. Chang, and D. McManus. 2012. "Alternative Lending Channels and the Crisis in U.S. Housing Markets." Real Estate Economics 40, Special Issue No. 1: S8-S31.

Bernadini, M., and L. Forni. 2017. "Private and Public Debt: Are Emerging Markets at Risk?" IMF Working Paper 17/61, International Monetary Fund, Washington, DC.

Bernanke, B. S. 2017a. "Monetary Policy in a New Era." Paper presented at the Peterson Institute conference on "Rethinking Macroeconomic Policy," Washington, October 12-13.

———. 2017b. "Temporary Price-Level Targeting: An Alternative Framework for Monetary Policy." Brookings Institution Blog, October 12, 2017. https://www.brookings.edu/blog/ben-bernanke/2017/10/12/temporary-price-level-targeting-an-alternative-framework-for-monetary-policy.

———. 2007. "Globalization and Monetary Policy," Speech at the Fourth Economic Summit, Stanford Institute for Economic Policy Research, Stanford, CA.

Bernanke, B. S., and M. Gertler. 1995. "Inside the Black Box: The Credit Channel of Monetary Policy Transmission." *The Journal of Economic Perspectives* 9 (4): 27-48.

Besley, T., and T. Persson. 2014. "Why do Developing Countries Tax So Little?" *Journal of Economic Perspectives*, 28 (4): 99-120.

Bi, H., W. Shen, and S. Yang. 2014. "Fiscal Limits, External Debt, and Fiscal Policy in Developing Countries." IMF Working Paper 14/49, International Monetary Fund, Washington, DC.

Bordo, M., and C. Meissner. 2016. "Fiscal and Financial Crises." NBER Working Paper 22059, National Bureau of Economic Research.

Bordo, M. D., and A. Orphanides. 2013. *The Great Inflation: The Rebirth of Modern Central Banking.* Chicago: University of Chicago Press.

Borensztein, E., and L. Ye. 2018. "Corporate Debt Overhang and Investment: Firm-Level Evidence." Policy Research Working Paper 8553, World Bank, Washington, DC.

Bown, C. 2018. "Protectionism Was Threatening Global Supply Chains Before Trump." VoxEU.org, CEPR Policy Portal, October 30, 2018. https://voxeu.org/article/protectionism-was-threatening-global-supply-chains-trump.

Bown, C., E. Jung, and Y. Zhang. 2018. "Trump's Steel Tariffs Have Hit Smaller and Poorer Countries the Hardest." Peterson Institute for International Economics, November 2018.

Bräuning, F., and V. Ivashina. 2018. "U.S. Monetary Policy and Emerging Market Credit Cycles." NBER Working Paper 25185, National Bureau of Economic Research, Cambridge, MA.

Bruhn, M. 2011. "Reforming Business Taxes: What is the Effect on Private Sector Development?" Viewpoint: Public Policy for the Private Sector, Note No. 330, World Bank, Washington, DC.

Brynjolfsson, E., and A. McAfee. 2014. *The Second Machine Age: Work, Progress, and Prosperity in a Time of Brilliant Technologies.* New York; W. W. Norton & Company.

Burger, M. J., and E. I. Ianchovichina. 2017. "Surges and Stops in Greenfield and M&A FDI Flows to Developing Countries: Analysis by Mode of Entry." *Review of World Economics* 153 (2): 411-432.

Buttiglione L., P. Lane, L. Reichlin, and V. Reinhart. 2014. "Deleveraging, What Deleveraging? The 16th Geneva Report on the World Economy," CEPR Press, Center for Economic and Policy Research, Washington, DC.

Caballero, J. 2014. "Do Surges in International Capital Inflows Influence the Likelihood of Banking Crises?" *Economic Journal* 136 (591): 281-316.

Caldara, D., and M. Iacoviello. 2017. "Measuring Geopolitical Risk." Working Paper, Board of Governors of the Federal Reserve System, Washington, DC.

Carney, M. 2015. "Inflation in a Globalised World." Remarks at the Economic Policy Symposium, Federal Reserve Bank of Kansas City, Jackson Hole, August 29.

Carstens, A. 2018. Interview with Börsen-Zeitung, May 22, 2018.

Castro, V. 2013. "The Duration of Business Cycle Expansions and Contractions: Are There Change-Points in Duration Dependence?" *Journal of Empirical Economics* 44 (2): 511-544.

CBO (Congressional Budget Office). 2018. *The Budget and Economic Outlook: 2018 to 2028.* Washington, DC: Congressional Budget Office.

CEWC (Central Economic Work Conference). 2018. Summary of Conference Proceedings. Available at https://news.sina.com.cn/o/2018-12-21/doc-ihqhqcir9028199.shtml (Chinese).

Cerutti, E., S. Claessens, and L. Laeven. 2015. "The Use and Effectiveness of Macroprudential Policies: New Evidence." IMF Working Papers 15/61, International Monetary Fund, Washington, DC.

Ciccarelli, M., and B. Mojon. 2010. "Global Inflation." *The Review of Economics and Statistics* 92 (3): 524-535.

Claessens, S., A. Kose, and M. Terrones. 2012. "How do Business and Financial Cycles Interact?" *Journal of International Economics* 87 (1): 178-190.

Clements, B., K. Dybczak, V. Gaspar, S. Gupta, and M. Soto. 2015. "The Fiscal Consequences of Shrinking Populations." IMF Staff Discussion Note 15/21, International Monetary Fund, Washington, DC.

Cline, W. R. 1981. *World Inflation and the Developing Countries.* Washington, DC: Brookings Institution.

Constantinescu, C., A. Mattoo, A. Mulabdic, and M. Ruta. 2018. "Global Trade Watch 2017: Trade Defies Policy Uncertainty—Will It Last?" World Bank, Washington, DC.

Corsetti, G., K. Kuester, A. Meier, and G. J. Müller. 2013. "Sovereign Risk, Fiscal Policy, and Macroeconomics." *Economic Journal* 123 (566): F99-F132.

Criscuolo, C., and J. Timmis. 2017. "The Relationship Between GVCs and Productivity." *International Productivity Monitor* 32 (Spring): 61-83.

Crump, R., S. Eusepi, and E. Moench. 2018. "The Term Structure of Expectations and Bond Yields." Federal Reserve Bank of New York Staff Reports 775, Federal Reserve Bank of New York, NY.

Cusolito A. P., R. Safadi, and D. Taglioni. 2017. "Inclusive Global Value Chains Policy Options for Small and Medium Enterprises and Low-Income Countries." A co-publication of the World Bank Group and the Organization for Economic Co-operation and Development.

Cusolito, A. P., and W. Maloney. 2018. *Productivity Revisited: Shifting Paradigms in Analysis and Policy.* Washington, DC: World Bank.

Dabla-Norris, M. E., L. Jaramillo, F. Lima, and A. Sollaci. 2018. "Size Dependent Policies, Informality and Misallocation." IMF Working Paper 18/179, International Monetary Fund, Washington, DC.

Davies, G., M. Obstfeld, A. M. Taylor, and D. Wilson. 2014. "Will Emerging Market Jitters Morph into a Crisis?" Fulcrum Research Paper. https://www.ambassadorfms.com/resources/201403-Fulcrum-Research-Paper---Will-emerging-market-jitters-morph-into-a-crisis.pdf.

Demirgüç-Kunt, A., L. Klapper, D. Singer, S. Ansar, and J. Hess. 2018. *The Global Findex Database 2017: Measuring Financial Inclusion and the Fintech Revolution.* Washington, DC: World Bank.

Devarajan, S., D. S. Go, C. Lakatos, S. Robinson, and K. Thierfelder. 2018. "Traders' Dilemma: Developing Countries' Response to Trade Disputes." Policy Research Working Paper 8640, World Bank, Washington, DC.

Diamandis, P., and S. Kotler. 2012. *Abundance: The Future is Better than You Think.* New York: Free Press.

Diebold, F., and G. Rudebusch. 1999. *Business Cycles: Durations, Dynamics, and Forecasting.* Princeton: Princeton University Press.

Dincer, N., and B. Eichengreen. 2014. "Central Bank Transparency and Independence: Updates and New Measures." *International Journal of Central Banking* 10 (1): 189-259.

Dobbs, R, S. Lund, J. Woetzel, and M. Mutafchieva. 2015. "Debt and (not much) Deleveraging." McKinsey Global Institute, Washington, DC.

Docquier, F., T. Müller, and J. Naval. 2017. "Informality and Long-Run Growth." *The Scandinavian Journal of Economics* 119 (4): 1040-1085.

Donaldson, D. 2018. "Railroads of the Raj: Estimating the Impact of Transportation Infrastructure." *The American Economic Review* 108 (4-5): 899-934.

Draghi, M. 2015. "Global and Domestic Inflation." Speech at the Economic Club of New York, December 4.

Du, W., and J. Schreger. 2016. "Sovereign Risk, Currency Risk, and Corporate Balance Sheets." Harvard Business School BGIE Unit Working Paper 17-024, Harvard University, Cambridge, MA.

ECB (European Central Bank). 2016. "Understanding the Weakness in Global Trade: What is the New Normal?" Occasional Paper Series Number 178, September, Frankfurt am Main.

———. 2018. *Financial Stability Review.* November. Frankfurt am Main: European Central Bank.

Eichengreen, B., and P. Gupta. 2016. "Managing Sudden Stops." Policy Research Working Paper 7639, World Bank, Washington, DC.

Elgin, C., M. A. Kose, F. Ohnsorge, and S. Yu. Forthcoming. "Measuring the Informal Economy and its Business Cycles." Mimeo, World Bank, Washington, DC.

Elms, D. K., and P. Low, eds. 2013. *Global Value Chains in a Changing World.* World Trade Organization, Fung Global Institute, Temasek Foundation Center for Trade and Negotiations. Geneva: WTO Publications.

Engen, E., T. Laubach, and D. Reifschneider. 2015. "The Macroeconomic Effects of the Federal

Reserve's Unconventional Monetary Policies." Board of Governors of the Federal Reserve System, Finance and Economics Discussion Series 2015-005, Washington, DC.

Feng, L., Z. Li, and D. Swenson. 2017. "Trade Policy Uncertainty and Exports: Evidence from China's WTO Accession." *Journal of International Economics* 106 (May): 20-36.

Fessehaie, J., and M. Morris. 2018. *Global Value Chains and Sustainable Development Goals: What Role for Trade and Industrial Policies*. Geneva: International Centre for Trade and Sustainable Development Report.

Filmer, D., H. Rogers, N. Angrist, and S. Sabarwal. 2018. "Learning-Adjusted Years of Schooling (LAYS): Defining A New Macro Measure of Education." Policy Research Working Paper 8591, World Bank, Washington, D.C.

Fischer, S. 2015. "Global and Domestic Inflation." Speech at Crockett Governors' Roundtable 2015 for African Central Bankers, University of Oxford, Oxford.

Flabbi, L., and R. Gatti. 2018. "A Primer on Human Capital." Policy Research Working Paper 8309, World Bank, Washington, DC.

FOMC (Federal Open Market Committee). 2018. "Economic Projections of Federal Reserve Board Members and Federal Reserve Bank Presidents Under their Individual Assessments of Projected Appropriate Monetary Policy, December 2018." Projection Materials, Board of Governors of the Federal Reserve System, Washington, DC.

Forbes, K. 2018. "Macroprudential Policy after the Crisis: Forging a Thor's Hammer for Financial Stability in Iceland." Mimeo, MIT-Sloan School of Management, Massachusetts Institute of Technology, Cambridge, MA.

Freund, C., M. J. Ferrantino, M. Maliszewska, and M. Ruta. 2018. "Impacts on Global Trade and Income of Current Trade Disputes." MTI Practice Notes, Number 2, World Bank, Washington, DC.

FSOC (Financial Stability Oversight Council). 2018. *Annual Report 2018*. December. Washington, DC: Financial Stability Oversight Council.

Gates, S., H. Hegre, H. Nygård, and H. Strand. 2012. "Development Consequences of Armed Conflict." *World Development* 40 (9): 1713-1722.

Gelain, P., K. J. Lansing, and G. J. Natvik. 2018. "Explaining the Boom-Bust Cycle in the U.S. Housing Market: A Reverse-Engineering Approach." *Journal of Money Credit and Banking* 50 (8): 1751-1783.

Gelos, G. 2012. "International Mutual Funds, Capital Flow Volatility, and Contagion—A Survey." In *The Evidence and Impact of Financial Globalization*, edited by G. Caprio Jr., T. Beck, S. Claessens, and S. L. Schmukler. Cambridge, MA: Academic Press.

Goldberg, P. K., and N. Pavcnik. 2003. "The Response of the Informal Sector to Trade Liberalization." *Journal of Development Economics* 72 (2): 463-496.

Gopalan, R., A. Mukherjee, and M. Singh. 2016. "Do Debt Contract Enforcement Costs Affect Financing and Asset Structure?" *Review of Financial Studies* 29 (10): 2774-2813.

Greenlaw, D., J. Hamilton, E. Harris, and K. West. 2018. "A Skeptical View of the Impact of the Fed's Balance Sheet." NBER Working Paper 24687, National Bureau of Economic Research, Cambridge, MA.

Ha, J., A. Ivanova, F. Ohnsorge, and F. Unsal. 2019. "Inflation: Concepts, Evolution and Correlates." In *Inflation in Emerging and Developing Economies: Evolution, Drivers and Policies*, edited by J. Ha, M. A. Kose, and F. Ohnsorge. Washington, DC: World Bank.

Ha, J., M. A. Kose, and F. Ohnsorge. 2019. *Inflation in Emerging and Developing Economies: Evolution, Drivers and Policies*. Washington, DC: World Bank.

Ha, J., M. A. Kose, F. Ohnsorge, and F. Unsal. 2019. "Understanding Global Inflation Synchronization." In *Inflation in Emerging and Developing Economies: Evolution, Drivers and Policies*, edited by J. Ha, M. A. Kose, and F. Ohnsorge. Washington, DC: World Bank.

Ha, J., M. Stocker, and H. Yilmazkuday. 2019. "Inflation and Exchange Rate Pass-Through." In *Inflation in Emerging and Developing Economies: Evolution, Drivers and Policies*, edited by J. Ha, M. A. Kose, and F. Ohnsorge. Washington, DC: World Bank.

Handley, K., and N. Limão. 2015. "Trade and Investment under Policy Uncertainty: Theory and Firm Evidence." *American Economic Journal: Economic Policy* 7 (4): 189-222.

H.M. Treasury. 2018. "EU Exit: Long-Term Economic Analysis." November. HM Government, London.

Hoekman, B. 2015. *The Global Trade Slowdown. A New Normal?* VoxEU ebook. London: CEPR Press.

Holston, K., T. Laubach, and J. Williams. 2016. "Measuring the Natural Rate of Interest: International Trends and Determinants." FRBSF Working Paper 2016-11, Federal Reserve Bank of San Francisco.

Huidrom, R., M. A. Kose, J. J. Lim, and F. L. Ohnsorge. 2016. "Do Fiscal Multipliers Depend on Fiscal Positions?" Policy Research Working Paper 7724, World Bank, Washington, DC.

Iacoviello, M., and G. Navarro. 2018. "Foreign Effects of Higher U.S. Interest Rates." International Finance Discussion Papers 1227, Board of Governors of the Federal Reserve System, Washington, DC.

IMF (International Monetary Fund). 2017. "People's Republic of China: Financial System Stability Assessment—Press Release and Statement by the Executive Director for People's Republic of China." IMF Country Report 17/358, International Monetary Fund, Washington, DC.

————. 2018a. "Challenges for Monetary Policy in Emerging Markets as Global Financial Conditions Normalize." Chapter in *World Economic Outlook*. Washington, DC: International Monetary Fund.

————. 2018b. "Capital Flows to Sub-Saharan Africa: Causes and Consequences." In *Sub-Saharan Africa Regional Economic Outlook: Capital Flows and the Future of Work*. Washington, DC: International Monetary Fund.

————. 2018c. *Fiscal Monitor: Capitalizing on Good Times. April 2018*. Washington, DC: International Monetary Fund.

————. 2018d. *World Economic Outlook October 2018: Challenges to Steady Growth*. October. Washington, DC: International Monetary Fund.

————. 2018e. *Global Financial Stability Report: A Decade after the Global Financial Crisis: Are We Safer?* October. Washington, DC: International Monetary Fund.

————. 2018f. "Saudi Arabia: Selected Issues." IMF Country Report 18/264, International Monetary Fund, Washington, DC.

Johnson, R., and G. Noguera. 2017. "A Portrait of Trade in Value Added over Four Decades." *Review of Economics and Statistics* 99 (5): 896-911.

Koepke, R. 2018. "Fed Policy Expectations and Portfolio Flows to Emerging Markets." *Journal of International Financial Markets, Institutions and Money* 55 (July): 170-194.

Koopman, R., Z. Wang, and S.-J. Wei. 2014. "Tracing Value-Added and Double Counting in Gross Exports." *The American Economic Review* 104 (2): 459-94.

Kopp, E., and P. Williams. 2018. "A Macroeconomic Approach to the Term Premium." IMF Working Paper 18/140, International Monetary Fund, Washington, DC.

Kose, M. A., S. Kurlat, F. L. Ohnsorge, and N. Sugawara. 2017. "A Cross-Country Database of Fiscal Space." Policy Research Working Paper 8157, World Bank, Washington, DC.

Kose, M. A., F. L. Ohnsorge, L. S. Ye, and E. Islamaj. 2017. "Weakness in Investment Growth: Causes, Implications and Policy Responses." Policy Research Working Paper 7990, World Bank, Washington, DC.

Kose, M. A., H. Matsuoka, U. Panizza, and D. Vorisek. 2019. "Inflation Expectations: Review and Evidence." In *Inflation in Emerging and Developing Economies: Evolution, Drivers and Policies*, edited by J. Ha, M. A. Kose, and F. Ohnsorge. Washington, DC: World Bank.

Kose, M. A., and M. E. Terrones. 2015. *Collapse and Revival. Understanding Global Recessions and Recoveries*. Washington, DC: International Monetary Fund.

Kose, M. A., C. Otrok, and E. Prasad. 2012. "Global Business Cycles: Convergence or Decoupling?" *International Economic Review* 53 (2): 511-538.

Kose, M. A., E. Prasad, K. Rogoff, and S.-J. Wei. 2010. "Financial Globalization and Economic Policies." In *Handbook of Development Economics* 5, edited by D. Rodrik, and M. Rosenzweig. Amsterdam: North-Holland.

Kowalski, P., J. L. Gonzalez, A. Ragoussis, and C. Ugarte. 2015. "Participation of Developing Countries in Global Value Chains." OECD Trade Policy Papers 179, Organisation for Economic Co-operation and Development, Paris.

Kraay, A. 2018. "Methodology for a World Bank Human Capital Index." Policy Research Working Paper 8593, World Bank, Washington, DC.

Kutlina-Dimitrova, Z., and C. Lakatos. 2017. "The Global Costs of Protectionism." Policy Research Working Paper 8277, World Bank, Washington, DC.

Laeven, L., and F. Valencia. 2018. "Systemic Banking Crises Revisited." IMF Working Paper 18/206, International Monetary Fund, Washington, DC.

La Porta, R., and A. Shleifer. 2014. "Informality and Development." *Journal of Economic Perspectives* 28 (3): 109-126.

Lindé, J., and A. Pescatori. 2017. "The Macroeconomic Effects of Trade Tariffs: Revisiting the Lerner Symmetry Result." IMF Working Paper 17/151, International Monetary Fund, Washington, DC.

Lodefalk, M. 2014. "The Role of Services for Manufacturing Firm Exports." *Review of World Economics* 150 (1): 59-82.

Lund, S., J. Woetzel, E. Windhagen, R. Dobbs, and D. Goldshtein. 2018. "Rising Corporate Debt: Peril or Promise?" Discussion Paper, McKinsey Global Institute.

Maestas, N., K. J. Mullen, and D. Powell. 2016. "The Effect of Population Aging on Economic Growth, the Labor Force and Productivity," NBER Working Papers 22452, National Bureau of Economic Research, Cambridge, MA.

Mai, N. 2018. "Global Debt and the New Neutral." VoxEU.org, CEPR Policy Portal, June 14 2018. https://voxeu.org/article/global-debt-and-equilibrium-interest-rates.

Maliszewski, W., S. Arslanalp, J. Caparusso, J. Garrido, S. Guo, J. S. Kang, and W. R. Lam. 2016. "Resolving China's Corporate Debt Problem." IMF Working Paper 16/203, International Monetary Fund, Washington, DC.

Melitz, M. J. 2003. "The Impact of Trade on Intra-Industry Reallocations and Aggregate Industry Productivity." *Econometrica* 71 (6): 1695-1725.

Mendoza, E., and M. Terrones, 2012. "An Anatomy of Credits Booms and their Demise." *Journal Economia Chilena* (The Chilean Economy): 15 (2): 4-32.

Mian, A., and A. Sufi. 2009. "The Consequences of Mortgage Credit Expansion: Evidence from the U.S. Mortgage Default Crisis." *The Quarterly Journal of Economics* 124 (4): 1449-1496.

Miroudot, S., and C. Cadestin. 2017. "Services in Global Value Chains: From Inputs to Value-Creating Activities." OECD Trade Policy Papers 197, Organization for Economic Co-operation and Development, Paris.

Miroudot, S., D. Rouzet, and F. Spinelli. 2013. "Trade Policy Implications of Global Value Chains." OECD Trade Policy Papers 161, Organization for Economic Co-operation and Development, Paris, France.

Moriconi, S., G. Peri, and R. Turati. 2018. "Skill of the Immigrants and Vote of the Natives: Immigration and Nationalism in European Elections 2007-2016." NBER Working Paper 25077, National Bureau of Economic Research, Cambridge, MA.

Obstfeld, M. 2015. "Trilemmas and Tradeoffs: Living with Financial Globalization." BIS Working Papers 480, Bank for International Settlements, Basel.

OECD (Organisation for Economic Co-operation and Development). 2018. *Compendium of Productivity Indicators*. Paris: Organisation for Economic Co-operation and Development.

Ohnsorge, F. L., M. Stocker, and Y. M. Some. 2016. "Quantifying Uncertainties in Global Growth Forecasts." Policy Research Working Paper 7770, World Bank, Washington, DC.

Ordóñez, J. 2014. "Tax Collection, the Informal Sector, and Productivity." *Review of Economic Dynamics* 17 (2): 262-286.

Osnago, A., R. Piermartini, and N. Rocha. 2018. "The Heterogeneous Effects of Trade Policy Uncertainty: How Much Do Trade Commitments Boost Trade?" Policy Research Working Paper 8567, World Bank, Washington, DC.

Oviedo, A., M. Thomas, and K. Karakurum-Ozdemir. 2009. "Economic Informality: Causes, Costs, and Policies—Literature Survey." World Bank Working Paper 167, World Bank, Washington, DC.

Park, C., and R. Mercado. 2014. "Determinants of Financial Stress in Emerging Market Economies." *Journal of Banking & Finance* 45 (August): 199-224.

Prichard, W. 2010. "Taxation and State Building: Towards a Governance Focused Tax Reform Agenda." IDS Working Paper 341, Institute of Development Studies, Brighton, United Kingdom.

Raschen, M., and T. Rehbock. 2016. "Common Challenges for Europe and Asia as Interdependence Grows." KfW Research Focus on Economics, Kreditanstalt für Wiederaufbau, Frankfurt am Main.

Rogoff, K. 2003. "Globalization and Global Disinflation." *Federal Reserve Bank of Kansas City Economic Review* 88 (4): 45-78.

———. 2014. "The Exaggerated Death of Inflation." Project Syndicate, September 2.

Rudebusch, G. 2016. "Will the Economic Recovery Die of Old Age?" FRBSF *Economic Letter* 2016-3, Federal Reserve Bank of San Francisco.

Sahay, R., and M. Čihák. 2018. "Women in Finance: A Case for Closing Gaps." IMF Staff Discussion Note. International Monetary Fund, Washington, DC.

Sahay, R., M. Čihák, P. N'Diaye, A. Barajas, R. Bi, D. Ayala, Y. Gao, et al. 2015. "Rethinking Financial Deepening: Stability and Growth in Emerging Markets." IMF Staff Discussion Note 15/08, International Monetary Fund, Washington, DC.

Schneider, F., and D. H. Enste. 2000. "Shadow Economies: Size, Causes, and Consequences." *Journal of Economic Literature* 38 (1): 77-114.

Shambaugh, J. C. 2004. "The Effect of Fixed Exchange Rates on Monetary Policy." *The Quarterly Journal of Economics* 119 (1): 301-352.

Sims, C., and Z. Tao. 2006. "Does Monetary Policy Generate Recessions?" *Macroeconomic Dynamics* 10 (2): 231-272.

Sobrun, J., and P. Turner. 2015. "Bond Markets and Monetary Policy Dilemmas for the Emerging Markets." BIS Working Papers 508, Bank for International Settlements, Basel.

Stocker, M., J. Baffes, Y. Some, D. Vorisek, and C. Wheeler. 2018. "The 2014-16 Oil Price Collapse in Retrospect: Sources and Implications." Policy Research Working Paper 8419, World Bank, Washington, DC.

Taglioni, D., and D. Winkler. 2016. *Making Global Value Chains Work for Development.* Washington, DC: World Bank.

Taylor, J. B. 2014. "Inflation Targeting in Emerging Markets: The Global Experience." Speech at the Conference on Fourteen Years of Inflation Targeting in South Africa and the Challenge of a Changing Mandate, South African Reserve Bank, Pretoria.

UNCTAD (United Nations Conference on Trade and Development). 2018. *World Investment Report— Investment and New Industrial Policies.* Geneva, Switzerland: UNCTAD.

UN and World Bank. 2018. *Pathways for Peace: Inclusive Approaches to Preventing Violent Conflict.* Washington, DC: World Bank.

Van Biesebroeck, J., and T. Sturgeon. 2011. "Global Value Chains in the Automotive Industry: An En-hanced Role for Developing Countries?" *International Journal of Technological Learning, Innovation and Development* 4 (1-3): 181-205.

Végh, C., G. Vuletin, D. Riera-Crichton, J. Medina, D. Friedheim, M. Diego, L. Morano, and L. Venturi. 2018. *From Known Unknowns to Black Swans: How to Manage Risk in Latin America and the Caribbean.* Washington, DC: World Bank.

Vorisek, D., G. Kambou, Y. Okawa, T. Taskin, E. Vashakmadze, and L. S. Ye. Forthcoming. "Potential Growth in Emerging Markets and Developing Economies: Regional Dimensions and Policy Options." Policy Research Working Paper, World Bank, Washington, DC.

Wang, Y. 2016. "What are the Biggest Obstacles to Growth of SMEs in Developing Countries?—An Empirical Evidence from an Enterprise Survey." *Borsa Istanbul Review* 16 (3): 167-176.

Williams, J. 2017. "Preparing for the Next Storm: Reassessing Frameworks & Strategies in a Low R-Star World." Remarks at the Shadow Open Market Committee, New York, New York, May 5.

World Bank. 2014. *World Development Report 2014: Risk and Opportunity, Managing Risk for Development.* Washington, DC: World Bank.

———. 2015. *Global Economic Prospects: Having Fiscal Space and Using It.* January. Washington, DC: World Bank.

———. 2016. *Global Economic Prospects: Spillovers and Weak Growth.* January. Washington, DC: World Bank.

———. 2017. *State of Electricity Access Report 2017.* May. Washington, DC: World Bank.

———. 2018a. *Global Economic Prospects: The Turning of the Tide?* June. Washington, DC: World Bank.

———. 2018b. "Navigating Uncertainty." In *East Asia and Pacific Economic Update.* October. Washington, DC: World Bank.

———. 2018c. *Migration and Remittances: Recent Developments and Outlook.* December. Washington, DC: World Bank.

———. 2018d. *Commodity Markets Outlook. The Changing of the Guard: Shifts in Industrial Commodity Demand.* October. Washington, DC: World Bank.

———. 2018e. "Critical Connections: Promoting Economic Growth and Resilience in Europe and Central Asia." *Europe and Central Asia Economic Update.* October. Washington, DC: World Bank.

———. 2018f. "A New Economy for the Middle East and North Africa." In *Middle East and North Africa Economic Monitor.* October. Washington, DC: World Bank.

―――. 2018g. "Boosting Access to Electricity in Africa through Innovation, Better Regulation." *Africa's Pulse*. Volume 17. April. Washington, DC: World Bank.

―――. 2018h. *South Asia Economic Focus*. Fall. Washington, DC: World Bank.

―――. 2018i. "Migration and Remittances: Developments and Outlook." In *Migration and Development Brief*. Washington, DC: World Bank.

―――. 2018j. "The Implications of Tariffs for Commodity Markets." In *Commodity Markets Outlook. The Changing of the Guard: Shifts in Industrial Commodity Demand*. October. Washington, DC: World Bank.

―――. 2018k. *Global Economic Prospects: Broad-Based Upturn, but for How Long?* January. Washington, DC: World Bank.

―――. 2018l. *Poverty and Shared Prosperity Report 2018: Piecing Together the Poverty Puzzle*. Washington, DC: World Bank.

―――. 2018m. *Moving for Prosperity: Global Migration and Labor Markets*. Policy Research Report. Washington, DC: World Bank.

―――. 2018n. *China—Systematic Country Diagnostic: Towards a More Inclusive and Sustainable Development*. Washington, DC: World Bank.

―――. 2018o. *Inflation in Emerging and Developing Economies: Evolution, Drivers and Policies*. Washington, DC: World Bank.

―――. 2018p. *Fiscal Adjustment in Latin America and the Caribbean: Short-Run Pain, Long-Run Gain?* Washington, DC: World Bank.

―――. 2018q. *The Human Capital Project*. Washington, DC: World Bank.

―――. 2019. Forthcoming. *World Development Report 2019: The Changing Nature of Work*. Washington, DC: World Bank.

World Bank, WTO, OECD, IDE-JETRO, and UIBE. 2017. *Global Value Chain Development Report: Measuring and Analyzing the Impact of GVCs on Economic Development*. Washington DC: World Bank.

Wyplosz, C. 2012. "Fiscal rules: Theoretical issues and historical experiences." In *Fiscal Policy after the Financial Crisis* (pp. 495-525). University of Chicago Press.

CHAPTER 2

REGIONAL OUTLOOKS

EAST ASIA and PACIFIC

Growth in the East Asia and Pacific region is expected to moderate to a still-robust 6 percent in 2019 and 2020. In China, policies aimed at rebalancing and countering external headwinds will continue to tilt activity toward domestic demand and away from exports. Risks to regional growth are to the downside and have intensified, including the possibility of further escalation of trade restrictions and faster-than-expected tightening of global financing conditions. Countries most vulnerable to disruptions in global trade and financial market activity are those with high debt, elevated current account deficits and high exposure to portfolio and bank inflows, and significant reliance on exports.

Recent developments

Growth in the East Asia and Pacific (EAP) region is estimated to have slowed to 6.3 percent in 2018 and momentum has weakened, reflecting diminishing support from exports partly offset by robust domestic demand (Figure 2.1.1; Table 2.1.1). External conditions have deteriorated, reflecting moderating global demand, heightened trade tensions, and a substantial tightening of financing conditions. This less favorable international environment has been accompanied by financial stress in some large emerging market and developing economies (EMDEs).

Several large economies in the region have faced some combination of capital outflows, currency depreciations, equity market corrections, and foreign reserve losses (e.g., China, Indonesia, Malaysia, the Philippines, Thailand). In addition to country-specific factors, the countries most affected were those with sizable or widening current account deficits and dependence on volatile portfolio flows, those with relatively high asset valuations, or those with exposure to trade disputes involving major economies (e.g., China, Indonesia, Myanmar, the Philippines). Bond spreads in these countries have generally widened, but less than during the last two financial stress

episodes and less than the EMDE average, reflecting continued strong investor confidence toward these economies.

China has been easing monetary and fiscal policies in anticipation of slowing export growth amid trade tensions, while at the same time making progress at reducing growth in non-bank financing. In contrast, several countries, such as Indonesia and the Philippines, have stemmed capital outflows by tightening monetary policy. Most EAP countries have taken advantage of flexible exchange rates, which has allowed their currencies to act as shock absorbers during times of stress. Indonesia has also implemented measures to curb imports while taking steps to increase coal exports, as part of an effort to reduce the current account deficit and relieve pressure on the rupiah (World Bank 2018a; World Bank 2018b).

Growth in China is estimated to have slowed to a still robust 6.5 percent in 2018, with resilient domestic demand helping to offset a deceleration of exports (Figure 2.1.2). Consumption has remained strong and private investment is recovering, partly in response to more supportive policies, as authorities attempt to offset the effects of various United States trade restrictions. The services sector has continued to outperform. Price growth of newly constructed residential buildings, most notably in Tier 1 cities, has rebounded following several years of correction.

Note: Ekaterine Vashakmadze. Research assistance was provided by Liu Cui.

FIGURE 2.1.1 **EAP: Recent developments**

Growth in EAP slowed to 6.3 percent in 2018, with robust domestic demand but softening export growth. Inflation has been trending up but is generally below targets. EAP economies faced some combination of capital outflows, currency depreciations, equity market corrections, and foreign reserve losses during the 2018 financial market stress episode. Regional bond spreads have generally widened but less than during the last two financial stress episodes and less than the EMDE average.

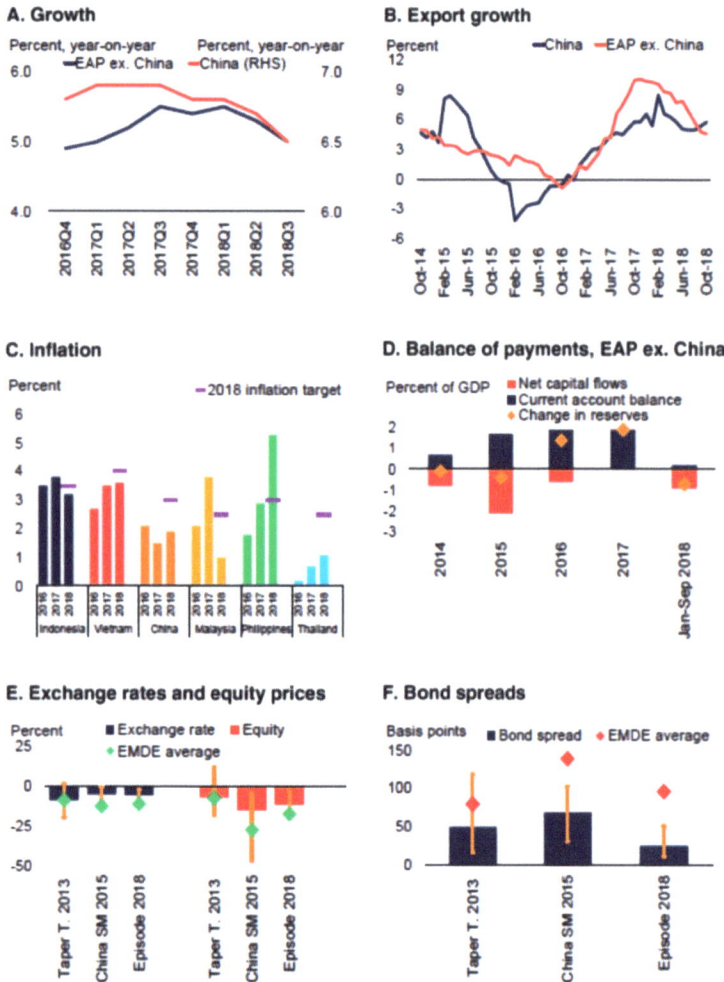

A. Growth

B. Export growth

C. Inflation

D. Balance of payments, EAP ex. China

E. Exchange rates and equity prices

F. Bond spreads

Source: Bloomberg, Haver Analytics, J.P. Morgan, World Bank.

E.F. "Taper T. 2013" refers to mid-2013 global financial market stress episode; "China SM 2015" refers to mid-2015 China stock market (SM) turbulence; "Episode 2018" refers to mid-2018 financial market volatility episode. The start dates for the stress episodes are: Taper Tantrum: May 23, 2013; China SM 2015: June 12, 2015; Episode 2018: April 15, 2018.

A. Aggregate growth rates are based on constant 2010 U.S. dollar GDP-weights and include Indonesia, Malaysia, Mongolia, Philippines, Thailand, and Vietnam. Last observation is 2018Q3.

B. Data include only goods. 12-month moving average. Aggregate growth rate excludes Cambodia, Fiji, Lao PDR, Mongolia, Myanmar, Solomon Islands, Papua New Guinea, Timor-Leste, Vanuatu, and Vietnam due to data limitations. Last observation is October 2018.

C. Average year-on-year growth. The midpoints of targeted ranges in 2018 in Indonesia (2.5-4.5 percent), Philippines (2-4 percent), Vietnam (4 percent), China (3 percent), and Thailand (1-4 percent). For Malaysia, the midpoint of Bank Negara's 2018 forecast of 2-3 percent is used. Last observation is November 2018.

D. Current account balance is based on non-seasonally adjusted data. The aggregate includes Indonesia, Malaysia, Philippines, and Thailand. Net capital flows and change in reserves are estimates. Last observation is 2018Q3.

E. Percent change of exchange rates (U.S. dollar vs. local currency) and equity prices in local currency over 247 days since the start dates of respective stress episodes. EAP aggregate exchange rate includes China, Indonesia, Malaysia, Mongolia, Philippines, Thailand and Vietnam. EAP aggregate equity price includes China, Indonesia, Malaysia, Philippines, Thailand and Vietnam. Orange lines denote minimum-maximum ranges. Green diamonds denote EMDE averages.

F. The change of bond spread over 247 days since the start dates of respective stress episodes. The average spread of a country's sovereign debt (as measured by J.P. Morgan's Emerging Markets Bond Index) over their equivalent maturity U.S. Treasury bond. EAP aggregate bond spread includes China, Indonesia, Malaysia, Philippines and Vietnam. Orange lines denote minimum-maximum ranges. Red diamonds denote EMDE averages.

On the external front, China's current account surplus has dissipated as import growth outpaced export growth. Export growth is estimated to have dropped from about 9 percent in 2017 to around 4-5 percent in 2018, reflecting the dampening effects of weaker global demand and new U.S. tariffs. Since the beginning of 2018, substantial new tariffs have been introduced on bilateral trade between China and the United States, accounting for about 11.4 percent of China's goods exports and about 6.5 percent of imports. Capital outflows have resumed, and equities and the renminbi have been under pressure, reflecting heightened trade tensions and diverging monetary policy: a loosening by the People's Bank of China (PBoC) and a tightening by the U.S. Federal Reserve.

Growth in commodity-importing economies excluding China is moderating. In the Philippines, activity has slowed as surging inflation, capacity constraints, and currency pressures have prompted authorities to hike policy rates. Growth in Vietnam remains robust, helped by booming exports, but authorities have tightened fiscal policy as part of their commitment to reduce the economic role of the state. In Thailand, a cyclical recovery continues, but its pace is moderating in response to tighter fiscal policies and the effects of softening global demand on export growth.

In commodity-exporting EAP economies, the investment-led cyclical recovery is maturing, and the pace and composition of growth continues to reflect country-specific factors. In Indonesia, growth last year was led by rising investment on the back of accelerated infrastructure spending and investment in the mining sector (World Bank 2018c). In Malaysia, lower public investment is weighing on growth, reflecting the completion of several infrastructure projects and a more prudent approach toward new ones (World Bank 2018d). In contrast to the regional trend, import growth in Malaysia has been weak, reflecting weak demand for capital goods imports combined with lower imports of intermediate goods.

Despite the slowdown, EAP remains one of the world's fastest-growing regions and has been relatively resilient to recent bouts of financial market volatility (Figure 2.1.3). One reason is that most EAP countries (with the exception of the Pacific Islands) continue to experience growth above the EMDE average and maintain mostly diminishing, but still positive current account balances net of foreign direct investment (e.g., China, Malaysia, Thailand, the Philippines, and Vietnam). Another reason is that policy frameworks across EAP region have improved over time with the shift to floating exchange rates, economic diversification, and solid buffers.

That said, many countries have pockets of vulnerabilities, including elevated levels of public and private debt (e.g., China, Lao PDR, Malaysia, Mongolia, Papua New Guinea, Vietnam), external debt (e.g., Malaysia, Mongolia, Lao PDR), foreign participation in local-currency sovereign bond markets (e.g., Indonesia, Malaysia), fiscal deficits (e.g., Cambodia, Lao PDR, Mongolia, Vietnam), and current account deficits and high reliance on volatile capital flows (e.g., Cambodia, Indonesia, Mongolia). In addition, deep regional and global integration makes the region vulnerable to trade shocks, as described in the risk section below.

Outlook

Regional growth is expected to moderate from 6.3 percent in 2018 to 6 percent in 2019 and stay at that pace in 2020—broadly unchanged from June forecasts (Tables 2.1.1 and 2.1.2; Figure 2.1.3). The outlook is predicated on broadly stable commodity prices in the next two years, a moderation in global demand and trade, and a gradual tightening of global financing conditions.

The structural slowdown in China is expected to continue. Growth is projected to slow from 6.5 percent in 2018 to 6.2 percent on average in 2019-20, and domestic and external rebalancing are expected to endure. Authorities in China have shifted to looser monetary and fiscal policies in response to a more challenging external environment, including heightened trade tensions. They have cut reserve requirements, reduced taxes and fees, increased export tax rebates, and accelerated issuance of special purpose local government bonds to bolster infrastructure spending. Authorities have also reiterated their commitment to growth stability and structural

FIGURE 2.1.2 China: Recent developments

In China, growth is slowing but remains robust amid resilient consumption. China's current account surplus has dissipated as import growth outpaced export growth. Equities and the renminbi have been under pressure throughout 2018. Bond spreads, which widened between late-2017 and early-2018 on trade concerns, have been stable since mid-2018, reflecting continued strong investor confidence. The PBoC has been easing monetary policy, but keeping credit growth in check, by reducing shadow financing. Prices of newly constructed residential buildings most notably in Tier 1 cities, have rebounded following several years of correction.

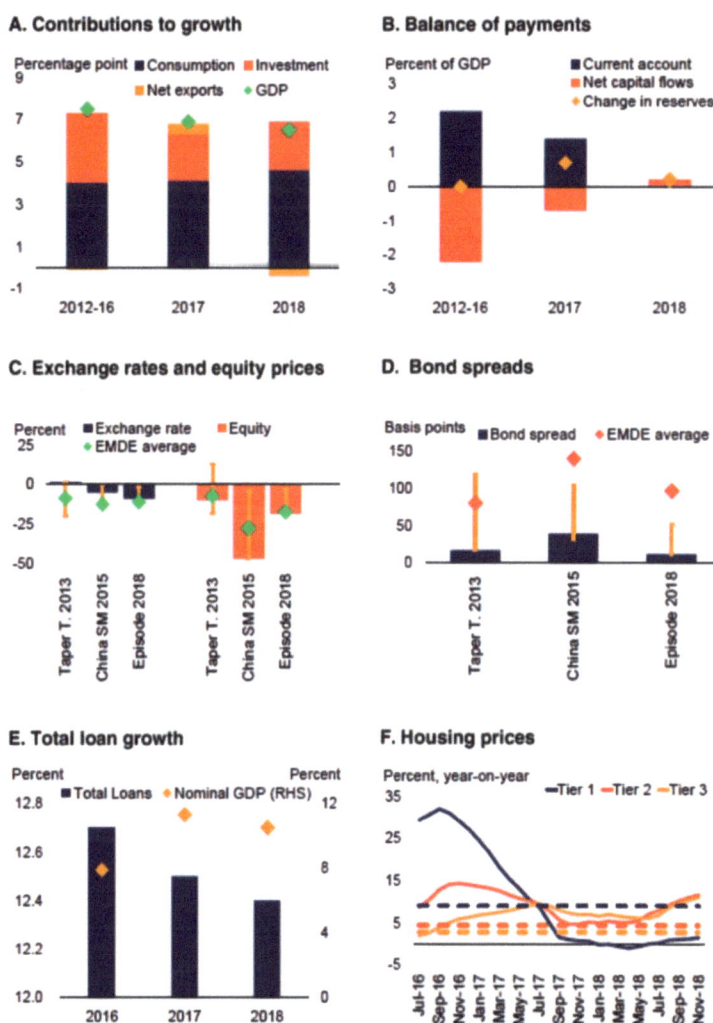

A. Contributions to growth

B. Balance of payments

C. Exchange rates and equity prices

D. Bond spreads

E. Total loan growth

F. Housing prices

Source: Bloomberg, Haver Analytics, J.P. Morgan, the National Bureau of Statistics of China, World Bank.

C.D. "Taper T. 2013" refers to mid-2013 global financial market stress episode; "China SM 2015" refers to mid-2015 China stock market (SM) turbulence; "Episode 2018" refers to mid-2018 financial market volatility episode. The start dates for the stress episodes are: Taper Tantrum: May 23, 2013; China stock market turbulence: June 12, 2015; Episode 2018: April 15, 2018.

A. Investment refers to gross capital formation, which includes change in inventories. Data for 2018 are estimates.

B. Net capital flows and change in reserves are estimates. Data for 2018 are estimates.

C. Percent changes of exchange rates (U.S. dollar vs. Chinese renminbi) and equity prices in Chinese renminbi over 247 days since the start dates of respective stress episodes. Orange lines denote EAP minimum-maximum ranges. Green diamonds denote EMDE averages.

D. Change of bond spread over 247 days since the start dates of respective stress episodes. Bond spread measures the average spread of a country's sovereign debt (as measured by J.P. Morgan's Emerging Markets Bond Index) over their equivalent maturity U.S. Treasury bond. Orange lines denote the EAP minimum-maximum ranges. Red diamonds denote EMDE averages.

E. Domestic and overseas loans. Data for 2018 is through November. Last observation is 2018Q3 for nominal GDP and November 2018 for total loan growth.

F. The National Bureau of Statistics of China surveys house prices in 70 cities and divides them into three tiers. The first tier includes Shanghai, Beijing, Guangzhou, and Shenzhen. The second tier includes 31 provincial capital and sub-provincial capital cities. The third tier includes 35 other cities. Dotted lines indicate February 2011-November 2018 averages. Last observation is November 2018.

FIGURE 2.1.3 Outlook and risks

EAP growth is projected to gradually decelerate, reflecting a structural slowdown in China. Excluding China, growth is expected to remain stable in 2019-20. The region is characterized by deep regional and global integration, which makes it vulnerable to external shocks. Domestic and external vulnerabilities would amplify the impact of external shocks, especially where policy buffers are limited.

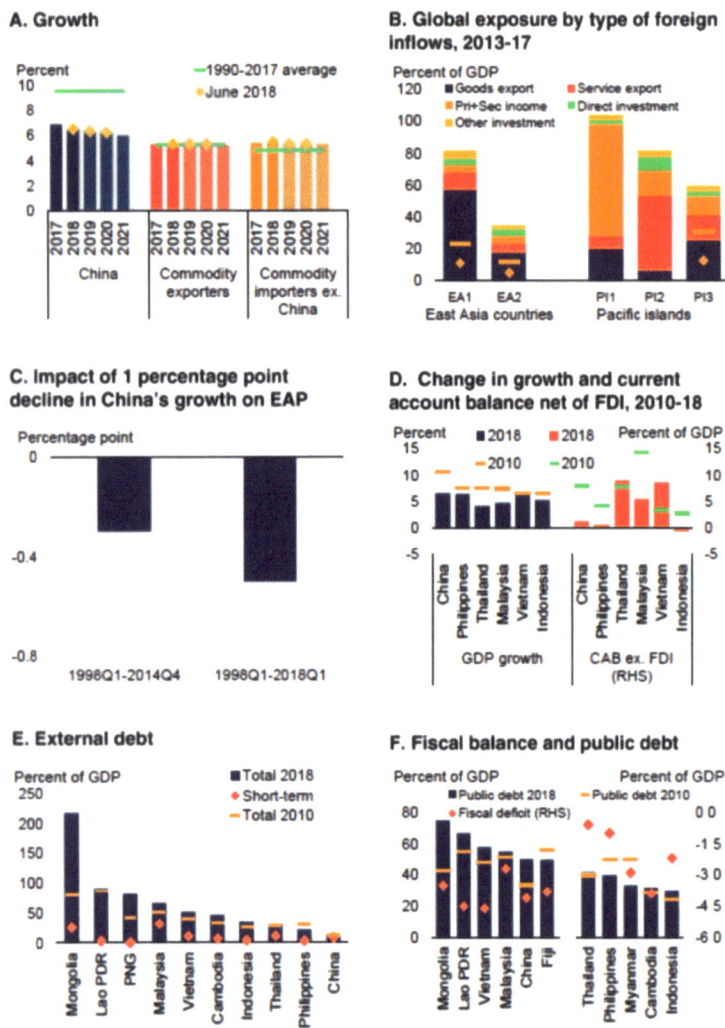

A. Growth

B. Global exposure by type of foreign inflows, 2013-17

C. Impact of 1 percentage point decline in China's growth on EAP

D. Change in growth and current account balance net of FDI, 2010-18

E. External debt

F. Fiscal balance and public debt

Source: Haver Analytics, International Monetary Fund, World Bank.
A. Commodity importers ex. China include Cambodia, Fiji, Philippines, Solomon Islands, Thailand, Vietnam, and Vanuatu. Commodity exporters include Indonesia, Lao PDR, Malaysia, Mongolia, Myanmar, Papua New Guinea, and Timor-Leste. Yellow diamonds denote forecasts in the June 2018 edition of the *Global Economic Prospects* report. Aggregates growth rates are calculated using 2010 U.S. dollar GDP-weights. Data in shaded areas are forecasts.
B. EA = East Asia. PI = Pacific Islands. EA1 includes Brunei Darussalam, Cambodia, Malaysia, Mongolia, Thailand and Vietnam; EA2 includes Indonesia, Lao PDR, Myanmar and Philippines. PI1 includes Kiribati, Marshall Islands, Micronesia, Timor-Leste, Tonga and Tuvalu; PI2 includes Palau and Vanuatu; PI3 includes Fiji, Papua New Guinea, Samoa and Solomon Islands.
The linkages presented in this chart only present direct channels. Spillovers may propagate via indirect channels such as global and regional value chains. Diamond denotes direct exposure to China. Hyphen denotes share of commodity exports in GDP. Direct exposure to China and the share of commodity exports in GDP is not shown for PI1 and PI2 country groups due to data limitations.
C. Median of posterior distribution. Estimates based on a Bayesian SVAR, using quarterly data for 1998Q1-2018Q1. The spillovers include the effects through indirect channels, including confidence and global and regional value chains. Cumulative impact on growth after two years. GDP weighted.
D. CAB ex. FDI = Current Account Balance excluding Foreign Direct Investment. Orange hyphen denotes GDP growth in 2010; green hyphen—CAB ex. FDI in 2010. Data for 2018 are estimates.
E. PNG = Papua New Guinea. External debt stock is defined as debt owed to nonresidents repayable in foreign currency, goods, or services. It is the sum of public, publicly guaranteed, and private nonguaranteed debt. Data are in current U.S. dollars. Short-term debt includes all debt having an original maturity of one year or less and interest in arrears on long-term debt. Diamond denotes short-term external debt as share of GDP in 2018; hyphen—total external debt as share of GDP in 2010.
F. Diamond denotes estimated fiscal balance as share of GDP in 2018; hyphen denotes public debt as share of GDP in 2010. The general government debt data for Mongolia is based on World Bank staff estimates.

reform objectives in late-2018 (CEWC 2018).

These policy steps are expected to largely offset the direct negative impact of higher tariffs on China's exports, which would otherwise lower growth by about 0.1-0.3 percentage point in 2019. In addition, the authorities have stepped up their structural reform efforts to improve the business environment, including for foreign firms, have lowered tariffs on imports, with the exception of some tariffs on U.S. imports in retaliation to U.S. tariffs on China's goods, and have strengthened intellectual property protection.

Growth in the rest of the region is projected to remain broadly unchanged at around 5.2 percent on average in 2019-20. Resilient domestic demand is expected to offset the negative impact of slowing exports. Growth among commodity importers is projected to moderate in 2019 as it converges with its potential rate. Excluding China, the 2018 growth outlook for EAP commodity importers has been downgraded because of a moderation in private consumption amid rising inflation in the Philippines.

Growth in commodity exporters is expected to remain broadly unchanged at about 5.1 percent in 2019, in line with potential, with significant cross-country differences. This forecast is slightly below that of June, reflecting a number of downward revisions (e.g., Lao PDR, Malaysia, Myanmar). Output gaps in most commodity exporting economies are expected to close over the forecast horizon, as investment growth stabilizes and trade flows decelerate. For both commodity exporters and importers, inflation pressures are expected to intensify over the forecast horizon, in part reflecting exchange rate pass-through as well as domestic demand pressures.

Despite the projected robust activity in the region in the near term, underlying potential growth—which has fallen considerably over the past decade—is likely to decline further over the long term. This reflects increasingly adverse demographic patterns and a projected slowdown in capital accumulation as credit growth is reined in.

Risks

Risks to the forecasts remain tilted to the downside and have intensified. Heightened trade tensions involving large economies continue to create uncertainty about the future of established trading relationships. A potential disruption of trade would disproportionately affect the more open economies in the region. The region is characterized by deep regional and global integration, which makes it vulnerable to external shocks. The region relies significantly on foreign income, mostly from exports but also from returns on foreign assets and direct investment. Total exports and gross capital inflows exceed 50 percent of GDP in more than two-thirds of the region's economies, and 100 percent in about one-third (Figure 2.1.3). In many regional economies, the cost of rising import tariffs may be magnified by participation in complex global value chains (e.g., Malaysia, Thailand, the Philippines; Chapter 1, World Bank 2018a). Furthermore, the impact of trade measures could be amplified regionally if it also weighs on investor confidence and reduces foreign direct investment (IMF 2018a; World Bank 2018a).

China's baseline projection assumes that the fiscal and monetary policy stimulus that has been introduced in response to rising U.S. tariffs will offset the immediate economic impact of trade-related headwinds. However, if authorities opt for additional and stronger fiscal and monetary stimulus initiatives—particularly in the form of unfunded mandates for local governments to increase public investment—the measures may also run counter to the needed deleveraging and de-risking process. These measures, could also undermine the efforts to contain credit growth and limit risks to corporate and bank balance sheets (Chapter 1; World Bank 2018a).

A continued intensification of trade tensions, along with the previously introduced measures, would affect close to all goods trade between China and the United States. In the extreme case scenario, further escalation of trade tensions, coupled with a downturn in confidence and investment, could reduce global exports by up to 3 percent and global income by 1.7 percent over the

medium term. The largest decline (up to 3.5 percent of income) would be felt in China (Freund et al. 2018).[1]

A significant disruption to activity in China would have large regional effects, propagating through bilateral trade, regional supply chains, and financial linkages (Figure 2.1.3). A one-off, unexpected 1 percentage-point drop in China's GDP growth would lower growth in the rest of the region by 0.5 percentage points after two years (World Bank 2016a, 2018a). Growth spillovers from China would be particularly large for commodity exporters, particularly Mongolia, due to their reliance on commodity exports to China, and for Cambodia and the Pacific Islands, which depend on China for tourism and FDI.

Risks of disorderly financial market developments have also intensified (Chapter 1). A further tightening of global financial conditions could be triggered by rising inflation, swelling fiscal deficits, or contagion from financial stress in other EMDEs, and could place further pressure on regional exchange rates and asset prices. High debt levels and external vulnerabilities among some EAP countries could amplify the impact of external shocks such as a sudden stop in capital flows or a rise in borrowing costs. If a combination of downside risks were to materialize, it could trigger an even sharper slowdown in regional growth.

---

[1] This scenario assumes a 25 percent tariff surcharge on all products traded between China and the United States, combined with a decline in investor confidence, resulting in a 0.5 percentage point drop in global investment to GDP (Freund et al. 2018).

TABLE 2.1.1 East Asia and Pacific forecast summary

(Real GDP growth at market prices in percent, unless indicated otherwise)

Percentage point differences
from June 2018 projections

	2016	2017	2018e	2019f	2020f	2021f	2018e	2019f	2020f
EMDE EAP, GDP[1]	6.3	6.6	6.3	6.0	6.0	5.8	0.0	-0.1	0.0
(Average including countries with full national accounts and balance of payments data only)[2]									
EMDE EAP, GDP[2]	6.3	6.6	6.3	6.0	6.0	5.8	0.0	-0.1	0.0
GDP per capita (U.S. dollars)	5.6	5.9	5.7	5.4	5.4	5.3	0.0	-0.1	-0.1
PPP GDP	6.3	6.5	6.3	5.9	5.9	5.8	0.1	-0.2	-0.1
Private consumption	6.8	6.5	7.7	7.4	7.1	7.2	0.7	0.6	0.1
Public consumption	9.3	8.5	7.6	7.3	7.1	7.1	0.0	-0.2	-0.3
Fixed investment	6.6	4.5	5.6	5.3	5.2	5.1	0.1	0.0	-0.3
Exports, GNFS[3]	3.3	9.4	4.8	4.7	4.4	4.3	-0.9	-1.3	-1.4
Imports, GNFS[3]	5.4	8.1	6.8	6.5	5.9	5.8	1.0	0.4	-0.5
Net exports, contribution to growth	-0.6	0.4	-0.6	-0.5	-0.5	-0.5	-0.6	-0.5	-0.3
Memo items: GDP									
East Asia excluding China	4.9	5.4	5.2	5.2	5.2	5.2	-0.2	-0.1	-0.1
China	6.7	6.9	6.5	6.2	6.2	6.0	0.0	-0.1	0.0
Indonesia	5.0	5.1	5.2	5.2	5.3	5.3	0.0	-0.1	-0.1
Thailand	3.3	3.9	4.1	3.8	3.9	3.9	0.0	0.0	0.1

Source: World Bank.

Note: e = estimate; f = forecast. EMDE = emerging market and developing economy. World Bank forecasts are frequently updated based on new information and changing (global) circumstances. Consequently, projections presented here may differ from those contained in other Bank documents, even if basic assessments of countries' prospects do not differ at any given moment in time.

1. GDP at market prices and expenditure components are measured in constant 2010 U.S. dollars. Excludes Democratic People's Republic of Korea and dependent territories.

2. Sub-region aggregate excludes Democratic People's Republic of Korea, dependent territories, Fiji, Kiribati, the Marshall Islands, the Federated States of Micronesia, Myanmar, Nauru, Palau, Papua New Guinea, Samoa, Timor-Leste, Tonga, and Tuvalu, for which data limitations prevent the forecasting of GDP components.

3. Exports and imports of goods and non-factor services (GNFS).

To download this data, please visit www.worldbank.org/gep.

TABLE 2.1.2 East Asia and Pacific country forecasts[1]

(Real GDP growth at market prices in percent, unless indicated otherwise)

Percentage point differences
from June 2018 projections)

	2016	2017	2018e	2019f	2020f	2021f	2018e	2019f	2020f
Cambodia	6.9	7.0	7.1	6.8	6.8	6.7	0.2	0.1	0.2
China	6.7	6.9	6.5	6.2	6.2	6.0	0.0	-0.1	0.0
Fiji	0.4	3.8	3.5	3.4	3.3	3.3	0.0	0.0	0.0
Indonesia	5.0	5.1	5.2	5.2	5.3	5.3	0.0	-0.1	-0.1
Lao PDR	7.0	6.9	6.5	6.6	6.7	6.6	-0.1	-0.3	-0.2
Malaysia	4.2	5.9	4.7	4.7	4.6	4.6	-0.7	-0.4	-0.2
Mongolia	1.4	5.4	5.9	6.6	6.3	6.2	0.6	0.2	-0.2
Myanmar	5.9	6.8	6.2	6.5	6.6	6.8	-0.5	-0.4	-0.5
Papua New Guinea	2.6	2.8	0.3	5.1	3.1	3.4	2.0	1.1	0.1
Philippines	6.9	6.7	6.4	6.5	6.6	6.6	-0.3	-0.2	0.0
Solomon Islands	3.5	3.5	3.4	2.9	2.8	2.7	0.4	0.0	0.0
Thailand	3.3	3.9	4.1	3.8	3.9	3.9	0.0	0.0	0.1
Timor-Leste[2]	5.3	-4.7	0.8	3.3	4.9	5.0	-1.4	-0.9	0.9
Vietnam	6.2	6.8	6.8	6.6	6.5	6.5	0.0	0.0	0.0

Source: World Bank.

Note: e = estimate; f = forecast. World Bank forecasts are frequently updated based on new information and changing (global) circumstances. Consequently, projections presented here may differ from those contained in other Bank documents, even if basic assessments of countries' prospects do not significantly differ at any given moment in time.

1. GDP at market prices and expenditure components are measured in constant 2010 U.S. dollars.

2. Non-oil GDP. Timor-Leste's total GDP, including the oil economy, is roughly a double of its non-oil economy and is highly volatile as a result of sensitivity to changes in global oil prices and local production levels.

To download this data, please visit www.worldbank.org/gep.

BOX 2.1.1 Informality in East Asia and Pacific

The share of informal output in East Asia and Pacific (EAP) region is below the EMDE average while the share of informal employment is above average. Within the region, informality is particularly high in lower-income countries, which are also characterized by a lack of diversification, large rural sectors, and weak institutions. Nonetheless, even higher-income economies within the region have urban informality. This diversity within the region argues for tailored policy approaches to address challenges associated with informality. Higher-income countries can prioritize urban planning and providing essential social protection to informal workers. Lower-income countries can focus on policies that increase productivity, lower costs, and increase the potential benefits of regulatory compliance.

Introduction

The share of informal output in East Asia and Pacific (EAP) is below the EMDE average.[1] Nevertheless, despite a downward trend over the past 30 years, informality remains high in the lower-middle-income economies, including Lao PDR, Myanmar, Cambodia. Higher-income countries in the region have made considerable progress in integrating rural migrants into urban labor markets, but face challenges related to urban informality, particularly in providing access to public services and essential social protection.

Against this backdrop, this box examines the following questions:

- How has informality evolved in East Asia and Pacific?

- What have been the macroeconomic and social implications of informality?

- What policy options are available to address challenges associated with informality?

Evolution of informality

In the EAP region, informal output accounted for about 30 percent of GDP on average in 2010-2016, slightly below the EMDE median (Figure 2.1.1.1). However, at 47 percent of total employment, informal employment in EAP was above the EMDE average during the same period.[2] About 73 percent of the labor force in EAP lacked basic pension coverage during 2001-10.

Informality in the EAP region has declined over the past two decades (Chapter 3; Schneider, Buehn, and Montenegro 2010). The share of informal output declined from 35 percent of official GDP to 27 percent between 1990-2000 and 2010-16—the fastest decline among EMDE regions. Survey-based measures of informality also suggest a moderate decline in acceptance and perception of informality.

The decline in informality has been accompanied by sustained growth, rapid industrialization, urbanization, and improvements in institutional quality (Loayza 2016; World Bank 2015). A large number of informal, mainly agricultural, workers in China have been successfully integrated into the formal labor force mainly by absorbing migrants into the urban labor market (World Bank 2014a). Total employment in China rose by about 250 million during 1990–2014, amid large-scale rural-to-urban migrant flows (Lam, Liu, and Schipke 2015). Between 1990-2000 and 2010-16, the share of informal output declined particularly rapidly in the fastest-growing countries, in part reflecting the effect of comprehensive reforms (Cambodia, Myanmar, Lao PDR). For example, the informal share of output has fallen by 33 percentage points in Myanmar (to below 30 percent in 2010-16) following broad-based liberalization measures.

The region is characterized by significant cross-country heterogeneity in terms of institutional and socio-economic indicators (Figure 2.1.1.1). Per capita GDP levels vary widely across EAP, and those economies with higher per capita GDP generally have lower levels of informality (ILO 2018a; Loayza and Rigolini 2006). The share of informal output in higher income countries is about 30 percentage points less than in lower-middle-income countries (Lao PDR and Myanmar). The share of informal employment is also about one-quarter that of lower-

---

Note: This box was prepared by Ekaterine Vashakmadze and Jinxin Wu.

[1] Informality is often defined as market-based legal production of goods and services that are hidden from public authorities for monetary, regulatory, and institutional reasons (Schneider, Buehn, and Montenegro 2010). Informal output is measured as a percent of total output in official GDP. In this box, informality is estimated based on the Dynamic General Equilibrium (DGE) model used in Elgin and Oztunali (2012) (for more detailed discussion see Chapter 3 and Annex 3.1).

[2] The most frequently used informal employment measure is the share of self-employment in total employment, which represents a lower bound of informal employment (La Porta and Shleifer 2014). Self-employed

workers are those workers who, working on their own account, with one or a few partners, or in a cooperative, hold the type of jobs defined as "self-employment jobs" (for more detailed discussion see Chapter 3 and Annex 3.1).

BOX 2.1.1 Informality in East Asia and Pacific *(continued)*

FIGURE 2.1.1.1 Informality in East Asia and Pacific

Compared with other EMDE regions, East Asia and Pacific (EAP)'s share of informal output is moderate whereas its share of informal employment is above average. Informality is particularly high in lower income countries, which are also characterized by stringent labor regulations and lack of enforcement.

A. Informal economy as share of total economic output

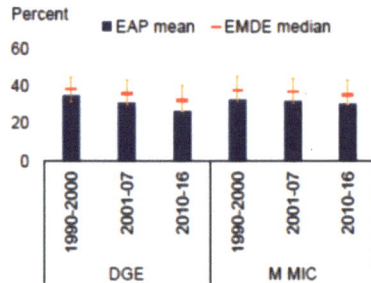

B. Share of labor force without pension; share of self-employed

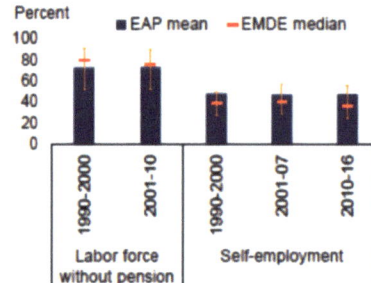

C. Perceived informal activities and attitudes towards informality

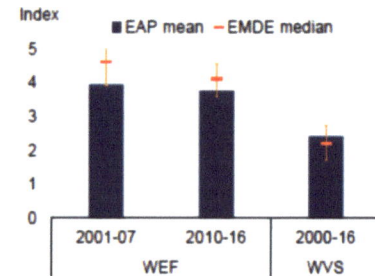

D. Informality by different measures

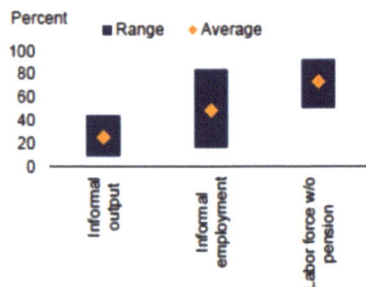

E. Cross country difference in informality

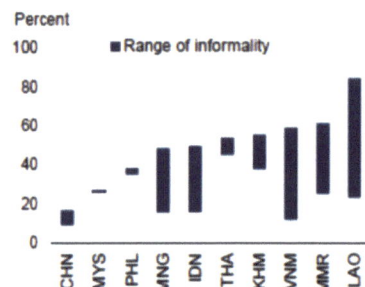

F. Institutional factors

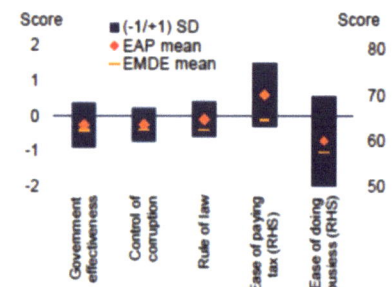

Sources: Elgin et al. (forthcoming), World Bank (Doing Business, World Development Indicators, World Governance Indicators), World Economic Forum, World Value Survey.

Note: Blue bars show simple averages of the informal economy of the region. Red markers show the median of all EMDEs and the vertical lines denote interquartile range of all EMDEs.

A. DGE = dynamic general equilibrium model. MIMIC = multiple indicators multiple causes model. The DGE model estimates the size of the informal sector as a percent of official GDP (see Elgin and Oztunali 2012). The MIMIC model is a structural equations model that considers multiple causes of informal activity and captures multiple outcome indicators of informal activity (see Schneider, Buehn, and Montenegro 2010). It also estimates the informal output as a percent of official GDP. DGE sample includes 12 EAP economies and 122 EMDEs; MIMIC sample includes 14 EAP economies and 124 EMDEs.

B. Labor force without pension is presented as the share of the labor force that does not contribute to a retirement pension scheme, derived from data on pension coverage obtained from WDI. Self-employed is the presented as the share of self-employment in total employment. Labor force without pension sample includes 8 EAP economies and 103 EMDEs; self-employed sample includes 19 EAP economies and 134 EMDEs.

C. WEF = World Economic Forum. WVS = World Values Survey. WEF index is the average response at the country-year level to the question: "In your country, how much economic activity do you estimate to be undeclared or unregistered? (1 = Most economic activity is undeclared or unregistered; 7 = Most economic activity is declared or registered)." WEF index is inverted; a higher average at the country level indicates a larger informal economy. The index does not use data for 2004–05 due to inconsistency in survey methods. The WVS asks whether respondents can justify cheating on taxes (1 = never justifiable; 10 = always justifiable). The average responses at the country-year level are used as a measure of attitude toward informality (or tax morality; Oviedo, Thomas, and Karakurum-Ozdemir 2009). WEF sample includes 12 EAP economies and 114 EMDEs; WVS sample includes 6 EAP economies and 66 EMDEs.

D. Diamonds represent the average level of EAP region; bars denote the range of EAP countries in each measure.

E. The upper bound of bar indicates the share of informal employment in total employment. The lower bound indicates the share of informal output in official GDP based on the Dynamic General Equilibrium (DGE) model. For Malaysia, the level of informal output is higher than the level of informal employment.

F. All measures are taken from the latest year available. The first three institutional measures are taken from World Bank's World Governance Indicators (World Bank 2018e), with a higher value indicating better institutional quality in year 2016. The "ease of doing business" and "ease of paying taxes" are taken from World Bank's Doing Business database (World Bank 2018f) and measured as distance to frontier, with a higher value indicating a more favorable business environment. Sample includes 22 EAP economies and 149 EMDEs. An economy's distance to frontier is reflected on a scale from 0 to 100, where 0 represents the lowest performance and 100 represents the frontier.

BOX 2.1.1 Informality in East Asia and Pacific *(continued)*

middle income economies.[3] Informality is most pervasive in Lao PDR and Myanmar, at around 60-80 percent of total employment. Indonesia, Mongolia, and Vietnam have below average informal output shares, but their informal employment shares are above the EAP average (ADB 2010; Handayani 2016).

Drivers and implications of informality

Informality has been attributed to several drivers. These included large agricultural sectors, rapid urbanization, low human capital, and overly burdensome regulations.

Size of agricultural sectors. People living in rural areas are almost twice as likely to be in informal employment as those in urban areas, and agriculture is the sector with the highest share of informal employment (ILO 2018a). The agricultural sector still accounts for about 30 percent of employment in EAP on average, and these shares are particularly high in Lao PDR, Myanmar, and Vietnam (ADB 2010; Figure 2.1.2). Informal workers constitute the vast majority of employment in the agriculture sector in Cambodia and Thailand, in part because high compliance costs discourage formal-sector activity of agricultural small enterprises (ILO 2018a).

Urbanization. Rapid urbanization in EAP has supported large-scale rural-to-urban migration, stimulated growth, productivity, and formal and informal job creation (Ghani and Kanbur 2013). The urbanization process has coincided with the rapid structural transformation of China and other fast-growing East Asian economies and the shift of activity from agriculture to manufacturing and services (McMillan, Rodrik, and Sepulveda 2017; Rodrik 2015). In general, a larger non-agricultural sector is associated with a smaller informal sector, and informality in manufacturing is significantly lower than in services (Atesagaoglu, Bayram, and Elgin 2017). Although the growth of urban areas provides opportunities for many, urban expansion, if not well planned, can also contribute to rising urban informality and policy challenges. In China, for example, unequal access to public services between citizens with urban household registrations (hukou) and those without, although diminishing, has led to unregistered urban households that lack essential social protection (Park, Wu, and Du 2012; World Bank 2014a).

Underinvestment in human capital. In EAP, investment in human capital and higher levels of educational attainment have increased labor productivity and have been closely associated with a smaller share of the informal economy (Figure 2.1.1.2; ILO 2018a; Moscoso-Boedo and D'Erasmo 2012). Workers with higher education levels are also more likely to be formally employed. This is also evident in cross-country comparisons. For example, in Indonesia, the results of the 2009 Informal Sector Survey (ISS) in Yogyakarta and Banten suggest that persons who are informally employed tended to have lower levels of education than those with formal jobs (ADB 2010). Malaysia is among the countries with the highest educational attainment and the lowest share of informal employment (25 percent). In contrast, Lao PDR, Myanmar and Cambodia are characterized by low educational outcomes and high informality.

Enterprise sector characteristics. In China and Vietnam, informal economies arose amid economic reforms that began in the 1970s and allowed the emergence of a private economy in the form of unregulated micro-enterprises, family enterprises, and individual entrepreneurs (Park, Wu, and Du 2012). The informal economy comprises more than 90 percent of micro and small enterprises worldwide (ILO 2018b). In EAP, informal workers tend to be employed in small, low-productivity firms. For example, in Indonesia, most informal firms are very small (micro) firms with less than five employees. These firms tend to be less productive than larger firms and pay lower wages. Their operations tend to be local, predominantly supplying local markets, with little desire for expansion (Rothenberg et al. 2015).

Taxes and labor regulations. Informality is also a consequence of higher tax burdens, stringent labor regulations, limited enforcement capacity, and poor governance (World Bank 2014a). In EAP, informality is higher in lower-income countries with markedly weaker institutional quality, cumbersome rules and procedures, and pervasive lack of awareness or adequate enforcement (Lao PDR, Myanmar; Figure 2.1.1.2). Within Malaysia, the Philippines, Thailand, and Vietnam, informality has been associated with more rigid business regulations and ineffective law enforcement (Loayza and Rigolini 2006).

Informality has been associated with a number of adverse economic outcomes. These include urban poverty, household vulnerability to shocks and lower productivity.

Urban poverty and income inequality. EAP is the world's most rapidly urbanizing region, with an average annual urbanization rate of 3 percent (World Bank 2017a). The

---

[3] Although the commonly observed link between income growth and informality generally holds in the EAP region, informality is nevertheless relatively high in Thailand despite its higher income status (Hassan and Schneider 2016).

BOX 2.1.1 Informality in East Asia and Pacific (continued)

FIGURE 2.1.1.2 Drivers and implications of informality in East Asia and Pacific

Better institutions and business environments, industrialization, and rapid urbanization are associated with low informality in higher-income economies. Countries with a high share of informality have higher income inequality and lower levels of educational attainment.

A. Informality and institutions

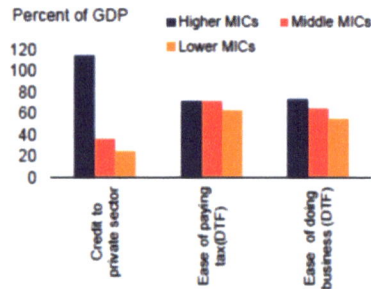

B. Institutional factors in countries with high and low informality

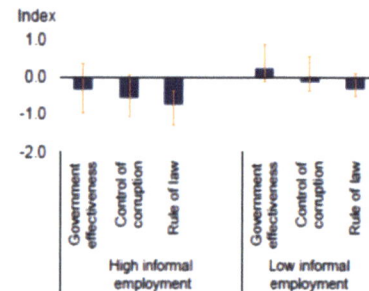

C. Employment in agriculture

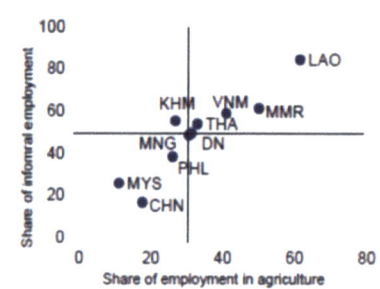

D. Urban population as percent of total population

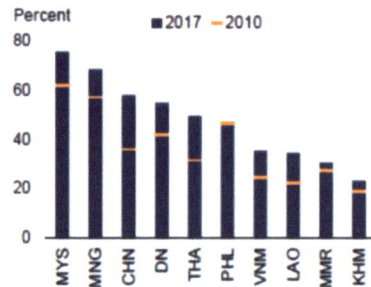

E. Year of total schooling

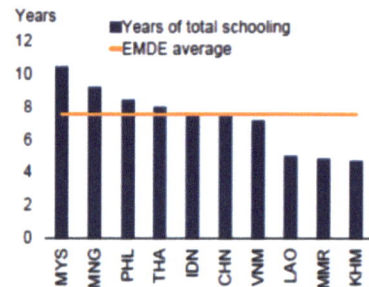

F. Human capital index

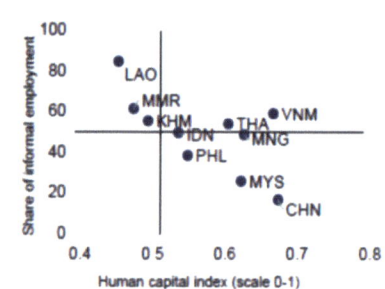

Sources: Barro-Lee (2013), Elgin et al. (forthcoming), World Bank (Doing Business, World Development Indicators, World Governance Indicators).

A. Higher MIC = China, Malaysia, and Thailand; Middle MICs = Indonesia, Mongolia, and the Philippines. Lower MICs = Cambodia, Lao PDR, Myanmar, and Vietnam.. The grouping of countries is based on GDP per capita.

B. All measures are taken from the latest year available. The first three institutional measures are taken from World Bank's World Governance Indicators (2017), with a higher value indicating better institutional quality in year 2016. Error bars reflect all EAP countries.

C.-F. CHN = China, IDN = Indonesia, KHM = Cambodia, LAO = Lao PDR, MMR = Myanmar, MNG = Mongolia, MYS = Malaysia, PHL = Philippines, THA = Thailand, VNM = Vietnam.

C. The vertical and horizontal lines denote EMDE averages.

D. Latest data available is 2014.

E. Data are from Barro-Lee (2013). Average years of total schooling is the average years of education completed among people over age 15.

F. The HCI calculates the contributions of health and education to worker productivity. The final index score ranges from zero to one and measures the productivity as a future worker of child born today relative to the benchmark of full health and complete education. The vertical and horizonal lines denote EMDE averages.

rapid growth of cities has created challenges that include the lack of affordable housing, resulting in increasing slums, poor provision of basic services, and widening inequality for urban dwellers. EAP hosts the world's largest slum population, many of them informally employed: around 35 percent of urban population (250 million people) live in slums. In Indonesia, 27 percent of the urban population do not have access to improved sanitation facilities (WHO and UNICEF 2015), followed by 21 percent in the Philippines (USAID 2017). The cities with the highest numbers of urban poor are in

China, Indonesia, and the Philippines, while the highest urban poverty rates are in the Pacific Island countries of Papua New Guinea, Timor-Leste, Vanuatu, and in Indonesia and Lao PDR (World Bank 2016b, World Bank 2017a).[4]

In China, the exceptional scale of rural to urban migration amplifies the challenges from informality. Many of these

_____

[4] Approximately 75 million people in EAP region live below the US$3.10/day poverty line.

BOX 2.1.1 Informality in East Asia and Pacific (continued)

workers—approximately 120-150 million— are migrant workers who are not registered to work in cities, and therefore lack a number of formal protections (Jutting and Xenogiani 2007, Huang 2009). These urban migrants gain a large wage premium by migrating; yet both rural and urban migrants tend to work in informal jobs and lack adequate social protection (Gagnon, Xenogiani, and Xing 2011). In Thailand, informally employed workers systematically present lower earnings at all earnings levels, and the difference increases with level of earnings (ILO 2015).

Household vulnerability to shocks. Informality may impose significant economic risk and result in underinvestment in human capital of current and future generations (Oviedo, Thomas, and Karakurum-Ozdemir 2009). It is characterized by a lack of adequate social protection coverage, which increases household vulnerability to shocks. For middle and lower income countries in EAP region, pension coverage is extremely low (Figure 2.1.1.2). In China, formal casual workers report lower monetary and subjective well-being than employees and business owners (Liang, Appleton, and Song 2016).

Low productivity. Countries characterized by larger informal sectors are associated with lower shares of skilled workers and weaker total factor productivity. At the firm level, entering and operating in the formal sector is costly, but provides firms with better access to technologies, skilled workers, and access to capital (Figure 2.1.1.2; D'Erasmo, Moscoso Boedo, and Senkal 2014). There exists a sharp productivity difference between firms of the same size in the formal and informal sector when measured in terms of value added per employee, with formal firms being, on average, 30 percent more productive (Fajnzylber, Maloney, and Montes-Rojas 2011; La Porta and Shleifer 2014; Monteiro and Assuncao 2012; Perry et al. 2007). Despite a well-documented gap between the performance of formal and informal firms, less is known about how the allocation of low-productivity firms in the informal sector affects productivity over time. If by operating informally firms are able to cut costs and stay more productive, then a shift from the informal to the formal sector will not necessarily lead to an increase in productivity. Indeed, some recent studies find evidence that a shift into the formal sector does not necessarily lead to an increase in productivity for firms (De Mel, McKenzie, and Woodruff 2013; Demenet, Razafindrakoto, and Roubaud 2016; McKenzie and Sakho 2010). Overall, while individual motivations to become or stay informal may differ, the aggregate outcome can be characterized as low scale output and low productivity.

Policy challenges

A tailored approach can help address the challenges associated with informality (OECD 2015; World Bank 2014a). Higher-income countries can prioritize providing essential social protection to informal workers; lower-income countries can focus on reforms to increase firm and worker productivity.

Essential social protection. In higher-income countries, essential social protection coverage can be expanded to shield informal workers from adverse shocks (Olivier, Masabo, and Kalula 2012). This would imply higher public expenditure on social protection to extend at least basic social protection coverage to all (ILO 2017).

Reforms to improve urban planning. Urban planning can help improve access to jobs, affordable housing, commercial services, public transportation, and health and education services to ensure equal opportunity for disadvantaged communities (World Bank 2015; Judy and Gadgil 2017). Examples of effective metropolitan governance include Beijing, Jakarta, Kuala Lumpur, Metro Manila Developments Authority (MMDA) and Shanghai (World Bank and DRCSC 2014; World Bank 2015).

Reforms to increase firm productivity. Agglomeration benefits can lower the unit costs of public service provision, enabling governments to extend access to basic services to more people (Ghani and Kanbur 2013; World Bank 2014a, 2018g). Policies to support small agricultural enterprises, which engage a large share of EAP's workforce, and other micro, small- or medium-sized enterprises include improving access to services, decreasing red tape and corruption, facilitating access to financial services, and offering better education and training (OECD 2009; World Bank 2018h).

Remove disincentives to formal employment. Removing disincentives to formal employment could encourage a shift of informal workers into formal employment. Reform options include lower registration costs; shorter registration procedures; streamlined registration services, for example, through information and communication technologies; lower compliance costs by introducing simplified tax assessment and payment regimes; improved access to financial services; and improved access to training, skills development, and business development services (ILO 2016). As small firms have different motivations to stay small and informal, measures to lower cost and increase the potential benefits of regulatory compliance can be combined with a more effective enforcement regime.

EUROPE and CENTRAL ASIA

Regional growth is estimated to have decelerated to an estimated 3.1 percent in 2018 and is projected to further slow to 2.3 percent this year, mainly because of weakness in Turkey. Regional growth is expected to pick up modestly in 2020-21, as a gradual recovery in Turkey offsets moderating activity in Central Europe. The main risks to the region are weaker-than-expected investment due to heightened policy uncertainty, and a renewal of financial pressure in Turkey combined with possible contagion to the rest of the region.

Recent developments

Activity in Europe and Central Asia (ECA) is estimated to have slowed to 3.1 percent in 2018 from 4 percent in 2017, reflecting the marked weakness in activity in Turkey in the second half of the year. Excluding Turkey, regional growth remained unchanged at an estimated 2.9 percent in 2018, as slowing activity in countries in the western part of the region, such as Bulgaria and Romania, offset an acceleration in the eastern part of the region that benefitted from higher oil prices (Figure 2.2.1). Regional trade growth declined during 2018.

In Turkey, the lira declined around 30 percent over the course of 2018, reflecting capital outflows in response to accelerating inflation, a perceived delay in monetary tightening, and rising private sector debt. The country accumulated a sizable current account deficit and a large foreign currency-denominated debt load, leaving it vulnerable to shifting investor sentiment and currency depreciation. Output shrank by 1.1 percent from the second quarter to the third quarter amid plummeting consumer confidence and credit scarcity. Despite this contraction, strong growth in the first half of the year will bring Turkish growth to an estimated 3.5 percent for 2018.

Growth among the Central European economies slowed in 2018. Softening exports and labor shortages restrained growth in Bulgaria, Croatia, and Romania. In contrast, despite labor shortages, growth in Poland accelerated slightly because of strong consumption and investment. Robust domestic demand supported activity in the Western Balkans, except for Montenegro. In the Former Yugoslav Republic of Macedonia, growth rebounded in 2018 as the formation of a new government ended a prolonged political crisis and improved investor sentiment (World Bank 2018i).

The Russian Federation and other oil exporters in Central Asia maintained steady growth in 2018, supported by a rise in oil prices. Although economic sanctions tightened, Russia experienced relatively low and stable inflation and increased oil production. As a result of robust domestic activity, the Russian economy expanded at a 1.6 percent pace in the year just ended (World Bank 2018j). Higher-than-expected production in the Kashagan oil field and strong domestic demand supported growth in Kazakhstan. A stabilization in the financial sector and higher oil prices contributed to a slow recovery of growth in Azerbaijan in 2018.

The stance of fiscal policy in the region varies. Turkey has committed to tight fiscal policy to help curb high inflation and currency depreciation. Romania's fiscal stance is mixed, with income tax reductions and increased public sector benefits offset by an increase in social contribution

---

Note: This section was prepared by Yoki Okawa. Research assistance was provided by Zhuo Chen and Mengyi Li.

FIGURE 2.2.1 ECA: Recent developments

Regional growth is estimated to have slowed in 2018 reflecting financial stress in Turkey and weak regional trade. Financial stress in Turkey, which experienced a sharp depreciation and an increase in bond spreads, does not appear to have spilled over to other countries in the region. Slowing inflation in the eastern ECA region led to loosening in monetary policy, while a pickup in inflation from 2016 level in the western ECA has not yet led to monetary tightening. The fiscal stance in the region is mixed.

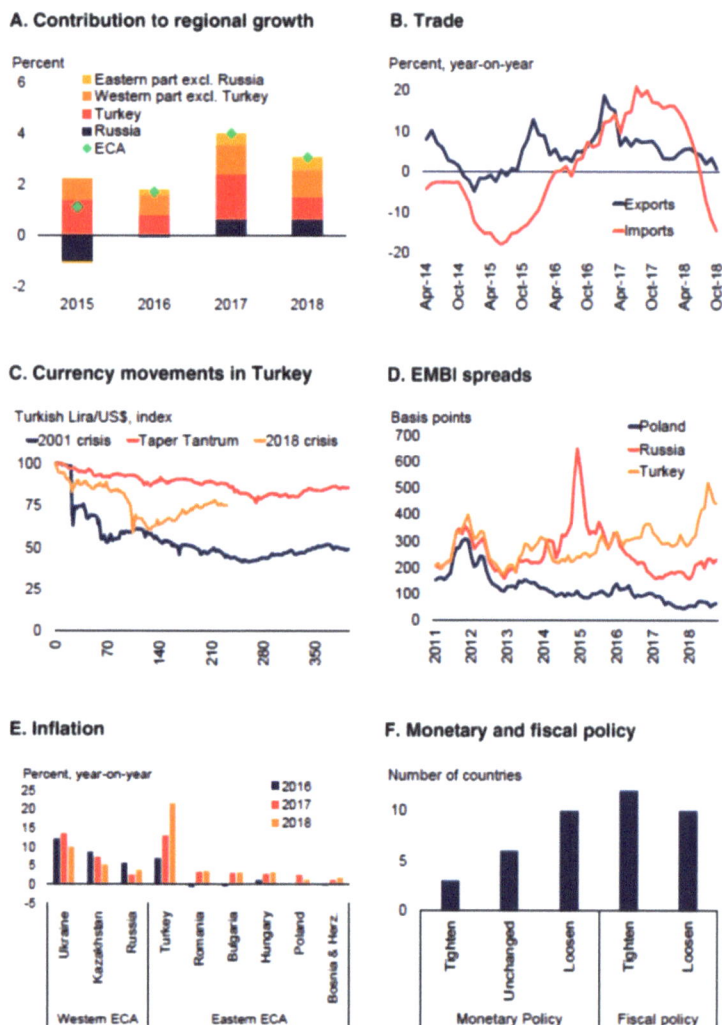

A. Contribution to regional growth

B. Trade

C. Currency movements in Turkey

D. EMBI spreads

E. Inflation

F. Monetary and fiscal policy

Source: Haver Analytics, World Bank.
A. Aggregates growth rates calculated using constant 2010 U.S. dollar GDP weights.
B. Three-month moving averages of GDP-weighted trade volume indexes for Russia, Turkey, Poland, Ukraine, Kazakhstan, Hungary, and Armenia.
C. Cumulative change of exchange rate for 400 days from the starting date. Starting dates are February 1, 2001, May 2, 2013 and May 2, 2018 for 2001 crisis, Taper Tantrum, and 2018 crisis, respectively. Last observation for the 2018 crisis is December 19, 2018.
E. Last observation is November for each year.
F. Monetary policy tightening/loosening is defined as increase/decrease of the central bank's policy rate between January and November 2018. Fiscal policy tightening/loosening is defined as increase/decrease of primary balance in estimated 2018 values compared to 2017.

revenue. Fiscal policy has become more procyclical in some Central European countries. In the eastern part of the region, the Russian government has implemented a new fiscal rule and is estimated

to have recorded its first surplus since 2012 in 2018. As fiscal stimulus measures are phased out, Kazakhstan has started to tighten its fiscal stance, resulting in improvements in its non-oil fiscal balance. Azerbaijan continues to rely on fiscal measures to support its economy.

For the majority of ECA countries, monetary policy is either stable or loosening. At the end of 2018, nine countries have policy rates lower than a year ago, while three countries have higher policy rates (Romania, Ukraine, Turkey). Inflation peaked at 25 percent in Turkey in October, significantly above the 5 percent target amid an overheating economy in the first half of 2018 and currency depreciation in the second. To ward off inflationary and currency pressures, Turkey's central bank increased the average cost of funding by more than 10 percentage points over the course of 2018. In Central Europe, tightening labor markets and increasing energy prices have pushed inflation up toward target, with monetary policy remaining stable in most countries. One exception is Romania, where robust domestic demand pushed inflation above the upper bound of the target band, prompting monetary policy tightening. Gradually accelerating inflation has also led to policy tightening in Ukraine. In the Western Balkans, Albania, FYR Macedonia, and Serbia have lowered policy rates amid stable and below-target inflation. For oil exporters, such as Azerbaijan and Kazakhstan, the stabilization of currency following the 2014-16 oil price plunge has resulted in lower inflation and looser monetary policy. In Russia, monetary policy was tightened in late 2018 amid pressures on the currency.

Outlook

The lingering effects of financial stress in Turkey are expected to further slow of regional growth in 2019. Growth is expected to slide to 2.3 percent, before recovering to 2.7 percent in 2020 (Figure 2.2.2). Excluding Turkey, regional growth is expected to average 2.6 percent during the forecast horizon, compared to 2.9 percent in 2018, with a gradual deceleration in Central Europe. This outlook is predicated on an orderly tightening of global financial conditions, oil prices averaging $67 in 2019-2021, a gradual slowdown in the

Euro Area, and the absence of heightened geopolitical tensions.

While the outlook for Turkey is subject to considerable uncertainty, the country is expected to be weighted down by high inflation, high interest rates, and low confidence, which will dampen consumption and investment. Turkish growth is expected to slow to 1.6 percent in 2019 and begin to recover by 2020 through a gradual improvement in domestic demand and continued strength in net exports. However, this outlook assumes that fiscal and monetary policy successfully avert further sharp falls in the lira and, that corporate debt restructurings help avert serious damage to the financial system. A comprehensive stabilization package with consistent policy framework, clear milestones, and effective communication would help reduce risks and support recovery.

Spillovers from Turkey to the rest of the region are expected to remain modest, as trade and financial linkages are relatively limited. On the trade side, Azerbaijan has the largest exposure, as 9 percent of its exports are directed to Turkey. Financial linkages are also small—only Georgia receives meaningful amounts of FDI from Turkey, and foreign bank ownership of Turkish assets is limited in scale.

Growth in western ECA, excluding Turkey, is projected to gradually slow toward potential, driven by a slowdown in Central European economies. Domestic demand in this sub-region will be constrained by tight labor markets, while a continued slowdown in the Euro Area will limit export growth. Poland is expected to slow from 5.0 percent in 2018 to 4.0 percent in 2019, as Euro Area growth slows.

Growth in eastern ECA is forecast to slow in 2019, as the large economies including Russia, Kazakhstan and Ukraine decelerate. The VAT in Russia is expected to rise from 18 to 20 percent in 2019, weighing on near term growth. Kazakhstan's economy is also expected to decelerate as oil production growth levels off and fiscal consolidation efforts continue (World Bank 2018k).

FIGURE 2.2.2 **ECA: Outlook and risks**

Regional growth is expected to slow notably in 2019 and gradually accelerate in 2020-21, partly reflecting a sharp decline and subsequent recovery in Turkish growth. A number of countries in the region appear vulnerable to shifts in investor sentiment, as reflected by their high current account deficits and corporate debt.

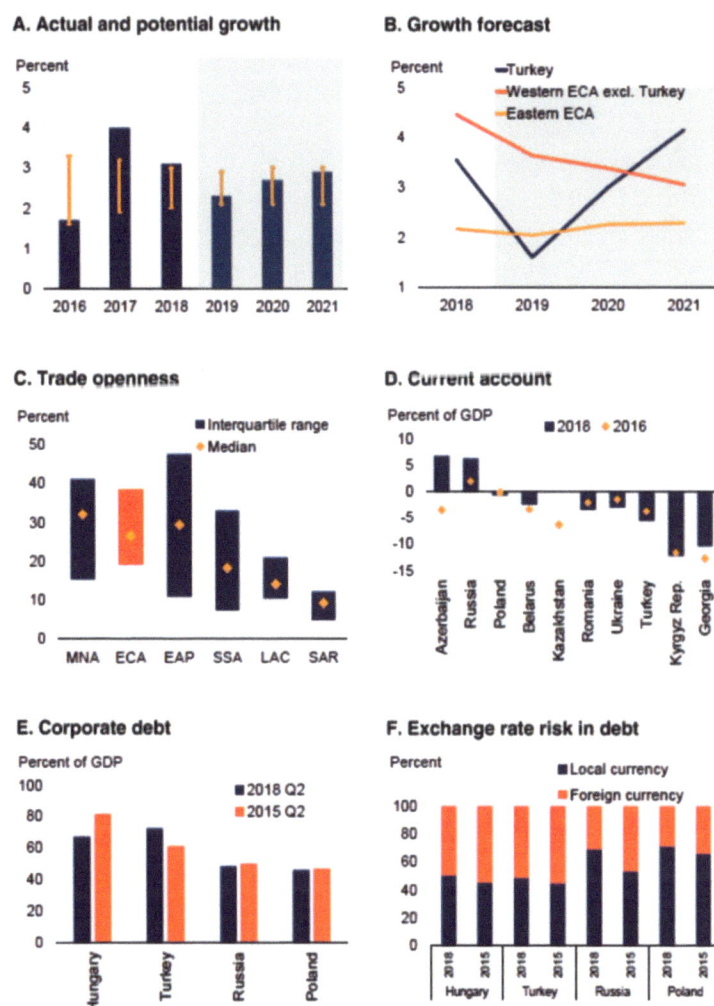

Source: Haver Analytics, Institute of International Finance, International Monetary Fund, World Bank.
A. Blue bars refer to GDP-weighted average actual growth and vertical orange line show minimum-maximum range of potential growth estimates based on five different methodologies (production function approach, multivariate filter, IMF World Economic Outlook five-year-ahead forecast, Consensus Forecasts, and potential growth estimates in OECD Economic Outlook and OECD Long-Term Baseline Projections).
A. B. Data in shaded area are forecasts.
C. Share of exports as a percentage of GDP in 2016. EAP = East Asia and Pacific, ECA = Europe and Central Asia, LAC = Latin America and the Caribbean, MNA = Middle East and North Africa, SAR = South Asia, and SSA = Sub-Saharan Africa.
D. Current account balance as a percentage of GDP.
E-F. The data used are IIF end-of-period estimates of non-financial corporate debt as a percentage of GDP.

Risks

While there are some upside risks to the forecasts —for example, that stronger-than-expected energy prices may support activity in Russia and other energy exporters—the balance of risks is increasingly tilted down. The most important downside risk is the possibility that the recent financial stress in Turkey worsens and triggers widespread bank failures. Turkish corporations carry significant debt, much of which is denominated in or linked to foreign currencies. Although many corporations are hedged against exchange rate risks, and corporate debt restructuring is on its way, falling domestic demand and forex exposure of the non-tradable sector pose risks. Currency depreciation and high interest rates could push corporate borrowers into bankruptcy and depleting banks' capital buffers. Renewed pressure in currency markets and increased uncertainty about the policy framework would increase the probability of a deepening crisis, implying a longer and more severe slowdown than currently forecast for Turkey (World Bank forthcoming). While direct linkages between Turkey and the rest of the region are small, an intensification of financial stress in Turkey or other EMDEs could also lead investors to re-evaluate their exposure in the region, which in turn could lead to capital outflows, currency depreciations, and rising borrowing costs.

The potential for financial stress is more elevated in countries with domestic vulnerabilities like Romania and Belarus, which have large current account deficits or large foreign-currency denominated debt. Public debt, which remains high despite recent declines, and private borrowing in foreign currencies makes Central European countries vulnerable to financial pressure. Public debt has also been trending up in Central Asia and the Western Balkans.

Increases in policy uncertainty could undermine confidence in the region and impact growth. A slowdown or reversal of ongoing structural reforms remains a risk in many countries in the region, especially in Armenia, Azerbaijan, Belarus, Ukraine, and Turkey. Tension concerning Syria or Ukraine could trigger new sanctions. Policy disagreements between the European Union and some Central European countries could deter international investors and reduce fiscal transfers. An escalation of trade restrictions between the United States and the Euro Area could have a negative impact on western ECA countries, as the Euro Area is the largest trading partner for all countries in the sub-region.

TABLE 2.2.1 Europe and Central Asia forecast summary

(Real GDP growth at market prices in percent, unless indicated otherwise)

Percentage point differences
from June 2018 projections

	2016	2017	2018e	2019f	2020f	2021f	2018e	2019f	2020f
EMDE ECA, GDP[1]	**1.7**	**4.0**	**3.1**	**2.3**	**2.7**	**2.9**	**-0.1**	**-0.8**	**-0.3**
EMDE ECA, GDP excl. Turkey	1.2	2.9	2.9	2.6	2.6	2.5	0.1	-0.2	-0.1
(Average including countries with full national accounts and balance of payments data only)[2]									
EMDE ECA, GDP[2]	1.6	4.0	3.0	2.3	2.7	2.9	-0.2	-0.8	-0.3
GDP per capita (U.S. dollars)	1.2	3.6	2.7	2.0	2.4	2.7	-0.1	-0.8	-0.3
PPP GDP	1.6	3.9	3.0	2.3	2.7	2.9	-0.2	-0.8	-0.3
Private consumption	1.2	4.8	3.0	2.4	3.2	2.9	-0.1	-0.8	0.1
Public consumption	2.9	2.1	1.9	2.5	2.2	2.1	0.4	1.1	0.9
Fixed investment	0.0	6.3	0.3	2.3	4.6	4.8	-4.9	-2.5	-0.1
Exports, GNFS[3]	3.4	6.9	5.5	5.3	4.3	4.5	0.7	0.6	-0.4
Imports, GNFS[3]	3.2	10.4	2.8	5.1	5.8	5.8	-2.7	-0.4	0.6
Net exports, contribution to growth	0.2	-0.7	1.1	0.3	-0.2	-0.2	1.1	0.3	-0.2
Memo items: GDP									
Commodity exporters[4]	0.3	2.0	2.1	2.0	2.2	2.3	0.1	-0.3	-0.1
Commodity importers[5]	3.1	6.0	4.0	2.6	3.2	3.6	-0.3	-1.2	-0.5
Central Europe[6]	3.4	4.9	4.5	3.6	3.3	3.0	0.3	-0.1	-0.2
Western Balkans[7]	3.0	2.5	3.5	3.5	3.8	3.8	0.3	0.1	0.0
Eastern Europe[8]	0.8	2.6	3.5	2.9	3.1	3.4	0.2	-0.7	-0.4
South Caucasus[9]	-1.6	2.0	2.5	4.0	3.8	3.4	-0.1	0.0	0.1
Central Asia[10]	3.3	4.8	4.4	4.2	4.0	4.1	0.0	0.0	0.0
Russia	-0.2	1.5	1.6	1.5	1.8	1.8	0.1	-0.3	0.0
Turkey	3.2	7.4	3.5	1.6	3.0	4.2	-1.0	-2.4	-1.0
Poland	3.1	4.8	5.0	4.0	3.6	3.3	0.8	0.3	0.1

Source: World Bank.
Note: e = estimate; f = forecast. EMDE = emerging market and developing economy. World Bank forecasts are frequently updated based on new information and changing (global) circumstances. Consequently, projections presented here may differ from those contained in other Bank documents, even if basic assessments of countries' prospects do not differ at any given moment in time.
1. GDP at market prices and expenditure components are measured in constant 2010 U.S. dollars.
2. Sub-region aggregate excludes Bosnia and Herzegovina, Kosovo, Montenegro, Serbia, Tajikistan, and Turkmenistan, for which data limitations prevent the forecasting of GDP components.
3. Exports and imports of goods and non-factor services (GNFS).
4. Includes Albania, Armenia, Azerbaijan, Kazakhstan, the Kyrgyz Republic, Kosovo, Russia, Tajikistan, Turkmenistan, Ukraine, and Uzbekistan.
5. Includes Belarus, Bosnia and Herzegovina, Bulgaria, Croatia, Georgia, Hungary, FYR Macedonia, Moldova, Montenegro, Poland, Romania, Serbia, and Turkey.
6. Includes Bulgaria, Croatia, Hungary, Poland, and Romania.
7. Includes Albania, Bosnia and Herzegovina, Kosovo, FYR Macedonia, Montenegro, and Serbia.
8. Includes Belarus, Moldova, and Ukraine.
9. Includes Armenia, Azerbaijan, and Georgia.
10. Includes Kazakhstan, the Kyrgyz Republic, Tajikistan, Turkmenistan, and Uzbekistan.
To download this data, please visit www.worldbank.org/gep.

TABLE 2.2.2 Europe and Central Asia country forecasts[1]

(Real GDP growth at market prices in percent, unless indicated otherwise)

Percentage point differences from June 2018 projections

	2016	2017	2018e	2019f	2020f	2021f	2018e	2019f	2020f
Albania	3.4	3.8	4.0	3.6	3.5	3.5	0.4	0.1	0.0
Armenia	0.2	7.5	5.3	4.3	4.6	4.6	1.2	0.3	0.6
Azerbaijan	-3.1	0.1	1.1	3.6	3.3	2.7	-0.7	-0.2	0.1
Belarus	-2.5	2.4	3.4	2.7	2.5	2.5	0.5	0.0	0.0
Bosnia and Herzegovina[2]	3.1	3.0	3.2	3.4	3.9	4.0	0.0	0.0	-0.1
Bulgaria	3.9	3.8	3.3	3.1	3.0	2.8	-0.5	-0.5	-0.6
Croatia	3.5	2.9	2.7	2.8	2.8	2.6	0.1	0.1	0.0
Georgia	2.8	4.8	5.3	5.0	5.0	5.0	0.8	0.2	0.0
Hungary	2.3	4.1	4.6	3.2	2.8	2.4	0.5	0.0	-0.2
Kazakhstan	1.1	4.1	3.8	3.5	3.2	3.2	0.1	0.2	0.4
Kosovo	4.1	4.2	4.2	4.5	4.5	4.5	-0.6	-0.3	-0.3
Kyrgyz Republic	4.3	4.6	3.1	3.4	3.9	4.0	-1.1	-1.4	-1.1
Macedonia, FYR	2.8	0.2	2.5	2.9	3.2	3.3	0.2	0.2	0.2
Moldova	4.5	4.5	4.8	3.8	3.5	3.2	1.0	0.1	0.0
Montenegro	2.9	4.7	3.8	2.8	2.5	2.5	1.0	0.3	0.4
Poland	3.1	4.8	5.0	4.0	3.6	3.3	0.8	0.3	0.1
Romania	4.8	6.9	4.1	3.5	3.1	2.8	-1.0	-1.0	-1.0
Russia	-0.2	1.5	1.6	1.5	1.8	1.8	0.1	-0.3	0.0
Serbia	2.8	1.9	3.5	3.5	4.0	4.0	0.5	0.0	0.0
Tajikistan	6.9	7.1	6.0	6.0	6.0	6.0	-0.1	0.0	0.0
Turkey	3.2	7.4	3.5	1.6	3.0	4.2	-1.0	-2.4	-1.0
Turkmenistan	6.2	6.5	6.2	5.6	5.1	4.9	-0.1	-0.7	-1.2
Ukraine	2.3	2.5	3.5	2.9	3.4	3.8	0.0	-1.1	-0.6
Uzbekistan	7.8	5.3	5.0	5.1	5.5	6.0	0.0	0.0	0.0

Source: World Bank.

Note: e = estimate; f = forecast. World Bank forecasts are frequently updated based on new information and changing (global) circumstances. Consequently, projections presented here may differ from those contained in other Bank documents, even if basic assessments of countries' prospects do not significantly differ at any given moment in time.

1. GDP at market prices and expenditure components are measured in constant 2010 U.S. dollars, unless indicated otherwise.
2. GDP growth rate at constant prices is based on production approach.
To download this data, please visit www.worldbank.org/gep.

BOX 2.2.1 Informality in Europe and Central Asia

The share of informal output in Europe and Central Asia (ECA) is larger than the EMDE average, even after a decline from elevated 1995 levels, but informality in the labor market is below average and there is wide heterogeneity within the region. Informality in ECA has been associated with weak institutions, sizeable agricultural sectors, and large-scale migration as well as low productivity, fiscal revenue losses, and poor job prospects for youth. In some ECA countries, declines in informality have accompanied the simplification of tax systems and labor market reforms, as well as reforms to reduce corruption.

Introduction

Informal output accounts for a larger share of official GDP (36 percent) in Europe and Central Asia (ECA) than in the average EMDE (Figure 2.2.1.1).[1] However, despite a widely shared history of transition from centrally planned to market economies, there is significant variation in informality within the region, ranging from 22 percent to 56 percent.

Against this backdrop, this box examines the following questions.

- How has informality evolved in Europe and Central Asia?

- What have been the macroeconomic and social correlates of informality?

- What policy options are available to address challenges associated with informality?

Evolution and drivers of informality

Evolution of informality. With the collapse of centrally planned economies in the late 1980s, many firms chose to operate in the informal sector to avoid burdensome regulations, taxation, or corruption. Estimates based on electricity consumption suggest that the average size of the informal economy more than doubled during 1989-95 (Johnson, Kaufmann, and Shleifer 1997). While informality declined in most countries once they began to recover, there was considerable heterogeneity across countries. In the western part of the region, where institutions are stronger, informality has declined steeply.[2] Notwithstanding this decline, one in ten formal employees

in Central Europe still received "envelope wages" as recently as 2006, and the informal economy accounted for 10 percentage points of GDP more than in the more advanced EU19 economies in 1999-2007 (Fialová and Schneider 2011).[3] In the eastern part of the region, the decline in informality has been considerably less pronounced, in part reflecting slower implementation of market liberalizing and other reforms, as well as persistently higher levels of corruption (Kaufmann and Kaliberda 1996).

Drivers of informality. Informality in ECA economies has typically been attributed to three factors:

- *Agriculture.* Higher labor market informality has been associated with a larger share of workers in the agricultural sector as they tend to be self-employed (Figure 2.2.1.2; Rutkowski 2006; World Bank 2011). A larger agricultural sector has also been correlated with greater informality in non-agricultural sectors (Atesagaoglu, Bayram, and Elgin 2017).

- *Remittances.* In countries with large diasporas, informal activity has been higher among workers in households that receive sizeable remittances (Chatterjee and Turnovsky 2018; Shapiro and Mandelman 2016). In Kazakhstan, FYR Macedonia, Moldova, Serbia, Tajikistan, and Ukraine, remittances provided the capital to establish small businesses, which tend to be informal, and the income support needed to accept less secure but often more lucrative informal work (Ivlevs 2016).

- *Institutions.* Institutional quality varies widely within the region. The east has considerably weaker institutional quality indicators than the west, which implemented substantial reforms in the context of the EU accession process (Figure 2.2.1.2; Kaufmann and Kaliberda 1996).[4] In general, a favorable business

---

Note: This section was prepared by Yoki Okawa. Research assistance was provided by Zhuo Chen and Mengyi Li.

[1] The methodology of informality estimates is discussed in Chapter 3.

[2] The western part of the region includes Central Europe (Bulgaria, Croatia, Hungary, Poland and Romania) and the Western Balkans (Albania, Bosnia and Herzegovina, Kosovo, the Former Yugoslav Republic of Macedonia, Montenegro, and Serbia), and Turkey. The eastern part of the region comprises Eastern Europe (Belarus, Moldova, and Ukraine), South Caucasus (Armenia, Azerbaijan and Georgia), Central Asia (Kazakhstan, Kyrgyz Republic, Tajikistan, Turkmenistan, and Uzbekistan) and Russia.

[3] "Envelope wages" refers to the practice of paying a portion of wages in undeclared cash to avoid tax and social contributions (see, for example, Horodnic 2016, and Williams and Padmore 2013).

[4] Institutional indicators include the World Bank's Doing Business Indicators and World Governance Indicators of government effectiveness, control of corruption, or rule of law.

BOX 2.2.1 Informality in Europe and Central Asia (*continued*)

FIGURE 2.2.1.1 Informality in Europe and Central Asia

The share of informal output in the ECA region is higher than the EMDE median throughout the sample period, and it declined at the roughly same pace as in the other EMDE regions. However, employment informality is low, in part reflecting a low share of agriculture in some countries in the region. Institutional quality is on par with other regions, albeit with considerable heterogeneity within the region.

A. Share of informal economy in output

B. Share of labor force without pension; share of self-employed

C. Institutional quality

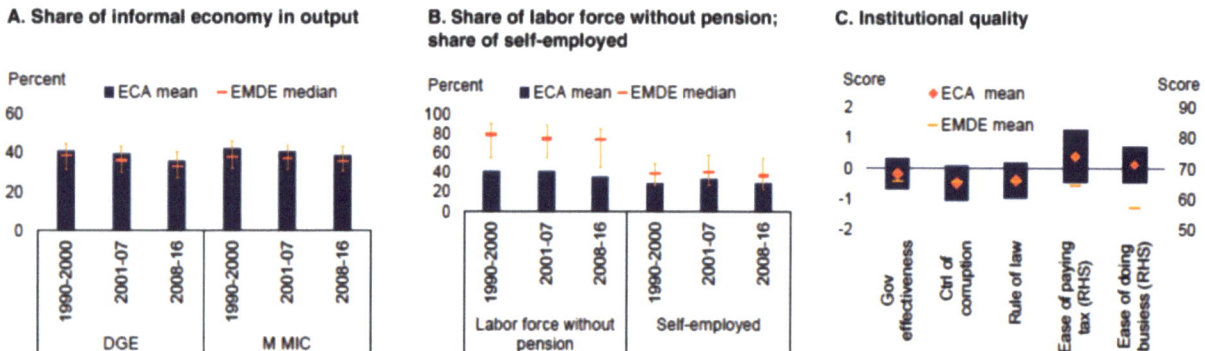

Source: Elgin et al. (forthcoming), World Bank.
Note: Blue bars show simple averages of the informal economy of the region. Red markers show the median average of all EMDEs and the vertical lines denote interquartile range of all EMDEs.
A. Both DGE and MIMIC estimates measure the informal output in percent of official GDP.
B. Labor force without pension is the fraction of the labor force that doesn't contribute to a retirement pension scheme, which is derived from the original data on pension coverage obtained from WDI. Self-employed is the share of self-employment in total employment.
C. All measures are taken from the latest year available. The first three institutional measures are taken from World Bank's World Governance Indicators (2017), with a higher value indicating better institutional quality in year 2016. The "Ease of doing business" (DB 2018) and "Ease of paying taxes" (DB 2017) are taken from World Bank's Doing Business database and measured as "Distance to Frontier", with a higher value indicating an easier environment for businesses.

environment encourages firms to do business in the formal sector (Chapter 3). However, the transition from economies dominated by large state-owned enterprises to more private-business friendly economies sometimes created more informal employment and larger informal sectors (Earle and Sakova 2000).

Correlates of informality

Firm productivity. Some country-specific studies suggest that informal firms tend to be less productive than formal firms. In Turkey, for example, after controlling for firm characteristics, informal firms in the manufacturing and services sectors had 16 percent and 38 percent lower total factor productivity than formal firms, respectively, with the productivity gap attributed to restricted access to public services and formal markets (Taymaz 2009). By these estimates, shifting all informal firms in the Turkish manufacturing and services sectors into the formal sector could raise total output by 5 percent and 25 percent, respectively (Taymaz 2009). In Kyrgyz Republic, productivity in the informal sector has declined significantly since 2009, despite robust productivity

growth in the formal sector (Sattar, Keller, and Baibagsy Uulu 2015).

Fiscal revenues. Large informal sectors erode tax revenues and hamper governments' ability to provide public goods. However, the magnitude of foregone revenues due to informality remains a matter of debate. One estimate suggests that tax revenue losses from informality could have been as high as 7 percent of GDP in Central Asia and the Caucasus in 2004 (Grigorian and Davoodi 2007). However, estimates based on micro survey data suggest only modest potential revenues gains (0.03-0.07 percentage points of GDP) from turning informal workers into formal workers in a country such as Ukraine in 2009, as newly formalized are mainly low-skilled and subject to low tax rates (World Bank 2011).

Labor market prospects. Informal employment is more common among young, low-skilled, and female workers. Some studies suggest that informal employment can damage long-term carrier prospects and entrench income differentials (Taymaz 2009; World Bank 2007, 2011). However, informal employment can also be an income source when formal employment opportunities are scarce,

BOX 2.2.1 Informality in Europe and Central Asia (*continued*)

as well as help develop human capital that can lead to formal employment or self-employment, as has been found for Turkey and Russia(Guariglia and Kim 2006; Taymaz 2009).[5] Better-paid informal activity may also encourage skilled professionals to forgo migration opportunities in highly regulated economies with large emigration, such as Tajikistan (Abdulloev, Gang, and Landon-Lane 2011).

Inequality. In some countries, the low wages paid to informal workers (the "wage penalty") compared with formal workers have contributed to inequality. In Serbia, the wage penalty contributed to rising inequality between 2002 and 2007 (Krstic and Sanfey 2010). A similar wage penalty in Turkey was found for less educated workers (Taymaz 2009). However, in some cases informal workers have been found to earn a wage premium, e.g., in Russia, Romania, Tajikistan, and Ukraine (Lehmann and Norberto 2018; Shehu and Nilsson 2014; Staneva and Arabsheibani 2014; Zahariev 2003). In those countries, the informal wage premium may compensate for the lack of social security and lower job security (Lehmann and Norberto 2018; Marcouiller, de Castrilla and Woodruff 1997).[6]

Policy challenges

The impact of policies on informality can depend on country characteristics such as labor market flexibility, efficiency of tax collection or control of corruption. This underscores the importance of ensuring that reform efforts are carefully tailored to country circumstances to avoid unintended increases in informality.

Labor market policies. The impact of labor market reforms on informality has been mixed in ECA, and appears to have depended on the types of the reform. In a cross-sectional study of ECA countries, more restrictive employment protection legislation has been associated with a higher share of the informal economy (both in terms of GDP and labor force; Fialová 2011; Lehmann and Muravyev 2009). In contrast, there was no robust association of informality with more generous unemployment benefits or higher minimum wages

(Fialová and Schneider 2011; Lehmann and Muravyev 2009).

Fiscal policy. Several countries have changed tax rates or tax enforcement, but the impact on informality has varied. That said, reducing the tax compliance burden and subsidizing the transition to formal sectors have typically been accompanied by declines in informality.[7]

- *Flat tax.* A flat labor income tax rate has been introduced in several ECA countries (e.g., Bulgaria, Poland, Russia, and Romania). The flat tax reform in Russia was followed by a decline in informal employment and informal activity, especially in the top income bracket (Slonimczyk 2012). A simulation suggests that the Polish flat tax reform in 2004 could have led to a 48 percent increase in reported business income and 25 percent higher tax revenue, despite a lower average marginal tax rate (Kopczuk 2012). However, flat tax structures can be regressive and need to be balanced with poverty fighting initiatives.

- *Preferential tax schemes.* Certain preferential tax schemes for the self-employed and small firms can encourage movement away from the informal sector. One such scheme, indirect assessments of tax liabilities, has been shown to encourage entrepreneurship, help revenue collection from hard-to-tax sectors, and ease the transition from informal to formal work. However, such preferential schemes can also encourage formal workers to pursue the preferential status and may encourage firms to remain small (Packard et al. 2014).

- *Shift from labor to other taxation.* Shifting from labor income taxes, which constitute a wedge between informal and formal employment, to less distorting and more easily enforced taxes, such as value-added taxes and progressive real estate taxes, can shrink the informal economy (Packard, Koettl, and Montenegro 2012).

- *Subsidies.* A formal employment subsidy, such as the one introduced in Turkey, can increase the number of registered jobs by encouraging informal workers to

[5] This is consistent with the finding that informally employed youth have lower job satisfaction relative to their peers with formal jobs (Shehu and Nilsson 2014).

[6] Controlling for worker characteristics and selection bias, the absence of male-female wage differentials in the informal economy—in the presence of large differentials in the formal economy—has been interpreted as sign of lesser gender discrimination in the informal economy than in the formal economy in Turkey (Tansel 2000).

[7] On the one hand, higher labor tax rates encourage a move of labor into untaxed informal employment, especially for low-wage earners (Koettl and Weber 2012). On the other hand, higher labor tax rates have in some cases been associated with a lower share of informal employment, because higher revenue allow governments to provide better public goods that can only be accessed in formal employment (Fialová and Schneider 2011, Friedman et al. 2000).

BOX 2.2.1 Informality in Europe and Central Asia (*continued*)

FIGURE 2.2.1.2 Correlates of informality in Europe and Central Asia

Informality as a percentage of GDP in the eastern part of the region is higher than the western part of the region, in part reflecting differences in institutional quality. Employment informality tends to be higher in countries with larger agricultural sectors.

A. Informality in output

B. Institutional quality

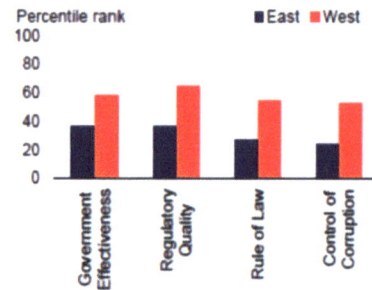

C. Labor market informality and agricultural employment

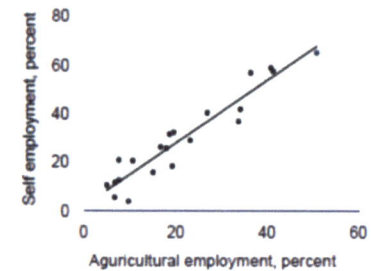

Source: Elgin et al. (forthcoming), European Bank of Reconstruction and Development, World Bank.
A-B. Data are from the latest year available, usually 2016. The western part of the region includes Central Europe (Bulgaria, Croatia, Hungary, Poland and Romania) and the Western Balkans (Albania, Bosnia and Herzegovina, Kosovo, the Former Yugoslav Republic of Macedonia, Montenegro, and Serbia), and Turkey. The eastern part of the region comprises Eastern Europe (Belarus, Moldova, and Ukraine), South Caucasus (Armenia, Azerbaijan and Georgia), Central Asia (Kazakhstan, Kyrgyz Republic, Tajikistan, Turkmenistan, and Uzbekistan) and Russia.
A. Orange diamonds indicate subsample average and blue bars indicate one standard deviation range.
C. Agricultural employment and self-employment are shares of employment in agriculture or share of self-employed in total employment.

transition to formal employment as well as provide better social protection (Betcherman, Daysal, Pagés 2010).

Control of corruption. Better governance and more effective tax authorities can reduce the size of the informal economy and increase tax revenue. Bureaucratic

corruption has been associated with greater informal activity in Poland, Romania, and Slovakia (Johnson et al. 2000). Conversely, better control of corruption has reduced the extent of informal activities in the countries that joined the European Union in the mid-2000s (Fialová and Schneider 2011).

LATIN AMERICA and THE CARIBBEAN

Growth in Latin America and the Caribbean was disappointingly weak in 2018, at an estimated 0.6 percent, and notably lower than previously expected. This reflected the impact of Argentina's currency crisis, a truckers' strike and policy uncertainty in Brazil, and worsening conditions in Venezuela. Growth is expected to pick up to 1.7 percent in 2019, as growth accelerates in Brazil and the recession in Argentina begins to fade. Per capita growth in LAC is projected to pick up moderately, and to outpace that in advanced economies starting in 2020, after six years of stalled convergence. Downside risks continue to dominate. Key external risks include further tightening of external financial conditions and additional escalation of international trade policy uncertainty. The region also faces intraregional and domestic risks, such as spillovers from larger-than-expected growth contractions in Argentina and Venezuela and the persistent threat of natural disasters and extreme weather.

Recent developments

Growth in Latin America and the Caribbean (LAC) stalled at a subdued 0.6 percent in 2018, substantially weaker than previously projected. The disappointing growth outcome reflected softening global trade growth and tighter external financing conditions. Developments in Argentina, Brazil, and Venezuela hindered regional growth, despite better performance in several mid-size economies (e.g., Chile, Colombia, Peru). Growth moderated in Central America, reflecting a variety of factors, while it strengthened in almost all Caribbean economies as the subregion began to recover from a severe 2017 hurricane season.

In Brazil, growth bounced back in the second half of 2018, following a strike-induced dip around mid-year, but remains subdued. In Argentina, the currency crisis and associated sharp tightening of monetary and fiscal policies, together with the effect of a severe drought on the agriculture sector, resulted in a contraction in activity. Venezuela's economic collapse has deepened, and there is no indication that the latest redenomination of the currency has had a major impact on ongoing hyperinflationary dynamics.

Commodity price developments are also affecting LAC economies. The decline in copper prices in the second half of 2018 contributed to slowing growth momentum in Chile and Peru, after a an acceleration in the first half. Rising oil prices underpinned accelerating growth in oil-producing Colombia, while they were one factor that inhibited growth in oil-importing Central America in 2018, despite the decline in prices at the end of the year. The Central American sub-region was also affected by weak confidence in Costa Rica and Panama, political uncertainty in Guatemala, and social unrest in Nicaragua.

A long-awaited rebound in regional fixed investment that began in 2017 was significantly weaker in 2018 than previously expected, after losing momentum in the first half of the year (Figure 2.3.1). Export growth in the region was also lower than expected, owing to the drought in Argentina and slowing global trade growth.

Nearly all LAC economies with floating exchange rates have experienced nominal depreciation against the U.S. dollar, particularly Argentina, Brazil, Chile, and Uruguay. The adjustment in effective terms has been more modest. In most of these economies, especially Argentina, depreciation is contributing to a rise in inflation. Recent interest-rate hikes (e.g., in Chile) were

---

Note: This section was prepared by Dana Vorisek. Research assistance was provided by Brent Harrison.

FIGURE 2.3.1 **LAC: Recent developments**

Investment and export momentum in LAC have slowed. Rising U.S. interest rates and weakening investor sentiment toward EMDEs has translated into diminished capital inflows and rising bond spreads and credit default swap spreads in LAC, while a strengthening U.S. dollar is putting upward pressure on inflation in some countries. Fiscal deficits narrowed in most LAC countries in 2018, mainly reflecting higher revenues, but debt continues to build.

A. Investment and export growth

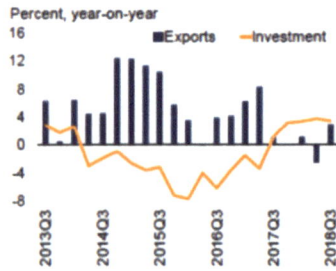

Percent, year-on-year

B. Exchange rates against the U.S. dollar

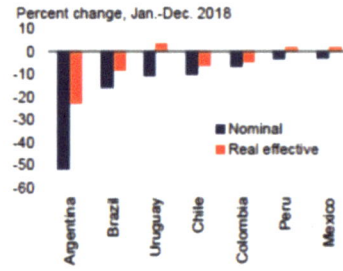

Percent change, Jan.-Dec. 2018

C. Inflation

Percent, year-on-year

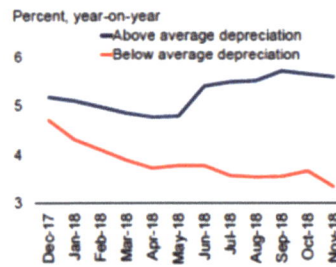

D. Bond spreads

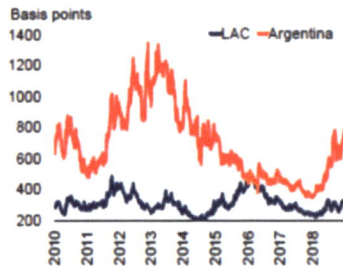

Basis points

E. Gross capital inflows

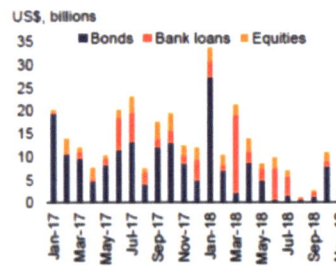

US$, billions

F. Fiscal balances and government debt

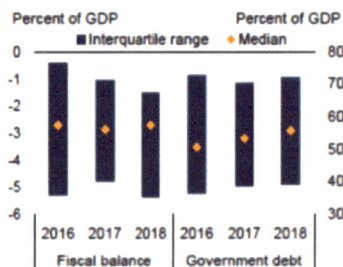

Percent of GDP   Percent of GDP

Sources: Bloomberg, CPB Netherlands Bureau for Economic Policy Analysis, Dealogic, Haver Analytics, International Monetary Fund, World Bank.
A. Investment growth is the GDP-weighted average of 15 economies, excluding Venezuela, that represent 93 percent of regional GDP. Investment for 2018Q3 is estimated using actual data for economies representing 87 percent of regional GDP. Last observation is 2018Q3.
B. Last observation is December 19, 2018.
C. Lines show group averages. Above average and below average groups are delineated according to currency depreciation against the U.S. dollar between January 2, 2018 and November 1, 2018. Sample includes 17 economies, excluding Argentina and Venezuela, and excluding those with conventional currency pegs and currency boards and those using the U.S. dollar as their official currency. Last inflation observation is November 2018.
D. LAC line shows median of 15 economies. Last observation is December 19, 2018.
E. Last observation is November 2018.
F. Sample includes 32 economies.

made partly in reaction to exchange rate pass-through to domestic inflation, despite falling pass-through ratios observed over the long term (Ha,

Stocker, and Yilmazkuday 2019). Central banks in several countries have intervened in foreign exchange markets using derivative instruments to reduce currency volatility (e.g., Brazil, Uruguay) or to build reserves (e.g., Colombia).

External financing conditions have tightened. Against the backdrop of rising U.S. interest rates, U.S. dollar appreciation, and weaker investor sentiment toward EMDEs, the region has experienced a generalized rise in bond and credit default swap spreads and a fall in equity prices. Capital inflows, particularly bond flows, steadily diminished through the third quarter of 2018. Current account deficits have widened in most commodity-exporting and commodity-importing economies. Several Caribbean economies that were not significantly damaged by hurricanes in 2017, however, registered narrowing deficits or widening surpluses as a share of GDP in 2018 on strong tourism inflows and rising oil prices (e.g., The Bahamas, Belize, St. Vincent and the Grenadines, and Trinidad and Tobago).

Fiscal conditions across the region remain fragile, and government debt continues to build. Fiscal deficits narrowed slightly in most countries in 2018, however. The improvement mainly reflected higher revenues, in part stemming from rising prices of key commodities. The fiscal austerity program in Argentina will be challenging to implement but should improve long-term fiscal sustainability, while a recently legislated fiscal reform in Costa Rica will boost revenues and should improve investor sentiment. In Colombia, a proposed tax reform would boost revenues in order to comply with fiscal targets. A proposed tax reform in Chile would integrate and streamline the tax system.

Outlook

Regional growth is projected to advance to a still modest 1.7 percent in 2019, lower than previously projected, and build to 2.5 percent in 2021 (Figure 2.3.2). The acceleration will be supported mainly by a pickup in private consumption. Investment growth will accelerate, though at a slower pace this year than previously expected, in view of tight financing conditions and planned public spending reductions in a number of countries. Decelerating global trade will limit export growth during the forecast period.

Although the prices of key non-oil commodities such as soybeans and copper are projected to continue rising through the forecast period, copper prices will increase at a much slower pace through 2021 than in 2017 and 2018. Oil prices are projected to be flat, on average, during 2019-21, at $67 per barrel, potentially limiting fiscal and export revenue increases in oil-producing economies.

In Brazil, growth is expected to steadily build momentum in 2019, from a weak base. The forecast of 2.2 percent for this year assumes that fiscal reforms are implemented expeditiously under the incoming administration, and that a recovery of consumption and investment, resulting from improving confidence and investor sentiment, will outweigh the negative growth effect of reduced government spending. In Mexico, policy uncertainty and the prospect of still subdued investment is expected to keep growth at a moderate 2.0 percent in 2019, despite the decrease in trade-related uncertainty following the announcement of the United States-Mexico-Canada Agreement. Argentina's economy is expected to continue contracting in 2019 as deep fiscal consolidation results in a loss of employment and reduction in consumption and investment, and as high interest rates place corporate balance sheets under stress and dampen private investment.

By 2020, a strengthening recovery in Brazil, modestly accelerating growth in Mexico, and solid performance in Chile, Colombia, and Peru, are expected to help push regional growth to 2.4 percent, consistent with potential. Per capita GDP growth in the region is also expected to accelerate moderately, and to outpace per capita growth in advanced economies starting in 2020, after six years of stalled convergence.

Achieving sustained improvements in potential growth in the region over the medium term will require implementing reforms in several areas. There is need to improve infrastructure and

FIGURE 2.3.2 LAC: Outlook and risks

Growth in LAC is projected to accelerate only moderately through 2021, and at a slower pace than previously expected. Risks to the regional outlook are predominantly to the downside. Further tightening of global financing conditions and escalation of trade tensions among major economies are key external risks. The region also faces intraregional and domestic risks, such as spillovers from a larger-than-expected growth contraction in Argentina or a worsening collapse in Venezuela, and unexpected disruptions from natural disasters and extreme weather.

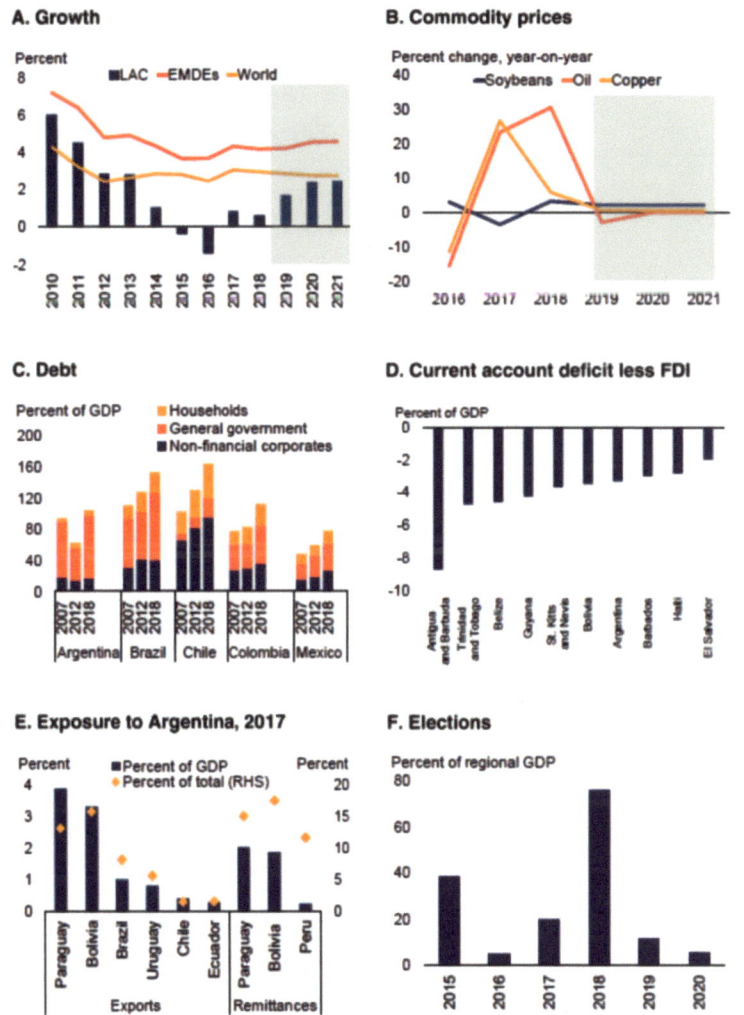

A. Growth

B. Commodity prices

C. Debt

D. Current account deficit less FDI

E. Exposure to Argentina, 2017

F. Elections

Sources: Bank for International Settlements, Comtrade, Haver Analytics, International Monetary Fund, World Bank.
B. Lines show change in nominal prices.
C. Bars show data for 2007Q4, 2012Q4, and 2018Q2.
F. Chart shows GDP of LAC countries holding presidential or parliamentary elections in a given year as a share of regional GDP. An economy is counted only once when both types of elections occur in a single year.

education attainment, reduce labor market inflexibility, deepen trade integration, and address the negative economic and social outcomes of informality, among other challenges (World Bank 2018l; Chapter 3; Box 2.3).

Risks

Risks to the regional outlook remain tilted to the downside. The experience of Argentina in 2018 is a stark reminder of the risk of sudden and widespread shifts in investor sentiment. Tightening global financing conditions are a particular concern for countries with large current account deficits or reliance on volatile capital inflows (e.g., Argentina, Bolivia, and several Caribbean countries), with high external debt loads (e.g., Jamaica, Nicaragua, Venezuela), or with sizable foreign-currency-denominated debt as a share of GDP (e.g., Costa Rica, Honduras, Nicaragua).

Trade tensions are another key external risk. Although trade diversion in response to rising trade restrictions in the United States and Canada may benefit some LAC economies in the short term, continued trade tensions may dampen regional growth in the medium term through export, confidence, and commodity market channels.

LAC economies also face intraregional and domestic sources of risk. Thus far, the recession in Argentina has had limited spillovers on the rest of the region. But a larger-than-expected contraction in Argentina could spill over to the rest of the region through trade and financial flows. Bolivia and Paraguay are most reliant on Argentina as a destination for goods exports and a source of remittance inflows. Although Uruguay has diversified its trading partners in recent years, it remains reliant on Argentina for services export revenues through tourism. Cross-border bank lending data for Latin American economies is patchy but suggests that Panama is most exposed, although with bank claims on Argentina still limited at approximately 0.6 percent of domestic GDP.

Continued outward migration from Venezuela is producing spillovers elsewhere in the region. In Colombia, the cost of providing basic public services to migrants and Colombian returnees at levels similar to those delivered to the local population is an estimated 0.2–0.4 percent of GDP per year in the short term (World Bank

2018m).[1] However, in the medium and long term, inward migration to Colombia could result in a growth boost as a result of a larger labor supply and higher consumption and investment.

Poor fiscal conditions and slow progress in addressing of fiscal imbalances are downside risks, and may have negative repercussions for debt sustainability and market confidence. In Argentina, for instance, adherence to the fiscal consolidation plan is key to a quick emergence from the recent currency crisis. Plans to implement fiscal reform in other countries (e.g., Costa Rica) need to be carried out to retain investor confidence. In Brazil, the new administration needs to urgently make plans to reduce fiscal vulnerabilities arising from an unsustainable pension system.

Election-related risks, which generated considerable uncertainty in countries such as Brazil and Mexico in 2018, are expected to recede, given that the elections scheduled in the next two years are in economies representing a much lower share of regional GDP. However, it will be incumbent on some new governments to implement challenging policy reforms.

Unexpected disruptions related to natural disasters and extreme weather represent a significant ongoing risk. Hurricanes, floods, droughts, and earthquakes have long had detrimental impacts on growth in several economies in the region in recent years. The region remains highly vulnerable to such events, underscoring the need to use risk instruments such as catastrophe bonds and domestic and multi-country catastrophe risk insurance funds (Végh et al. 2018).

---

[1] Calculations of the cost of public services are made using the number of migrants and returnees in Colombia as of September 2018.

TABLE 2.3.1 Latin America and the Caribbean forecast summary

(Real GDP growth at market prices in percent, unless indicated otherwise)

Percentage point differences
from June 2018 projections

	2016	2017	2018e	2019f	2020f	2021f	2018e	2019f	2020f
EMDE LAC, GDP[1]	-1.5	0.8	0.6	1.7	2.4	2.5	-1.1	-0.6	-0.1
(Average including countries with full national accounts and balance of payments data only)[2]									
EMDE LAC, GDP[2]	-1.4	0.8	0.6	1.7	2.4	2.5	-1.1	-0.6	-0.1
GDP per capita (U.S. dollars)	-2.5	-0.2	-0.4	0.7	1.4	1.5	-1.1	-0.6	-0.1
PPP GDP	-0.8	1.2	0.9	1.8	2.5	2.6	-1.0	-0.6	-0.1
Private consumption	-1.6	1.6	0.5	1.8	2.7	2.8	-1.6	-0.7	0.0
Public consumption	0.1	-0.7	0.1	-0.1	0.1	0.4	0.3	-0.3	-0.6
Fixed investment	-7.0	-0.6	1.4	2.1	4.8	4.6	-2.3	-1.9	0.2
Exports, GNFS[3]	1.2	2.4	3.3	4.0	3.6	3.6	0.1	0.3	-0.3
Imports, GNFS[3]	-3.1	5.2	2.7	3.7	4.8	4.9	-1.6	-0.4	0.2
Net exports, contribution to growth	0.9	-0.6	0.2	0.1	-0.2	-0.3	0.4	0.2	0.0
Memo items: GDP									
South America[4]	-3.1	0.3	-0.1	1.4	2.3	2.4	-1.4	-0.7	0.0
Central America[5]	3.9	3.8	2.7	3.4	3.5	3.6	-1.0	-0.5	-0.4
Caribbean[6]	4.4	3.4	4.4	4.0	4.0	3.8	0.9	0.5	0.2
Brazil	-3.3	1.1	1.2	2.2	2.4	2.4	-1.2	-0.3	0.0
Mexico	2.9	2.1	2.1	2.0	2.4	2.4	-0.2	-0.5	-0.3
Argentina	-1.8	2.9	-2.8	-1.7	2.7	3.1	-4.5	-3.5	-0.1

Source: World Bank.

Note: e = estimate; f = forecast. EMDE = emerging market and developing economy. World Bank forecasts are frequently updated based on new information and changing (global) circumstances. Consequently, projections presented here may differ from those contained in other Bank documents, even if basic assessments of countries' prospects do not differ at any given moment in time.

1. GDP at market prices and expenditure components are measured in constant 2010 U.S. dollars.
2. Aggregate includes all countries in notes 4, 5, and 6, and Mexico, except those for which data limitations prevent the forecasting of demand-side GDP components: Dominica, Grenada, Guyana, St. Kitts and Nevis, St. Lucia, St. Vincent and the Grenadines, Suriname, and Trinidad and Tobago.
3. Exports and imports of goods and non-factor services (GNFS).
4. Includes Argentina, Bolivia, Brazil, Chile, Colombia, Ecuador, Paraguay, Peru, Uruguay, and Venezuela.
5. Includes Costa Rica, El Salvador, Guatemala, Honduras, Nicaragua, and Panama.
6. Includes Antigua and Barbuda, The Bahamas, Barbados, Belize, Dominica, Dominican Republic, Grenada, Guyana, Haiti, Jamaica, Suriname, St. Kitts and Nevis, St. Lucia, St. Vincent and the Grenadines, and Trinidad and Tobago.

To download this data, please visit www.worldbank.org/gep.

TABLE 2.3.2 Latin America and the Caribbean country forecasts[1]

(Real GDP growth at market prices in percent, unless indicated otherwise)

Percentage point differences from June 2018 projections

	2016	2017	2018e	2019f	2020f	2021f	2018e	2019f	2020f
Argentina	-1.8	2.9	-2.8	-1.7	2.7	3.1	-4.5	-3.5	-0.1
Belize	-0.5	1.2	1.5	1.9	1.7	1.7	-0.5	0.0	0.0
Bolivia	4.3	4.2	4.5	4.3	3.8	3.4	0.6	0.7	0.4
Brazil	-3.3	1.1	1.2	2.2	2.4	2.4	-1.2	-0.3	0.0
Chile	1.3	1.5	3.9	3.5	3.3	3.2	0.6	0.1	-0.2
Colombia	2.0	1.8	2.7	3.3	3.7	3.6	0.0	0.0	0.1
Costa Rica	4.2	3.3	2.7	2.7	2.8	3.0	-0.7	-0.9	-0.8
Dominican Republic	6.6	4.6	5.8	5.1	5.0	4.8	0.8	0.4	0.4
Ecuador	-1.2	2.4	1.0	0.7	0.7	1.2	-1.2	-0.8	-0.2
El Salvador	2.6	2.3	2.8	2.5	2.4	2.4	0.5	0.3	0.2
Grenada	3.7	5.1	5.2	4.2	2.8	2.8	1.9	1.4	0.0
Guatemala	3.1	2.8	2.7	2.9	3.0	3.1	-0.4	-0.4	-0.3
Guyana	2.6	2.1	3.4	4.6	30.0	24.8	-0.4	0.8	1.0
Haiti[2]	1.5	1.2	1.6	2.3	2.4	2.5	-0.2	-0.1	0.0
Honduras	3.8	4.8	3.6	3.8	3.8	3.7	0.1	0.2	0.0
Jamaica	1.4	1.0	1.7	1.8	2.0	2.0	0.0	-0.1	0.0
Mexico	2.9	2.1	2.1	2.0	2.4	2.4	-0.2	-0.5	-0.3
Nicaragua	4.7	4.9	-3.8	-0.5	2.6	3.6	-8.5	-5.0	-1.8
Panama	5.0	5.3	4.0	6.0	5.4	5.2	-1.6	0.4	-0.2
Paraguay	4.3	5.0	4.0	3.9	4.0	4.0	-0.3	-0.3	-0.2
Peru	4.0	2.5	3.9	3.8	3.8	3.7	0.4	0.0	0.0
St. Lucia	3.4	3.8	1.5	2.7	2.8	2.3	-1.3	0.4	0.5
St. Vincent and the Grenadines	1.3	0.5	1.2	1.6	1.6	2.0	-0.9	-0.9	-1.1
Suriname	-5.6	1.7	1.4	1.6	1.8	1.9	0.3	-0.1	-0.3
Trinidad and Tobago	-6.1	-2.6	1.0	0.9	1.2	1.2	-0.6	-1.0	0.0
Uruguay	1.7	2.7	2.1	2.1	2.3	2.5	-1.2	-1.0	-0.6
Venezuela	-16.5	-14.5	-18.0	-8.0	-5.0	-4.0	-3.7	-1.0	-1.0

Source: World Bank.

Note: e = estimate; f = forecast. World Bank forecasts are frequently updated based on new information and changing (global) circumstances. Consequently, projections presented here may differ from those contained in other Bank documents, even if basic assessments of countries' prospects do not significantly differ at any given moment in time.

1. GDP at market prices and expenditure components are measured in constant 2010 U.S. dollars.

2. GDP is based on fiscal year, which runs from October to September of next year.

To download this data, please visit www.worldbank.org/gep.

BOX 2.3.1 Informality in Latin America and the Caribbean

Informal sector output in Latin America and the Caribbean, equivalent to about one-third of GDP, is slightly higher than in the median emerging market and developing economy, despite a steady decline during recent decades. Roughly six out of ten of those employed in the region are employed informally. Informality has been associated with lower growth, weaker productivity, and higher levels of inequality. Policies to reduce payroll taxes and increase labor inspections have been found to reduce informality.

Introduction

Informality in Latin America and the Caribbean (LAC) during the past decade was slightly higher than in the median emerging market and developing economy (EMDE), whether measured in terms of informal output or the share of self-employment (Figure 2.3.1.1; Box 3.2). Yet there is substantial heterogeneity in the incidence of informality within the region. Informality tends to be higher in countries with poorer institutional environments.

Against this backdrop, this box addresses the following questions:

- How has informality evolved in Latin America and the Caribbean?

- What have been the macroeconomic and social correlates of informality?

- What policy options are available to address challenges associated with informality?

Evolution and drivers of informality

Moderate informality. On average, the informal economy in LAC was equivalent to 34 percent of official GDP in 2016, slightly above the median EMDE.[1] Informal employment averaged 62 percent of total employment in 2016 (slightly below the EMDE median), while 38 percent of those employed were self-employed. Within the region, informality varies considerably.

Regional heterogeneity. The amount of output generated by the informal sector (output informality) ranged from 16 percent of GDP in Chile, in line with rates observed in advanced economies, to 56 percent in Bolivia. Haiti also has very high informality, at 61 percent of GDP.[2] Survey-based measures of labor informality show a similarly wide range. For Caribbean countries with available data, self-

employment as a share of formal employment tends to be very low: 12 percent in Suriname (2014), 14 percent in The Bahamas (2011), and 17 percent in Barbados (2013). Again, Bolivia appears at the top end of the spectrum, with self-employment equivalent to 64 percent of formal employment in 2015. In most countries, labor informality is higher than output informality, although Brazil, Guatemala, and several Caribbean countries are exceptions.

Trend decline in output informality. Output informality in the region has steadily declined since the early 2000s (Figure 2.3.1.2). Several of the countries with the highest incidence of output informality (e.g., Bolivia, Panama, Peru) have also experienced some of the largest declines during the past two decades, in part due to rapid formal job creation in the context of strong output growth. Yet even where labor informality has fallen, the decline did not necessarily affect all workers equally. In Argentina and Brazil, two of the largest economies in LAC, middle-aged men, the highly skilled, and those working full time were the most likely to shift from informal to formal employment during the 2000s (Maurizio 2015). Moreover, the decline in output informality has not always been accompanied by a similar decline in labor informality, which has been persistently high in countries such as Bolivia, Colombia, Honduras, Jamaica, Nicaragua, and Peru.

Correlates of informality

Informality has been associated with weak institutions and business climates as well as poor macroeconomic, microeconomic, and social outcomes in LAC. These include lower output and productivity growth, weaker financial resilience of households, and greater poverty.

Weak governance and business climates. Most of the institutional factors associated with informality are at or slightly above the EMDE average in LAC. However, LAC economies with below-average institutional quality have also tended to be those with high informality. For instance, Peru's higher labor informality compared to

---

Note: This box was prepared by Dana Vorisek. Research assistance was provided by Brent Harrison and Jinxin Wu.

[1] Output informality based on DGE estimates of Elgin and Oztunali (2014), unless otherwise specified.

[2] For lack of data on DGE estimates, this figure refers to MIMIC estimates (Chapter 3). DGE and MIMIC estimates are similar at the country level.

[3] Dougherty and Escobar (2013); Estevão and de Carvalho Filho (2012); Loayza (1997); Loayza, Servén, and Sugawara (2010); Vuletin (2008).

BOX 2.3.1 Informality in Latin America and the Caribbean (*continued*)

FIGURE 2.3.1.1 Informality in Latin America and the Caribbean

Output-based informality in LAC has fallen since the 1990s, on average, yet remains above the median in EMDEs. Employment-based informality in the region has risen slightly, to about the EMDE median. The key institutional factors that are often associated with informality, other than the difficulty of paying taxes, are slightly better in LAC than in all EMDEs.

A. Informal activity as share of total economic output

B. Share of self-employed; perceived informal activity

C. Institutional quality

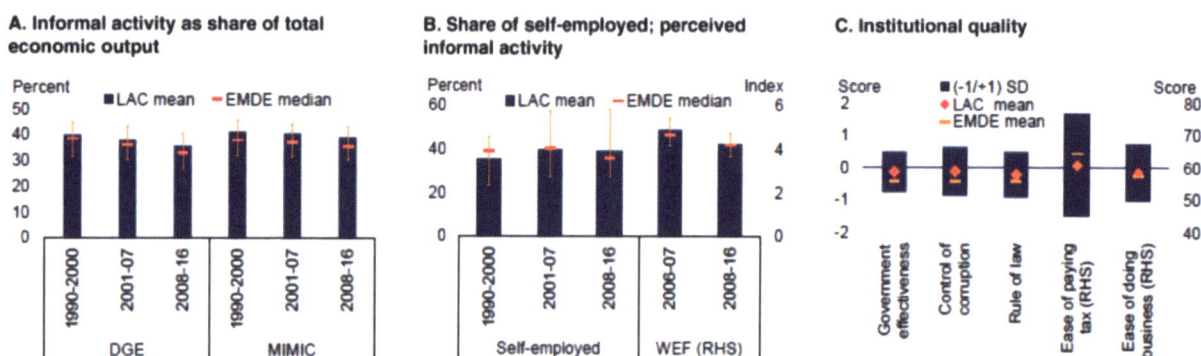

Sources: Elgin et al. (forthcoming), Eurostat; Haver Analytics, Inter-American Development Bank, national statistical bureaus and offices, Organisation for Economic Co-operation and Development, World Bank (Doing Business, World Development Indicators, and World Governance Indicators).

A.-C. Blue bars show simple averages of economies in the region. Red markers show the median of all EMDEs. Vertical lines denote interquartile range of all EMDEs.

A. DGE = dynamic general equilibrium model. MIMIC = multiple indicators multiple causes model. The DGE model estimates the size of the informal sector as a percent of official GDP (see Elgin and Oztunali 2012). The MIMIC model is a structural equations model that considers multiple causes of informal activity and captures multiple outcome indicators of informal activity (see Schneider, Buehn, and Montenegro 2010). It also estimates the informal output as a percent of official GDP. DGE sample includes 26 LAC economies and 122 EMDEs; MIMIC sample includes 25 LAC economies and 124 EMDEs.

B. Self-employed is the presented as the share of self-employment in total employment. WEF = World Economic Forum. WEF index is the average response at the country-year level to the question: "In your country, how much economic activity do you estimate to be undeclared or unregistered? (1 = Most economic activity is undeclared or unregistered; 7 = Most economic activity is declared or registered)." WEF index is inverted; a higher average at the country level indicates a larger informal economy. The index does not use data for 2004–05 due to inconsistency in survey methods. The WVS asks whether respondents can justify cheating on taxes (1 = never justifiable; 10 = always justifiable). The average responses at the country-year level are used as a measure of attitude toward informality (or tax morality; Oviedo, Thomas, and Karakurum-Ozdemir 2009). Self-employed sample includes 32 LAC economies and 134 EMDEs; WEF sample includes 25 LAC economies and 114 EMDEs.

C. All measures are taken from the latest year available. The first three institutional measures are taken from World Bank's World Governance Indicators (2017), with a higher value indicating better institutional quality in 2016. The "ease of doing business" and "ease of paying taxes" are taken from World Bank's Doing Business database and measured as distance to frontier, with a higher value indicating a more favorable business environment. Sample includes 32 LAC economies and 149 EMDEs.

Chile has been mostly attributed to poor governance (Loayza and Wada 2010a). One of the most common explanations for informality in LAC countries has been restrictive business and labor regulations, which discourage firms from entering the formal sector.[3]

High tax burdens. High tax rates or burdensome tax regulations have also encouraged informality in the region (Loayza 1997; Ordóñez 2014; Vuletin 2008). Both corporate and personal income tax rates tend to be higher in LAC than in the average EMDE—indeed, LAC is the only EMDE region where the average personal income tax rate has risen since the early 2000s.

Trade liberalization amid inflexible labor markets. Some instances of trade liberalization have also been associated with rising informality in LAC. The reduction of trade barriers in the 1980s and 1990s led to fears that domestic firms in the formal sector would be rendered uncompetitive and shift to the informal sector. In Brazil,

the association between trade liberalization and informality was ambiguous in the early literature (Bosch, Goñi-Pacchioni, and Maloney 2012; Goldberg and Pavcnik 2003; Menezes-Filho and Muendler 2011). However, recent research has established that trade liberalization was followed by increased informality in Brazil, though only in the long run (Dix-Carneiro and Kovak 2017; Dix-Carneiro et al. 2018). In Colombia, trade liberalization was associated with slightly higher informality, yet only prior to a subsequent reform that increased labor market flexibility (Goldberg and Pavcnik 2003).

Sectoral and worker characteristics. Informality has been shown to be higher in the presence of large agricultural sectors. Other structural factors, such as poor education and skills, have also been identified as underlying reasons for labor informality (Fernandez and Villar 2016). In some LAC countries, a considerable share of people working informally entered the informal sector voluntarily. Switching between the formal and informal sectors has

BOX 2.3.1 **Informality in Latin America and the Caribbean** (*continued*)

FIGURE 2.3.1.2 **Evolution and correlates of informality in Latin America and the Caribbean**

Although output-based informality in LAC has fallen, the incidence of informality still varies considerably within the region. In LAC economies where corruption and the burden of paying taxes is high, output-based informality tends to be high. Self-employment tends to be high where labor market efficiency is low. Both corporate and personal income tax rates are higher in LAC than in all EMDEs.

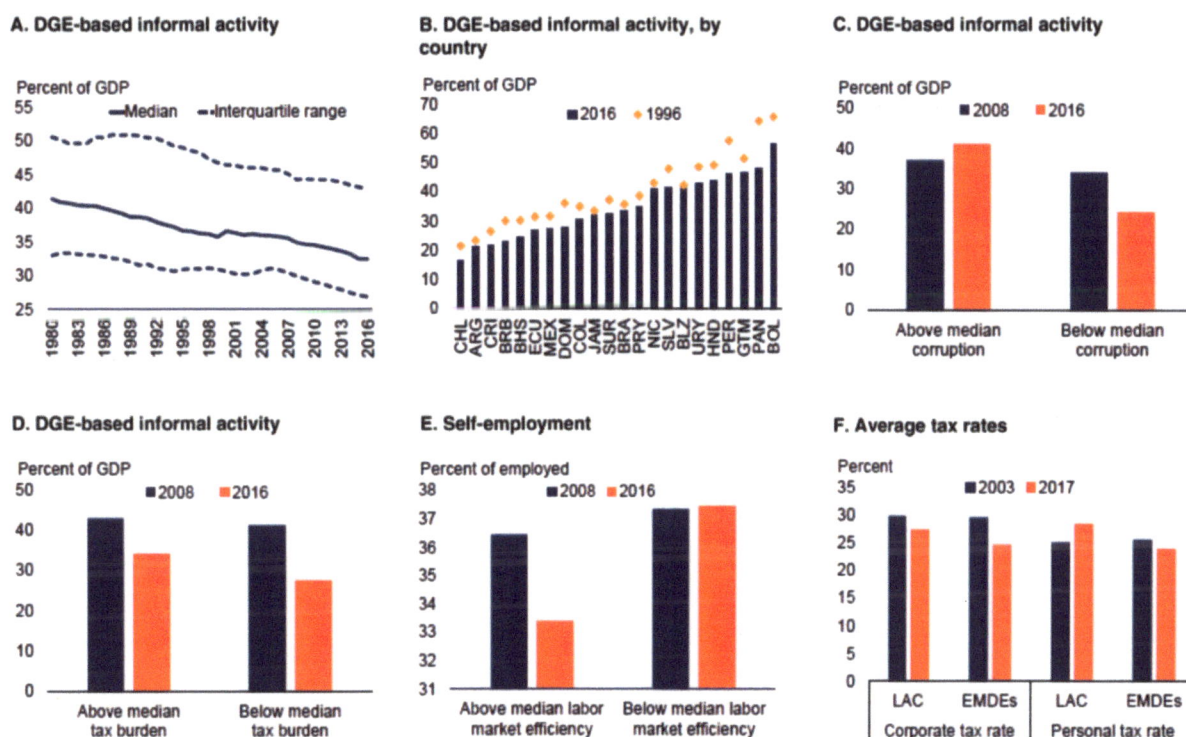

A. DGE-based informal activity

B. DGE-based informal activity, by country

C. DGE-based informal activity

D. DGE-based informal activity

E. Self-employment

F. Average tax rates

Source: Elgin et al. (forthcoming), Haver Analytics, Inter-American Development Bank, national statistical bureaus and offices, Organisation for Economic Co-operation and Development, Végh and Vuletin (2015), World Bank (Doing Business, World Development Indicators, and World Governance Indicators), World Economic Forum (Global Competitiveness Index).
A. Sample includes 23 economies. The median of the MIMIC-based estimate of informality shows a similar downward trend.
B. CHL = Chile, ARG= Argentina, CRI= Costa Rica, BRB = Barbados, BHS = The Bahamas, ECU = Ecuador, MEX = Mexico, DOM = Dominican Republic, COL = Colombia, JAM = Jamaica, SUR = Suriname, BRA = Brazil, PRY = Paraguay, NIC = Nicaragua, SLV = El Salvador, BLZ = Belize, URY = Uruguay, HND = Honduras, PER = Peru, GTM = Guatemala, PAN = Panama, BOL = Bolivia.
C. Bars show medians. Sample includes 21 LAC economies.
D. Bars show medians. Sample includes 20 LAC economies. Tax burden is measured as the ease of paying taxes in the World Bank's Doing Business indicators.
E. Bars show medians. Sample includes 16 LAC economies.
F. Corporate tax rate sample includes 17 LAC economies and 49 EMDEs; personal tax rate sample includes 17 LAC economies and 47 EMDEs.

been common in the largest economies in the region (Bosch and Maloney 2010; Fiess, Fugazza, and Maloney 2008; Perry et al. 2007). This may reflect a higher regard for self-employment in LAC relative to other regions, or a response to adverse employment and income shocks in the formal sector.

Lower output growth. In studies of a large number of LAC economies, informality has been negatively associated with growth, even after controlling for country characteristics (Loayza 1997; Loayza, Servén, and Sugawara 2010). However, studies at the country level are

less conclusive. In Mexico, for instance, informality has been accompanied by slowing growth, yet in Brazil, falling informality may not be associated with higher GDP (Levy 2008; Ulyssea 2018).

Lower productivity growth. The informality literature on LAC has established a link between informality and aggregate productivity (Loayza, Servén, and Sugawara 2010). Linkages between informality and productivity have also been identified at the firm level. Informal firms in Brazil, for instance, have been less productive than formal firms (de Paula and Scheinkman 2011). In

BOX 2.3.1 Informality in Latin America and the Caribbean (*continued*)

Paraguay, not only are informal firms less productive, but their low productivity has had negative spillovers to formal firms (Vargas 2015).

Lower savings and access to finance for households and firms. For workers and firms, there are negative financial implications of informality. Informal workers in Chile, for instance, have not been able to save as much as formal workers, and have had less access to finance than formal firms (Schlcarek and Caggia 2015). In Brazil, poor access to finance was the key reason for informal firms being small and unproductive: their cost of capital was at least 1.3 times that of formal firms (de Paula and Scheinkman 2011). Similarly, in Ecuador, lower productivity and profitability in informal firms was due in part to worse access to credit (Medvedev and Oviedo 2013). Across the region, rising informality has been associated with lower pension contributions (Vuletin 2008).

Higher poverty and inequality. Informality in LAC has also been associated with inequality and poverty, in part reflecting the wage gap between the informal and formal sectors. In Argentina, past poverty has been associated with current informal employment, and past informality has been associated with current poverty (Devicienti, Groisman, and Poggi 2015). The process of increasing formal-sector employment contributed significantly to the decline in inequality in Argentina and Uruguay during the 2000s (Aramante, Arim, and Yapor 2016; Beccaria, Maurizio, and Vazquez 2015). In Colombia, informal workers received lower wages than formal workers due not only to lower returns to their education, but also to educational mismatches (Herrera-Idárraga, López-Bazo, and Motellón 2015).

Policy options

Designing policies to address informality requires an understanding of its causes and characteristics. These vary considerably, even within individual countries in LAC (Fernandez and Villar 2016; Perry et al. 2007).

Tax system. Making tax policy less restrictive, by lowering tax rates or simplifying tax systems, could incentivize firms to become formal and increase demand for formal workers.

Indeed, a large reduction in payroll tax rates in Colombia in 2012 reduced labor informality in the main metropolitan areas by about 7 percentages points (Fernandez and Villar 2016). The results of Brazil's reduction and simplification of business taxes in 1996 have been more ambiguous. Early studies found that the reform was associated with a significant increase in the incidence of formal firms, and that newly formalized firms achieved higher revenue and profits than those operating informally, although the impact of the reform on informality varied across economic sectors (Fajnzylber, Maloney, and Montes-Rojas 2011; Monteiro and Assuncão 2012). Recent studies have found no evidence of increased formalization as a result of the reform (e.g., Piza 2016).

Labor market regulation. Tighter labor inspections have been effective in reducing informality in the region, through a variety of mechanisms. In Brazil, tighter enforcement of labor market regulations raised wages and output by improving the allocation of workers between the formal and informal sectors (Meghir, Narita, and Robin 2015). More frequent labor inspections in Brazil also induced some informal workers to become formal, albeit due to wage rigidity in the formal sector (Almeida and Carneiro 2012). Inspections were also more effective than incentives in convincing firms in Brazil to operate in the formal sector (de Andrade, Bruhn, and McKenzie 2013).

Other regulations. Policy reforms intended to ease barriers to entering the formal sector have had diverse outcomes. A reform that simplified the process of opening a business in Mexico was successful in increasing the number of registered businesses (Bruhn 2011; Kaplan, Piedra, and Seira 2011). However, the reform had no impact on informality: the owners of the new businesses were former employees of formal firms, rather than informal workers. Financial deepening contributed to a reduction in informality in Uruguay, particularly for women and older workers (Gandelman and Rasteletti 2016). Finally, the emerging "gig" economy presents unique policy challenges that may require regulatory changes to smooth economic risks for "gig" workers (World Bank 2014b, 2016c, and 2018n).

MIDDLE EAST and NORTH AFRICA

percent in 2019, supported by improvements in both oil exporters and oil importers. Rising investment and easing fiscal consolidation are supporting the recovery of some oil exporters, while oil importers continue to benefit from policy reforms. Regional growth is projected to reach 2.7 percent in 2020, as domestic demand remains generally resilient. Risks are tilted to the downside, including the possibility that activity will be constrained by intensified geopolitical tensions, stronger external trade headwinds, abrupt tightening of global financing conditions, and slower-than-expected reform pace.

Recent developments

Growth in the Middle East and North Africa (MENA) region is estimated to have improved to 1.7 percent in 2018, rebounding from a sharp deceleration a year earlier driven by oil production cuts in oil exporters and fiscal tightening (Figure 2.4.1).[1] Growth among oil importers has picked up in the past two years and continues to garner positive momentum. Although positive spillovers to the region via external demand are softening amid weaker global economic prospects, domestic factors continue to support growth. These include generally resilient domestic demand and policy reforms that are helping the region's transition away from dependence on commodity exports and the public sector.

Growth in oil exporters is estimated to have recovered further in 2018. In the Gulf Cooperation Council (GCC), increased oil production and prices have eased the pressure for fiscal consolidation, enabled higher public spending, and supported higher current account balances. Non-oil sector activity in the GCC has largely been stable. Among non-GCC oil exporters, activity in Iran has been severely affected by U.S. sanctions and has been a significant drag on oil exporters' and regional growth. Growth in other non-GCC oil exporters has been supported by public spending and investment.

Among oil importers, growth has been steadily improving as reforms proceed. In Egypt, the largest country in this group, tourism and natural gas activity have continued to show strength. Its unemployment rate has generally fallen, and policy reforms have contributed to an upgrade of its sovereign rating in August 2018. Fiscal adjustments in Egypt have also been steadily progressing. More generally, robust agricultural production and tourism have helped support growth of the oil importers in the region, especially Morocco and Tunisia. However, while international reserves have strengthened in Egypt, they have declined in other oil importers amid higher external vulnerabilities. Policy reforms in oil importers have helped promote innovation capacity among firms, but the scope for improvement remains large, given fundamental challenges like the quality of electricity supply that hinder the potential for private sector dynamism

---

Note: This section was prepared by Lei Sandy Ye. Research assistance was provided by Mengyi Li.

[1] The World Bank's Middle East and North Africa aggregate includes 16 economies and is grouped into three subregions. Bahrain, Kuwait, Oman, Qatar, Saudi Arabia, and the United Arab Emirates comprise the Gulf Cooperation Council (GCC); all are oil exporters. Other oil exporters in the region are Algeria, the Islamic Republic of Iran, and Iraq. Oil importers in the region are Djibouti, the Arab Republic of Egypt, Jordan, Lebanon, Morocco, Tunisia, and West Bank and Gaza. Syrian Arab Republic, the Republic of Yemen, and Libya are excluded from regional growth aggregates due to data limitations.

FIGURE 2.4.1 MENA: Recent developments

Growth in the MENA region is estimated to have improved to 1.7 percent in 2018, supported by increased oil production and eased fiscal stance in the GCC. Growth among oil importers has been supported by policy reforms, contributing to greater capacity to innovate. The region continues to tackle long-term challenges, such as high youth unemployment and electricity access, through structural adjustment programs. Inflation has been volatile in Egypt and Iran, but remains generally stable in the region. High public debt is a significant headwind to growth for oil importers.

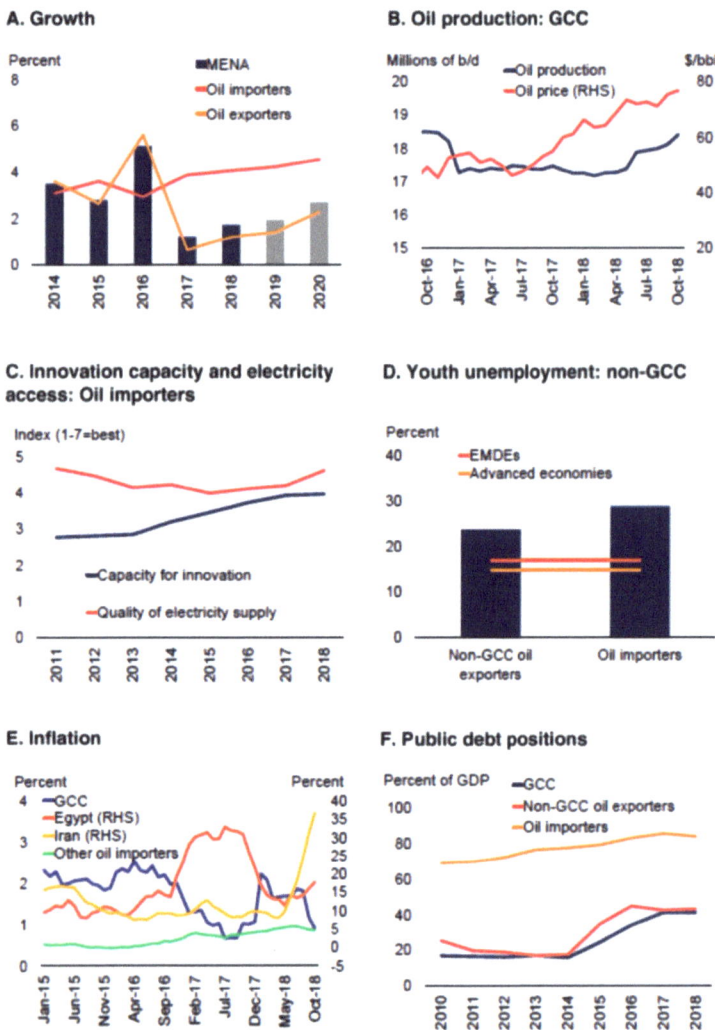

A. Growth

B. Oil production: GCC

C. Innovation capacity and electricity access: Oil importers

D. Youth unemployment: non-GCC

E. Inflation

F. Public debt positions

Source: Bank for International Settlements, Haver Analytics, International Energy Agency, International Monetary Fund, World Bank, World Economic Forum.
A. Weighted average growth rates of real GDP. Gray denotes forecasts.
B. Sum of production in Bahrain, Kuwait, Oman, Qatar, Saudi Arabia, and the UAE. Oil price denotes average of Brent, Dubai, and WTI.
C. Based on World Economic Forum surveys. "Capacity for Innovation" denotes response to the question: "In your country, to what extent do companies have the capacity to innovate? [1 = not at all; 7 = to a great extent]." "Quality of Electricity Supply" denotes response to the question "In your country, how reliable is the electricity supply (lack of interruptions and lack of voltage fluctuations)? [1 = extremely unreliable; 7 = extremely reliable]." Unweighted averages. Years denoted refer to edition year of data. Includes 5 oil importers.
D. Youth unemployment as a percent of youth labor force (age 15-24). Includes 10 MENA economies. Unweighted averages. Based on 2017 data.
E. Monthly year-on-year growth rates of CPI inflation. Last observation is October 2018.
F. General government debt as a ratio to GDP. 2018 data are estimates. Unweighted averages. Includes 6 GCC economies, 3 non-GCC oil exporters, and 6 oil importers.

(Arezki et al. 2018). These reforms also address challenges in the labor market, including high youth unemployment (Purfield et al. 2018; Schiffbauer et al. 2015).

Headline inflation in Egypt remains near its end-2018 target level of 13 percent, despite edging up recently. Core inflation has been contained and the central bank has conducted two policy rate cuts in 2018, despite tighter external financing conditions. In Iran, inflation rose sharply in the second half of 2018, partly reflecting the depreciation of the rial in the parallel market relative to early 2018. Inflation is generally contained across the rest of the MENA region, averaging less than 3 percent in the GCC, and rising moderately in smaller oil importers.

Bond issuance across the region, particularly in the GCC, was robust at the start of 2018, but slowed around mid-year amid tighter external financing conditions and rising investor risk aversion. Although international financing conditions have become less favorable, investor confidence in the region were supported by efforts by GCC countries to diversify their economies as well as their recent inclusion in the MSCI Emerging Markets Index (Saudi Arabia) or JP Morgan EMBI bond indexes (5 GCC economies). These developments kept the region somewhat insulated from the turmoil affecting many emerging markets and developing economies (EMDEs) in the second half of 2018.

Outlook

GDP growth is projected to rise slightly to 1.9 percent in 2019 and pick up to 2.7 percent later in the forecast horizon. Both oil exporters and oil importers will show steady growth improvement over the forecast period. Despite the headwinds from a less favorable international economic environment, which is expected to be marked by slower global trade growth and tighter external financing conditions, domestic factors—in particular, policy reforms—continue to bolster growth in the region.

Among oil exporters, growth in 2019 is expected to improve slightly, supported by continued strengthening in the GCC that is partly offset by weakness among the large non-GCC oil exporters. Higher investment and improved regulatory environments are expected to support higher growth in GCC economies. Over the medium term, growth among the GCC economies will remain steady, underpinned by planned diversification programs, infrastructure projects, and medium-term reform plans (World Bank 2018o, 2018p). Outside of the GCC, activity in Iran is expected to contract as U.S. sanctions bite. Algeria's growth is projected to moderate after its budgeted strong increase in government spending in 2018 tapers.

Among oil importers, growth is forecast to rise further, led by improvements among the larger economies. Investment will be further supported by reforms that strengthen the business climate and a pickup in domestic demand (World Bank 2018q). Tourism is envisioned to continue supporting activity in Egypt, Morocco, and Tunisia. Positive spillovers via external demand in the Euro Area are likely to taper somewhat amid the area's weaker growth prospects. While smaller oil importers' growth is envisioned to pick up slightly, these economies continue to grapple with elevated public debt, and in some cases, the challenges associated with the ongoing refugee crisis.

Medium-term growth forecasts for the MENA region are predicated on the assumption that there will not be a significant escalation of geopolitical conflicts and that there will be limited regional spillovers from conflict-ridden economies. Continued IMF and World Bank programs in many economies (e.g., Egypt, Morocco) are expected to provide a basis for needed structural adjustments (e.g., stronger fiscal management frameworks, higher public infrastructure quality), as well as steps to address the vulnerabilities associated with the informal sector (Chapter 3; Box 2.4.1). Financial reforms—such as newly approved bankruptcy laws in Egypt, Saudi Arabia, and the United Arab Emirates—should help relieve financial constraints in the corporate sector and support investor confidence (World Bank

FIGURE 2.4.2 MENA: Outlook and risks

Heightened geopolitical tensions have been associated with volatile sovereign default spreads and may amplify fragile economies' significant income losses. Trade disputes involving major economies may weigh on external demand of both oil exporters and importers, while a more abrupt-than-expected tightening of global financing costs may raise external debt vulnerabilities, especially if accompanied by sharp dollar appreciation.

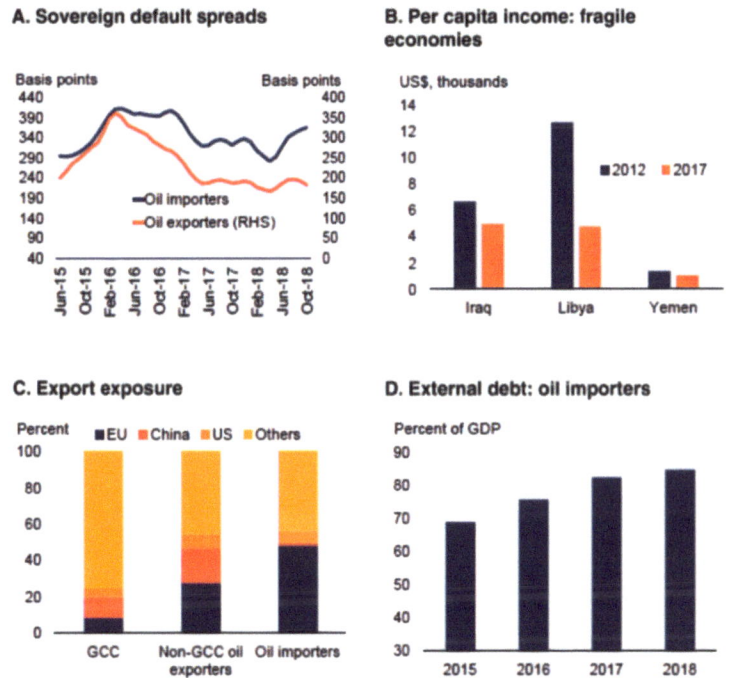

Source: Haver Analytics, International Monetary Fund, World Bank.
A. Denotes 5 Year USD Credit Default Swap Par Mid Rate. Oil importers include 4 economies. Oil exporters include 6 economies. Three month-rolling unweighted averages. UAE denotes average of Abu Dhabi and Dubai.
B. Estimated per capita income in thousands of US dollars. Data not available for Syria.
C. Share of goods exports to respective economies denoted as a ratio to each country group's total exports. Denotes latest available data in 2017. Includes 6 GCC economies, 3 non-GCC oil exporters, and 7 oil importers.
D. Unweighted averages. 2018 data are estimates. Includes 6 oil importers.

2014b). Multilateral efforts to promote rural transportation, electricity access, and private sector financing (e.g., Gaza Solar Fund, Compact with Africa) are likely to enhance the business climate. Collectively, policy reforms across the region are expected to improve growth potential in the medium term.

Risks

Risks to the regional outlook are tilted to the downside. A diverse range of geopolitical risks have been associated with volatile sovereign default spreads in both oil exporters and importers (Figure 2.4.2). New conflicts in fragile economies illustrate the potential for an escalation of military conflicts to inflict even greater damage to incomes and economic activity (Devarajan and Mottaghi 2017). These conflicts may also diminish access to health and water services in fragile economies, as well as compound the impact of the refugee crisis on host and origin economies. Regional conflicts could also deter tourism, foreign direct investment, and remittances. A substantial further escalation of U.S.-Iran tensions could have adverse spillovers to the rest of the region.[2] Geopolitical factors, as well as uncertainty in oil production in response to these factors, could trigger volatility in oil prices. Together, these could complicate or stall fiscal and current account adjustments in both oil exporters and importers.

Escalating global trade tensions may negatively impact the MENA region. Although direct trade exposure with the United States is low, the region is tightly interconnected to the European Union and, to a lesser degree, China. A further rise of trade tensions could weigh heavily on the demand for exports from the MENA region (World Bank 2016a). This risk may be slightly mitigated by deeper trade integration across regional neighbors (e.g., Djibouti-Ethiopia).

Abrupt tightening of global financing conditions may affect both oil exporters and importers. Interest rates in GCC economies have moved broadly in tandem with advanced economies' policy rates, especially that of the U.S., and their net external assets positions are strong. Combined with the gradual nature of advanced economy monetary policy normalization, the dampening effect on borrowing costs and non-oil activity associated with higher interest rates have so far been modest. However, a more abrupt tightening of advanced economy monetary policy could weigh on capital flows to the region and dampen foreign investor confidence in large GCC economies, which had recently relaxed foreign investment restrictions (World Bank 2018p). High external debt denominated in foreign currency in some oil importers implies that they are also vulnerable to unexpected sharp appreciation of the U.S. dollar.

Post-election political uncertainty in some economies delayed the formation of new governments. This may slow the pace of reforms. Several oil importers also depend on IMF/WB multi-year fiscal adjustments programs, which hinge on progress in the pace of reforms. Potential delays in reforms may also be reflected in some oil exporters through inefficiencies in management of contingent liabilities and large investment projects.

On the upside, rising reconstruction spending in conflict affected economies (e.g., Iraq) may have positive spillovers to neighboring economies, supporting higher investment in physical infrastructure as well as soft infrastructure (e.g., broadband internet, mobile telephony) (Arezki et al. 2018).

---

[2] The current sanctions feature waivers from eight economies that import oil from Iran, as well as proposed Special Purpose Vehicles designed by the EU to facilitate transactions with Iran.

TABLE 2.4.1 Middle East and North Africa forecast summary

(Real GDP growth at market prices in percent, unless indicated otherwise)

Percentage point differences from June 2018 projections

	2016	2017	2018e	2019f	2020f	2021f	2018e	2019f	2020f
EMDE MENA, GDP[1]	5.1	1.2	1.7	1.9	2.7	2.7	-1.3	-1.4	-0.5
(Average including countries with full national accounts and balance of payments data only)[2]									
EMDE MENA, GDP[2]	4.8	1.4	1.7	1.6	2.7	2.7	-1.3	-1.7	-0.6
GDP per capita (U.S. dollars)	3.0	-0.3	0.1	0.1	1.3	1.4	-1.3	-1.7	-0.6
PPP GDP	5.1	1.7	1.8	1.6	2.8	2.8	-1.4	-1.8	-0.7
Private consumption	2.8	2.2	1.5	1.6	2.3	2.3	-1.9	-1.9	-1.2
Public consumption	-6.3	2.3	3.4	1.1	1.9	1.9	2.1	-0.3	0.3
Fixed investment	-2.0	1.0	2.8	3.6	4.7	4.8	-2.3	0.0	-0.1
Exports, GNFS[3]	8.5	2.9	1.9	1.8	3.4	3.4	-1.8	-2.3	-0.6
Imports, GNFS[3]	-1.2	5.1	1.3	1.9	3.1	3.1	-2.4	-1.2	-0.3
Net exports, contribution to growth	4.2	-0.4	0.5	0.2	0.5	0.5	0.0	-0.7	-0.3
Memo items: GDP									
Oil exporters[4]	5.6	0.6	1.2	1.4	2.3	2.3	-1.5	-1.7	-0.6
GCC countries[5]	2.4	-0.3	2.0	2.6	2.7	2.7	-0.1	-0.1	0.0
Saudi Arabia	1.7	-0.9	2.0	2.1	2.2	2.2	0.2	0.0	-0.1
Iran	13.4	3.8	-1.5	-3.6	1.1	1.1	-5.6	-7.7	-3.1
Oil importers[6]	2.9	3.9	4.1	4.2	4.6	4.7	0.1	-0.2	0.0
Egypt	4.3	4.7	5.5	5.7	5.9	6.0	0.2	0.0	0.1
Fiscal year basis[7]	4.3	4.2	5.3	5.6	5.8	6.0	0.3	0.1	0.0

Source: World Bank.

Note: e = estimate; f = forecast. EMDE = emerging market and developing economy. World Bank forecasts are frequently updated based on new information and changing (global) circumstances. Consequently, projections presented here may differ from those contained in other Bank documents, even if basic assessments of countries' prospects do not differ at any given moment in time.

1. GDP at market prices and expenditure components are measured in constant 2010 U.S. dollars. Excludes Libya, Syria, and Yemen due to data limitations.
2. Aggregate includes all countries in notes 4 and 6 except Djibouti, Iraq, Qatar, and West Bank and Gaza, for which data limitations prevent the forecasting of GDP components.
3. Exports and imports of goods and non-factor services (GNFS).
4. Oil exporters include Algeria, Bahrain, Iran, Iraq, Kuwait, Oman, Qatar, Saudi Arabia, and the United Arab Emirates.
5. The Gulf Cooperation Council (GCC) includes Bahrain, Kuwait, Oman, Qatar, Saudi Arabia, and the United Arab Emirates.
6. Oil importers include Djibouti, Egypt, Jordan, Lebanon, Morocco, Tunisia, and West Bank and Gaza.
7. The fiscal year runs from July 1 to June 30 in Egypt; the column labeled 2017 reflects the fiscal year ended June 30, 2017.
To download this data, please visit www.worldbank.org/gep.

TABLE 2.4.2 Middle East and North Africa economy forecasts[1]

(Real GDP growth at market prices in percent, unless indicated otherwise)

Percentage point differences from June 2018 projections

	2016	2017	2018e	2019f	2020f	2021f	2018e	2019f	2020f
Algeria	3.2	1.4	2.5	2.3	1.8	1.8	-1.0	0.3	0.5
Bahrain	3.2	3.9	3.2	2.6	2.8	2.8	1.5	0.5	0.7
Djibouti	8.6	5.7	6.7	7.3	7.5	7.5	0.2	0.9	1.2
Egypt	4.3	4.7	5.5	5.7	5.9	6.0	0.2	0.0	0.1
Fiscal year basis[2]	4.3	4.2	5.3	5.6	5.8	6.0	0.3	0.1	0.0
Iran	13.4	3.8	-1.5	-3.6	1.1	1.1	-5.6	-7.7	-3.1
Iraq	13.0	-2.1	1.9	6.2	2.9	2.8	-0.6	2.1	1.0
Jordan	2.0	2.0	2.1	2.3	2.4	2.7	-0.1	-0.1	0.0
Kuwait	2.9	-3.5	1.7	3.6	3.6	3.6	-0.2	0.1	0.6
Lebanon	1.7	1.5	1.0	1.3	1.5	1.5	-1.0	-0.7	-0.5
Morocco	1.1	4.1	3.2	2.9	3.5	3.5	0.2	-0.6	-0.2
Oman	5.0	-0.9	1.9	3.4	2.8	2.8	-0.4	0.9	-0.1
Qatar	2.1	1.6	2.3	2.7	3.0	3.0	-0.5	-0.5	0.2
Saudi Arabia	1.7	-0.9	2.0	2.1	2.2	2.2	0.2	0.0	-0.1
Tunisia	1.1	2.0	2.6	2.9	3.4	3.6	0.2	0.0	0.0
United Arab Emirates	3.0	0.8	2.0	3.0	3.2	3.2	-0.5	-0.2	-0.1
West Bank and Gaza	4.7	3.1	1.7	1.9	1.9	1.9	-0.8	-0.4	-0.4

Source: World Bank.
Note: e = estimate; f = forecast. World Bank forecasts are frequently updated based on new information and changing (global) circumstances. Consequently, projections presented here may differ from those contained in other Bank documents, even if basic assessments of economies' prospects do not significantly differ at any given moment in time.
1. GDP at market prices and expenditure components are measured in constant 2010 U.S. dollars. Excludes Libya, Syria, and Yemen due to data limitations.
2. The fiscal year runs from July 1 to June 30 in Egypt; the column labeled 2017 reflects the fiscal year ended June 30, 2017.
To download this data, please visit www.worldbank.org/gep.

BOX 2.4.1 Informality in the Middle East and North Africa

Middle East and North Africa's (MENA's) informal sector output, on average, amounts to nearly one quarter of official GDP. However, there is wide heterogeneity across the region. Informality is high among non-GCC economies, the young population, as well as the agricultural workforce. Levels of informality in the region are closely linked to its economic structure and governance climate, including low private sector vibrancy and limited economic diversification. Policy options that reduce regulatory barriers, streamline public sector efficiency, and enhance workforce skills can help improve access to the formal sector and unlock the potential of a relatively young informal workforce.

Introduction

The extent of informal output in the Middle East and Africa region amounts to nearly one quarter of official GDP during 2008-16, lower than in other EMDE regions. However, there is considerable heterogeneity within the region, with higher informality among non-Gulf Cooperation Council (GCC) economies. Moreover, although the share of informal activity in MENA has been steady over the past two decades, perceptions of informality in the MENA region have edged upward. Employment informality is high among lower-skilled workers and the youth, which poses important challenges for MENA's ongoing transition to a more diversified economic structure and jobs-oriented growth.

Against this backdrop, this box examines the following questions:

- How has informality evolved in the Middle East and North Africa?

- What are the macroeconomic and social correlates of informality?

- What policy options are available to address challenges associated with informality?

Evolution of informality

On average during 2008-2016, informal sector output in MENA amounted to about one quarter of official GDP, lower than other EMDE regions (Figure 2.4.1.1; Chapter 3). During the same period, about 24 percent of the labor employment are reported to be self-employed.

Broadly stable over time. The extent of informal sector output in MENA appears to have remained steady over the past two decades, although survey-based measures of informality suggest that perceived informality may have increased. The persistence of informality is linked to the long-standing economic structure of MENA economies, including dependence on commodities production in oil

exporters, a limited private sector, low labor mobility, and lack of economic diversification.

Regional heterogeneity. The moderate average level of informality masks disparate trends within the region. The share of informal output in GCC economies is about 8 percentage points less than in non-GCC economies (18 percent and 26 percent, respectively), and the share of self-employment to total employment in non-GCC economies is about 10 times that of the GCC.

Correlates of informality

Informality in MENA has reflected a number of economic and development challenges. These ranged from limited private sector activity to conflict situations. Large informal sectors have been associated with lower productivity, low wages, and less inclusive growth. Although informality can provide helpful employment opportunities where the formal sector features distortions and governance is poor, the structural, policy, and institutional features that foster informality in MENA poses challenges for the region's efforts to diversify and reduce its reliance on commodity production and the public sector.

Economic structure. Low informality in the GCC reflects high reliance on expatriate workers and high public employment for nationals (World Bank 2018o). In the non-GCC economies, informal workers constitute the vast majority of the employed in the agriculture and mining sectors. Across countries, a higher share of agricultural employment had been associated with higher informality (Elshamy 2015; Gatti et al. 2014; UNDP 2013; World Bank 2014c). Urban workers were also 5-12 percent less likely to be informally employed than rural workers (Angel-Urdinola and Tanabe 2012), altogether consistent with the negative correlation between stage of development and informality.

Governance and business climates. Informality in MENA is closely linked to governance quality, which has been negatively correlated with informality (Elbadawi and Loayza 2008). In non-GCC economies, where informality is higher, institutional quality indicators also tend to be markedly lower than in the GCC. This issue is further

Note: This box was prepared by Lei Sandy Ye. Research assistance was provided by Mengyi Li and Jinxin Wu.

BOX 2.4.1 Informality in the Middle East and North Africa (*continued*)

FIGURE 2.4.1.1 Informality in the Middle East and North Africa

MENA's informal sector output comprises nearly one quarter of official GDP, lower than other EMDE regions. However, perceptions of informality in MENA has risen somewhat while they have declined in the median EMDE.

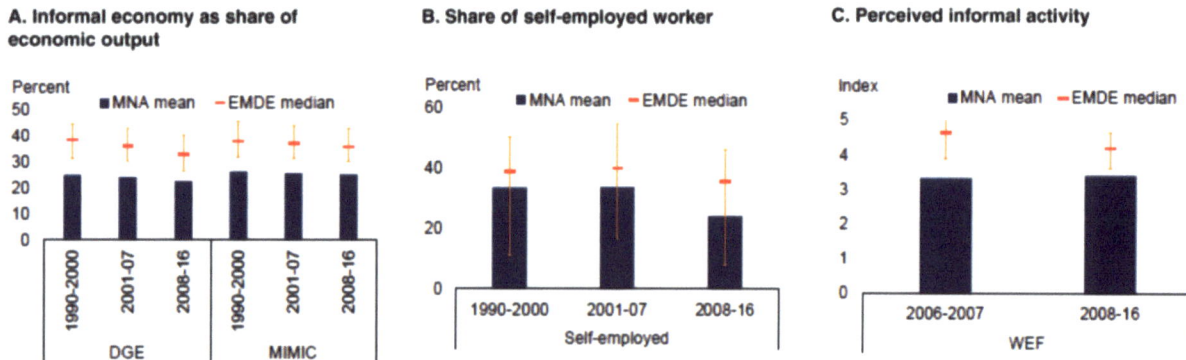

A. Informal economy as share of economic output

B. Share of self-employed worker

C. Perceived informal activity

Source: Elgin et al. (forthcoming), International Labor Organization, World Bank, World Economic Forum.
A.-C. Blue bars show simple averages of economies in the region. Red markers show the median of all EMDEs. Vertical lines denote interquartile range of all EMDEs.
A. DGE = dynamic general equilibrium model. MIMIC = multiple indicators multiple causes model. The DGE model estimates the size of the informal sector as a percent of official GDP (see Elgin and Oztunali 2012). The MIMIC model is a structural equations model that considers multiple causes of informal activity and captures multiple outcome indicators of informal activity (see Schneider, Buehn, and Montenegro 2010). It also estimates the informal output as a percent of official GDP. DGE measure includes 6 GCC economies and 9 non-GCC economies. MIMIC measure includes 6 GCC economies and 10 non-GCC economies. Excludes Djibouti, Iraq, Libya (DGE only), and West Bank and Gaza.
B. Self-employed is the share of self-employment in total employment. Includes 6 GCC economies and 10 non-GCC economies (excludes Djibouti, Iraq, and Libya).
C. WEF index is the average responses at the country-year level to the following question (surveyed by World Economic Forum): "In your country, how much economic activity do you estimate to be undeclared or unregistered? (1=Most economic activity is undeclared or unregistered; 7 = Most economic activity is declared or registered)." WEF indices are re-ordered (i.e. 1= Most economic activity is declared or registered; 7= Most economic activity is undeclared or unregistered) so that a higher average at the country level indicates a larger informal economy. The index does not use data for year 2004-2005 due to inconsistency in survey methods. Includes 6 GCC economies and 10 non-GCC economies (excludes Djibouti, Iraq, and West Bank and Gaza).

compounded by poor public services and burdensome regulatory environment, which raise the costs of operating in the formal sector (World Bank 2016d).

Conflict. In a number of countries (e.g., Syrian Arab Republic), wars and violent conflicts have severely limited the number of public sector jobs, which also led workers to shift into the informal sector for lack of alternatives (Devarajan and Mottaghi 2017; Ianchovichina and Ivanic 2014). In neighboring countries of fragile and war-torn economies (e.g., Jordan, Lebanon), the massive influx of refugees—many of whom are unregistered—has boosted the informal sector, where jobs tend to be labor intensive and low skilled.

Lower productivity. High informality has been associated with lower labor productivity and more limited export potential, partly reflected in its relatively low informal share of output compared to that of employment (Box 3.2; Elbadawi and Loayza 2008; Gatti et al. 2014). Hindrances in the formal sector, including regulatory barriers to entry and burdensome taxation, divert otherwise productive firms and workers to enter and remain in the informal

sector where productivity is lower.[1] Moreover, based on enterprise survey data, a sizable portion of firms in oil importers (e.g., Morocco, Tunisia) consider competitors' practices in the informal sector as hindering their own business operations (Figure 2.4.1.2; World Bank 2004).[2]

Restricted market access. Informal workers in the region tend to be concentrated in small and medium-sized firms, which constitute more than 90 percent of MENA's private enterprises (Purfield et al. 2018). Although these firms can include young start-ups with high entrepreneurial potential, they have tended to be oriented toward local markets, with limited regional or global market access (World Bank 2004, 2016d). Among these enterprises, a 1 percentage point increase in the share of informal workers was associated with a 6-percentage-points lower

---

[1] Within small and medium-sized enterprises in MENA, a 1 percentage point increase in the share of informal workers was associated with 3 percentage point lower relative wages (Elbadawi and Loayza 2008).

[2] Informal business operations may also imply lower contributions to government revenues, while possibly raising resource utilization on public services, such as infrastructure use (Galal 2005; Gatti et al. 2014).

BOX 2.4.1 Informality in the Middle East and North Africa (*continued*)

FIGURE 2.4.1.2 Correlates of informality and policy challenges

Informal activity is higher among non-GCC economies in the MENA region, and competition from the informal sector presents a major obstacle to businesses in several large economies. Low wages for informal sector women workers have been associated with particularly low female labor force participation rates in the region. Informality is also high among the youth in MENA, a group that often has insufficient access to education and training programs. In non-GCC economies, where informality is more pervasive, policies that improve access to finance and public-sector effectiveness can help increase mobility from the informal to the formal sector.

A. Informality in regional subgroups

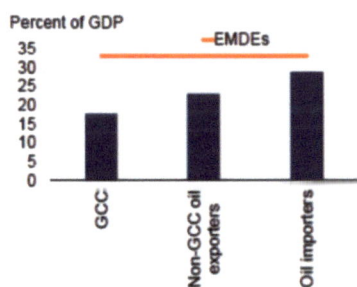

B. Firms citing informal sector competitor business practices as biggest obstacle

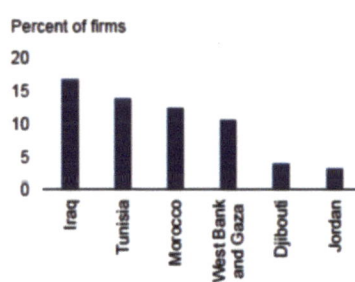

C. Female labor force participation

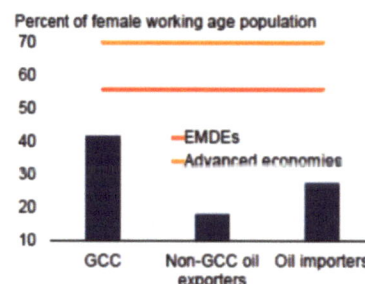

D. Youth unemployed or not in education

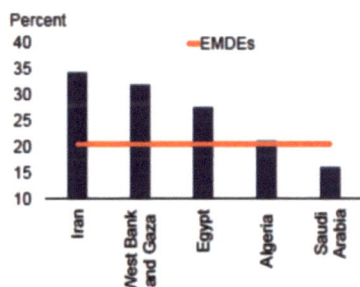

E. Firms citing access to finance as a major constraint

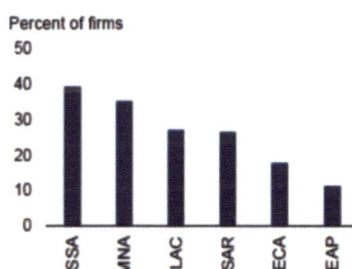

F. Public sector effectiveness: non-GCC

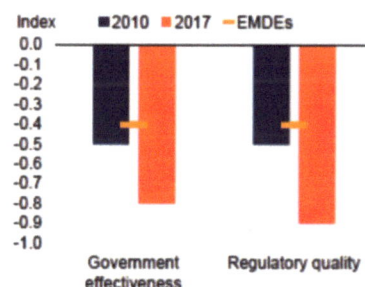

Source: Elgin et al. (forthcoming), International Labor Organization, World Bank, World Economic Forum.

A. Based on DGE estimates of informal output in percent of official GDP (chapter 3). 2008-16 averages. "EMDEs" denote the median of all EMDEs during the same period. Includes 6 GCC economies, 2 non-GCC oil exporters, and 5 oil importers. Excludes Djibouti, Iraq, Libya, Syria, Yemen, and West Bank and Gaza.

B. Columns denote the percent of firms citing "informal business practices" as the biggest obstacle to their business. Based on the latest available World Bank Enterprise Survey year since 2013 for each economy denoted.

C. Workforce as a percent of female population ages 15-64. Based on 2017 data. Unweighted averages. Includes 6 GCC economies, 3 Non-GCC oil exporters, and 7 oil importers.

D. Denotes share of youth (aged 15-24 years) not in education, employment, or training in percent of youth population. Based on latest available data since 2010 for each country.

E. Percent of firm citing access to finance as a major constraint to business, based on World Bank enterprise surveys (surveys in the MENA region only include non-GCC economies). EAP = East Asia and Pacific, ECA = Europe and Central Asia, LAC = Latin America and the Caribbean, MNA=Middle East and North Africa, SAR = South Asia, and SSA = Sub-Saharan Africa. Based on latest survey year since 2010 for each country. Includes 9 MNA economies.

F. Based on the Worldwide Governance Indicators of regulatory quality and government effectiveness, in which a lower index denotes weaker regulatory quality and weaker effectiveness. Index ranges from -2.5 to 2.5. Includes 13 non-GCC economies. Unweighted averages. "EMDEs" denotes the year 2017.

revenue share destined for non-local markets (Elbadawi and Loayza 2008).

Wage differentials. Informality presents a source of employment but also income vulnerability among women and the youth. The wage gap between informal and formal workers (i.e., formality premium) has been higher for women than men. For example, in Egypt, the formal wage

premium was about 20 percent for males but more than 50 percent for females (Gatti et al. 2014). Informality rates are higher among the young workers, who often do not enter public sector jobs until later in age (Angel-Urdinola and Tanabe 2012; Elbadawi and Loayza 2008). In Morocco, the formal wage premium among the youth was more than 50 percent (Gatti et al. 2014). Further, returns to education have been lower in the informal sector than

BOX 2.4.1 Informality in the Middle East and North Africa (*continued*)

the formal sector, which has discouraged skills acquisition (Angel-Urdinola and Tanabe 2012).[3]

Less inclusive growth. High informality in the region is associated with lower levels of educational attainment and enrollment, as in many economies a majority of informal workers are school dropouts or have not received a secondary education (Gatti et al. 2014). High informality is associated with limited access to health care and legal services, especially in fragile areas (Cho 2011). Workers in the informal sector have also reported harsher job conditions and poorer work safety, and among young informal workers, lower levels of job satisfaction (Gatti et al. 2014). These social disparities have the potential to slow reform momentum in the region by constraining consensus-building.

Policy challenges

Informality in non-GCC MENA countries, where informality is widespread, reflects deep-rooted economic structures. These economies have some of the highest youth unemployment rates and lowest female labor force participation rates among all EMDEs. Public sector employment constitutes more than 15 percent of total employment, about twice the EMDE average (IMF 2018b). Multi-pronged policies can aim to create a more vibrant private sector and strengthen human capital of workers, part of building a new social contract in the region (Devarajan and Mottaghi 2015). Policies targeting specific vulnerable groups can lessen the negative externalities associated with informality.

Fiscal reforms. Burdensome taxation has been a key constraint to formal sector firms in MENA (Gatti et al. 2014). In non-GCC MENA economies where informality is more pervasive, reforms to align tax systems with international best practices and strengthen enforcement could further attract informal firms to productive formal activity while also raising revenue collection. Such reforms may include reducing excessive corporate tax rate burdens and enhancing revenue collection through harmonized electronic filing systems (e.g., Morocco).

Access to finance. Access to finance is a larger obstacle to doing business in non-GCC MENA than in most other EMDE regions. Boosting access to finance, including through a stronger legal framework and improved credit protection regimes, can help promote private sector activity by increasing transparency of firms to investors and facilitating investment (Farazi 2014; Straub 2005). A number of economies in MENA have recently adopted policies in this area, such as new insolvency resolution laws in Egypt, Saudi Arabia, and the United Arab Emirates. The adoption of financial technologies (Fintech), such as innovations that automate financial transactions, can also facilitate financial services to informal unbanked individuals or small and medium-sized enterprises (Arezki et al. 2018; Lukonga 2018).

Regulatory effectiveness. Beyond its large size, public sector effectiveness and regulatory quality in non-GCC MENA countries have deteriorated in the last decade. Corruption is cited among the biggest hindrances to MENA firm operations and increases incentives for firms and workers to operate informally (World Bank 2016d). Together with low regulatory efficiency, corruption reduces the effectiveness of labor market regulations and enforcement (Gatti et al. 2014). Policies that reduce regulatory costs help increase mobility of MENA firms between the informal and formal sector, while those that strengthen property rights may assist the rural or agricultural-sector populations to access financing (e.g., enabling collateralized loans). Policies to promote entrepreneurial activities, such as easing of business licensing requirements, can also facilitate entry of informal workers into more productive jobs in the formal sector.

Education. Policies that encourage higher education and expand job training can be especially relevant for younger workers by facilitating their entry into more productive formal jobs. Training programs may be particularly effective if coupled with mechanisms to increase women's mobility, which is constrained in the region, and offer a combination of soft and hard skills. Training is also more effective if extended to areas (e.g., rural) where educational levels are lower, as MENA region's training programs tended to serve higher income and more educated individuals (Angel-Urdinola, Semlali, and Brodmann 2010). A holistic approach that combines job training with job creation efforts, such as through public-private sector programs, can also be effective; given higher unemployment rates for university graduates than low-skilled workers in the region (World Bank 2018r).

---

[3] Evidence from Egypt, for example, suggests that a worker in the formal sector who has completed 5 years of education earns comparable wages to those of an informal sector worker with 12-14 years of education (Angel-Urdinola and Tanabe 2012).

SOUTH ASIA

outlook are tilted down. On the domestic side, vulnerabilities are being exacerbated by fiscal slippages and rising inflation, and the possibility of delays in needed structural reforms to address weaknesses in the balance sheets of banks and non-financial corporates. Key external risks include a further deterioration in current accounts and a faster-than-expected tightening of global financing conditions.

Recent developments

Growth in South Asia accelerated to an estimated 6.9 percent in 2018 from 6.2 percent the previous year, with domestic demand strengthening in India as temporary disruptions fade and the benefits from ongoing structural reforms start to materialize. The recovery was in line with expectations, and recent high frequency data–including purchasing managers' indices and industrial production–have broadly remained solid (Figure 2.5.1).

Throughout the region, private consumption picked up in 2018 while investment remained solid. The solid investment was supported by the fading of a number of temporary disruptions, a revival of credit growth, and ongoing infrastructure projects. Strong domestic demand boosted imports, while exports remained subdued amid weak global trade sentiment, causing current account deficits to widen (World Bank 2018s).

India's growth accelerated to an estimated 7.3 percent in FY2018/19 (April to March) as economic activity continued to recover with strong domestic demand. While investment

continued to strengthen amid GST harmonization and a rebound of credit growth, consumption remained the major contributor to growth (Ahmad et al. 2018).

Excluding India, regional growth moderated slightly in 2018. Pakistan's GDP (factor cost) is estimated to have grown 5.8 percent in FY2017/18 (July 16 to July 15), with solid contributions from consumption and investment. Activity was supported by strengthening in the agricultural and industrial sectors, and a sustained acceleration in services.

In Bangladesh, growth was broad-based, remaining strong at an estimated 7.9 percent in FY2017/18 (July 1 to June 30). Private consumption was the main driver of growth, supported by strong remittance inflows. Net exports turned negative because of rising food and capital machinery imports and weak exports (World Bank 2018t).

In Sri Lanka, activity accelerated to an estimated 3.9 percent in 2018 on the back of a recovery in the agriculture and services sectors. In Nepal, economic activity remained solid with a 6.3 percent growth in FY2017/18 (July 16 to July 15). Less favorable monsoons led to weakness in agricultural activity, but this was offset by a recovery in remittances and robust industrial

---

Note: This section was prepared by Temel Taskin. Research assistance was provided by Ishita Dugar and Brent Harrison.

FIGURE 2.5.1 SAR: Recent developments

South Asia remains the fastest growing EMDE region. High frequency indicators of economic activity are mixed across the region but are broadly consistent with the recovery underway. Remittance inflows are an important source of income in the region. Inflation is below official targets in general despite a recent acceleration in some countries. Sovereign credit default spreads have been rising as the Federal Reserve continues to tighten monetary policy and U.S. dollar appreciates.

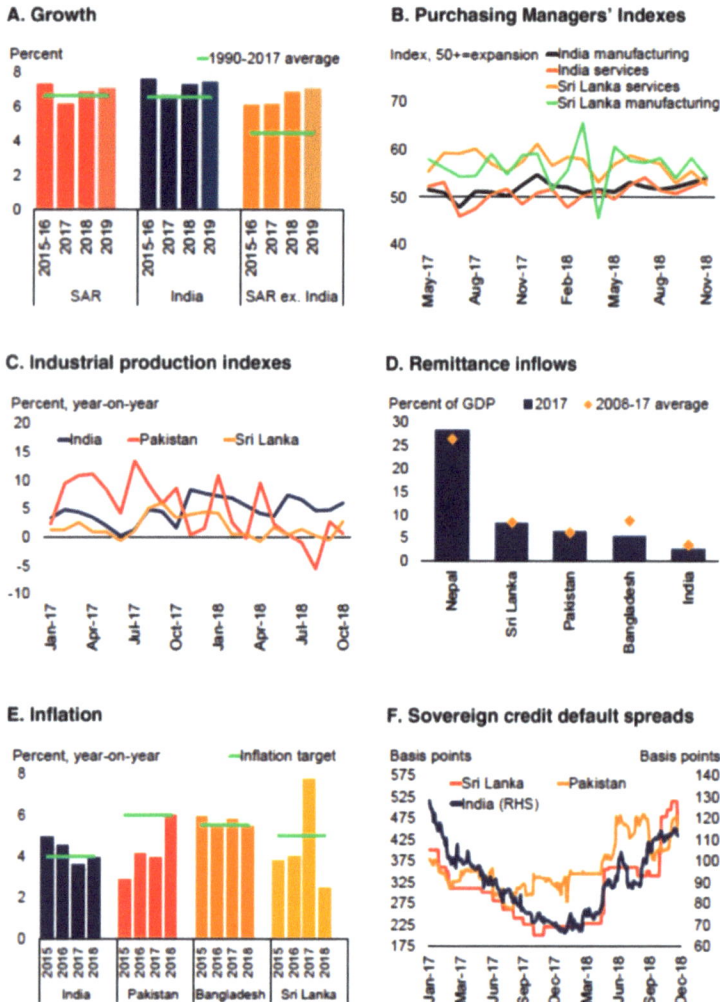

A. Growth

B. Purchasing Managers' Indexes

C. Industrial production indexes

D. Remittance inflows

E. Inflation

F. Sovereign credit default spreads

Source: Haver Analytics, International Monetary Fund, World Bank.
A. SAR = South Asia Region. Aggregate growth rates are calculated using constant 2010 U.S. dollar GDP-weights. Data for 2018 are estimates. Shaded areas indicate forecasts.
B. PMI readings above 50 indicate expansion in economic activity; readings below 50 show contraction. Last observation is November 2018.
C. Last observation is October 2018.
D. Data present the workers' remittances and compensation received by countries. Last observation is 2017.
E. Last observation is October 2018.
F. Data present five-year U.S. dollar credit default swap (mid-rate). Last observation is December 2018.

sector growth, particularly for manufacturing activities (World Bank 2018u).

Investment and services remained the major contributor to economic activity in Bhutan and the Maldives. In Bhutan, hydropower and other infrastructure projects supported investment, and GDP expanded by an estimated 4.6 percent in FY2017/18 (July 1 to June 30). Maldives' GDP accelerated to an estimated 8.0 percent in 2018, reflecting strength in tourism and construction. Growth in Afghanistan is estimated to have edged down to 2.4 percent. Although activity was supported by agriculture and services, subdued business confidence and security challenges continued to weigh on growth.

There were some signs of rising inflation pressure across the region, and both India and Pakistan raised rates in 2018 to counter the effects of currency depreciation, rising energy prices, and domestic capacity constraints.

Sovereign bond yields surged in the region last year. Fiscal consolidation stalled owing to elections in several countries, contributing further to the region's high levels of government debt. In India, the government deficit was higher than planned, reflecting lower-than-expected revenues from telecom spectrum auctions and low dividends from public sector enterprises (World Bank 2018v). The central government is budgeting a reduction in the fiscal deficit for next fiscal year. Pakistan's fiscal deficit rose to 6.6 percent of GDP last year, well above the government's target of 4.1 percent, as tax collection fell short of expectations.

External vulnerabilities are also rising in the region. In Sri Lanka and to some extent in Pakistan, external debt is sizable and current account deficits have deteriorated considerably. Recent currency pressures have eroded Pakistan's foreign exchange reserves significantly—they currently amount to only around two months of imports.

Outlook

The outlook for South Asia is robust, despite the financial stress that has affected a number of EMDEs and continued trade disputes. Regional growth is expected to accelerate in 2019, to 7.1 percent (Figure 2.5.2). Economic activity will be underpinned by solid investment and robust consumption. While exports and imports will be held back owing to slowing global trade, the region's relatively low exposure to international trade will mitigate the impact of this slowdown on the regional outlook.

India's GDP is forecast to grow by 7.3 percent in FY2018/19 and 7.5 percent thereafter, in line with June forecasts. Private consumption is projected to remain robust and investment growth is expected to continue as the benefits of recent policy reforms begin to materialize and credit rebounds. Strong domestic demand is envisioned to widen the current account deficit to 2.6 percent of GDP next year. Inflation is projected to rise somewhat above the midpoint of the Reserve Bank of India's target range of 2 to 6 percent, mainly owing to energy and food prices.

In the rest of the region, economic activity will average 5.6 percent over the forecast horizon. In Pakistan, macroeconomic imbalances weigh on growth outlook. Pakistan is expected to face financing needs due to large current account and fiscal deficits combined with low international reserves. GDP growth is projected to decelerate to 3.7 percent in FY2018/19, with financial conditions tightening to help counter rising inflation and external vulnerabilities. Activity is projected to rebound and average 4.6 percent over the medium term with support from stabilizing macroeconomic conditions (World Bank 2018u).

In Bangladesh, robust economic activity is expected to be sustained. GDP growth is forecast at 7.0 percent in FY2018/19 and is expected to decelerate only slightly over the forecast horizon. Activity will be supported by strong private consumption and investment on the back of infrastructure projects. Net exports are projected to contribute negatively to GDP growth as imports outpace exports in response to strong domestic demand.

In Sri Lanka, last year's recovery from adverse weather conditions is expected to continue in 2019, with 4.0 percent GDP growth. Activity will be supported by robust domestic demand as consumption rebounds following natural disasters, and investment is boosted by infrastructure projects. Nepal's strong post-earthquake momentum is expected to moderate—GDP

FIGURE 2.5.2 SAR: Outlook and risks

Economic activity is projected to remain strong. Possible fiscal slippages could further worsen already-high public debt positions. Non-performing assets remain high despite recent efforts to improve the quality of financial sector balance sheets. External imbalances pose a risk to the outlook. Major economies in the region have tightened their monetary stance to stabilize inflation and mitigate external risks.

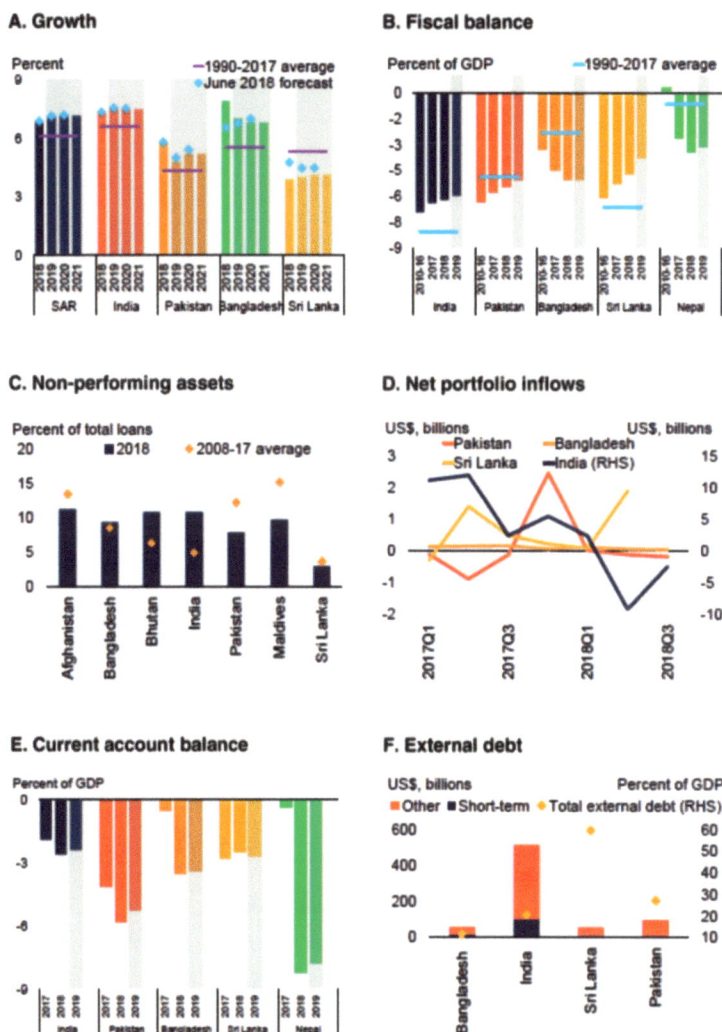

A. Growth

B. Fiscal balance

C. Non-performing assets

D. Net portfolio inflows

E. Current account balance

F. External debt

Source: Haver Analytics, World Bank.
A. SAR = South Asia Region. Aggregate growth rates are calculated using constant 2010 U.S. dollar GDP-weights. 2018 data are estimates. Shaded areas indicate forecasts.
B.E. 2018 data are estimates. Shaded areas indicate forecasts. The data represent fiscal years of countries except for Sri Lanka, as described in Table 2.5.1.
C. Data present the ratio of bank non-performing loans to total gross loans. Last observation is 2017.
D. Last observation is 2018 Q3 for Bangladesh and Pakistan, and 2018 Q2 for India and Sri Lanka.
F. Gross external debt position including both public and private sectors, as of 2018 Q2.

growth is forecast to decelerate to 5.9 percent in FY2018/19. Activity will be underpinned by strong infrastructure investment and consumption.

In Bhutan and the Maldives, activity will remain reliant on construction and tourism. Bhutan's growth is projected to accelerate to 7.6 percent 2018/19, supported by ongoing infrastructure projects and rising tourism. In the Maldives, growth is expected to moderate to 6.3 percent in 2019 as construction activity returns to long-term averages, and capital investment projects gradually slow down. Afghanistan's economy is expected to remain subdued, expanding 2.7 percent in 2019, as a result of security challenges ahead of elections, declining business confidence, and worsening drought conditions.

In South Asia, a large proportion of activity is informal, which may constrain productivity, wages, and access to social protection systems (Kanbur 2017). Investing in education and skills, improving the business environment by enhancing regulatory frameworks and boosting the quality of government services provided to formal firms are among the policy measures which can encourage formal activity (Box 2).

Risks

The risks to the outlook are tilted downside. Domestic vulnerabilities are being exacerbated by fiscal slippages and rising inflation, escalation in political uncertainty, and the possibility of delays in the needed structural reforms to address weaknesses in balance sheets of banks and non-financial corporates. Key external risks include a further deterioration in current accounts and a faster-than-expected tightening of global financing conditions.

South Asian economies have high levels of public debt in general. Fiscal slippages could further worsen already-precarious public debt positions and result in a costly rise in already- elevated interest payments.

The upcoming election cycle next year elevates political uncertainty in the region. The challenging political environment could adversely affect the ongoing reform agenda and economic activity in some countries (e.g. Afghanistan, Sri Lanka).

In South Asia, non-performing assets (NPAs) are still high despite recent measures taken to improve the recognition of these assets (Figure 2.5.2). Especially, public sector banks in India, which represent roughly 70 percent of the banking sector assets, still report low profitability and high NPAs. Credit expansion could be limited in some major South Asia economies unless further steps are taken to deal with financial and corporate balance sheets.

On the external front, the region has relatively low exposure to international trade, which limits the benefits from trade over the long term. However, the low exposure also suggests that that it could be more insulated from the effects rising trade protectionism than other regions. Moreover, the region may even benefit from trade diversion amid the recent dispute between some major economies (World Bank 2017b).

Persistent current account deficits and high levels of external debt make the region more vulnerable to a faster-than-expected tightening of global financial conditions.

South Asia is one of the most vulnerable regions to natural disasters (World Bank 2017c). In recent years, the number of affected people and geographical areas from natural disasters such as drought, floods, and earthquakes have risen in the region. Increasingly common natural disasters could disrupt infrastructure, agricultural output, and economic activity in general. The realization of these domestic or external risks could weaken investor confidence and result in capital outflows, currency depreciation leading to rising external debt, a tightening of domestic financing conditions, and a slowdown in regional growth (Eichengreen and Gupta 2015; Kose et al. 2017).

TABLE 2.5.1 South Asia forecast summary

(Real GDP growth at market prices in percent, unless indicated otherwise)

Percentage point differences
from June 2018 projections

	2016	2017	2018e	2019f	2020f	2021f		2018e	2019f	2020f
EMDE South Asia, GDP[1,2]	7.5	6.2	6.9	7.1	7.1	7.1		0.0	0.0	-0.1

(Average including countries with full national accounts and balance of payments data only)[3]

	2016	2017	2018e	2019f	2020f	2021f		2018e	2019f	2020f
EMDE South Asia, GDP[3]	7.6	6.2	6.9	7.1	7.2	7.1		0.0	-0.1	0.0
GDP per capita (U.S. dollars)	6.2	4.9	5.7	5.9	6.0	6.0		0.1	0.0	0.0
PPP GDP	7.6	6.2	6.9	7.1	7.2	7.1		0.0	0.0	0.0
Private consumption	7.6	6.0	6.9	7.0	7.0	7.0		0.3	0.1	0.0
Public consumption	8.5	11.1	10.7	9.1	8.5	8.5		1.0	0.3	0.0
Fixed investment	9.4	8.0	8.2	8.0	7.8	7.5		0.6	0.3	0.1
Exports, GNFS[4]	1.9	6.2	5.6	5.6	5.9	6.0		-0.1	-0.5	-0.2
Imports, GNFS[4]	2.6	14.6	8.5	6.3	6.7	6.8		1.0	-0.2	0.6
Net exports, contribution to growth	-0.3	-2.3	-1.1	-0.6	-0.6	-0.6		-0.4	-0.2	-0.3

Memo items: GDP[2]	16/17	17/18	18/19e	19/20f	20/21f	21/22f		18/19e	19/20f	20/21f
South Asia excluding India	5.8	5.9	5.7	5.5	5.6	5.6		0.1	-0.1	-0.1
India	7.1	6.7	7.3	7.5	7.5	7.5		0.0	0.0	0.0
Pakistan (factor cost)	5.4	5.8	3.7	4.2	4.8	4.8		-1.3	-1.2	-0.6
Bangladesh	7.3	7.9	7.0	6.8	6.8	6.8		0.3	-0.2	-0.2

Source: World Bank.
Note: e = estimate; f = forecast. EMDE = emerging market and developing economy. World Bank forecasts are frequently updated based on new information and changing (global) circumstances. Consequently, projections presented here may differ from those contained in other Bank documents, even if basic assessments of countries' prospects do not differ at any given moment in time.
1. GDP at market prices and expenditure components are measured in constant 2010 U.S. dollars.
2. National income and product account data refer to fiscal years (FY) for the South Asian countries, while aggregates are presented in calendar year (CY) terms. The fiscal year runs from July 1 through June 30 in Bangladesh, Bhutan, and Pakistan, from July 16 through July 15 in Nepal, and April 1 through March 31 in India.
3. Sub-region aggregate excludes Afghanistan, Bhutan, and Maldives, for which data limitations prevent the forecasting of GDP components.
4. Exports and imports of goods and non-factor services (GNFS).
For additional information, please see www.worldbank.org/gep.

TABLE 2.5.2 South Asia country forecasts

(Real GDP growth at market prices in percent, unless indicated otherwise)

Percentage point differences
from June 2018 projections

Calendar year basis[1]	2016	2017	2018e	2019f	2020f	2021f		2018e	2019f	2020f
Afghanistan	2.4	2.7	2.4	2.7	3.2	3.2		0.2	0.2	-0.1
Maldives	6.2	7.1	8.0	6.3	5.6	5.6		2.5	1.8	0.7
Sri Lanka	4.5	3.3	3.9	4.0	4.1	4.1		-0.9	-0.5	-0.4

Fiscal year basis[1]	16/17	17/18	18/19e	19/20f	20/21f	21/22f		18/19e	19/20f	20/21f
Bangladesh	7.3	7.9	7.0	6.8	6.8	6.8		0.3	-0.2	-0.2
Bhutan	5.8	4.6	7.6	6.4	6.4	6.4		2.2	0.4	-2.3
India	7.1	6.7	7.3	7.5	7.5	7.5		0.0	0.0	0.0
Nepal	7.9	6.3	5.9	6.0	6.0	6.0		1.4	1.8	1.8
Pakistan (factor cost)	5.4	5.8	3.7	4.2	4.8	4.8		-1.3	-1.2	-0.6

Source: World Bank.
Note: e = estimate; f = forecast. World Bank forecasts are frequently updated based on new information and changing (global) circumstances. Consequently, projections presented here may differ from those contained in other Bank documents, even if basic assessments of countries' prospects do not differ at any given moment in time.
1. Historical data is reported on a market price basis. National income and product account data refer to fiscal years (FY) for the South Asian countries with the exception of Afghanistan, Maldives, and Sri Lanka, which report in calendar year (CY). The fiscal year runs from July 1 through June 30 in Bangladesh, Bhutan, and Pakistan, from July 16 through July 15 in Nepal, and April 1 through March 31 in India.
For additional information, please see www.worldbank.org/gep.

BOX 2.5.1 Informality in South Asia

South Asia's share of informal employment is the largest among EMDE regions, despite a below-average share of informal output. Heavy tax burdens, above-average corruption, and low government effectiveness have contributed to high employment informality. Informal employment is concentrated among low-skilled, young, female and rural workers. The sizable informal sector is associated with lower productivity, lower government revenues, and higher poverty in the region. Policy options to address these challenges include investing in human capital in the form of training programs and improving access to finance.

Introduction

South Asia (SAR) is the EMDE region with the highest average share of informal employment among EMDE regions, despite a below-median and declining share of informal output. Nonetheless, there is significant heterogeneity in the share of employment as well as output informality among South Asian countries.

Against this backdrop, this Box examines the following questions:

- How has informality evolved in South Asia?

- What have been the macroeconomic and social correlates of informality?

- What policy options are available to address challenges associated with informality?

Evolution of informality

Informality in SAR. In aggregate, output informality in the SAR region is below the average of other EMDE regions—the size of informal sector relative to official GDP was on average 30 percent in South Asia compared with 35 percent in average EMDE during 2008-2016 (Figure 2.5.1.1). During the same period, 96 percent of workers lacked pension coverage and 63 percent were self-employed.

Evolution of informality in SAR. Output informality declined from 37 percent in 1990s to 32 percent in the 2010s, broadly in line with the decline in informality in other EMDEs. However, labor informality over the same period persisted or rose depending on the measure of informality. For example, the share of the labor force without pension coverage rose from 88 percent to 96 and self-employment remained around 63 percent.

Regional heterogeneity. The extent of informality varies substantially across countries in South Asia. Sri Lanka had

the highest degree of informality (output in the informal sector is about 40 percent of total output) in 2016 and India had the lowest share (below 20 percent). However, this ranking is reversed using labor market indicators of informality: Sri Lanka has the lowest share of self-employment (42 percent) and India the highest (76 percent) as of 2016. These differences are reflected in lower labor productivity in the informal sector (relative to the formal sector) in India than in Sri Lanka.

Correlates of informality

Business climates. Costs to doing business—such as tax burdens, labor regulation, and cost of starting business— are among the main drivers of informality identified in the empirical literature (FICCI 2017; Goldar and Aggarwal 2012). Over the past decade, SAR has suffered from greater corruption and weaker government effectiveness than other EMDE regions (Figure 2.5.1.2). Tax burdens and indicators of ease of doing business have also been less favorable than in the average EMDE (World Bank 2017c). Among costs to doing business, heavy tax burdens were particularly strongly associated in India and Pakistan with a larger fraction of firms operating unregistered (Ghani, Kerr, O'Connell 2013; Waseem 2013).

Worker characteristics. South Asia's informal labor force consists predominantly of low-skilled, female, rural, and young workers (Bahadur and Parajuli 2014; Goldar and Agarwal 2012; Gunatikala 2008; Williams, Shahid, and Martinez 2015). The intensity of informal employment in South Asia reflects a lack of formal jobs and skills, as well as a preference towards self-employment (Arby, Malik, and Hanif 2010; Williams, Shahid, and Martinez 2015). This means that informal firms are usually small, agricultural, and consist mostly of self-employed workers (FICCI 2017).

Lower productivity and incomes. In South Asia, informal workers have had lower earnings, fewer skills, and less access to social protection systems; this has been reflected in lower productivity and higher poverty (Kanbur 2017; Likhi 2013). Informal employment among underrepresented groups in labor markets, such as women and the young, has grown over the past decade and

Note: This box was prepared by Temel Taskin. Research assistance was provided by Brent Harrison and Jinxin Wu.

BOX 2.5.1 Informality in South Asia (*continued*)

FIGURE 2.5.1.1 Informality in South Asia

South Asia's share of informal employment is the largest among EMDE regions, despite a below-average share of informal output.

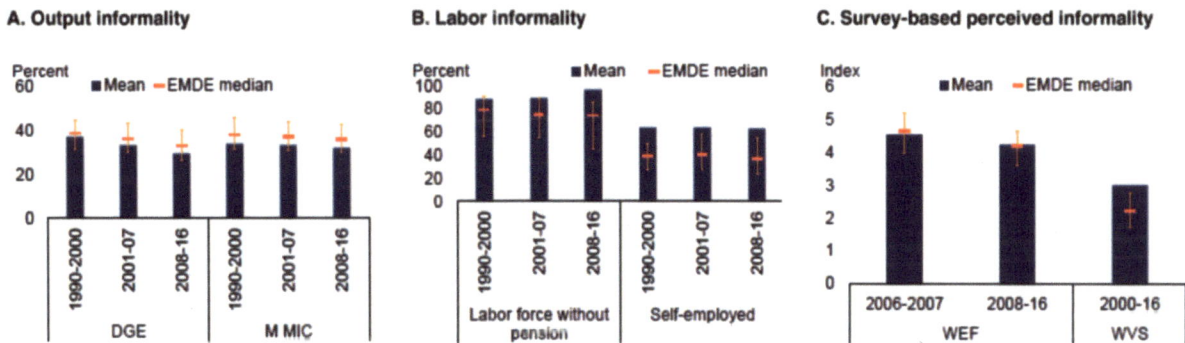

A. Output informality

B. Labor informality

C. Survey-based perceived informality

Source: Elgin et al. (forthcoming); World Bank.

A. DGE = dynamic general equilibrium model. MIMIC = multiple indicators multiple causes model. Both DGE and MIMIC estimates measure the informal output in percent of official GDP.

B. Labor force without pension is the fraction of the labor force that doesn't contribute to a retirement pension scheme, which is derived from the original data on pension coverage obtained from WDI. Self-employed is the share of self-employment in total employment.

C. WEF = World Economic Forum. WVS = World Values Survey. WEF index is the average responses at the country-year level to the following question (surveyed by World Economic Forum): "In your country, how much economic activity do you estimate to be undeclared or unregistered? (1=Most economic activity is undeclared or unregistered; 7 = Most economic activity is declared or registered)." WEF indices are re-ordered (i.e. 1= Most economic activity is declared or registered; 7= Most economic activity is undeclared or unregistered) so that a higher average at the country level indicates a larger informal economy. The index does not use data for year 2004-2005 due to inconsistency in survey methods. The World Value Survey asks whether respondents can justify cheating on taxes, with responses ranging from 1 (never justifiable) to 10 (always justifiable). The average responses at the country-year level are used as a measure for attitudes towards informality (or tax morality, Oveido et al. 2009), labeled as WVS. A higher average at the country level implies that people find cheating on taxes more justifiable.

constrained these groups' income security. Low earnings and limited options available to informal workers constrain their benefit from economic growth, which means that growth has been less inclusive than otherwise (ADB 2016; Heintz 2012). Conversely, in India, an easing of labor market restrictions and measures to foster gender equality—such as increasing female education and strengthening law enforcement against gender discrimination—have been associated with stronger growth as well as larger formal employment (Goldar and Aggarwal 2012; Khera 2016).

Lower government revenues. Large informal sectors—in addition to other factors such as inefficient tax administration and narrow tax base—weigh on tax revenues in South Asian economies (Cevik 2016; Ilzetzki and Lagakos 2017). On average, tax revenues as a percent in GDP have historically been below the EMDE average. The lack of tax revenues ultimately affects the ability of governments to fund its infrastructure investment, social programs, etc., and therefore limiting their ability to tackle poverty and inequality (Chapter 3).

Policy challenges

In South Asia, informal employment is concentrated among young, low-skilled, female, and rural workers. Policies targeting training and education of these groups, especially in rural areas, could help their transition to formal employment (Khera 2016).

There is significant room to improve the ease of doing business in South Asia. This could reduce informality by reducing the cost of entry and cost of operating in formal sector. Measures to reduce the time, cost, and complexity of registration would also improve the business climate and foster growth (FICCI 2017).

High quality public services can also provide an incentive for informal firms to become formal in order to access these services. Enhanced monitoring and enforcement, including of tax regulations, could help discourage informality (Ilzetzki and Lagakos 2017). Also, in India the recent introduction of a Goods and Services Tax and steps toward demonetization are expected to encourage a shift from the informal to the formal sector.

BOX 2.5.1 Informality in South Asia *(continued)*

FIGURE 2.5.1.2 Drivers of informality in South Asia

Heavy tax burdens, above-average corruption, and low government effectiveness likely have contributed to high employment informality. The sizable informal sector is associated with weaker government revenues and higher poverty in the region. Youth unemployment is much higher among women who represent a higher share of informal workers than men.

A. Doing business tax burden indicator: DTF

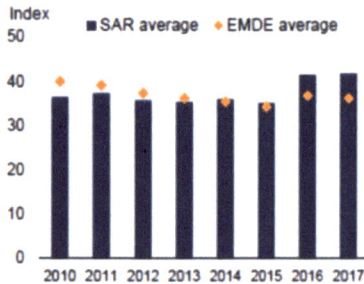

B. Doing business overall indicator

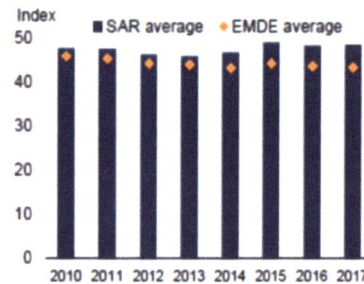

C. Government effectiveness and control of corruption

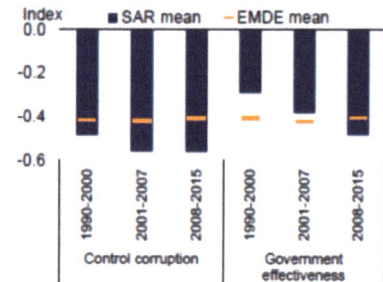

D. Poverty

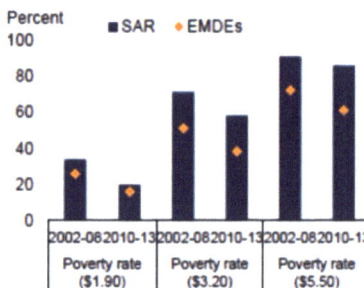

E. Government revenues

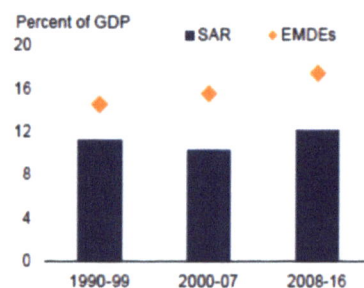

F. Youth employment and NEET

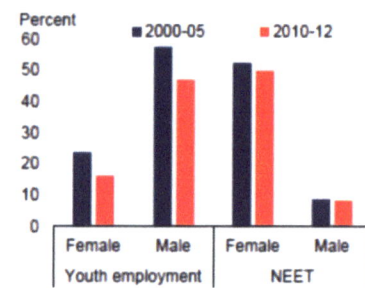

Source: World Bank, World Development Indicators.
A.B. Index denotes Distance to Frontier Score (100-regional score), where 100 equals international best practices. Greater distance indicates further below best practice score.
D.E. Episodes are determined based on data availability.
F. NEET stands for the share of youth Not in Employment, Education, or Training. Youth is defined as the population between ages of 15 and 24.

South Asia's self-employed, which account for about 80 percent of informally employed, have limited access to financial resources that could finance growth- or productivity-enhancing investment (Ghani, Kerr, and O'Connell 2013). Greater access to credit for the self-employed and household enterprises could help them grow into formality (Beck and Hoseini 2014). Microfinance can be an effective instrument for providing financial access to informal firms, as many of them are self-employed enterprises (ILO 2013; Likhi 2013).

SUB-SAHARAN AFRICA

The recovery in Sub-Saharan Africa continues, albeit at a softer pace. Growth in the region is estimated at 2.7 percent in 2018, significantly slower than expected, partly due to weaknesses in Angola, Nigeria, and South Africa. Growth is foreseen to rise to 3.4 percent in 2019 and 3.7 percent in 2020-21, as reduced policy uncertainty helps support a cyclical rebound in these large economies. However, per capita income growth will remain modest, and progress in poverty reduction limited. Risks to the outlook are tilted to the downside. Key external risks include an unexpectedly sharp decline in commodity prices, an abrupt tightening of global financial conditions, and escalating trade tensions involving major economies. Domestic risks pertain to fiscal slippage, political uncertainty, domestic conflicts, and adverse weather conditions.

Recent developments

The recovery in Sub-Saharan Africa (SSA) continued in 2018, but activity lost momentum in several countries. Growth in the region is estimated to have risen marginally from 2.6 percent in 2017 to 2.7 percent in 2018, slower than expected and still below potential. This reflected a sluggish expansion in the region's three largest economies—Angola, Nigeria, and South Africa (Figure 2.6.1). The region faced a more difficult external environment last year as global trade growth moderated, financing conditions tightened, and the U.S. dollar strengthened. Commodity prices diverged, with metals and agriculture prices dampened by weakening global demand, while oil prices were higher in most of 2018, mainly due to supply factors.

In Nigeria, oil production fell, partly owing to pipeline closures in mid-2018, while non-oil activity was dampened by lackluster consumer demand, as well as conflicts over land between farmers and herders that disrupted crop production. In Angola—the region's second largest oil exporter—stagnant non-oil activity was aggravated by a contraction in oil production,

which fell sharply due to underinvestment and to key oil fields reaching maturity. South Africa's economy emerged from a technical recession in the second half of 2018, in part due to improved activity in the agricultural and manufacturing sectors. However, growth remains subdued, as challenges in the mining sector and weak construction activity are compounded by policy uncertainty and low business confidence. Against this backdrop, the South African government announced measures to support the economy through reprioritized spending and structural reforms to improve the business environment and infrastructure delivery.

Growth in the rest of the region was broadly steady, although performance varied between country groups. While growth among metals exporters was subdued in 2018, activity in several oil exporters rebounded. In the Central African Economic and Monetary Community (CEMAC), growth benefitted from an increase in oil production and higher oil prices. Economic activity in non-resource-intensive countries remained robust, supported by agricultural production and services on the production side, and household consumption and public investment on the demand side. Several countries in the West African Economic and Monetary Union (WAEMU) grew at 6 percent or more, including Benin, Burkina Faso, Côte d'Ivoire, and

Note: This section was prepared by Gerard Kambou and Rudi Steinbach. Research assistance was provided by Mengyi Li.

FIGURE 2.6.1 **SSA: Recent developments**

The recovery in Sub-Saharan Africa has continued. However, growth remains well below its long-term average due to a sluggish expansion in Angola, Nigeria, and South Africa—the region's largest economies. The current account deficit has narrowed in oil exporters but deteriorated among metals exporters due to weaker export growth. Fiscal deficits have narrowed, mainly reflecting consolidation measures in some oil exporters. Public debt remains elevated, especially among non-resource-intensive countries due to their continued reliance on public investment to boost growth.

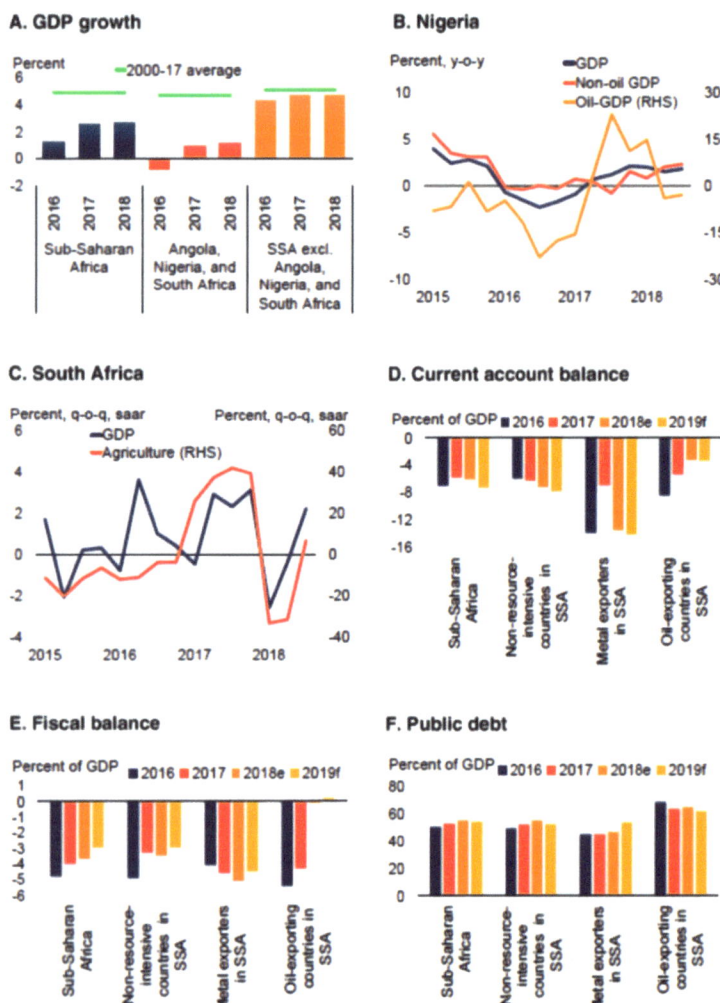

A. GDP growth

B. Nigeria

C. South Africa

D. Current account balance

E. Fiscal balance

F. Public debt

Source: Haver Analytics; International Monetary Fund, *World Economic Outlook*; National Bureau of Statistics (Nigeria); Statistics South Africa; World Bank.
A. Aggregate growth rates calculated using constant 2010 U.S. dollar weights.
D.-F. Median of groups. Non-resource-intensive countries include agricultural exporters and commodity importers.

Senegal. A strong rebound in agriculture in Kenya, Rwanda, and Uganda, following prior droughts, underpinned the pickup in activity in East Africa.

The median current account deficit is estimated to have widened from 5.8 percent of GDP in 2017 to 6.1 percent in 2018, but sizable differences persist

across countries. For large oil exporters (e.g., Angola, Nigeria), external balances improved, driven by higher oil prices and soft import demand. The current account deficit also narrowed significantly in CEMAC, underpinned by strong fiscal adjustments. By contrast, external balances in metals exporters deteriorated amid weaker exports in some countries and higher imports in others. In non-resource-intensive countries, current account deficits remained elevated due to high fuel imports and capital goods imports related to public infrastructure projects. Across the region, balance of payments financing became more difficult against the backdrop of rising external borrowing costs and weakening capital inflows. Eurobond issuance slowed markedly in the second half of the year, while FDI inflows remained subdued (UNCTAD 2018).

Currencies in the region depreciated in effective terms amid a broad-based strengthening of the U.S. dollar and weaker investor sentiment toward emerging markets. Investors' renewed focus on country-specific vulnerabilities contributed to a rapid sell-off of the South African rand and the Zambian kwacha since mid-2018. Elsewhere in the region, the pace of currency depreciation has been more modest.

Inflationary pressures persist in the region. Despite steep declines, inflation in Angola and Nigeria remained in double digits, partly due to continued exchange rate depreciation (Angola) and elevated food price inflation (Nigeria). In South Africa, inflation stayed within the 3 to 6 percent target range. Among non-resource-intensive countries, inflation rose sharply in Ethiopia and Sudan, due to a rapid expansion in credit and currency depreciation (Ethiopia) and the monetization of a large fiscal deficit (Sudan).

The median fiscal deficit for the region is estimated to have narrowed from 4 percent of GDP in 2017 to 3.7 percent in 2018. The fiscal balance improved sharply among many oil exporters. The narrower deficit in Angola partly stemmed from higher oil prices. CEMAC countries substantially reduced their fiscal deficits through revenue mobilization efforts and cuts in capital expenditures. By contrast, the fiscal deficit remained elevated in Nigeria, due to low tax revenue collection.

In metals exporters, the median fiscal deficit is estimated to have deteriorated sharply, as spending levels remain elevated in some countries, while revenues are suppressed. In non-resource-intensive countries, the median fiscal deficit is estimated to have widened modestly, reflecting continued public investment supported by enhanced revenue mobilization efforts.

In all, vulnerabilities remain: government debt-to-GDP ratios are estimated to have risen in more than half of the countries in 2018 and were above 60 percent in one-third (World Bank 2018w). Exchange rate depreciations (e.g., Zambia), negative growth (e.g., Equatorial Guinea, Republic of Congo), and the reporting of previously undisclosed debt (e.g., Mozambique, Republic of Congo) contributed to the deterioration.

In addition to the rise in debt ratios, changes in the composition of debt have made many countries more vulnerable to sharp movements in financing conditions (Chapter 4). As countries have gained access to international capital markets, and non-resident participation in domestic debt markets expanded, non-concessional debt has increased. Non-concessional financing accounted for more than half of total public debt in many countries (e.g., Cote d'Ivoire, Ghana, Republic of Congo, Sudan, Zambia, Zimbabwe).

Outlook

Growth in Sub-Saharan Africa is expected to pick up to 3.4 percent in 2019, rising to an average of 3.7 percent in 2020-21 (Figure 2.6.2). This is predicated on diminished policy uncertainty and improved investment in large economies, together with continued robust growth in non-resource-intensive countries. However, external headwinds have intensified, as growth among main trading partners moderates, global financial conditions tighten, and trade policy uncertainty persists (Chapter 1). Per capita income growth is predicted to remain well below its long-term average in many countries, yielding little progress in poverty reduction, and highlighting the need

FIGURE 2.6.2 SSA: Outlook and risks

A gradual recovery is expected, as an increase in oil production supports a modest growth pickup in Angola and Nigeria, and easing drought conditions boosts agricultural production. A rise in investment, as policy uncertainty gradually recedes, should further boost growth in the large economies. Activity in the rest of the region is expected to expand at a solid pace. Nevertheless, sluggish per capita growth implies continued slow progress in poverty reduction. A significant amount of international bonds are maturing, posing refinancing risks. Rising non-concessional debt is making countries more vulnerable to changes in international financial conditions.

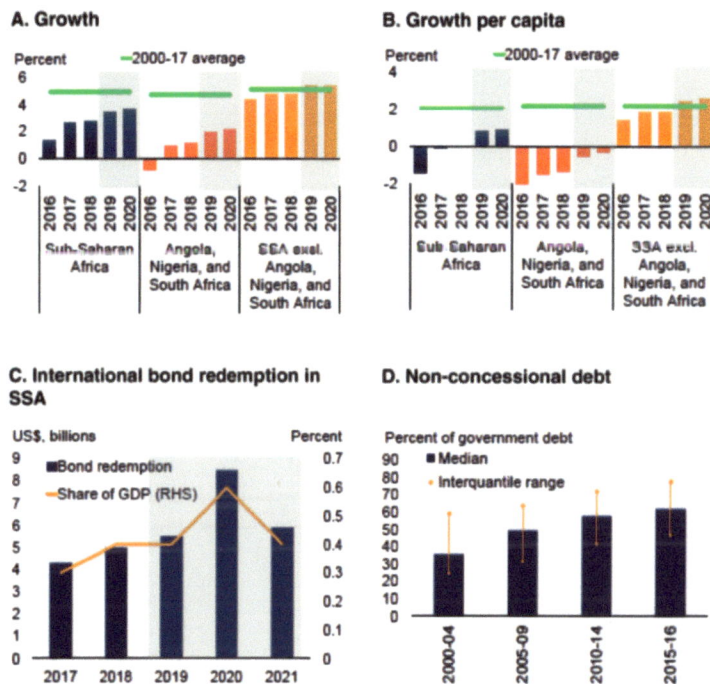

A. Growth

B. Growth per capita

C. International bond redemption in SSA

D. Non-concessional debt

Source: Dealogic, World Bank.
A.B. Aggregate growth rates calculated using constant 2010 U.S. dollar weights. Shaded areas represent forecasts.
C. Data reflects the principal amount at date of maturity, and excludes any interest payments.
D. Excludes Equatorial Guinea, Eswatini, Namibia, Seychelles, Somalia, and South Sudan due to data limitations.

for policy measures to raise potential output while raising the productive capacity of the poor (World Bank 2018x).

Growth in Nigeria is projected to rebound to 2.2 percent in 2019 and 2.4 percent in 2020-21. These forecasts are unchanged from June and assume that oil production will recover, but peak below government targets, while a slow improvement in private demand will constrain growth in the non-oil industrial sector. In Angola, the growth forecast has been upgraded to 2.9 percent in 2019, moderating to an average of 2.7 percent in 2020-21. A recovery in the oil sector, as new oil fields come on stream, is expected to boost growth, along with a pickup in activity in the non-oil sector as reforms bolster the business environment.

Growth in South Africa is projected to recover more slowly than previously expected, to 1.3 percent in 2019, before rising to 1.7 percent in 2020-21. High unemployment and slow growth in household credit extension are expected to constrain domestic demand in 2019, while fiscal consolidation limits government spending. Higher growth in 2020 reflects the expectation that the government's structural reform agenda will gradually gather speed, helping to boost investment growth, as policy uncertainty recedes and investor sentiment improves.

Excluding Angola, Nigeria, and South Africa, growth in the rest of Sub-Saharan Africa is expected to remain relatively solid, but with significant variation between country groups. Economic activity in CEMAC should benefit from higher oil production and an increase in domestic demand as fiscal tightening eases.

Growth is expected to rise moderately among metals exporters, supported in part by stronger mining activity. However, non-mining activity remains subdued owing to weak business confidence, accelerating inflation in some countries, and sluggish credit growth.

Among non-resource-intensive countries, economic activity is expected to remain robust in fast-growing countries, such as Cote d'Ivoire, Kenya, and Tanzania, boosted by public investment and strong agricultural production, and in smaller economies, such as Madagascar, on the back of solid export performance. While growth in Ethiopia is expected to remain strong, it will be weighed down by fiscal consolidation efforts to stabilize public debt.

Inflation is expected to pick up across the region in 2019, reflecting the pass-through of currency depreciations during 2018 and domestic price pressures among metals exporters and non-resource-intensive countries. Notably, inflation is envisioned to continue to recede in Angola and Nigeria. However, it may rise temporarily in Angola if the anticipated increases in utility tariffs and fuel prices are implemented. In addition,

price pressures are likely to intensify in Kenya, Tanzania, and Uganda.

Fiscal balances are expected to improve further, reflecting fiscal consolidation efforts among the large oil exporters and continued adjustment in CEMAC. Policy tightening is likely to yield smaller fiscal deficits in metals exporters, while fiscal deficits in non-resource-intensive countries should also continue to narrow as public investment spending slows to stabilize public debt.

Risks

Risks to the regional outlook are tilted to the downside. On the external front, slower-than-projected growth in China and the Euro Area, which have strong trade and investment links with Sub-Saharan Africa, would adversely affect the region through lower export demand and investment. Moreover, Sub-Saharan African metals producers would likely be among the hardest hit by escalating trade tensions between China and the United States, as metals prices would fall faster than other commodity prices as a result of weakening demand from China (World Bank 2018y). Furthermore, a faster-than-expected normalization of advanced-economy monetary policy could result in sharp reductions in capital inflows, higher financing costs, and disorderly exchange rate depreciations, especially in countries with weaker fundamentals or higher political risks (Arteta et al. 2015; IMF 2018c). Sharp currency declines would make the servicing of foreign-currency-denominated debt, already a rising concern in the region, more challenging.

The increased reliance on foreign currency borrowing has heightened refinancing and interest rate risk in debtor countries (Chapter 4). Furthermore, the rise in non-resident participation in domestic debt markets has exposed some countries to the risk of sudden capital outflows. In some countries, sizable loans to state-owned enterprises, backed by commodity exports, have increased the risk that a negative commodity price shock could trigger financial crises.

Domestic risks, in particular, remain elevated. Political uncertainty and a concurrent weakening of economic reforms could continue to weigh on the economic outlook in many countries. In countries holding elections in 2019 (e.g., Malawi, Mozambique, Nigeria, South Africa), domestic political considerations could undermine the commitment needed to rein in fiscal deficits or implement structural reforms, especially where public debt levels are high and rising. Insurgencies and armed conflicts, with their adverse effects on economic activity, remain an important risk in several countries. Adverse weather shocks and rising financial sector stress are additional risks.

TABLE 2.6.1 Sub-Saharan Africa forecast summary

(Real GDP growth at market prices in percent, unless indicated otherwise)

Percentage point differences from June 2018 projections

	2016	2017	2018e	2019f	2020f	2021f	2018e	2019f	2020f
EMDE SSA, GDP[1]	1.3	2.6	2.7	3.4	3.6	3.7	-0.4	-0.1	-0.1
(Average including countries with full national accounts and balance of payments data only)[2]									
EMDE SSA, GDP[2,3]	1.3	2.6	2.7	3.4	3.6	3.7	-0.4	-0.1	-0.1
GDP per capita (U.S. dollars)	-1.4	-0.1	0.0	0.8	0.9	1.0	-0.4	0.0	-0.1
PPP GDP	1.6	2.8	3.0	3.7	3.8	3.9	-0.4	0.0	-0.1
Private consumption	0.5	1.8	2.5	2.8	2.9	2.5	-0.1	0.0	0.0
Public consumption	1.3	2.8	2.6	2.9	3.0	2.8	0.1	0.0	0.0
Fixed investment	1.5	4.5	5.2	6.9	7.0	7.5	-1.6	-0.5	-0.6
Exports, GNFS[4]	2.4	3.6	2.4	3.1	3.4	3.1	-0.8	-0.4	-0.4
Imports, GNFS[4]	-0.4	3.1	3.2	3.5	3.6	3.8	0.2	0.2	0.2
Net exports, contribution to growth	0.8	0.2	-0.2	-0.1	-0.1	-0.3	-0.3	-0.2	-0.3
Memo items: GDP									
SSA excluding Nigeria, South Africa, and Angola	4.3	4.7	4.7	5.4	5.4	5.4	-0.2	0.1	-0.1
Oil exporters[5]	-0.7	1.4	1.7	2.9	2.8	2.8	-0.6	0.3	0.0
CFA countries[6]	2.9	3.3	3.8	4.9	4.7	4.6	-0.3	0.4	-0.2
CEMAC	-0.8	-0.2	1.0	3.0	2.6	2.3	-0.4	0.7	-0.4
WAEMU	6.5	6.6	6.3	6.4	6.4	6.3	-0.1	0.1	0.0
SSA3	-0.8	0.9	1.1	1.9	2.1	2.1	-0.6	-0.1	-0.1
Nigeria	-1.6	0.8	1.9	2.2	2.4	2.4	-0.2	0.0	0.0
South Africa	0.6	1.3	0.9	1.3	1.7	1.8	-0.5	-0.5	-0.2
Angola	-2.6	-0.1	-1.8	2.9	2.6	2.8	-3.5	0.7	0.2

Source: World Bank.

Note: e = estimate; f = forecast. EMDE = emerging market and developing economy. World Bank forecasts are frequently updated based on new information and changing (global) circumstances. Consequently, projections presented here may differ from those contained in other Bank documents, even if basic assessments of countries' prospects do not differ at any given moment in time.

1. GDP at market prices and expenditure components are measured in constant 2010 U.S. dollars. Excludes Central African Republic, São Tomé and Príncipe, Somalia, and South Sudan.
2. Sub-region aggregate excludes Central African Republic, São Tomé and Príncipe, Somalia, and South Sudan, for which data limitations prevent the forecasting of GDP components.
3. Sub-region historical growth rates may differ from the most recent edition of *Africa's Pulse* (https://www.worldbank.org/en/region/afr/publication/africas-pulse) due to data revisions and the inclusion of the Central African Republic and São Tomé and Príncipe in the sub-region aggregate of that publication.
4. Exports and imports of goods and non-factor services (GNFS).
5. Includes Angola, Cameroon, Chad, Republic of Congo, Gabon, Ghana, Nigeria, and Sudan.
6. Includes Benin, Burkina Faso, Cameroon, Central African Republic, Chad, Republic of Congo, Côte d'Ivoire, Equatorial Guinea, Gabon, Mali, Niger, Senegal, and Togo.
To download this data, please visit www.worldbank.org/gep.

TABLE 2.6.2 Sub-Saharan Africa country forecasts[1]
(Real GDP growth at market prices in percent, unless indicated otherwise)

Percentage point differences from June 2018 projections

	2016	2017	2018e	2019f	2020f	2021f	2018e	2019f	2020f
Angola	-2.6	-0.1	-1.8	2.9	2.6	2.8	-3.5	0.7	0.2
Benin	4.0	5.8	6.0	6.2	6.5	6.6	0.0	0.1	0.2
Botswana[2]	4.3	2.4	4.4	3.9	4.1	4.1	1.4	0.6	0.3
Burkina Faso	5.9	6.3	6.0	6.0	6.0	6.0	0.0	0.0	0.0
Burundi	-0.6	0.5	1.9	2.3	2.5	2.8	0.0	0.0	0.0
Cabo Verde	4.7	4.0	4.5	4.7	4.9	4.9	0.3	0.7	0.9
Cameroon	4.6	3.5	3.8	4.2	4.5	4.5	-0.1	0.1	0.2
Chad	-6.3	-3.0	3.1	4.6	6.1	4.9	0.5	2.1	0.3
Comoros	2.2	2.7	2.7	3.1	3.1	3.1	-0.2	0.1	0.1
Congo, Dem. Rep.	2.4	3.4	4.1	4.6	5.5	5.9	0.3	0.5	1.1
Congo, Rep.	-2.8	-3.1	1.0	3.2	-0.1	-1.5	0.3	-1.4	1.1
Côte d'Ivoire	8.0	7.7	7.5	7.3	7.4	6.8	0.1	0.1	0.2
Equatorial Guinea	-8.5	-4.9	-8.8	-2.1	-5.8	-5.8	-2.4	4.9	-5.3
Eswatini[3]	3.2	1.9	-0.6	1.7	1.8	1.8	-1.7	0.0	0.0
Ethiopia[2]	8.0	10.1	7.7	8.8	8.9	8.9	-1.9	-0.9	-1.0
Gabon	2.1	0.5	2.0	3.0	3.7	3.7	-0.6	-0.7	-0.2
Gambia, The	0.4	4.6	5.3	5.4	5.2	5.2	-0.1	0.2	0.3
Ghana[4]	3.7	8.5	6.5	7.3	6.0	6.0	-0.4	0.6	0.6
Guinea	10.5	8.2	5.8	5.9	6.0	6.0	-0.2	0.0	0.0
Guinea-Bissau	5.8	5.9	3.9	4.2	4.4	4.5	-1.2	-1.0	-1.0
Kenya	5.9	4.9	5.7	5.8	6.0	6.0	0.2	-0.1	-0.1
Lesotho	3.1	-1.7	1.2	1.2	0.2	1.8	-0.6	-1.4	-2.6
Liberia	-1.6	2.5	3.0	4.5	4.8	4.8	-0.2	-0.2	0.0
Madagascar	4.2	4.2	5.2	5.4	5.3	5.3	0.1	-0.2	0.0
Malawi	2.5	4.0	3.5	4.3	5.3	5.5	-0.2	0.2	0.4
Mali	5.8	5.4	4.9	5.0	4.9	4.8	-0.1	0.3	0.2
Mauritania	2.0	3.5	3.0	4.9	6.9	6.9	-0.6	0.3	1.7
Mauritius	3.8	3.9	3.9	4.0	3.6	3.6	-0.1	-0.1	-0.2
Mozambique	3.8	3.7	3.3	3.5	4.1	4.1	0.0	0.1	0.5
Namibia	0.6	-0.9	0.7	1.8	2.1	2.1	-0.8	-0.5	-0.9
Niger	4.9	4.9	5.2	6.5	6.0	5.6	-0.1	1.1	0.2
Nigeria	-1.6	0.8	1.9	2.2	2.4	2.4	-0.2	0.0	0.0
Rwanda	6.0	6.1	7.2	7.8	8.0	8.0	0.4	0.7	0.5
Senegal	6.2	7.2	6.6	6.6	6.8	6.9	-0.2	-0.2	-0.2
Seychelles	4.5	5.3	3.6	3.4	3.3	2.9	-0.4	-0.4	-0.2
Sierra Leone	6.3	3.7	3.7	5.1	6.3	6.3	-1.4	-0.6	-0.2
South Africa	0.6	1.3	0.9	1.3	1.7	1.8	-0.5	-0.5	-0.2
Sudan	4.7	4.3	3.1	3.6	3.8	3.8	0.5	0.5	0.3
Tanzania	7.0	7.1	6.6	6.8	7.0	7.0	0.0	0.0	0.0
Togo	5.1	4.4	4.5	4.8	5.1	5.1	-0.3	-0.2	0.1
Uganda[2]	4.8	3.9	6.1	6.0	6.4	6.5	0.6	0.0	-0.1
Zambia	3.8	3.5	3.3	3.6	3.8	3.8	-0.8	-0.9	-1.0
Zimbabwe	0.6	3.2	3.0	3.7	4.0	4.0	0.3	-0.1	0.0

Source: World Bank.
Note: e = estimate; f = forecast. World Bank forecasts are frequently updated based on new information and changing (global) circumstances. Consequently, projections presented here may differ from those contained in other Bank documents, even if basic assessments of countries' prospects do not significantly differ at any given moment in time.
1. GDP at market prices and expenditure components are measured in constant 2010 U.S. dollars. Excludes Central African Republic, São Tomé and Príncipe, Somalia, and South Sudan.
2. Fiscal-year-based numbers.
3. Formerly known as Swaziland.
4. Growth rates reflect GDP data prior to recent rebasing.

To download this data, please visit www.worldbank.org/gep.

BOX 2.6.1 Informality in Sub-Saharan Africa

Sub-Saharan Africa has high levels of informality, especially in West and East Africa, low-income countries, fragile states, and commodity exporters. Policies to increase human capital and foster productivity, improve access to resources, reduce regulatory burdens, and strengthen governance have been associated with a decline in informality, which in turn has been associated with better macroeconomic and social outcomes. However, for these policies to be effective, they need to be tailored to the specific nature of informality and types of informal firms.

Introduction

Despite a decline over the past three decades, employment informality in Sub-Saharan Africa (SSA) remains among the highest in emerging market and developing economies (EMDEs), with nine out of ten workers informally employed (of which six are self-employed). Output informality (around 40 percent of official GDP) and perceptions of informality are also high compared to other regions. Yet, there is considerable heterogeneity within the region—informality is higher in West and East Africa, low-income countries, fragile states, and commodity exporters. Pervasive informality contributes to lower government tax revenues, which limits the fiscal resources available for much-needed public investment and social programs.

Against this backdrop, this box examines the following questions:

- How has informality evolved?

- What are the macroeconomic and social correlates of informality?

- What are the policy options to address challenges associated with informality?

Evolution of informality

High average informality. On average in 2010-16, the informal economy in SSA countries amounted to 36-40 percent of official GDP, informal employment made up 90 percent of employment and, more narrowly, self-employment accounted for 58 percent of total employment (ILO 2018a; Figure 2.6.1.1).[1] Alternative measures of informality, such as the share of the labor force without pension coverage and perceptions of informal activity, were also high compared with other EMDE regions.

Heterogeneity. There is wide cross-country heterogeneity. West and East Africa had much higher average shares of

self-employed workers in total employment during 2010-16, at 80 percent and 68 percent, respectively. In contrast, the shares of self-employed workers in Central and Southern Africa were 48 and 43 percent respectively, only slightly above the EMDE average. Self-employment made up more than 85 percent of employment in Benin, Burundi, Madagascar, and Uganda whereas it was less than 20 percent in South Africa and Mauritius.

Evolution of informality in SSA. Informality in SSA has declined gradually over the past three decades, broadly in line with the EMDE trend. Some countries, however, have made significant progress in lowering the shares of informal output and employment, such as Botswana, Ethiopia, Ghana, Malawi, Rwanda, and Tanzania.

Correlates of informality

High informality in SSA reflects wide-ranging economic and development challenges in the region. It also reflects economic structures and a dearth of skilled labor.

Weak growth and conflict. SSA hosts all but seven of the world's 34 low-income countries and nearly half of the world's 36 fragile states (World Bank 2018z, 2018aa). In general, informality is higher in low-income SSA countries and, especially, fragile states. Economic disruptions during conflict and violence have forced people to earn their livelihoods in the informal economy (Heintz and Valodia 2008). Employment losses during recessions or shocks to crop production have also been associated with increases in informal labor supply (Calvés and Schoumaker 2004; Daniels 2003; Otsuka and Yamano 2006).

Economic structure. In commodity-exporting countries, the capital-intensive mining sector creates few formal employment opportunities, and economies in most countries in SSA have large agricultural sectors that have high rates of informal self-employment. In the non-agricultural sector, there is also considerable self-employment in labor-intensive services such as street vendors, craftsmen, and home-based activities (Fox and Sohnesen 2012). Rural-urban migration and increased labor force participation, especially among women, was mostly absorbed by the informal sector (Kessides 2005). In some societies, informal businesses are hereditary in

Note: This box was prepared by Wee Chian Koh with research assistance from Jinxin Wu.

[1] A recent enterprise census in Senegal finds that 97 percent of firms are informal (ANSD 2017).

BOX 2.6.1 Informality in Sub-Saharan Africa *(continued)*

FIGURE 2.6.1.1 Informality in Sub-Saharan Africa

Informality has declined in Sub-Saharan Africa, but remains among the highest in the world. Informality is higher in West and East Africa, low-income countries, fragile states, and commodity exporters.

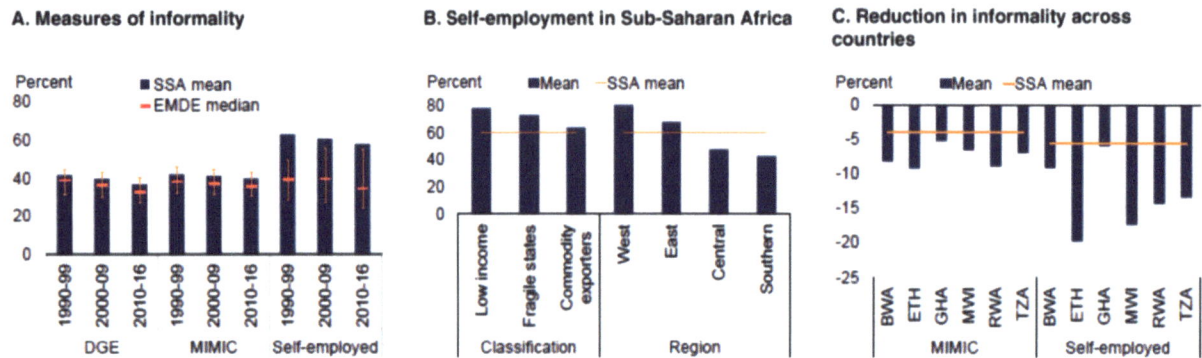

A. Measures of informality

B. Self-employment in Sub-Saharan Africa

C. Reduction in informality across countries

Source: Elgin et al. (forthcoming), International Labor Organization, World Development Indicators.
Note: A. Orange lines are the inter-quartile ranges for EMDEs.
A. DGE = dynamic general equilibrium model. MIMIC = multiple indicators multiple causes model. The DGE model estimates the size of the informal sector as a percent of official GDP (see Elgin and Oztunali 2012). The MIMIC model is a structural equations model that considers multiple causes of informal activity and captures multiple outcome indicators of informal activity (see Schneider, Buehn, and Montenegro 2010). It also estimates the informal output as a percent of official GDP. Self-employed is the share of self-employment in total employment.
B. World Bank classifications. Data for the period 1990-2016.
C. BWA = Botswana, ETH = Ethiopia, GHA = Ghana, MWI = Malawi, RWA = Rwanda, TZA = Tanzania. Percent change between 1990-2009 and 2010-16.

nature, where businesses are passed down to the next generation (Chen 2012). In others, social norms restrict the mobility of women, compelling them to be informally employed (ILO 2009).

Low human capital. The average years of schooling in SSA are well below those in any other EMDE regions (Figure 2.6.1.2). Informal workers in SSA tend to be lower skilled and less educated than formal workers (Adams, de Silva, and Razmara 2013). This limits opportunities for wage employment in the formal economy. Self-employed workers with low human capital, and hence low productivity, have an incentive to operate in the informal economy to avoid paying taxes and incurring other administrative costs (Oviedo, Thomas, and Karakurum-Özdemir 2009). Informal firms often have lower managerial ability and tend to produce low-quality inexpensive products with little demand from the formal sector (La Porta and Shleifer 2016). The HIV/AIDS pandemic has also taken a large toll on human capital and forced workers into less secure informal employment where discrimination is sometimes less pronounced (ILO 2009).

Limited access to resources and markets. Informality is associated with restricted access to electricity, finance, and

land (Ingram, Ramachandran, and Desai 2007). Limited availability of resources curtails informal firms' growth and productivity improvements (Steel and Snodgrass 2008). There are also obstacles to market access, such as lack of telecommunications or transport infrastructure, which is particularly important for firms that need to frequently interact with suppliers and customers. Access to public space and urban amenities are also important (Heintz and Valodia 2008).

High regulatory burden. Compared with other EMDEs, SSA has considerably higher regulatory burdens. Burdensome regulations such as lengthy processes in registering a business, complicated procedures in filing taxes, high costs of export and import documentary compliance, strict labor regulations, and high tax burdens can make it prohibitively expensive to operate in the formal economy (Mbaye and Benjamin 2015).

Weak governance. Compared with other EMDEs, SSA has considerably weaker governance and institutions. Poor governance and institutions may result in failures in enforcing regulations and containing corruption. This creates an environment for informal enterprises to easily conceal their activities and evade taxes (Mbaye and Benjamin 2015).

BOX 2.6.1 Informality in Sub-Saharan Africa (continued)

FIGURE 2.6.1.2 Economic and institutional indicators in Sub-Saharan Africa

Low human capital, limited access to resources, heavy regulatory burden, and weak governance are potentially important drivers of informality.

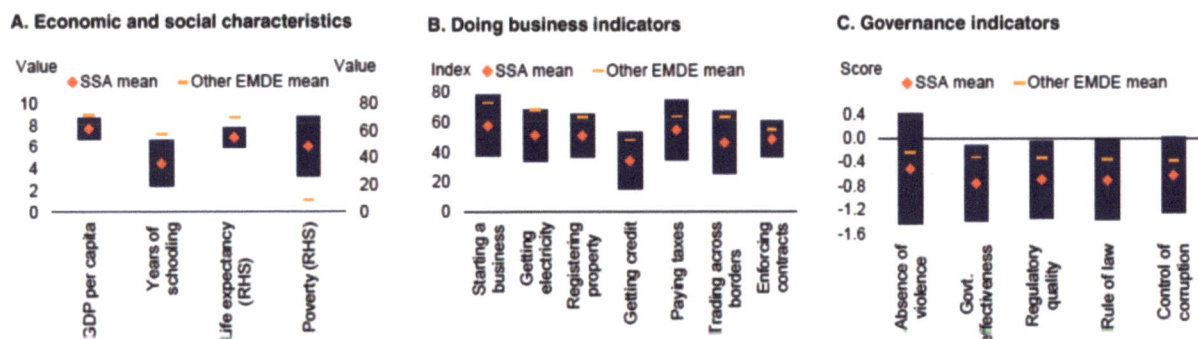

A. Economic and social characteristics

B. Doing business indicators

C. Governance indicators

Source: Barro and Lee (2013), World Bank (Doing Business, World Development Indicators, Worldwide Governance Indicators).

Note: A.-C. Blue bars are +/- one standard deviation of SSA mean. Other EMDE refers to all EMDEs except SSA countries.

A. GDP per capita is based on 2011 PPP in thousand dollars, expressed in logarithm. Life expectancy at birth is in years. Poverty is the headcount at $1.90 a day (2011 PPP) in percent of population.

B. The index represents the distance to the frontier (100) in the World Bank's Doing Business database. A higher index represents better performance. Data for the period 2004-16.

C. The score is based on Worldwide Governance Indicators. It ranges from -2.5 to 2.5. A higher score represents better performance. Data for the period 1996-2016.

Low productivity. Productivity differentials between the formal and informal sectors are large: value added per worker of informal firms is only 14 percent that of formal firms in the median SSA country, lower than the median in other EMDEs (La Porta and Shleifer 2014). Competition from informal firms, which do not shoulder the cost of compliances with taxes and regulations, also weigh on the profitability and investment of formal firms (Oosthuizen et al. 2016; Box 3.3). Although practices of competitors in the informal sector is only the third biggest reported obstacle in SSA, after electricity and access to finance, it is more problematic in SSA compared to other EMDEs (Dinh, Mavridis, and Nguyen 2010; La Porta and Shleifer 2016). In addition, since informal firms do not pay taxes, governments' ability to provide quality public services is constrained.

Poverty and social outcomes. While the informal economy can provide important opportunities for employment, the majority of those engaged in informal activities lack income security, employment benefits, and social protection. Moreover, higher informality in SSA is associated with lower life expectancy and worse poverty outcomes (Figure 2.6.1.3). Gender inequality is also prevalent in the informal economy in SSA: women are often placed in the most hazardous jobs with no access to occupational health and safety measures (ILO 2009).

Policy challenges

Unlocking the potential of the informal economy. While informality is more pervasive in SSA than in other EMDE regions, the move from informality to formality is more dynamic: more SSA formal firms started out as informal and the duration of informality is shorter than in other EMDEs (Figure 2.6.1.4). SSA also possesses a more positive attitude toward business opportunities than other EMDE regions, despite a higher proportion of people who became entrepreneurs out of necessity. Two-thirds (65 percent) of survey respondents believe they have the required skills and knowledge to start a business, 59 percent indicate they see good opportunities to start a firm, and 42 percent intend to start a business within three years. This intrinsic entrepreneurial spirit, despite high regulatory burdens and a weak entrepreneurship ecosystem, could render the informal sector a reservoir of untapped economic potential (De Soto 1989; Grimm, Knorringa, and Lay 2012).

To unlock this potential, both broad-based policy tools—such as increasing human capital—and policy tools targeted at specific parts of the informal sector are available. In Kenya, for example, improved managerial skills and new marketing channels induced by competition helped metalwork enterprises in the Kariobangi Light

BOX 2.6.1 Informality in Sub-Saharan Africa *(continued)*

FIGURE 2.6.1.3 Correlates of informality in Sub-Saharan Africa

Improvements in economic and institutional factors are associated with a reduction in informality. High informality is associated with worse macroeconomic and social outcomes. Years of schooling and primary school learning assessment scores in Sub-Saharan Africa are among the lowest in the world. Investing in human capital is critical to improve labor skills.

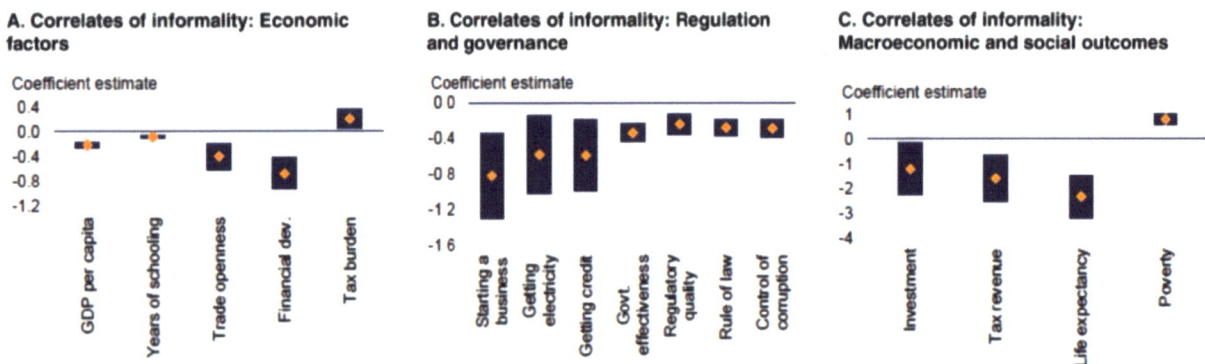

A. Correlates of informality: Economic factors

B. Correlates of informality: Regulation and governance

C. Correlates of informality: Macroeconomic and social outcomes

Source: Barro and Lee (2013), Elgin et al. (forthcoming), World Bank (Doing Business, World Development Indicators, Worldwide Governance Indicators).
Note: The orange diamonds are the coefficient estimates and the blue bars denote the 90 percent confidence intervals. OLS estimators are applied, with country means over the sample period used for both the dependent and independent variables. The share of self-employed in total employment is the measure of informality. Informality is the dependent variable in A.-B., and it is the independent variable in C. 37 SSA countries are included in the regressions. The coefficient estimate measures the effect on the dependent variable of a unit change in the independent variable. For example, in A., a 1 percent increase in the tax rate is associated with a 0.2 percent increase in informality. In C., a 1 percent increase in informality is associated with a 1.6 percent decline in government tax revenue.
A. GDP per capita is based on 2011 PPP in thousand dollars, expressed in logarithm. Trade openness is total trade (exports + imports) as a share of GDP. Financial development is proxied by private credit as a percentage of GDP. Tax burden is the total tax rate using data from Doing Business. Data for the period 1990-2016.
B. The correlates are the distance to the frontier in Doing Business (data for the period 2004-16) and the scores based on Worldwide Governance Indicators (data for the period 1996-2016).
C. Investment is gross fixed capital formation as a percentage of GDP. Tax revenue is expressed as a share of GDP. Life expectancy at birth is in years. Poverty is the headcount at $1.90 a day (2011 PPP) in percent of population.

Industries grow and transition to the formal economy (Sonobe, Akoten, and Otsuka 2011). The local government provided little support other than designating an area for these artisans to operate, but that proved to be sufficient.[2]

Investing in human capital. Policies should be prioritized toward increasing human capital. Less than 20 percent of primary school students in Sub-Saharan Africa—typically from poor households—pass a minimum proficiency threshold in learning assessment, which is the lowest among EMDEs (World Bank 2018n). Teachers are also often absent from classrooms. These learning deficiencies amplify over time and eventually show up as weak labor skills. Although technically and politically difficult, serious efforts must be made to improve learning outcomes.

─────────────
[2] Also in Kenya, the M-Pesa mobile money transfer system, combined with affordable ICT services, increased microenterprises' profitability (Mbogo 2010). Improving the survival chances of these microenterprises is one pathway toward growing the formal economy. David et al. (2012) provide other examples of successes at the local government level.

Increasing firm productivity. Small informal firms, lacking in human capital, would not sharply increase their productivity by merely registering (La Porta and Shleifer 2016). In contrast, large informal firms resemble formal firms much more than their small informal counterparts: productivity differentials of large informal firms relative to formal firms are minor (Benjamin and Mbaye 2012). In West Africa, the largest and fastest growing sectors are, in fact, dominated by large informal firms. This argues for policies to encourage small firms to grow into more productive formal firms, through skills upgrading and better access to inputs and resources such as business development services, transport and communications connectivity, financial services, health services, land and property rights, infrastructure, technology, and product markets (Oosthuizen et al. 2016). As these firms become more productive and produce higher quality products, they may be able to participate in supply chains in the formal sector (La Porta and Shleifer 2016). For large firms or those that voluntarily remain informal to evade taxes or avoid labor codes, incentives to encourage formal

BOX 2.6.1 Informality in Sub-Saharan Africa *(continued)*

FIGURE 2.6.1.4 Entrepreneurial conditions, entrepreneurship attitude, and informality indicators in Sub-Saharan Africa

Despite a higher proportion of necessity-driven informal entrepreneurs, Sub-Saharan Africa benefits from more dynamic entrepreneurial attitudes. More formal firms in Sub-Saharan Africa than in other EMDE regions started out as informal firms. However, small informal firms often lack managerial skills and resources. Skills upgrading and improving access to resources can help informal firms become more productive and therefore compete in the formal sector.

A. Entrepreneurial framework conditions

B. Entrepreneurship attitude

C. Informality indicators

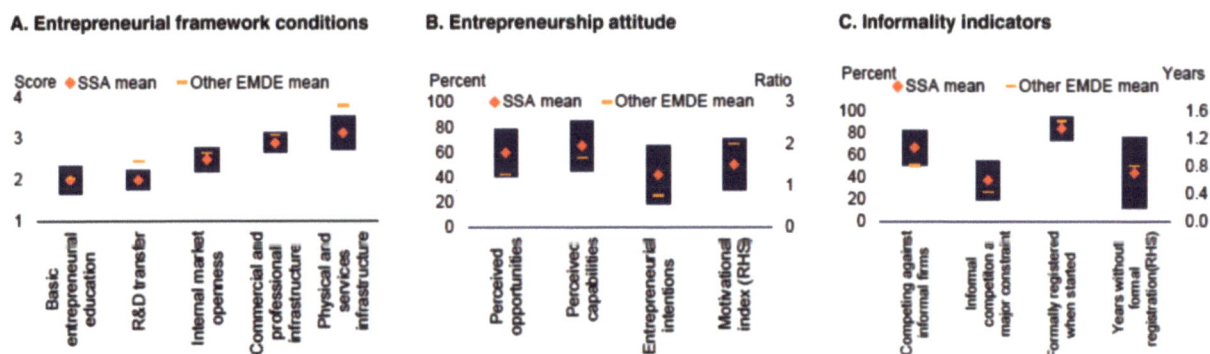

Source: Global Entrepreneurship Monitor, World Bank Enterprise Surveys.
Note: Blue bars are +/- one standard deviation of SSA mean. Other EMDE refers to all EMDEs except SSA countries.
A. The score is based on National Expert Survey of the Global Entrepreneurship Monitor. It ranges from 1 to 9. A higher score represents better perceived condition.
B. Data from the Adult Population Survey of the Global Entrepreneurship Monitor for the period 2001-16. Motivation index is the percentage of those who have recently started a business that are improvement-driven opportunity motivated divided by the percentage that is necessity-motivated. A lower ratio indicates a higher proportion that is necessity-driven.
C. Data from the World Bank Enterprise Surveys for the period 2006-16.

registration can be combined with tighter enforcement (Mbaye and Benjamin 2015).

Building institutions. Regulatory and institutional reforms to build public trust can strengthen incentives for firms to operate formally (Mbaye and Benjamin 2015). This includes improving the business environment by removing unnecessary regulatory barriers, strengthening monitoring and enforcement capabilities, and upholding legal and judicial systems. These policies apply equally to formal firms as an enabling environment is critical for investment and employment generation. Improving macroeconomic stability with sound fiscal and monetary policy frameworks is also essential.

Stakeholder engagement. Governments can actively engage with the informal community to encourage a shift towards greater formality (ILO 2009). This can involve educating informal firms on the benefits of formal registration, providing information on the procedures, participating in social dialogues to understand pressing issues for informal firms, customizing household surveys to better capture important aspects of informality, and collaborating with informal actors to design and implement effective development policies.

References

Abdulloev, I., I. N. Gang, and J. Landon-Lane. 2011. "Migration as a Substitute for Informal Activities: Evidence from Tajikistan." *Research in Labor Economics* 34 (6236): 205–227.

Adams, A. V., S. J. de Silva, and S. Razmara. 2013. *Improving Skills Development in the Informal Sector: Strategies for Sub-Saharan Africa. Directions in Development.* Washington, DC: World Bank.

AfDB (African Development Bank). 2016. "Addressing Informality in Egypt." North Africa Policy Series Working Paper, African Development Bank, Côte d'Ivoire.

ADB (Asian Development Bank). 2010. *The Informal Sector and Informal Employment in Indonesia.* Manila: Asian Development Bank.

———. 2016. *Social Protection for Informal Workers in Asia.* Edited by S. W. Handayani. Mandaluyong, Philippines: Asian Development Bank.

Ahmad, J. K., F. Blum, P. Gupta, and D. Jain. 2018. "India's Growth Story." Policy Research Working Paper 8599, World Bank, Washington, DC.

Almeida, R., and P. Carneiro. 2012. "Enforcement of Labor Regulation and Informality." *American Economic Journal: Applied Economics* 4 (3): 64–89.

ANSD (Agence Nationale de la Statistique et de la Démographie). 2017. *Rapport Global du Recensement Général des Entreprises.* Dakar: Agence Nationale de la Statistique et de la Démographie.

Angel-Urdinola, D. F., A. Semlali, and S. Brodmann. 2010. "Non-Public Provision of Active Labor Market Programs in Arab-Mediterranean Countries: An Inventory of Youth Programs." Social Protection Discussion Papers 55673, World Bank, Washington, DC.

Angel-Urdinola, D. F., and K. Tanabe. 2012. "Micro-Determinants of Informal Employment in the Middle East and North Africa Region." Social Protection Discussion Paper 1201, World Bank, Washington, DC.

Aramante, V., R. Arim, and M. Yapor. 2016. "Decomposing Inequality Changes in Uruguay: The Role of Formalization in the Labor Market." *IZA Journal of Development Economics* 5: 13.

Arby, M. F., M. J. Malik, and M. N. Hanif. 2010. "Size of Informal Economy in Pakistan." Working Paper 33, State Bank of Pakistan.

Arezki, R., L. Mottaghi, A. Barone, R. Y. Fan, A. A. Harb, O. M. Karasapan, H. Matsunaga, et al. 2018. *Middle East and North Africa Economic Monitor: A New Economy for Middle East and North Africa.* October. Washington, DC: World Bank.

Arteta, C., M. A. Kose, F. L. Ohnsorge, and M. Stocker. 2015. "The Coming U.S. Interest Rate Tightening Cycle: Smooth Sailing or Stormy Waters?" Policy Research Note 2, World Bank, Washington, DC.

Atesagaoglu, O., D. Bayram, and C. Elgin. 2017. "Informality and Structural Transformation." *Central Bank [of Turkey] Review* 17 (4): 117-126.

Bahadur, R. 2014. "Determinants of Informal Employment and Wage Differential in Nepal." *The Journal of Development and Administrative Studies* 22 (1-2): 37-50.

Barro, R., and J-W. Lee. 2013. "A New Data Set of Educational Attainment in the World, 1950-2010." *Journal of Development Economics* 104 (September): 184-198.

Beccaria, L., R. Maurizio, and G. Vazquez. 2015. "Recent Decline in Wage Inequality and Formalization of the Labour Market in Argentina." *International Review of Applied Economics* 29 (5): 677–700.

Beck, T., and M. Hoseini. 2014. "Informality and Access to Finance: Evidence from India." Mimeo. City University London.

Benjamin, N., and A. A. Mbaye. 2012. *The Informal Sector in Francophone Africa: Firm Size, Productivity and Institutions.* Washington, DC: World Bank.

Betcherman, G., N. M. Daysal, and C. Pagés. 2010. "Do Employment Subsidies Work? Evidence from Regionally Targeted Subsidies in Turkey." *Labour Economics* 17 (4): 710–722.

Bosch, M., E. Goñi-Pacchioni, and W. Maloney. 2012. "Trade Liberalization, Labor Reforms, and Formal-Informal Employment Dynamics." *Labour Economics* 19 (5): 653–667.

Bosch, M., and W. F. Maloney. 2010. "Labor Dynamics in Developing Countries: Comparative Analysis Using Markov Processes: An Application to Informality." *Labour Economics* 17 (4): 621–631.

Bruhn, M. 2011. "License to Sell: The Effect of Business Registration Reform on Entrepreneurial Activity in Mexico." *The Review of Economics and Statistics* 93 (1): 382–386.

Calvés, A. E., and B. Schoumaker. 2004. "Deteriorating Economic Context and Changing Patterns of Youth Employment in Urban Burkina Faso: 1980-2000." World Development 32 (8): 1341-1354.

Cevik, S. 2016. "Unlocking Pakistan's Revenue Potential." IMF Working Paper 16/182, International Monetary Fund, Washington, DC.

Chatterjee, S., and S. J. Turnovsky. 2018. "Remittances and the Informal Economy." Journal of Development Economics 133 (July): 66-83.

Chen, M. 2012. "The Informal Economy: Definitions, Theories and Policies." WIEGO Working Paper 1, Women in Informal Employment: Globalizing and Organizing, Cambridge, MA.

CEWC (Central Economic Work Conference). 2018. Summary of conference proceedings. Available at https://news.sina.com.cn/o/2018-12-21/doc-ihqhqcir9028199.shtml (Chinese).

Cho, Y. 2011. "Informality and Protection from Health Shocks: Lessons from Yemen." Policy Research Working Paper 5746, World Bank, Washington, DC.

Daniels, L. 2003. "Factors that Influence the Expansion of the Microenterprise Sector: Results from Three National Surveys in Zimbabwe." Journal of International Development 16 (6): 675-714.

David, S., O. Ulrich, S. Zelezeck, and N. Majoe. 2012. Managing Informality: Local Government Practices and Approaches Towards the Informal Economy in Africa. Pretoria: SA LED Network / SALGA and LEDNA.

de Andrade, G. H., M. Bruhn, and D. McKenzie. 2013. "A Helping Hand or the Long Arm of the Law? Experimental Evidence on What Governments Can Do to Formalize Firms." Policy Research Working Paper 6435, World Bank, Washington, DC.

De Mel, S., D. McKenzie, and C. Woodruff. 2013. "The Demand for, and Consequences of, Formalization Among Informal Firms in Sri Lanka." American Economic Journal: Applied Economics 5 (2): 122–150.

de Paula, A., and J. Scheinkman. 2011. "The Informal Sector: An Equilibrium Model and Some Empirical Evidence from Brazil." Review of Income and Wealth 57: 10–24.

De Soto, H. 1989. The Other Path: The Invisible Revolution in the Third World. New York: Harper and Row.

Demenet, A., M. Razafindrakoto, and F. Roubaud. 2016. "Do Informal Businesses Gain from Registration and How? Panel Data Evidence from Vietnam." World Development 84 (August): 326-341.

D'Erasmo, P. N., H. J. Moscoso Boedo, and A. Şenkal. 2014. "Misallocation, Informality, and Human Capital: Understanding the Role of Institutions." Journal of Economic Dynamics & Control 42 (May): 122-142.

Devarajan, S., and L. Mottaghi. 2015. "Towards a New Social Contract." Middle East and North Africa Economic Monitor. Washington, DC: World Bank.

Devarajan, S., and L. Mottaghi. 2017. "The Economics of Post-Conflict Reconstruction in MENA." Middle East and North Africa Economic Monitor. Washington, DC: World Bank.

Devicienti, F., F. Groisman, and A. Poggi. 2010. "Are Informality and Poverty Dynamically Interrelated? Evidence from Argentina." In Studies in Applied Welfare Analysis: Papers from the Third ECINEQ Meeting, edited by J. A. Bishop, 79–106. Bingley, U.K.: Emerald Group Publishing.

Dinh, H. T., D. A. Mavridis, and H. B. Nguyen. 2010. "The Binding Constraint on the Growth of Firms in Developing Countries." Policy Research Working Paper 5485, World Bank, Washington, DC.

Dix-Carneiro, R., P. K. Goldberg, C. Meghir, and G. Ulyssea. 2018. "Trade and Informality in the Presence of Labor Market Frictions and Regulations." Working paper, Center for Monetary and Financial Studies, Madrid.

Dix-Carneiro, R., and B. Kovak. 2017. "Margins of Labor Market Adjustment to Trade." Working Paper 23595, National Bureau for Economic Research, Cambridge, MA.

Dougherty, S., and O. Escobar. 2013. "The Determinants of Informality in Mexico's States." OECD Economics Department Working Papers 1043, Organisation for Economic Co-operation and Development, Paris.

Earle, J. S., and Z. Sakova. 2000. "Business Start-ups or Disguised Unemployment? Evidence on the Character of Self-employment from Transition Economies." Labour Economics 7 (5): 575-601.

Eichengreen, B., and P. Gupta. 2015. "Tapering Talk: The Impact of Expectations of Reduced Federal Reserve Security Purchases on Emerging Markets." Emerging Markets Review 25 (December): 1-15.

Elbadawi, I., and N. Loayza. 2008. "Informality, Employment and Economic Development in the Arab World." *Journal of Development and Economic Policies* 10 (2): 27-75.

Elgin, C., M. A. Kose, F. Ohnsorge, and S. Yu. Forthcoming. "Measuring the Informal Economy and its Business Cycles." Mimeo, World Bank, Washington, DC.

Elgin, C., and O. Oztunali. 2012. "Shadow Economies Around the World: Model Based Estimates." Working Paper 2012/05, Bogazici University, Department of Economics.

———. 2014. "Institutions, Informal Economy, and Economic Development." *Emerging Markets Finance and Trade* 50 (4): 117–134.

Elshamy, H. M. 2015. "Measuring the Informal Economy in Egypt." *International Journal of Business Management and Economic Research* 6 (2): 137 – 142.

Estevão, M., and I. de Carvalho Filho. 2012. "Institutions, Informality, and Wage Flexibility: Evidence from Brazil." IMF Working Paper 12/84, International Monetary Fund, Washington, DC.

Fajnzylber, P., W. F. Maloney, and G. V. Montes-Rojas. 2011. "Does Formality Improve Micro-Firm Performance? Evidence from the Brazilian SIMPLES Program." *Journal of Development Economics* 94 (2): 262 – 276.

Farazi, S. 2014. "Informal Firms and Financial Inclusion: Status and Determinants." Policy Research Working Paper 6778, World Bank, Washington, DC.

Fernández, C., and L. Villar. 2016. "Informality and Inclusive Growth in Latin America: The Case of Colombia." IDS Working Paper 469, Institute of Development Studies, Brighton, U.K.

Fialová, K., and O. Schneider. 2011. "Labor Institutions and Their Impact on Shadow Economies in Europe." Policy Research Working Paper 5913, World Bank, Washington, DC.

FICCI (Federation of Indian Chambers of Commerce and Industry). 2017. *Informal Economy in India: Setting the Framework for Formalisation*. Edited by J. Vij, A. Khanna, and P. Srivastava. New Delhi: Konrad-Adenauer-Stiftung.

Fiess, N., M. Fugazza, and W. Maloney. 2008. "Informality and Macroeconomic Fluctuations." IZA Discussion Paper 3519, Institute for the Study of Labor, Bonn.

Fox, L., and T. P. Sohnesen. 2012. "Household Enterprises in Sub-Saharan Africa: Why They Matter for Growth, Jobs, and Livelihoods." Policy Research Working Paper 6184, World Bank, Washington, DC.

Freund, C., M. J. Ferrantino, M. Maliszewska, and M. Ruta. 2018. "Impacts on Global Trade and Income of Current Trade Disputes." MTI Practice Note No. 2, World Bank, Washington, DC.

Friedman, E., S. Johnson, D. Kaufmann, and P. Zoido-Lobatón. 2000. "Dodging the Grabbing Hand: The Determinants of Unofficial Activity in 69 Countries." *Journal of Public Economics* 76 (3): 459–493.

Gagnon, J., T. Xenogiani, and C. Xing. 2011. "Are All Migrants Really Worse Off in Urban Labour Markets? New Empirical Evidence from China." IZA Discussion Paper 6268, Institute for the Study of Labor, Bonn.

Galal, A. 2005. "The Economic of Formalization: Potential Winners and Losers from Formalization in Egypt." In *Investment Climate, Growth, and Poverty*, edited by G. Kochendorfer-Lucius and B. Pleskovic. Washington, DC: World Bank.

Gandelman, N., and A. Rasteletti. 2016. "The Impact of Bank Credit on Employment Formality: Evidence from Uruguay." *Emerging Markets Finance and Trade* 52 (7): 1661–1678.

Gatti, R., D. F. Angel-Urdinola, J. Silva, and A. Bodor. 2014. *Striving for Better Jobs: The Challenge of Informality in the Middle East and North Africa*. Washington, DC: The World Bank.

Ghani, E., and R. Kanbur. 2013. "Urbanization and (In)Formalization." Policy Research Working Paper 6374, World Bank, Washington, DC.

Ghani, E., W. Kerr, and S. O'Connell. 2013. "The Exceptional Persistence of India's Unorganized Sector." Policy Research Paper 6454, World Bank, Washington, DC.

Goldar, B., and S. C. Aggarwal. 2012. "Informalization of Industrial Labor in India: Effects of Labor Market Rigidities and Import Competition." *The Developing Economies* 50 (2): 141-69.

Goldberg, P., and N. Pavcnik. 2003. "The Response of the Formal Sector to Trade Liberalization." *Journal of Development Economics* 72 (2): 463–496.

Grigorian, D. A., and H. R. Davoodi. 2007. "Tax Potential vs. Tax Effort: A Cross-Country Analysis of Armenia's Stubbornly Low Tax Collection." IMF Working Paper 07/106, International Monetary Fund, Washington, DC.

Grimm, M., P. Knorringa, and J. Lay. 2012. "Constrained Gazelles: High Potential in West Africa's Informal Economy." *World Development* 40 (7): 1352-1368.

Guariglia, A., and B.-Y. Kim. 2006. The Dynamics of Moonlighting in Russia: What is Happening in the Russian Informal Economy? *Economics of Transition* 14 (1): 1-45.

Gunatilaka, R. 2008. "Informal Employment in Sri Lanka: Nature, Probability of Employment, and Determinants of Wages." ILO Asia-Pacific Working Paper Series, International Labour Organization, New Delhi.

Ha, J., M. Stocker, and H. Yilmazkuday. 2019. "Inflation and Exchange Rate Pass-Through." In *Inflation: Evolution, Drivers, and Policies*, edited by J. Ha, M. A. Kose, and F. Ohnsorge, 273–319. Washington, DC: World Bank.

Handayani, S. W. 2016. *Social Protection for Informal Workers in Asia*. Manila: Asian Development Bank.

Hassan, M., and F. Schneider. 2016. "Size and Development of the Shadow Economies of 157 Countries Worldwide: Updated and New Measures from 1999 to 2013." IZA Discussion Paper 10281, IZA - Institute of Labor Economics, Bonn, Germany.

Heintz, J., and I. Valodia. 2008. "Informality in Africa: A Review." WIEGO Working Paper 3, Women in Informal Employment: Globalizing and Organizing, Cambridge, MA.

Herrera-Idárraga, P., E. López-Bazo, and E. Motellón. 2015. "Double Penalty in Returns to Education: Informality and Educational Mismatch in the Colombian Labour Market." *The Journal of Development Studies* 51 (12): 1683-1701.

Huang, P. 2009. "China's Neglected Informal Economy. Reality and Theory." *Modern China* 35 (4): 405-438.

Ianchovichina, E., and M. Ivanic. 2014. "Economic effects of the Syrian war and the spread of the Islamic state on the Levant (English)." Policy Research Working Paper 7135, World Bank, Washington, DC.

ILO (International Labour Organization). 2009. *The Informal Economy in Africa: Promoting Transition to Formality: Challenges and Strategies*. Geneva: International Labor Office.

———. 2013. *The Informal Economy and Decent Work: A Policy Resource Guide Supporting Transitions to Formality*. Geneva: International Labour Organization.

———. 2015. "Earnings Differentials Between Formal and Informal Employment in Thailand." ILO Asia-Pacific Working Paper Series, International Labour Organization, Bangkok.

———. 2016. "Policies, Strategies and Practices for the Formalisation of Micro and Small Enterprises." International Labour Organization, Geneva, Switzerland.

———. 2017. *World Social Protection Report 2017-19: Universal Social Protection to Achieve the Sustainable Development Goals*. Geneva: International Labour Organization.

———. 2018a. *Women and Men in The Informal Economy: A Statistical Picture*. Geneva: International Labour Organization.

———. 2018b. *World Employment and Social Outlook: Trends 2018*. Geneva: International Labour Organization.

Ilzetzki, E., and D. Lagakos. 2017. "The Macroeconomic Benefits of Tax Enforcement in Pakistan." International Growth Centre, London School of Economics.

IMF (International Monetary Fund). 2018a. *World Economic Outlook: Challenges to Steady Growth*. October. Washington, DC: International Monetary Fund.

———. 2018b. "Public Wage Bill in the Middle East and Central Asia Region." IMF Departmental Paper, International Monetary Fund, Washington, DC.

———. 2018c. "Capital Flows to Sub-Saharan Africa: Causes and Consequences." In *Sub-Saharan Africa Regional Economic Outlook: Capital Flows and the Future of Work*. Washington, DC: International Monetary Fund.

Ingram, M., V. Ramachandran, and V. Desai. 2007. "Why Do Firms Choose to be Informal? Evidence from Enterprise Surveys in Africa." RPED Paper 134, World Bank, Washington, DC.

Ivlevs, A. 2016. "Remittances and Informal Work." *International Journal of Manpower* 37 (7): 1172–1190.

Johnson, S., D. Kaufmann, and A. Shleifer. 1997. "The Unofficial Economy in Transition." *Brookings Papers on Economic Activity* 1997 (2): 159-239.

Judy, L., and B. G. U. Gadgil. 2017. *East Asia and Pacific Cities: Expanding Opportunities for the Urban Poor*. Washington, DC: World Bank.

Jutting, J., and T. Xenogiani. 2007. "Informal Employment and Internal Migration: The Case of China." OECD Publishing, Paris.

Kanbur, R. 2017. "Informality: Causes, Consequences and Policy Responses." *Review of Development Economics* 21 (4): 939-961.

Kaplan, D. S., E. Piedra, and E. Seira. 2011. "Entry Regulation and Business Start-Ups: Evidence from Mexico." *Journal of Public Economics* 95 (11-12): 1501-1515.

Kaufmann, D., and A. Kaliberda. 1996. "Integrating the Unofficial Economy into the Dynamics of Post-Socialist Economies: A Framework of Analysis and Evidence." Policy Research Working Paper 1691, World Bank, Washington, DC.

Kessides, C. 2005. "The Urban Transition in Sub-Saharan Africa: Implications for Economic Growth and Poverty Reduction." Africa Region Working Paper 97, World Bank, Washington, DC.

Khera, P. 2016. "Macroeconomic Impacts of Gender Inequality and Informality in India." IMF Working Paper 16/16, International Monetary Fund, Washington, DC.

Koettl, J., and M. Weber. 2012. "Does Formal Work Pay? The Role of Labor Taxation and Social Benefit Design in the New EU Member States." *Research in Labor Economics* 34 (April): 167–204.

Kopczuk, W. 2012. "The Polish Business 'Flat' Tax and its Effect on Reported Incomes: A Pareto Improving Tax Reform." Columbia University Working Paper, Columbia University, New York.

Kose, M. A., F. L. Ohnsorge, L. S. Ye, and E. Islamaj. 2017. "Weakness in Investment Growth: Causes, Implications and Policy Responses." Policy Research Working Paper 7990, World Bank, Washington, DC.

Krstic, G., and P. Sanfey. 2010. "Earnings Inequality and the Informal Economy: Evidence from Serbia." Working Paper 114, European Bank for Reconstruction and Development, London.

La Porta, R., and A. Shleifer. 2014. "Informality and Development." *Journal of Economic Perspectives* 28 (3): 109-126.

———. 2016. "The Unofficial Economy in Africa." In *African Successes, Volume 1: Government and Institutions*, edited by Edwards, S., S. Johnson, and D. N. Weil. Chicago: University of Chicago Press.

Lam, R., X. Liu, and A. Schipke. 2015. "China's Labor Market in the "New Normal." IMF Working Paper 15/151, International Monetary Fund, Washington, DC.

Lehmann, H., and A. Muravyev. 2009. "How Important are Labor Market Institutions for Labor Market Performance in Transition Countries?" Discussion Paper 4673, The Institute for the Study of Labor (IZA), Bonn, Germany.

Lehmann, H., and P. Norberto. 2018. "Informal Employment Relationships and the Labor Market: Is There Segmentation in Ukraine?" *Journal of Comparative Economics* 46 (3): 838-857.

Levy, S. 2008. *Good Intentions, Bad Outcomes: Social Policy, Informality, and Economic Growth in Mexico.* Washington, DC: Brookings Institution.

Liang, Z., S. Appleton, and L. Song. 2016. "Informal Employment in China: Trends, Patterns and Determinants of Entry." IZA Discussion Paper 10139, Institute for the Study of Labor, Bonn.

Likhi, A. 2013. "Employment and Participation in South Asia: Challenges for Productive Absorption." *People, Spaces, Deliberation* (blog), October 23. https://blogs.worldbank.org/publicsphere/employment-and-participation-south-asia-challenges-productive-absorption.

Loayza, N. V. 1997. "The Economics of the Informal Sector: A Simple Model and Some Empirical Evidence from Latin America." Policy Research Working Paper 1727, World Bank, Washington, DC.

———. 2016. "Informality in the Process of Development and Growth." Policy Research Working Paper 7858, World Bank, Washington, DC.

Loayza, N. V., and J. Rigolini. 2006. "Informality Trends and Cycles." Policy Research Working Paper 4078, World Bank, Washington, DC.

Loayza, N. V., and T. Wada. 2010a. "Informal Labor: Basic Measures and Determinants." Mimeo, World Bank, Washington, DC.

———. 2010b. "Informal Labor in the Middle East and North Africa: Basic Measures and Determinants." Mimeo, World Bank, Washington, DC.

Loayza, N. V., L. Servén, and N. Sugawara. 2010. "Informality in Latin America and the Caribbean." In *Business Regulation and Economic Performance*, edited by N. Loayza and L. Servén, 157–196. Washington, DC: World Bank.

Lukonga, L. 2018. "Fintech, Inclusive Growth and Cyber Risks: Focus on the MENAP and CCA Regions." IMF Working Paper 18/201, International Monetary Fund, Washington, DC.

Marcouiller, D., V. R. de Castilla, and C. Woodruff. 1997. "Formal Measures of the Informal-Sector Wage Gap in Mexico, El Salvador, and Peru." *Economic Development and Cultural Change* 45 (2): 367-392.

Maurizio, R. 2015. "Transitions to Formality and Declining Inequality." *Development and Change* 46 (5): 1047–1079.

Mbogo, M. 2010. "The Impact of Mobile Payments on the Success and Growth of Micro-Business: The Case of M-Pesa in Kenya." *Journal of Language, Technology &Entrepreneurship in Africa* 2 (1): 182-203.

Mbaye, A. A., and N. Benjamin. 2015. "Informality, Growth, and Development in Africa." In *The Oxford Handbook of Africa and Economics*, edited by C. Monga and J. Y. Lin. New York: Oxford University Press.

McKenzie, D., and Y. S. Sakho. 2010. "Does it Pay Firms to Register for Taxes? The Impact of Formality on Firm Profitability." *Journal of Development Economics* 91 (1): 15-24.

McMillan, M., D. Rodrik, and C. Sepúlveda. 2017. *Structural Change, Fundamentals, and Growth: A Framework and Case Studies.* Washington, DC: International Food Policy Research Institute.

Medvedev, D., and A. M. Oviedo. 2013. "Informality and Productivity: Evidence from a New Firm Survey in Ecuador." Policy Research Working Paper 6431, World Bank, Washington, DC.

Meghir, C., R. Narita, and J.-M. Robin. 2015. "Wages and Informality in Developing Countries." *The American Economic Review* 105 (4): 1509–1546.

Menezes-Filho, N. A., and M.-A. Muendler. 2011. "Labor Reallocation in Response to Trade Reform." Working Paper 17372, National Bureau for Economic Research, Cambridge, MA.

Monteiro, J. C. M., and J. J. Assunção. 2012. "Coming Out of the Shadows? Estimating the Iimpact of Bureaucracy Simplification and Tax Cut on Formality in Brazilian Microenterprises." *Journal of Development Economics* 99 (1): 105-115.

Moscoso-Boedo, H. J., and P. N. D'Erasmo, 2012. "Misallocation, Informality, and Human Capital." Virginia Economics Online Paper 401, University of Virginia.

OECD (Organisation for Economic Co-operation and Development). 2009. *Is Informal Normal? Towards More and Better Jobs in Developing Countries.* Paris: OECD Publishing.

———. 2015. "Strengthening Institutions to Address Informality in Emerging Asia." In *Economic Outlook for Southeast Asia, China and India 2015, Strengthening Institutional Capacity.* Paris: OECD Publishing.

———. 2017. *A Decade of Social Protection Development in Selected Asian Countries.* Paris: OECD Publishing.

Olivier, M., J. Masabo, and E. Kalula. 2012. "Informality, Employment and Social Protection: Some Critical Perspectives for/from Developing Countries." https://www.researchgate.net.

Oosthuizen, M., K. Lilenstein, F. Steenkamp, and A. Cassim. 2016. "Informality and Inclusive Growth in Sub-Saharan Africa." ELLA Regional Evidence Paper, ELLA Network, Lima.

Ordóñez, J. C. L. 2014. "Tax Collection, the Informal Sector, and Productivity." *Review of Economic Dynamics* 17 (2): 262–286.

Otsuka, K., and T. Yamano. 2006. "The Role of Non-Farm Income to Poverty Reduction: Evidence from Asia and East Africa." *Agricultural Economics* 35 (s3): 393-397.

Oviedo, A. M., M. R. Thomas, and K. Karakurum-Özdemir. 2009. "Economic Informality: Causes, Costs, and Policies: A Literature Survey." Working Paper 167, World Bank, Washington, DC.

Packard, T., J. Koettl, and C.E. Montenegro. 2012. *In from the Shadow: Integrating Europe's Informal Labor.* Washington, DC: World Bank.

Park, A., Y. Wu, and Y. Du. 2012. "Informal Employment in Urban China: Measurement and Implications." World Bank, Washington, DC.

Perry, G. E., W. F. Maloney, O. S. Arias, P. Fajnzylber, A. D. Mason, and J. Saavedra-Chanduvi. 2007. *Informality: Exit and Exclusion.* Washington, DC: World Bank.

Piza, C. 2016. "Revisiting the Impact of the Brazilian SIMPLES Program on Firms' Formalization Rates. Policy Research Working Paper 7605, World Bank, Washington, DC.

Purfield, C., H. Finger, K. Ongley, B. Baduel, C. Castellanos, G. Pierre, V. Stepanyan, and E. Roos. 2018. "Opportunity for All: Promoting Growth and

Inclusiveness in the Middle East and North Africa." Departmental Paper 18/11, International Monetary Fund, Washington, DC.

Rodrik, D. 2015. "Premature Deindustrialisation." NBER Working Paper 20935, National Bureau of Economic Research, Cambridge, MA.

Rothenberg, A. D., A. Gaduh, N. E. Burger, C. Chazali, I. Tjandraningsih, R. Radikun, C. Sutera, and S. Weilant. 2015. "Rethinking Indonesia's Informal Sector." *World Development* 80 (April): 96–113.

Rutkowski, J. 2006. "Labor Market Developments During Economic Transition." Policy Research Working Paper 3894, World Bank, Washington, DC.

Sattar, S., J. L. Keller, and A. Baibagysh Uulu. 2015. "Transitioning to Better Jobs in the Kyrgyz Republic: A Jobs Diagnostic." World Bank, Washington, DC.

Schiffbauer, M., A. Sy, S. Hussain, H. Sahnoun, and P. Keefer. 2015. *Jobs or Privileges: Unleashing the Employment Potential of the Middle East and North Africa.* MENA Development Report. Washington, DC: World Bank.

Schlcarek, A., and M. Caggia. 2015. "Household Saving and Labor Productivity: The Case of Chile." IDB Working Paper 581, Inter-American Development Bank, Washington, DC.

Schneider, F., A. Buehn, and C. Montenegro. 2010. "Shadow Economies All over the World: New Estimates for 162 Countries from 1999 to 2007." Policy Research Working Paper 5356, World Bank, Washington, DC.

Shapiro, A. F., and F. S. Mandelman. 2016. "Remittances, Entrepreneurship, and Employment Dynamics over the Business Cycle." *Journal of International Economics* 103 (November): 184-199.

Shehu, E., and B. Nilsson. 2014. *Informal Employment Among Youth: Evidence from 20 School-to-work Transition Surveys.* Geneva: International Labour Organization.

Slonimczyk, F. 2012. "The Effect of Taxation on Informal Employment: Evidence from the Russian Flat Tax Reform." In *Informal Employment in Emerging and Transition Economies,* edited by H. Lehmann and K. Tatsiramos. Bingley, England: Emerald Group Publishing Limited.

Sonobe, T., J. E. Akoten, and K. Otsuka. 2011. "The Growth Process of Informal Enterprises in Sub-Saharan Africa: A Case Study of a Metalworking Cluster in Nairobi." *Small Business Economics* 36 (3): 323-335.

Staneva, A. V., and G. R. Arabsheibani. 2014. "Is There an Informal Employment Wage Premium? Evidence from Tajikistan." *IZA Journal of Labor and Development* 3 (1): 1–24.

Steel, F. W., and D. Snodgrass. 2008. "Raising Productivity and Reducing Risks of Household Enterprises—Diagnostic Methodology Framework." WIEGO Network and World Bank, Washington, DC.

Straub, S. 2005. "Informal Sector: The Credit Market Channel." *Journal of Development Economics* 78 (2): 299-321.

Tansel, A. 2000. "Wage Earners, Self-Employment and Gender in the Informal Sector in Turkey Wage Earners, Self-Employment and Gender in the Informal Sector in Turkey." Working Paper 24, Policy Research Report on Gender and Development, World Bank, Washington, DC.

Taymaz, E. 2009. "Informality and Productivity: Productivity Differentials between Formal and Informal Firms in Turkey." Economic Research Center Working Paper 9(01), World Bank, Washington, DC.

Ulyssea, G. 2018. "Firms, Informality, and Development: Theory and Evidence from Brazil." *The American Economic Review* 108 (8): 2015–2047.

UN (United Nations Development Programme). 2013. "The Informal Sector in the Jordanian Economy." United Nations Development Programme.

UNCTAD (United Nations Conference on Trade and Development). 2018. *World Investment Report – Investment and New Industrial Policies.* Geneva, Switzerland: UNCTAD.

USAID (United States Agency for International Development). 2017. *Philippines National Demographic and Health Survey.* Rockville, MD: USAID.

Vargas, M. 2015. "Informality in Paraguay: Macro-Micro Evidence and Policy Implications." IMF Working Paper 15/245, International Monetary Fund, Washington, DC.

Végh, C., and G. Vuletin. 2015. "How Is Tax Policy Conducted over the Business Cycle?" *American Economic Journal* 7 (3): 327–370.

Végh, C. A., G. Vuletin, D. Riera-Crichton, J. P. Medina, D. Friedheim, L. Morano, and L. Venturi. 2018. *From Known Unknowns to Black Swans: How to Manage Risk in Latin America and the Caribbean.* LAC Semiannual Report. Washington, DC: World Bank.

Vuletin, G. 2008. "Measuring the Informal Economy in Latin America and the Caribbean." IMF Working Paper 08/102, International Monetary Fund, Washington, DC.

Waseem, M. 2013. "Taxes, Informality and Income Shifting: Evidence from a Recent Pakistani Tax Reform." Mimeo, London School of Economics.

WHO (World Health Organization) and UNICEF. 2015. *Progress on Sanitation and Drinking Water: 2015 Update and MDG Assessment*. Geneva, Switzerland: WHO and UNICEF.

Williams, C., M. Shahid, and A. Martinez. 2015. "Determinants of the Level of Informality in Informal Micro-Enterprises: Some Evidence from the City of Lahore, Pakistan." *World Development* 84 (August): 312-325.

World Bank and DRCSC (Development Research Center of the State Council, the People's Republic of China). 2014. *Urban China: Toward Efficient, Inclusive, and Sustainable Urbanization*. Washington, DC: World Bank.

World Bank. Forthcoming 2019. "Walking a Tightrope." *Turkey Economic Monitor*. Washington, DC: World Bank.

———. 2004. Unlocking the Employment Potential in the Middle East and North Africa. MENA Development Report. Washington, DC: The World Bank.

———. 2007. Informality: Exit and Exclusion. Washington, DC: World Bank.

———. 2011. "The Scope and Main Characteristics of Informal Employment in Ukraine." Technical Note for the Government of Ukraine, World Bank, Washington, DC.

———. 2014a. *East Asia Pacific at Work: Employment, Enterprise, and Well-being*. Washington, DC: World Bank.

———. 2014b. *World Development Report: Risk and Opportunity, Managing Risk for Development*. Washington, DC: World Bank.

———. 2014c. *Arab Republic of Egypt. More Jobs, Better Jobs: A Priority of Egypt*. Poverty Reduction and Economic Management Department Report 88447, Middle East and North Africa Region. Washington, DC: World Bank.

———. 2015. *East Asia's Changing Urban Landscape: Measuring a Decade of Spatial Growth*. Washington, DC: World Bank.

———. 2016a. *Global Economic Prospects: Spillovers amid Weak Growth*. January. Washington, DC: World Bank.

———. 2016b. "Indonesia's Urban Story." World Bank, Washington, DC.

———. 2016c. *World Development Report 2016: Digital Dividends*. Washington, DC: World Bank.

———. 2016d. *What's Holding Back the Private Sector in MENA? Lessons from the Enterprise Survey*. Washington, DC: World Bank.

———. 2017a. *East Asia and Pacific Cities: Expanding Opportunities for the Urban Poor*. Washington, DC: World Bank.

———. 2017b. *South Asia Economic Focus: Globalization Backlash*. Spring. Washington, DC: World Bank.

———. 2017c. *Global Economic Prospects: A Fragile Recovery*. June. Washington, DC: World Bank.

———. 2018a. *East Asia and Pacific Economic Update: Navigating Uncertainty*. October. Washington, DC: World Bank.

———. 2018b. *China Economic Update*. December. Washington, DC: World Bank.

———. 2018c. "Strengthening Competitiveness." *Indonesia Economic Quarterly*. December. Washington, DC: World Bank.

———. 2018d. "Realizing Human Potential." *Malaysia Economic Monitor*. December. Washington, DC: World Bank.

———. 2018e. "World Governance Indicators" (database). Available at http://info.worldbank.org/governance/wgi. Accessed on December 6, 2018.

———. 2018f. "Doing Business" (database). Available at http://www.doingbusiness.org/. Accessed on December 6, 2018.

———. 2018g. *World Development Indicators*. Washington, DC: World Bank.

———. 2018h. *World Development Report 2019: The Changing Nature of Work*. Washington, DC: World Bank.

———. 2018i. *Western Balkan Regular Economic Report: Higher but Fragile Growth*. Washington, DC: World Bank.

————. 2018j. *Russia Economic Report: Preserving Stability; Doubling Growth; Halving Poverty -- How?* November. Washington, DC: World Bank.

————. 2018k. *Kazakhstan Economic Update.* Washington, DC: World Bank.

————. 2018l. *Global Economic Prospects: Broad-Based Upturn, but for How Long?* January. Washington, DC: World Bank.

————. 2018m. "Migración desde Venezuela a Colombia: Impactos y Estrategia de Respuesta en el Corto y Mediano Plazo." World Bank, Washington, DC.

————. 2018n. *World Development Report 2018: Learning to Realize Education's Promise.* Washington, DC: World Bank.

————. 2018o. "Deepening Reforms; In Focus: Pension Systems in the Gulf." *Gulf Economic Monitor.* February. Washington, DC: World Bank.

————. 2018p. "Staying the Course on Reforms: In Focus: Water for Prosperity and Development." *Gulf Economic Monitor.* November. Washington DC: World Bank.

————. 2018q. *Doing Business: Reforming to Create Jobs.* Washington, DC: World Bank.

————. 2018r. *Expectations and Aspirations: A New Framework for Education in the Middle East and North Africa.* Washington, DC: World Bank.

————. 2018s. *South Asia Economic Focus: Budget Crunch.* Fall. Washington, DC: World Bank.

————. 2018t. "Nepal Development Update." November. World Bank, Washington DC.

————. 2018u. "Bangladesh Development Update: Building on Resilience." World Bank, Washington DC.

————. 2018v. *Global Economic Prospects: The Turning of the Tide.* June. Washington, DC: World Bank.

————. 2018w. *Africa's Pulse.* October. Washington, DC: World Bank.

————. 2018x. "Piecing Together the Poverty Puzzle." In *Poverty and Shared Prosperity.* October. Washington, DC: World Bank.

————. 2018y. "The Implications of Tariffs for Commodity Markets." In *Commodity Markets Outlook. The Changing of the Guard: Shifts in Industrial Commodity Demand.* October. Washington, DC: World Bank.

————. 2018z. "World Bank Country and Lending Groups." Accessed October 1, 2018. https://datahelpdesk.worldbank.org/knowledgebase/articles/906519-world-bank-country-and-lending-groups.

————. 2018aa. "Harmonized List of Fragile Situations." Accessed October 1, 2018. http://www.worldbank.org/en/topic/fragilityconflictviolence/brief/harmonized-list-of-fragile-situations.

Zahariev, A. 2003. "Tax Avoidance in Bulgaria: The Human Capital Approach." *SSRN Electronic Journal* 2003 (5).

CHAPTER 3

GROWING IN THE SHADOW

Challenges of Informality

The informal sector accounts for about a third of GDP and 70 percent of employment (of which self-employment is more than a half) in emerging market and developing economies. Informality is more widespread in lower-income countries with a large agricultural sector and a high share of unskilled workers. While offering the advantage of flexibility and employment in some economies, a larger informal sector is associated with lower productivity, reduced tax revenues, and greater poverty and inequality. Overcoming the challenges of informality requires a balanced mix of policies that carefully take into account country-specific drivers. A well-designed policy framework could complement lowering regulatory and tax burdens with increasing the efficiency of public revenue collection and regulatory frameworks. It could also include expanded access to finance, markets, and inputs to foster firm productivity and growth; better education to facilitate formal sector employment; improved public services to bolster tax morale; and enhanced safety nets to cushion household risks.

Introduction

The livelihoods of the poor in emerging market and developing economies (EMDEs) often depend on informal activity. In these economies, informal sector output on average accounts for about one-third of GDP and informal employment constitutes about 70 percent of employment (of which self-employment accounts for more than a half; Figure 3.1). In some countries in Sub-Saharan Africa, informal employment accounts for more than 90 percent of employment and informal output is as much as 62 percent of official GDP (ILO 2018a).

Informality is a multidimensional concept, differing in nature across workers and countries (Perry et al. 2007). Some workers and firms are "excluded" from the modern economy or critical state benefits by tax and regulatory burdens (de Soto 1989; Loayza, Oviedo, and Servén 2006). This type of informality is frequently associated with low productivity and poorly paid low-skilled employment (La Porta and Shleifer 2014; Loayza 2018). Other informal workers voluntarily "exit" the formal sector and choose informal activity for its flexibility and independence (Maloney 2004; Günther and Launov 2012).[1] In lower-income

countries, the informal sector is a major source of income to many low-skilled individuals whose income would otherwise fall below subsistence (Docquier, Müller, and Naval 2017). These reasons for participating in the informal economy mean informal workers range from agricultural day laborers to self-employed lawyers with a few employees.[2]

Regardless of the reason why individual workers or firms choose between formal and informal activity, a large informal sector has been associated with unfavorable macroeconomic and development outcomes. On average, economies with larger informal sectors tend to have lower productivity, slower physical and human capital accumulation, higher poverty and inequality, and smaller fiscal resources.[3] The informal sector itself has, on average, lower productivity than the

---

Note: This chapter was prepared by a team led by M. Ayhan Kose, Franziska Ohnsorge and Shu Yu, and including Mohammad Amin, Sinem Kilic Celik, Gene Joseph Kindberg Hanlon, Ergys Islamaj, Sergiy Kasyanenko, Cedric Okou, Naotaka Sugawara, Temel Taskin, and Collette Wheeler.

[1] Several studies find that some informal workers in EMDEs operate voluntarily in the informal sector. For instance, Falco et al. (2015) use survey data from Ghana and find little evidence for the overall inferiority of working in the informal sector compared with the formal sector. Falco and Haywood (2016) report that returns to productive characteristics in self-employment have increased significantly in Ghana between 2004 and 2011 whilst self-

employment has attracted increasingly skilled workers. Blanchflower, Oswald, and Stutzer (2001) note that many workers in advanced economies, such as the United States and Portugal, report preferring to be self-employed.

[2] Research suggests the coexistence of both "excluded" and "exiting" types of informality (e.g., Perry et al. 2007; Hazans 2011; Bosh and Maloney 2008, 2010; Lehmann and Pignatti 2007; Fiess, Fugazza, and Maloney 2010; Nordman, Rakotomanana, and Roubaud 2016).

[3] La Porta and Shleifer (2014) provide evidence that informality is associated with lower productivity, less access to financing, and less-educated managers. Some studies show that informality is associated with higher income inequality and poverty (Rosser, Rosser, and Ahmed 2000; Perry et al. 2007; Chong and Gradstein 2007; Loayza, Servén, and Sugawara 2010). Lower physical investment in the informal sector could reflect an unwillingness of informal firms to adopt technologies or scale up that would make them visible to tax and other authorities (Dabla-Norris and Inchauste 2008; Gandelman and Rastelletti 2017). Docquier, Müller, and Naval (2017) develop a model that predicts that the informal sector would lead to slower human capital formation. Less educated managers partially explain lower labor productivity observed in informal firms (Cirera and Maloney 2017). Benjamin et al. (2014) show that informality is associated with weaker international competitiveness.

formal sector because it tends to employ less-skilled workers, have restricted access to funding, services and markets, and lack economies of scale.[4] Employment in the informal sector can provide a safety net by keeping or creating employment during periods when the formal sector is shedding jobs (Loayza and Rigolini 2011). However, workers in the informal economy are largely excluded from the social security system and less protected against negative shocks than workers in the formal sector (Box 3.1).

Against this backdrop, this chapter examines the main features of informal economies and possible policies to address the challenges associated with informality. Specifically, it addresses the following questions:

- What are the main features of the informal economy?

- What are the empirical linkages between informality and development outcomes?

- Which policies can mitigate the adverse effects of informality?

The chapter makes the following contributions to the literature on informality:

- **Broad database on informality.** The chapter compiles a new database from a wide range of informality measures. It employs these measures to provide a rich set of stylized facts on informality that are robust to the choice of measure.

- **Informality, poverty, and income (wage) inequality.** The chapter documents that higher informality is associated with greater poverty. This may, in part, reflect lower wages for informal workers than formal workers. While many survey-based studies have documented the existence of such wage differentials (especially at the country-level), this chapter distills broader lessons from a large number of studies.

- **Informality and fiscal indicators.** The chapter is the first to document the empirical link between higher informality and unfavorable aggregate fiscal outcomes, including revenues and expenditures. This goes beyond previous studies that have focused on the implications for specific tax categories, such as value-added taxes (Keen 2008).

- **Informal competition and formal firm productivity.** The chapter presents the first cross-country study that quantifies the lower productivity of formal firms that face competition from informal firms. This adds to the rich literature that documents the sizable productivity differential between formal and informal firms.

- **Policy implications.** The chapter analyzes the implications of country-specific policy changes for the informal sector and synthesizes the lessons from these changes to offer a menu of policy options that takes into account the importance of complementarities.

The chapter reports the following main findings:

- **Main features of the informal economy.** In EMDEs, the informal economy in 2016 on average accounts for 32 percent of GDP and, 70 percent of employment, with self-employment accounting for 43 percent of employment (Figure 3.1). Informality tends to be higher in lower-income economies that are less open to international trade, have larger agricultural sectors, and have larger pools of young and unskilled workers. Both informal output and employment have declined since 1990. Informality declined faster in countries with higher output growth, rapid physical capital accumulation, and stronger improvements in governance and business climates.

- **Prevalence of informality.** One-half of the world's informal output and 95 percent of its informal employment is in EMDEs. Three EMDE regions (East Asia and Pacific (EAP), Latin America and the Caribbean (LAC), and Europe and Central Asia (ECA)) accounted for more than one-third of the world's informal output, but only one-quarter of its

---

[4] For details, see Jovanovic (1982), Amaral and Quintin (2006), Galiani and Weinschelbaum (2012), Loayza (2018).

formal output. Meanwhile, South Asia (SAR) hosts almost half of the world's informal workers, although the region accounts for less than one-tenth of the world's formal employment and less than one-twentieth of the world's formal output. Another 14 percent of the world's informally employed are in Sub-Saharan Africa (SSA), two to five times the region's share of the world's formal output or formal employment.

- **Informality and development outcomes.** Higher informality is associated with lower output growth, lower productivity, and higher poverty and income inequality. Potential reasons for greater poverty in economies with higher informality may include a lack of fiscal resources to fund public services or wage differentials between informal and formal workers. Workers in the formal economy earn, on average, about 19 percent more than workers in the informal economy. These wage differentials largely reflect the characteristics of informal workers, who tend to be lower-skilled than formal workers.

- **Informality and firm productivity.** The average informal firm in EMDEs is only one-quarter as productive as the average firm operating in the formal sector. Moreover, firms in the formal sector that face informal competition are, on average, only three-quarters as productive as those that do not. Better business climates can mitigate some of these productivity differentials.

- **Informality and fiscal indicators.** In EMDEs with the most pervasive informality, government revenues are lower by 5-10 percentage points of GDP (and expenditures lower by 4-10 percentage points of GDP) than in those with the lowest levels of informality. In developing economies, pervasive informality further limits governments' limited ability to implement redistributive measures, invest in public infrastructure, or carry out other growth-enhancing policies.

- **Policy implications.** A review of studies of policy measures that have had repercussions

FIGURE 3.1 Informality: Magnitude and correlates

The informal sector accounts for about a third of GDP and 70 percent of employment (of which self-employment is more than a half) in emerging market and developing economies (EMDEs). A large informal sector is associated with slower GDP growth and weaker governance as well as greater poverty and income inequality. Widespread informality is also seen in economies with lower government expenditures and revenues, and a skew towards trade-based taxation.

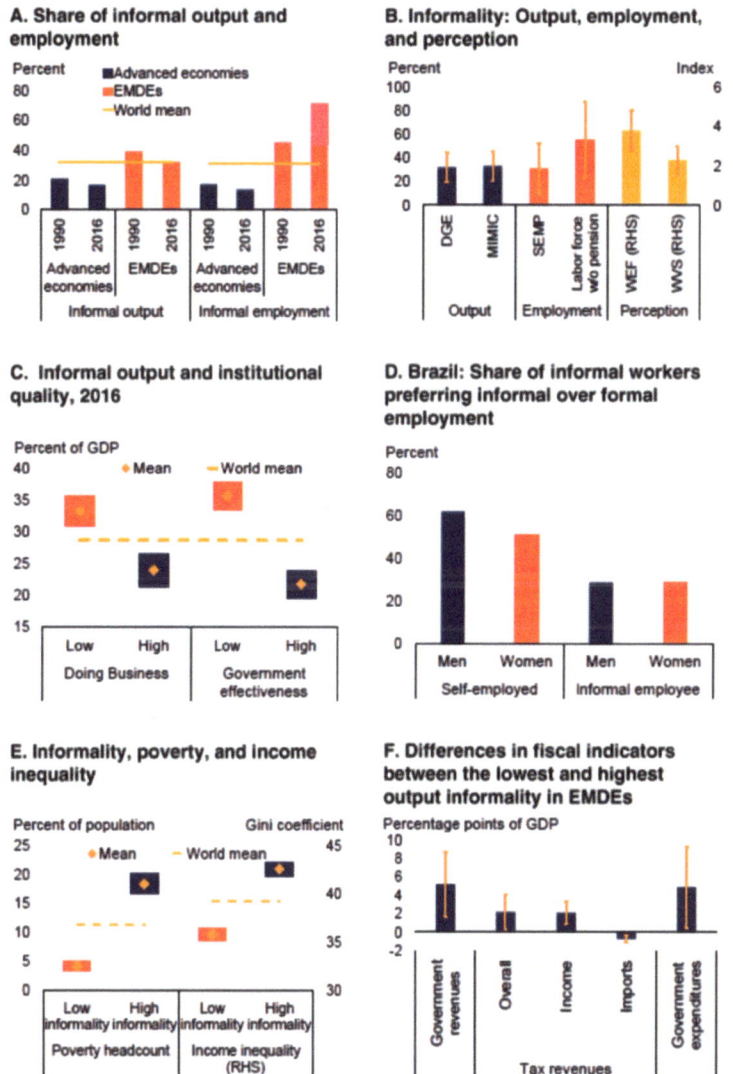

A. Share of informal output and employment

B. Informality: Output, employment, and perception

C. Informal output and institutional quality, 2016

D. Brazil: Share of informal workers preferring informal over formal employment

E. Informality, poverty, and income inequality

F. Differences in fiscal indicators between the lowest and highest output informality in EMDEs

Source: Elgin et al. (forthcoming a); International Monetary Fund, World Economic Outlook; Maloney (2004); International Labour Organization; World Bank (Doing Business, World Development Indicators, World Governance Indicators); World Economic Forum; World Value Survey.

A. Unweighted averages. Informal employment (in red) uses self-employment shares (with additional informal employment shares in shaded red) in the closest (latest) available year around 1990 and 2016. World averages between 1990-2016 are in orange. EMDEs= Emerging market and developing economies.

B. Unweighted average for each informality measure for latest available year (with the corresponding +/-1 standard deviation shown in vertical bars). See Annex 3.1 for details.

C. Group averages of DGE-based informal output in percent of official GDP in year 2016 are shown in diamonds, with bars showing 95 percent confidence intervals. The dashed line shows the world average. "High" ("Low") indicates countries with above- (below-) median values in the following two measures: Doing Business distance-to-frontier and governance effectiveness (WGI).

D. The shares of informal workers preferring informal over formal employment (Maloney 2004).

E. Data are for 1990-2016. Group means (diamonds) and 95 percent confidence intervals (bars) are shown for poverty headcount ratio at $1.90 a day (2011 PPP, percent of population) and Gini coefficients. "High informality" ("Low informality") indicates countries with above- (below-) median informal output (DGE-based estimates).

F. Differences in the 2000-16 average fiscal indicators among the third of EMDEs with the highest and lowest informality (measured by the share of DGE-based informal output averaged during 2000-16). Vertical bars indicate 90 percent confidence intervals of the difference. Sample includes 70 non-energy exporting EMDEs with populations above 3 million people.

BOX 3.1 Linkages between formal and informal sectors

Empirical evidence on the degree of cyclicality of the informal economy with the formal economy is mixed. The cyclicality and sensitivity of informal employment to formal business cycles depends on the sources of shocks driving business cycles, the presence of rigidities in the formal sector, the initial extent of informality, and the availability of informal jobs.

While there is broad consensus that the informal economy is sizable in emerging market and developing economies (EMDEs), evidence for its behavior over the business cycles remains inconclusive. An informal economy that expands while the formal economy contracts may support household incomes during economic downturns and could serve as a safety net (Loayza and Rigolini 2011). An informal economy that behaves procyclically could function as a "growth engine" by providing more services and intermediate inputs to the formal economy during economic expansions but, conversely, could also amplify the adverse effect of recessions (Dell'Anno 2008; Chen 2005; Meagher 2013).[1] Earlier work suggests that the degree of cyclicality of the informal economy depends on the measure of informality, the types of shocks causing business cycles, and country characteristics.

Against this backdrop, this box reviews the literature and presents results from a set of empirical exercises to address the following questions:

- What conclusions does the literature offer about the cyclical behavior of the informal economy?

- How synchronized have been movements in informal and formal economies?

- What are the policy implications of cyclicality?

Literature review

The literature on the cyclical behavior of the informal economy offers mixed conclusions. Studies focusing on the share of the informal economy in total output or employment tend to find countercyclical behavior whereas studies focusing on output or employment levels tend to find procyclical behavior. The theoretical literature suggests that the degree of procyclicality depends on the source of shocks causing business cycle fluctuations and on the presence of labor market rigidities. This section summarizes this literature.[2]

Informal economy as a countercyclical safety net

The informal sector can serve as buffers and safety nets for the poor if it absorbs labor during recessions.[3] This can facilitate an economic recovery provided that re-entry into the formal sector is possible when the formal economy returns to expansion (Colombo, Onnis, and Tirelli 2016; IMF 2017; Loayza and Rigolini 2011).

Macroeconomic evidence. Macroeconomic studies suggest that the informal economy can behave "countercyclically" in the sense that the share of informal employment indeed rises during business cycle downturns.[4] Using data from 54 countries for 1984-2008, Loayza and Rigolini (2011) show that, on average, a one standard deviation slowdown in GDP per capita growth (i.e., 3 percentage points) is linked with a short-run increase in the share of self-employment in the total labor force by 1.2 percentage points. However, they also find considerable heterogeneity across countries—the counter-cyclicality of informal employment is much weaker in economies with more pervasive informality.[5]

Using quarterly data for Mexico, Fernández and Meza (2015) find that the correlation between informal employment and official GDP is modest (about -0.3), whereas the correlation between formal employment and formal output is strongly positive. The authors argue that this lowers cyclicality of total employment. Colombo, Onnis, and Tirelli (2016) use electricity consumption as a proxy for total economic activity to study cyclical properties of informality in 48 countries over the period

---

Note: This box was prepared by Sergiy Kasyanenko and Shu Yu.

[1] See Meagher (2013) for a literature review on studies concerning the linkage between formal and informal economy.

[2] Several recent studies also argue that pervasive informality may influence the measured cyclicality of the formal economy. For example, Restrepo-Echavarria (2014) and Horvath (2018) show that models with a large and poorly measured informal sector can generate excess volatility of formal consumption relative to formal output – a common feature of business cycles in many EMDEs.

[3] Due to its flexibility, the informal sector is able to adjust in wages rather than employment during recessions, which explains the informal employment's lack of responses to economic downturns (Maloney 2004; Guriev, Speciale and Tuccio 2016).

[4] Remittances, as a buffer against shocks to formal economy, may also influence the cyclicality of the informal sector. Remittances appear to be largely absorbed by the informal sector as Ivlevs (2016) finds that high level of remittances tends to be associated with more informality. Shapiro and Mandelman (2016) and Chatterjee and Turnovsky (2018) show that countercyclical remittances are associated with higher informal employment during recessions as formal employment declines.

[5] The extent of countercyclicality drops as the share of informal employment in total employment increases and disappears when informal employment accounts for more than 42-43 percent of total employment. Theoretically, Shapiro (2014) suggest that while the share of self-employment tends to decline during economic upturns, the ease of entry into self-employment explains the differences in cyclical behavior across countries.

BOX 3.1 Linkages between formal and informal sectors *(continued)*

1984-2005 and illustrate that the informal economy expands following a banking crisis. Finally, Kaufmann and Kaliberda (1996), Busato and Chiarini (2004) and Elgin (2012) present empirical evidence that the informal economy acts as a buffer, increasing its share of official GDP during economic downturns.[6]

More procyclical fiscal policy in less developed economies with weaker institutions may contribute to counter-cyclicality of informal activity. Fiscal policy tends to be more procyclical in countries with higher informality (Çiçek and Elgin 2011). In particular, procyclical fiscal consolidation during recessions, including through higher taxes, may encourage more informal employment and strengthen the counter-cyclicality of informal activity.

Microeconomic evidence. In work flow data for Brazilian metropolitan labor markets between 1983 and 2002, Bosch, Goni, and Maloney (2007) find that the informal sector is able to absorb more labor during economic downturns as jobs became scarce in the formal sectors. Bosch and Esteban-Pretel (2012) use the same data and find that the share of formal employment falls as formal-economy output contracts, in part because the rate at which workers find formal jobs plummets while that at which they find informal jobs remains broadly stable.[7]

Informal economy as an engine of growth

Since informal firms provide services, as well as final and intermediate goods to the formal sector, one would expect a positive correlation between formal and informal sector activity (Lubell 1991; Arvin-Rad, Basu, and Willumsen 2010; Moreno-Monroy, Pieters, and Erumban 2014). In addition, informal-economy income can support formal-economy demand.[8]

Macroeconomic evidence. Using informal output levels (as opposed to the share of the informal economy), Bajada (2003), Giles (1997), Tedds and Giles (2000), and Dell'Anno (2008) find that informal-economy output movements correlate positively (i.e., move pro-cyclically) with formal-economy output movements in Australia, New Zealand, Canada, and a group of 19 Latin American countries. In a group of developing countries, Fiess, Fugazza, and Maloney (2010) identify episodes where relative demand or productivity shocks to the non-tradables sector (as opposed to the tradables sector) are associated with higher informal employment (hence, pro-cyclicality). In Brazil and Mexico, higher separation rates from informal jobs and a large drop of the formal job finding rate may induce labor outflows from the informal sector during recessions (Bosch and Maloney 2008). Arvin-Rad, Basu, and Willumsen (2010) develop a theoretical model that establishes procyclical informal-formal sector linkages, particularly when formal firms sub-contract labor-intensive stages of production to the informal sector.

Microeconomic evidence. Schneider (1998) reports that in Germany and Austria at least two-thirds of the income earned in the informal economy is immediately spent in the official economy resulting in considerable (positive) stimulating effects on the official economy. In firm-level data for India, Moreno-Monroy, Pieters, and Erumban (2014) find that formal and informal sector employment are positively correlated, in part because subcontracting by formal-sector firms to informal firms contributes to job creation in the informal sector. Data from Indian manufacturing firms show that the gross value added for several predominantly informal industries is positively correlated with that in the formal sector and FDI. This may be indicative of technological spillovers contributing to both formal and informal sectors (Beladi, Dutta, and Kar 2016).

Factors determining the degree of procyclicality of the informal economy

Cross-country heterogeneity. There is considerable cross-country heterogeneity in the degree of pro-cyclicality of informal employment. It tends to be higher when informality is greater (Loayza and Rigolini 2011), when informal employment is more common (Shapiro 2014), when there are stronger informal-formal sector linkages such as through subcontracting (e.g., Moreno-Monroy, Pieters, and Erumban 2014; Mbaye, Benjamin, and Gueye 2017).

Source of shocks causing business cycles. The informal economy can move procyclically or countercyclically,

---

[6] This empirical relationship between informal and formal activities appears to be present in both advanced economies and EMDEs. For example, Kaufmann and Kaliberda (1996) cover a panel of 16 Central and Eastern European countries in 1989-1994; Busato and Chiarini (2004) used data on the share of informal output in total GDP from the United States, Italy, the United Kingdom, and New Zealand over the period 1960-1997; Elgin (2012) utilizes a panel of 152 countries from 1999 to 2007.

[7] Job separation rates are countercyclical (i.e rise during recessions) for both sectors, with a much higher probability of losing an informal job during recessions.

[8] See Schneider (1998), Gibson (2005), Docquier, Müller, and Naval (2017), Kanbur (2017), Eliat and Zinnes (2002), and World Bank (2014). Although the relationship between formal and informal sectors may be symbiotic in the short run especially when policymakers are concerned about the welfare of low-skilled working poor, argue that in the long-run pervasive informality may create poverty traps and stymie economic development.

BOX 3.1 Linkages between formal and informal sectors *(continued)*

depending on the sectoral origin of the shocks that generate business cycles in the presence of wage rigidities, especially in the formal sector (Fiess, Fugazza, and Maloney 2010). Positive relative demand or productivity shocks to the non-tradable (largely informal) sector could increase informal employment, i.e. generate procyclicality in informal employment, especially when combined with wage rigidities in the formal sector. For instance, in Colombia, capital account liberalization in the context of broader reforms during 1991-1996 raised permanent income and constituted a positive demand shock to the non-tradeable sector. This upturn resulted in an expanding non-tradable informal sector. Conversely, in the presence of wage rigidities, a negative shock to the tradables sector would expand informal (nontradables) employment and thus appear as countercyclicality.

Synchronization in formal and informal-economy movements

As in other studies that examine levels of employment and output, the data set used in this chapter suggests that, at the macroeconomic level, *formal employment* levels and *informal output* levels comove with formal output levels but *informal employment* levels do not. Several methodologies point to this finding, including analyses of volatility, business cycle turning points, correlations and factor models.

- *Macroeconomic volatility.* Since formal and informal employment move marginally (but statistically significantly) in opposite directions, the volatility of total (formal and informal) employment is somewhat lower than the volatility of each type of employment in isolation (Figure 3.1.1, Elgin et al. forthcoming a; Loayza and Rigolini 2011; Fernández and Meza 2015).[9] Self-employment (as a proxy for informal employment) is somewhat less volatile than formal employment. In contrast, informal output is somewhat less volatile than formal output, possibly reflecting flexible adjustments in hours worked in the informal economy (Meghir, Narita, and Robin 2015; Guriev, Speciale, and Tuccio 2016).

- *Business cycle turning points.* About three fourths of business cycle troughs in formal output coincide with a trough in the informal output; seven out of ten formal output peaks coincide with informal output peaks (Elgin et al. forthcoming b). In contrast, turning points in self-employment, as a proxy for informal employment, rarely coincide with turning points in formal employment or formal output.

- *Correlations.* Lead, lag, and contemporaneous correlations of formal-economy output with informal-economy output are highly and statistically significant whereas those between formal output and informal employment are statistically insignificant (Figure 3.1.1; Elgin et al. forthcoming b). This is consistent with studies that find countercyclicality in the share of the informal economy and those show that informal firms are flexible enough to adjust in wages rather than employment during economic downturns (Maloney 2004; Loayza and Rigolini 2011; Guriev, Speciale and Tuccio 2016).[10]

- *Common factors.* A dynamic factor model applied to formal and informal output and employment finds that a single common factor accounts for 38 and 40 percent of the output variance of the informal and formal economies, respectively (Kose, Prasad, and Terrones 2003; Elgin et al. forthcoming b). This common factor explains only a negligible share of the variance in informal employment.

Policy implications

A large degree of comovement of informal employment and formal output in and of itself may not warrant policy action for two reasons. First, the direction of comovement can change over time if business cycle fluctuations are caused by changing sources of sectoral shocks. Second, the appropriate policy response would depend on the source of the shock that generates comovement. If a procyclical expansion in informal employment is largely the reflection of shocks in the nontradable sector, such as in construction, no policy response specifically related to informality may be needed. In contrast, if a countercyclical expansion in informal employment reflects a downturn in the tradable sector, such as in manufacturing, in the presence of labor market rigidities, measures to ease labor market rigidities may be the appropriate response (Fiess, Fugazza, and Maloney 2010).

---

[9] The correlation between formal and informal employment growth rates is above 0.2 and significant at 1 percent level.

[10] This lack of comovement between formal output and informal employment is particularly pronounced in EMDEs, possibly reflecting data challenges in EMDEs, genuinely lesser synchronicity between formal economic output and formal employment in advanced economies, or higher labor market rigidities in EMDEs (Neumeyer and Perri 2005; Botero et al. 2004; Campos and Nugent 2012).

BOX 3.1 Linkages between formal and informal sectors *(continued)*

FIGURE 3.1.1 Interaction between formal and informal economies

Formal employment and informal output levels tend to comove with formal output levels, whereas informal employment levels do not. Since formal and informal employment are marginally negatively correlated, total (formal and informal employment) is less volatile than each in isolation.

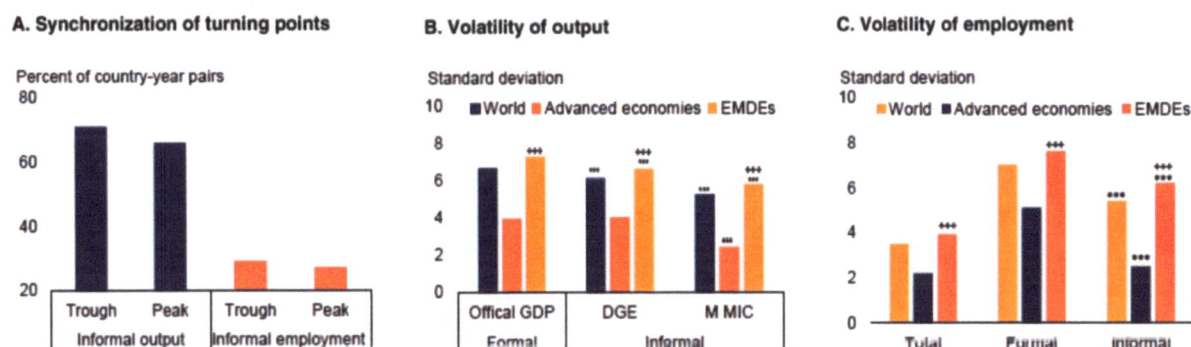

A. Synchronization of turning points

B. Volatility of output

C. Volatility of employment

Source: Elgin et al. (forthcoming a, forthcoming b).
Note: Data are from 1990 to 2016. DGE-based estimates are used for informal output in A-B, while data on self-employment are used for informal employment.
A. Troughs and peaks are identified as in Harding and Pagan (2002). The bars show the share of formal peaks (or troughs) that coincide with informal peaks (or troughs).
B-C. Standard deviations in annual growth rates are shown in bars. "***" indicates statistically significant differences at least at 10 percent level between informal and informal output (employment). "+++" indicates statistically significant differences at least at 10 percent level between advanced economies and EMDEs.

In addition to measures taken explicitly to address informality, many measures undertaken for other reasons, such as tax measures, may have implications for informality. The discussion in this box highlights that these implications warrant a carefully calibrated policy mix.

The resilience of informal employment to business cycle swings, juxtaposed with the weaker development outcomes associated with informality (discussed in the main text), suggests a trade-off. In the short run, informal activity can provide a safety net during business cycle swings and labor dislocations caused by major structural changes such as trade liberalizations; in the long term, however, the informal sector can be a source of poverty and stymie development (Docquier, Müller, and Naval 2017; Dix-

Carniero, Goldberg and Meghir 2018). Policy measures that—deliberately or inadvertently—reduce informality can therefore protect vulnerable population groups better if they are accompanied by strengthened social safety nets that can fulfill some of the roles of the informal sector.

Similarly, if comovement between formal and informal output reflects synergies, such as through subcontracting, policy measures aimed at curtailing informal activity can disrupt formal activity.

These effects could be mitigated if measures that reduce informality were accompanied by greater labor and product market flexibility in the formal sector that facilitates a reallocation of informal workers and firms.

for informality highlights the need for a comprehensive policy package that takes into account country-specific features that lead to informality and determine its consequences. First, strategies to reduce informality outright may hurt vulnerable groups and disrupt formal activity that relies on informal-economy inputs. These effects can be mitigated by stronger safety nets, greater labor

and product market flexibility, and better access to resources for informal firms. Second, policies to spur development, as a collateral benefit, can help reduce informality. Specific measures discussed in this chapter include simplification of tax codes and enhanced enforcement of revenue collection, which can reduce the incentive to operate informally depending on country-specific circumstances;

easing of labor market regulations to lower the relative cost of employing formal workers and create a level playing field for formal and informal firms and workers; as well as greater access to finance and public services to help increase productivity in the informal sector and encourage a shift of activity to the formal sector.

Informality: Conceptual considerations and measurement

Definition of informality

Informality is often defined as market-based legal production of goods and services that are hidden from public authorities for monetary, regulatory, and institutional reasons (Schneider, Buehn, and Montenegro 2010).[5] This general definition encompasses many types of informal activity among workers and firms.[6] Some studies distinguish different types of informality by the motives of participating in the informal economy. For example, some classify informal workers and firms into those that are "excluded" and those that "voluntarily exit" from the formal sector (Perry et al. 2007). Others focus on "subsistence informality," which is pervasive in lower-income countries and characterized by low-skill technology. In the absence of such an informal economy, the income of low-skilled workers would fall below subsistence levels (Docquier, Müller, and Naval 2017).

Some others classify informal workers and firms into evaders, avoiders, and outsiders depending on their compliance with regulations and regulations' applicability (Kanbur and Keen 2015; Kanbur

2009). Evaders are firms that are covered by the regulation but do not comply; avoiders are firms that adjust to be outside the remit of the regulation; outsiders are firms that are simply not covered by the regulation. More recent studies distinguish different types of informality by the entities engaged in informal activity, separate from their motivation: within firms, formal and informal workers or activities ("interfirm margin") and, within sectors, informal and formal firms or workers ("intersectoral margin," Maloney 2006; Ulyssea 2018).[7] Individual country practices vary widely but typically adhere to these broad principles.

- **Informal workers.** Informal employment covers all workers of the informal sector and informal workers outside the informal sector (ILO 2018a).[8] The former comprises all persons who were employed in at least one informal firm. The latter group includes both self-employed and workers that are not employed in formal contractual arrangements or not subject to social protection or employment benefits. Some have defined informal employment more specifically as that of workers without pension coverage, which is a part of social protection (Loayza, Servén, and Sugawara 2010).

- **Informal firms.** An informal firm satisfies the following criteria (ILO 2018a).[9] First, it is not

---

[5] Monetary reasons include avoiding taxes and social security contributions; regulatory reasons include avoiding government bureaucracy or regulatory burdens, while institutional reasons include corruption, the quality of political institutions and weak rule of law. For the purposes of this chapter, the informal economy reflects activities that, if recorded, would contribute to GDP, and does not cover illegal activities or household production (Schneider, Buehn, and Montenegro 2010; Medina and Schneider 2018). The difference between informal production and household production is that the latter does not encounter monetary transactions.

[6] The definition and classification of informality is deeply context specific. Similarly, the choice of informality measures largely depends on the research question (see Elgin et al. forthcoming a, for details).

[7] See Perry et al. (2007, p.27) for a more detailed description of informal employment and different types of informal employment.

[8] The most frequently used informal employment measure is the share of self-employment in total employment, which is a lower bound of informal employment (e.g., La Porta and Shleifer 2014). As defined by the 1993 International Classification of Status in Employment (ICSE-93), self-employed workers are those workers who, working on their own account or with one or a few partners or in a cooperative, hold the type of jobs defined as "self-employment jobs." The other measure, informal employment, comprises all workers of the informal sector and informal workers outside the informal sector. The former covers all persons who, during a given reference period, were employed in at least one informal sector enterprise, irrespective of their status in employment and whether it was their main or a secondary job. The latter covers self-employment and employees holding informal jobs. See Annex 3.1 for details. For the remainder of the chapter, informal employment will be proxied by self-employment since data on informal employment is not available for advanced economies. The numbers here refer to the latest available years.

[9] Benjamin and Mbaye (2012) and Mbaye, Benjamin, and Gueye (2017) provide an alternative definition of informal firms as a continuum depending on size, registration, honest accounting, tax payments, mobility of work-place and access to bank credit.

an incorporated enterprise that is a legal entity separate from its owners, has its own complete set of accounts, but is not owned nor controlled by one or a few household members. Second, it is a market enterprise that sells its goods or services. Third, it falls into one of the following categories: it keeps the number of workers employed on a continuous basis and below a threshold determined by the country; it is not registered; or its workers are not registered.

Measurement of informality

Reflecting the difficulty of measuring informality, the literature has developed a wide range of estimation methods to capture its extent. In this chapter, a database of all commonly used measures of informality is compiled (summarized in Annex Table 3.1.1), ranging from model-based estimates of the share of informality in official GDP (MIMIC and DGE estimates), to survey-based measures of the share of informality in total employment (share of self-employed and share of workers covered by pension schemes), and public perceptions of the extent of informality (World Economic Forum index, World Value Survey index, and Enterprise Surveys).[10] The database includes up to 196 economies (36 advanced and 160 emerging market and developing economies) over the 1990-2016 period. Both cross-country rankings and time trends are consistent for most countries. That said, the chapter relies mainly on the two model-based (DGE and MIMIC) estimates of the share of informal output and the share of self-employed (from International Labour

Organization, World Development Indicators, and national statistical offices' databases), which stand out in their time and country coverage.[11]

Main features of the informal economy

Informality: Lower in advanced economies than in EMDEs. On average, the size of the informal economy is about 32 percent of official GDP and, in EMDEs, 71 percent of total employment in 2016, of which self-employment accounts for 43 percent of total employment (based on latest available data for each country). A higher level of development, e.g., as measured by per capita income, is associated with lower informality, regardless of the measure of informality or the year chosen (La Porta and Shleifer 2014; Figure 3.2). As a result, informality tends to be considerably more pervasive in EMDEs than in advanced economies: in advanced economies, informal output accounts for about 17 percent of output and self-employment accounts for 14 percent of employment. Perceptions from business owners and managers about the pervasiveness of informality also suggest greater informal activity in EMDEs than in advanced economies.

Cross-country heterogeneity: Pronounced in EMDEs. The size of the informal economy varies widely across countries (Figure 3.2). In EMDEs, the informal economy ranged from around 10 (in China) to 69 (in Equatorial Guinea) percent of GDP—depending on the measure used—and self-employment ranged from near-zero (Qatar) to around 90 (Burundi) percent of employment. Among advanced economies, the share of informal output in GDP has varied from less than 12 percent, in Switzerland and Singapore, to about 32 percent in Estonia. During 2006-16, Greece registered the highest share of informal employment (37 percent) among advanced economies.

---

[10] For the compiled data set, see Elgin et al. (forthcoming-a). In the data set, the Multiple Indicators Multiple Causes (MIMIC) model is a model of structural equations that use observable causes and indicators to capture the latent level of informal output. Elgin et al. (forthcoming a) follow Schneider, Buehn, and Montenegro (2010) closely when estimating the MIMIC model for 160 countries over the period 1993-2015. The dynamic general equilibrium (DGE) model of Elgin and Oztunali (2014) provides an alternative estimate of the size of the informal sector for 158 countries (36 AEs and 122 EMDEs) over the period 1950-2016. To make the measures comparable with those in the literature, both measures are reported in percent of official GDP. In the following sections, "in percent of GDP or output" is used as the equivalent of "in percent of official GDP" in the context of the share of informal output (both DGE-based and MIMIC-based estimates), while "in percent of employment" is used as the equivalent of "in percent of total employment."

[11] For presentational simplicity, throughout this chapter, the output share of informality refers to the share of informal output based on DGE model estimates, unless otherwise noted. The main results for features of informality, correlates of informality, and developmental implications are robust to the use of MIMIC-based estimates.

FIGURE 3.2 Informality in advanced economies and EMDEs

There is wide cross-country heterogeneity in informality, especially among EMDEs. Since 1990, the share of informal employment and output has declined in both advanced economies and EMDEs, despite largely unchanged perceptions of the size of the informal sector.

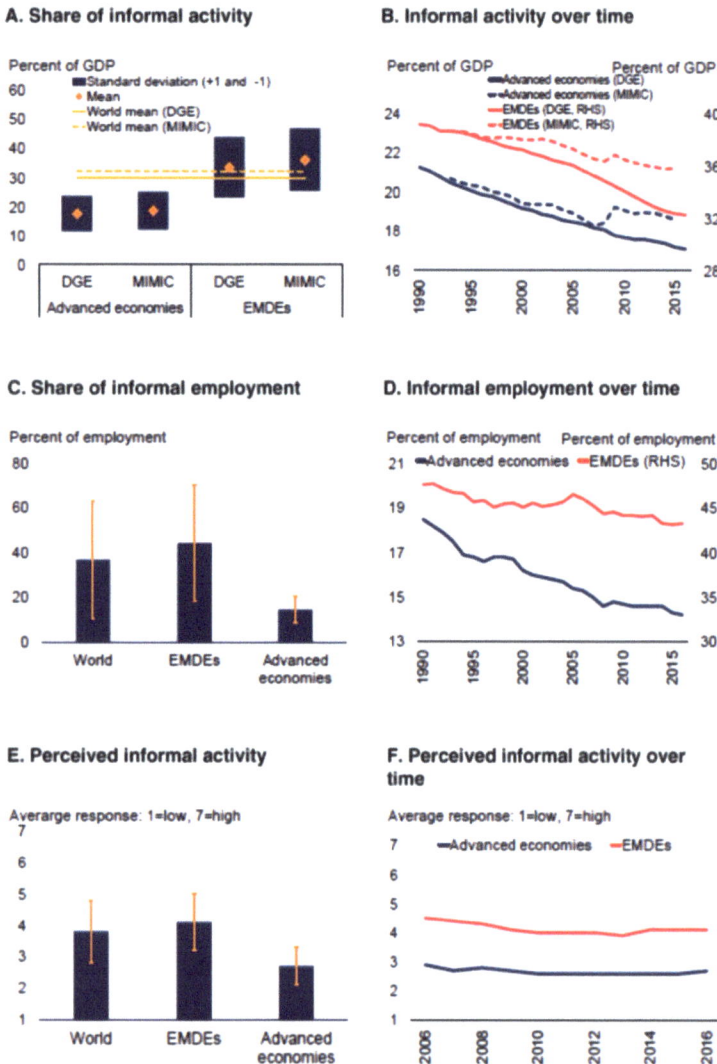

A. Share of informal activity

B. Informal activity over time

C. Share of informal employment

D. Informal employment over time

E. Perceived informal activity

F. Perceived informal activity over time

Source: Elgin et al. (forthcoming a); International Labour Organization; World Bank, World Development Indicators; World Economic Forum.
Note: See Annex 3.1 for data definitions.
A.C.E. Group means for the period 2006-16 are shown in blues with +/-1 standard deviation shown in orange vertical bars. World means are shown in yellow lines (dashed line for MIMIC estimates in A). The group statistics are calculated for the world, advanced economies (AEs) and emerging market and developing economies (EMDEs).
B.D.F. Group means are calculated for advanced economies (AEs, in blue) and emerging and developing economies (EMDEs, in red). Dashed lines are for MIMIC estimates in B. In D, missing data for informal employment are extrapolated in EMDEs for earlier years and filled using the latest available observation in recent years.
E.F. WEF (World Economic Forum) index of informality.

Regional informality: Common in all EMDE regions. Informality is common in all EMDE regions but takes different forms (World Bank 2012). On average, the informal economy's share of output is highest in Sub-Saharan Africa (SSA), Europe and Central Asia (ECA), and Latin America and the Caribbean (LAC). The share of self-employment, however, is highest in Sub-Saharan Africa (SSA), South Asia (SAR), and East Asia and the Pacific (EAP; Figure 3.3).

Two country examples illustrate differences across regions. In Brazil, the informal sector employs one-third of total employment and produces one-third of GDP. In Pakistan, the informal sector provides two-thirds of total employment but produces only about one-third of GDP. This difference points to considerably lower informal labor productivity relative to total labor productivity in Pakistan than in Brazil, in part reflecting lower educational attainment of informal workers (La Porta and Shleifer 2014; Loayza 2018).

Three EMDE regions (EAP, LAC and ECA) alone accounted for more than one-third of the world's informal output in 2016, but only one-quarter of the world's formal output. Almost half (42 percent) of the world's informal workers can be found in South Asia (SAR), although the region only accounts for 9 percent of the world's formal employment and 3 percent of the world's formal output (Box 3.2). Another 14 percent of the world's informally employed are in Sub-Saharan Africa (SSA), well above SSA's share of the world's formal output (2 percent) or formal employment (5 percent).

Informality over time: Downward trend. The shares of both informal output and self-employment have declined since 1990, especially in EMDEs (Figure 3.2 and 3.4). Between 1990-16, on average, the share of informal output fell by about 7 percentage points of GDP in EMDEs (to 32 percent of GDP) and by about 4 percentage points (to 17 percent of GDP) in advanced economies. Over the same period, the average share of self-employment declined by about 4 percentage points (to 14 percent of total employment) in advanced economies and by about 4.5 percentage points (to 43 percent of total employment) in EMDEs. These declines were broad-based: the share of informal output declined by 5 percentage points of output or more between 1990 and 2016 in all advanced economies and 86 percent of EMDEs.[12]

In EMDEs, the largest declines in the shares of informal output and employment occurred from the mid-2000s onwards in a reversal of a decade of rising informal employment and barely shrinking informal output.[13] In advanced economies, the largest declines in the share of informal employment occurred between the late 1990s and the global financial crisis; they have since partly reversed, amid anemic post-crisis growth (Figure 3.2).[14] Among EMDE regions, the informal economy's share of output dropped most in EAP, LAC, and SAR, while the share of self-employment dropped most in EAP, ECA, and the Middle East and North Africa (MENA; Box 3.2).

Characteristics of informal sector business cycles. The main features of recessions and recoveries in the formal economy, defined as in Harding and Pagan (2002) and Claessens, Kose, and Terrones (2012), do not differ statistically significantly from those in the formal economy (Figure 3.5; Elgin et al. forthcoming a). On average, both formal and informal recessions last about 1.5 years, which are about 0.5 years shorter than formal and informal recoveries. The speeds of adjustment in recessions (about 4 percentage points decline per year) and of recoveries do not differ statistically significantly between formal and informal sector.

---

[12] The DGE-based measure of informal output shows that between 1990 and 2016, the share of informal output over official GDP fell in 140 (36 AEs and 104 EMDEs) out of 158 countries where data are available. Similar results are found in MIMIC-based measure on informal output. During the same period, 84 (18 AEs and 66 EMDEs) out of 127 countries experienced a drop in the share of self-employment.

[13] The small-scale decline in the beginning of the 1990s is also driven by the expanding informal sector in countries in Eastern and Central Europe during their economic transition (Kaufmann and Kaliberda 1996).

[14] A country-specific regression of the share of the informal economy in GDP and employment on a time trend over the period 1990-2016 captures this secular decline. In 50 (WEF)-100 (DGE) percent of advanced economies (depending on the measure) and 48 (WEF)-81 (MIMIC) percent of EMDEs, there has been a significant downward trend in the share of the informal economy in GDP and employment.

FIGURE 3.3 Informality by EMDE region

Informality is common in all EMDE regions but takes different forms. On average, the share of informal output is highest in Sub-Saharan Africa, Europe and Central Asia, and Latin America and the Caribbean. The share of self-employment is highest in Sub-Saharan Africa, South Asia, and East Asia and the Pacific.

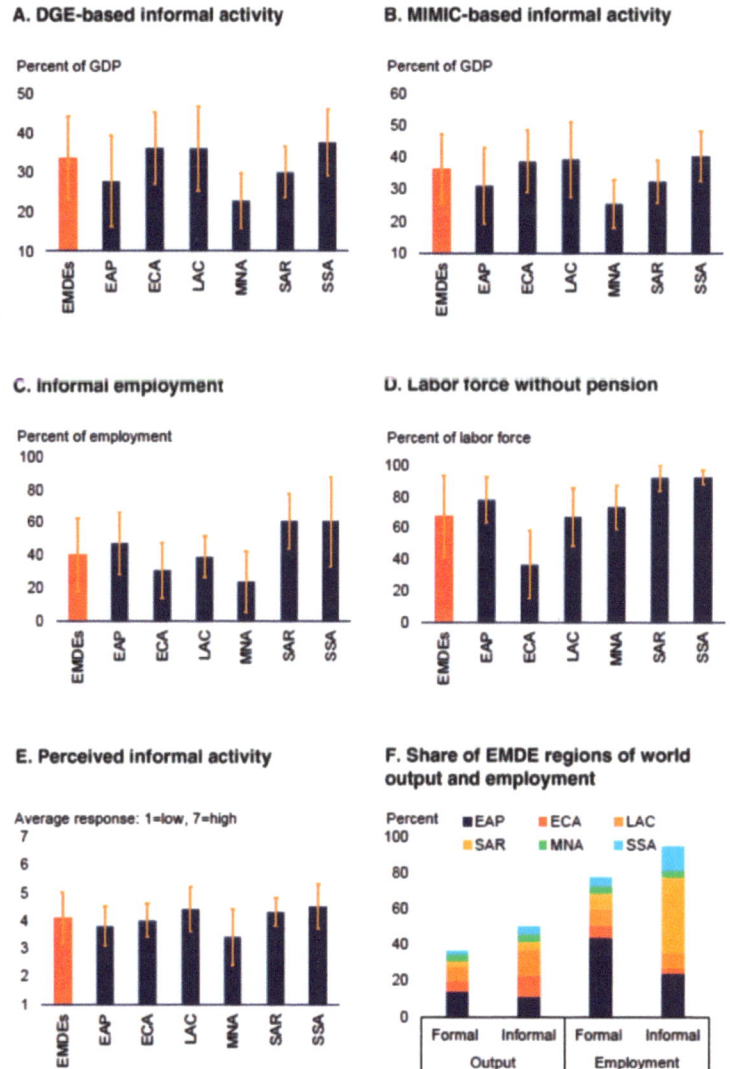

A. DGE-based informal activity

B. MIMIC-based informal activity

C. Informal employment

D. Labor force without pension

E. Perceived informal activity

F. Share of EMDE regions of world output and employment

Source: Elgin et al. (forthcoming a); International Labour Organization; World Bank, World Development Indicators; World Economic Forum.
Note: See Annex 3.1 for data definitions. Blue and red bars indicate group means for 2006-16, with orange vertical bars indicating +/-1 standard deviation. EAP = East Asia and Pacific, ECA = Europe and Central Asia, LAC = Latin America and the Caribbean, MNA = Middle East and North Africa, SAR = South Asia, and SSA = Sub-Saharan Africa. EMDEs = Emerging market and development economies.
C. Self-employment shares are used here.
E. Informality index provided by World Economic Forum (a higher value indicates more informality).
F. DGE-based estimates of informal output in each region as a proportion of total estimated informal GDP. Shares of self-employment are used as proxies for shares of informal employment. Formal output is equivalent to official GDP. Estimates are based on their respective average shares of output and employment during 2010-16.

BOX 3.2 Regional dimensions of informality: An overview

Informality, especially employment informality, is most prevalent in less developed EMDE regions. Together, South Asia and Sub-Saharan Africa account for nearly 60 percent of all informal workers in EMDEs. However, even in some wealthier EMDE regions, such as Latin America and the Caribbean and Europe and Central Asia, informality remains significant in part due to weak institutions and high levels of taxation and regulation. Both the drivers and implications of informality vary across and within regions, suggesting the need for tailored policy responses.

The informal economy accounts for a significant proportion of both employment and output across EMDEs. Around three-quarters of EMDE employment is estimated to be in the informal sector. Self-employment, which is relatively easy to measure and provides a lower bound estimate of informality, is 43 percent of total employment in the average EMDE, although this proportion ranges from 22 percent in the Middle East and North Africa (MENA), to 62 percent in Sub-Saharan Africa (SSA).[1]

Informality has both costs and benefits. It can provide an important source of income in EMDEs, often to those with few available alternatives. That said, informal employment is often associated with lower and more uncertain incomes for workers and lower revenues available for governments to fund their development objectives.

The regional disparities in the scale of informality depend on a wide range of factors. To summarize these regional distinctions, this box addresses the following questions:

- Where is global informality concentrated?

- What have been the correlates of informality across EMDE regions?

- What policy options are available?

Where is global informality concentrated?

Regional composition of EMDE informal sectors. One-half of the world's informal output and 95 percent of informal employment is located in EMDEs. Three EMDE regions alone accounted for one-third of the world's informal output in 2016: East Asia and Pacific (EAP), Latin America and the Caribbean (LAC), and Europe and Central Asia (ECA). They are also the largest EMDE

regions by formal GDP, accounting for one-quarter of the world's formal output.

In terms of employment, almost half (42 percent) of the world's informal workers can be found in South Asia (SAR), although the region accounts for just 9 percent of the world's formal employment and 3 percent of the world's formal output (Figure 3.2.1). Sub-Saharan Africa (SSA) is also over-represented in its share of informal employment, accounting for 14 percent of the world's total, well above its share of the world's formal output (2 percent) or formal employment (5 percent).

Informal-sector productivity in EMDE regions. In all EMDE regions, the proportion of informal employment exceeded the share of informal output, reflecting a tendency for the informal sector to be less productive than the formal sector (La Porta and Shleifer 2014; Fajnzylber, Maloney, and Montes-Rojas 2011). This difference is particularly pronounced for SAR and SSA, where the informal *employment* share is approximately double the informal output share.

Trend decline in informality. In all EMDE regions, the informal sector has steadily declined in relative importance since the 1990s. On average, informality has fallen by 5 percentage points of GDP since the 1990s, partially driven by economic development and improvement in governance. The decline in relative importance was largest in EAP and SAR with informality falling by 8 percentage points in both regions. Faster-than-average formalization of the economy in these two regions is likely to in part reflect faster-than-average per capita GDP growth since the 1990s. Conversely, informality in the Middle East and North Africa (MENA) decreased only modestly amid persistently weak growth and entrenched weak governance.

Within-region heterogeneity. The regions with the widest per capita income heterogeneity were also those with the widest range of informality as a share of output or employment. Informality is significantly more prevalent in lower-income economies within EAP despite the relatively low share of informal output for the region as a whole. In MENA, the non-Gulf Cooperation Council (GCC) economies have elevated levels of informality while the share for MENA as a whole is the lowest of all EMDE regions (Box 2.4). In contrast, in SSA, where the variation

---

Note: This box was prepared by Gene Kindberg-Hanlon with research assistance from Jinxin Wu and Zhuo Chen. It summarizes six boxes on the regional dimensions of informality featured in Chapter 2.

[1] For the purposes of this box, informal employment is proxied by self-employment because of good data coverage, and the regional disparities identified in this box are robust to other measures.

BOX 3.2 Regional dimensions of informality: An overview *(continued)*

FIGURE 3.2.1 Informality in EMDE regions

Informality is pervasive across all EMDEs—although the share of informal output in GDP has been falling over time, its incidence is higher in the poorest regions.

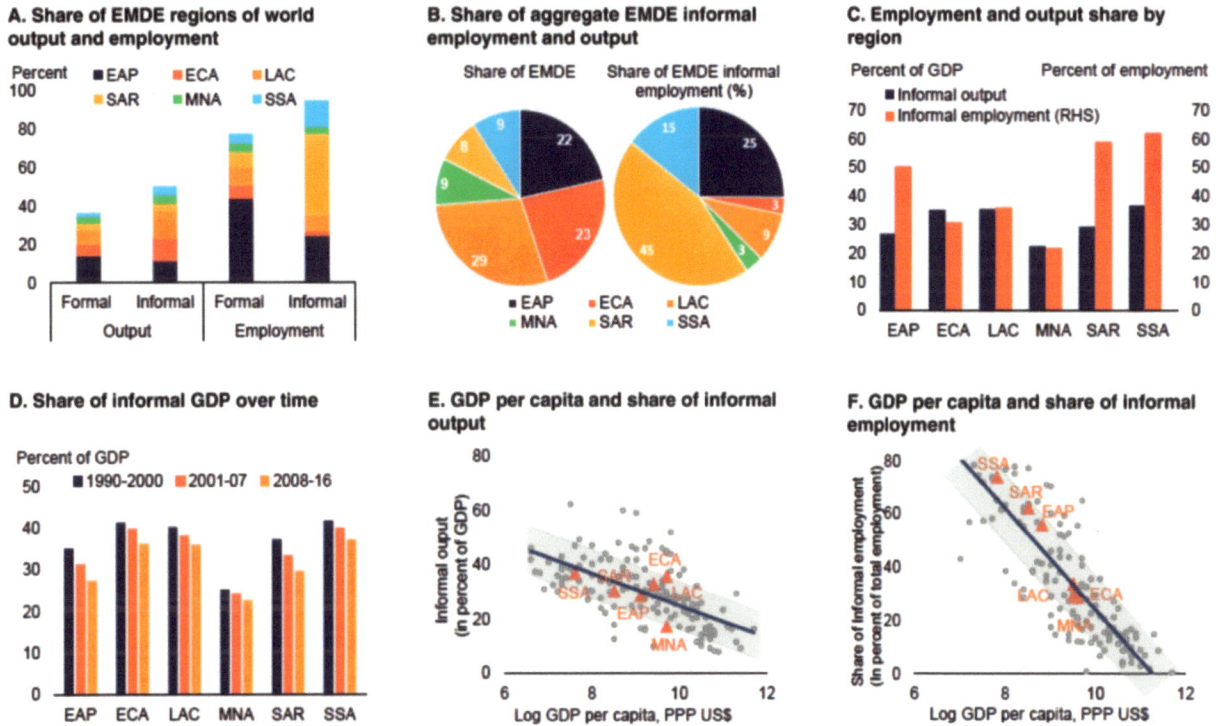

A. Share of EMDE regions of world output and employment

B. Share of aggregate EMDE informal employment and output

C. Employment and output share by region

D. Share of informal GDP over time

E. GDP per capita and share of informal output

F. GDP per capita and share of informal employment

Source: Elgin et al. (forthcoming a), World Bank.
Note: Data are between 2010 and 2016. EAP = East Asia and Pacific, ECA = Europe and Central Asia, LAC = Latin America and the Caribbean, MNA = Middle East and North Africa, SAR = South Asia, and SSA = Sub-Saharan Africa.
A.B. DGE-based estimates of informal output in each region as a proportion of total estimated informal GDP. Estimates of self-employment shares are used to proxy informal employment. Formal output equals official GDP. Estimates are based on their respective average shares of output and employment.
C. Mean of informal output (DGE-based estimates, percent of official GDP) and employment estimate (self-employment, percent of total employment) in each region.
D. Average DGE estimate of informal output relative to total output in each time period.
E.F. Grey markers show average log GDP (2011 PPP $ - averaged 2010-16) relative to DGE/SEMP estimate of informal output/employment for 154 and 147 economies respectively, with the fitted lines shown in blue and the corresponding +1 and -1 standard errors shown in shaded gray areas. Regional markers show median GDP per capita and median informal output/employment in EMDE regions.

of per capita incomes is one-fifth that of MENA (the EMDE region with the largest per capita income heterogeneity), informality amounted to over 30 percent of output and 39 percent of employment in three-quarters of countries.

What have been the correlates of informality across regions?

Informality is concentrated in countries which are less developed and suffer from a range of institutional weaknesses. Poverty and low human capital are strongly associated with those regions with the highest incidence of informality. In contrast, in wealthier regions such as LAC and ECA, institutional weaknesses and tax policy have contributed to elevated levels of informality.

Economic development. Informality is most prevalent in EMDE regions with low income per capita, reflecting the role of informality as both a driver and consequence of poverty (La Porta and Shleifer 2014). None of the regional shares of informal output or employment deviates statistically significantly from what might have been expected based on average per capita incomes alone (Figure 3.2.1).

Low human capital. Informality is also more prevalent where educational attainment is weak.[2] In SSA, where

_____

[2] Docquier, Müller, and Naval (2017) demonstrates that a sizeable informal sector that competes with the formal sector for low-skilled workers reduces the incentives to invest in human capital in the long run. In addition, weak educational attainment is a feature of lack of development, which contributes to informality (Loayza 2016).

BOX 3.2 Regional dimensions of informality: An overview (continued)

FIGURE 3.2.2 Regional correlates of informality

Informality is most prevalent in regions with poor educational attainment and large agricultural sectors. In some regions where tax avoidance is relatively easy, there is a strong relationship between the region's above-average tax rates and the level of informality.

A. Years of schooling, by EMDE region

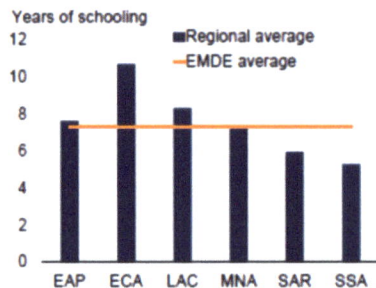

B. Share of agricultural sector in total output, by EMDE region

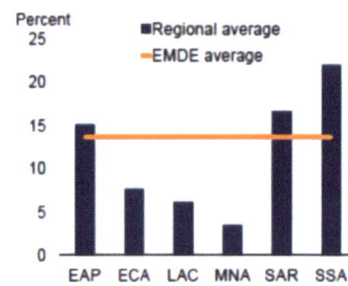

C. Corporate tax rates

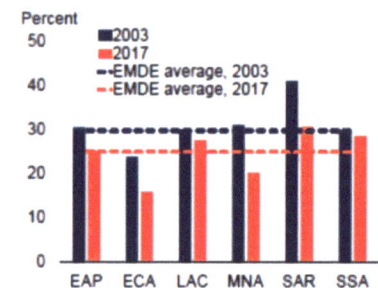

Sources: Barro and Lee (2013), Végh and Vuletin (2015), World Development Indicators, World Bank.
Note: EAP = East Asia and Pacific, ECA = Europe and Central Asia, LAC = Latin America and the Caribbean, MNA = Middle East and North Africa, SAR = South Asia, and SSA = Sub-Saharan Africa.
A. Average years of schooling for those aged 15 and older, taken from Barro and Lee (2013).
B. Average agricultural output as a percentage of total GDP.
C. Corporate tax rates are constructed as regional averages using Végh and Vuletin (2015).

educational attainment is the lowest on average among EMDEs, informal sector workers are much less likely to have completed primary education than those in the formal sector (Figure 3.2.2; Adams, de Silva, and Razmara 2013). Education levels have also been found to be an important correlate of informality in SAR, where attainment is also below the EMDE average.[3]

High regulatory and tax burdens. In LAC, several studies have found a strong relationship between the region's above-average tax rates and ease of tax avoidance, and the level of informality (Figure 3.2.2; Loayza 1996; Vuletin 2008; Ordóñez 2014). For ECA, labor market regulations that are more restrictive than elsewhere have been identified as drivers of informal employment (Fialová and Schneider 2011).

Weak institutions. Some economies in ECA have below-average institution quality, which may explain the region's slightly above-average degree of output informality despite ECA's relatively high per capita income. In non-GCC MENA economies, corruption has been cited among the biggest hindrances to firms which may increase incentives to operate informally (World Bank 2016).

Region-specific factors. A number of region-specific factors have contributed to informality.

- In ECA, a high share of informal output is partly a legacy of the collapse of the Soviet Union in the late 1980s and early 1990s as well large remittance inflows that have financed informal sector activity (Box 2.2).

- In some LAC economies, the trade liberalizations of the 1990s have been identified as contributors to growing informality, as formal firms that were unable to compete in a liberalized formal economy retreated into informality (Box 2.3).

- In MENA, although informality is particularly pronounced in non-GCC economies, in the GCC informality is low partly because of its heavy reliance on documented foreign workers and government employment (Box 2.4; World Bank 2018c).

- In SSA, large agricultural sectors help explain widespread informal employment as does the conflict and violence that have afflicted the region and forced people to earn their livelihoods in the informal economy (Box 2.6).

What policy options are available?

To mitigate the damaging effects associated with informality, policy responses can be tailored to the circumstances and drivers of informality in that economy. Policy options can be broadly split into several categories:

---

[3] Williams, Shahid, and Martinez (2016), Bahadur and Parajuli (2014), and Gunatikala (2008).

BOX 3.2 Regional dimensions of informality: An overview *(continued)*

Improving human capital. By investing in education and social services to improve human capital, policy makers can improve the productive capacity of workers that are currently uncompetitive in the formal sector. Training has been found to boost worker income and firm revenue in studies in the informal sectors of SSA and SAR (Verner and Verner 2005; Burki and Abbas 1991).

Improving access to public services and finance. Efforts to facilitate informal sector business can benefit informal sector workers and make them more competitive (Box 2.6; Sonobe, Akoten, and Otsuka 2011). For example, in SSA, providing informal traders public goods, such as a market to trade in or access to water and sanitation, has helped increase informal firm profitability and product quality. In SAR, a lack of access to financial resources is common for the self-employed (Ghani, Kerr, and O'Connell 2013; Box 2.5). Enabling access to microfinance has been found to increase investment and productivity in the informal sector (Likhi 2013; Donou-Adonsou and Sylwester 2017; Imai and Azam 2012).

Easing tax and regulatory burdens. Several studies in LAC have found that policies to reduce tax rates and simplify tax systems have incentivized firms to transition to the formal sector. Payroll or business tax cuts in Colombia, Brazil and Uruguay have been associated with higher formal employment and firm registration.[4] However, in regions where tax rates or tax compliance costs are not elevated, cutting taxes can be counterproductive in

reducing informality. In ECA, where corporate tax rates are lower than the EMDE average, *higher* taxation was associated with increased formalization in some studies because of the lack of public goods provided in regions with insufficient tax revenue (Fialová and Schneider 2011; Friedman et al. 2000). Separately, less restrictive employment protection has been associated with a smaller informal economy (both in employment and output) in ECA countries (Fialová and Schneider 2011: Lehmann and Muravyev 2009).

Tightening enforcement. Enforcement that is economically and socially sensible can help reduce the presence of the informal sector (Loayza 2018). In LAC, policies such as labor inspections have been found to induce informal workers and firms to formalize (De Andrade, Bruhn, and McKenzie 2013; and Almeida and Carneiro 2012). Studies in ECA, SAR and EAP have also found that lower levels of enforcement are associated with higher rates of informality (Box 3.4). Regulatory and tax compliance rates increase more if increased labor or tax inspections are accompanied by other measures such as awareness campaigns (Rani et al. 2013).

Reducing corruption. In ECA, where informality rose considerably following the disruptions associated with the collapse of the Soviet Union, higher corruption has been linked with higher informality (Friedman et al. 2000). Economies in ECA that were slower to implement structural reforms and control corruption in the 1990s saw a smaller-than-average decline in informality (Kaufmann and Kaliberda 1996). Corruption is also a key disincentive to enter the formal sector in MENA according to firm surveys.

[4] See Fernández and Villar (2016), Fajnzylber, Maloney, and Montes-Rojas (2011), and Monteiro and Assunção (2012).

Causes and implications of informality

Causes of informality. Theoretical models present two major reasons for the emergence of informal activity: lack of development (Harris and Todaro 1970; Loayza 2016), and poor governance including burdensome regulations, corruption, or poor public services (de Soto 1989).

- **Lack of development.** Informality has often been attributed to under-development. This reflects an inability of an urban modern

formal sector to absorb rural migrants during the urbanization process (Harris and Todaro 1970; Fields 1975; Loayza 2016). Development can further shrink the informal sector because households tend to shift away from agricultural and informal sector goods as their incomes grow (Saracoglu 2008). Finally, limited access to credit, often associated with less development, constrains informal firms' ability to overcome barriers to entry into the formal sector.[15]

[15] See Ferreira-Tiyaki (2008), D'Erasmo and Moscoso Boedo (2012), and Capasso and Jappelli (2013).

FIGURE 3.4 Changes in informality

Informality declined in EMDEs during the period 1990-2016, with the share of output dropping especially in East Asia and the Pacific, Latin America and Caribbean, and South Asia.

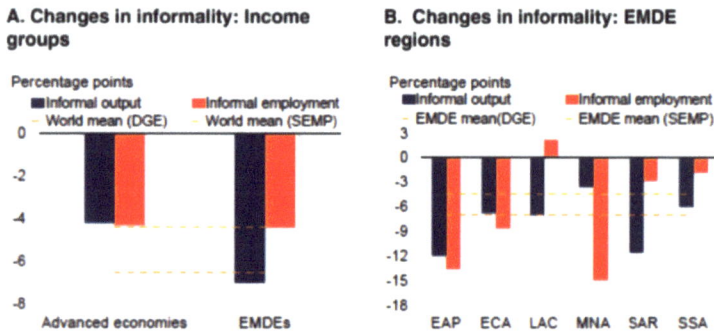

A. Changes in informality: Income groups

B. Changes in informality: EMDE regions

Source: Barro and Lee (2013), Elgin et al. (forthcoming a), World Bank (World Development Indicators).
Note: See Annex 3.1 for data definitions. Data are 1990-2016 group averages. EAP = East Asia and Pacific, ECA = Europe and Central Asia, LAC = Latin America and the Caribbean, MNA = Middle East and North Africa, SAR = South Asia, and SSA = Sub-Saharan Africa.
A. Unweighted group averages for advanced economies and EMDEs, with self-employment (in percent of total employment) shown in red and DGE-based informal output (in percent of official GDP) shown in blue. Unweighted world averages are shown in dashed lines.
B. Unweighted group averages for EMDE regions, with self-employment (in percent of total employment) shown in red and DGE-based informal output (in percent of official GDP) shown in blue. Unweighted EMDE averages are shown in dashed lines.

- **Heavy-handed regulation.** Higher taxation and heavy-handed regulation increases firms' incentives to reduce taxation or the cost of regulatory compliance by remaining informal (Ihrig and Moe 2004; Amaral and Quintin 2006; D'Erasmo and Moscoso Boedo, 2012; Auriol and Warlters, 2005; Prado 2011; Kanbur 2017; Dabla-Norris et al. 2018; Ulyssea 2018).[16] Excessive labor regulations encourage informal employment by increasing the cost of formal employment (Rauch 1991; Loayza 2016).

- **Poor governance.** Corruption and rent-seeking bureaucracies increase firms' incentives to avoid interaction with the state by remaining informal (Sarte 2000; Choi and Thum 2005; Freidman et al. 2000). Conversely, access to productivity-enhancing public goods, such as to electricity or the court system, can lead to an increase in the share of formal production (Mendicino and Prado 2014).

Implications of informality. A sizeable informal sector could impede growth, encourage poor governance, and limit a government's ability to reduce income inequality.

- **Slower growth.** A sizeable informal sector that competes with the formal sector for low-skilled workers reduces the incentives to invest in human and physical capital and new technologies and slows growth in the long run (Docquier, Müller, and Naval 2017; Loayza 1996; Sarte 2000).

- **Poor governance.** Several theoretical models attribute corruption and excessive regulations to the presence of an informal economy. Government officials are incentivized to impose excessive regulations and permits to have the power to collect bribes in return for providing permits (Shleifer and Vishny 1993). Others have argued that the government strategically designs a system of poor governance to promote informality for the poor, which acts as an alternative redistributive strategy (Marjit, Mukherjee, and Kolmar 2006).

Correlates of informality

The causes and implications of informality predicted by theoretical models are also confirmed by empirical studies as many correlates of informality are symptoms of under-development. A large informal economy is associated with weaker economic outcomes, such as a under-development, less access to credit, limited trade openness, less skilled labor force, as well as weaker output, investment and productivity growth (Box 3.3). Informality is also associated with less effective institutions, such as weak governance and excessive tax and regulatory burdens (Loayza, Oviedo, and Servén 2006; Enste and Schneider 1998).

Under-development. A lower level of development, as measured by per capita income, is associated with higher informality (Figure 3.6).[17]

---

[16] Also see Busato and Chiarini (2004), Charlot, Malherbet, and Terra (2015), Saracoğlu (2008), and Ordóñez (2014).

[17] See also Loayza, Servén, and Sugawara (2006) and La Porta and Shleifer (2014).

In the case of both output and employment informality, GDP per capita in countries with below-median ("low") informality is about 2-3 times of those in countries with above-median ("high") informality (Figure 3.6).[18] The lower productivity and resource misallocation associated with higher informality may also be reflected in slower output growth.[19]

Slower accumulation of physical and human capital. A larger informal economy is associated with a lower rate of output growth. This may reflect slower accumulation of physical or human capital (Ovedio, Thomas, and Karakurum-Ozdemir 2009). At the firm level, informality can limit access to conventional bank credit, because of a lack of documentation for assets and inadequate financial statements.[20] Investment activity in the informal sector may also be subdued because informal firms may be unwilling to adopt technologies that would make them more visible to tax and other authorities (Dabla-Norris and Inchauste 2008; Gandelman and Rasteletti 2017). For example, about 11,600 firms that participated in Enterprise Surveys in 18 countries during 2007-2014, the fraction of firms that invested in any given year in the formal sector was significantly higher than that in the informal sector. In the long run, the tendency to hire less skilled workers in the informal sector may slow human capital accumulation. Indeed, countries with below-median informality tend to have significantly higher levels of human capital (Maloney, 2004; Docquier, Müller, and Naval 2017; Figure 3.6).

Slower productivity growth. At the macroeconomic level, the evidence for a correlation between productivity growth and informality has been mixed (Perry et al. 2007; D'Erasmo and Moscoso Boedo 2012). At the firm level, in contrast, many studies have shown that informal firms tend to be less productive than

FIGURE 3.5 Characteristics of informal- and formal-economy business cycles

Informal-economy business cycles are not significantly different from formal-economy business cycles.

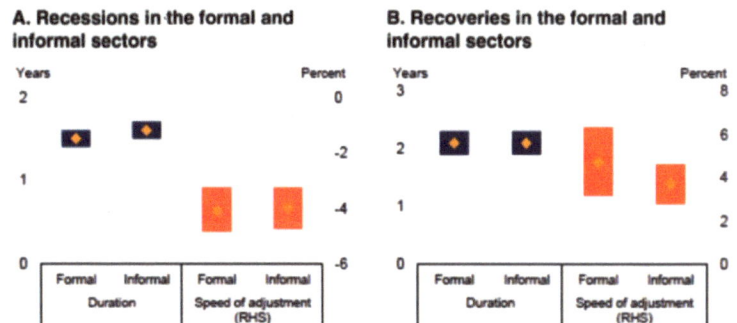

A. Recessions in the formal and informal sectors

B. Recoveries in the formal and informal sectors

Source: Elgin et al. (forthcoming a); Penn World Table; World Bank, World Development Indicators.
Note: Data are for the period 1990-2016. Diamonds indicate sample means; bars indicate 95 percent confidence intervals. Business cycle turning points are determined based on formal and informal GDP levels (i.e., official GDP statistics, DGE estimates) using the algorithm of Harding and Pagan (2002). Recession is defined as the phase from peak to trough, and recovery as the phase from trough to a return to pre-recession output levels. "Duration", and "Speed of adjustment" (often termed as "Slope") are defined as in Annex 3.2.

their formal counterparts; although this productivity differential in part reflects the characteristics of informal firms.[21] On average, informal labor productivity is lower than total labor productivity in EMDEs, although not in advanced economies (Figure 3.6; Loayza 2018). In addition, competition from informal firms has been associated with lower productivity of formal firms. The presence of informal competitors, which do not shoulder regulatory and tax burdens, can reduce formal firms' profitability, thus eroding their ability to invest in productivity-enhancing technologies or human capital (Perry et al. 2007; Box 3.3).

Less trade openness. A smaller informal sector is associated with greater economic openness, especially to trade.[22] On average, the trade-to-GDP ratio is lower by 17 percentage points in

---

[18] Median informality amounts to about 32 percent of GDP for DGE-based informal output and 34 percent of total employment for self-employment.

[19] See Hsieh and Klenow (2009), Loayza and Rigolini (2011), Docquier, Müller, and Naval (2017), Cirera and Maloney (2017), Levy (2018), and Bachas, Jaef, and Jensen. (2018).

[20] See Koeda and Dabla-Norris (2008) for details. Empirically, greater access to credit has been associated with lower informality (Maloney 2004; Straub 2005; La Porta and Shleifer 2014).

[21] La Porta and Shleifer (2014), Fajnzylber, Maloney, and Montes-Rojas (2011), de Mel, McKenzie, and Woodruff (2012), Demenet, Razafindrakoto, and Roubaud (2016), and McKenzie and Sakho (2010).

[22] Empirical studies, such as Goldberg and Pavcnik (2004, 2007), Sharma (2009), Boly (2018), and McCaig and Pavcnik (2018), show that informality declined following some trade liberalization episodes. Conversely, a short-term increase in informality has been attributed to trade liberalization amid inflexible labor markets in studies such as Goldberg and Pavcnik (2003), Attanasio, Goldberg and Pavcnik (2004), and Bosch, Goñi-Pacchioni, and Maloney (2012).

BOX 3.3 Casting a shadow: Productivity in formal and informal firms

The average informal firm in emerging market and developing economies (EMDEs) is only one-quarter as productive as the average firm operating in the formal sector. Moreover, firms in the formal sector that face informal competition are, on average, only three-quarters as productive as those that do not. This suggests that competition from the informal sector can erode formal firms' market share and resources available to boost productivity where formal firms shoulder the additional cost of regulatory compliance. More effective governance and stronger control of corruption can help mitigate these effects.

The productivity differential between formal and informal firms is well established in the literature (Loayza and Rigolini 2006; Oviedo 2009). However, there is mixed evidence on the impact of a large informal sector on formal firms' productivity. Some studies suggest that the informal and formal sectors operate independently so that there are no productivity spillovers (La Porta and Shleifer 2014). Others report that competition from the informal sector may erode the profitability of firms that operate in the formal sector, which leads to limited resources to enhance firm productivity.[1] The aggregate effect depends on country characteristics.

Against this backdrop, this box documents the productivity gap between formal and informal firms and their interactions. Specifically, it addresses the following questions:

- How large is the productivity differential between formal and informal firms?

- To what extent are formal firms exposed to informal competition?

- How does informal competition affect the productivity of formal firms?

Productivity differential between formal and informal firms

Literature review. The literature documents that informal firms in EMDEs are less productive than formal firms, with a productivity gap ranging between 30 to 216 percent (Perry et al. 2007; La Porta and Shleifer 2008). This productivity gap between informal and formal firms is attributed to modest technological improvements, reliance on unskilled labor, limited economies of scale, and restricted access to services, markets, and funding.[2] Moreover, labor productivity varies within the informal sector along different dimensions such as firm size

and type of activity (Amin and Huang 2014; Amin and Islam 2015).

Methodology. In this box, the productivity gap between formal and informal firms is estimated using World Bank's Enterprise Survey data collected over a period spanning 2007 to 2014 for a cross-section of 4,036 informal firms and 7,558 formal firms in 18 EMDEs (Annex Table 3.1). Formal firms are those that comply with tax, customs, labor, and licensing regulations and register with the relevant authorities; unregistered firms belong to the informal sector. To estimate the productivity gap, a measure of labor productivity—log annual sales in 2009 U.S. dollars per worker—is regressed on a dummy variable that takes the value 1 for informal firms and 0 otherwise and a set of control variables capturing additional firm characteristics (employment size, time in business, location, sector, country).[3]

Lower productivity in informal than formal firms. Virtually across the board, firm-level labor productivity is much lower in the informal sector than in the formal sector (Annex Table 3.1).[4] The productivity differentials vary widely in this sample, from 48 (Côte-d'Ivoire) to 93 percent (Argentina). On average across the whole sample, the productivity of informal firms is only one-quarter of the productivity of formal firms (Figure 3.3.1).

Drivers of productivity gap between informal and formal firms. Firm size, age, location in the capital city and manager experience are associated with significantly larger productivity gaps between informal and formal sectors (Figure 3.3.1, Annex Table 3.2).[5] Formal firms appear to be better equipped to reap the productivity benefits from size, age, and location than informal firms.

Note: This box was prepared by Mohammad Amin and Cedric Okou.

[1] Gonzalez and Lamanna (2007), Heredia et al. (2017), Mendi and Costamagna (2017).

[2] Jovanovic (1982), Amaral and Quintin (2006), Galiani and Weinschelbaum (2012).

[3] Commonly used revenue-based measures of productivity may conflate efficiency and price effects. Disentangling efficiency and price effects, by relying on physical productivity measures, may shed new light on productivity patterns, especially at the firm level (Jones and Nordhaus 2008; Cusolito and Maloney 2018).

[4] Exceptions are Democratic Republic of Congo and Cabo Verde possibly due to a low productivity of formal firms.

[5] The results are robust to comparing the coefficient estimates for the informal-firm dummy between a baseline regression including all controls and an alternative regression dropping each dummy one at a time (Annex Table 3.2).

BOX 3.3 Casting a shadow: Productivity in formal and informal firms *(continued)*

FIGURE 3.3.1 **Characteristics of informal firms**

Among informal firms, those with managers with higher education and those without any employees other than the owner are significantly more productive. The average informal firm in emerging market and developing economies has only one-quarter of the productivity of the average firm operating in the formal sector. This productivity differential between formal and informal firms is particularly pronounced among larger and older firms that operate in the capital city and are led by experienced managers.

A. Average productivity in formal and informal firms

B. Productivity differential between different types of informal firms

C. Productivity differential between formal and informal firms, by type of informal firms

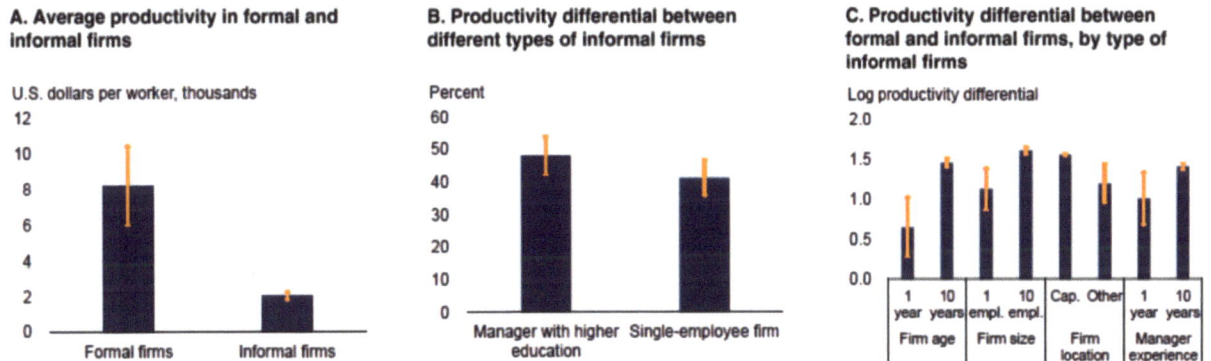

Source: World Bank.

Notes: World Bank's Enterprise Survey data for 135 countries (2008-18). Labor productivity is proxied by the annual sales in 2009 U.S. dollars per worker. Bars show the estimates with the corresponding +/- 2 standard errors shown in whiskers.

A. Labor productivity in the average formal and average informal firm, controlling for firm characteristics (firm size and age, manufacturing sector activity, location in the capital city and country fixed effects) as shown in column (1) in Annex Table 3.2.

B. Cross-country average of percent difference between labor productivity in the median informal firm with a manager with higher education or without any employees other than the owner, and the median informal firm with a manager without higher education or with more employees than the owner. Estimates from Annex Table 3.1.

C. Difference in log of labor productivity between the average formal and average informal firm in each group, as estimated in coefficient estimates of Annex Table 3.2. "Other" stands for "not located in capital city"; "Cap." stands for "located in capital city."

- *Firm age.* As firms grow older, they are either sufficiently productive to survive or they disappear ("selection effect"; Brandt, Van Biesenbroeck, and Zhang 2012). In addition, learning from experience may have taught older firms productivity gains ("learning effect"; Luttmer 2007). These effects appear to be much more pronounced among formal firms than among informal firms. As a result, the productivity differential between formal and informal firms widens as the age of firms increases. Among one-year-old firms, informal firms have about half the productivity of formal firms. Among ten-year-old firms, informal firms have less than one-quarter the productivity of formal firms.

- *Firm size.* Larger firms can reap economies of scale that raise their productivity compared to smaller firms. Again, in this sample, this effect appears to be stronger among formal firms than among informal firms. Among firms with one employee, informal firms have just under one-third the productivity of formal firms; among firms with ten employees, informal firms have less than one-quarter the productivity of formal firms.

- *Firm location.* Capital cities are typically among countries' largest economic centers and so can offer agglomeration benefits: larger markets, better infrastructure to access markets and operate, a larger pool of workers, greater technology spillovers (Rosenthal and Strange 2004; Duranton and Puga 2004). Again, formal firms appear to be better able to benefit from these locational advantages, but the effect is economically modest (although statistically significant). Among firms operating inside the capital city, informal firms' productivity is 31 percent that of similar formal firms; outside the capital city, informal firms' productivity is 30 percent that of similar formal firms.

- *Manager experience.* Managerial ability has been associated with higher productivity, through a variety of channels including hiring decisions and input choices (Fernandes 2008). Again, managerial experience appears to benefit formal firms' productivity more than informal firms' productivity. Among firms managed by managers with one year of experience, informal firms' productivity is just over one-third that of formal firms; among firms with

BOX 3.3 Casting a shadow: Productivity in formal and informal firms *(continued)*

managers with ten years of experience, informal firms' productivity is less than one-quarter that of formal firms.

Productivity differentials across informal firms. Labor productivity also differs across different types of informal firms, although the characteristics that are associated with higher labor productivity of informal firms differ across countries.[6] In two-fifths of countries, informal firms managed by a manager with higher education or without any employees other than the owner are significantly more productive than other informal firms (column (1) in Annex Table 3.2). Other informal firm characteristics, such as operating in the services sector or being a startup, are accompanied by higher productivity in some countries but lower productivity in other countries.

Productivity of formal firms amid high informality

Impact of informal competition on formal firms: Theory. The extent of competition between formal and informal firms depends on the underlying reasons for the existence of informal firms.[7]

Informality as a survival strategy of unproductive firms. Low-productivity firms may be forced into informal operations or, even if they operate formally, employing informal workers because this may reduce their costs (Ulyssea 2018; Boly 2018). Operating in the informal sector and employing informal labor may, therefore, be a survival strategy for less-productive firms that belong to fundamentally different markets (La Porta and Shleifer 2014). "Surviving" informal firms are likely to operate in very different markets and sell different products than formal firms (La Porta and Shleifer 2014). In such circumstances, competition between informal and formal firms and its impact on formal firms may be limited.

Informality as an evasion strategy of productive firms. Some informal firms may be sufficiently productive to survive in

the formal sector yet choose to remain informal to benefit from the cost advantage of noncompliance with (possibly excessive) taxes and regulations (Maloney 2004; de Mel, McKenzie, and Woodruff 2011).[8] Such informal firms could constitute an untapped potential for a productivity boost (de Soto 1989). On the other hand, they can create aggressive competition with formal firms that do shoulder the additional cost of tax and regulatory compliance. Such informal competition can reduce the profitability necessary for formal firms to invest in productivity-enhancing new technologies or to innovate, especially in a context of weak property rights enforcement.[9] Alternatively, this very competition could force formal firms to increase productivity or, for the lowest-productivity ones, to exit.[10]

Extent of informal-firm competition for formal firms. In the World Bank's nationally representative survey data for 75,137 formal (registered) firms in 135 countries between 2008 and 2018, about 55 percent of formal firms reported facing competition form informal firms.[11] The share of informal firms competing against formal firms was about 60 percent in EMDEs, 13 percentage points higher than in advanced economies. The level of competition varied widely across countries, ranging from about 7 percent in Bhutan to 95 percent in Uganda. Smaller firms were significantly more likely to be exposed to informal competition than larger firms but there is little evidence of any other systematic difference between firms that were exposed and those that were not (Figure 3.3.2).

Impact of informal competition on the productivity of formal firms

Methodology. OLS regressions are used to estimate the difference in labor productivity between formal firms that compete against informal firms and those that do not. In the baseline specification, the dependent variable is again

---

[6] Haltiwanger, Lane, and Spletzer (1999), Maloney (2004), |Deininger, Jin, and Sur (2007), de Mel, McKenzie, and Woodruff (2011), Grimm et al. (2012), Amin and Huang (2014), Amin and Islam (2015), Islam (2018).

[7] This discussion assumes that firms are either formal or informal. In practice, the degree of informality can vary (Perry et al 2007; Ulyssea 2018). At the extensive margin are firms that operate fully informally, in product markets and labor markets. They sell their output informally and employ informal labor. At the intensive margin are firms that operate semi-formally: they sell their output into formal product markets but employ, in part, informal labor, as observed in EMDEs and LICs.

[8] Such circumstances are likely to be associated with an environment of weak regulatory and tax enforcement (Quintin 2008; Dabla-Norris, Gradstein, and Inchauste 2008; Ulyssea 2010; Benjamin and Mbaye 2012).

[9] This has been documented for some Latin America countries, India, Poland, Portugal, Russia, and Turkey. For evidence, see Heredia et al. (2017), Perry et al. (2007), Farrell (2004), Capp, Elstrodt, and Jones (2005), Cunha (2006), Gonzalez and Lamanna (2007), Friesen and Wacker (2013), Allen and Schipper (2016), Iriyama, Kishore, and Talukda (2016), and Distinguin, Rugemintwari, and Tacneng (2016).

[10] This has been documented for Egypt, see Ali and Najman (2017); Melitz (2003); Schipper (2016).

[11] In the World Bank's Enterprise Surveys, formal firms are asked the following question: "Does this establishment compete against unregistered or informal firms?"

BOX 3.3 Casting a shadow: Productivity in formal and informal firms (continued)

FIGURE 3.3.2 Formal firms facing informal competition

On average, more than half (55 percent) of formal firms reported facing informal competition. Nearly 60 percent of formal firms in EMDEs were exposed to informal competition whereas 47 percent of formal firms in advanced economies reported facing informal competition. The degree of informal competition reported by formal firms was higher for smaller than larger firms, but comparable across sectors or formal firms' productivity.

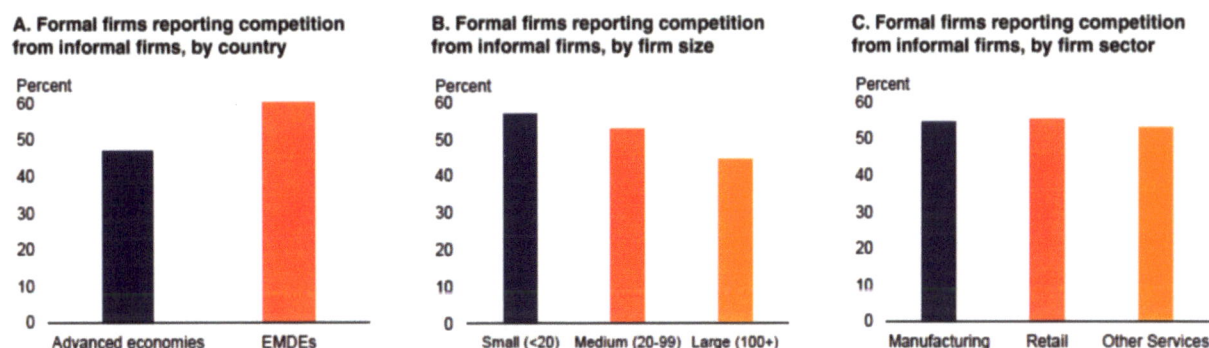

A. Formal firms reporting competition from informal firms, by country

B. Formal firms reporting competition from informal firms, by firm size

C. Formal firms reporting competition from informal firms, by firm sector

Source: World Bank.
Note: World Bank's Enterprise Survey data for 135 countries (2008-18). Figures show the shares of formal firms.

labor productivity measured by the (log of) annual sales in 2009 U.S. dollars per worker. The main explanatory variable is the informal competition indicator proxied by the proportion of formal firms in a cell that report facing competition from informal firms. A cell is defined as a group of firms of similar size and in the same region and sector.[12]

Productivity gap between formal firms with and without informal competition. Formal firms that face informal competition are, on average, 24 percent less productive than those that do not (Figure 3.3.3; Annex Table 3.3). After controlling for the informal competition, formal firms in the manufacturing and retail industries have higher productivity than those in other services. Older, exporting, and foreign-owned formal firms also have higher productivity even if they face competition from informal firms.

Role of the business climate and development. Economic development and the business climate may substantially

shape the productivity gap between formal firms that face informal competition and those that do not. This is captured in interaction terms between the share of similar formal firms reporting informal competition and indicators of development (the logarithm of per capita GDP), the quality of business climate as proxied by the distance to the frontier in the Doing Business Index, the control of corruption of the World Governance Indicators, and the Business Freedom index of the Economic Freedom indicators (Annex Table 3.3). Higher GDP per capita, better control of corruption, and a business environment that is freer and closer to best-practices dampen the detrimental impact of informal competition on formal firm productivity.

- *Development.* The sample is split into those countries with per capita income in the highest quartile in the sample and those in the lowest quartile in the sample. Formal firms that face informal competition in the average country with the highest per capita incomes are only 14 percentage point less productive than formal firms that do not face such competition. In contrast, on average in countries in the lowest quartile of per capita incomes, formal firms facing informal competition are 30 percent less productive than those firms that do not face such competition.

- *Control of corruption.* Again, the sample is split into those countries in the quartile of countries with the

---

[12]As a caveat, the informal competition faced by a specific firm may also be driven by its productivity, thus generating endogeneity concerns. To address possible endogeneity issue, we use the proportion of formal firms facing informal competition in a group of firms of similar size in the same region and sector (a "cell") rather than a firm dummy. A cell proportion should be much less correlated with the productivity of a specific firm, and therefore, should be more robust to endogeneity concerns.

BOX 3.3 Casting a shadow: Productivity in formal and informal firms *(continued)*

FIGURE 3.3.3 Productivity of formal firms facing informal competition

On average, formal firms that face informal competition have only three-quarters of the productivity of firms that do not face informal competition, after controlling for firm characteristics. Better business climates and governance and more economic development can narrow this productivity differential.

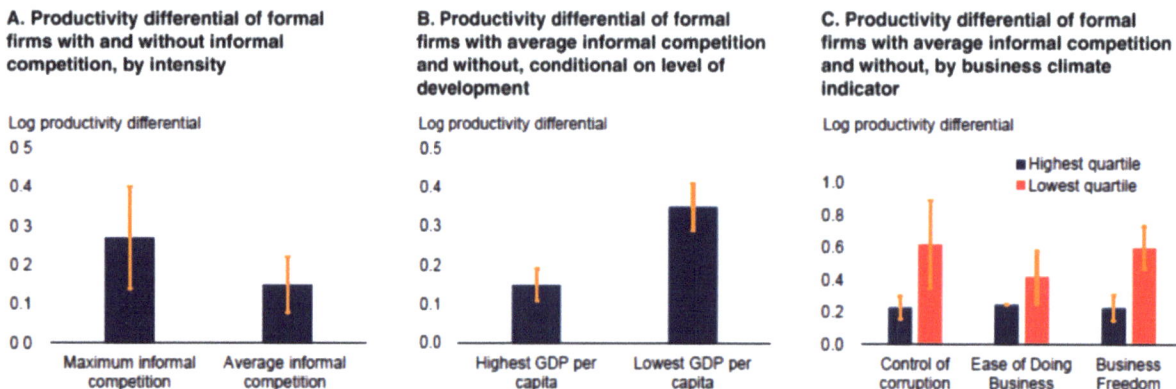

A. Productivity differential of formal firms with and without informal competition, by intensity

B. Productivity differential of formal firms with average informal competition and without, conditional on level of development

C. Productivity differential of formal firms with average informal competition and without, by business climate indicator

Source: World Bank.

Note: Based on coefficient estimates from Annex Table 3.3, which shows results from an OLS regression with labor productivity as the dependent variable, as proxied by annual sales (in 2009 U.S. dollars, in thousands, logs) per worker, in a sample of World Bank's Enterprise Survey data collected during 2007-14 for 4,036 informal firms and 7,558 formal firms in 18 countries. Bars show the estimates with the corresponding +/- 2 standard errors shown in whiskers.

A. Log productivity differential between formal firms facing informal competition and formal firms not facing informal competition. Maximum informal competition assumes that all firms in a cell face informal competition. Average informal competition assumes that 55 percent of firms in a cell face informal competition.

B-C. Log productivity differential between formal firms facing informal competition and formal firms not facing informal competition, conditional on development and institutional quality. It is assumed that 55 percent of firms in a cell face informal competition. Each bar conditions on the GDP per capita (B), control of corruption (C), ease of Doing Business (C), or Business Freedom index (C) of the median country in the top ("highest quartile") or bottom ("lowest quartile") quarter of countries in terms of GDP per capita, control of corruption, ease of Doing Business, or Business Freedom index.

strongest control of corruption and those in the quartile with the weakest control of corruption. In countries with the strongest control of corruption, on average, formal firms that face informal competition are only 22 percentage point less productive than formal firms that do not face such competition, whereas in the countries with the weakest control of corruption, this differential grows to 35 percent.

- ***Ease of Doing Business.*** Similarly, the productivity differential between formal firms that face informal competition and those that do not might halve (to 21 percent) if a country like Angola (in the quartile of countries with the most difficult business climates) were to improve its business climate to the level of a country like the Former Yugoslav Republic of

Macedonia (among the countries with the most conducive business climates).

Conclusion

The productivity gap between informal and formal firms is substantial in EMDEs, averaging 75 percent in a sample of 18 EMDEs between 2007-14. Competition from informal firms also appears to weigh on the productivity of exposed formal firms: the productivity of formal firms that compete with informal firms is only three-quarters that of formal firms that do not compete with informal firms, after controlling for other firm characteristics. Improvements in the business climate, and economic development more broadly, can mitigate some of these negative productivity spillovers from informal to formal firms.

countries with a greater share of self-employment than countries with a smaller share of self-employment (Figure 3.6).[23] Similarly, higher capital account openness is associated with less output and employment informality. That said, the impact of major trade liberalization episodes on informality varies across countries and differs between the short and the long term (Box 3.4; Goldberg and Pavcnik 2003; Fugazza and Fiess 2010; Dix-Carneiro and Kovak 2017).

Heavier regulatory burden. Both empirical and theoretical studies suggest that heavier regulatory (or administrative) burdens may encourage informality as workers and firms join the informal sector to avoid regulatory and administrative compliance costs.[24] The Doing Business distance-to-frontier scores for countries with below-median informality (by DGE estimates) is 60 points—which is significantly higher (by about 6 points or three-fifths of a standard deviation) than in countries with high (above-median) output informality (Figure 3.6). Similarly, the Business Freedom index is 7.5 points (about half of a standard deviation) higher in countries with low (below-median) output informality than in countries with high (above-median) informality.

Weaker governance. Research points to the contribution of poor governance to the pervasive informality in some EMDEs, especially in Latin America and the Caribbean and Europe and Central Asia regions (Box 3.2).[25] On average, countries with above-median informality over the period 1990-2016 have had weaker government

FIGURE 3.6 Correlates of informality: Economic and institutional factors

Higher informality is associated with lower levels of development, poorer access to credit, heavier regulatory burdens, and weaker governance.

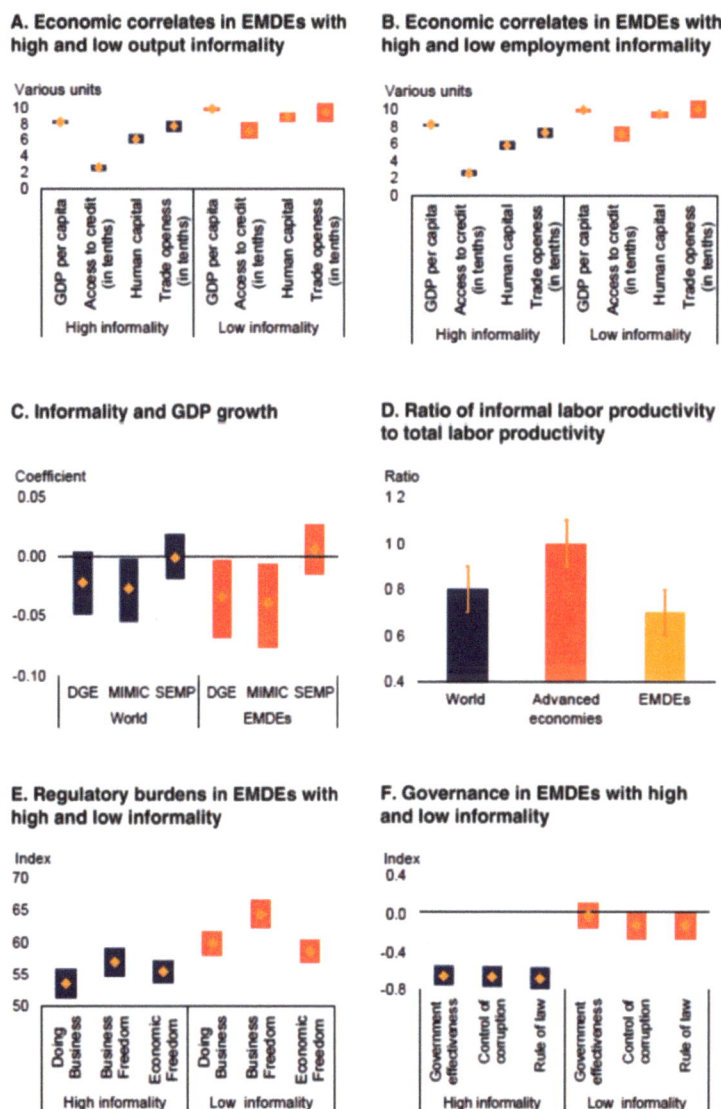

A. Economic correlates in EMDEs with high and low output informality

B. Economic correlates in EMDEs with high and low employment informality

C. Informality and GDP growth

D. Ratio of informal labor productivity to total labor productivity

E. Regulatory burdens in EMDEs with high and low informality

F. Governance in EMDEs with high and low informality

Source: Barro and Lee (2013), Elgin et al. (forthcoming a), Heritage Foundation, World Bank (Doing Business, World Development Indicators, World Governance Indicators).
Note: Data are between 1990 and 2016.The corresponding 90 percent confidence intervals are shown as bars (except in D).
A.-B. The group means for the following correlates are calculated for EMDEs with "high informality" (i.e., above median DGE-based informal output measure, A; above median self-employment share, B) and those with "low informality" (i.e., below median DGE-based informal output measure, A; below median self-employment share, B) over the period 1990-2016: GDP per capita (in logs, PPP, constant 2011 international $, WDI), access to credit (i.e., private sector credit in percent of GDP); human capital (i.e., average years of schooling), trade openness (i.e. the sum of exports and imports in percent of GDP).
C. Annual GDP growth rates are regressed against the six measures of informality while controlling for real GDP per capita (in logs, WDI).
D. The average relative ratio of informal labor productivity over total labor productivity in 2016 are shown in bars for advanced economies, EMDEs, and world, with corresponding 95 percent confidence interval shown in orange vertical bars. The relative ratio is calculated using DGE-based estimates and the share of self-employment following the method in Loayza (2018).
E.-F. Unweighted group averages over the period 1990-2016 (shown as the orange diamonds) for EMDEs with high informality (above median DGE-based informal output measure) and those with low informality are shown for the following correlates: Doing Business (measured as the overall distance to frontier with 100 being the frontier and 0 being the farthest from the frontier, Doing Business); Business Freedom and Economic Freedom (Heritage Foundation); government effectiveness, control of corruption, and rules of law (as defined in World Governance Indicators).

---

[23] However, the trade-to-GDP ratio is not different between countries with a greater share of informal output than countries with a smaller share of informal output.

[24] Perry et al. (2007), Ulyssea (2010), Bruhn (2011), de Mel, McKenzie, and Woodruff (2013), Rocha, Ulyssea, and Rachter (2018).

[25] Loayza, Oviedo, and Servén (2006) find that poorer bureaucratic quality is associated with more informality. Choi and Thum (2005) and Dreher and Schneider (2010) report an association between higher informality and weaker law and order and control of corruption. Iriyama, Kishore, and Talukda (2016) show that firms are more likely to engage in corruption when facing competition from informal firms. Dabla-Norris, Gradstein, and Inchauste (2008) show that the quality of the legal framework is important in determining the size of the informal sector. Loayza and Wada (2010) estimate, for example, that 75 percent of the difference in labor informality between Peru and Chile is due to causes related to poor governance.

FIGURE 3.7 EMDEs: Correlates of changes in informality

Among EMDEs, countries with larger declines in informality also have faster physical accumulation, improved access to credit, and better governance.

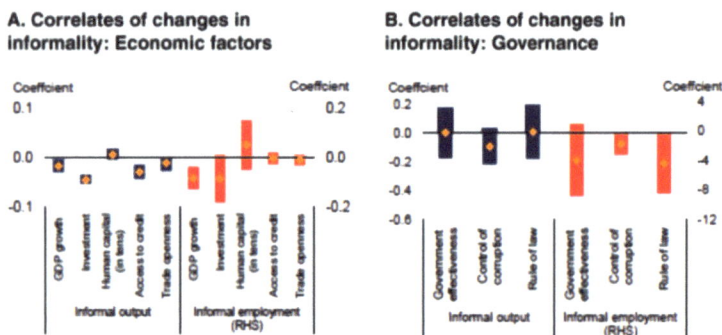

A. Correlates of changes in informality: Economic factors

B. Correlates of changes in informality: Governance

Source: Barro and Lee (2013), Elgin et al. (forthcoming a), World Bank (World Development Indicators, World Governance Indicators).
Note: See Annex 3.1 for data definitions. Data between 1990 and 2016 in EMDEs are used here.
A-B. Diamonds show the coefficient estimates obtained from regressing the annual change in informal output (DGE-based estimates in percent of official GDP) or informal employment (self-employment in total employment) upon annual changes in various economic and governance indicators, with the corresponding 90 percent confidence intervals shown in bars. The indicators include real GDP growth, investment (in percent of GDP), access to credit (private sector credit in percent of GDP), human capital (average years of schooling), trade openness (the sum of exports and imports in percent of GDP) and three measures from WGI (2018). Fixed-effects estimators are used here.

effectiveness (by about 0.6 points, or three-quarters of a standard deviations) than countries with below-median informality (Figure 3.6). Similar differences are found in the case of control of corruption and rule of law. For example, in Georgia, during the period 1996-2016, the transition to a market economy brought significant improvements in government effectiveness, control of corruption, and rule of law. With output growth averaging about 6 percent per year, the share of informal output fell by 9 percentage points of GDP, and the share of informal employment in total employment fell by a similar magnitude.

Correlates of the decline in informality since 1990. The decline in informality was larger in countries with the bigger improvements in governance and, for output informality, faster growth in GDP and investment, and better access to credit (Figure 3.7).[26] Perceptions of informality appear to change much more slowly than actual

informal output and employment shares. Since 2000, perceptions have shifted significantly (into a different quartile of informality) in only 14 percent of all EMDEs (Elgin et al. forthcoming a).

Informality, poverty, and income inequality

Many studies document that informal-sector wages are below those in the formal sector, for a variety of reasons.[27] This raises concerns that, over the long term, informality may entrench earnings differentials and income inequality and may contribute to greater poverty in countries with high informality.[28]

Worker earnings differentials

Causes of wage differentials. Lower wage in the informal sector could result from different worker characteristics in the formal and informal sectors, possibly in response to the comparative advantage that some workers might have in informal sector activities, or to non-wage benefits that might accrue to work in the informal sector (Maloney 2004; Heckman and Li 2003). Alternatively, wage differentials could stem from rigidities and other factors that create a wedge in wages between similar workers in informal and formal employment. These factors can include labor regulations or tax provisions that force workers into the informal sector (Harris and Todaro 1970). An alternative to measuring wage differentials could be an assessment of the subjective well-being or job satisfaction of workers in the formal and informal sectors where workers benefit from flexibility and independence (e.g., Blanchflower, Oswald, and Stutzer 2001; Sanfey and Teksoz 2007; Falco et al. 2015).

---

[26] A panel regression suggests that faster declines in the share of agricultural employment and faster increases in the share of industrial employment are associated with larger long-term reductions in informality, controlling for per capita GDP.

[27] Perry et al. (2007), Marcouiller, de Castilla, and Woodruff (1997), Tansel and Kan (2012), Bargain and Kwenda (2014), Goldberg and Pavcnik (2003), Pavcnik et al. (2004), Goldberg and Pavcnik (2003, 2007), and Paz (2014) all document the existence of wage premia. Pratap and Quintin (2006), El Badaoui, Strobl, and Walsh (2008), El Badaoui, Strobl, and Walsh (2010) caution that this premium disappears depending on model specifications, estimation methods or country samples.

[28] The linkage between informality and poverty could also be due to the absence of better formal jobs in underdeveloped countries (Perry et al. 2007).

Methodology: Meta-Regression Analysis. A meta-regression analysis is employed to aggregate estimates of the formal wage premium from a set of studies to obtain a quantitative assessment of the sources of cross-study variation. The analysis focuses on 18 studies that test for the presence of significant wage differentials between formal and informal jobs, and its main sources (a detailed review of literature and methodology are presented in Annex 3.3). As is common practice in such meta-regression analyses, no study is excluded ex ante based on its source or its results, but rather the selection of studies is constrained to those that present numerical estimates with confidence bands for country samples since 2000.

Empirical estimates of wage differentials. The estimates of the wage differential between informal and formal workers in the 18 studies selected here range from a formal sector wage penalty of 50 percent in Tajikistan (Huber and Rahimov 2014) to a premium of 113 percent in South Africa (El Badaoui, Strobl, and Walsh 2008). The average formal wage premium in the studies is 19 percent (Figure 3.8). This wage differential between formal and informal jobs is particularly wide in LAC and SSA but below-average in ECA and SAR. It is also larger for informally employed than self-employed workers. Self-employed and contributing family members (predominantly women) constitute the majority of informal workers in developing Asia and Africa, whereas informal employees dominate the informal sector in ECA and in LAC (ILO 2018b).[29] Wage premia in the formal sector tend to be higher where informality is more widespread.[30]

Sources of observed wage differentials. The formal wage premium largely disappears in studies that control for unobserved characteristics of workers. Informal employment tends to be associated with lower education and with workers

FIGURE 3.8 EMDEs: Estimates of informal-formal wage gap

Estimates of informal-formal wage gaps vary considerably across countries and definitions of informality. Countries in Latin America and the Caribbean and Sub-Saharan Africa tend to exhibit both a higher incidence of informality and a larger wage premium in the formal sector.

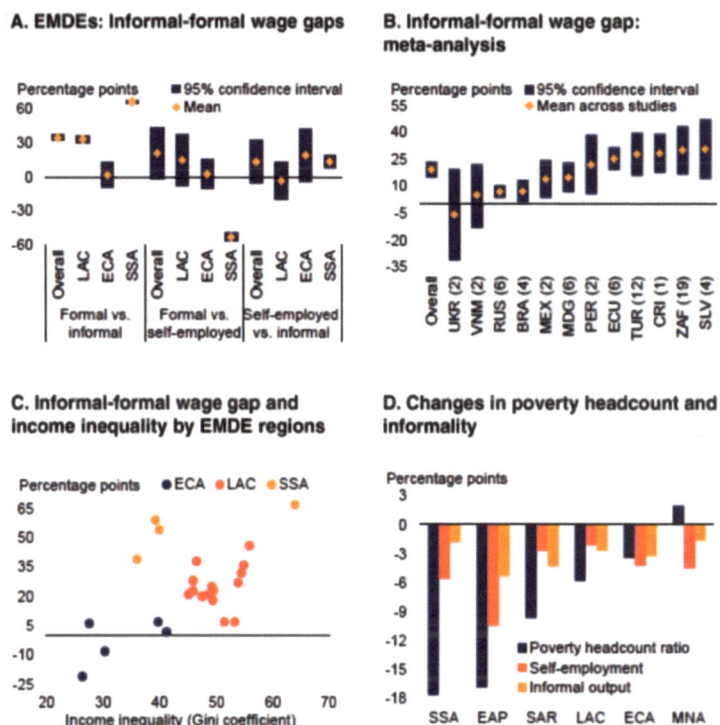

A. EMDEs: Informal-formal wage gaps

B. Informal-formal wage gap: meta-analysis

C. Informal-formal wage gap and income inequality by EMDE regions

D. Changes in poverty headcount and informality

Source: Elgin et al. (forthcoming a); Gindling, Mossaad, and Newhouse (2016); World Bank, World Development Indicators.
Note: A positive wage gap indicates a penalty for working informally—a lower wage for informal workers than for comparable formal workers; a negative wage gap indicates a premium for working informally—a higher wage for informal workers than for comparable formal workers. EMDE regions include ECA=Europe and Central Asia, EAP=East Asia and Pacific, LAC=Latin America and the Caribbean, MNA=Middle East and North Africa, SAR=South Asia Region, and SSA=Sub-Saharan Africa. Wage gap between wage employees in the informal and formal sectors is displayed on the vertical axis in A-C.
A. Formal vs. informal=a wage gap between wage employees in the formal and informal sectors; formal vs. self-employed=a wage gap between workers with formal jobs and self-employed workers; self-employed vs. informal: a wage gap between self-employed workers and wage employees in the informal sector.
B. UKR=Ukraine, VNM=Vietnam, RUS=Russia, BRA=Brazil, MEX=Mexico, MDG=Madagascar, PER=Peru, ECU=Ecuador, TUR=Turkey, CRI=Costa Rica, ZAF=South Africa, SLV=El Salvador. The number of studies or estimates for each country is shown in parenthesis; country means are calculated using a random-effects meta-analysis model.
C. Income inequality is measured as Gini coefficient provided by WDI.
D. Self-employment is the percent of self-employed in total employment. Poverty headcount is the poverty headcount ratio at $1.90 a day (2011 PPP, percent of population). Informal output is the GDP weighted average of the World Bank country estimates of the informal output as a percent of official output. Average changes for these measures during the period 2005-15 are shown here.

---

[29] In many EMDEs, informal employment is generally a more important source of employment for women than men and, for women, a more important source than formal employment (Chen, Vanek, and Heintz 2006; ILO 2017).

[30] The association between the level of wage premia in the formal sector and the level of informality could be driven by the stricter labor regulations that raise both wages and informality (Rauch 1991; Loayza 2016).

that are, on average, either younger or older than in the formal sector. It is also more prevalent in rural areas, where there are fewer alternatives in the formal sector, and among women (Hazans 2011; Gasparini and Tornarolli 2007). The informal sector employs more low-skilled labor than the formal sector, which can slow human

FIGURE 3.9 Informality, poverty, and income inequality

A larger informal economy is associated with higher poverty rates and income inequality. It is also linked with smaller declines in poverty rates.

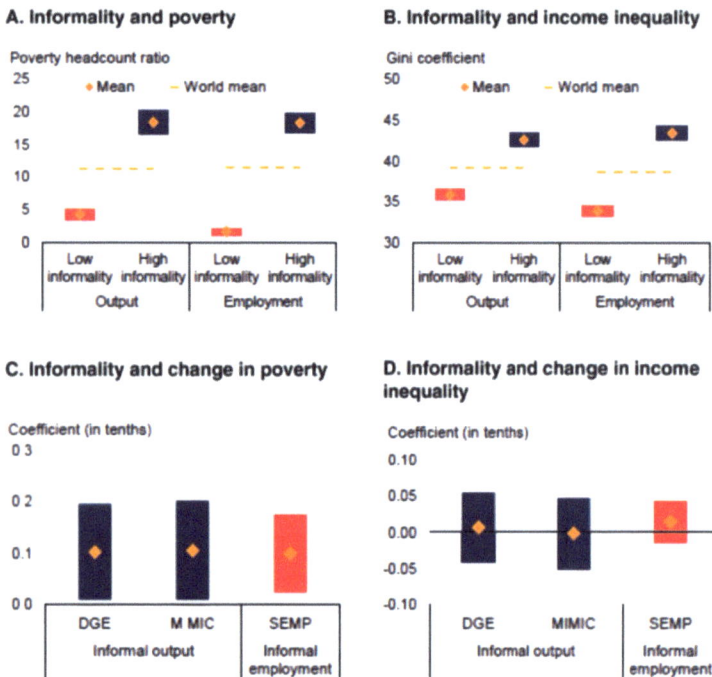

A. Informality and poverty

B. Informality and income inequality

C. Informality and change in poverty

D. Informality and change in income inequality

Source: Elgin et al. (forthcoming a); World Bank, World Development Indicators.
Note: See Annex 3.1 for data definitions. "SEMP" is the share of self-employment in percent of total employment.
A.B. The average measure of poverty (i.e. the poverty headcount ratio at $1.90 a day at 2011 PPP exchange rate in percent of the population) and Gini coefficient (World Bank estimates) over 1990-2016 for countries with higher informality (above median) and those with lower informality (below median) are shown in diamonds with the 95 percent confidence intervals shown in bars. Output informality is measured as DGE-based informal output in percent of official GDP, while employment informality is measured as self-employment in percent of total employment.
C.D. Estimates from Annex Table 3.4.1. Informality indicators are averages over 1990-2005. Control variable, initial level of poverty rate (earliest year over 1990-2005), is included (the same applies to Gini index). The dependent variable is an annual change in poverty headcount ratio at $1.90 a day (2011 PPP, percent of population) over the earliest year and the latest year (as in C; or the annual change in Gini index over the earliest and the latest year in D). For the comparison and scaling issues, coefficients of DGE, MIMIC, and self-employment are multiplied by 10. Estimated coefficients are shown in diamonds while the corresponding 90 percent confidence intervals (calculated from robust standard error) are shown in bars. The results are robust when controlling for initial GDP per capita.

capital accumulation in the long run (Docquier, Müller, and Naval 2017). Thus, differences in characteristics of workers (e.g., education) largely account for the formal sector wage premium.

Aggregate income inequality and poverty

The wage gap between the formal economy and the informal economy has been associated with persistent income inequality and poverty.[31]

Conversely, the decline in poverty rates across all EMDEs regions (and especially in SAR and SSA) during 2005-15 was accompanied by a contraction of informal activities (Figure 3.8). At the country-level, a larger informal economy is associated with a higher poverty headcount (Figure 3.9). However, the direction of causality between informality and poverty remains an open question.

Regression analysis. The relationship between pre-existing informality and changes in the share of the population living in extreme poverty (i.e., the poverty headcount ratio at $1.90 a day at 2011 PPP exchange rate in percent of the population) or the Gini coefficient (World Bank estimates) is estimated in an ordinary least squares regression. Specifically, the annual average change in the poverty headcount ratio (or Gini coefficient) between the latest (in the period 2011-16) and earliest available data (in the period 1990-2005) for up to 74 countries is regressed on 1990-2005 average informality. To mitigate concerns about endogeneity, time horizons considered for informality measures precede those for the change in the poverty rate or Gini coefficient (Loayza, Servén, and Sugawara 2010; Annex 3.4). The regression controls for the initial level of poverty (or Gini coefficient) and income per capita, using the earliest available income data.

Pre-existing informality and changes in poverty. The estimated impact of pre-existing informality on changes in the poverty rate (but in this sample not on inequality) is statistically significant (Figure 3.9).[32] The association with changes in poverty is similar for employment and output informality. In the average EMDE, the share of extreme poor in the population (the headcount ratio) declined by about 0.8 percentage point between 2011 and 2016. These estimates imply that a country with a 10 percentage points higher share of informal output than its peers witnessed 0.1 percentage point slower poverty reduction per year.

---

[31] Chong and Gradstein (2007), Amaral and Quintin (2006); Pratap and Quiten (2006), and Loayza, Servén, and Sugawara (2010).

[32] This is in line with other studies that find an insignificant relationship between inequality and informality after controlling for institutional outcomes (Perry et al. 2007) or focus on causality running from inequality to informality (Chong and Gradstein 2007).

BOX 3.4 Under the magnifying glass: How do policies affect informality?

Country-specific studies have found that reductions in tax and regulatory burdens have often been associated with lower informality. In contrast, trade liberalization that raised the competition level in the tradable sector has been associated with greater informality in the short run, unless it was accompanied by measures that increase labor market flexibility. The reduction in informality was greater for reforms accompanied by business development and training programs, public awareness campaigns and stronger enforcement.

Cross-country studies have identified a range of policies associated with lowering informality. These policies have typically fallen into three categories: tax reform, regulatory reform, and trade liberalization.[1]

- **Tax reform.** Lower tax rates, simplified tax systems, harmonized tax regulations, technology-based monitoring and consolidated electronic tax payment systems can encourage firms and workers in the informal sector to move to the formal sector.

- **Regulatory reform.** Lower minimum wages and lower barriers to worker recruitment and dismissal have been associated with lower informal activity. In addition, a wide range of institutional factors have been associated with reduced informality: more efficient legal systems, better property rights protection, lower regulatory burdens, less cumbersome registration processes, easier access to credit, and lower corruption.

- **Trade liberalization.** In Latin America, trade liberalization has often been followed by an increase in informal activity in the short run, unless accompanied by complementary measures to increase labor market flexibility. Trade liberalization raises real wages, by depressing prices, and thus encourages worker entry into the informal economy where entry cost is lower than in the formal economy (Arias et al. 2018).

Many EMDEs have implemented these types of reforms either with the explicit purpose of reducing informal activity, or for other purposes with collateral effects on informal activity. Many of these reforms were implemented as part of broad-based, multi-pronged reform packages. Against this backdrop, this box compiles a comprehensive review of single-country studies on the impact of policy changes on informal activity. Specifically, the box addresses the following questions:

- Which policy changes have been studied?

- What are the common lessons from these policy changes?

- What is the role of complementary policy measures?

Studies of policy changes

Selection of studies. 19 studies are selected based on two criteria: (1) they examine specific policy changes in a single EMDE and (2) they measure an outcome that relates to informal activity, such as the share of informal workers or firms.[2] These studies cover 15 policy changes in Brazil (mid-1980s, 1990s, 2003), Colombia (1980s, 1990s), Egypt (1998, 2004), Georgia (2010), India (1988-2000, 2017), Indonesia (1996-2004), Mexico (2002-06), Pakistan (2009), Russia (2001), Turkey (2004-05), and Vietnam (1999-2013). Five of these country cases implemented tax changes, four implemented regulatory changes in labor markets, two implemented other regulatory changes, and four implemented trade liberalization measures (Annex Table 3.4).[3]

Tax reform. The studies examined both tax rate changes and tax simplification. In 2017, India streamlined and

Note: This box was prepared by Cedric Okou.

[1] Lower tax rates have been associated with smaller informal sectors (Loayza and Rigolini 2006; Loayza 1996). Greater labor market flexibility has been associated with lower informality (Maloney 1999; Heckman and Pagés 2004; Oviedo 2009). Institutional reforms that improve the business climate have been accompanied by lower informal activity (Beck, Demirgüç-Kunt, and Maksimovic 2006; Bosch, Goni, and Maloney 2007; Friedman et al. 2000; Loayza 1996; Loayza, Oviedo, and Servén 2005; Loayza and Rigolini 2006; Monteiro and Assunção 2012; Perry et al. 2007; Rocha, Ulyssea, and Rachter 2018; Schneider and Enste 2000; Ulyssea 2018; Wellalage and Locke 2016). Trade liberalization in a context of labor market rigidity has been associated with higher informality in the short run (Goldberg and Pavcnik 2004, 2007).

[2] Studies are identified from the English-language repositories of academic articles and working papers, including EconLit, JSTOR, EBSCO, Google Scholar, RePEc, Social Science Research Network (SSRN), the National Bureau of Economic Research (NBER), World Bank Policy Research Working Paper Series, International Monetary Fund Working Paper Series, and IZA Working Papers.

[3] Other studies documented the outcomes of randomized experiments and counterfactual prototypical policies in Benin, Brazil, Cameroon, Malawi, Sri Lanka and several other Sub-Saharan Africa countries (Nguimkeu 2015; Bandaogo 2016; Benhassine et al. 2016; Ulyssea 2018; Campos, Goldstein, and McKenzie 2015; de Mel, McKenzie, and Woodruff 2012).

BOX 3.4 Under the magnifying glass: How do policies affect informality? *(continued)*

lowered the average tax rate of goods and services (Government of India 2017). Georgia introduced a preferential tax regime for small businesses in 2010 (Bruhn and Loeprick 2014). Russia introduced a flat personal income tax and cut payroll taxes and social security contributions in 2001 (Slonimczyk 2012). Conversely, Pakistan raised income taxes on noncorporate partnership firms in 2009 (Waseem 2018). In addition to lowering the average tax rate for small firms, the SIMPLES reform in Brazil in 1996 simplified the tax and social security contributions regime for small firms (Fajnzylber, Maloney, and Montes-Rojas 2011; Maloney and Mendez 2004).[4]

Regulatory changes. A few episodes of labor market and other regulatory reforms have been studied. In 2001, as part of fiscal decentralization in Indonesia, minimum-wage setting responsibilities were transferred to provinces and local governments. The move was accompanied by a sharp increase in the average real minimum wage (Comola and Mello 2011). In 2004-05, Turkey implemented two employment subsidy schemes that strengthened incentives to register for the social security system (Betcherman, Daysal, and Pagés 2010). Mexico simplified business registration by introducing its Rapid Business Opening System (SARE) in various municipalities during 2002-06 (Fajnzylber, Maloney, and Montes-Rojas 2011).

Trade liberalization. Several studies have examined episodes of major trade liberalization. Comprehensive trade liberalizations with drastic tariff reductions were implemented in Colombia in the late 1980s and early 1990s. They followed Colombia's GATT accession in 1981 (Goldberg and Pavcnik 2003; Attanasio, Goldberg and Pavcnik 2004). Egypt introduced gradual trade liberalization measures in 1998 and, more comprehensively, again in 2004 in the context of macroeconomic stabilization plans (Selwaness and Zaki 2015). In Vietnam, the U.S.-Vietnam bilateral trade agreement (BAT) came into effect in 2001 (McCaig and Pavcnik 2015, 2018) and, in the span of ten years, turned the United States from Vietnam's fifth-largest to its largest export destination between 1998 and 2008. The trade agreement was followed by reforms in 2006 to increase labor market flexibility. In 1988, Brazil took initial steps to liberalize trade but at the same time restricted labor market flexibility in its Constitutional Reform. The 1988 reform included cuts in maximum work hours, higher vacation pays, longer maternity leave, higher dismissal cost, and

limits on union power (Busch, Goni and Maloney 2007).[5] In 1991, India liberalized trade, removed price controls, and removed license requirements in most industries (Sharma 2009).

Common lessons

Most studies have found the expected impact of these policy changes on informality (Figure 3.4.1). Tax simplification, tax cuts and regulatory easing tended to reduce informality. Trade liberalization tended to increase informality unless it was accompanied by increased labor market flexibility.

Tax simplification and tax cuts were associated with lower informality in India, Russia, Georgia and Mexico—in the form of greater formal firm registration (India, Brazil, Georgia), greater income reporting (Brazil, Russia), greater or a greater share of formal employment (Brazil, Russia). The reforms were followed by an increase in the number of registered firms by about 5 percent in Brazil and by 18-30 percent in Georgia (Bruhn and Loeprick 2014; Fajnzylber, Maloney, and Montes-Rojas 2011). In India, the introduction of the Goods and Services Tax has been accompanied by a 50 percent increase in the number of indirect taxpayers (Government of India 2017). Conversely, Pakistan's corporate tax hike was followed by rising informality as firms switched business models and reported lower earning.

Regulatory changes to encourage reporting (Turkey) or simplify business registration (Mexico) were associated with greater formal employment and firm registration, whereas higher minimum wages were associated with greater informal employment. Employment subsidy schemes in Turkey were followed by an increase in the number of registered jobs in eligible provinces by up to 13 percent (Betcherman, Daysal and Pagés 2010). In India, following broad-based industrial liberalization measures, the number of informal establishments fell faster (by 25 percentage points) in states with more pro-employer labor laws than in states with less flexible labor laws (Sharma 2009). A 5 percent increase in the number of registered firms was attributed to simplified business registration procedures in Mexico (Bruhn 2011, 2013). Conversely, in Indonesia a 10 percentage point increase in the minimum

---

[4] Recent studies (e.g., Piza 2016) found mixed results regarding robustness of Fajnzylber, Maloney and Montes-Rojas (2011)'s finding.

[5] Recent Bosch, Goni, and Maloney (2007) focus on this initial reform phase. From 1990-1997, the pace of trade liberalization picked up significantly (Ferreira and Rossi 2003) and was accompanied by the 1994 Plano Real of fiscal reform, social security reform, state monopoly reform, and civil service reform.

BOX 3.4 Under the magnifying glass: How do policies affect informality? *(continued)*

FIGURE 3.4.1 Overview of policy changes

Most surveyed policy changes, including five tax reforms, six regulatory reforms, and four trade reforms were conducted in Latin America and the Caribbean, East Asia and Pacific, and Europe and Central Asia. The bulk of these reforms delivered the expected outcomes and were implemented post-2000.

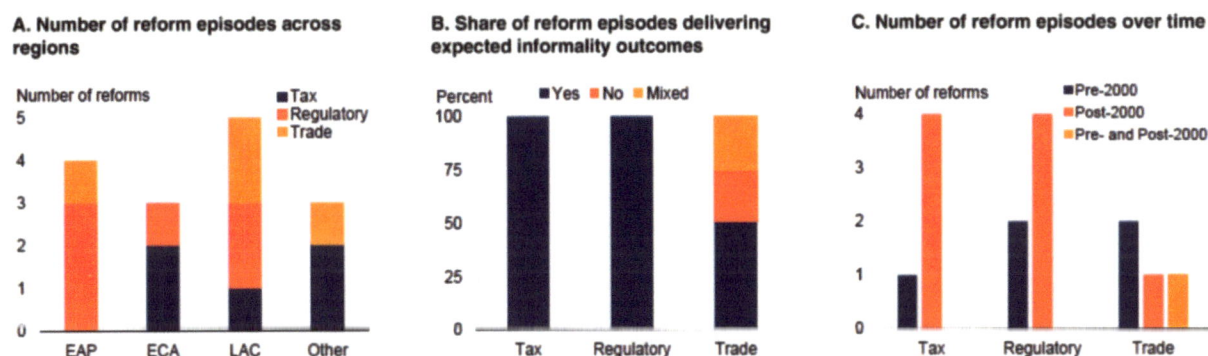

A. Number of reform episodes across regions

B. Share of reform episodes delivering expected informality outcomes

C. Number of reform episodes over time

Source: World Bank.

Note: Descriptive summary of surveyed reform episodes.

A. Number of surveyed policies across regions. EAP = East Asia and Pacific, ECA = Europe and Central Asia, LAC = Latin America and the Caribbean, MNA = Middle East and North Africa, SAR = South Asia, and SSA = Sub-Saharan Africa. "Other" includes MNA, SAR and SSA.

B. "Yes (No)" means that the outcome of a policy intervention is (not) consistent with the expected impact. "Mixed" means that the outcome of a policy intervention varies over time. The expected impacts of reforms are: (1) reduced tax burden would reduce informality; (2) increased labor market flexibility would reduce informality; (3) lowered entry and exit barriers in formal sector would reduce informality; (4) trade liberalization would increase informality due to intense foreign competition that disrupts existing formal firms.

C. Number of surveyed policies implemented before and after 2000. Waves of trade liberalization in Egypt were fielded pre- (1998) and post-2000.

wage over the mean wage was associated with a 0.9-1.1 percent increase in informal employment (Comola and Mello 2011).

Trade liberalizations in Brazil, Colombia, and Egypt were typically associated with greater informality in the short run—unless accompanied by measures to improve labor market flexibility. During Colombia's trade liberalization in the 1980s and 1990s, a 10-percentage-point decline in tariffs in a given industry was associated with a 1 percentage point increase in the probability of informal employment—but only for the period preceding a major labor market reform that increased labor market flexibility (Goldberg and Pavcnik 2003; Attanasio, Goldberg, and Pavcnik 2004). In Egypt, the trade liberalization of 1998 was associated with increased informal employment whereas the trade liberalization measures of 2004—which were preceded by 2003 reforms to increase labor market flexibility—were not (Selwaness and Zaki 2015). Similarly, trade liberalization accompanied by measures to reduce labor market flexibility, such as in Brazil in the late 1980s and early 1990s was accompanied by rising informal employment (Bosch, Goni, and Maloney 2007). In Vietnam, rapid export growth was associated with a 5 percentage point higher share of formal manufacturing

employment, a growing share of formal employment, and shrinking informal employment (McCaig and Pavcnik 2018; Boly 2008).

Role of complementary policy measures

Several of the policies discussed above were not primarily implemented with informality in mind. Yet, they had the unintended consequence of raising informality: tax increases in Pakistan, decentralization of minimum wage regulation in Indonesia, and trade liberalization in Egypt, Brazil and Colombia. Other reforms did not have as large an effect on informality as expected, such as the tax reform in Georgia. Three factors accounted for these: interactions between multiple reforms; scale of reform; and enforcement.

Interactions between multiple reforms. In Egypt, trade liberalization implemented in a supportive environment, with reforms to increase labor market flexibility, was associated with lower informality in 2004 but, in the absence of labor reforms, informality increased following the 1998 trade liberalization. Similarly, trade liberalization combined with increased labor market rigidities raised

BOX 3.4 Under the magnifying glass: How do policies affect informality? *(continued)*

informality in Brazil in the late 1980s and early 1990s. When product markets were restructured, such as during trade liberalization, greater labor market flexibility facilitated the reallocation of workers to more competitive industries. A large share of unskilled labor may also have increased the likelihood that trade liberalization raised informal employment (Loayza and Rigolini 2006; Selwaness and Zaki 2015). In Brazil, Colombia, and Vietnam, the short-term increase in informal employment was particularly pronounced among less skilled workers (Goldberg and Pavcnik 2003; McCaig and Pavcnik 2015).

Scale of reform and persistence of effects. Some reforms were simply too narrowly targeted to have a sizeable or lasting impact on informality. For example, the short-lived impact of tax reform found by some studies—only in the first year—has been attributed to the modest scale of the reform (Bruhn and Loeprick 2014). Moreover, policy reforms may have different short- and long-run effects on informality. For instance, trade liberalization may increase informality in the short run, but not necessarily in the long run (Goldberg and Pavcnik 2003; Dix-Carneiro and Kovak 2017).

Weak enforcement. Particularly in environments with weak enforcement of firm and employment regulation, higher taxes or minimum wages can encourage informal activity. In Pakistan, Turkey, and Indonesia, weaker enforcement was associated with greater informality.[6]

Conclusion

The studies of microeconomic impacts of policy changes are a reminder of the importance of comprehensive reform packages. Several of the packages discussed above, as an unintended consequence, raised informal employment or firm activity. Such unintended reform impacts can be mitigated by bundling mutually reinforcing reforms, such as trade liberalization with labor market reform, or tax and minimum wage hikes with strengthened enforcement and public awareness campaigns.

---

[6] Oviedo (2009), Betcherman, Daysal, and Pagés (2010), Vargas (2015), Waseem (2018), Comola and Mello (2011), and Loayza (1996).

Informality and fiscal outcomes

A large informal economy erodes the tax base and constrains governments' ability to provide public services, conduct countercyclical policies, serve debt, and implement redistributive measures (Chapter 4; Ordóñez 2014; Besley and Persson 2014). This puts a premium on designing tax and social security systems that avoid unintended incentives to shift activity from the formal to the informal sector and level the playfield for both formal and informal sectors (Perry et al. 2007; Djankov et al. 2010; Loayza 2018; Dabla-Norris et al. 2018).

Revenue outcomes. Regardless of the measure of informality, on average, government revenues in EMDEs with the most pervasive informality have been 5-10 percentage points of GDP below those with the least pervasive informality (Figure 3.10). The composition of tax revenues is tilted towards trade taxes in economies with more pronounced informality. Revenues from trade taxes have been 0.7-1.0 percentage points of GDP higher in EMDEs with greater informality compared with those with the lowest levels of informality. Income tax revenues, in contrast, tend to be lower in the EMDEs with the highest output informality. Greater reliance on indirect taxation makes the tax system less progressive and, hence, less redistributive than a system based on more progressive direct taxation.

Expenditure outcomes. Revenue weakness is also reflected in lower government expenditures. In EMDEs with the most pervasive informality, government expenditures were 4-10 percentage points of GDP lower than in those with the lowest informality (Figure 3.10). Insufficient resources for redistributive policies may contribute to the correlation between informality and poverty.

Policy options

Many EMDE governments implemented policies at the microeconomic level and found that the implications for informality were more benign when these reforms were implemented in a supportive institutional and macroeconomic environment. For instance, trade liberalization programs that raised real wages and reduced firms' profitability in the tradable sector were associated with greater informality in the short term—unless they were accompanied by higher labor market flexibility and more skilled labor force (Box 3.4; Goldberg and Pavcnik 2003; McCaig and Pavcnik 2015).

Country experiences suggest the need for a comprehensive development strategy that is informed by the drivers of and challenges posed by informality and carefully tailored to country circumstances. Policies that seek to improve fiscal accounts, such as strengthened tax administration or streamlined tax regulations, can be associated with lowering informality in some economies. Separately, policies that aim at invigorating private sector activity and productivity and leveling the playfield for all workers and firms, particularly measures to make the labor market more flexible, the regulatory framework more adaptable, and governance more effective, can lower informality and/or improve the working conditions in the informal sector. Finally, supportive macroeconomic and social policies (such as enhancing public service and social protection) can ease the implementation of these reforms and facilitate a smoother transition from the informal sector to the formal sector.

These policy measures can help lower informality while also spurring growth more broadly. They should be accompanied by strengthening the basic social safety nets to preserve incomes of vulnerable groups. Disruptions to formal activity from interventions to lower informality could be mitigated by reforms to increase labor and product market flexibility.

Fiscal policy measures

Some countries have implemented reforms to address the fiscal challenges associated with informality, including, in the collection process, to reduce fiscal barriers or incentives for firms to operate informally.

- *Tax compliance* has been encouraged by simplifying tax codes, improving tax enforcement (e.g., via the use of information

FIGURE 3.10 EMDEs: Informality and fiscal outcomes

Widespread informality is associated with lower government revenues, a skew towards trade-based taxation, and lower government expenditures.

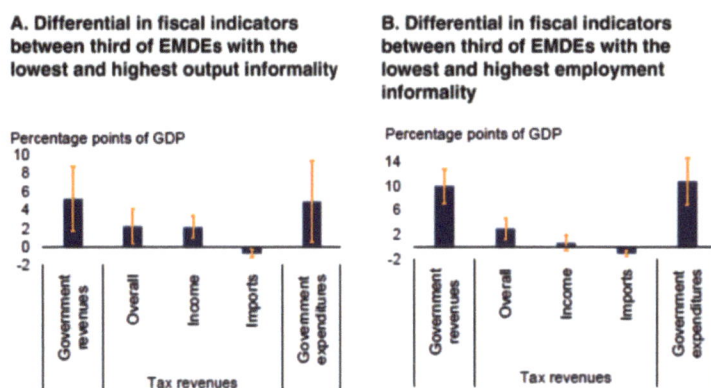

Source: Elgin et al. (forthcoming a); International Monetary Fund, World Economic Outlook; World Bank, World Development Indicators
Note: Fiscal indicators and informality measures are 2000-16 averages. Sample includes 70 non-energy exporting EMDEs with populations above 3 million people.
A.B. Difference (in percentage points of GDP) between the average fiscal indicators among the third of EMDEs with the highest and lowest informality by the share of informal output (as measured by the DGE methodology) in percent of official GDP (A) or by the share of self-employment in percent of total employment (B). Vertical bars indicate 90 percent confidence intervals of the differences.

technology and communication tools), building tax administrations' capacity, harmonizing tax regulations or forms (e.g., across firms of different sizes), limiting the use of cash transactions, and encouraging the use of bank-based tax payments (Morales and Medina 2016; Ulyssea 2018; Rocha, Ulyssea, and Rachter 2018; Awasthi and Engelschalk 2018).

- *Tax burdens* have been reduced for formal firms by offering tax relief for new employees or simplifying tax bases in industries with a high percentage of undeclared workers (e.g., domestic work). Reducing tax burdens has been among the most common policy reforms in EMDEs, especially in East Asia and Pacific (EAP) and Latin America and Caribbean (LAC; Figure 3.11).[33]

- *Value-added taxation (VAT)* can help strengthen tax collection even in the presence of a sizable informal sector (World Bank 2018

---

[33] In China, for example, the computerization of VAT invoices between 1998-2007 explained roughly 15 percent of cumulative VAT revenues and increased the effective average tax rate by approximately 5-14 percent paid by firms (Fan, et al. 2018).

FIGURE 3.11 EMDEs: Policies to address challenges of informality

Governments have implemented a wide range of reforms that could affect informality.

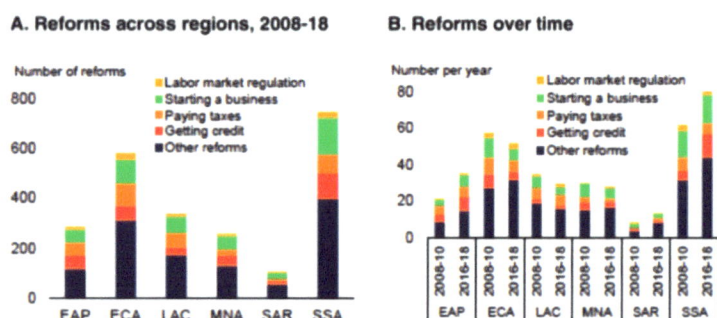

A. Reforms across regions, 2008-18

B. Reforms over time

Source: World Bank, Doing Business.
Note: See Doing Business 2008-18 for reform details.
A. The number of policy reforms that have been implemented after year 2008 and are regarded as "improvement" in the ease of doing business or "neutral" (which only applies to "labor market regulation") by Doing Business 2008-18.
B. The annual average number of policy reforms that have been implemented during 2008-10 in comparison to the annual average number of reforms conducted during 2016-18 (shown in bars).

b). Since informal firms would not be allowed to claim VAT refunds on taxed inputs, the VAT would implicitly serve as an input tax (de Paula and Scheinkman 2010; Loayza 2018). Conversely, more effective VAT administration, including through digitalization of receipts, could raise tax revenues while also increasing incentives to register for tax refunds.[34]

- *Better tax morale*, reflecting the perception that tax dollars are spent judiciously (for the appropriate objectives and in the correct way), can encourage greater tax compliance and lessen informality (Sung, Awasthi, and Lee 2017). Measures to cultivate better tax morale include appeals to people to declare their activities, campaigns to encourage a culture of commitment to declaration, and efforts to change perceptions of the tax system's fairness (Williams and Schneider 2016). Tax systems that create an unlevel playfield for different types of firms (e.g., size-dependent tax

policies) and encourage informality may warrant reform.

- *An improved provision of public goods and services*, such as better education or infrastructure, could help improve the productivity in both formal and informal sectors (Oviedo, Thomas, and Karakurum-Ozdemir 2009; Benjamin and Mbaye 2012; Kim, Loayza, and Meza-Cuadra 2016; World Bank 2018b).

- *Social security systems* can be reformed to reduce the incentives to hire informal workers.[35] Measures include steps to shift the burden of payments of contributions from employers to employees (e.g., in Latvia, Poland, Slovenia), to reduce employers' social security contributions (e.g., in Bulgaria), and to link social benefits to personal contributions (e.g., in most EU 27 countries; Oviedo, Thomas, and Karakurum-Ozdemir 2009). Transitions from an employment-based social security system to a well-designed model of risk sharing can provide a better safety net for informal workers and help protect both formal and informal workers during economic downturns (World Bank 2013, 2018a; Box 3.1).

Business climate and governance measures

Many reforms that are designed to invigorate private sector growth can also help reduce informality, such as reducing corruption, improving business climates and governance, strengthening enforcement, or liberalizing labor and product markets, including through trade liberalization.[36] Policy measures that narrow the earnings gap between informal and formal workers or those that reduce the productivity gap between informal and formal firms (for example, through measures to improve education or expand access to conventional sources of credit) can also help lower the extent of informal activity. Trade

---

[34] See Loayza (2018) for a detailed discussion on how to reform the social security system to reduce informality. See World Bank (2018b) for a discussion on how to provide better social security to informal workers. Levy (2008) and Maloney (2004) suggest that establishing parallel non-contributory systems in the presence of informality could further encourage informality.

[35] See Johnson, Kaufman and Zoido-Lobaton (1998), Djankov et al. (2002), Prado (2011), USAID (2015), Baksi and Bose (2016), Kanbur (2017), and Divanbeigi and Ramalho (2015).

[36] Kuddo (2018) shows that about 60 percent of the reforms passed between 2007 and 2017 throughout the world aimed at improving labor market flexibility.

liberalization, however, may encourage informality in the short term unless complementary reforms are implemented (Box 3.4; Figure 3.11).

Labor regulations. Over the past decade, governments—especially in ECA, SSA and, more recently, LAC—have implemented reforms to increase labor market flexibility.[37] These include less restrictive regulations with respect to hiring and firing, to working arrangements, and to wage rates. Other types of policy changes, such as providing incentives for worker registration (e.g., legalization of undocumented workers) and improved enforcement of existing labor laws, may also encourage workers to move to the formal sector (Anand and Khera 2016; Munkacsi and Saxegaard 2017). For example, Japan has allowed undeclared workers to claim certain social benefits, thereby improving the monitoring of their employment. In rapidly urbanizing countries with still-large rural populations, easing labor market regulation could play an important role in enabling workers to move into the urban, more productive and more modern sectors (Annex Figure 3.5.1; Annex 3.5; Loayza 2016).[38]

Firm regulations. A variety of measures can encourage firms to participate in the formal sector. For example, formal entry of firms can be facilitated and encouraged by creating "one-stop-shop" registration to simplify the process (e.g., in Australia, Belgium, Ukraine), training and business services can be provided to firms that register (e.g., in Mexico and Malawi; Campos, Goldstein, and McKenzie 2018), and access to credit can be made easier for firms in the formal sector. EMDEs in the ECA and SSA regions have implemented an above-average number of reforms to reduce the costs of starting a business during the past decade (Figure 3.11). Easier firm

registration and lower registration costs can also encourage the entry of young and productive firms, which can boost the productivity of the economy (Haltiwanger, Jarmin, and Miranda 2013; Nguimkeu 2015; Loayza 2018).

Regulatory enforcement. While other policy options increase the benefits of joining the formal economy, stricter enforcement can increase the cost of remaining in the informal economy. Policy options include increasing the frequency of inspections (in most EU15 countries and Bangladesh), creating a national-level firm or employee registry (in Poland), and launching public awareness campaigns regarding tax compliance (e.g., in China and Korea).[39] However, these enforcement measures tend to be most effective when implemented in conjunction with steps to improve the governance and business climate (e.g., making the labor market flexible) and when they are applied even-handedly to both formal and informal firms (Loayza 2018).

Education. Informal workers tend to be less productive than formal workers. To the extent that workers remain in the informal sector for lack of human capital or skills, better and more accessible public education may help workers (or their dependents) to move into better paid formal employment (Maloney 2004; Perry et al. 2007; Andrews, Sánchez, and Johansson 2011). This can also have the benefit of reducing income inequality and poverty.

Access to finance. Firms in the informal sector have more limited access to credit from the banking sector and capital markets, which restricts their ability to invest in productivity-enhancing new technologies (Ferreira-Tiyaki 2008; D'Erasmo 2016; Capasso and Jappelli 2013). One of the options to have greater access to finance is to improve personal property registration, which makes loans more accessible for firms operating in the informal economy (e.g., Czech Republic; Doing Business 2012). Improving access to credit has been a common policy reform in EAP, MENA, SAR and, more recently, in SSA. Separately, digital payment systems can provide an

---

[37] Loayza (2016) develops a theoretical model that traces informality, government regulations, economic growth and urban migration through the process of development. The model highlights the potential effect of the minimum wage on labor misallocation and on capital accumulation. A higher minimum wage slows capital accumulation and pushes workers into the informal economy. See Annex 3.5 for details. Caballero et al. (2013) show that job security regulation hampers the creative-destruction process, which could impede growth.

[38] See, for instance, Oviedo, Thomas, and Karakurum-Ozdemir (2009), Bruhn and McKenzie (2014), Awasthi and Engelschalk (2018), and De Giorgi, Ploenzke, and Rahman (2018).

[39] See, for instance, Oviedo, Thomas, and Karakurum-Ozdemir (2009), Bruhn and McKenzie (2014), Awastchi and Engelschalk (2018), and De Giorgi, Ploenzke, and Rahman (2018).

entry point to the formal financial system and encourage a shift away from informal finance (World Bank 2017).

From a comprehensive strategy to implementation

A comprehensive strategy: The right policy mix. Policy interventions in isolation may only have a limited impact on informality but can have unintended consequences (Box 3.4; Ulyssea 2018; Oviedo, Thomas, and Karakurum-Ozdemir 2009).[40] A coherent reform strategy calls for well-integrated reforms that complement each other and address the complexity of informality (Loayza 2018).

Tailoring implementation. Cross-country experiences also highlight the importance of a country-specific implementation plan: each reform component requires a diagnosis of the country's current situation, followed by specific reforms to address the main weaknesses associated with and underlying sources of informality (Loayza 2018). In SSA, SAR, and the non-GCC economies of MENA, for example, general education and training programs to raise human capital could be prioritized (Box 3.2; Boxes 2.1-2.6). In LAC, reducing particularly high tax and regulatory costs to businesses could incentivize firms to join the formal sector. In ECA, improving government effectiveness and reducing corruption could be policy priorities. The success of implementation also depends on careful monitoring of potential unintended consequences and a supportive macroeconomic, political and institutional environment. The latter ensures the political and fiscal viability of the implementation and reduces the transition costs for workers moving from the informal sector to the formal sector.

Emerging policy opportunities and challenges

Human capital adaptability. The emerging "gig" economy poses opportunities and policy challenges with its higher accessibility, more fluid labor arrangements, and greater reliance on digital technology than more traditional forms of informality. Since "gig" workers do not fully participate in the social security system, they are, by some definitions, informal workers (Loayza, Servén, and Sugawara 2010). Regulatory changes, especially in the context of social security systems, may be needed to ensure that "gig" workers' economic risks are manageable and that they do not permanently lose access to the formal economy (World Bank 2014, 2016, 2018b). Since these workers will likely take on many different assignments over the course of their careers, the ability to learn and adapt will be essential. Policies can support this adaptability with more provision of education and (re)training programs (World Bank 2019; Card, Kluve, and Weber 2018). Emphasis should also be given to the development of cognitive skills in primary and secondary education or via intentional instruction at earlier ages, and the improvement of the terms of employment (Almeida, Behrman and Robalino, 2012; World Bank, 2018a, 2018b).

Harnessing new technology. New technologies offer governments an opportunity to both reduce the incentives for and increase the cost of operating informally. For example, new technologies can also help strengthen tax administration and improve access to finance, including by improving the ability to broaden the tax net and assess credit worthiness (Gupta et al. 2017; Junquera-Varela et al. 2017; Awasthi and Engelschalk 2018; Capasso, Monferra, and Sampagnaro 2018). Digitalization can lower regulatory burdens, thus reducing the cost of operating in the formal economy. For example, Costa Rica reduced the time required to register a business by digitizing tax registration records and company books in 2009 (Doing Business 2009). This was followed by a drop in the share of informal employment by 4 percentage points of total employment and a fall in the share of informal output by about 2 percentage points of official GDP during 2009-16. Similar reforms have been carried out in Guyana (2010) and Kenya (2011) (Doing Business 2010, 2011).

---

[40] Ulyssea (2018) shows that formalization policies differ in their impact on informality and GDP. For instance, reducing form sector's entry costs is not as effective in reducing informality as other formalization policies, but it leads to greater GDP and wages. The reverse holds for increasing enforcement.

ANNEX 3.1 Measures of informality

The database includes most informality measures employed by the literature. These measures cover up to 196 economies (36 advanced economies and 160 emerging market and developing economies) for as much as 1950-2016 (Annex Table 3.1.1). Measures can be divided into indirect (model-based) estimates and direct (survey-based) estimates.

Indirect estimates

Previous studies use various indirect approaches to estimate the size of the informal sector, including the currency-demand approach (e.g., Ardizzi et al. 2014), and the electricity-demand approach (e.g., Johnson, Kaufmann, and Shleifer 1997; Lackó 2000), the Multiple Indicators Multiple Causes (MIMIC) model (e.g., Schneider, Buehn, and Montenegro 2010), and the Dynamic General Equilibrium (DGE) model (e.g., Ihrig and Moe 2004; Elgin and Oztunali 2014; Orsi, Raggi, and Turino 2014). Among all indirect estimation methods, the MIMIC and DGE models stand out in their year and country coverage. The other two indirect approaches, that is, the electricity-demand approach and the currency-demand approach, suffer from limited data availability and theoretical caveats (see Ahumada, Alvaredo, and Canavesa 2007; Schneider and Buehn 2016 for details). Therefore, the MIMIC and DGE models are used here to estimate the size of the informal sector.

The multiple indicators multiple causes model (MIMIC).[1] The Multiple Indicators Multiple Causes model is a model of structural equations that can be applied to estimate the size of informal economic activity. There are two features of MIMIC that make it a preferred estimation approach for some researchers. First, it explicitly considers multiple causes of informal activity and captures multiple outcome indicators of informal activity.[2] Second, it estimates informal activity across country and over time. The data on causes and indicators of informal activity identified in the literature are largely based on macroeconomic series in a panel setting and updated annually.

To estimate the size of the informal sector (i.e., in percent of official GDP) with the MIMIC model, this study closely follows Schneider, Buehn, and Montenegro (2010). Six causes and three indicators are used in the estimation to capture the hypothesized relationships between the informal sector (the latent variable) and its causes and indicators. Once the relationships are identified and the parameters are estimated, the estimation results are used to calculate the MIMIC index, which gives the absolute values of the size of the informal sector after a benchmarking procedure. The MIMIC approach delivers a panel of estimates (labelled as MIMIC) for 160 economies over the period 1993-2015.

Six causes and three indicators are used in the estimation (as in Schneider, Buehn, and Montenegro 2010). The six cause variables used are: (1) size of government (general government final consumption expenditure, as a percent of GDP, obtained from UN, spliced with WDI) as proxy for indirect taxation; (2) share of direct taxation (direct taxes in percent of overall taxation, WDI); (3) Fiscal Freedom index obtained from Heritage Foundation as a tax burden variable in a wide sense; (4) Business Freedom index provided by Heritage Foundation; (5) the unemployment rate and GDP per capita to capture the state of the economy (obtained from WDI, the latter is spliced with IMF World Economic Outlook (WEO)); and (6) a measure on government effectiveness provided by Worldwide Governance Indicators. The three indicator variables include: (1) growth rate of GDP per capita (WDI, spliced with IMF WEO); (2) the labor force participation rate (people over 15 economically active as a

---

[1] The limitations of the standard MIMIC model of Schneider, Buehn, and Montenegro (2010) and others include (e.g., Medina and Schneider 2018; Feige 2016): (1) the use of GDP (GDP per capita and growth of GDP per capita) as both cause and indicator variables, (2) its reliance on another independent study's base-year estimates on the informal economy to calibrate the size of informal economy in percent of GDP, and (3) the estimated coefficients are sensitive to alternative model specifications and sample coverage.

[2] Indirect approaches like the currency demand approach or the electricity approach condense the full range of informal activity across product and factor markets into just one indicator. However, the informal sector shows its effects in various markets (Schneider, Buehn, and Montenegro 2010), which would be captured better in a MIMIC model.

percentage of total population, WDI, spliced with Haver Analytics), and (3) currency as a ratio of M0 (currency outside the banks) over M1 (IMF International Financial Statistics).

The estimation results from the model specification that ensures maximum data coverage (Annex Table 3.1.2) are used to generate the MIMIC index of the share of informal output relative to official GDP ($\tilde{\eta}_t$).[3] Then we conduct an additional benchmarking procedure where $\tilde{\eta}_t$ is converted into absolute values of the informal sector ($\hat{\eta}_t$) using the following equation:[4]

$$\hat{\eta}_t = \frac{\tilde{\eta}_t}{\tilde{\eta}_{2000}} \ \eta^*_{2000}, \qquad (1)$$

where t denotes year, $\tilde{\eta}_{2000}$ is the value of the estimated index in the base year 2000, and η^*_{2000} is the exogenous estimate (base value) of the informal economies in 2000. While the estimates ($\tilde{\eta}_t$) determine the movement of the absolute values of the informal sector over time, the base values η^*_{2000} decide the rankings of the countries' informal sector within the sample in year 2000. The base values η^*_{2000} are taken from Schneider (2007) or, for another 10 countries, from Schneider, Buehn, and Montenegro (2010).

The DGE model (DGE). A Dynamic General Equilibrium (DGE) model (e.g., Ihrig and Moe 2004; Elgin and Oztunali 2014; Orsi et al. 2014; Loayza 2016) typically considers how households allocate labor between formal and informal economies within each period and how the allocation changes over time. In comparison to other methods, the DGE approach stands out in its comprehensive country-year coverage, clear economic reasoning, and its applicability in policy experiments and projection (e.g., Loayza 2016).

The deterministic DGE model of Elgin and Oztunali (2014) is used to estimate the size of the informal sector. The model captures the essence of labor allocation between the formal and informal sector and allows the estimation of 158 economies

(36 AEs and 122 EMDEs) over the period 1950-2016. In the model, an infinitely lived representative household is endowed with certain units of productive capital and time. The household has access to two productive technologies, denoted formal and informal, and maximizes its lifetime utility by allocating labor between the informal and formal economies and allocating income between consumption and investment.

In model, an infinitely lived representative household is endowed with units of productive capital and a total of $H_t > 0$ units of time. The household has access to two productive technologies, denoted formal and informal, and maximizes its lifetime utility by solving the following optimization problem:

$$\begin{array}{c} max \\ \{C_t, I_t, K_{t+1}, N_{It}, N_{Ft}\}_{t=0}^{\infty} \end{array} \sum_{t=0}^{\infty} \beta^t U(C_t)$$

$$s.t. C_t + I_t = (1 - \tau_t) A_{Ft} K_t^\alpha N_{Ft}^{1-\alpha} + A_{It} N_{It}^\gamma \qquad (2)$$

$$K_{t+1} = I_t + (1 - \delta) K_t \qquad (3)$$

$$N_{It} + N_{Ft} = H_t \qquad (4)$$

$\beta < 1$ is the discount factor and the instantaneous utility function U(.) is strictly increasing and strictly concave. Eq(2) defines the household's resource feasibility constraint: the sum of consumption C_t and investment I_t should equal the amount produced using the formal and informal technologies. The right-hand side of equation (2) shows that the formal technology follows a standard Cobb-Douglas specification, where A_{Ft} is the level of productivity exclusive to the formal sector. K_t is the household's capital stock while N_{It} is the number of hours the household devotes to the formal sector. τ_t captures the tax rate imposed on formal output. Informal economy depends on the number of hours the household devotes to the informal sector, N_{It} and its exclusive level of technology, A_{It}. Assuming no cost for hiding and the government cannot enforce payment, the household will attempt to hide the income received from the informal sector.

The rest of the household's problem is standard: equation (3) specifies the law of motion for capital, where $\delta \in [0; 1]$ is the depreciation rate.

---

[3] See the model specification in column (5) in Annex Table 3.1.2.

[4] Calibration is performed separately for each country. Following Schneider, Buehn, and Montenegro (2010), the MIMIC index has been adjusted to the positive range by adding a positive constant.

equation (4) is the household's time constraint. In this simple model, the government's policy τ_t is assumed to be exogenously given and the tax revenue is assumed to be used to finance an exogenous stream of government spending, G_t. Then, given the government policy variable tax burden $\{\tau_t\}$, a competitive equilibrium of the two-sector model is a set of sequences $\{C_t, I_t, K_{t+1}, N_{It}, N_{Ft}, G_t\}_{t=0}^{\infty}$ that maximize expected utility from consumption (i.e., $\sum_{t=0}^{\infty} \beta^t U(C_t)$).

The model provides a reasonable mapping between formal economy and informal economy in a dynamic setting. The two key equilibrium conditions are the equilibrium condition that connects formal and informal economy through labor allocation, and the equilibrium condition that captures the intertemporal substitution. The calibration and data construction rely on these two conditions to estimate the ratio, $\frac{Y_{It}}{Y_{Ft}}$, which can be further expressed as $\frac{A_{It} N_{It}^{\gamma}}{A_{Ft} K_t^{\alpha} N_{Ft}^{1-\alpha}}$.

The calibration takes parameter values suggested by the earlier literature (e.g., α is assumed to be equal to 0.36; and γ takes 0.425; Ihrig and Moe 2004) and uses data from PWT 9.0 for capital stock (K_t), private consumption (C_t), formal employment (N_{Ft}), depreciation rates (δ, country averages), and tax rates (τ_t).[5] By matching the productivity in the informal sector to the informal economy size in 2007 of the series reported in Schneider, Buehn, and Montenegro (2010) and assuming that A_{It} grows at the average growth rate of K_t and A_{Ft},[6] the DGE estimates are computed for 158 countries over the period 1950-2016.

Survey-based estimates

Labor force surveys (LFS) and household surveys (HS) on labor related measures. Four existing informality measures are labor related, out of which three are related to employment and one to pension coverage. These measures are mainly

gathered from labor force surveys and sometimes covered by household surveys. Labor related measures have the advantages of not replying on strong assumptions, having no need for based-year estimates for calibration, and having sufficient time variation for time-series analysis.[7]

The most frequently used measure is the share of self-employment in total employment, which is a lower bound of informal employment (e.g., La Porta and Shleifer 2014; Maloney 2004).[8] As defined by the 1993 International Classification of Status in Employment (ICSE-93), self-employed workers are those workers who, working on their own account or with one or a few partners or in a cooperative, hold the type of jobs defined as "self-employment jobs." These are jobs where the remuneration is directly dependent upon the profits derived from the goods and services produced. WDI and ILO further classify them into the following four sub-categories: employers, own-account workers, members of producers' cooperatives, and contributing family workers.

The two other measures are informal employment (*Informal employment*) and employment outside the formal sector (*Employment (excl. formal sector)*). These two measures are usually expressed in percent of total employment and refer to different aspects of informality. While employment in the informal sector is an enterprise-based concept, informal employment is a job-based concept and has a broader definition than self-employment. Informal employment comprises all workers of the informal sector and informal workers outside the informal sector. The former covers all persons who, during a given reference period, were employed in at least one informal sector enterprise, irrespective of their status in employment and whether it was their main or a secondary job a job-based concept. The latter

---

[5] The estimation results are qualitatively robust to different model specifications such as using alternative values for δ, α, γ, adding labor-leisure choice, tax enforcement parameter to informal sector income (for example, using revenue in percent of GDP rather than government spending in percent of GDP for τ_t), see Elgin and Oztunali (2014) for details.

[6] This assumption implies that growth in the formal sector can spillover to the informal sector via capital accumulation and technological diffusion.

[7] They also have the following limitations: (1) the data are costly to gather, which results in limited country and year coverage; (2) survey methodologies may vary across time and countries, making the measures incomparable; (3) the typical drawbacks of survey-based estimates (such as sample bias) may make the data quality questionable; and (4) employment measures cannot reflect other changes in the informal sector, such as productivity.

[8] Among all labor-related measures, self-employment stands out in its time and country coverage and sufficient level of time variation, making it suitable for time-series analysis and cross-country comparison.

covers self-employment and employees holding informal jobs. ILO presents a detailed definition of these two measures (http://www.ilo.org/ilostat-files/Documents/description_ IFL_EN.pdf).

Combining various cross-country databases and additional data from the national statistical offices and other sources, the resulting data set on self-employment is a panel of 180 economies over the period 1955-2016. The data set on informal employment covers 53 countries/regions from various years during 2001-2016 while the data set on employment outside the formal sector contains 57 countries/regions from various years during 1999-2016.

Data on pension coverage (labeled as *Pension coverage*) are also gathered from various issues of the World Bank's World Development Indicators (WDI book version, reported until 2012). The measure is defined as the fraction of the labor force that contributes to a retirement pension scheme Loayza, Oviedo, Servén 2010; WDI). It yields a panel that covers 135 countries from 1990 to 2010.

Firm surveys. Two data sets of firm surveys have comprehensive coverage: World Bank Enterprise Surveys, and Executive Opinion Surveys conducted by World Economic Forum. World Bank Enterprise Surveys cover 139 economies over the period 2006-2016 while Executive Opinion Surveys cover 151 countries over the period 2006-2016.

Both surveys are answered by top managers and business owners, who are business experts and should be familiar with the business climate in a country. The surveys could reflect some dimensions of informality (e.g., the extent of competition from the informal sector) that are not captured in the other informality measures. Similar to labor-related measures, measures from firm surveys also have the advantages of being free of strong assumptions and base-year estimates for calibration.[9]

World Bank Enterprise Surveys compile responses on various topics (including informality) from face-to-face interviews with top managers and business owners in over 130,000 companies in 146 countries. The surveys yield the following measures of informality (e.g., used in Amin and Islam 2015; La Porta and Shleifer 2014): percent of firms competing against unregistered or informal firms (*WB1*), percent of firms formally registered when they started operations in the country (*WB2*), (average) number of years firms operating without formal registration (*WB3*), and percent of firms identifying practices of competitors in the informal sector as a major constraint (*WB4*). A higher value of *WB1*, *WB3* and *WB4* indicates a higher level of informality, while the reverse holds for *WB2*.

In comparison to Enterprise Surveys, Executive Opinion Surveys provide a more balanced panel data set, making them more suitable for business cycle analysis. World Economic Forum has been conducting the Executive Opinion Survey every year since 1979. As reported in the 2014 edition, over 13,000 executives in 144 economies were surveyed. From year 2006, when conducting the survey, the following question is asked, "In your country, how much economic activity do you estimate to be undeclared or unregistered? (1=Most economic activity is undeclared or unregistered; 7 = Most economic activity is declared or registered)." The average responses at the country-year level constitute a series of informality measures, labeled as *WEF*. A lower average at the country level indicates a larger informal economy.

Household surveys (HS). Household surveys either report the extent of informality in an economy or report people's opinions on informal economic activities. Among all, World Value Surveys (WVS) stand out in their country and year coverage with others focusing on European countries. It asks whether respondents can justify

---

[9] There are two drawbacks of informality measures from firm surveys. First, firm surveys tend to have limited year coverage. Second, since people's perception does not move much over time, this type of measures do not have much time variation. Both drawbacks limit their application in time-series analysis. However, they shed light on the perceived extent of informality in a country and provide guidance for constructing and validating indirect model estimates.

cheating on taxes in five waves from 1981-1984 to 2010-2014. The responses range from 1 (never justifiable) to 10 (always justifiable). In total, 94 economies participated in the survey. The average responses at the country-year level are used as a measure for attitudes towards informality (or tax morality; Oviedo, Thomas, and Karakurum-Özdemir 2009), labeled as WVS. A higher average at the country level implies that people find cheating on taxes more justifiable. Former studies show that the lack of tax morality is associated with a higher level of informality.

ANNEX 3.2 Characteristics of informal-economy business cycles

Harding and Pagan (2002)'s approach is used to identify business cycle turning points in formal and informal sectors in annual data: Peaks (troughs) are identified in years when output is higher (lower) than the two subsequent and two preceding years. A recession is defined as the period from a business cycle peak to a trough. An expansion is the converse, the period from a business cycle trough to its peak. A recovery is the early part of an expansion and is defined as the period from the business cycle trough to the year in which the output level recovers to that of the most recent business cycle peak (Claessens, Kose, and Terrones 2012). The main characteristics of recessions and recoveries include duration and speed of adjustment (often termed as "slope") are defined as in Claessens, Kose, and Terrones (2012).

- **Duration** captures, for a recession, the period from peak to trough, for a recovery, the period it takes for output to return to its pre-trough peak, and for an expansion the period from trough to peak.

- **Speed of adjustment** ("slope") measures the speed of a cyclical phase and is defined as the ratio of amplitude over duration for a recession and the ratio of the change from the trough to the last peak divided by duration for a recovery (Claessens, Kose, and Terrones 2012).

ANNEX 3.3 Informality and earnings inequality: A meta-analysis approach

Selection of studies. The collection of the representative sample of studies on informality and wage inequality follows selection guidelines outlined in Stanley et al. (2013) and is broadly similar to criteria applied by van der Sluis, van Praag, and Vijverberg (2005). An initial search was conducted in the major English language repositories of academic articles and working papers.[10] A study was included in the database if it: (1) provided a quantitative estimate of the informal-formal wage gap and a corresponding standard error or a t-statistic; (2) used data from micro-level household or labor surveys to obtain these estimates; (3) analyzed a developing country or a group of developing economies as defined by the World Bank classification; and (4) was published after 1990.[11] The resulting database included 18 studies with a total of 83 individual coefficient estimates covering 20 emerging market and developing economies (Annex Table 3.3.1).

Definitions matter. Differences in estimates of the incidence of informal employment and the wage differentials between formal and informal workers in part reflect differences in data coverage and definitions of informal workers.[12] Self-employed workers constitute the core of informal employment since they typically lack registration at the national level, do not contribute to social security and are not entitled to paid annual and sick leave.[13] However, not all informal workers are self-employed, while the informal sector itself may be divided into several tiers such as informal self-

---

[10] Covered online databases include EconLit, JSTOR, EBSCO, Google Scholar, RePEc, Social Science Research Network (SSRN), the National Bureau of Economic Research (NBER), World Bank Policy Research Working Paper Series, International Monetary Fund Working Paper Series, and IZA Working Papers.

[11] Prior to 1990, reliable and comparable individual or household level survey data, which is used to estimate wage gaps between the formal and informal sectors, is very limited for developing countries.

[12] Perry et al. (2007), Hussmanns (2004), ILO (2013).

[13] According to ILO 2018, nearly 90 percent of all own-account workers—the largest component of self-employed, in the emerging markets and developing economies—are in the informal sector accounting for over 45 percent of all informal jobs.

employed entrepreneurs or professional workers and informal non-professional employees.[14] In developing economies, about half of informal workers are non-professional self-employed workers—who migrate to formal employment as per capita incomes grow—-and the majority of the remainder are informal employees (Gindling, Mossaad, and Newhouse 2016). Studies typically find that self-employed informal workers earn the same or more than formal workers, but employed informal workers earn less than formal workers, especially in the lower tail of the wage distribution (Figure 3.8).[15] Given data constraints, most studies on wage differentials between formal and informal sectors look at gross reported earnings. Several studies use imputed net wages calculated based on the national income tax tables. Their conclusions are broadly in line with the rest of the literature (El Badaoui, Strobl, and Walsh 2008, 2010).

Methodology matters. Empirical research of the wage differential between informal and formal workers has largely relied on estimating "Mincerian" wage regressions conditional on the observed characteristics of workers, although more recent studies have used quantile regressions to assess sector wage gaps along the wage distribution.[16] Such cross-sectional wage regressions are biased when workers' unobserved characteristics affect both their choice of sector and their wage. For example, several studies find workers transitioning from the formal sector into the informal sector after spending several years accumulating experience and knowledge in the formal sector (Maloney 2004; Gong et al. 2004). Hence, studies that rely on panel data to control for time-invariant unobserved worker charac-teristics find much smaller informal-formal wage differentials (El Badaoui, Strobl, and Walsh, 2008; Cho and Cho 2011; Botelho and Ponczek 2011). Similarly, semiparametric matching methods, such as propensity score matching and difference-in-difference estimators that are immune to the

misspecification of the wage regressions, find modest or insignificant wage differentials between formal and informal jobs (Pratap and Quintin 2006).

Meta Regression Analysis of informal-formal wage gap. A random-effects model assumes that there is a distribution of true effects rather than a common fixed effect across the studies (DerSimonian and Laird 1986). In particular, a study-specific estimate of the informal-formal wage gap has a sampling distribution $\hat{\theta}_i \sim N(\theta_i, \sigma^2)$, where σ^2 is the within study variance of the estimate due to a sampling error; while the true effect has the following distribution $\hat{\theta}_i \sim N(\mu, \tau^2)$. Meta-analysis pools information across many studies to estimate μ and τ^2, where τ^2 measure the degree of across-study variations.[17] The proportion of total variation in study estimates is equal to $I^2 = \tau^2/(\tau^2 + \sigma^2)$ and reflects the impact of across-study heterogeneity (Higgins and Thompson 2002). The meta-regression analysis (MRA) can be performed to associate this variation with any characteristics of the study or sample.

The MRA of estimated wage differentials between formal and informal jobs uses estimates of the wage gap drawn from each study as the dependent variable. The set of regressors, or moderator variables, includes study characteristics that are deemed consequential for the reported results, for example, identification and estimation methods, study design and data sources. This, in particular, helps clarify the diversity of research outcomes on the size of the informal-formal wage gap and identify the sensitivity of reported wage gaps to study-specific methods and data. A random-effects MRA is performed by estimating the following regression:

$$\hat{\theta}_i = \mu + \sum_j^k \alpha_j X_{ij} + \epsilon_i + \vartheta_i$$

where $\hat{\theta}_i$ is a study-specific estimate of the informal-formal wage gap, ϵ_i is a sampling error

---

[14] Fields (1990, 2005), Cunningham and Maloney (2001), Günther and Launov (2006).

[15] Arias and Khamis (2008), Nguyen et al. (2013), Lehmann and Pignatti (2007), Maloney (1999).

[16] Tansel and Kan (2012), Lehmann and Zaiceva (2013), Bagain and Kwenda (2014).

[17] The random-effects meta-analysis estimate is a special case of a generalized method of moments estimator, where each estimate is weighted proportionally to its sampling error. Thus, it can only be applied to studies that reported standard errors of their inform-formal wage gap estimates

with a standard deviation that may vary across studies, ϑ_i is an error term reflecting across-study variation of true effects with a constant across-study variance τ^2; finally, the set of moderator variables, $X_{(ij)}$, includes:

- A dummy variable accounts for differences in methodology: FE_i is 1 if fixed effects were used to correct for unobserved workers' characteristics and 0 otherwise.

- Two dummy variables reflect the gender composition of the sample: $FEMALE_i$ is 1 if estimates were obtained for female workers only and 0 otherwise, $MALE_i$ is 1 if estimates were obtained for male workers only and 0 otherwise, the reference category for this set of dummy variables are estimates obtained with samples containing both female and male workers.

- Regional dummy variables are included to account for regional heterogeneity.

- *Self-employed_i* is a dummy variable indicating that a study measured the wage gap between self-employed and formal employees.

The sample coverage is reported in Annex Table 3.3.1, while the regression results are reported in Annex Table 3.3.2.

ANNEX 3.4 Pre-existing informality and changes in poverty and income inequality

Following Loayza, Servén, and Sugawara (2010), the following OLS model is estimated to gauge the impact of informality on changes in poverty and income inequality:

$$\Delta \overline{y}_i = \alpha_0 + \theta_1 \overline{x_{i,1990-2005}} + \theta_2 Initial\ y_i + \epsilon_i$$

The results are reported in Annex Table 3.4.1. Dependent variable ($\Delta \overline{y}_i$) in column [1]-[3] is annual change in poverty headcount ratio (i.e. Poverty headcount ratio at \$1.90 a day (2011 PPP), percent of population) over the earliest year and the latest year, in percentage points, in country i (over the period 2011-2016). In column [4]-[6], the dependent variable ($\Delta \overline{y}_i$) is annual

change in Gini index over the earliest year and the latest year, in percentage points, (over the period 2011-2016). The average measure for pre-existing informality in country i (i.e. $\overline{x_{i,1990-2005}}$) over the period 1990-2005—including the share of DGE/MIMIC-based estimates of informal output in official GDP, the share of self-employed in employed, — is the variable of interest. The initial condition of poverty or income inequality (*Initial y_i*, i.e., the level of poverty / income inequality in the earliest available year between 1990 and 2005) is controlled for. The results do not change when controlling for the initial level of GDP per capita (i.e. the level of real GDP per capita in the earliest available year between 1990 and 2005).

The proxies for poverty and income inequality (Gini coefficient) are taken from World Development Indicators (WDI). The former is Poverty headcount ratio at \$1.90 a day (2011 PPP), percent of population.

ANNEX 3.5 Labor legislation and informality

The implications of labor market deregulation for informality can be traced out in the theoretical model of Loayza (2016). It is shown that minimum wage restraint will speed up formalization of economies in Europe and Central Asia and Middle East and North Africa and modernization—whether informal or formal—of economies in South Asia and Sub-Saharan Africa.

Theoretical mechanism for empirical link

Loayza (2016) develops a theoretical model that traces informality, government regulations, economic growth and urban migration through the process of development. The model highlights the doubly distortionary effect of the minimum wage on labor misallocation and on capital accumulation. A higher minimum wage slows capital accumulation and pushes workers into the informal economy.

A developing economy can be interpreted as consisting of two coexisting economies: a *modern* economy that is organized in firms using a high-productivity technology and employing both capital and labor and a *rudimentary, informal* economy that represents the self-employed using only labor with a low-productivity technology. The *modern* economy, itself, consists of two sectors: a capital-intensive *modern formal* sector that complies with government-mandated labor costs including the minimum wage; and a *modern informal* sector that is less capital intensive, pays low labor costs and high capital costs and produces with lower productivity by contravening labor regulations.

A developing economy passes through three stages of development as it becomes richer. In the first phase, *modern informal* employment expands as falling relative cost of urban living encourage rural workers (in the rudimentary informal sector) to migrate to cities. In the second phase, rural-urban migration slows, the relative shares of the modern informal and formal sectors stabilize, but the relative size of the rudimentary informal sector shrinks.[18] In the third phase, *modern informal* employment declines as rural-urban migration stalls and a rising capital-labor ratio reduces the relative (and absolute) size of the modern informal sector.[19]

Theoretical impact of changes in minimum wages on informality

The model provides a framework for tracing out the implications for growth and informality of changes to labor market regulations, here represented by the minimum wage.[20] When the minimum wage is higher than the unregulated market wage, it creates a distortion in the labor market, which moves labors to the modern informal sector where the minimum wage is not binding. For 127 economies, of which 28 are advanced and 99 are EMDEs, the evolution of the relative size of informal output and employment over 2015-2035 is considered for two scenarios.[21]

- **Baseline scenario**. The minimum wage rises at the rate of labor productivity.

- **Reformist scenario**. The minimum wage rises one percentage point more slowly than labor productivity growth.

The outcomes of both scenarios depend on the initial conditions of the country, future population and TFP growth rates, and the rate of change of the minimum wage.[22] In the baseline scenario, the minimum wage is assumed to grow in line with labor productivity growth, such that informal rudimentary employment shrinks while the formal and informal modern employment expand at a similar rate. In the reformist scenario, slower minimum wage growth will speed up capital accumulation, increase rural-urban migration, raise capital-labor ratio, reduce the wage distortion created by the minimum wage, and result in an expanding modern and formal sector.

Global implications in theory: Employment in the modern economy. On average, in both the baseline and reformist scenarios, the employment share of the modern economy is predicted to expand, by, respectively, 18 (more than one-quarter) and 23 (more than one-third) percentage points (Annex Figure 3.5.1). In both scenarios, capital accumulation attracts rural workers from the rudimentary informal sector, reduces the wage distortion created by the minimum wage, and results in allocating more labor in the modern formal sector. In the baseline scenario, capital accumulation encourages rural-urban migration and modern employment. Employment in both formal and informal modern sectors grow at similar rates. As a result, share of informal modern employment in modern employment remains steady but its share in total (modern and rudimentary) employment increases by 9 percentage points.

In the reformist scenario, the slower growth in the minimum wage encourages faster capital accumu-

---

[18] The relative shares of modern informal sector remain stable due to the constant urban capital-labor ratio during the second phase.

[19] The size of the modern informal sector diminishes when the rate of natural increase in urban population is not too large and when the minimum legal wage is no longer binding.

[20] The relative sizes of different sectors are projected using the parameter values, population projections and total factor productivity growth from Loayza and Meza-Suadra (2016). 2015 is taken as the starting year and the relative sizes of the three sectors are projected for year 2015-2035. The real cost of capital are assumed to match labor productivity growth.

[21] The country classification is listed in Annex 3.5.1. See Loayza (2016) for the list of countries.

[22] The initial conditions include the capital stock, total factor productivity, and the labor force, and the share of formal and informal labor, both rudimentary and modern (See Loayza 2016 for details).

lation and migration to the modern economy, which speeds up the modernization process. Minimum wage growth below productivity growth in the formal sector gradually widens the wage gap between the formal and informal wages in the modern sector and encourages more formal, modern employment. As a result, the share of formal modern employment in modern employment rises by 22 percentage points and the share of formal modern employment in total (modern and rudimentary) employment increases by 33 percentage points.

Differences between advanced economies and EMDEs. Advanced economies have small rural and modern informal sectors compared with EMDEs, to begin with. The rural sector is already negligible in advanced economies, accounting for 9 percent of employment, whereas it accounts for 44 percent of employment in EMDEs. The modern informal sector already accounts for a similarly modest 8 percent of employment in advanced economies, but 28 percent of employment in EMDEs. Under the baseline scenario, and even more quickly and comprehensively under the reformist scenario, the modern informal and rudimentary sectors will virtually disappear in advanced economies, together accounting for about 10 percent of employment from 18 percent initially. In EMDEs, the rural sector will continue to play an important, albeit shrinking, role, accounting for 15-22 percent of employment. Rural-urban migration will continue to fuel the expansion of the modern economy, but only in the reformist scenario will this migration ensure that the modern formal sector grows more rapidly than the modern informal sector.

Differences across EMDE regions. EMDE regions differ widely in their initial conditions, hence also in the implications of policy changes. In 2015, Sub-Saharan Africa (SSA) and South Asia (SAR) had large rural economies, accounting for more than 60 percent of employment, whereas Europe and Central Asia (ECA) and the Middle East and North Africa (MNA) had predominantly modern economies, which accounted for about 80 percent of employment. Over the next two decades, reformist or baseline policies would reduce the

ANNEX FIGURE 3.5.1 Implications of relaxing the minimum wage restraint

Over the next two decades, according to the model, the employment share of the modern economy is expected to expand. In the baseline scenario, the informal economy would grow faster than the formal economy, whereas the informal economy would shrink in the minimum wage restraint scenario. The theoretical model suggests that lowering the minimum wage would speed up formalization in regions like Europe and Central Asia and Middle East and North Africa and accelerate economic modernization in South Asia and Sub-Saharan Africa.

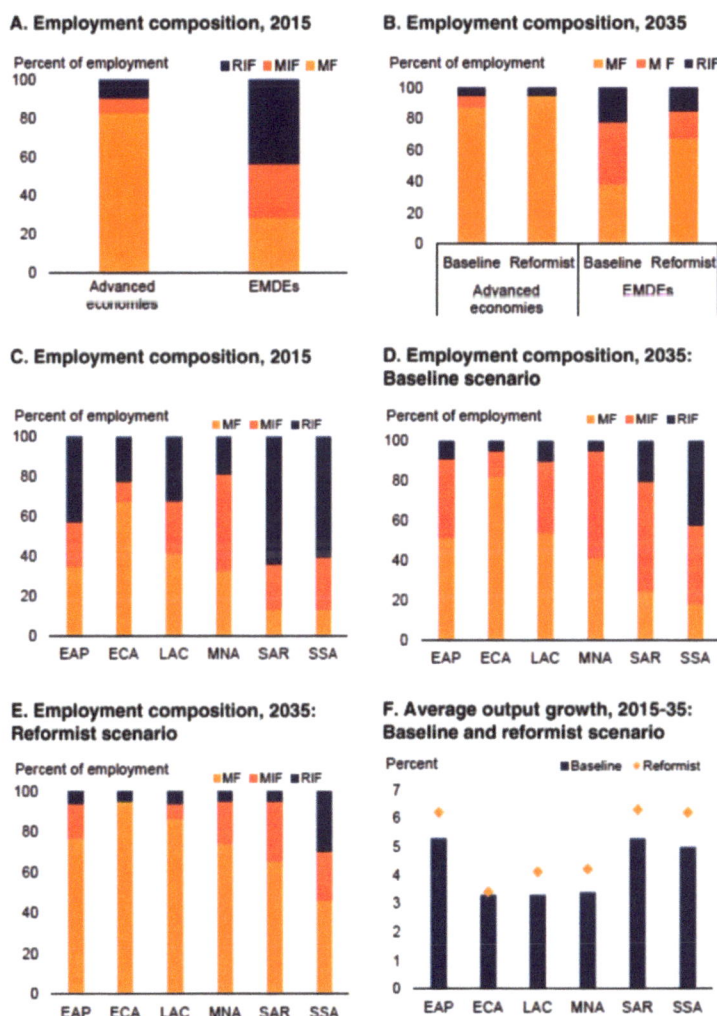

A. Employment composition, 2015

B. Employment composition, 2035

C. Employment composition, 2015

D. Employment composition, 2035: Baseline scenario

E. Employment composition, 2035: Reformist scenario

F. Average output growth, 2015-35: Baseline and reformist scenario

Source: World Bank staff calculation using the model of Loayza (2016).
Note: "MF" stands for employment in the modern formal sector (in orange), "MIF" stands for employment in the modern informal sector (in red), while "RIF" stands for employment in the rudimentary informal sector (in blue). The relative sizes of different sectors are projected using the parameter values, population projections and total factor productivity growth from Loayza (2016). Under the baseline scenario, the minimum wage rises at the rate of labor productivity. Under the reformist scenario, the minimum wage rises one percentage point more slowly than the rate of labor productivity growth. 2015 is taken as the starting year for the projection exercise. "Advanced economies" represents the unweighted average of the 28 advanced economies in the sample, while "EMDEs" represents the unweighted average of the 99 emerging markets and developing economies in the sample. These group averages are calculated for East Asia and Pacific (EAP), Europe and Central Asia (ECA), Latin America and Caribbean (LAC), Middle East and North Africa (MNA), South Asia (SAS), and Sub-Saharan Africa (SSA).
A. The stacked bars show the average employment shares in 2015 for each sector in advanced economies and in EMDEs.
B. The stacked bars show the average employment shares projected for 2035 in advanced economies and in EMDEs.
C. The stacked bars show the average employment shares across all EMDE regions in the sample for each sector in 2015.
D.E. The stacked bars show the average employment shares across all EMDE regions in the sample for each sector in 2035 under baseline and reformist scenario.
F. The diamond shows average annual GDP growth between 2015-35 across all EMDE regions for the reformist scenario. The blue bars show the growth rate for the baseline scenario.

share of rural employment in SSA below the current EMDE regional median and would virtually eliminate rural employment in ECA and MNA (under reformist policies, also in East Asia and Pacific, EAP, Latin America and the Caribbean, LAC, and South Asia, SAR). The reformist scenario would speed up this formalization process, especially in MNA and LAC, where the migration to the modern economy is almost coming to a halt and further

capital accumulation will raise the unregulated market wage, making minimum wage no longer binding in the formal modern sector and allocating more labor in the formal modern sector. The reformist scenario could raise growth by 0.1-1.2 percentage point per year over the baseline scenario. In SAR and SSA, the reformist scenario could generate the largest boosts to output growth because of their initially large rural sectors increase the potential for rural-urban migration.

ANNEX TABLE 3.1 **Labor productivity differential between types of firms (percent)**

	Informal firms						Informal versus formal firms
	Manager has higher education	Main owner is male	Services sector	Firm has bank loan	Single-employee firm	Young firm (<=5 years)	
Angola	45.8	70.0	44.9	-60.0	225.0	20.0	-75.5***
Argentina	25.0	200***	0.0	0.0	11.1	-16.7	-92.5***
Burkina Faso	-6.2	-6.2	28.6	6.7	66.7	-10.0	-79.8***
Botswana	89.4*	72.7**	-29.1	100.0	-35.0	-18.2	-89.8***
Côte d'Ivoire	0.0	25.0	66.7**	-40.0	50.0	40.0	-47.5*
Cameroon	-41.7*	36.4	77.8**	-24.0	140.0***	56.2**	-55.8***
Congo, Dem. Rep.	33.3	0.0	36.0**	50.0	50.0***	0.0	10.7
Cabo Verde	133.3	-25.0	185.7	1585**	566.7*	100.0	0.89
Ghana	0.0	12.5	0.0	25.0	66.7***	0.0	-51.8***
Guatemala	25.0	46.7***	33.3**	50.0	57.1***	-20.0	-86.0***
Kenya	50.0***	6.7	-40***	44.0**	12.0	-20.0**	-81.6***
Madagascar	40.0	-33.3	100***	33.3	60.0*	8.3	-88.1***
Mali	13.2	14.3	-19.4	31.4	57.1	-46.2**	-71.3***
Myanmar	80.0*	-11.1	63.6***	11.3	31.2	0.0	-89.1***
Mauritius	66.7*	6.7	114.3***	25.0	6.7	25.0	-82.9***
Nepal	11.1	0.0	0.0	33.3	150.0***	-16.7	-56.5***
Peru	28.6*	12.5	-50***	-11.1	2.9	-7.4	-74.2***
Rwanda	50.0***	28.6**	25.0*	-25.9	50.0***	-11.1	-91.4***
All countries	48.1***	10.2	8.2	20.0**	41.2***	-6.7	-79.4***

Source: World Bank.

Note: Productivity differential between the median informal and the median formal firm (last column) or between median informal firms among different groups of firms (all other columns). For example, "Manager has higher education" shows the difference in the median productivity among informal firms with managers with higher education and the median productivity among informal firms with managers without higher education. Other firm characteristics are not controlled for, hence results are similar but not identical to column (1) in Annex Table 3.2. Productivity is defined as annual sales (in 2009 U.S. dollars) relative to the number of workers. "All countries" is the unweighted average across each column. ***, **, * indicates statistical significance at the 1, 5, and 10 percent level.

ANNEX TABLE 3.2 Labor productivity of formal and informal firms

	[1]	[2]	[3]	[4]	[5]
Informal firm Y:1 N:0	-1.400***	-0.648***	-1.131***	-1.200***	-1.008***
	(0.091)	(0.184)	(0.131)	(0.121)	(0.160)
Firm age (logs)	0.120***	0.285***	0.118***	0.116**	0.137***
	(0.045)	(0.053)	(0.045)	(0.045)	(0.045)
Firm size (logs, workers)	-0.102***	-0.119***	-0.056*	-0.104***	-0.108***
	(0.027)	(0.027)	(0.032)	(0.028)	(0.028)
Manufacturing Y:1 N:0	-0.402***	-0.407***	-0.401***	-0.401***	-0.399***
	(0.056)	(0.056)	(0.056)	(0.056)	(0.056)
Capital city Y:1 N:0	0.201***	0.190***	0.187***	0.394***	0.201***
	(0.061)	(0.061)	(0.061)	(0.087)	(0.061)
Manager experience (logs, years)	0.094**	0.141***	0.107***	0.091**	0.190***
	(0.040)	(0.041)	(0.040)	(0.040)	(0.055)
Informal firm * Firm age (logs)		-0.353***			
		(0.069)			
Informal firm * Firm size (logs, workers)			-0.208***		
			(0.066)		
Informal firm * Capital city Y:1 N:0				-0.360***	
				(0.114)	
Informal firm * Manager experience (logs, years)					-0.176***
					(0.060)
Country fixed effects	Yes	Yes	Yes	Yes	Yes
Constant	9.013***	8.552***	8.859***	8.909***	8.748***
	(0.131)	(0.164)	(0.149)	(0.139)	(0.162)
Number of observations	10,527	10,527	10,527	10,527	10,527
R-squared	0.291	0.296	0.293	0.293	0.292

Source: World Bank.

Note: Standard errors in brackets. Significance is denoted by *** (1 percent), ** (5 percent), * (10 percent). OLS regression with labor productivity as dependent variable, as proxied by annual sales (in 2009 U.S. dollars, in thousands, in logs) per worker, based on a sample using World Bank's Enterprise Survey data collected during 2007-14 for 4,036 informal firms and 7,558 formal firms in 18 countries. "Informal firm" is a dummy variable taking the value of 1 if a firm is unregistered and 0 otherwise. "Manufacturing" is a dummy variable taking the value of 1 if a firm operates in the manufacturing sector and 0 otherwise. "Capital city" is a dummy variable taking the value of 1 if a firm is located in the capital city and 0 otherwise.

ANNEX TABLE 3.3 Labor productivity of formal firms facing informal competition

	[1]	[2]	[3]	[4]	[5]
Informal Competition	-0.268***	-1.642***	-1.919***	-0.574***	-1.657***
(Proportion of firms in the cell that report competing with informal firms)	(0.067)	(0.602)	(0.618)	(0.059)	(0.307)
Number of workers (logs)	-0.197***	-0.150***	-0.175***	-0.166***	-0.179***
	(0.016)	(0.017)	(0.019)	(0.019)	(0.020)
Firm's age (logs)	0.208***	0.215***	0.296***	0.286***	0.356***
	(0.023)	(0.026)	(0.032)	(0.029)	(0.032)
Firm belongs to manufacturing sector: Yes 1 No 0	0.137***	0.077*	0.164***	0.157***	0.139***
	(0.044)	(0.046)	(0.052)	(0.048)	(0.053)
Firm belongs to retail sector: Yes 1 No 0	0.695***	0.747***	0.896***	0.862***	0.879***
	(0.045)	(0.047)	(0.053)	(0.049)	(0.054)
Top manager is female: Yes 1 No 0	-0.051	-0.125**	-0.128*	-0.086	-0.063
	(0.048)	(0.058)	(0.073)	(0.067)	(0.070)
Exports (proportion of sales)	0.268**	0.403***	0.431***	0.385***	0.397***
	(0.114)	(0.117)	(0.145)	(0.133)	(0.148)
Firm has foreign owners: Yes 1 No 0	0.638***	0.836***	0.821***	0.658***	0.781***
	(0.063)	(0.062)	(0.070)	(0.066)	(0.074)
Log GDP per capita (PPP, 2009 Int'l Dollars)		0.631***			
		(0.043)			
Informal Competition * Log GDP per capita		0.138**			
		(0.067)			
Distance to Frontier (Doing Business)			0.031***		
(Higher values imply better regulatory practices)			(0.006)		
Informal Competition * DTF			0.022**		
			(0.010)		
Corruption (Governance Indicators)				0.574***	
(Higher values imply less corruption)				(0.048)	
Informal Competition * Corruption				0.177**	
				(0.085)	
Business Freedom index (Economic Freedom of the World)					0.015***
(Higher values imply less regulation and more freedom for businesses)					(0.003)
Informal Competition * Business Freedom index (Economic Freedom of the World)					0.016***
					(0.005)
Constant	8.771***	3.818***	7.469***	9.410***	8.163***
	(0.178)	(0.390)	(0.381)	(0.088)	(0.224)
Country fixed effects	YES	NO	NO	NO	NO
Number of observations	45,996	45,996	44,770	45,996	43,760
R-squared	0.404	0.259	0.184	0.191	0.154

Source: World Bank.

Note: Standard errors in brackets. Significance is denoted by *** (1 percent), ** (5 percent), * (10 percent). OLS regression with labor productivity as dependent variable, as proxied by annual sales (in 2009 U.S. dollars, in thousands, in logs) per worker, based on a sample of formal firms only using World Bank's Enterprise Survey data collected during 2007-14 for 4,036 informal firms and 7,558 formal firms in 18 countries. "Informal competition" is the share of firms in a cell (a group of firms of similar size in the same region and sector) that report competition from informal firms. It is worth mentioning that one could use a firm-level dummy rather than the proportion of formal firms in a cell to proxy informal competition. However, endogeneity concerns may arise because the informal competition faced by a specific firm may also be driven by its productivity. Therefore, the proportion of formal firms facing informal competition in a cell, which would be uncorrelated with the productivity of a specific firm, should be more robust to endogeneity concerns. "Manufacturing" is a dummy variable taking the value of 1 if a firm operates in the manufacturing sector and 0 otherwise. "Capital city" is a dummy variable taking the value of 1 if a firm is located in the capital city and 0 otherwise.

ANNEX TABLE 3.4 Survey of policy changes

Study	Country	Years	Methodology	Policy change	Estimated impact as expected
Tax reforms					
Bruhn and Loeprick (2014)	Georgia	2010	Regression Discontinuity Design (RDD) regression	Introduction of preferential tax regimes for micro and small businesses in 2010.	**YES.** The introduction of preferential tax regimes for micro and small businesses in 2010 increased the number of newly registered formal firms by 18-30 percent below the eligibility threshold during the first year of the reform. No significant effect was seen in subsequent years.
Fajnzylber, Maloney, and Montes-Rojas (2011); Maloney and Mendez (2004)	Brazil	1996	OLS regression on firm-level survey data	The SIMPLES program introduced in November 1996 consolidated multiple taxes and social security contributions into a single payment and reduced tax burdens (on average 8 percent) for eligible small firms.	**YES.** SIMPLES raised the proportion of firms that have a license to operate by 4.5 percent (20.8 to 25.3 percent), are registered as a legal entity, pay taxes and make social security contributions. Newly created firms (with employees) that opted for operating formally achieved higher levels of revenue and profits, employed more workers and were more capital intensive. This occurred, not through greater access to credit or contracts with larger firms, but through lower cost of contracting labor that allowed the adoption of more productive technologies.
Keats (2017)	India	2017	descriptive	The GST reform introduced in 2017 simplified the taxation of goods and services and reduced the incidence of taxation from 26.5 percent to 15-20 percent.	**YES.** The GST reform reduced the percentage of informal firms by 50 percent.
Slonimczyk (2012)	Russia	2001	Difference-In-Differences (DID) estimation	The fiscal reform implemented in 2001 reduced payroll and social taxes. The reform lowered the average personal income tax (PIT) to a flat rate of 13 percent.	**YES.** The tax reform reduced the share of informal labor. The decline was sharpest among individuals with the largest gains from the tax reform.
Waseem (2018)	Pakistan	2009	Difference-In-Differences (DID) estimation	The tax reform implemented in 2009 raised the income tax rate on earnings for noncorporate partnership firms from 5 to 25 percent.	**YES.** In a context of weak enforcement and widespread informality, an increase in the tax rate (from 5 to 25 percent) on noncorporate partnership income led firms to report significantly lower earnings (roughly half), migrate into informality, and switch business form to avoid the additional tax burden.

ANNEX TABLE 3.4 Survey of policy changes *(continued)*

Regulatory (labor and business) reforms

Study	Country	Years	Methodology	Policy change	Estimated impact as expected
Bosch, Goni, and Maloney (2007)	Brazil	Mid 1980s and 1990s	Cross-section weighted least squares	The constitutional reform in 1988 cut maximum work hours, raised vacation pay, extended maternity leave, and raised dismissal cost.	**YES.** A large fraction of the 10 percentage point rise in informal employment in Brazil during 1990-2000 was driven by rising labor costs and reduced flexibility.
Betcherman, Daysal, and Pagés (2010)	Turkey	2004 and 2005	Difference-In-Differences (DID) estimation	Two employment subsidy schemes were introduced in 2004 and 2005.	**YES.** Employment subsidies significantly raised the number of registered jobs in eligible provinces (5-13 percent for the first program and 11-15 percent for the second).
Comola and Mello (2011)	Indonesia	1996 to 2004	seemingly unrelated regression (SUR)	As part of fiscal decentralization, the central government transferred minimum-wage setting responsibilities to provinces and local governments after 2001.	**YES.** The fiscal decentralization led to a sharp increase in the real value of the minimum wage. District-level survey data suggests that an increase in the ratio of the minimum wage to the mean wage by 10 percentage point was associated with a rise in informal sector employment by 0.9-1.1 percentage point and a drop in formal sector employment by 0.5-0.7 percentage point.
McCaig and Pavcnik (2015); and Boly (2018)	Vietnam	1999 to 2009 and 2005 to 2013	Linear probability model	Labor market reforms in 2006 established a new flexible system in which minimum wages vary according to location and sector of employment.	**YES.** From 1999 to 2009, the labor force surged (up by 35 percent) in a fast-growing Vietnamese economy (with 78 percent increase in GDP per capita). This economic upturn led to a contraction of the informal employment (from 86 to 79 percent). Younger and more educated male workers were more likely to migrate from informal to formal activities, in sharp contrast to older and poorly educated females. Firms opting out of informality achieved higher profit and greater value added.
Sharma (2009)	India	1988 to 2000	OLS regression on firm-level survey data	The major deregulation in 1991 in India removed license requirements on the setup and expansion of factories in nearly half of all industries.	**YES.** Informality dropped, and the reduction in informality was greatest in states with more pro-employer labor laws. In states with pro-employer labor laws, the number of informal establishments declined by 25 percent more than in states with less flexible labor laws.
Bruhn (2011, 2013)	Mexico	2002 to 2006	OLS regression on firm-level survey data	The business registration reform established a Rapid Business Opening System (SARE) in various municipalities in Mexico from 2002 to 2006.	**YES.** SARE was exclusively implemented for eligible low-risk industries such as commerce and restaurants, excluding high-risk industries (e.g., chemical plants, transportation). The reform induced a 5 percent increase in the number of registered businesses. This increase was mainly driven by former wage earners switching from ineligible industries to launch eligible businesses, rather than the registration of existing informal businesses.

ANNEX TABLE 3.4. Survey of policy changes (*continued*)

Study	Country	Years	Methodology	Policy change	Estimated impact as expected
Trade liberalization					
Bosch, Goni, and Maloney (2007)	Brazil	Mid 1980s and 1990s	Cross-section weighted least squares	In addition to major changes in labor legislation, the constitutional reform in 1988 introduced trade liberalization policies.	**YES.** A small fraction of the 10 percentage point rise in informal employment in Brazil during 1990-2000 was driven by trade liberalization in the mid1980s and 1990s.
Goldberg and Pavcnik (2003); Attanasio, Goldberg, and Pavcnik (2004)	Colombia	1980s and 1990s	Two-step restricted least squares estimation	Trade liberalization measures were implemented in the 1980s and 1990s.	**YES.** Employment informality expanded (i.e. a 1-percentage point decline in a tariff in a given industry is associated with a 0.1 percentage point increase in the probability of informal employment), but only for the period preceding a major labor market reform that increased labor market flexibility.
Selwaness and Zaki (2015)	Egypt	1998 and 2004	OLS regression on individual-level survey data	Waves of trade liberalization in 1998 and 2004 reduced tariffs nearly by 70 percentage points, from 110 percent at the end of the 1980s to reach 40 percent by the end of 1990's.	**MIXED (YES in 1998, NO in 2004).** The impact depended on the observation period and the degree of labor market rigidity. Trade liberalization reforms increased informality among workers in 1998, but lowered the likelihood of informal employment post-2004. This difference may be attributed to labor reforms implemented in 2003 that added flexibility to the market during the second wave liberalization.
McCaig and Pavcnik (2018)	Vietnam	2001/2002 and 2003/2004	on household survey data	US-Vietnam bilateral trade agreement (BAT) went into effect in 2001.	**NO.** Evidence from household surveys in 2001/2002 and 2003/2004 shows that US tariffs reduction (20.9 percent average annual drop) induced a sharp increase in exports to the US, which grew from 3.6 to 10.4 percent of Vietnam's GDP. This positive export shock generated 5 percentage point increase in the share of manufacturing workers in the formal sector. In addition, the prevailing labor productivity gap of 3.7 (when heterogeneity and measurement errors are accounted for) between the informal and the formal sector induced a reallocation of labor towards the formal sector, and increased the aggregate labor productivity within manufacturing by 2.8 percent per year.

Source: World Bank.
YES (NO) means that the outcome of a policy intervention is (not) consistent with the expected impact. MIXED means that the outcome of a policy intervention varies over time. The expected impacts of reforms are: (i) reduced tax burden would reduce informality; (ii) increased labor market flexibility would reduce informality; (iii) lowered entry and exit barriers in formal sector would reduce informality; (iv) trade liberalization would increase informality due to intense foreign competition that disrupts existing formal firms.

ANNEX TABLE 3.1.1 Data coverage

Estimation method	Aspect			Measures	# of AE	# of EMDE	Time period
Indirect	Output			DGE (percent of GDP)	36	122	1950-2016
				MIMIC (percent of GDP)	36	124	1993-2015
Direct (survey-based)	Labor Force Surveys	Employment		Pension coverage (percent of labor force)	31	104	1990-2010
				Self-employment (percent of total employment)	36	144	1955-2016
				Informal employment (percent of total employment)	0	53	2001-2016
				Employment outside the formal sector (percent of total employment)	0	57	1999-2016
	Firm surveys	Perception	(a)	WEF(1-7=Most informal)	36	115	2006-2016
			Firms	WB: percent Competing against informal firms	8	131	2006-2016
				WB: percent firms formally registered when founded	7	129	2006-2016
				WB: Number of years operated without registration	7	129	2006-2016
				WB: percent firms that found competitors in the informal sector as a constraint	7	131	2006-2016
	HS		(b)	WVS: Justifiable (Cheating on taxes)	26	68	1981-2010

Note: DGE is benchmarked to Schneider, Buehn, and Montenegro (2010). World Value Survey (WVS) asks whether cheating on taxes is justifiable (1 is "never justifiable" and 10 is "always justifiable") and reports average responses at the country-year level, with a higher level suggesting that the country is more tolerant towards the informal sector. World Economic Forum (WEF) asks "In your country, how much economic activity do you estimate to be undeclared or unregistered? (1= Most economic activity is undeclared or unregistered; 7= Most economic activity is declared or registered)" and reports average responses at the country-year level. Here the average responses have been reordered to make "7= Most economic activity is undeclared or unregistered; 1= Most economic activity is declared or registered" where a higher level suggesting a larger informal sector in the country. The WEF data for year 2004 and 2005 are dropped since different ordering were used before 2006, which makes the numbers incomparable over time. WB shows the results for World Bank Enterprise Surveys. "HS" stands for "Household surveys". "(a)" stands for "Output, and "(b)" stands for "Opinions/Tax Morality". See Elgin et al (forthcoming a) for detailed information.

ANNEX TABLE 3.1.2. MIMIC model estimation results (1993-2015)

	[1] 88 Developing Countries	[2] 98 Developing Countries	[3] 120 Countries	[4] 151 Countries	[5] 161 Countries
Size of government	0.133***	0.143***	0.157***	0.152***	0.145***
	(0.023)	(0.021)	(0.024)	(0.019)	(0.019)
Share of direct taxation	0.035		0.009		
	(0.023)		(0.022)		
Business Freedom	0.035	0.040**	0.058**		
	(0.021)	(0.020)	(0.024)		
Fiscal Freedom	0.002	-0.010	-0.038		
	(0.023)	(0.020)	(0.025)		
Unemployment rate	0.078***	0.105***	0.055**	0.067***	0.066***
	(0.023)	(0.021)	(0.022)	(0.019)	(0.019)
GDP per capita	-0.342***	-0.324***	-0.393***	-0.381***	-0.385***
	(0.035)	(0.027)	(0.029)	(0.022)	(0.022)
Government effectiveness			-0.069***	-0.043**	-0.042**
			(0.020)	(0.018)	(0.018)
Growth rate of GDP per capita	-0.835***	-0.618***	-0.362***	-0.310***	-0.306***
	(0.119)	(0.085)	(0.079)	(0.064)	(0.064)
Labor force participation rate	-0.321***	-0.219***		-0.167***	-0.155***
	(0.091)	(0.073)		(0.053)	(0.052)
Growth rate of labor force			-0.091		
			(0.064)		
Currency (M0/M1)	1.000	1.000	1.000	1.000	1.000
	(0.000)	(0.000)	(0.000)	(0.000)	(0.000)
Statistical tests					
RMSEA	0.061	0.057	0.070	0.087	0.089
p(RMSEA<=0.05)	0.097	0.190	0.002	0.000	0.000
Chi-squared (p)	63.922 (0.00)	60.646 (0.000)	124.517 (0.000)	153.29 (0.000)	160.63 (0.000)
AIC	27388.448	33527.217	41436.305	43231.405	44080.904
BIC	27464.278	33602.241	41522.616	43306.446	44156.205
CFI	0.820	0.852	0.761	0.771	0.764
TLI	0.685	0.734	0.590	0.571	0.558
SRMR	0.033	0.030	0.041	0.046	0.047
CD	0.846	1	1	1	1
Number of observations	1,159	1,570	1,627	2,374	2,422

Note: Absolute z-statistics in parentheses. ***, **, * denote significance at the 1, 5, and 10 percent significance levels. All variables are used as their standardized deviations from the mean. Data sources for variables used in the model are listed in Section II footnote 6. Following the MIMIC models' identification rule, the currency (M0/M1) variable is fixed to an a priori value. The currency variable shows the level of money (cash) in circulation. "AIC" stands for "Akaike's information criterion" and "BIC" stands for "Bayesian information criterion." "RMSEA" stands for "Root Mean Square Error of Approximation." "TLI" stands for "Tucker Lewis Index." "CFI" stands for "Comparative Fit Index." "SRMR" stands for "Standardized Root Mean Square Residual" and "CD" shows the coefficient of determination. These are goodness-of-fit statistics.

ANNEX TABLE 3.3.1 **Database of studies for meta regressions analysis**

Study	Countries / Estimates	Sample period	Methodology	Mean wage gap*
Aydin, Hisarciklilar, Ilkkaracan (2010)	1/4	1998-2007	OLS, ML logit	57.75
Baskaya and Hulagu (2011)	1/2	2005-2009	OLS, PSM	15.45
Bargain and Kwenda (2014)	3/6	2001, 2005	OLS, FE	19.19
Botelho and Ponczek (2011)	1/2	1995-2001	OLS, FE	11.76
Earle and Sakova (2000)	6/6	1993, 1994	ML Logit	-13.33
El Badaoui, Strobl, and Walsh (2008)	1/17	2001-2003	OLS, DID, PSM	28.48
El Badaoui, Strobl, and Walsh (2010)	1/6	1994	OLS, PSM	25.65
Funkhouser (1997)	1/4	1991-1992	OLS	23.82
Gindling (1991)	1/1	1982	OLS	28.50
Huber and Rahimov (2014)	1/2	2007	OLS	-34.98
Lehmann and Pignatti (2007)	1/2	2004	OLS	-6.80
Lehmann and Zaiceva (2013)	1/5	2003-2011	OLS, QR, FE	6.90
Magnac (1991)	1/1	1980	OLS	30.30
Marcouiller, de Castilla, and Woodruff (1997)	3/6	1990	OLS	16.50
Nguyen, Nordman, and Roubaud (2013)	1/4	2002-2006	OLS, FE	4.83
Nordman, Rakotomanana, and Roubaud (2016)	1/6	2000-2004	OLS, FE	15.33
Pratap and Quintin (2006)	1/3	1993-1995	OLS, FE	28.49
Tansel and Kan (2012)	1/6	2006-2009	OLS, FE	11.56

Source: World Bank.
Note: OLS=pooled ordinary least squares, FE=fixed effects regression, ML logit=multinomial logit regression, PSM=propensity score matching, DID=difference-in-difference estimators, QR=quantile regression. The sample covers these EMDE countries: Argentina, Brazil, Columbia, Costa Rica, Czech Republic, Ecuador, El Salvador, Hungary, Madagascar, Mexico, Peru, Poland, Russia, Slovakia, South Africa, Tajikistan, Turkey, Ukraine and Vietnam.
*Average formal sector premium across all estimates, percent; a negative number indicates a wage penalty for formal sector workers.

ANNEX TABLE 3.3.2 Meta regression analysis summary

Moderator variables	[1]	[2]	[3]	[4]	[5]	[6]	[7]	[8]
μ	0.195***	0.11**	0.23***	0.21***	0.14***	0.24***	0.17***	0.18***
	(0.03)	(0.04)	(0.03)	(0.03)	(0.04)	(0.04)	(0.05)	(0.06)
Female		0.16*			0.15*		0.12	0.12
		(0.08)			(0.08)		(0.08)	(0.08)
Male		0.14**			0.13**		0.11*	0.10
		(0.06)			(0.06)		(0.06)	(0.06)
Fixed Effects			-0.15**		-0.13**	-0.14**	-0.13**	-0.13**
			(0.07)		(0.06)	(0.06)	(0.06)	(0.07)
Self-employed				-0.34*		-0.32**	-0.25*	-0.26*
				(0.14)		(0.13)	(0.14)	(0.14)
Latin America and the Caribbean								0.00
								(0.07)
Europe and Central Asia								-0.03
								(0.07)
Adjusted *R-squared*		7.8	5.8	6.4	12.0	11.4	14.8	12.4
Number of observations	83	83	83	83	83	83	83	83
τ^2	0.06	0.05	0.05	0.05	0.05	0.05	0.05	0.05
I^2	99.6	99.5	99.4	99.5	99.4	99.4	99.4	99.1

Source: World Bank.
Note: *** p<0.01, ** p<0.05, * p<0.1; standard errors are in parenthesis. Within study standard errors of the estimates are used as weights to correct for the heterodasticity. The dependent variable is the informal-formal wage gap estimates by former studies (listed in Annex Table 3.3.1). τ^2 captures the degree of across-study variations, and I^2 reflects the impact of across-study heterogeneity.

ANNEX TABLE 3.4.1 **Pre-existing informality and changes in poverty and income inequality: OLS**

Moderator variables	[1]	[2]	[3]	Moderator variables	[4]	[5]	[6]
	Annual change in poverty				Annual change in income inequality		
Initial poverty rate	-0.024	-0.025	-0.029	Initial Gini index	-0.020	-0.020	-0.017
	(7.90)***	(7.94)***	(7.31)***		[-5.58]***	[-5.51]***	[-5.58]***
DGE	0.010			DGE	0.001		
	(1.84)*				[0.24]		
MIMIC		0.011		MIMIC		-0.000	
		(1.83)*				[-0.04]	
Self-employment			0.010	Self-employment			0.001
			(2.23)**				[0.84]
Constant	-0.507	-0.533	-0.466	Constant	0.671	0.705	0.534
	(2.13)**	(2.13)**	(2.81)***		[4.72]***	[4.91]***	[3.45]***
R-squared	0.48	0.47	0.45	R-squared	0.28	0.26	0.26
Number of observations	73	74	71	Number of observations	72	73	69

Source: World Bank.
Note: Estimated by ordinary least squares method. Dependent variable in column [1]-[3]: Annual change in poverty headcount ratio (i.e., Poverty headcount ratio at $1.90 a day (2011 PPP), percent of population) over the earliest year and the latest year, in percentage points. Dependent variable in column [4]-[6]: Annual change in Gini index over the earliest year and the latest year, in percentage points. Annual change in poverty headcount ratio (i.e., Poverty headcount ratio at $1.90 a day (2011 PPP), percent of population) over the earliest year and the latest year, in percentage points. Initial poverty rate (or Gini index for column [4]-[6]) is the earliest available year between 1990-2005. Informality indicators are averages over 1990-2005. *, **, and *** denote that the coefficients are statistically significant at the 10 percent, 5 percent, and 1 percent levels, respectively. Heteroskedasticity-robust standard errors are estimated with t-statistics presented below the corresponding coefficients.

ANNEX TABLE 3.5.1 **Sample**

EMDEs (99)			Advanced Economies (27)
Angola	Eswatini	Niger	Australia
Albania	Gambia, The	Nigeria	Austria
Algeria	Ghana	Oman	Belgium
Argentina	Guatemala	Pakistan	Canada
Bahamas, The	Guinea	Panama	Cyprus
Bahrain	Guinea-Bissau	Paraguay	Denmark
Bangladesh	Haiti	Peru	Finland
Barbados	Honduras	Philippines	France
Belize	Hungary	Poland	Germany
Benin	India	Qatar	Greece
Bhutan	Indonesia	Romania	Iceland
Bolivia	Iran	Rwanda	Ireland
Botswana	Iraq	Saudi Arabia	Israel
Brazil	Jamaica	Senegal	Italy
Brunei Darussalam	Jordan	Sierra Leone	Japan
Bulgaria	Kenya	South Africa	Korea, Rep.
Burkina Faso	Kuwait	Sri Lanka	Luxembourg
Burundi	Lao PDR	St. Lucia	Malta
Cabo Verde	Lebanon	St. Vincent and the Grenadines	Netherlands
Cambodia	Liberia	Sudan	Norway
Cameroon	Madagascar	Tanzania	Portugal
Central African Republic	Malawi	Thailand	Singapore
Chad	Malaysia	Togo	Spain
Chile	Mali	Trinidad and Tobago	Sweden
China	Mauritania	Tunisia	Switzerland
Colombia	Mauritius	Turkey	United Kingdom
Congo, Dem. Rep.	Mexico	Uganda	United States
Congo, Rep.	Mongolia	Uruguay	
Côte d'Ivoire	Morocco	Venezuela	
Dominican Republic	Mozambique	Vietnam	
Ecuador	Namibia	West Bank and Gaza	
Egypt	Nepal	Zambia	
El Salvador	Nicaragua	Zimbabwe	

Source: World Bank.
Note: The country sample and classification are taken from Loayza (2016).

References

Adams, A. V., S. J. de Silva, and S. Razmara. 2013. *Improving Skills Development in the Informal Sector: Strategies for Sub-Saharan Africa.* Directions in Development series. Washington, DC: World Bank,.

Ahumada, H., F. Alvaredo, and A. Canavesa. 2007. "The Monetary Method and the Size of the Shadow Economy: A Critical Assessment." *Review of Income and Wealth* 53 (2): 363–371.

Ali, N., and B. Najman. 2017. "Informal Competition, Firms' Productivity and Policy Reforms in Egypt." In *The Informal Economy: Exploring Drivers and Practices*, edited by I. A. Horodnic, P. Rodgers, C. C. Williams and L. Momtazian. Abingdon, UK: Routledge.

Allen, J., and T. Schipper. 2016. "Understanding the Informal Sector: Do Formal and Informal Firms Compete?" Mimeograph.

Almeida, R., and P. Carneiro. 2012. "Enforcement of Labor Regulation and Informality." *American Economic Journal: Applied Economics* 4 (3): 64-89.

Almeida, R., J. Behrman, and D. Robalino. 2012. "The Right Skills for the Job? Rethinking Training Policies for Workers." *Human Development Perspectives.* Washington, DC: World Bank.

Amaral, P. S., and E. Quintin. 2006. "A Competitive Model of the Informal Sector." *Journal of Monetary Economics* 53 (7): 1541-1553.

Amin, M., and X. Huang. 2014. "Does Firm-size Matter in the Informal Sector?" Enterprise Note 28, World Bank, Washington, DC.

Amin, M., and A. Islam. 2015. "Are Large Informal Firms More Productive than the Small Informal Firms? Evidence from Firm-level Surveys in Africa." *World Development* 74 (October): 374-385.

Anand, R., and P. Khera. 2016. "Macroeconomic Impact of Product and Labor Market Reforms on Informality and Unemployment in India." IMF Working Paper 1647, International Monetary Fund, Washington, DC.

Andrews, D., A. C. Sánchez, and Å. Johansson. 2011. "Towards a Better Understanding of the Informal Economy." OECD Economics Department Working Paper 873, OECD Publishing, Paris.

Ardizzi, G., C. Petraglia, M. Piacenza, and G. Turati. 2014. "Measuring the Underground Economy with the Currency Demand Approach: A Reinterpretation of the Methodology, With an Application to Italy." *Review of Income and Wealth* 60 (4): 747-772.

Arias, O., and M. Khamis. 2008. "Comparative Advantage, Segmentation and Informal Earnings: A Marginal Treatment Effects Approach." IZA Discussion Paper 3916, IZA-Institute of Labor Economics, Bonn, Germany.

Arias, J., E. Artuc, D. Lederman, and D. Rojas. 2018. "Trade, Informal Employment and Labor Adjustment Costs." *Journal of Development Economics* 133 (July): 396-414.

Arvin-Rad, H., A. K. Basu, and M. Willumsen. 2010. "Economic Reform, Informal–Formal Sector Linkages and Intervention in the Informal Sector in Developing Countries: A Paradox." *International Review of Economics & Finance* 19 (4): 662–70.

Attanasio, O., P. Goldberg, and N. Pavcnik. 2004. "Trade Reforms and Wage Inequality in Colombia." *Journal of Development Economics* 74 (2): 331-366.

Auriol, E., and M. Warlters. 2005. "Taxation Base in Developing Countries." *Journal of Public Economics* 89 (4): 625–46.

Awasthi, R., and M. Engelschalk. 2018. "Taxation and the Shadow Economy: How the Tax System Can Stimulate and Enforce the Formalization of Business Activities." Policy Research Working Paper 8391, World Bank, Washington, DC.

Aydin, E., M. Hisarciklilar, and I. Ilkkaracan. 2010. "Formal versus Informal Labor Market Segmentation in Turkey in the Course of Market Liberalization." *Topics in Middle Eastern and North African Economies*, 12 (September): 1-44.

Bachas, P., R. N. F. Jaef, and A. Jensen. 2018. "Size-Dependent Tax Enforcement and Compliance: Global Evidence and Aggregate Implications." Policy Research Working Paper 8363, World Bank, Washington, DC.

Bahadur, R. 2014. "Determinants of Informal Employment and Wage Differential in Nepal." *The Journal of Development and Administrative Studies* 22 (1-2): 37-50.

Bajada, C. 2003. "Business Cycle Properties of the Legitimate and Underground Economy in Australia." *Economic Record* 79 (247): 397-411.

Baksi, S., and P. Bose. 2016. "Informal Sector, Regulatory Compliance, and Leakage." *Journal of Development Economics* 121 (July): 166-176.

Bandaogo, M. S. 2016. "Fiscal and Monetary Policy in the Presence of Informality and the Incentive to Join a

Currency Union." Working Paper, University of Washington, Seattle.

Bargain, O., and P. Kwenda. 2014. "The Informal Sector Wage Gap: New Evidence Using Quantile Estimations on Panel Data." *Economic Development and Cultural Change* 63 (1): 117–53.

Barro, R., and J. Lee. 2013. "A New Data Set of Educational Attainment in the World, 1950-2010." *Journal of Development Economics* 104 (September): 184 -198.

Baskaya, Y. S., and T. Hulagu. 2011. "Informal-Formal Worker Wage Gap in Turkey: Evidence from A Semi-Parametric Approach." Working Paper 11/15, Central Bank of the Republic of Turkey, Ankara.

Beck, T., A. Demirguc-Kunt, and V. Maksimovic. 2006. "The Influence of Financial and Legal Institutions on Firm Size." *Journal of Banking and Finance* 30 (11): 2995-3015.

Beladi, H., M. Dutta, and S. Kar. 2016. "FDI and Business Internationalization of the Unorganized Sector: Evidence from Indian Manufacturing." *World Development* 83 (July): 340–49.

Benhassine, N., D. McKenzie, V. Pouliquen, and M. Santini. 2016. "Can Enhancing the Benefits of Formalization Induce Informal Firms to Become Formal? Experimental Evidence from Benin." Policy Research Working Paper 7900, World Bank, Washington, DC.

Benjamin, N., and A. A. Mbaye. 2012. *The Informal Sector in Francophone Africa: Firm Size, Productivity, and Institutions.* Washington, DC: World Bank.

Benjamin, N., K. Beegle, F. Recanatini, and M. Santini. 2014. "Informal Economy and the World Bank." Policy Research Working Paper 6888, World Bank, Washington, DC.

Besley, T., and T. Persson. 2014. "Why do Developing Countries Tax so Little?" *Journal of Economic Perspectives* 28 (4): 99-120.

Betcherman, G., N. M. Daysal, and C. Pagés. 2010. "Do Employment Subsidies Work? Evidence from Regionally Targeted Subsidies in Turkey." *Labour Economics* 17 (4): 710-722.

Blanchflower, D. G, A. Oswald, and A. Stutzer. 2001. "Latent Entrepreneurship across Nations." *European Economic Review* 45 (4): 680–91.

Boly, A. 2018. "On the Short- and Medium-Term Effects of Formalisation: Panel Evidence from

Vietnam." *The Journal of Development Studies* 54 (4): 641–656.

Bosch, M., and J. Esteban-Pretel. 2012. "Job Creation and Job Destruction in the Presence of Informal Markets." *Journal of Development Economics* 98 (2): 270–86.

Bosch, M., E. Goni, and W. Maloney. 2007. "The Determinants of Rising Informality in Brazil: Evidence from Gross Worker Flows." Policy Research Working Paper 4347, World Bank, Washington, DC.

Bosch, M., E. Goñi-Pacchioni, and W. Maloney, 2012. "Trade Liberalization, Labor Reforms and Formal–Informal Employment Dynamics." *Labour Economics* 19 (5): 653-667.

Bosch, M., and W. F. Maloney. 2008. "Cyclical Movements in Unemployment and Informality in Developing Countries." Policy Research Working Paper 4648, World Bank, Washington, DC.

———. 2010. "Comparative Analysis of Labor Market Dynamics Using Markov Processes: An Application to Informality." *Labour Economics* 17 (4): 621-631.

Botelho, F., and V. Ponczek. 2011. "Segmentation in the Brazilian Labor Market." *Economic Development and Cultural Change* 59 (2): 437–63.

Botero, J., S. Djankov, R. La Porta, F. Lopez-de-Silanes and A. Shleifer. 2004. "The Regulation of Labor." *Quarterly Journal of Economics* 119 (4): 1339-1382.

Brandt, L., J. Van Biesenbroeck, and Y. Zhang. 2012. "Creative Accounting or Creative Destruction? Firm-level Productivity Growth in Chinese Manufacturing." *Journal of Development Economics* 97 (2): 339-351.

Bruhn, M. 2011. "License to Sell: The Effect of Business Registration Reform on Entrepreneurial Activity in Mexico." *The Review of Economics and Statistics* 93 (1): 382-386.

———. 2013. "A Tale of Two Species: Revisiting the Effect of Registration Reform on Informal Business Owners in Mexico." *Journal of Development Economics* 103 (July): 275-283.

Bruhn, M., and J. Loeprick. 2014. "Small Business Tax Policy, Informality, and Tax Evasion: Evidence from Georgia." Policy Research Working Paper 7010, World Bank, Washington, DC.

Bruhn, M., and D. McKenzie. 2014. "Entry Regulation and the Formalization of Microenterprises in Developing Countries." *The World Bank Research Observer* 29 (2): 186–201.

Burki, A. and Q. Abbas. 1991. "Earnings Functions in Pakistan's Urban Informal Sector: A Case Study." *The Pakistan Development Review* 30 (4): 695-706.

Baskaya. Y.S., and T. Hulagu. 2011. "Informal-Formal Worker Wage Gap in Turkey : Evidence From A Semi-Parametric Approach." Working Papers 1115, Research and Monetary Policy Department, Central Bank of the Republic of Turkey.

Busato, F., and B. Chiarini. 2004. "Market and Underground Activities in a Two-Sector Dynamic Equilibrium Model." *Economic Theory* 23 (4): 831–61.

Caballero, R., K. Cowan, E. Engel, and A. Micco. 2013. "Effective Labor Regulation and Microeconomic Flexibility." *Journal of Development Economics* 101 (C): 92-104.

Campos, F., M. Goldstein, and D. McKenzie. 2015. "Short-Term Impacts of Formalization Assistance and a Bank Information Session on Business Registration and Access to Finance in Malawi." Policy Research Working Paper 7183, World Bank, Washington, DC.

Campos, F., M. Goldstein, and D. McKenzie. 2018. "How Should the Government Bring Small Firms into the Formal System? Experimental Evidence from Malawi." Policy Research Working Paper 8601, World Bank, Washington, DC.

Campus, N., and J. Nugent. 2012. "The Dynamics of the Regulation of Labor in Developing and Developed Countries Since 1960," IZA Discussion Paper 6881, IZA-Institute of Labor Economics, Bonn, Germany.

Capasso, S., and T. Jappelli. 2013. "Financial Development and the Underground Economy." *Journal of Development Economics* 101 (March): 167-178.

Capasso, S. S. Monferra, and G. Sampagnaro. 2018. "The Shadow Economy and Banks' Lending Technology." Mimeo.

Capp, J., H. Elstrodt, and W. Jones Jr. 2005. "Reining in Brazil's Informal Economy." *McKinsey Quarterly.* Available at http://www.mckinseyquarterly.com.

Card, D., J. Kluve, and A. Weber. 2018. "What Works? A Meta-Analysis of Recent Active Labor Market Program Evaluations." *Journal of the European Economic Association* 16 (3): 894-931.

Charlot, O., F. Malherbet, and C. Terra. 2015. "Informality in Developing Economies: Regulation and Fiscal Policies." *Journal of Economic Dynamics and Control* 51 (1): 1–27.

Chatterjee S., and S. J. Turnovsky. 2018. "Remittances and the Informal Economy." *Journal of Development Economics* 133: 66-83.

Chen, M. 2005. "Rethinking the Informal Economy: Linkages with the Formal Economy and the Formal Regulatory Environment." Working Paper 2005/10. Research Paper, UNU-WIDER, United Nations University (UNU).

Chen, M., J. Vanek, and J. Heintz. 2006. "Informality, Gender and Poverty: A Global Picture." Economic *and Political Weekly* 41 (21): 2131-2139.

Cho, J., and D. Cho. 2011. "Gender Difference of the Informal Sector Wage Gap: A Longitudinal Analysis for the Korean Labor Market." *Journal of the Asia Pacific Economy* 16 (4): 612–29.

Choi, J., and M. Thum. 2005. "Corruption and the Shadow Economy." *International Economic Review* 46 (3): 817-836.

Chong, A., and M. Gradstein. 2007. "Inequality and Informality." *Journal of Public Economics* 91(1-2): 159-179.

Çiçek, D., and C. Elgin. 2011. "Cyclicality of Fiscal Policy and the Shadow Economy." *Empirical Economics* 41 (3): 725-737.

Cirera, X., and W. Maloney. 2017. *The Innovation Paradox: Developing-Country Capabilities and the Unrealized Promise of Technological Catch-Up.* Washington, DC: World Bank.

Claessens, S., M. A. Kose, and M. E. Terrones. 2012. "How Do Business and Financial Cycles Interact?" *Journal of International Economics* 87 (1): 178-190.

Colombo, E., Onnis, L. and P. Tirelli. 2016. "Shadow Economies at Times of Banking Crises: Empirics and Theory." *Journal of Banking and Finance* 62 (C): 180-190.

Comola, M., and L. Mello. 2011. "How Does Decentralized Minimum Wage Setting Affect Employment and Informality? The Case of Indonesia." *Review of Income and Wealth* 57 (5): S79-S99.

Cunha, B. 2006. "Informality, Productivity and Growth." World Bank, Washington, DC.

Cunningham, W., and W. Maloney. 2001. "Heterogeneity among Mexico's Microenterprises: An Application of Factor and Cluster Analysis." *Economic Development and Cultural Change* 50 (1): 131-56.

Cusolito, A. P., and W. F. Maloney. 2018. "Productivity Revisited: Shifting Paradigms in Analysis and Policy." World Bank, Washington, DC.

Dabla-Norris, E., M. Gradstein, and G. Inchauste. 2008. "What Causes Firms to Hide Output?" *Journal of Development Economics* 85 (1-2): 1-27.

Dabla-Norris, E., and G. Inchauste. 2008. "Informality and Regulations: What Drives the Growth of Firms?" *IMF Staff Papers* 55 (1): 50-82.

Dabla-Norris, E., L. J. Mayor, F. Lima, and A. Sollaci. 2018. "Size Dependent Policies, Informality, and Misallocation." IMF Working Paper 18/179, International Monetary Fund, Washington DC.

Dell'Anno, R., 2008. "What is the Relationship Between Unofficial and Official Economy? An Analysis in Latin American Countries." *European Journal of Economics, Finance and Administrative Sciences* 12: 185-203.

De Andrade, G. H., M. Bruhn, and D. McKenzie. 2013. "A Helping Hand or the Long Arm of the Law? Experimental Evidence on What Governments Can Do to Formalize Firms." Policy Research Working Paper 6435, World Bank, Washington, DC.

Deininger, K., S. Jin, and M. Sur. 2007. "Sri Lanka's Rural Non-Farm Economy: Removing Constraints to Pro-Poor Growth," *World Development* 35 (12): 2056-2078.

Demenet, A., M. Razafindrakoto, and F. Roubaud. 2016. "Do Informal Businesses Gain from Registration and How? Panel Data Evidence from Vietnam." *World Development* 84 (August): 326-341.

D'Erasmo, P. N. 2016. "Access to Credit and the Size of the Formal Sector." *Economía* 16 (2): 143-199.

D'Erasmo, P. N., and H. J. Moscoso Boedo. 2012. "Financial Structure, Informality and Development." *Journal of Monetary Economics* 59 (3): 286-302.

De Giorgi, G., M. Ploenzke, and A. Rahman. 2018. "Small Firms' Formalisation: The Stick Treatment." *The Journal of Development Studies* 54 (6): 983–1001.

De Mel, S., D. McKenzie, and C. Woodruff. 2011. "What is the Cost of Formality? Experimentally Estimating the Demand for Formalization." Working Paper, University of Warwick, Coventry, England.

———. 2012. "The Demand for, and Consequences of, Formalization Among Informal Firms in Sri Lanka." Policy Research Working Paper 5991, World Bank, Washington, DC.

De Paula, Á., and J. Scheinkman. 2010. "Value-Added Taxes, Chain Effects, and Informality." *American Economic Journal: Macroeconomics* 2 (4): 195-221.

DerSimonian, R., and N. Laird. 1986. "Meta-Analysis in Clinical Trials." *Controlled Clinical Trials* 7 (3): 177–88.

De Soto, Hernando. 1989. *The Other Path: The Invisible Revolution in the Third World.* New York: Harper & Row.

Distinguin, I., C. Rugemintwari, and R. Tacneng. 2016. "Can Informal Firms Hurt Registered SMEs' Access to Credit?" *World Development* 84 (August): 18-40.

Divanbeigi, R. and R. Ramalho. 2015. "Business Regulations and Growth." Policy Research Working Paper 7299, World Bank, Washington DC.

Dix-Carniero, R., P. K. Goldberg, and C. Meghir. 2018. "Trade and Informality in the Presence of Labor Market Frictions and Regulations." Unpublished manuscript https://www.cemfi.es/ftp/pdf/papers/pew/DGMU.pdf .

Dix-Carneiro, R., R. R. Soares, and G. Ulyssea. 2018. "Economic Shocks and Crime: Evidence from the Brazilian Trade Liberalization." *American Economic Journal: Applied Economics* 10 (4): 158-95.

Dix-Carneiro, R., and B. K. Kovak. 2017. "Trade Liberalization and Regional Dynamics" *The American Economic Review* 107 (10): 2908-46.

Djankov, S., T. Ganser, C. McLiesh, R. Ramalho, and A. Shleifer. 2010. "The Effect of Corporate Taxes on Investment and Entrepreneurship." *American Economic Journal: Macroeconomics* 2 (3): 31-64.

Djankov, S., R. La Porta, F. López de Silanes, and A. Shleifer. 2002. "The Regulation of Entry." *Quarterly Journal of Economics* 117 (1): 1-37.

Docquier, F., T. Müller, and J. Naval. 2017. "Informality and Long-Run Growth." *The Scandinavian Journal of Economics* 119 (4): 1040-1085.

Donou-Adonsou, F. and K. Sylwester. 2017. "Growth Effect of Banks and Microfinance: Evidence from Developing Countries." *The Quarterly Review of Economics and Finance* 64 (May): 44-56.

Dreher, A., and F. Schneider. 2010. "Corruption and The Shadow Economy: An Empirical Analysis." *Public Choice* 144 (1-2): 215-238.

Duranton, G. and D. Puga. 2004. "Chapter 48— Micro-Foundations of Urban Agglomeration Economies." Chapter 48 in *Handbook of Regional and Urban Economics 4*. Amsterdam: Elsevier.

Earle, J. S., and Z. Sakova. 2000. "Business Start-Ups or Disguised Unemployment? Evidence on the Character of Self-Employment from Transition Economies." *Labour Economics* 7 (5): 575–601.

Eilat, Y., and C. Zinnes. 2002. "The Shadow Economy in Transition Countries: Friend or Foe? A Policy Perspective." *World Development* 30 (7): 1233–54.

El Badaoui, E., E. Strobl, and F. Walsh. 2008. "Is There an Informal Employment Wage Penalty? Evidence from South Africa." *Economic Development and Cultural Change* 56 (3): 683–710.

El Badaoui, E., E. Strobl, and F. Walsh. 2010. "The Formal Sector Wage Premium and Firm Size." *Journal of Development Economics* 91 (1): 37–47.

Elgin, C. 2012. "Cyclicality of the Informal Economy." Working Paper 02, Department of Economics, Bogazici University, Istanbul.

Elgin, C., and O. Oztunali. 2014. "Institutions, Informal Economy, and Economic Development." *Emerging Markets Finance and Trade* 50 (4): 117-134.

Elgin, C., A. Kose, F. Ohnsorge, and S. Yu. Forthcoming a. "Measuring the Informal Economy and its Business Cycles." Mimeo, World Bank, Washington, DC.

Elgin, C., A. Kose, F. Ohnsorge, and S. Yu. Forthcoming b. "Synchronization of Informal and Formal Business Cycles." Mimeo, World Bank, Washington, DC.

Enste, D., and F. Schneider. 1998. "Increasing Shadow Economies all over the World - Fiction or Reality." IZA Discussion Paper 26, IZA-Institute of Labor Economics, Bonn, Germany.

Fajnzylber, P., W. Maloney, and G. Montes-Rojas, 2011. "Does Formality Improve Micro-Firm Performance? Evidence from the Brazilian SIMPLES Program." *Journal of Development Economics* 94 (2): 262–276.

Falco, P., W. Maloney, B. Rijkers, and M. Sarrias. 2015. "Heterogeneity in Subjective Wellbeing: An Application to Occupational Allocation in Africa."

Journal of Economic Behavior and Organization 111 (March): 137-153.

Falco, P., and L. Haywood. 2016. "Entrepreneurship versus Joblessness: Explaining the Rise in Self-Employment." *Journal of Development Economics* 118 (January): 245–65.

Fan, H., Y. Liu, N. Qian, and J. Wen. 2018. "The Dynamic Effects of Computerized VAT Invoices on Chinese Manufacturing Firms." NBER Working Paper 24414. National Bureau of Economic Research.

Farrell, D. 2004. "The Hidden Dangers of Informal Economy." *McKinsey Quarterly* 3: 27-37.

Feige, E. L. 2016. "Reflections on the Meaning and Measurement of Unobserved Economies: What Do We Really Know about the "Shadow Economy"?" *Journal of Tax Administration* 2 (1): 1-37.

Fernandes, A. M. 2008. "Firm Productivity in Bangladesh Manufacturing Industries." *World Development* 36 (10): 1725-1744.

Fernández, A., and F. Meza. 2015. "Informal Employment and Business Cycles in Emerging Economies: The Case of Mexico." *Review of Economic Dynamics* 18 (2): 381–405.

Fernández, C., and L. Villar. 2016. "Informality and Inclusive Growth in Latin America: The Case of Colombia." IDS Working Paper 469, Institute of Development Studies, Brighton, U.K.

Ferreira, P. C., and J. L. Rossi. 2003. "New Evidence from Brazil on Trade Liberalization and Productivity Growth." *International Economic Review* 44 (4): 1383-1405.

Ferreira-Tiryaki, G. 2008. "The Informal Economy and Business Cycles." *Journal of Applied Economics* 11 (1): 91-117.

Fialová, K., and O. Schneider. 2011. "Labor institutions and their impact on shadow economies in Europe," Policy Research Working Paper 5913, World Bank, Washington, D.C.

Fields, G. S. 1975. "Rural-Urban Migration, Urban Unemployment and Underemployment, and Job-Search Activity in LDCs." *Journal of Development Economics* 2 (2): 165–87.

———. 1990. "Labour Market Modeling and the Urban Informal Sector: Theory and Evidence." In *The Informal Sector Revisited*, edited by D. Turnham, B. Salomé, and A. Schwarz. Paris: Organisation for Economic Co-Operation and Development.

———. 2005. "A Guide to Multisector Labor Market Models," Social Protection Discussion Paper 0505, World Bank, Washington, DC.

Fiess, N. M., M. Fugazza, and W. F. Maloney. 2010. "Informal Self-Employment and Macroeconomic Fluctuations." *Journal of Development Economics* 91 (2): 211–226.

Friedman, E., S. Johnson, D. Kaufmann, and P. Zoido-Lobatón. 2000. "Dodging the Grabbing Hand: The Determinants of Unofficial Activity in 69 Countries." *Journal of Public Economics* 76 (3): 459–493.

Friesen, J., and K. Wacker. 2013. "Do Financially Constrained Firms Suffer from More Intense Competition by the Informal Sector? Firm-Level Evidence from the World Bank Enterprise Surveys." Courant Research Centre Discussion Paper 139, University of Göttingen, Germany.

Fugazza, M., and N. Fiess. 2010. "Trade Liberalization and Informality: New Stylized Facts." Policy Issues in International Trade and Commodities Study Series No. 43, United Nations, New York and Geneva.

Funkhouser, E. 1997. "Mobility and Labor Market Segmentation: The Urban Labor Market in El Salvador." *Economic Development and Cultural Change* 46 (1): 123–53.

Galiani, S., and F. Weinschelbaum. 2012. "Modeling Informality Formally: Households and Firms." *Economic Inquiry* 50 (3): 821–838.

Gandelman, N., and A. Rasteletti. 2017. "Credit Constraints, Sector Informality and Firm Investments: Evidence from a Panel of Uruguayan Firms." *Journal of Applied Economics* 20 (2): 351–72.

Gasparini, L., and L. Tornarolli. 2007. "Labor Informality in Latin America and the Caribbean: Patterns and Trends from Household Survey Microdata." CEDLAS Working Papers, Universidad Nacional de La Plata, Argentina.

Ghani, E., W. Kerr, and S. O'Connell. 2013. "The Exceptional Persistence of India's Unorganized Sector." Policy Research Paper 6454, World Bank, Washington, DC.

Gibson, B. 2005. "The Transition to a Globalized Economy: Poverty, Human Capital and the Informal Sector in a Structuralist CGE Model." *Journal of Development Economics* 78 (1): 60–94.

Giles, D. E. A. 1997. "Causality between the Measured and Underground Economics in New Zealand." *Applied Economics Letters* 4 (1): 63-67.

Gindling, T. H. 1991. "Labor Market Segmentation and the Determination of Wages in the Public, Private-Formal, and Informal Sectors in San José, Costa Rica." *Economic Development and Cultural Change* 39 (3): 585–605.

Gindling, T., N. Mossaad, and D. Newhouse. 2016. "Earnings Premiums and Penalties for Self-Employment and Informal Employees around the World." Policy Research Working Paper 7530, World Bank, Washington, DC.

Goldberg, P. K., and N. Pavcnik. 2003. "The Response of the Informal Sector to Trade Liberalization. *Journal of Development Economics* 72 (2): 463-496.

———. 2004. "Trade, Inequality, and Poverty: What Do We Know? Evidence from Recent Trade Liberalization Episodes in Developing Countries." Working Paper 10593. National Bureau of Economic Research, Cambridge, MA.

Goldberg, P. K., and N. Pavcnik. 2007. "Distributional Effects of Globalization in Developing Countries." *Journal of Economic Literature* 45 (1): 39–82.

Gong, X., A. van Soest, and E. Villagomez. 2004. "Mobility in the Urban Labor Market: A Panel Data Analysis for Mexico." *Economic Development and Cultural Change* 53 (1): 1–36.

Gonzalez, A., and F. Lamanna. 2007. "Who Fears Competition from Informal Firms?" Policy Research Working Paper Series 4316, World Bank, Washington DC.

Government of India. 2017. "A New, Exciting Bird's-Eye View of the Indian Economy Through the GST." Chapter 2 in *Economic Survey 2017-18*. New Delhi: Ministry of Finance.

Grimm, M., P. Knorringa, and J. Lay. 2012. "Constrained Gazelles: High Potentials in West Africa's Informal Economy." *World Development* 40 (7): 1352-1368.

Guriev, S, B Speciale, and M Tuccio. 2016. "How do Regulated and Unregulated Labor Markets Respond to Shocks? Evidence from Immigrants During the Great Recession", CEPR Discussion Paper 11403, Centre for Economic Policy Research, Washington, DC.

Gupta, S., M. Keen, A. Shah, and G. Verdier. 2017. *Digital Revolutions in Public Finance*. Washington, DC: International Monetary Fund.

Gunatilaka, R. 2008. "Informal Employment in Sri Lanka: Nature, Probability of Employment, and Determinants of Wages." ILO Asia-Pacific Working

Paper Series, International Labour Organization, Geneva.

Günther, I., and A. Launov. 2006. "Competitive and Segmented Informal Labor Markets." IZA Discussion Paper 2349, IZA-Institute of Labor Economics, Bonn, Germany.

Günther, I., and A. Launov. 2012. "Informal Employment in Developing Countries: Opportunity or Last Resort?" *Journal of Development Economics* 97 (1): 88–98.

Guriev, S, B Speciale, and M Tuccio. 2016. "How do Regulated and Unregulated Labor Markets Respond to Shocks? Evidence from Immigrants during the Great Recession." CEPR Discussion Paper 11403, Centre for Economic Policy Research, Washington, DC.

Haltiwanger, J., R. Jarmin, and J. Miranda. 2013. "Who Creates Jobs? Small versus Large versus Young." *Review of Economics and Statistics* 95 (2): 347–361.

Haltiwanger, J. C., J. I. Lane, and J. R. Spletzer. 1999. "Productivity Differences Across Employers: The Roles of Employer Size, Age, and Human Capital." *The American Economic Review* 89 (2): 94-98.

Harding, D., and A. Pagan. 2002. "Dissecting the Cycle: A Methodological Investigation." *Journal of Monetary Economics* 49 (2): 365-381.

Harris, J. R. and M. P. Todaro. 1970. "Migration, Unemployment, and Development: A Two Sector Analysis." *The American Economic Review* 60 (1): 126-142.

Hazans, M. 2011. "Informal Workers Across Europe: Evidence from 30 European Countries." Policy Research Working Paper 5912, World Bank, Washington, DC.

Heckman, J., and X. Li. 2004. "Selection Bias, Comparative Advantage and Heterogeneous Returns to Education: Evidence from China in 2000." *Pacific Economic Review*, 9: 155-171.

Heckman, J., and C. Pagés (eds.). 2004. *Law and Employment. Lessons for Latin America and the Caribbean.* Chicago: The University of Chicago Press,.

Heredia, J., A. Flores, C. Geldes, and W. Heredia. 2017. "Effects of Informal Competition on Innovation Performance: The Case of Pacific Alliance." *Journal of Technology Management and Innovation* 12 (4): 22-28.

Higgins, J. P. T., and S. G. Thompson. 2002. "Quantifying Heterogeneity in a Meta-Analysis." *Statistics in Medicine* 21 (11): 1539–58.

Hsieh, C., and P. Klenow. 2009. "Misallocation and Manufacturing TFP in China and India." *The Quarterly Journal of Economics* 124 (4): 1403–48.

Huber, P., and U. Rahimov. 2014. "Formal and Informal Sector Wage Differences in Transition Economies: Evidence from Tajikistan." Working Papers in Business and Economics 48/2014, Mendel University in Brno, Czech Republic.

Hussmanns, R. 2004. "Measuring the Informal Economy: From Employment in the Informal Sector to Informal Employment." ILO Working Paper 42, International Labor Office, Geneva.

Horvath, J. 2018. "Business Cycles, Informal Economy, and Interest Rates in Emerging Countries." *Journal of Macroeconomics* 55 (March): 96-116.

Ihrig, J., and K. S. Moe. 2004. "Lurking in The Shadows: The Informal Sector and Government Policy." *Journal of Development Economics* 73 (2): 541-557.

Imai, S., and S. Azam. 2012. "Does Microfinance Reduce Poverty in Bangladesh? New Evidence from Household Panel Data." *The Journal of Development Studies* 48 (5): 633-653.

International Labor Organization (ILO). 2013. *Measuring Informality: A Statistical Manual on The Informal Sector and Informal Employment.* International Labor Office, Geneva.

International Labor Organization (ILO). 2018a. *Informal Economy.* Geneva: International Labor Office.

———. 2018b. *Women and Men in the Informal Economy: A Statistical Picture.* Geneva: International Labor Office.

International Monetary Fund (IMF). 2007. *Indonesia: 2007 Article IV Consultation.* Washington, DC: International Monetary Fund.

Iriyama, A., R. Kishore, and D. Talukda. 2016. "Playing Dirty or Building Capability? Corruption and HR Training as Competitive Actions to Threats from Informal and Foreign Firm Rivals." *Strategic Management Journal* 51 (2): 315-334.

Islam, A. 2018. "The Burden of Water Shortages on Informal Firms." Policy Research Working Paper 8457, World Bank, Washington, DC.

Ivlevs, A. 2016. "Remittances and Informal Work." IZA Discussion Paper 10196, IZA-Institute of Labor Economics, Bonn, Germany.

Johnson, S., D. Kaufmann, and A. Shleifer. 1997. "The Unofficial Economy in Transition." *Brookings Papers on Economic Activity* (Fall): 159-240.

Johnson, S., D. Kaufmann, and P. Zoido-Lobaton. 1998. "Regulatory Discretion and the Unofficial Economy." *The American Economic Review* 88 (2): 387 –92.

Jones, I. C., and W. Nordhaus. 2008. "Comment on" A. Shleifer and R. La Porta's "The Unofficial Economy and Economic Development." *Brookings Papers on Economic Activity* 2008 (2): 353-363.

Jovanovic, B. 1982. "Selection and Evolution of Industry." *Econometrica* 50 (3): 649–70.

Junquera-Varela R. F., M. Verhoeven, G. P. Shukla, B. Haven, R. Awasthi, and B. Moreno-Dodson. 2017. *Strengthening Domestic Resource Mobilization: Moving from Theory to Practice in Low- and Middle-Income Countries*. Directions in Development series. Washington, DC: World Bank.

Kanbur, R. 2009. "Conceptualizing Informality: Regulation and Enforcement." IZA Discussion Paper 4188, IZA-Institute of Labor Economics, Bonn, Germany.

———. 2017. "Informality: Causes, Consequences and Policy Responses." *Review of Development Economics* 21 (4): 939-961.

Kanbur, R., and M. Keen. 2015. "Rethinking Informality." Voxeu (blog), June 15, https://voxeu.org/article/rethinking-informality.

Kaufmann, D., and A. Kaliberda. 1996. "Integrating the Unofficial Economy into the Dynamics of Post-Socialist Economies: A Framework of Analysis and Evidence." Policy Research Working Paper 1691, World Bank, Washington DC.

Keen, M. 2008. "VAT, Tariffs, and Withholding: Border Taxes and Informality in Developing Countries." *Journal of Public Economics* 92 (10-11): 1892–1906.

Kim, Y., N. Loayza, and C. Meza-Cuadra, 2016. "Productivity as the Key to Economic Growth and Development," Research and Policy Briefs 108092, The World Bank, Washington DC.

Koeda, J., and E. Dabla-Norris, 2008. "Informality and Bank Credit; Evidence from Firm-Level Data." IMF Working Papers 08/94, International Monetary Fund, Washington DC.

Kuddo, A. 2018. "Labor Regulations Throughout the World: An Overview". Jobs Working Paper No. 16, World Bank, Washington DC.

La Porta, R., and A. Shleifer. 2008. "The Unofficial Economy and Economic Development." *Brookings Papers on Economic Activity* 2008 (2): 275-352.

La Porta, R., and A. Shleifer. 2014. "Informality and Development." *Journal of Economic Perspectives* 28 (3): 109-126.

Lackó, M. 2000. "Hidden Economy—An Unknown Quantity? Comparative Analysis of Hidden Economics in Transition countries 1989-95." *Economics of Transition* 8 (1): 117-149.

Lehmann, H., and A. Muravyev. 2009. "How Important are Labor Market Institutions for Labor Market Performance in Transition Countries?." IZA Discussion Paper 4673, IZA-Institute of Labor Economics, Bonn, Germany.

Lehmann, H., and N. Pignatti. 2007. "Informal Employment Relationships and Labor Market Segmentation in Transition Economies: Evidence from Ukraine." IZA Discussion Paper 3269, IZA-Institute of Labor Economics, Bonn, Germany.

Lehmann, H., and A. Zaiceva. 2013. "Informal Employment in Russia: Incidence, Determinants and Labor Market Segmentation." DSE Working Paper 903, Department of Economics, University of Bologna, Bologna, Italy.

Levy, S. L. 2008. *Good Intentions, Bad Outcomes: Social Policy, Informality and Economic Growth in Mexico*. Washington, DC: Brookings Institution Press.

Levy, S. 2018. *Under-Rewarded Efforts: The Elusive Quest for Prosperity in Mexico*. Washington, DC: Inter-American Development Bank.

Likhi, A. 2013. "Employment and Participation in South Asia: Challenges for Productive Absorption." *People, Spaces, Deliberation* (blog), October 24. https://blogs.worldbank.org/publicsphere/employment-and-participation-south-asia-challenges-productive-absorption.

Loayza, N. V. 1996. "The Economics of the Informal Sector: A Simple Model and Some Empirical Evidence from Latin America." *Carnegie-Rochester Conference Series on Public Policy* 45: 129-162.

————. 2016. "Informality in the Process of Development and Growth." *The World Economy* 39 (12): 1856-1916.

————. 2018. "Informality: Why Is It So Widespread and How Can It Be Reduced?" *Research & Policy Brief,* World Bank, Kuala Lumpur.

Loayza, N., and C. Meza-Cuadra. 2016. "A Toolkit for Informality Scenario Analysis." Available at: http://www.worldbank.org/en/research/brief/a-toolkit-for-informality-scenario-analysis. Updated version, accessed on June 24, 2018.

Loayza, N., A. M. Oviedo, and L. Servén. 2006, "The Impact of Regulation on Growth and Informality – Cross-country Evidence." In *Linking the Formal and Informal Economy,* edited by B. Guha-Khasnobis, R. Kanbur and E. Ostrom. New York: Oxford University Press.

Loayza, N. V., and J. Rigolini. 2006. "Informality Trends and Cycles." Policy Research Working Paper 4078, World Bank, Washington, DC.

————. 2011. "Informal Employment: Safety Net or Growth Engine?" *World Development* 39 (9): 1503-1515.

Loayza, N., L. Servén, and N. Sugawara. 2010. "Informality in Latin America and the Caribbean." In *Business Regulation and Economic Performance,* edited by N. Loayza and L. Servén. Washington, DC: World Bank.

Loayza, N., and T. Wada. 2010. "Informal Labor in the Middle East and North Africa: Basic Measures and Determinants." Mimeo. World Bank, Washington, DC.

Lubell, H. 1991. *The Informal Sector in the 1980s and 1990s.* Paris: OECD.

Luttmer, E. G. J. 2007. "Selection, Growth, and the Size Distribution of Firms." *The Quarterly Journal of Economics* 122 (3): 1103-1144.

Magnac, T. 1991. "Segmented or Competitive Labor Markets." *Econometrica* 59 (1): 165-87.

Maloney, W. F. 1999. "Does Informality Imply Segmentation in Urban Labor Markets? Evidence from Sectoral Transitions in Mexico." *World Bank Economic Review* 13: 275-302.

————. 2004. "Informality Revisited." *World Development* 32 (7): 1159-1178.

————. 2006. "Informality Deconstructed." Mimeo. World Bank, Washington, DC.

Maloney, W. F., and J. Mendez. 2004. "Measuring the Impact of Minimum Wages: Evidence from Latin America." In *Law and Employment: Lessons from Latin America and the Caribbean,* edited by J. J. Heckman and C. Pagés. Chicago: University of Chicago Press.

Marcouiller, D., V. R. de Castilla, and C. Woodruff. 1997. "Formal Measures of the Informal-Sector Wage Gap in Mexico, El Salvador, and Peru." *Economic Development and Cultural Change* 45 (2): 367–92.

Marjit S., V. Mukherjee and M. Kolmar. 2006. "Poverty, Taxation, and Governance." *The Journal of International Trade & Economic Development* 15 (3): 325-333.

Mbaye, A., N. Benjamin, and F. Gueye. 2017. "The Interplay Between Formal and Informal Firms and Its Implications on Jobs in Francophone Africa: Case studies of Senegal and Benin." In *The Informal Economy in Global Perspective* edited by A. Polese, C. C. Williams, I. O. Horodnic, and P. Bejakovic. Basingstoke, UK: Palgrave Macmillan.

McCaig, B., and N. Pavcnik. 2015. "Informal Employment in a Growing and Globalizing Low-Income Country." *The American Economic Review* 105 (5): 545-550.

McCaig, B., and N. Pavcnik. 2018. "Export Markets and Labor Allocation in a Low-Income Country." *The American Economic Review* 108 (7): 1899-1941.

McKenzie, D., and Y. Sakho. 2010. "Does it Pay Firms to Register for Taxes? The Impact of Formality on Firm Productivity." *Journal of Development Economics* 91 (1): 15-24.

Meagher, K. 2013. "Unlocking the Informal Economy: A Literature Review on Linkages between Formal and Informal Economies in Developing Countries." WIEGO *Working Paper* 27, Women in Informal Employment: Globalization and Organization, Manchester, England.

Medina, M., and F. Schneider. 2018. "Shadow Economies around the World: What Did We Learn Over the Last 20 Years?" IMF Working Paper 18/17, International Monetary Fund, Washington, DC.

Meghir, C., R. Narita, and J. Robin. 2015. "Wages and Informality in Developing Countries." *American Economic Review* 105 (4): 1509-46.

Melitz, M. J. 2003. "The Impact of Trade on Intra-Industry Reallocations and Aggregate Industry Productivity." *Econometrica* 71 (6): 1695-1725.

Mendi, P., and R. Costamagna. 2017. "Managing Innovation Under Competitive Pressure from Informal Producers." *Technological Forecasting and Social Change* 114 (January): 192–202.

Mendicino C., and M. Prado. 2014. "Heterogeneous Firms and the Impact of Government Policy on Welfare and Informality." *Economics Letters* 124 (1): 151-156.

Monteiro, J. C. M., and J. J. Assuncão. 2012. "Coming Out of the Shadows? Estimating the Impact of Bureaucracy Simplification and Tax Cut on Formality in Brazilian Microenterprises." *Journal of Development Economics* 99 (1): 100 – 115.

Morales, L., and C. Medina. 2017. "Assessing the Effect of Payroll Taxes on Formal Employment: The Case of the 2012 Tax Reform in Colombia." *Economía* 18(1): 75-124.

Munkacsi, Z., and M. Saxegaard. 2017. "Structural Reform Packages, Sequencing, and the Informal Economy." IMF Working Paper 17/125, International Monetary Fund, Washington DC.

Nguyen, H. C., C. J. Nordman, and F. Roubaud. 2013. "Who Suffers the Penalty? A Panel Data Analysis of Earnings Gaps in Vietnam." *The Journal of Development Studies* 49 (12): 1694–1710.

Nordman, C., F. Rakotomanana, and F. Roubaud. 2016. "Informal versus Formal: A Panel Data Analysis of Earnings Gaps in Madagascar." *World Development* 86 (October): 1–17.

Nguimkeu, P. E. 2015. "An Estimated Model of Informality with Constrained Entrepreneurship." Working Paper, Georgia State University, Atlanta.

Neumeyer, P., and F. Perri. 2005. "Business Cycles in Emerging Economies: the Role of Interest Rates." *Journal of Monetary Economics* 52 (2): 345-380.

Ordóñez, J. 2014. "Tax Collection, the Informal Sector, and Productivity." *Review of Economic Dynamics* 17 (2): 262-286.

Orsi, R., D. Raggi, and F. Turino. 2014. "Size, Trend, and Policy Implications of the Underground Economy." *Review of Economic Dynamics* 17 (3): 417-436.

Otobe, N. 2017. "Gender and the Informal Economy: Key Challenges and Policy Response." Employment Policy Department Employment Working Paper No. 236. International Labour Organization, Geneva.

Oviedo, A. M. 2009. "Economic Informality: Causes, Costs, and Policies, A Literature Survey of International Experience." World Bank, Washington, DC.

Oviedo, A., M. Thomas, and K. Karakurum-Özdemir. 2009. "Economic Informality: Causes, Costs, and Policies – A Literature Survey." Working Paper 167, World Bank, Washington, DC.

Pavcnik, N. and A. Blom and P. Goldberg and N. Schady. 2004. "Trade Liberalization and Industry Wage Structure: Evidence from Brazil." *World Bank Economic Review* 18 (3): 319-344.

Paz, L. 2014. "The Impacts of Trade Liberalization on Informal Labor Markets: A Theoretical and Empirical Evaluation of the Brazilian Case." *Journal of International Economics* 92(2): 330-348.

Perry, G. E., W. F. Maloney, O. S. Arias, P. Fajnzylber, A. D. Mason, and J. Saavedra-Chanduvi. 2007. *Informality: Exit and Exclusion*. Washington, DC: World Bank.

Piza, C. 2016. "Revisiting the Impact of the Brazilian SIMPLES Program on Firms' Formalization Rates." Policy Research Working Paper 7605, World Bank, Washington, DC.

Prado, M. 2011. "Government Policy in the Formal and Informal Sectors." *European Economic Review* 55 (8): 1120–36.

Pratap, S., and E. Quintin. 2006. "Are Labor Markets Segmented in Developing Countries? A Semiparametric Approach." *European Economic Review* 50 (7): 1817-1841.

Quintin, E. 2008. "Contract Enforcement and the Size of the Informal Economy." *Economic Theory* 37 (3): 395-416.

Rani, U., P. Belser, M. Oelz, and S. Ranjbar. 2013. "Minimum Wage Coverage and Compliance in Developing Countries." *International Labor Review* 152 (3-4): 381-410.

Rauch, J. E. 1991. "Modelling the Informal Sector Formally." *Journal of Development Economics* 35 (1): 33-47.

Restrepo-Echavarria, P. 2014. "Macroeconomic Volatility: The Role of the Informal Economy." *European Economic Review* 70 (August): 454-469.

Rocha, R., G. Ulyssea, and R. Rachter. 2018. "Do Lower Taxes Reduce Informality? Evidence from Brazil." *Journal of Development Economics* 134 (September): 28-49.

Rosenthal, S. S., and W. C. Strange. 2004. "Evidence on the Nature and Source of Agglomeration Economies." Chapter 49 in *Handbook of Regional and Urban Economics 4*. Amsterdam: Elsevier.

Rosser B., M. Rosser, and E. Ahmed. 2000." Income Inequality and the Informal Economy in Transition Economies." *Journal of Comparative Economics* 28 (1): 156-171.

Sanfey, P., and U. Teksoz. 2007. "Does Transition Make You Happy?" *Economics of Transition* 15 (4): 707–31.

Saracoğlu, D. S. 2008. "The Informal Sector and Tax on Employment: A Dynamic General Equilibrium Investigation." *Journal of Economic Dynamics and Control* 32 (2): 529–49.

Sarte, P.-D. G. 2000. "Informality and Rent-Seeking Bureaucracies in a Model of Long-Run Growth." *Journal of Monetary Economics* 46 (1): 173–97.

Schipper, T. 2016. "Informality, Innovation, and Aggregate Productivity Growth." Mimeograph.

Schneider, F. 1998. "Further Empirical Results of the Size of the Shadow Economy of 17 OECD Countries over Time." Discussion Paper, Department of Economics, University of Linz, Austria.

———. 2005. "Shadow Economies Around the World: What do we Really Know?" *European Journal of Political Economy* 21: 598-642.

Schneider, F. and A. Buehn. 2016. "Estimating the Size of the Shadow Economy: Methods, Problems and Open Questions." IZA Discussion Paper 9820, IZA-Institute of Labor Economics, Bonn, Germany.

Schneider, F., A. Buehn, and C. E. Montenegro. 2010. "Shadow Economies All over the World: New Estimates for 162 Countries from 1999 to 2007." Policy Research Working Paper 5356, World Bank, Washington, DC.

Schneider, F., and D. H. Enste. 2000. "Shadow Economies: Size, Causes, and Consequences." *Journal of Economic Literature* 38 (1): 77-114.

Selwaness, I., and C. Zaki. 2015. "Assessing the Impact of Trade Reforms on informal employment in Egypt." *The Journal of North African Studies* 20 (3): 391-414.

Shapiro, A. F. 2014. "Self-employment and Business Cycle Persistence: Does the Composition of Employment Matter for Economic Recoveries?" *Journal of Economic Dynamics and Control* 46 (September): 200-218.

Shapiro, A. F., and F. S. Mandelman. 2016. "Remittances, Entrepreneurship, and Employment Dynamics over the Business Cycle." *Journal of International Economics* 103 (November): 184-199.

Sharma, S. 2009. "Entry Regulation, Labor Laws and Informality." Working Paper, Enterprise Analysis Unit, World Bank, Washington, DC.

Shleifer, A., and R. W. Vishny. 1993. "Corruption." *The Quarterly Journal of Economics* 108 (3): 599–617.

Slonimczyk, F. 2012. "The Effect of Taxation on Informal Employment: Evidence from the Russian Flat Tax Reform." Chapter 2 in *Informal Employment in Emerging and Transition Economies*, edited by H. Lehmann and K. Tatsiramos. Bingley, UK: Emerald Group Publishing Company.

Stanley, T., H. Doucouliagos, M. Giles, H. Heckemeyer, R. Johnston, P. Laroche, and J. Nelson. 2013. "Meta-Analysis of Economics Research Reporting Guidelines: Reporting Guidelines for Meta-Regression Analysis in Economics." *Journal of Economic Surveys* 27 (2): 390–94.

Straub, S. 2005. "Informal Sector: The Credit Market Channel." *Journal of Development Economics* 78 (2): 299-321.

Sonobe, T., J. E. Akoten, and K. Otsuka. 2011. "The Growth Process of Informal Enterprises in Sub-Saharan Africa: A Case Study of a Metalworking Cluster in Nairobi." *Small Business Economics* 36 (3): 323-335.

Sung, M. J., R. Awasthi, and H. C. Lee. 2017. "Can Tax Incentives for Electronic Payments Reduce the Shadow Economy? Korea's Attempt to Reduce Underreporting in Retail Businesses." Policy Research Working Paper 7936, World Bank, Washington, DC.

Tansel, A., and E. Kan. 2012. "The Formal/Informal Employment Earnings Gap: Evidence from Turkey." ERC Working Paper 1204, Economic Research Center, Middle East Technical University, Ankara.

Tedds, L., and D. A. Giles. 2000. "Modelling the Underground Economies in Canada and New Zealand: A Comparative Analysis." Econometrics Working Papers 3. Department of Economics, University of Victoria.

Ulyssea, G. 2010. "Regulation of Entry, Labor Market Institutions and the Informal Sector." *Journal of Development Economics* 91 (1): 87-99.

Ulyssea, G. 2018. "Firms, Informality, and Development: Theory and Evidence from Brazil." *The American Economic Review* 108 (8): 2015-47.

Ulyssea, G., and V. Ponczek. 2018. "Enforcement of Labor Regulation and the Labor Market Effects of Trade: Evidence from Brazil." IZA Discussion Paper 11783, IZA-Institute of Labor Economics, Bonn, Germany.

USAID (U.S. Agency for International Development). 2005. *Removing Barriers to Formalization: The Case for Reform and Emerging Best Practice.* Washington, DC.: USAID.

Van der Sluis, J., M. van Praag, and W. Vijverberg. 2005. "Entrepreneurship Selection and Performance: A Meta-Analysis of the Impact of Education in Developing Economies." *World Bank Economic Review* 19 (2): 225-261.

Vargas, J. P. M. 2015. "Informality in Paraguay: Macro-Micro Evidence and Policy Implications." Working Paper 15/245, IMF, Washington, DC.

Vegh, C., and G. Vuletin. 2015. "How Is Tax Policy Conducted over the Business Cycle?" *American Economic Journal: Economic Policy* 7 (3): 327-70.

Verner, D., and M. Verner. 2000. "Economic Impacts of Professional Training in the Informal Sector of Cote d'Ivoire: Evaluation of the PAFPA." Policy Research Working Paper 3668, World Bank, Washington, DC.

Vuletin, G. 2008. "Measuring the Informal Economy in Latin America and the Caribbean." IMF Working Paper 08/102, International Monetary Fund, Washington, DC.

Waseem, M. 2018. "Taxes, Informality and Income Shifting: Evidence from a Recent Pakistani Tax Reform." *Journal of Public Economics* 157 (January): 41-77.

Wellalage, N. H., and S. Locke. 2016. "Informality and Credit Constraints: Evidence from Sub-Saharan African MSEs." *Applied Economics* 48 (29): 2756-2770.

Williams, C. C., and F. Schneider. 2016. *Measuring the Global Shadow Economy: The Prevalence of Informal Work and Labour.* Cheltenham, GL, and Northampton, MA: Edward Elgar Publishing.

Williams, C., M. Shahid, and A. Martinez. 2015. "Determinants of the Level of Informality in Informal Micro-Enterprises: Some Evidence from the City of Lahore, Pakistan." World Development 84 (August): 312-325.

World Bank. 2012. *Jobs – World Development Report 2013.* Washington, DC: World Bank.

World Bank. 2013. *Risk and Opportunity – World Development Report 2014.* Washington, DC: World Bank.

World Bank. 2014. *World Development Report 2014: Risks and Opportunities.* Washington, DC: World Bank.

World Bank. 2016. *World Development Report 2016: Digital Dividends.* Washington, DC: World Bank.

World Bank. 2017. *The Global Findex Database 2017: Measuring Financial Inclusion and the Fintech Revolution.* Washington, DC: World Bank.

World Bank. 2018a. *Risk Sharing for a Diverse and Diversifying World of Work.* Social Protection and Jobs White paper. (Forthcoming). Washington, DC: World Bank.

World Bank. 2018b. *World Development Report 2018: Learning to Realize Education's Promise.* Washington, DC: World Bank.

World Bank. 2018c. *Gulf Economic Monitor: Deepening Reforms.* Washington, DC: World Bank.

World Bank. 2019. *World Development Report 2019: The Changing Nature of Work.* Washington, DC: World Bank.

World Governance Indicators (database), World Bank, Washington, DC. http://info.worldbank.org/govern ance/wgi/#home.

CHAPTER 4

TWO TOPICAL ESSAYS

Debt in Low-Income Countries: Evolution, Implications, and Remedies

Poverty Impact of Food Price Shocks and Policies

Debt in Low-Income Countries: Evolution, Implications, and Remedies

Debt vulnerabilities in low-income countries (LICs) have increased substantially in recent years. Since 2013, median government debt has risen by about 20 percentage points of GDP and increasingly comes from non-concessional and private sources. As a result, in most LICs interest payments are absorbing an increasing proportion of government revenues. The majority of LICs would be hard hit by a sudden weakening in trade or global financial conditions given high levels of external debt, lack of fiscal space, low foreign currency reserves, and undiversified exports. A proactive effort to identify and reduce debt-related vulnerabilities is a priority for many LICs. Policymakers should focus on mobilizing domestic resources, improving debt transparency, and strengthening debt management practices. These efforts should be complemented by measures to strengthen fiscal frameworks, improve the efficiency of public expenditures and public investment management, and develop domestic financial systems.

Introduction

In recent years, many low-income countries (LICs) have gained access to additional sources of finance, including private and non-Paris Club creditors.[1] While this has enabled these countries to fund important development needs, it has also led to higher levels of public debt. The increasing share of market-based debt exposes many LICs to interest rate, and refinancing risks. These trends take place as the external environment is becoming more challenging and borrowing costs are expected to rise around the world, as described in Chapter 1. This means that, in the event of an abrupt deterioration in market conditions, some LICs may struggle to refinance debts from foreign sources and are at risk of capital flow reversals and dislocating currency depreciations. In this context, it is important for LICs to develop their domestic financial systems, strengthen capacity for domestic resource mobilization, improve macro-fiscal frameworks, and improve their resilience to shocks through the sound management of public debt and investment.

Against this backdrop, this essay addresses the following questions:

- What are the key characteristics of the recent rise in LIC debt?

- How does rising debt relate to other LIC vulnerabilities?

- How can better debt management help reduce LIC vulnerabilities?

- How can complementary policy measures reduce LIC vulnerabilities?

Key characteristics of the recent rise in LIC debt

A recent sharp rise. Debt relief under the Heavily Indebted Poor Countries (HIPC) initiative and the Multilateral Debt Relief Initiative (MDRI) helped to reduce public debt among LICs from a median debt-to-GDP ratio of close to 100 percent in the early 2000s to a median of just over 30 percent in 2013.[2] This downward trend reversed sharply thereafter, with the median debt ratio rising to above 50 percent by 2017 (Figure 4.1.1). The increase was large relative to other EMDEs, whose median debt rose by less than 11 percentage points of GDP from 2013 to 2017, compared to 20 percentage points for LICs. It was also broad-based: debt ratios rose in almost 90 percent of LICs, and a third experienced debt increases of more than 20 percentage points.

This essay was prepared by Sinem Kilic Celik and Patrick Kirby in collaboration with Andre Proite and Sebastian Essl from the Global Macro and Debt Analytics Group of the Macro, Trade, and Investment Global Practice.

[1] LICs refers to countries meeting the World Bank Group's definition of countries with per capita gross national income below $995 per year in 2017. This group includes 33 countries (Annex 4.1.1).

---

[2] Most LICs—27 out of 33—benefited from one or both of the HIPC and MDRI programs.

FIGURE 4.1.1 LIC government finances

LIC government debt ratios have risen since 2013, in part because of widening fiscal deficits, but still remain well below levels in the early 2000s.

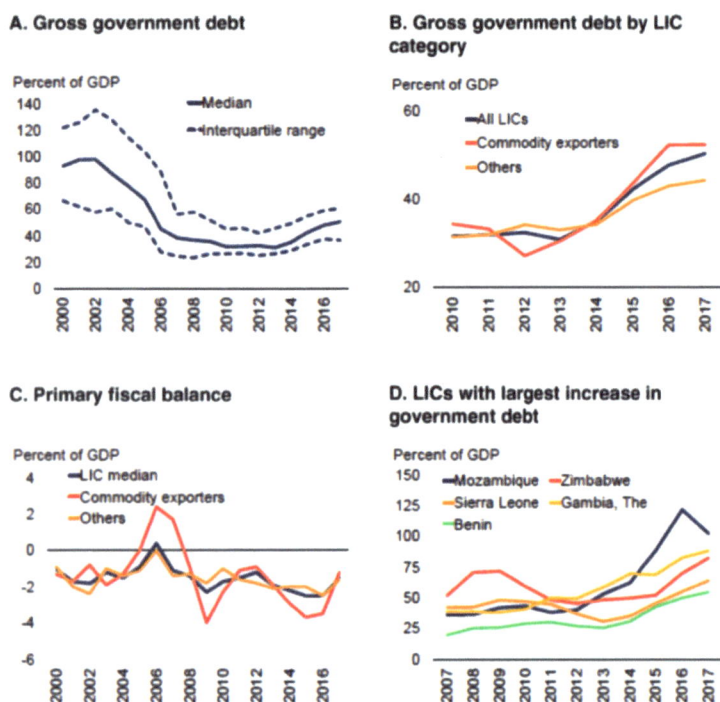

A. Gross government debt

B. Gross government debt by LIC category

C. Primary fiscal balance

D. LICs with largest increase in government debt

Source: International Monetary Fund, World Bank.
A. Dashed blue lines denote the interquartile range, while the solid blue line is the median.
A.B.C. The sample includes 30 low-income countries, of which 2 are oil exporters, 8 metals exporters, and the remaining 20 are non-resource-intensive. It excludes Somalia, South Sudan, and Syria due to data restrictions.
A.B. Figure shows median gross government debt in percent of GDP.
B.C.D. LICs= Low-income countries.

The key role of fiscal deficits. Primary fiscal deficits had largely been closed among LICs by 2006, but widened steadily following the global financial crisis, especially among commodity exporters suffering from falling commodity prices. Rising deficits may also be the result of LICs' increased ability to borrow as a result of HIPC and MDRI debt relief (Bayraktar and Fofack 2011; Marcelino and Hakobyan 2014). The primary balance of most LICs has been negative since the mid-2000s, and all but five (of 31 with available data) LICs had primary deficits in 2017, with a third carrying a primary deficit exceeding 3 percent of GDP.

Uses of borrowed funds. A rising debt burden is typically less of a reason for concern if it is used to finance investment that raises a country's potential output, and therefore its ability to repay loans in the future (World Bank 2017). In some LICs,

growing deficits reflected a push to finance public investment, as suggested by the doubling of median LIC public investment as a share of GDP from 3 percent in 2000 to 6 percent in 2015. This was the experience of Guinea-Bissau, Madagascar, Mali, and Nepal, where wider fiscal deficits were matched by higher public investment (IMF 2018a). These countries form a minority, however, as a substantial part of LIC borrowing has been used to finance a rise in current consumption. In resource-intensive countries in Sub-Saharan Africa, for example, the bulk of increased spending enabled by a rise in commodity prices went to public sector wages (World Bank 2018a). Some borrowing may also have been redirected toward the accumulation of private assets stored abroad.[3]

Dependence on external debt. Given their typically small local creditor base, a significant share of LIC borrowing comes from abroad and is denominated in foreign currencies. The resulting currency mismatch poses a challenge to LICs, as a depreciating currency can lead to a rise in the domestic value of the country's debt burden and interest payments. This challenge is more severe in countries with a significant share of external debt priced at market rates, and less so for countries benefiting from the low interest rates on concessional debt.

The median LIC carries external debt, including both public and private debt, equivalent to 28 percent of GDP and almost half of total debt. Median external debt as a share of GDP has risen about 3 percentage points since 2012, with several important outliers. Commercial debt issuances have contributed to especially sharp rises in external debt burdens in Mozambique and Tajikistan. In Uganda, external debt as a share of GDP has more than doubled since 2012, to more than 40 percent of GDP in 2017. The maturity composition of LIC external debt has remained broadly stable—short-term debt remained moderate at 5 percent of total external debt in 2016.

---

[3] Ndikumana and Boyce (2011) find that for every dollar in external loans to Sub-Saharan Africa, capital outflows increased by roughly 60 cents in the same year.

Shift toward non-traditional creditors. The composition of public debt has shifted over the last decade, becoming increasingly non-concessional as LICs have increased their reliance on financing from non-traditional sources (Figure 4.1.2). The median share of non-concessional debt in public debt rose to 55 percent in 2016 (the latest year for which data are available), an increase of nearly 8 percentage points since 2013, and 15 percentage points compared with a decade earlier. Commercial creditors have become an important source of credit for some countries (World Bank and IMF 2018a). Ethiopia, Mozambique, Rwanda, Senegal, Tajikistan, and Tanzania have all issued commercial public debt since 2010, generally denominated in U.S. dollars.[4]

Non-Paris Club creditors, notably China, have also become a more important source of financing over the past decade, especially in Sub-Saharan Africa (World Bank 2015a). In 2016, non-Paris Club debt accounted for more than a fifth of the median LIC's external debt, and about 13 percent of their public debt (World Bank 2018b). Major recipients of lending from non-Paris Club creditors include the Democratic Republic of Congo, Ethiopia, Mozambique, Tanzania, Uganda, and Zimbabwe (Atkins et al. 2017; Eom, Brautigam and Benabdallah 2018).

Lending arrangements for commercial and non-Paris Club debt are often not public, and they can be complex and varied (World Bank and IMF 2018b). Some of this debt is collateralized, which could reduce budget flexibility by earmarking revenues, could weaken the creditor's incentive to assess the borrower's debt sustainability, and (if large) could increase funding costs from other creditors who may reassess the probability of being repaid. Moreover, increased exposure to non-Paris Club and commercial creditors may pose coordination challenges for debt resolutions in the future, making the consequences of debt distress even more disruptive, especially if debt is collateralized (World Bank and IMF 2018c).

FIGURE 4.1.2 **Public debt in LICs**

Higher debt, and the shift from concessional to market financing, makes LICs more vulnerable to rising interest rates.

A. **Change in creditor composition of public and publicly guaranteed external debt, 2007-16**

B. **Share of non-concessional debt**

C. **Interest payments**

D. **Share of LICs in debt distress or at high risk of distress**

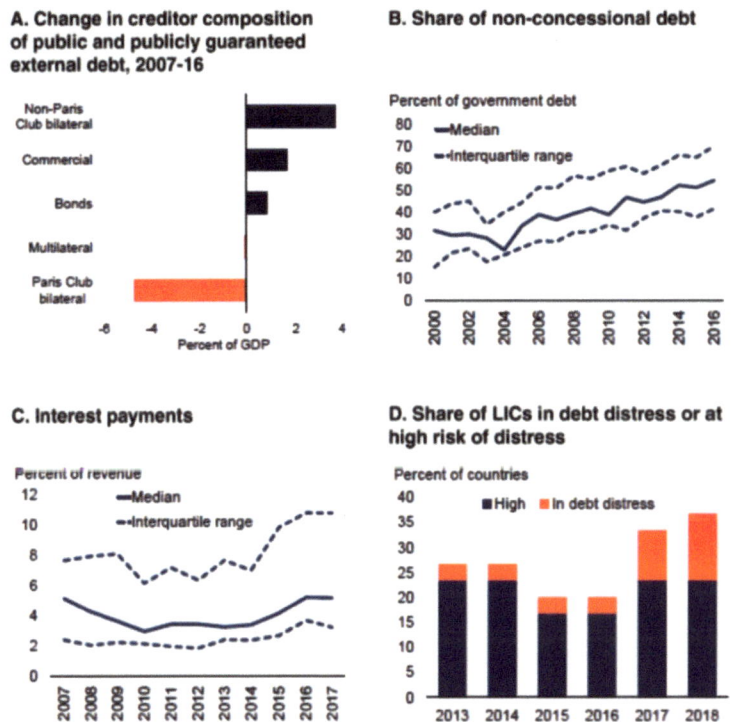

Source: International Monetary Fund, World Bank.
A. GDP-weighted average across 32 low-income countries. "Bilateral" includes public and publicly guaranteed (PPG) loans from governments and their agencies (including central banks), loans from autonomous bodies, and direct loans from official export credit agencies. "Multilateral" includes PPG loans and credits from the World Bank, regional development banks, and other multilateral and intergovernmental agencies. It excludes loans from funds administered by an international organization on behalf of a single donor government. "Bonds" include PPG bonds that are either publicly issued or privately placed. "Commercial" includes PPG debt from commercial bank loans from private banks and other private financial institutions, as well as export and supplier credits.
B.C. Dashed blue lines denote the interquartile range, while solid blue line is the median. Includes 30 low-income countries and excludes Somalia, South Sudan, and Syria due to data restrictions.
D. Figure shows the percent of low-income countries eligible to access the IMF's concessional lending facilities that are either at high risk of, or in, debt distress. A country is considered to be in debt distress if it is experiencing difficulties in servicing its debt, as evidenced, for example, by the existence of arrears, ongoing or impending debt restructuring, or if there are indications that a future debt distress event is probable. The sample includes 30 low-income countries.

Rising cost of debt service. As debt loads have grown and become less concessional, interest payments have absorbed a growing share of government revenues. Among LICs, the median interest payments-to-revenue ratio rose to over 5 percent in 2017, up from just over 3 percent in 2013. The increase in the ratio was due to rapidly rising interest payments, with median interest payments among LICs having grown by over 128 percent versus 31 percent growth in government revenues.

Drivers of rising debt. Countries with the fastest rise in debt were often fragile and affected by a

---

[4] Of 11 LIC debt issuances since 2010, all were denominated in U.S. dollars, with the exception of one of Senegal's two issuances in 2018, which was euro-denominated.

combination of conflict, weak governance, or commodity-dependence (World Bank 2018c). In The Gambia, government debt increased from nearly 60 percent of GDP in 2013 to an estimated 88 percent in 2017, with interest payments absorbing 42 percent of revenue. The rise in debt was a result of loose fiscal policy, bailouts of state-owned enterprises, and widespread misman-agement by the previous government prior to a transition to democracy in early 2017 (IMF 2018b).

In Mozambique, the government debt-to-GDP ratio has increased by close to 50 percentage points since 2013, reaching an estimated 102 percent in 2018, with interest payments rising from 2.6 percent of revenues to 16.5 percent over the same period. The deterioration was underpinned by rising deficits as fiscal policy remained loose amid lower commodity prices and subdued growth, and was aggravated by the inclusion of previously undisclosed external commercial debt in 2016 (IMF 2018c). The country is in debt distress, and several payments to external borrowers have been missed.

Zimbabwe is also classified as being in debt distress. Over the last five years, government debt has risen substantially from just over 48 percent of GDP in 2013 to an estimated 82 percent in 2017. Persistently large fiscal deficits have partly been the result of an elevated public wage bill, which absorbed 90 percent of revenues in 2017 (IMF 2017). In addition, revenues remain subdued amid weak growth and structural rigidities, while transfers to the agricultural sector have kept non-wage expenditure elevated. Moreover, the deficits have partly been financed through an overdraft facility at the Reserve Bank of Zimbabwe that, given insufficient reserves, has led to money creation and exacerbated foreign-currency shortages.

Risk of debt distress. Higher levels of public debt, much of it external, and an increased reliance on commercial loans make many LICs vulnerable to currency, interest rate, and refinancing risks (Devarajan 2018; Gill and Karakülah 2018a,b).[5]

LIC vulnerabilities are reflected by the fact that almost all LICs have the lowest or second lowest grade in the OECD's country credit risk classification.[6] Because of rising arrears or the need for debt restructuring, eleven LICs were assessed as being in debt distress or at a high risk of debt distress as of November 2018, compared to only six in 2015.[7] For LICs assessed at low or moderate risk of debt distress, safety margins have eroded.

Other LIC vulnerabilities

Private debt. Due to shallow domestic capital markets and limited access to international finance, the median LIC has total private debt equivalent to only 18 percent of GDP, significantly less than the 41 percent ratio for the median non-LIC EMDE (Figure 4.1.3).[8] Nonetheless, LIC private sector debt has been on a steady upward trend since 2005, rising by almost 8 percentage points. Excess private debt can sometimes be transformed into public debt, either directly through bailouts or indirectly through countercyclical government spending in response to private deleveraging, suggesting that the line between public and private debt can blur (Mbaye, Badia and Chae 2018).

Growth subject to downside risks. Growth in LICs is expected to remain resilient, supporting their ability to service debt, but risks are tilted to the downside. LIC growth is expected to average 5.6 percent in 2018 and accelerate to just over 6 percent in 2019-20, supported by rising agricultural output and continued infrastructure investment (Chapter 1). However, over the next

---

[6] There is one exception: The credit rating for Senegal has improved recently in the OECD credit risk classification, improving from 6 to 5 in a 0-7 rating system, with a higher number indicating higher credit risk (OECD 2018).

[7] A country is considered to be in debt distress if it is experiencing difficulties in servicing its debt, as evidenced, for example, by the existence of arrears, ongoing or impending debt restructuring, or if there are indications that a future debt distress event is probable. LICs in debt distress are The Gambia, Mozambique, South Sudan, and Zimbabwe. LICs at high risk of debt distress are Afghanistan, Burundi, Central African Republic, Chad, Ethiopia, Haiti, and Tajikistan. There is a total of 30 LICs who have a debt sustainability analysis (DSA) available under the Joint World Bank / IMF debt sustainability framework (DSF).

[8] Private sector debt refers to the sum of commercial banks' and other financial corporations' claims on the non-financial private sector, in percent of GDP.

---

[5] Separately, some countries such as The Gambia are vulnerable to rollover risk because of heavy reliance on short-term domestic debt (IMF 2018d).

decade, weaker growth in major emerging markets may slow global demand for metals, which dampens growth prospects for LICs that depend on metals for government and export revenues (World Bank 2018c). Downside risks to this outlook predominate and include the possibility of a faster-than-expected slowdown among major trading partners (including China, a major commodity consumer); a renewed plunge in commodity prices; a deterioration in international financial conditions; and the possibility of natural disasters, conflict, or severe weather events.

Elevated debt, lower investment growth, increased risks. Rising levels of non-concessional public debt, often at variable rates, make some LICs susceptible to a sudden increase in borrowing costs, especially when they have substantial refinancing needs in coming years or have borrowed in foreign currencies. As advanced economies continue to withdraw monetary policy accommodation, new debt issuances and debt rollovers may become more expensive, resulting in rising LIC debt service costs that could weaken investment and lower medium-term growth (World Bank 2015b, 2016, and 2017). Fiscal consolidation, while often necessary, can also dampen growth in the short term.

In the absence of sufficient lending made available at concessional terms, there is a risk that high public debt will lead to higher interest rates, crowding out private investment and slowing growth.[9] Similarly, rising interest payments to domestic creditors may encourage policymakers to engage in financial repression—using admin-istrative or other means to channel domestic savings toward the purchase of public debt—which can dampen private sector investment and limit the development of domestic financial markets (Fry 1997).

Substantial current account deficits. Almost all LICs carry persistent, substantial current account deficits, with an estimated median of 6.8 percent of GDP in 2017 (Figure 4.1.4). Forty percent of

---

[9]Bevan (2012) argues that although evidence in the literature for the crowding out effect on investment in LICs is weak, it may be more important where financial depth is low.

FIGURE 4.1.3 Risks to LIC debt sustainability

Private sector debt has risen alongside public debt in LICs. LIC exports tend to be concentrated in a few products, generally commodities. LIC growth is accelerating but risks are tilted to the downside. Over the medium term, demand for many commodities is expected to slow, which may pose a challenge for exporters.

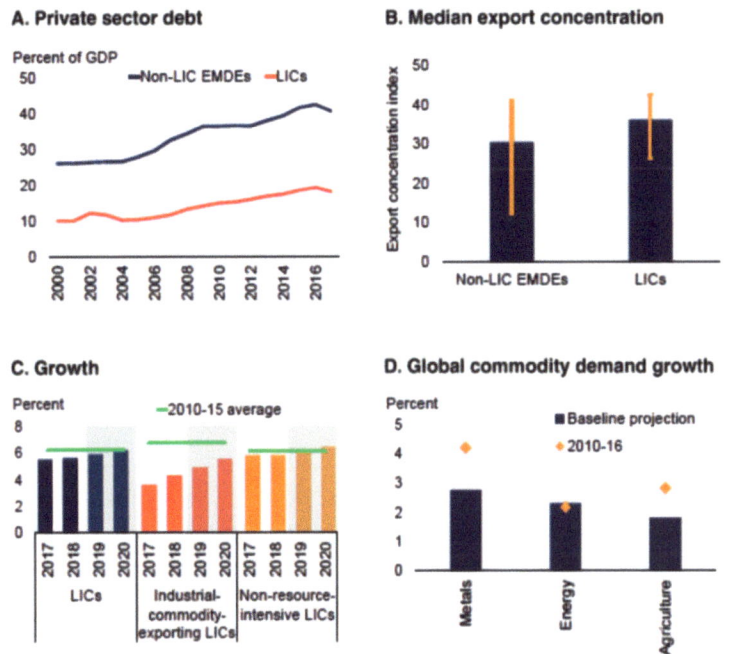

Source: BP Statistical Review, Haver Analytics, United Nations, United States Department of Agriculture, World Bank, World Bureau of Metals Statistics.
A. Domestic credit to the non-financial private sector provided by commercial banks and, if data are available, by other financial corporations. Median debt, based on 148 EMDEs and 29 LICs.
A.B. Non-LIC EMDEs= Emerging market and developing economies excluding LICs; LICs= Low-income countries.
B. Orange lines indicate interquartile ranges of Herfindahl-Hirschmann concentration index, which measures the degree of product concentration, with values closer to 100 indicating a country's exports are highly concentrated in a few products.
D. To ensure comparability, 2010-16 is model-predicted commodity demand growth.

LICs had current account deficits that widened by at least 3 percentage points of GDP over the last decade. Among metals exporters, rising deficits reflected the pickup in import-intensive mining investment, while in non-resource-intensive countries it often reflected high public investment.

Countries relying on capital inflows to finance a large and persistent current account can be more vulnerable to currency crises, as weaker investor confidence can result in a slowdown in capital inflows, leading to higher borrowing costs, downward currency pressures, difficulties in rolling over debt, and possible macroeconomic and financial market stress (Roubini and Wachtel 1999). Current account deficits in LICs, however, are typically financed by capital inflows from development assistance, remittances, foreign lending, and foreign direct investment. The stable, long-term and often concessional nature of this financing mitigates some of the risks usually associated with large current account deficits. Foreign direct investment and development assistance flows were generally more than adequate to finance LICs' current account deficits—the median LIC received inflows of these types 1.6 times as large as its current account deficit. In more than half of LICs, development assistance alone was greater than the total current account deficit. Median FDI inflows were equal to about half the current account, except for metals exporters where it was considerably more.

FDI flows to LICs, however, are particularly sensitive to fluctuations in global growth and liquidity (Burger and Ianchovichina 2017). Among these countries, commodity exporters, particularly metals exporters, are particularly vulnerable to sudden swings in FDI flows that accompany changes in the external environment—FDI flows are more than twice as volatile in metal-exporting LICs than in other EMDEs. While external vulnerabilities can be mitigated by a strong foreign reserve position, more than 40 percent of LICs with available data have reserves close to or below three months of imports.

Role of better debt management

Goal of sound debt management. In most LICs, government debt is the largest domestic financial portfolio, and debt management operations can be substantial relative to public spending and economic activity. A sound macro-fiscal policy framework requires that public debt is sustainable and can be serviced under a wide range of circumstances at reasonable costs. While ex ante the level of debt is mainly determined by fiscal policy, ex post the composition of debt can play an important role in safeguarding debt sustainability. Effective debt management plays a critical role in funding the government's financing needs in a timely fashion, helping ensure low debt servicing costs at an acceptable degree of risk, and supporting the development of domestic securities markets. In addition, debt management can help

minimize fiscal risks stemming from contingent liabilities, such as guarantees or on-lending to state-owned enterprises or through public-private partnerships, through effective monitoring and reporting.

The benefits of sound debt management are fourfold:

- **Lowers debt servicing costs.** In many LICs, debt service payments absorb a significant share of public revenues (notably in Burundi, the Central African Republic, and Chad), reflecting a combination of low revenue bases, sizable debt loads, and a shift toward non-concessional terms. Effective debt management can help avoid excessive debt service costs by increasing awareness of the financial options available, enabling countries to borrow at competitive costs with a prudent degree of risk.

- **Supports financial sector development.** More developed local-currency bond markets can promote economic stability by reducing the reliance on external debt, facilitating the implementation of counter-cyclical fiscal policies, and enhancing resilience to sudden reversals of capital flows. Public debt instruments can serve as a benchmark for pricing of private sector debt instruments. Local-currency bond markets can enable diversification from bank financing and provide a savings vehicle for a variety of investors to support growth (World Bank and IMF 2014).

- **Reduces economic volatility.** Effective debt management can reduce economic volatility by selecting debt instruments that help insulate the government balance sheet from uncertainties. Both currency and interest rate shocks can be mitigated in this fashion, making a country less susceptible to contagion and financial risks, and supporting cheaper and more stable funding for the private sector.

- **Enhances public sector transparency and medium-term planning.** A key element of sound public debt management is the public and comprehensive reporting of government debt, which improves the capacity of policymakers and the broader public to assess the fiscal position and appropriately weigh public balance sheet risks alongside spending and revenue priorities.

Evolution of debt management in LICs. Despite some improvements, debt management in LICs still suffers from substantial deficiencies. Weaknesses in debt transparency, notably in monitoring and reporting, are pervasive. Medium-term debt strategies are becoming more common but have shortcomings in quality and implementation. Capacity and institutional set-up are often lagging.

- **Debt transparency.** Better compilation and monitoring of public debt and guarantees are needed to ensure that risks are detected before they materialize (World Bank 2007). Recent examples of hidden debt and discrepancies among debt statistics point to continued low debt recording capacity, weak legal frameworks, and governance challenges. Debt Management Performance Assessments (DeMPA) suggest that, of the seventeen LICs with available data, minimum requirements in debt recording are met by only eight, and monitoring guarantees are met by only four. Due to shortcomings in accuracy, timeliness, coverage and completeness of debt records, only four of these seventeen countries met the minimum requirements for debt reporting and evaluation (Figure 4.1.5). Only a third of the 59 countries eligible for International Development Association borrowing report private sector external debt statistics (World Bank and IMF 2018d).

- **Debt management strategies.** A growing number of countries are producing medium-term debt management strategies. However, their quality varies significantly, and implementation is often lagging. Few countries are aligning the processes for managing medium-term debt with their budget process.[10]

---

[10] The World Bank, in partnership with the IMF, has been supporting increasing debt management capacity in LICs through its Debt Management Facility (DMF). Building on the progress achieved and on lessons learned in recent years, this involves

FIGURE 4.1.4 External positions in LICs

LICs carry persistent current account deficits, largely financed by development assistance and FDI. However, FDI flows can be volatile, especially for metals exporters. Modest foreign exchange reserves make some countries vulnerable to changes in foreign investor sentiment.

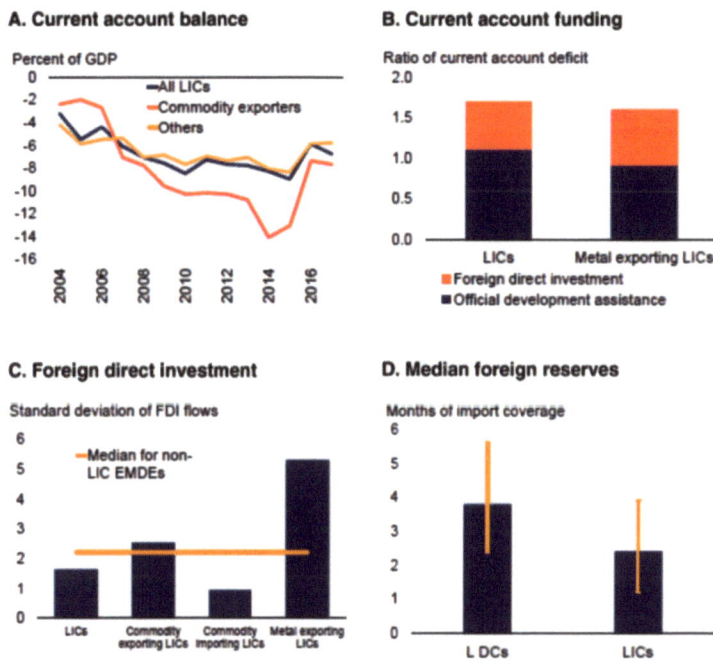

A. Current account balance

B. Current account funding

C. Foreign direct investment

D. Median foreign reserves

Source: International Monetary Fund, World Bank.
A. LICs= Low-income countries. Figure shows median current account balance in percent of GDP. The sample represents a total of 30 low-income countries, of which 2 are oil exporters, 8 are metals exporters, and the remaining 20 are non-resource-intensive. It excludes Somalia, South Sudan, and Syria due to data restrictions.
B. The sample represents a total of 21 low-income countries, including 6 metals-exporting LICs, with current account deficits in 2016.
C. EMDEs= Emerging market and developing economies. Standard deviation represents the median standard deviation of foreign direct investment in percent of GDP from 2000 to 2017.
D. LIDCs=Low-income developing countries; LICs=Low-income countries. See Annex 41 for details. Orange lines indicate interquartile range. Data is as of the last reported year, mostly 2016.

- **Broader issues.** Some of the most pressing challenges include insufficient legal frame-works, weak capacity, lack of coordination between fiscal and monetary policy, inefficient

---

supporting further improvements in debt recording and monitoring, increasing debt transparency, and adding to debt management capacity. The DMF also seeks to strengthen macro-fiscal frameworks, including through improved domestic revenue mobilization, and to advance the implementation of growth-enhancing structural reforms. Since 2009, the DMF has supported over 280 Technical Assistance missions in 75 countries and 14 subnational governments, trained client practitioners and hosted around 40 debt management practitioners. A growing number of countries prepare and publish debt management strategies, the quality of debt records in many LICs has improved, and many countries have well-structured debt management offices. Several countries have strengthened their legal framework and improved their operational risks management with the support of the DMF.

FIGURE 4.1.5 **LIC policy frameworks**

Debt management capacity in many LICs is low, especially in the areas of debt reporting and monitoring. Policy frameworks have improved in LICs, with several countries adopting flexible exchange rates and strengthening their central banks' independence.

A. Countries meeting DeMPA minimum requirements, select categories

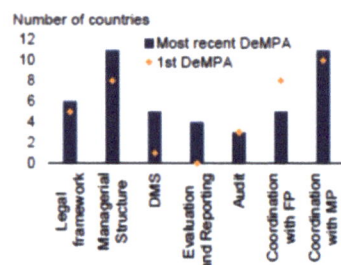

B. Countries meeting DeMPA minimum requirements, select categories

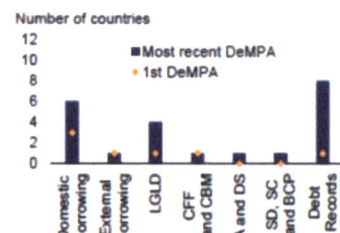

C. Central bank transparency index

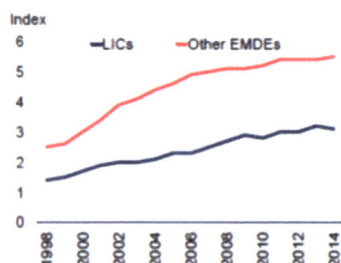

D. Exchange rate regimes

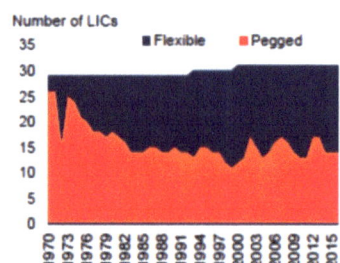

Source: Bloomberg, Debt Management Performance Assessments (DeMPA), Dincer and Eichengreen (2014), International Monetary Fund, Shambaugh (2004), World Bank.

A.B. BCP=Business Continuity Planning; CBM=Cash Balance Management; CFF=Cash Flow Forecasting; DA=Debt Administration; DMS=Debt Management Strategy; DS=Data Security; FP=Fiscal Policy; LGLD=Loan Guarantees, On lending Derivatives; MP=Monetary Policy; SD=Segregation of Duties; SC=Staff Capacity. Sample covers 17 low-income countries.

C. Unweighted averages. The range of the index is from 0-15, 0=least transparent and 15=most transparent.

D. De facto exchange rate regime from the Exchange Rate Regime Classification of Shambaugh (2004) is used to determine whether a country has a pegged or flexible exchange rate. The original classification has four categories: "1" reflects no fluctuation at all, "2" indicates movements within 1 percent bands, "3" indicates movements within 2 percent bands, and "4" indicates a one-time devaluation with 0 change in the remaining 11 months of the year. Shambaugh (2004) assesses these movements against relevant base currencies. The constructed dummy variable indicating a pegged exchange rate regime was defined to equal 1 for countries classified as 1, 2, 3, or 4. A value of 0 is assigned to flexible exchange rates—i.e., exchange rates that routinely fluctuate outside a 2 percent band. Based on 31 LICs.

management of cash and fiscal risks, and poor audit and risk control procedures.

Complementary policy measures

Domestic resource mobilization. Among LICs, there is considerable scope to enhance tax revenues and reduce the need to rely on debt financing (Baum et al. 2017). In the median LIC, government revenues accounted for only 19 percent of GDP in 2017, well below 28 percent of

GDP in the median non-LIC EMDE, reflecting the prevalence of informal activity (Chapter 3). This highlights the need to broaden tax bases, especially for higher-income households, in a way that minimizes economic distortions and that carefully manages trade-offs between efficiency and equity (World Bank 2018d). Unexpected revenue windfalls from sudden improvements in a country's terms of trade can be set aside to reduce fiscal deficits and debt.

Improving spending efficiency. LICs have significant infrastructure needs that require debt financing. However, debt sustainability concerns associated with the financing of infrastructure may be lessened if these expenditures are accompanied by stronger long-term growth and better macro-fiscal, budgeting, and financing frameworks. There may also be room to cut unproductive spending (often subsidies) in order to allow for more growth-enhancing or better-targeted programs.[11] Debt used to finance projects that generate a revenue stream is less likely to be unsustainable. There is also often considerable scope to improve the efficiency of investment spending by improving the institutions and procedures governing project appraisal, procurement, and monitoring. By one estimate, a country moving from the lowest quartile to the highest quartile in the efficiency of public investment could double the impact of that investment on growth (IMF 2015).

Development of local financial markets. Reliance on external funding means that there is often a currency mismatch in LIC borrowing and revenues, leaving countries vulnerable to swings in the value of the currency. The development of local currency bond markets can help mitigate this risk, though they are often a relatively high-cost option. These markets require a functional money market, primary and secondary markets, a diverse base of investors, a stable regulatory system which includes reliable custody and settlement systems,

---

[11] Credible and well-designed institutional arrangements—such as fiscal rules, stabilization funds, and medium-term expenditure frameworks—can help build fiscal space, improve the management of revenue windfalls, and strengthen policy outcomes (Huidrom, Kose, and Ohnsorge 2016).

and a significant improvement in debt management capacity. Sound macroeconomic policy and financial sector stability are also critical, as is transparent and effective communication by the government. Alongside improved debt management, growing local financial markets can help countries graduate from concessional lending by mitigating some of the costs and risks associated with non-concessional debt.

Better data collection. Transparency about balance sheets is a pre-requisite for sound debt management. Among other gaps, there is often limited data on contingent liabilities (especially those arising from state-owned enterprises and public-private partnerships) and the assets held by LIC governments. These data limitations are especially acute for debt issued by commercial and non-Paris Club creditors. Improving data collection practices for LIC debt would help policymakers make informed and appropriate borrowing decisions and allow the public to hold the government accountable for its fiscal management (World Bank and IMF 2018d).

Monetary policy and exchange rate regimes. More resilient monetary policy frameworks and foreign reserve buffers can help mitigate the impact of terms-of-trade and other shocks, including on the fiscal position (Adler, Magud, and Werner 2017). More LICs could join the growing number of EMDEs where improvements in the monetary policy regime have reduced inflation and, where appropriate, allow greater exchange rate flexibility to absorb shocks.

Rigorous and transparent lending standards. Creditors also have a role to play in containing debt vulnerabilities. The Addis Ababa Action Agenda calls for debtors and creditors to work together to prevent and resolve unsustainable debt situations. Creditors can aim for good practice in lending, drawing on principles for sustainable lending such as those being championed by G20 countries (G20 2018).

Conclusion

In recent years, a broad-based rise in borrowing has increased public debt vulnerabilities in LICs. The composition of debt has also shifted, as many LICs have increased their exposure to non-Paris Club creditors and market-based debt, which may pose coordination challenges for any future debt resolution. While increased access to market funding has provided LICs with opportunities to address development needs, it has also exposed some countries to currency, interest rate, and refinancing risks.

The number of LICs at high risk of debt distress or in debt distress has increased significantly, and safety margins in many LICs currently assessed at low or moderate risks of debt distress have eroded. External gross financing needs are likely to rise further as current account deficits widen and large international bonds fall due. By increasing the effectiveness of resource mobilization, public spending, and debt management—supported by better data collection—LICs can reduce the probability of costly defaults, enhance debt transparency, support sustainable financial sector development, and reduce economic volatility.

ANNEX 4.1 Comparison of LIDCs and LICs

This essay discusses LICs following the World Bank Group definition of countries with per capita gross national income below $995 per year. This group includes 33 countries. It differs from other reports (such as IMF 2018a and World Bank and IMF 2018c), which include additional middle-income countries following the IMF definition of low-income developing countries (LIDCs). The term "LIDC" refers to countries with low per capita gross national income and comparatively weak socioeconomic indicators.

ANNEX TABLE 4.1 List of countries in LIDCs and LICs

Low-income developing countries (LIDCs)	Low-income countries (LICs)	Low-income developing countries (LIDCs)	Low-income countries (LICs)
1 Afghanistan	1 Afghanistan	31 Malawi	17 Malawi
2 Bangladesh		32 Mali	18 Mali
3 Benin	2 Benin	33 Mauritania	
4 Bhutan		34 Moldova	
5 Burkina Faso	3 Burkina Faso	35 Mozambique	19 Mozambique
6 Burundi	4 Burundi	36 Myanmar	
7 Cambodia		37 Nepal	20 Nepal
8 Cameroon		38 Nicaragua	
9 Central African Republic	5 Central African Republic	39 Niger	21 Niger
10 Chad	6 Chad	40 Nigeria	
11 Comoros	7 Comoros	41 Papua New Guinea	
12 Congo, Dem. Rep. of	8 Congo, Dem. Rep. of	42 Rwanda	22 Rwanda
13 Congo, Republic of		43 São Tomé and Príncipe	
14 Côte d'Ivoire		44 Senegal	23 Senegal
15 Djibouti		45 Sierra Leone	24 Sierra Leone
16 Eritrea	9 Eritrea	46 Solomon Islands	
17 Ethiopia	10 Ethiopia	47 Somalia	25 Somalia
18 Gambia, The	11 Gambia, The	48 South Sudan	26 South Sudan
19 Ghana			27 Syrian Arab Republic
20 Guinea	12 Guinea	49 Sudan	
21 Guinea-Bissau	13 Guinea-Bissau	50 Tajikistan	28 Tajikistan
22 Haiti	14 Haiti	51 Tanzania, United Rep. of	29 Tanzania, United Rep. of
23 Honduras		52 Timor-Leste	
24 Kenya		53 Togo	30 Togo
25 Kiribati		54 Uganda	31 Uganda
26 Kyrgyz Republic		55 Uzbekistan	
27 Lao P.D.R.		56 Vietnam	
28 Lesotho		57 Yemen, Rep. of	32 Yemen, Rep. of
29 Liberia	15 Liberia	58 Zambia	
30 Madagascar	16 Madagascar	59 Zimbabwe	33 Zimbabwe

(continues in the next column)

Source: International Monetary Fund, World Bank.

Poverty Impact of Food Price Shocks and Policies

In the event of large swings in world food prices, countries often intervene to dampen the impact of international food price spikes on domestic prices and to lessen the burden of adjustment on vulnerable population groups. While individual countries can succeed at insulating their domestic markets from short-term fluctuations in global food prices, the collective intervention of many countries may exacerbate the volatility of world prices. Insulating policies introduced during the 2010-11 food price spike may have accounted for 40 percent of the increase in the world price of wheat and one-quarter of the increase in the world price of maize. Combined with government policy responses, the 2010-11 food price spike tipped 8.3 million people (almost 1 percent of the world's poor) into poverty. Instead of trade policies, targeted safety net interventions such as cash transfers, food and in-kind transfers, and risk management instruments can be more effective in mitigating the negative effects of food price shocks on poor households.

Introduction

In August 2011, nominal international food prices hit an all-time high.[1] This followed shortly after the 2007-08 food price spike, which pushed an estimated 105 million people into extreme poverty (Ivanic and Martin 2008). This event also prompted widespread concerns about the food security of the poorest and fears over a potential world food crisis. Although food prices have declined considerably since then, in real terms, they are still significantly above their lows in 2000 (Figure 4.2.1).

Food price spikes such as in 2010-11 may materialize again as the growing frequency of extreme weather events increases the risk of disruption to food production, setbacks in food availability and access to food. World hunger and severe food insecurity rose during 2014-17, reversing the decline of the previous decade. In 2017, the number of undernourished people reached 821 million, up by 5 percent since 2014 and a setback in achieving the Sustainable Development Goal of eradicating hunger by 2030 (FAO et al. 2018). G20 policy makers have recently reiterated the urgency of tackling the challenges to achieving food security (G20 2018).

While agricultural and food prices are expected to rise only moderately in 2019, significant upside risks could materialize as a result of higher-than-expected energy prices, El Niño events, or trade tensions. First, higher-than-expected energy prices, a key input in the production of most agricultural commodities, could raise grain and oilseed prices. Energy prices affect agricultural production costs directly (through fuel use) and indirectly (through fertilizer and other chemicals use and an incentive to shift production to biofuels). Second, an El Niño event is expected with an 80 percent probability during December 2018-February 2019. Should this materialize, heavier-than-expected rains could occur in Central Asia, South America, and East Africa, while drier-than-normal conditions could affect Central America, the Caribbean, and Southern Africa, affecting the prices of many agricultural commodities. Finally, although the escalation of existing trade frictions represents a downside risk for the price of agricultural commodities, policy measures introduced by major producers and exporters in response to higher tariffs could also affect prices (World Bank 2018e).

Several forces have raised food prices during the 2000s. A dramatic increase in demand for feedstock for biofuel production in the early 2000s put considerable pressure on markets for grain and contributed to a rundown in stocks (Akiyama et al. 2001; Wright 2014). Population growth and urbanization, as well as a shift in diets toward animal-based foods, created demand pressures despite an increase in agricultural productivity in emerging market and developing economies (EMDEs; Fukase and Martin 2017). Slowing yield growth and declining availability of agricultural land constrained food production

---

Note: This essay was prepared by David Laborde, Csilla Lakatos, and Will Martin. Research assistance was provided by Xinyue Wang and Heqing Zhao.

[1] Unless otherwise stated, the concept of food prices as used in this essay refers to the commodity price of major staple foods such as rice, wheat, and maize.

FIGURE 4.2.1 **Global food prices**

In August 2011, shortly after the 2007-08 food price spike, international nominal food prices hit an all-time high. Although food prices have declined considerably since then, in real terms, they are still significantly above their lows in the 2000s. Evidence points to a rise in world hunger and severe food insecurity between 2014 and 2017, reversing the declining trend observed in the previous decade.

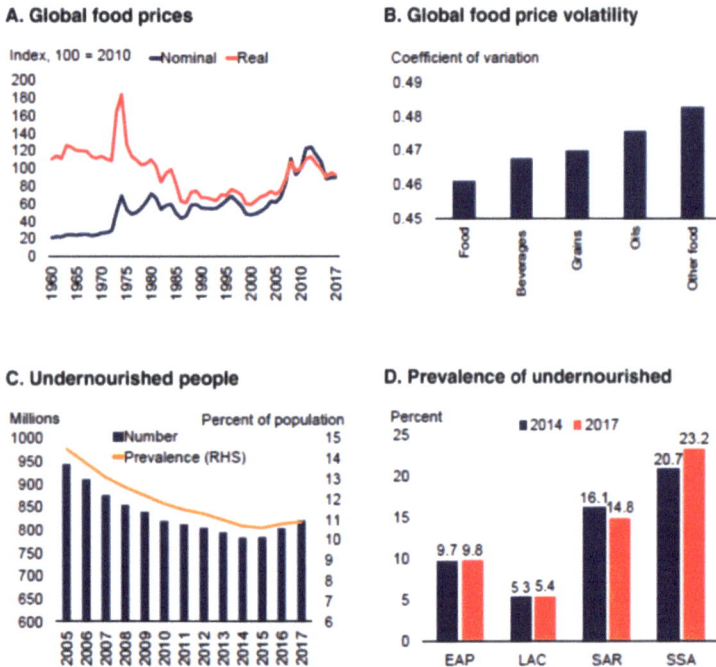

A. Global food prices

B. Global food price volatility

C. Undernourished people

D. Prevalence of undernourished

Source: Food and Agriculture Organization of the United Nations, World Bank.
A. Based on yearly commodity price indexes between 1960-2017.
B. Based on monthly commodity price indexes between January 1960 – November 2017.
C.D. Undernourishment is defined a state, lasting for at least one year, of inability to acquire enough food, defined as a level of food intake insufficient to meet dietary energy requirements.

growth. Extreme climate events (e.g., El Niño, droughts, and natural disasters), particularly when agricultural stocks are low, and the financialization of agricultural futures markets have also contributed to food price volatility.

Food price increases have important macro- and microeconomic impacts through several channels. At the macroeconomic level, food price increases result in higher inflation, which can reduce household real incomes. For food-importing countries, high food prices can also result in terms of trade shocks that lower growth and reduce government policy space.

The microeconomic impact of food price increases on poverty and inequality depends on the net food seller/buyer status of the poorest households. For households that are net sellers of food products

(such as farmers, agricultural workers, and small land owners), rising food prices increase real incomes. By contrast, they lower the real incomes of households that are net buyers of food. On average, sharp increases in food prices raise poverty, reduce nutrition, and curtail the consumption of essential services such as education and health care (World Bank 2011).[2]

Countries often use policy interventions to dampen the domestic impact of international food price spikes and lessen the burden on vulnerable population groups. For example, during the 2007-08 food price spike, close to three-quarters of EMDEs took policy action to insulate their domestic prices from the sharp increase in international food prices (World Bank 2009). In the event of food price spikes, net food-importing countries usually intervene by lowering trade protection (typically tariffs) on food items, while net food-exporting countries impose export restrictions or bans. These policies are often complemented with social safety net programs such as cash transfers or school feeding programs.

To the extent that policy interventions reduce the transmission of international price spikes to domestic markets, they may appear to be successful for individual countries. However, the combined intervention of many countries raises international prices. These insulating policies tend to encourage consumption and reduce production during price spikes. This, in turn, results in higher import demand and reduced export supply that further drive up global prices. During price plunges, government interventions encourage greater exports and greater global supply that further depresses prices. Only countries that insulate themselves to an above-average degree can reduce price volatility in their domestic markets (Anderson, Martin, and Ivanic 2017).

The international community has recognized the importance of ensuring the stability and availability of food supplies as key to addressing several development objectives. The Sustainable

---

[2] In the longer term, once producers and consumers have adjusted to the increases and wage rates have responded, sustained increases in food prices may lower poverty by raising incomes of poor food producing households (Ivanic and Martin 2014a; Gillson and Fouad 2014).

Development Goals (SDGs) give food security a high priority: the second SDG sets out explicitly the goal to "end hunger, achieve food security and improved nutrition, and promote sustainable agriculture." Other SDGs are strongly interconnected: food, agriculture and nutrition play an important role in SDGs on ending poverty, improving health, fostering sustainable consumption and production, and encouraging climate change adaptation and mitigation.

In this context, this essay addresses the following questions:

- How do food price shocks affect EMDEs?

- How do countries intervene to reduce the impact of food price shocks?

- What was the impact of the 2010-11 food price shock on poverty?

The essay presents the following findings:

- At the macroeconomic level, a high share of agriculture and food in total output, consumption, employment, trade, and government revenues heighten countries' vulnerability to volatility in international food prices. At the microeconomic level, food price spikes are felt most severely by the poorest segments of the population who tend to be net food buyers.

- Governments in EMDEs tend to respond particularly strongly to sharp changes in world prices for staple foods—such as rice, wheat and maize—to smooth volatility. Domestic food prices are considerably less volatile than world food prices in the short run, but over the longer term, there is a tendency for domestic and world prices to return to their original relationship. In the short run, a 1 percent increase in the world price of rice, wheat and maize is associated with an increase in domestic prices by 0.6 percent, 0.7 percent, and 0.8 percent, respectively.

- While individual countries can succeed at insulating their domestic markets from short-term fluctuations in global food prices, their

combined interventions make global food prices more volatile. Insulating policies introduced during the 2010-11 food price spike accounted for 40 percent of the increase in the world price of wheat and one-quarter of the increase in the world price of maize. In contrast, a reversal of earlier government interventions in rice markets dampened the degree to which world prices increased by about 50 percent.

- The 2010-11 food price spike, and the wide-spread government intervention that accompanied it, increased the number of poor living on less than $1.90 per day by almost 1 percent or 8.3 million.

Food price shocks and their effects

At the macroeconomic level, a high share of agriculture and food in total output, consumption, employment, trade, and government revenues heighten countries' vulnerability to volatility in international food prices. At the microeconomic level, a high share of net food buyers among the poorest segments of society heightens the adverse effects of food price spikes on poverty and income inequality.

Macroeconomic channels

Reliance on food imports and production. Agriculture accounts for close to one-third of total value added and two-thirds of total employment in LICs. This is almost three times their shares in the average EMDE (Figure 4.2.2; Aksoy and Beghin 2004). For example, in Burkina Faso and Burundi, agriculture accounts for more than four-fifths of total employment. In Chad and Sierra Leone, it accounts for more than half of domestic value added. In addition, more than three-quarters of LICs are net food importers compared to only half of EMDEs.[3] In these net food-importing LICs, net food imports amount to 5.4 percent of private consumption. Benin and Gambia are

---

[3] High trade costs, such as tariffs and border delays, can bias downwards estimates of the share of food imports (Tombe 2015).

FIGURE 4.2.2 Macroeconomic channels of transmission from global food prices

At the macroeconomic level, a high share of agriculture and food in total output, consumption, employment, trade, and government revenues heighten countries' vulnerability to volatility in international food prices.

A. Share of agriculture in economy

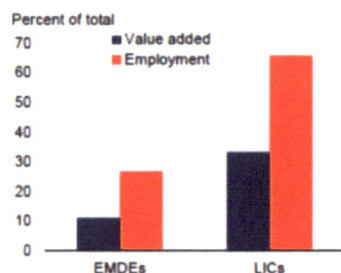

B. Net food imports and exports

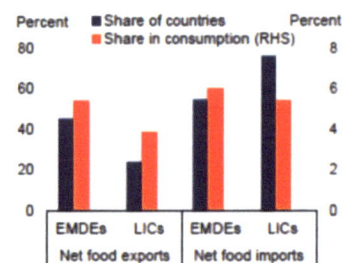

C. Inflation in LICs

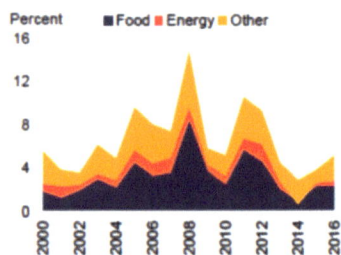

D. Contribution of food prices to inflation

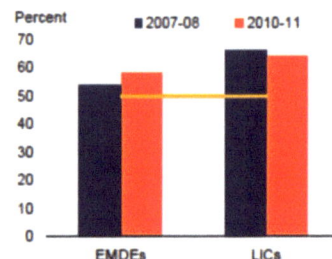

E. Terms of trade in LICs

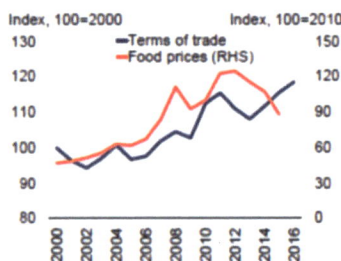

F. Fiscal balance in LICs

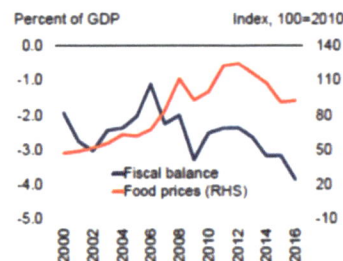

Source: Kose et al. (2017), World Bank.
A. Based on a sample of 93 non-LIC EMDEs and 21 LICs. Averages for 2010-16.
B. Blue bars show the share of non-LIC EMDEs or LICs in which food imports exceed food exports ("Net food importers") or food imports fall short of food exports ("Net food exporters"). Red bars show net food imports relative to consumption in non-LIC EMDE and LIC food exporters and importers.
C. Average inflation based on a sample of 12 LICs.
D. Share of inflation accounted for by food price inflation. Yellow line indicates half.
E. Net barter terms-of-trade index, 100=2000.
F. Median based on a sample of 26 LICs.

Inflation. A surge in food prices increases consumer price inflation. For example, the 2007-08 and 2010-11, LIC inflation more than doubled, from 7 to 15 percent during 2007-2008 and from 5 to 11 percent during 2010-2011. The increase in EMDE inflation was less pronounced, from 7 to 11 percent during 2007-2008 and from 5 to 6 percent during 2010-2011. Food prices accounted disproportionately for these increases in inflation—for about two-thirds in LICs and more than half in EMDEs. In vulnerable LICs such as Benin and Niger, where net food imports amount to 15 and 7 percent of household consumption, respectively, inflation surged from 1 percent to 8 percent and 0.2 percent to 11 percent, respectively, during the 2007-08 food price spike.

Terms of trade. Sharp increases in food prices can constitute significant adverse terms of trade shocks that lower growth, especially in countries that are large net importers of food. More than three-quarters of LICs are net food importers. The median LIC's terms of trade declined by 2 percent and 4 percent during the 2007-08 and 2010-11 food price spikes, respectively. In some, the deterioration was much steeper. For example, the terms of trade of Sierra Leone, a LIC highly reliant on food imports, weakened by 10 percent during each of these food price spike episodes.[5] In heavy food importers, the exchange rate depreciation typically associated with adverse terms of trade shocks can compel central banks to tighten monetary policy and further lower growth. Indeed, during the 2007-08 food price spike, close to half of EMDE central banks responded to rising inflation and depreciation by tightening monetary policy.[6]

Fiscal policy constraints. Absent stabilizing fiscal arrangements, heavy reliance on food and agricultural trade can contribute to volatility in public finances and erode fiscal sustainability: rising food prices may increase tax revenues from the agricultural sector and encourage governments to spend. Conversely, when food prices fall,

particularly vulnerable to high food prices, with net food imports adding up to more than 10 percent of private consumption.[4]

---

[4] Conversely, heavy reliance on food exports heightens vulnerability to food price declines. For example, in Malawi, net food exports amount to 12 percent of total private consumption.

---

[5] Severe terms of trade shocks are considerably more common in LICs than in advanced economies and, of all possible external shocks, tend to have the most severe output cost in LICs (IMF 2011; Becker and Mauro 2006).

[6] Based on a sample of 54 EMDEs.

revenue losses in the agricultural sector are exacerbated by political pressures to subsidize food production. During the sharp rise in food prices in 2007-08, LICs' fiscal balances deteriorated, on average, by close to 1 percentage point of GDP, in part due to higher food import bills. Food price spikes may also cause sociopolitical instability, including political unrest and food riots (Barrett 2013).

Microeconomic channels

Rising food prices impact households through price and income effects. They reduce households' purchasing power but raise income generated from food production. The overall impact on poverty and income inequality depends on the relative magnitude of these effects for households in different segments of the income distribution.

In LICs, households spend on average close to 60 percent of their income on food, more than one-third more than in EMDEs (Figure 4.2.3). In countries such as Burundi and Guinea, the share of food expenditures is even higher, accounting for more than 70 percent of total consumption of households. In LICs, more than one-third of households' consumption expenditure on food is spent on staple foods such as cereals and vegetables. These staple foods are considerably more exposed to international price volatility than domestically processed food products (Figure 4.2.1).

For households that are net sellers of agricultural and food products (e.g., farmers), rising food prices raise incomes. More than one-fifth of households around and below the poverty line of $1.90 per day are net food sellers in the average EMDE and LIC. Households around and below the poverty line in these countries tend to generate about one-quarter of their incomes from food production. In contrast, poor urban households are typically net buyers of food that spend a large share of their consumption expenditure on food (Aksoy and Hoekman 2010).

On average, many of the poor in EMDEs and LICs are net buyers of food. As a result, food price spikes tend to raise poverty, reduce nutrition and

FIGURE 4.2.3 Microeconomic channels of transmission from global food prices

At the microeconomic level, a high share of net food buyers among the poorest segments of the population heightens the adverse effects of food price spikes on income distribution and poverty.

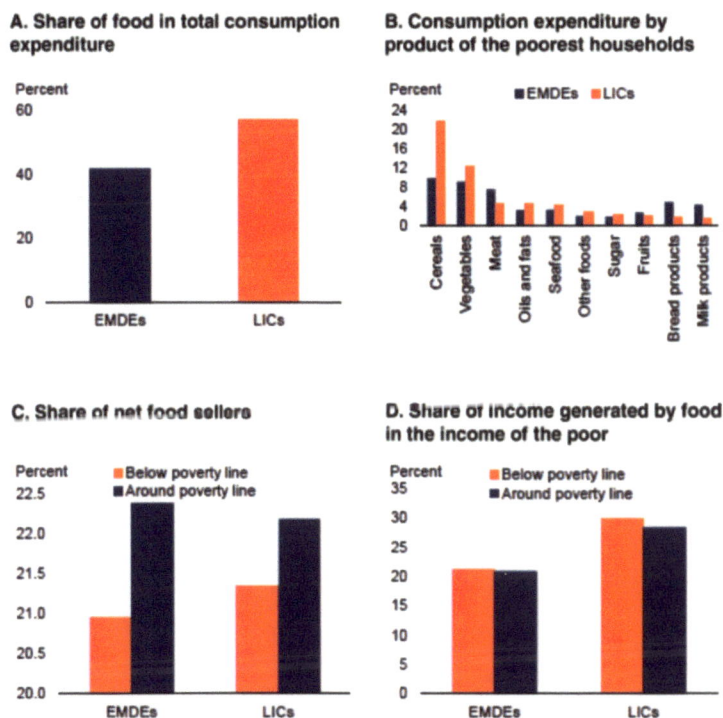

A. Share of food in total consumption expenditure

B. Consumption expenditure by product of the poorest households

C. Share of net food sellers

D. Share of income generated by food in the income of the poor

Source: International Food Policy Research Institute, World Bank.
A. Based on data from the Global Consumption Database reflecting on the share of food in total consumption expenditure of households. Data is available for 63 non-LIC EMDEs and 25 LICs. The base year of the household surveys differs but the data has been converted to a common reference year, 2010. The share of income spent on food is likely to be different.
B. Based on data from the Global Consumption Database on the share of products in total household consumption expenditure. Data is available for 63 non-LIC EMDEs and 25 LICs. The base year of the household surveys differs but the data has been converted to a common reference year, 2010. The share of income spent on food is likely to be different.
C.D. Averages weighted by the number of poor for a sample of 22 non-LIC EMDEs and 7 LICs. Poverty line is defined as $1.90/day.

cut consumption of essential services such as education and health care.[7] For example, the 2007-08 rise in food prices is estimated to have raised the number of poor by 105 million (10 percent of the people living on less than a one dollar a day; Ivanic and Martin 2008). In extreme cases, food price spikes can lead to food insecurity and hunger, with severely adverse long-term impacts on human capital.

_____

[7] Vulnerable groups such as women and children, are more likely to be disproportionately affected.

Government interventions during food price shocks

In the event of large swings in global food prices, governments are confronted with difficult policy choices. One option is to allow domestic prices to adjust to world food price changes, exposing domestic consumers and producers to changes in their real incomes. Even if a sizable non-tradeable service component in the cost of providing consumers with food such as transportation, storage and retail dampens the pass-through of world food price shocks into domestic markets, allowing domestic food prices to adjust may raise inflation in the short run and, in countries where inflation expectations are poorly anchored, in the medium to long run.[8]

Alternatively, governments can spare consumers or producers from these losses by reducing the transmission of international food price shocks to domestic markets.[9] As measured in this essay, policy intervention is reflected in the ratio of domestic to world prices—the "protection rate." During a period of rising world prices, the protection rate declines when a country seeks to insulate its domestic markets from the increase in world prices. If the protection rate rises, policymakers are compounding the increase in world prices.

In practice, during the 2007-08 food price spike, close to three-quarters of EMDEs took policy action to insulate their economies from the sharp increase in international food prices (World Bank

---

[8] The decline in real incomes associated with higher inflation would entail welfare losses, especially when consumers are loss- and risk-averse (Gouel and Jean 2015; Freund and Ozden 2008; Giordani, Rocha, and Ruta 2016; Easterly and Fischer 2001). In principle, monetary policy tightening can offset inflationary effects from rising global food prices to ensure that rising food prices remain a purely relative price change and do not become entrenched in higher inflation. However, this would come at the cost of reduced economic activity (Lustig 2009).

[9] Policymakers may also have a longer-term goal to protect (or to tax) domestic agents (Grossman and Helpman 1994). In empirical work based on political economy models, protection rates vary to reduce both the costs associated with adjusting prices and the costs of providing a rate of protection that differs from the long-run political equilibrium (Anderson and Nelgen 2011; Ivanic and Martin 2014b). The less than perfect pass-through world price shocks into domestic markets is explicitly considered.

2009). The most commonly used interventions were reductions in taxes, including import duties and consumer taxes (Figure 4.2.4).[10] Net importers frequently intervened by lowering import tariffs or even by introducing import subsidies, while net exporters imposed export restrictions or bans to dampen the increase in domestic prices.[11]

Domestic and world food price dynamics

Domestic food prices are considerably less volatile than global food prices in the short run, but over the longer term, there is a tendency for domestic prices to return to their original relationship with international prices (Figure 4.2.5). This does not necessarily imply that protection rates become zero, but that they return to their pre-spike levels.

Governments in EMDEs tend to respond particularly strongly to sharp changes in the world prices of staple foods—such as rice, wheat and maize—to reduce the volatility of domestic prices. For staple foods, domestic price movements can diverge substantially from international price movements in the short run, but converge in the longer term.

The movements of world and domestic staples food prices during the latest two food price spikes (2007-08 and 2010-11) resembled similar earlier episodes: world prices rose rapidly, while domestic prices rose only gradually. However, the 2010-11 spike was different from previous episodes in several aspects. The 2007-08 increase in food prices came after a long period of stability in food prices. In 2007-08, world prices of all staple foods increased steeply, led by the strong increase in the world price of rice. Most countries reacted strongly by introducing insulating policies. In contrast, the 2010-11 episode occurred when world markets and policies were still normalizing from the 2007-08 episode. Government

---

[10] If countries are insulating primarily through subsidies and are fiscally constrained, their ability to insulate will be limited (Ianchovichina, Leoning, and Wood 2014).

[11] For net importers, untargeted food subsidies have implications for government revenues and fiscal space. If financed by aid, the impact on fiscal space is limited. Alternatively, targeted transfers may be more effective in protecting vulnerable groups with limited macroeconomic repercussions.

interventions differed considerably across countries and across commodities. On average, government interventions (or the unwinding of earlier interventions) actually contributed to a decline in the world price of rice.

Rice. Rice was the staple food with the largest price increase during the 2007-08 food price spike. Between January 2007 and May 2008, world rice prices almost tripled.[12] This sharp increase reflected export restrictions introduced by major producers (e.g., India and Vietnam) motivated by food security concerns, panic buying by several large importers, a weak dollar, and record high prices of oil, which is a major input into food production (Childs and Kiawu 2009). During this episode, domestic markets were largely insulated from this global rice price spike (Ivanic and Martin 2008). By contrast, during the 2010-11 price spike, rice prices increased much less, by about 30 percent between June 2010 and May 2012. In some countries, adverse supply conditions combined with changes in non-tariff trade policies resulted in domestic rice prices rising above world prices.[13] Instead of insulating policies, on average, EMDEs implemented policies that raised domestic prices relative to world prices (Figure 4.2.5).

Wheat. Between February 2007 and March 2008, world wheat prices more than doubled, partly in response to lower-than-anticipated wheat production caused by drought in Australia, Ukraine and other major exporters.[14] Strong policy intervention partially insulated domestic markets from the global wheat price spike and their subsequent collapse in the aftermath of the global financial crisis in 2009-10. Similarly, during the 2010-11 event, world wheat prices more than doubled between June 2010 and May 2011.[15] This time, the increase in world prices was

---

[12] The world price of 5 percent broken white Thai rice increased from $313/mt to $902/mt.

[13] In Vietnam, for instance, domestic rice prices rose by 41 percent between July-October 2010 due to lower-than-expected production, prior commitments on exports, and high inflation from a depreciating currency.

[14] The world price of U.S. Hard Red Wheat (HRW) increased from $196/mt to $440/mt.

[15] The world price of U.S. Hard Red Wheat (HRW) increased from $158/mt to $355/mt.

FIGURE 4.2.4 Food-related government policies

Countries often use policy interventions to dampen the domestic impact of international food price spikes and lessen the burden on vulnerable population groups. In the short run, domestic markets for key staple foods, such as rice and wheat, are highly insulated from global food price swings. Insulation policies undertaken during the 2010-11 episode exacerbated the volatility of world prices and accounted for about 40 percent of the increase in the world price of wheat and one-quarter of the increase in the world price of maize.

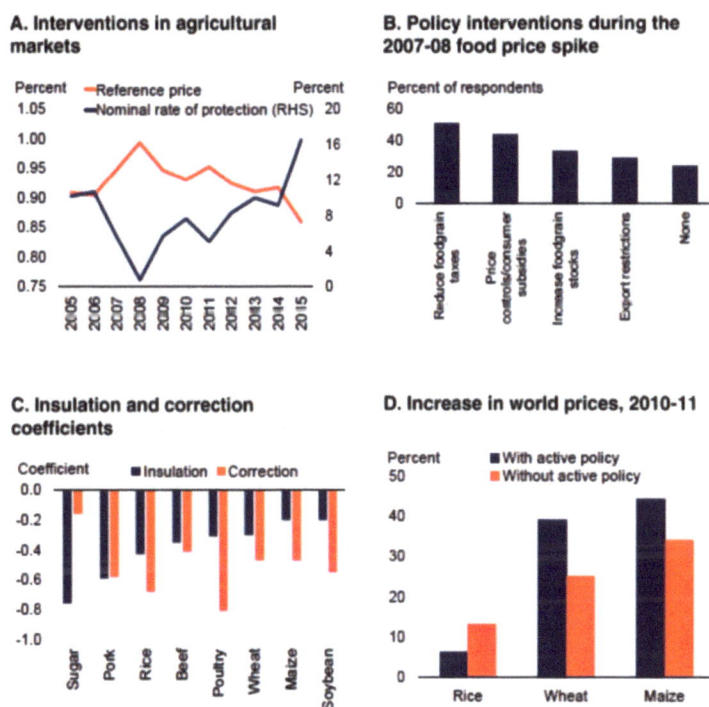

A. Interventions in agricultural markets

B. Policy interventions during the 2007-08 food price spike

C. Insulation and correction coefficients

D. Increase in world prices, 2010-11

Source: Ag-Incentives Database, Ivanic and Martin (2014b), World Bank.
A. Nominal Rate of Protection (NRP) is computed as the price difference between the farm gate price received by producers and an undistorted reference price at the farm gate level. The reference price at the farm gate level is defined as the net price of the product when it leaves the farm, after marketing costs have been subtracted. The undistorted farm gate price is defined as the price prevailing in competitive world markets.
B. Percent of respondents based on a survey of 80 EMDEs.
C. Estimates based on an Error Correction Model described in Annex 4.2.1. The coefficient of price insulation ranges from 0 for countries that do not insulate against the rise in world prices, to -1 for countries that adopt policies that fully insulate domestic markets. The error correction term represents the cost of being out of equilibrium or the speed with which polices achieve the target level of protection or at which policymakers move back toward this equilibrium after being forced away from it by a shock to world prices. Based on data for 82 countries, of which 26 advanced economies, 44 non-LIC EMDEs, and 12 LICs for the period 1955-2011.
D. Real terms. Estimates derived based on the methodology described in Annex 4.2.1.

partly driven by lower-than-expected production and exports in Kazakhstan, Russia, and Ukraine and excessive rains in Australia that damaged wheat crops (World Bank 2010). Large orders from major wheat importers in the Middle East and North Africa added to price pressures. Since 2011, global and domestic wheat prices have fluctuated, broadly synchronously.

Maize. During the 2007-08 food price spike, the world price of maize almost doubled, partly as a

FIGURE 4.2.5 Domestic and global food prices

Domestic food prices tend to be less volatile than global food prices. This partly reflects a sizeable services component in the cost of providing domestic consumers with food, but also policy intervention.

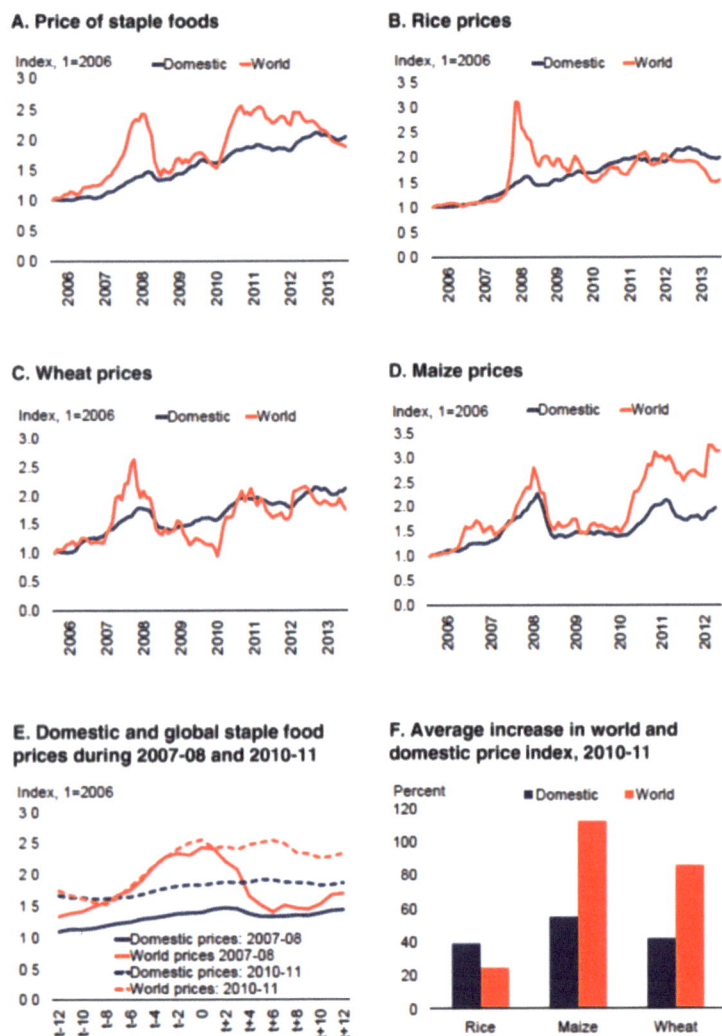

A. Price of staple foods

B. Rice prices

C. Wheat prices

D. Maize prices

E. Domestic and global staple food prices during 2007-08 and 2010-11

F. Average increase in world and domestic price index, 2010-11

Source: Ivanic and Martin (2014b), World Bank.
Note: Trade-weighted averages.
A. Rice, wheat, maize, oil, and sugar prices.
E. Event study based on monthly cross-country average domestic staples prices (average of wheat, rice and maize prices) and global staples prices (average of wheat, rice and maize) during 2007-08 and 2010-11. Period 0 represents the month of the peak of the world food price spike.
F. Average percent increase in the price index.

result of increasing U.S. demand for maize stimulated by mandatory targets for ethanol production.[16] Similarly, during the 2010-11 episode, the world price of maize increased significantly. As in the case of wheat, adverse weather-related events in major maize exporting countries contributed to the spike in world prices.

---

[16] Between January 2007 and June 2008, the world price of maize increased from $165/mt to $287/mt.

In contrast, many countries in Sub-Saharan Africa benefitted from excellent maize harvests, which in combination with unpredictable trade policies led to sharp falls in domestic prices.

Insulation of domestic food markets

Measuring the insulation of domestic markets. The degree of insulation of domestic markets from world food price swings can be quantified using an Error Correction Model (Annex 4.2.1). The model regresses the log of the protection rate on the log of world prices and the deviation from long-term "equilibrium" food prices. The model estimates the degree of insulation to global price changes in both the short run (specifically, a negative coefficient on short-term changes in global food prices) and long run (specifically, a negative coefficient on the long-term relationship between domestic and global food prices). The sample used here includes annual data for 8 food commodity prices in 82 countries, of which 44 are EMDEs and 12 are LICs, during 1955-2011.

Estimates of short-term insulation. Estimates point to considerable short-term insulation in markets for key staple foods such as rice and wheat (Figure 4.2.4). Among these key staples, insulation is the highest for rice. In the short run, a 1 percent increase in global rice, wheat, and maize prices is associated with an increase in domestic prices of 0.6 percent, 0.7 percent, and 0.8 percent, respectively.

Effectiveness of insulating policy measures. Certain types of interventions in markets for staple foods have raised volatility in domestic markets. For example, during the 2008-09 food price spike, several African countries intervened using food pricing, marketing, and trade policies to stabilize domestic maize markets. Countries that intervened most intensively experienced the highest domestic price volatility, mostly because of the ad hoc and unpredictable nature of these interventions (Chapoto and Jayne 2009).[17] The

---

[17] After abstaining from the use of interventions in staple food markets for several years, policymakers in Eastern and Southern Africa used extensively pricing, marketing, and trade policy tools during the 2015-16 agricultural season to contain the impact of an El Niño-induced decline in output and food security (Al-Mamun et al. 2017; Tschirley and Jayne 2010).

use of an export ban during food price spikes, possibly related to a domestic drought, illustrates the trade off between different policy instruments:

- **Ensuring food security.** By restricting the sale of food for exports, an export ban increases domestic supply and dampens domestic food price increases. This can help net-food buyers access food.

- **Alleviating poverty.** Net food-selling farmers are likely to be hardest-hit by a drought. An export ban reduces their ability to mitigate their production losses with higher incomes from higher prices. If these farmers are among the poorer segments of the income distribution, the export ban will likely increase poverty, as it did in Zambia during the 2016-17 El Niño event (Al-Mamun et al. 2017).

- **Volatility.** While export bans may alleviate pressures during a specific situation, they heighten domestic price volatility by preventing domestic shocks from being dissipated through changes in trade. If bans are backed up by stockholding measures such as those used in India, they can be consistent with domestic price stabilization, although the fiscal costs of this policy approach tends to be high relative to that of price insulation (Gouel, Gautam, and Martin 2016).

Synchronous policy measures. While individual countries can succeed at insulating their domestic markets from short-term fluctuations in global food prices, their combined policies may make global food prices more volatile. Government interventions tend to increase consumption and reduce production during price spikes and support production and discourage consumption during price plunges. During price spikes, this results in higher import demand and, hence, higher global demand that further drives up global prices. During price plunges, it encourages greater exports from each country and, hence, greater global supply that further depresses prices. Only countries that insulate themselves to an above-average degree are able to reduce the transmission of international price volatility to their domestic markets (Anderson, Martin and Ivanic 2017;

Martin and Anderson 2012; Ivanic and Martin 2014b).[18]

Poverty impact of the 2010-11 food price shock

The impact of the 2010-11 food price shock on poverty is quantified in two steps. The first step estimates the degree of policy intervention by countries (Anderson, Ivanic, and Martin 2014). In the second step, these estimates are fed into a computable general equilibrium (CGE) model in combination with household models for 285,000 households from 31 countries to determine the impact of policy interventions on poverty (Annex 4.2.1; Laborde, Robichaud and Tokgoz 2013). Two scenarios are compared. In the first scenario, the impact of countries' own interventions on poverty is considered. In the second scenario, the combined effect of all policy interventions on global food markets and their feedback to domestic poverty is quantified.

Impact of policy interventions on global and domestic prices

Quantifying policy interventions. A primary shock, such as a weather shock, is assumed to generate initial production shortfalls that are calibrated to match the observed changes in protection rates and world prices shown in Figure 4.2.6.[19] In attempting to insulate domestic markets from the increase in world prices, governments take offsetting trade measures, such as the introduction of export bans (food exporters) or the reduction of import duties (food importers). These policy responses are calibrated to match the observed protection rates and world price increases in 2010-11. As the model distinguishes between domestic and imported goods, two potential policy instruments are considered—an import duty (or subsidy) and an

---

[18] Consistent with Martin and Anderson (2012) and Anderson, Ivanic, and Martin (2014).

[19] For example, a negative production shock of 55 percent for rice, 27 percent for wheat, and 35 percent for maize in advanced economies and Russia generates an increase of 10 percent in average world prices for these commodities.

FIGURE 4.2.6 The extent of government interventions during the 2010-11 food price spike

Some countries reduced trade barriers to insulate themselves from increasing world prices. Others resorted to policy interventions that ultimately raised domestic prices more than the increase in world prices.

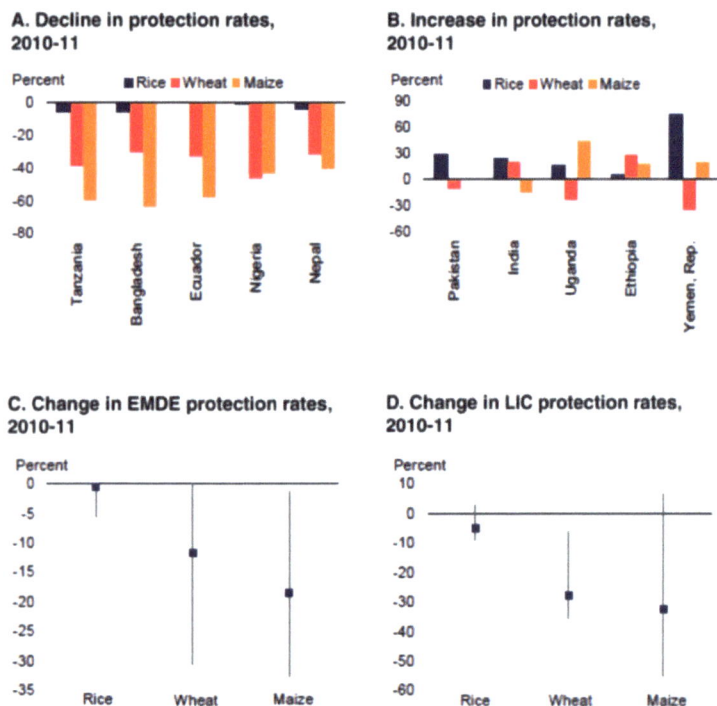

A. Decline in protection rates, 2010-11

B. Increase in protection rates, 2010-11

C. Change in EMDE protection rates, 2010-11

D. Change in LIC protection rates, 2010-11

Source: Ag-Incentives Database.

Note: Estimates based on the methodology described in Annex 4.2.1. Changes in the rates of protection are presented in the form: $T_i = \Delta t/(1+t_0)$, where t is the initial rate of protection (positive if an import tariff or export subsidy) and Δt is the change in this rate of protection. If the change in the rate of protection is negative during a period of rising world prices, countries are seeking to insulate their markets from the increase in prices. If it is positive, policymakers are compounding the increase in world prices with an increase in protection, which may be due to the correction of past "errors": If domestic prices fall below policymakers' desired long-run level of protection, or if a policy that insulated the domestic market from world markets and a subsequent exogenous shock—such as a harvest shortfall—has caused the domestic price to rise relative to the world price.

C.D. Median and interquartile range in the change for protection rates for rice, wheat, and maize in non-LIC EMDEs (C) and LICs (D).

export subsidy (or tax).[20] These measures, in turn, reinforce the original shock to world prices. The data used for quantifying the extent of trade policy interventions are taken primarily from the Ag-Incentives Consortium database reflecting changes

in domestic and world prices for 57 countries and 68 agricultural and food commodities during 2005-2015.[21] Where data from the Ag-Incentives database were unavailable, alternative data were used from FAOSTAT, GIEWS and Fewsnet. Overall, this analysis covers 24 major food producing and consuming countries, using data on household income sources and spending patterns from 2011. Of these, 18 are EMDEs and 6 are LICs.

Impact of policy interventions on global prices. During the food price spike of 2010-11, world prices of maize, wheat and rice rose by 44, 39, and 6 percent, respectively, but domestic prices considerably less (Figure 4.2.4). Model results suggest that the combined action of government policies amplified global wheat and maize price increases, accounting for about 40 percent of the increase in world price of wheat and one-quarter of the increase in the price of maize. In contrast, combined policy action reduced the rice price surge compared to a non-action scenario.[22]

Wheat. Most EMDEs took measures to offset the increase in global wheat prices in 2010-11, broadly similar to those employed during the spike in wheat prices in 2007-08. Policymakers justified efforts to dampen the impact of the global wheat price spike by noting that the world wheat price spike partly reflected a catching up with rising domestic wheat prices.[23] The combined intervention of countries accounted for close to 50 percent of the increase in the world price of wheat.

Maize. Although most countries insulated their domestic maize markets against maize price increase during 2010-11, there was considerable

---

[20] Many countries typically put in place flanking policies. In 2007-08, for example, Indonesia subsidized imports of wheat and rice, respectively, to hold down domestic consumer prices. To avoid subsidizing exports of the same goods, export restrictions were also introduced. Because rice, wheat, and maize are bulk commodities that are less strongly differentiated than manufactured products, two-way trade in these goods is unusual—except when there are regional differences in varieties (for example, Indian exports of Basmati rice and imports of Jasmine rice). Models of differentiated products are needed to adequately capture actual bilateral trade flows in these commodities (Thursby, Johnson, and Grennes 1986).

[21] The data is available at www.ag-incentives.org.

[22] This primarily reflects the elimination of export restrictions in India and the increased import protection in Pakistan, Indonesia, Uganda, and Yemen.

[23] Ethiopia is an exception, where domestic wheat prices rose 28 percentage points more than world prices during 2010-11. This reflected domestic supply shocks, combined with limited access to global wheat markets to alleviate shortages. In particular, wheat output fell by 10 percent in 2010-11 as a result of a fungus that destroyed the wheat harvest and lowered stocks in 2011. Wheat imports rose but were constrained by tight foreign exchange controls, effectively stopping private sector imports and ensuing that all grain imports are channeled through the state-owned Ethiopian Grain Trade Enterprise (Wakeyo and Lanos 2014; Negassa and Jayne 1997).

heterogeneity in policy responses. In Bangladesh, Ecuador, Malawi, Tanzania, and Zambia, protection rates fell, fully offsetting the rise in global maize prices. Ethiopia, Uganda, and Yemen increased protection rates or used policies that, in combination with domestic output shocks, amplified the increase in domestic prices.

Rice. Some countries (e.g., Bangladesh, Nepal, Panama, Tanzania and Zambia) reduced trade barriers to partially offset the rise in world rice prices. However, important net rice exporters such as India, Pakistan, and Yemen implemented policy interventions that, ultimately, raised domestic rice prices more than the increase in world prices. In India, the world's second-largest rice producer, quantitative restrictions imposed in 2007 initially prevented domestic price increases. However, the subsequent abolition of export quotas in September 2011 resulted in a surge in exports and a rise in domestic prices. In Pakistan, heavy summer flooding that affected one-fifth of the country's land area and inflicted extensive damage to crops raised domestic rice prices relative to the world price over the same period. A large increase in domestic prices relative to external prices occurred in Yemen, amid persistent water shortages and a shift to less water-intensive non-staple crops and, in Ethiopia and Uganda, amid drought. The combined intervention of all countries dampened the increase in the world price of rice by about 50 percent compared to a scenario without insulation policies.

Impact of policy intervention on poverty

Poverty impact of hypothetical food price spikes without policy intervention. A hypothetical 10 percent surge in rice, wheat, and maize prices raises the number of extreme poor living on less than $1.90 per day by 0.22 percent or 2.1 million. Among staple foods, an increase in wheat prices raises the number of poor most (by 0.01 percentage points for a 10 percent wheat price increase). Rice price increases cause particularly large increases in the number of poor in Sub-Saharan Africa (0.13 percentage points). Finally, maize price increases tend to have a lesser impact on the number of poor.

FIGURE 4.2.7 Poverty impact of policies implemented during the 2010-11 food price spike

The 2010-11 food price spike raised global poverty. The combined impact of all government interventions raised poverty worldwide, except in a few countries. Due to the dampening effect of interventions on the world price of rice, however, the impact of the combined interventions is found to have raised poverty about 14 percent less than individual action.

Source: World Bank.
Note: Based on estimates using the MIRAGRODEP computable general equilibrium model described in Annex 4.2.1.
A. Change in the poverty headcount measured at $1.90 per day.
B. Poverty impact measured at $1.90 per day.
A.C. EAP = East Asia and Pacific; LAC = Latin America and the Caribbean; MNA = Middle East and North Africa; SAR = South Asia; and SSA = Sub-Saharan Africa.
C.D. Assuming increases in the price of maize, rice, and wheat as represented in Figure 4.4.D and based on a poverty line of $1.90/day.

Poverty impact of 2010-11 food price spike with policy intervention. When incorporating the effects of government intervention to reduce the pass-through of rising global to domestic prices, model results suggest that the food price spikes of 2010-11 still raised poverty in most countries (Figure 4.2.7). On average, the share of extreme poor living on less than $1.90 per day increased by 0.12 percentage point from 13.7 percent. This is equivalent to an additional 8.3 million, or a 1 percent increase in the number of extreme poor.

Heterogeneity in poverty impact. The increase in world food prices, combined with government intervention, was most strongly felt in countries such as India and Uganda, where the extreme poor tend to be net food-buyers whose real incomes declined.[24] The poverty impact of the 2010-11 food price spike on some regions such as East Asia and the Pacific (EAP), and Latin America and the Caribbean (LAC) is estimated to have been limited: low rates of poverty combined with the benefits of the price increase for countries that are heavy exporters of rice (EAP) or maize (LAC) offset some of the losses incurred due to the increase in prices. Even in Sub-Saharan Africa—the region that accounts for two-thirds of the global increase in poverty—countries like Ethiopia and Nigeria implemented insulation policies that reduced poverty.

Comparison with 2007-08 food price shock. These poverty impacts are less pronounced than those induced by the 2007-08 food price shock. The 2007-08 food price shocks may have increased extreme poverty by 105 million (Ivanic and Martin 2008). Government policies reduced poverty impacts and their combined effect was close to zero (Anderson, Ivanic, and Martin 2014). The difference in poverty impacts reflects the greater severity of the 2007-08 price shocks, the stronger transmission of price changes from world to domestic markets and higher initial poverty rates (the poverty headcount in India, for instance, fell from 31 percent in 2009 to 21 percent in 2011).[25] While the 2007-08 event was led by rice prices, exacerbated by export restrictions imposed by major rice producers, the 2010-11 food price surge was led by maize and wheat prices, triggered by adverse weather events in major wheat and maize producers in Australia and the Black Sea Basin. During 2007-08, large rice consumers, such

as India, imposed export restrictions to contain domestic rice price increases. These were gradually unwound over the following years. In 2010-11, some large wheat and maize producers, such as Russia and Ukraine, introduced export restrictions and import bans to contain domestic price pressures.

Conclusions

During the 2010-11 food price shock, coming in short succession after the 2007-08 surge in food prices, many countries used trade policies to insulate domestic markets from the increase in world prices. While each country's policies can dampen domestic price movements, the combined use of policies by many countries increases global food price volatility. For example, widespread insulation policies accounted for 40 percent of the increase in world wheat prices and one-quarter for world maize prices. The increase in food prices combined with government policy responses in 2010-11 raised global poverty by almost 1 percent (8.3 million).

These findings highlight that the use of trade policy interventions to insulate domestic markets from food price shocks compounds the volatility of international prices and may not be effective in protecting the most vulnerable populations groups. Instead, targeted safety net interventions such as cash transfers, food and in-kind transfers, school feeding and public works programs can mitigate the negative impact of food price shocks on poor households. Measures such as crop and weather insurance, warehouse receipt systems, commodity exchanges and futures markets could also be used as risk management instruments. Additional policy interventions such as targeted nutrition and health programs can contribute to improving health outcomes in the medium term, while regulatory interventions (taxing unhealthy food) can improve health outcomes in the longer term.

More generally, in addition to targeted interventions it is important to ensure that countries have detailed strategic framework for food crisis response in place and that these programs are sufficiently resourced with administrative budgets. International financial

[24] Results reported here do not take into account the impact of safety-net programs such as India's Public Distribution System, which distributes food to poor households at fixed prices and so automatically makes larger transfer to the poor when food prices rise.

[25] World Bank (2012) estimate that the 2010-11 food price spike increased the number of poor by 50 million in the short run, and by 34 million in the long run. These higher estimates do not explicitly account for insulation policies and consider price increases of a wider range of food commodities (also beef, chicken, dairy, vegetable oils and soybean prices). In addition, there is uncertainty around poverty estimates due to systematic measurement errors in household surveys that may bias the poor's dependence on food purchases (Headey and Martin 2016). Finally, Jacoby (2016) and Jacoby and Dasgupta (2018) highlight the importance of accounting for the endogenous agricultural wage response and spillover effects to non-agricultural wages (also accounted for in this essay).

institutions (IFIs) can assist countries to better target the people most vulnerable to a food price crisis. IFIs can also help countries identify practical mechanisms (including indicators) for monitoring nutritional and welfare outcomes, in measuring the impacts of food crises and mitigation programs, and work with them to implement those mechanisms. The private sector can play a crucial role in enhancing investments in food supply in the short and medium term (World Bank 2013), while better collaboration among public and private stakeholders can improve risk management and provide effective responses to reduce the impacts of extreme weather on agriculture (G20 2018).

ANNEX 4.2 **Methodology**

Error Correction Model

The analytical framework used to represent the imperfect transmission of changes in international prices into domestic markets relies on an Error Correction Model (ECM) as described in Ivanic and Martin (2014a). As noted by Nickell (1985), this model represents a situation in which policymakers seek to reduce both the costs of change, and the costs of being out of equilibrium. A simplified version model used by Ivanic and Martin (2014a), expressed in logs, is:

$$\Delta\tau = \alpha\,(p^w - p^w_{t-1}) + \beta\,[p_{t-1} - \gamma\,p^w_{t-1}],$$

where p represents domestic prices; pw world prices; τ the rate of protection, approximated by $(p - p^w)$; α, $\alpha < 0$, the coefficient of price insulation ranging from 0 for countries that do no insulate against the rise in world prices, to -1 for countries that adopt policies that fully insulate domestic markets;

β, $\beta < 0$, the cost of being out of equilibrium or the speed with which polices achieve the target level of protection or at which policymakers move back toward this equilibrium after being forced away from it by a shock to world prices; γ determines the long-run relationship between a country's protection and the global level of agricultural protection; and $[p_{t-1} - \gamma \times p^w_{t-1}]$ is the deviation from the political-economy equilibrium. It depends on factors like income levels,

exportable/importable status, the elasticity of import demand, and the share of real incomes gains from higher protection that will accrue to politically organized producers (Anderson 1995; Grossman and Helpman 1994).

The database on Distortions to Agricultural Incentives (Anderson and Valenzuela 2008; Anderson and Nelgen 2013) is the main data source for estimating the ECM model. It includes estimates of domestic and world price levels, which also determine the level of protection. The price data used in the model capture natural shocks (oil prices, weather events) and the impact of trade policy interventions, the separate impact of which is not possible to disentangle. The model is estimated for eight food commodities with data for 82 countries, of which 26 are advanced economies, 44 EMDEs, and 12 LICs.

Measuring trade policy interventions

The approach to quantify the extent of trade policy interventions builds on that used in Anderson, Ivanic, and Martin (2014). It is assumed that a primary shock, such as weather shock, generates an initial change in domestic and world prices. In attempting to insulate consumers and producers from price increases, governments make offsetting changes in protection measures, such as the introduction of export bans or reduction in import duties. These measures, in turn, reinforce the original shock to world prices. When a country imposes an export restriction, the availability of food to the rest of the world is reduced, what tends to push up world price. Similarly, when an importing country reduces its import tariffs, it increases the demand for imports and hence puts upward pressure on the world price.

The impact of the changes in trade policies can be distinguished from those of the primary shocks by in the following equation:

$$\Sigma_i S_i(\,p_i\,) + v_i = \Sigma_i D_i(\,p_i\,),$$

where S_i is supply in region i; D_i is demand in region i; $p_i = p^*\,(1 + t_i)$ is the domestic price; p^* is the world price; t_i is a country-specific trade barrier, such as a proportional tariff; and v_i is a random production shift variable for region i. Totally differentiating the equation above, rearranging, and expressing the results in percentage changes yields an expression of the impact of a set of changes in trade distortions on the world price:

$$\hat{p}^* = \frac{\Sigma_i\,(G_i\,\eta_i - H_i\,\gamma_i)}{\Sigma_i\,H_i\,\hat{v}_i + \Sigma_i\,(H_i\gamma_i - G_i\eta_i)\,\hat{T}_i}$$

where $\hat{p}^*$ is the proportional change in the international price; $\hat{v}_i$ is an exogenous output shock such as might result from good or bad seasonal conditions; η_i is the elasticity of demand in market i; γ_i is the elasticity of supply in market i; G_i is the share at world prices of country i in global demand; H_i is the share of country i in global production, and $\hat{T}_i = (1 + t_i)$.

In other words, the impact on the world price of a change in trade policies in country is given as a weighted average of the changes in trade distortions in different markets, with the weight on region i depending on the importance of that country in global supply and demand, as well as the responsiveness of its production and consumption to price changes in the country, as represented by γ_i and η_i.

It is thus assumed that elasticities of demand are equal between countries, i.e., that imported and domestic goods are perfect substitutes, and that there are no supply responses. Alternatively, one could allow for differentiation between imported and domestic products, as well as a limited supply response (Jensen and Anderson 2017). The result would be an expression with weights that depend on, for instance, the shares of imports in consumption in each market. However, the overall result is similar in expressing the change in world prices as a weighted sum of changes in trade distortions.

To avoid having to deal with difficult-to-interpret interaction terms, all proportional changes are converted into log changes in T_i, p_i's, and p as:

$$\hat{p}_i = \hat{p} + \hat{T}_i$$

Changes in relative prices are measured as in the Agricultural Incentives database and capture a wide range of policy measures used to assess agricultural trade distortions—including tariffs, export subsidies, export taxes, export bans and import subsidies.

If products are homogeneous, and a country is small, the change in Δt represents the change in the domestic price of the good. Additionally, if $\hat{T}_i$ is negative in a period of rising world prices, countries are seeking to insulate their markets from the increase in prices. If it is positive, policymakers are compounding the increase in world prices with an increase in protection. This may be due to the correction of past "errors". This might occur if domestic prices fall below policymakers' desired long-run level, or if policy insulated the domestic market from world markets and an exogenous shock—such a harvest shortfall—has caused the domestic price to rise relative to the world price. Such insulation patterns have been observed in the maize markets in many African countries (Chapoto and Jayne 2009).

The MIRAGRODEP model

The analytical framework to measure the poverty implications of the 2010-11 food price spike relies on the MIRAGRODEP model (Laborde, Robichaud, and Tokgoz 2013) complemented with household surveys for more than 31 countries and 285,000 representative households. MIRAGRODEP is a dynamic, multi-country, and multi-sector computable general equilibrium (CGE) model. The model relies on GTAP 9, a global database for 2011. The GTAP database includes input-output tables linked by bilateral trade flows for 140 regions (countries or country aggregates) and 57 sectors. For the purposes of the simulations these countries and sectors were aggregated into 31 countries/regions and 15 sectors among which rice, wheat, and maize are represented separately.

On the supply side, the production function is a Leontief function of value-added and intermediate inputs. The intermediate inputs are represented by a nested, two-level constant elasticity of substitution (CES) function of all goods. Based on this, substitutability exists between intermediate goods, but these are more substitutable when they are in a same category (such as agricultural inputs or service inputs). Value-added is also represented by a nested structure of CES functions of unskilled labor, land, natural resources, skilled labor, and capital. This nesting allows the modeler to incorporate some intermediate goods that are substitutes of factors, such as energy or fertilizers.

On the demand side, a representative consumer is assumed to have a constant propensity to save. The remaining national income is used for the purchase of consumption goods. Consumers' preferences are represented by a linear expenditure system–constant elasticity of substitution (LES–CES) function, calibrated based on the U.S. Department of Agriculture Economic Research Service income and price elasticities to best reflect non-homothetic demand patterns with changes in revenue. Given an increase in the price staple foods, consumers substitute away to consume other food products. Armington elasticities, which measure the elasticity of substitution between products of different countries, are drawn from the GTAP database and are assumed to be the same across regions.

Factor endowments are assumed to be fully employed. The supply of capital goods is modified each year because of depreciation and investment. New capital is allocated among sectors according to an investment function. Growth rates of labor supply are fixed exogenously. Land supply is endogenous and depends on the real remuneration of land. Skilled labor is the only factor that is perfectly mobile; unskilled labor is imperfectly mobile between agricultural and nonagricultural sectors according to a constant elasticity of transformation (CET) function. Unskilled labor's remuneration in agricultural activities is different from that of nonagricultural activities. The only factor whose supply is constant is the natural resources factor. It is, however, possible to endogenously change the factor endowment in the baseline in order to reflect long-term depletion of resources with respect to a price trajectory.

The poverty impact is captured through a top-down approach using a data set of household surveys for more than 31 countries and 285,000 representative households. The impact of a policy shock on poverty depends on price changes, the relative reliance of households on the consumption of individual staple foods and the net food buying status of households in different segments of the distribution (Deaton 1989).

Beyond the standard features of a global dynamic CGE model, the MIRAGRODEP model includes several improvements: sub-national land markets (agro-ecological zones or administrative districts) and endogenous land supply; poverty analysis through either a top-down approach for global coverage or a bottom-up approach (for a subset of countries); dual-dual approach for formal/informal and rural/urban labor markets (Stifel and Thorbecke 2003); a consistent aggregator for trade policies (Laborde, Martin, and van der Mensbrugghe 2017); differentiated data sets on actual trade and farm policies and existing policy space for scenario design and endogenous policy responses; macro nutrient (calories, fats, proteins) accounting system based on FAOSTAT food balance sheets and a global Input-Output matrix; and sensitivity analysis framework based on Monte-Carlo simulations.

While the elasticities of substitution for rice, wheat, and maize used in this model, are higher than for manufactured goods, they are not infinite as assumed using the perfect substitutes model (Thursby, Johnson, and Grennes 1986). This specification has important implications for both the economy-wide analysis and at the household level. Given these assumptions, an increase in the price of an imported good has a muted impact on the domestic consumer price of that good. Since, with the Armington assumption—imported goods differentiated based on their country of origin—, the composite price of the consumer good is weighted by the shares of domestic and imported goods, the impact of a unit change in the world price, or in trade policy, is given by the share of imports in total consumption. Because the share of imports in total consumption of staple foods is typically small, the impact of trade policy on consumer prices is much more muted than under the assumption of perfect substitution used in Anderson, Ivanic, and Martin (2014). On the production side, the assumption that each country's export product is the same as the products sold domestically means that changes in export trade policies will have a more direct impact on producer prices if the country is an exporter and not too large in the markets it supplies.

References

Adler, G., N. E. Magud, and A. Werner. 2017. "Terms-of-Trade Cycles and External Adjustment." IMF Working Paper 17/29, International Monetary Fund, Washington DC.

Akiyama, T., J. Baffes, D. F. Larson, and P. Varangis. 2001. *Commodity Market Reforms: Lessons of Two Decades*. Washington, DC: World Bank.

Aksoy, M. A., and J. C. Beghin. 2004. *Global Agricultural Trade and Developing Countries*. Washington, DC: World Bank.

Aksoy, M. A., and B. Hoekman. 2010. *Food Price and Rural Poverty*. Washington, DC: World Bank.

Al-Mamun, A., A. Chapoto, B. Chisanga, W. Martin, and P. Samboko. 2017. "El Niño Impacts and Trade Policy Responses on Grain Markets and Trade in Eastern and Southern Africa." Mimeo. International Food Policy Research Institute, Washington, DC.

Anderson, K. 1995. "Lobbying Incentives and the Pattern of Protection in Rich and Poor Countries." *Economic Development and Cultural Change* 43 (2): 401 -23.

Anderson, K., M. Ivanic, and W. Martin. 2014. "Food Price Spikes, Price Insulation and Poverty." In *The Economics of Food Price Volatility*, edited by J. P. Chavas, D. Hummels, and B. Wright. Chicago: University of Chicago Press.

Anderson, K., W. Martin, and M. Ivanic. 2017. "Food Price Changes, Domestic Price Insulation and Poverty (When All Policymakers Want to be Above-Average)." In *Agriculture and Rural Development in a Transforming World*, edited by P. Pingali, and G. Feder. London: Routledge.

Anderson, K., and S. Nelgen. 2011. "Trade Barrier Volatility and Agricultural Price Stabilization." *World Development* 40 (1): 36-48.

———. 2013. "Updated National and Global Estimates of Distortions to Agricultural Incentives, 1955 to 2011." World Bank, Washington, DC.

Anderson, K., and E. Valenzuela. 2008. "Estimates of Global Distortions to Agricultural Incentives, 1955 to 2007." World Bank, Washington, DC.

Atkins, L., D. Brautigam, Y. Chen, and J. Hwang. 2017. "China-Africa Economic Bulletin #1: Challenges of and Opportunities from the Commodity Price Slump." China Africa Research Initiative, Johns Hopkins University School of Advanced International Studies, Washington, DC.

Barrett, C. 2013. *Food Security and Sociopolitical Stability*. Oxford: Oxford University Press.

Baum, A., A. Hodge, A. Mineshima, M. M. Badia, and R. Tapsoba. 2017. "Can They Do It All? Fiscal Space in Low-Income Countries." IMF Working Paper 17/110, International Monetary Fund, Washington, DC.

Bayraktar, N., and H. Fofack. 2011. "Capital Accumulation in Sub-Saharan Africa: Income-Group and Sector Differences." *Journal of African Economies* 20 (4): 531-561.

Becker, T., and P. Mauro. 2006. "Output Drops and the Shocks that Matter." IMF Working Paper 06/172, International Monetary Fund, Washington, DC.

Bevan, D. 2012. "Aid, Financial Policy, Climate Change, and Growth." Working Paper 77, United Nations University, World Institute for Development Economic Research, New York.

Burger, M. J., and E. I. Ianchovichina. 2017. "Surges and Stops in Greenfield and M&A FDI Flows to Developing Countries: Analysis by Mode of Entry." *Review of World Economics* 153 (2): 411-432.

Chapoto, A., and T. S. Jayne. 2009. "Effects of Maize Marketing and Trade Policy on Price Unpredictability in Zambia." Food Security Collaborative Working Papers 54499, Michigan State University.

Childs, N. W., and J. Kiawu. 2009. "Factors Behind the Rise in Global Rice Prices in 2008." U.S. Department of Agriculture, Economic Research Service.

Deaton, A. 1989. "Rice Prices and Income Distribution in Thailand: A Non-Parametric Analysis." *Economic Journal* 99 (395): 1–37.

Devarajan, S. 2018. "Low-Income Country Debt: Déjà Vu All Over Again?" Washington, DC: Future Development, Brookings Institution.

Dincer, N., and B. Eichengreen. 2014. "Central Bank Transparency and Independence: Updates and New

Measures." *International Journal of Central Banking* 10 (1): 189-253.

Easterly, W., and S. Fischer. 2001, "Inflation and the Poor." *Journal of Money, Credit and Banking* 33 (2): 160-78.

Eom, J., D. Brautigam, and L. Benabdallah. 2018. "The Path Ahead: The 7th Forum on China-Africa Cooperation." China-Africa Research Initiative Briefing Paper 1, Johns Hopkins School of Advanced International Studies, Washington DC.

FAO, IFAD, UNICEF, WFP, and WHO. 2018. *The State of Food Security and Nutrition in the World 2018: Building Climate Resilience for Food Security and Nutrition.* Rome: FAO.

Freund, C., and C. Ozden. 2008. "Trade Policy and Loss Aversion." *The American Economic Review* 98 (4): 1675–91.

Fry, M. J. 1997. "In Favour of Financial Liberalisation." *The Economic Journal* 107 (442): 754-770.

Fukase, E., and W. Martin. 2017. "Agro-Processing and Horticultural Exports from Africa." International Food Policy Research Institute, Washington, DC.

Gill, I., and K. Karakülah. 2018a. "Is Africa Headed for Another Debt Crisis?" Duke Center for International Development, Durham NC.

———. 2018b. "Sounding the Alarm on Africa's Debt." Washington, DC: Future Development, Brookings Institution.

Gillson, I., and A. Fouad. 2014. *Trade Policy and Food Security: Improving Access to Food in Developing Countries in The Wake of High World Prices.* Washington DC: World Bank.

Giordani, P., N. Rocha, and M. Ruta. 2016. "Food Prices and the Multiplier Effect of Trade Policy." *Journal of International Economics* 101 (1): 102–22.

Gouel, C., M. Gautam, and W. Martin. 2016. "Managing Food Price Volatility in a Large Open Country: The Case Of Wheat In India." *Oxford Economic Papers* 68 (3): 811–35.

Gouel, C., and S. Jean. 2015. "Optimal Food Price Stabilization in a Small Open Developing Country." *World Bank Economic Review* 29 (1): 74-101.

G20 (Group of 20). 2018. "G20 Leaders' Declaration Building Consensus for Fair and Sustainable Development." G20 Meeting, Buenos Aires, Argentina.

Grossman, G., and E. Helpman. 1994. "Protection for Sale." *The American Economic Review* 84 (4): 833-50.

Headey, D., and W. Martin. 2016. "The Impact of Food Prices on Poverty and Food Security." *Annual Review of Resource Economics* 8 (1): 329-351.

Huidrom, R., M. A. Kose, and F. L. Ohnsorge. 2016. "Challenges of Fiscal Policy in Emerging and Developing Economies." Policy Research Paper 7725, World Bank, Washington, DC.

Ianchovichina, E., Loening, J., and C. A. Wood. 2014. "How Vulnerable are Arab Countries to Global Food Price Shocks?" *The Journal of Development Studies* 50 (9): 1302-1319.

IMF (International Monetary Fund). 2011. "Managing Volatility: A Vulnerability Exercise for Low-Income Countries." International Monetary Fund, Washington, DC.

———. 2015. *Making Public Investment More Efficient.* Washington, DC: International Monetary Fund.

———. 2017. *Zimbabwe. Staff Report for the 2017 Article IV Consultation.* Washington, DC: International Monetary Fund.

———. 2018a. *Macroeconomic Developments and Prospects in Low-Income Developing Countries.* Washington, DC: International Monetary Fund.

———. 2018b. *The Gambia 2017 Article IV Consultation—Staff Report.* Washington, DC: International Monetary Fund.

———. 2018c. *Mozambique 2017 Article IV Consultation—Staff Report.* Washington, DC: International Monetary Fund.

———. 2018d. *IMF Fiscal Monitor: Capitalizing on Good Times, April 2018.* Washington, DC: International Monetary Fund.

Ivanic, M., and W. Martin. 2008. "Implications of Higher Global Food Prices for Poverty in Low-Income Countries." Policy Research Working Paper 4594, World Bank, Washington, DC.

————. 2014a. "Short- and Long-Run Impacts of Food Price Changes on Poverty." Policy Research Working Paper 7011, World Bank, Washington, DC.

————. 2014b. "Implications of Domestic Price Insulation for Global Food Price Behavior." *Journal of International Money and Finance* 42 (1): 272-288.

Jacoby, H. G. 2016. "Food Prices, Wages, and Welfare in Rural India." *Economic Inquiry* 54 (1): 159–76.

Jacoby, H. G., and B. Dasgupta. 2018. "Changing Wage Structure in India in the Post-Reform Era: 1993–2011." *IZA Journal of Migration* 8 (1): 1-26.

Jensen, H. G., and K. Anderson. 2017. "Grain Price Spikes and Beggar-Thy-Neighbor Policy Responses: a Global Economywide Analysis." *World Bank Economic Review* 31 (1): 158-175.

Kose, M. A., S. Kurlat, F. L. Ohnsorge, and N. Sugawara. 2017. "A Cross-Country Database of Fiscal Space." Policy Research Working Paper 8157, World Bank, Washington, DC.

Laborde, D., W. Martin, and D. Van der Mensbrugghe. 2017. "Measuring the Impacts of Global Trade Reform with Optimal Aggregators of Distortions." *Review of International Economics* 25 (2): 403-425.

Laborde, D., V. Robichaud, and S. Tokgoz. 2013. "MIRAGRODEP 1.0: Documentation." AGRODEP Technical Note, International Food Policy Research Institute, Washington, DC.

Lustig, N. 2009. "Coping with Rising Food Prices: Policy Dilemmas in the Developing World." Institute for International Economic Policy, George Washington University, Washington, DC.

Marcelino, S., and M.I. Hakobyan. 2014. "Does Lower Debt Buy Higher Growth? The Impact of Debt Relief Initiatives on Growth." IMF Working Paper 14/230, International Monetary Fund, Washington, DC.

Martin, W., and K. Anderson. 2012. "Export Restrictions and Price Insulation During Commodity Price Booms." *American Journal of Agricultural Economics* 94 (2): 422-7.

Mbaye, S., M. M. Badia, and K. Chae. 2018. "Bailing Out the People? When Private Debt Becomes Public." Working Paper 18/141, International Monetary Fund, Washington, DC.

Ndikumana, L., and J. Boyce. 2011. "Capital Flight from Sub-Saharan Africa: Linkages with External Borrowing and Policy Options." *International Review of Applied Economics* 25 (2): 149-170.

Negassa, A., and T. S. Jayne. 1997. "The Response of Ethiopian Grain Markets to Liberalization." Food Security Collaborative Working Papers 55595, Michigan State University.

Nickell, S. 1985. "Error Correction, Partial Adjustment and All That: An Expository Note." *Oxford Bulletin of Economics and Statistics* 47 (2): 119–29.

OECD (Organization for Economic Co-operation and Development. 2018. *Country Risk Classifications of the Participants to the Arrangement on Officially Supported Export Credits.* Paris: Organization for Economic Co-operation and Development.

Roubini, N., and P. Wachtel. 1999. "Current-Account Sustainability in Transition Economies." In *Balance of Payments, Exchange Rates, and Competitiveness in Transition Economies*, edited by M. I. Blejer and M Skreb, 19-93. Boston, MA: Springer.

Shambaugh, J. C. 2004. "The Effect of Fixed Exchange Rates on Monetary Policy." The *Quarterly Journal of Economics* 119 (1): 301-352.

Stifel, D. C., and E. Thorbecke. 2003. "A Dual-Dual CGE Model of an Archetype African Economy: Trade Reform, Migration and Poverty." *Journal of Policy Modeling* 25 (3): 207-235.

Thursby, M., P. Johnson, and T. Grennes. 1986. "The Law of One Price and the Modelling of Disaggregated Trade Flows." *Economic Modelling* 3 (4): 293-302.

Tombe, T. 2015. "The Missing Food Problem: Trade, Agriculture, and International Productivity Differences." *American Economic Journal: Macroeconomics* 7 (3): 226-58.

Tschirley, D., and T. Jayne. 2010. "Exploring the Logic Behind Southern Africa's Food Crises." *World Development* 38 (1): 76–87.

Wakeyo M., and B. Lanos. 2014. "Analysis of Price Incentives for Wheat in Ethiopia." Food and Agriculture Organization of the United Nations, Rome.

World Bank. 2007. *Managing Public Debt: From Diagnostics to Reform Implementation.* Washington, DC: World Bank.

———. 2009. *Global Economic Prospects January: Commodities at Crossroads.* January. Washington, DC: World Bank.

———. 2010. "Commodity Market Review." December. World Bank, Washington, DC.

———. 2011. "Responding to Global Food Price Volatility and Its Impact on Food Security." World Bank, Washington, DC.

———. 2012. *Global Monitoring Report 2012: Food Prices, Nutrition, and the Millennium Development Goals.* Washington, DC: World Bank.

———. 2013. "The World Bank Group and the Global Food Crisis: An Evaluation of the World Bank Group Response." World Bank, Washington, DC.

———. 2015a. *Global Economic Prospects: The Global Economy in Transition.* June. Washington, DC: World Bank.

———. 2015b. *Global Economic Prospects: Having Fiscal Space and Using It.* January. Washington, DC: World Bank.

———. 2016. *Global Economic Prospects: Spillovers Amid Robust Growth.* January. Washington, DC: World Bank.

———. 2017. *Global Economic Prospects: Weak Investment in Uncertain Times.* January. Washington, DC: World Bank.

———. 2018a. *Africa's Pulse, No. 17, April 2018.* Washington, DC: World Bank,.

———. 2018b. *International Debt Statistics 2019.* Washington, DC: World Bank.

———. 2018c. "Are Poor Countries Headed Towards Another External Debt Crisis?" Internal note.

———. 2018d. "Approach Paper: Public Finance for Development Evaluation." Internal note.

———. 2018e. *Commodity Market Outlook. The Changing of the Guard: Shifts in Commodity Demand.* October. Washington, DC: World Bank.

World Bank and IMF (International Monetary Fund). 2014. *Revised Guidelines for Public Debt Management.* Washington, DC: World Bank and International Monetary Fund.

———. 2018a. *Debt Vulnerabilities in IDA Countries.* Washington DC: World Bank and International Monetary Fund.

———. 2018b. *G-20 Note: Improving Public Debt Recording, Monitoring and Reporting Capacity in Low and Lower Middle-Income Countries: Proposed Reforms.* Washington, DC: World Bank and International Monetary Fund.

———. 2018c. *Debt Vulnerabilities in Emerging and Low-Income Economies.* October 2018 Meeting of the Development Committee. Washington DC: World Bank and International Monetary Fund.

———. 2018d. *G-20 Note: Strengthening Public Debt Transparency: The Role of the IMF and the World Bank.* Washington, DC: World Bank and International Monetary Fund.

———. 2018e. *Commodity Market Outlook. The Changing of the Guard: Shifts in Commodity Demand.* October. Washington, DC: World Bank.

Wright, B. 2014. "Global Biofuels: Key to the Puzzle of Grain Market Behavior." *Journal of Economic Perspectives* 28 (1): 73–98.

STATISTICAL APPENDIX

Real GDP growth

	Annual estimates and forecasts[1]						Quarterly growth[2]					
	2016	2017	2018e	2019f	2020f	2021f	17Q2	17Q3	17Q4	18Q1	18Q2	18Q3e
World	2.4	3.1	3.0	2.9	2.8	2.8	2.9	3.2	3.2	3.0	3.2	2.9
Advanced economies	1.7	2.3	2.2	2.0	1.6	1.5	2.1	2.5	2.4	2.2	2.4	2.0
United States	1.6	2.2	2.9	2.5	1.7	1.6	2.1	2.3	2.5	2.6	2.9	3.0
Euro Area	1.9	2.4	1.9	1.6	1.5	1.3	2.5	2.8	2.7	2.4	2.2	1.6
Japan	0.6	1.9	0.8	0.9	0.7	0.6	1.8	2.1	2.4	1.2	1.4	0.0
United Kingdom	1.8	1.7	1.3	1.4	1.7	1.8	1.9	2.0	1.6	1.3	1.4	1.5
Emerging market and developing economies	3.7	4.3	4.2	4.2	4.5	4.6	4.4	4.7	4.7	4.7	4.8	4.5
East Asia and Pacific	6.3	6.6	6.3	6.0	6.0	5.8	6.6	6.6	6.5	6.6	6.4	6.2
Cambodia	6.9	7.0	7.1	6.8	6.8	6.7	..	..	..	..	..	..
China	6.7	6.9	6.5	6.2	6.2	6.0	6.9	6.8	6.8	6.8	6.7	6.5
Fiji	0.4	3.8	3.5	3.4	3.3	3.3	..	..	..	..	..	..
Indonesia	5.0	5.1	5.2	5.2	5.3	5.3	5.0	5.1	5.2	5.1	5.3	5.2
Lao PDR	7.0	6.9	6.5	6.6	6.7	6.6	..	..	..	..	..	..
Malaysia	4.2	5.9	4.7	4.7	4.6	4.6	5.8	6.2	5.9	5.4	4.5	4.4
Mongolia	1.4	5.4	5.9	6.6	6.3	6.2	6.2	5.3	6.3	6.3	6.1	6.6
Myanmar	5.9	6.8	6.2	6.5	6.6	6.8	..	..	..	..	..	..
Papua New Guinea	2.6	2.8	0.3	5.1	3.1	3.4	..	..	..	..	..	..
Philippines	6.9	6.7	6.4	6.5	6.6	6.6	6.6	7.2	6.5	6.6	6.2	6.1
Solomon Islands	3.5	3.5	3.4	2.9	2.8	2.7	..	..	..	..	..	..
Thailand	3.3	3.9	4.1	3.8	3.9	3.9	3.9	4.3	4.0	4.9	4.6	3.3
Timor-Leste	5.3	-4.7	0.8	3.3	4.9	5.0	..	..	..	..	..	..
Vietnam	6.2	6.8	6.8	6.6	6.5	6.5	6.2	7.5	7.7	7.4	6.7	6.9
Europe and Central Asia	1.7	4.0	3.1	2.3	2.7	2.9	3.3	3.5	2.5	2.7	3.1	3.0
Albania	3.4	3.8	4.0	3.6	3.5	3.5	4.2	3.6	3.6	4.5	4.3	..
Armenia	0.2	7.5	5.3	4.3	4.6	4.6	..	..	..	..	..	..
Azerbaijan	-3.1	0.1	1.1	3.6	3.3	2.7	..	..	..	..	..	..
Belarus	-2.5	2.4	3.4	2.7	2.5	2.5	1.7	3.0	4.3	5.2	4.0	..
Bosnia and Herzegovina[7]	3.1	3.0	3.2	3.4	3.9	4.0	3.2	2.8	3.3	2.0	3.4	..
Bulgaria	3.9	3.8	3.3	3.1	3.0	2.8	3.8	4.3	3.3	3.5	3.2	2.7
Croatia	3.5	2.9	2.7	2.8	2.8	2.6	3.2	3.4	2.2	2.5	2.9	2.8
Georgia	2.8	4.8	5.3	5.0	5.0	5.0	4.8	4.0	5.3	5.2	5.6	3.7
Hungary	2.3	4.1	4.6	3.2	2.8	2.4	3.5	4.1	4.5	4.5	4.9	4.9
Kazakhstan	1.1	4.1	3.8	3.5	3.2	3.2	5.3	4.2	3.1	4.1	4.3	..
Kosovo	4.1	4.2	4.2	4.5	4.5	4.5	..	..	..	..	..	..
Kyrgyz Republic	4.3	4.6	3.1	3.4	3.9	4.0	..	..	..	..	..	..
Macedonia, FYR	2.8	0.2	2.5	2.9	3.2	3.3	-1.8	0.1	1.6	0.9	3.0	3.0
Moldova	4.5	4.5	4.8	3.8	3.5	3.2	..	..	..	..	..	..
Montenegro[5]	2.9	4.7	3.8	2.8	2.5	2.5	5.0	4.8	3.9	4.5	4.9	..
Poland	3.1	4.8	5.0	4.0	3.6	3.3	4.4	5.4	4.5	5.1	5.1	5.1
Romania	4.8	6.9	4.1	3.5	3.1	2.8	6.1	8.8	6.7	4.0	4.1	4.3
Russia	-0.2	1.5	1.6	1.5	1.8	1.8	2.5	2.2	0.9	1.3	1.9	1.5
Serbia	2.8	1.9	3.5	3.5	4.0	4.0	1.8	2.2	2.5	4.8	4.9	3.8
Tajikistan	6.9	7.1	6.0	6.0	6.0	6.0	..	..	..	..	..	..
Turkey	3.2	7.4	3.5	1.6	3.0	4.2	5.3	11.5	7.3	7.2	5.3	1.6
Turkmenistan	6.2	6.5	6.2	5.6	5.1	4.9	..	..	..	..	..	..
Ukraine	2.3	2.5	3.5	2.9	3.4	3.8	2.6	2.5	2.3	3.1	3.8	2.8
Uzbekistan	7.8	5.3	5.0	5.1	5.5	6.0	..	..	..	..	..	..

Real GDP growth *(continued)*

	Annual estimates and forecasts[1]						Quarterly growth[2]					
	2016	2017	2018e	2019f	2020f	2021f	17Q2	17Q3	17Q4	18Q1	18Q2	18Q3e
Latin America and the Caribbean	-1.5	0.8	0.6	1.7	2.4	2.5	1.5	1.9	2.3	1.9	1.6	1.6
Argentina	-1.8	2.9	-2.8	-1.7	2.7	3.1	3.0	3.8	3.9	3.9	-4.0	-3.5
Belize	-0.5	1.2	1.5	1.9	1.7	1.7	..	..	..	..	..	..
Bolivia	4.3	4.2	4.5	4.3	3.8	3.4	3.8	4.3	5.2	4.4	4.4	..
Brazil	-3.3	1.1	1.2	2.2	2.4	2.4	0.6	1.4	2.2	1.2	0.9	1.3
Chile	1.3	1.5	3.9	3.5	3.3	3.2	0.5	2.5	3.3	4.5	5.4	2.8
Colombia	2.0	1.8	2.7	3.3	3.7	3.6	1.7	1.7	1.8	2.2	2.8	2.7
Costa Rica	4.2	3.3	2.7	2.7	2.8	3.0	3.7	2.7	3.0	2.8	3.6	..
Dominican Republic	6.6	4.6	5.8	5.1	5.0	4.8	3.1	3.1	6.5	6.4	7.1	..
Ecuador	-1.2	2.4	1.0	0.7	0.7	1.2	2.1	2.9	2.8	1.6	0.9	..
El Salvador	2.6	2.3	2.8	2.5	2.4	2.4	0.3	3.2	2.5	2.7	2.9	..
Grenada	3.7	5.1	5.2	4.2	2.8	2.8	..	..	..	..	..	..
Guatemala	3.1	2.8	2.7	2.9	3.0	3.1	2.2	2.7	2.9	2.0	3.3	..
Guyana	2.6	2.1	3.4	4.6	30.0	24.8	..	..	..	..	..	..
Haiti[3]	1.5	1.2	1.6	2.3	2.4	2.5	..	..	..	..	..	..
Honduras	3.8	4.8	3.6	3.8	3.8	3.7	3.5	5.9	4.2	3.0	4.0	..
Jamaica	1.4	1.0	1.7	1.8	2.0	2.0	0.1	1.0	1.2	1.4	2.2	..
Mexico	2.9	2.1	2.1	2.0	2.4	2.4	1.9	1.5	1.5	1.2	2.6	2.5
Nicaragua	4.7	4.9	-3.8	-0.5	2.6	3.6	4.1	3.2	4.7	2.5	-4.4	..
Panama	5.0	5.3	4.0	6.0	5.4	5.2	5.1	5.2	4.4	4.0	3.1	3.6
Paraguay	4.3	5.0	4.0	3.9	4.0	4.0	2.8	5.8	5.4	4.7	6.2	...
Peru	4.0	2.5	3.9	3.8	3.8	3.7	2.5	2.9	2.4	3.2	5.5	2.3
St. Lucia	3.4	3.8	1.5	2.7	2.8	2.3	..	..	..	..	..	..
St. Vincent and the Grenadines	1.3	0.5	1.2	1.6	1.6	2.0	..	..	..	..	..	..
Suriname	-5.6	1.7	1.4	1.6	1.8	1.9	..	..	..	..	..	..
Trinidad and Tobago	-6.1	-2.6	1.0	0.9	1.2	1.2	..	..	..	..	..	..
Uruguay	1.7	2.7	2.1	2.1	2.3	2.5	2.8	1.9	2.0	2.2	2.6	2.1
Venezuela	-16.5	-14.5	-18.0	-8.0	-5.0	-4.0	..	..	..	..	..	..
Middle East and North Africa	5.1	1.2	1.7	1.9	2.7	2.7	1.3	2.3	1.1	2.3	2.6	2.6
Algeria	3.2	1.4	2.5	2.3	1.8	1.8	..	..	..	..	..	..
Bahrain	3.2	3.9	3.2	2.6	2.8	2.8	..	..	..	..	..	..
Djibouti	8.6	5.7	6.7	7.0	7.5	7.5	..	..	..	..	..	..
Egypt[3]	4.3	4.2	5.3	5.6	5.8	6.0	5.0	5.2	5.3	5.4	5.4	..
Iran	13.4	3.8	-1.5	-3.6	1.1	1.1	3.5	6.1	2.4	2.9	2.5	..
Iraq	13.0	-2.1	1.9	6.2	2.9	2.8	..	..	..	..	..	..
Jordan	2.0	2.0	2.1	2.3	2.4	2.7	..	..	..	..	..	..
Kuwait	2.9	-3.5	1.7	3.6	3.6	3.6	-2.9	-3.6	-2.7	-0.5	1.9	..
Lebanon	1.7	1.5	1.0	1.3	1.5	1.5	..	..	..	..	..	..
Morocco	1.1	4.1	3.2	2.9	3.5	3.5	..	..	..	..	..	..
Oman	5.0	-0.9	1.9	3.4	2.8	2.8	..	..	..	..	..	..
Qatar	2.1	1.6	2.3	2.7	3.0	3.0	0.8	0.7	3.3	2.0	2.5	..
Saudi Arabia	1.7	-0.9	2.0	2.1	2.2	2.2	-0.8	-0.3	-1.4	1.2	1.6	..
Tunisia	1.1	2.0	2.6	2.9	3.4	3.6	1.8	2.1	2.0	2.3	2.9	2.6
United Arab Emirates	3.0	0.8	2.0	3.0	3.2	3.2	..	..	..	..	..	..
West Bank and Gaza	4.7	3.1	1.7	1.9	1.9	1.9	..	..	..	..	..	..

Real GDP growth *(continued)*

	Annual estimates and forecasts[1]						Quarterly growth[2]					
	2016	2017	2018e	2019f	2020f	2021f	17Q2	17Q3	17Q4	18Q1	18Q2	18Q3e
South Asia	7.5	6.2	6.9	7.1	7.1	7.1	5.5	6.2	6.8	7.6	8.1	7.0
Afghanistan	2.4	2.7	2.4	2.7	3.2	3.2	..	..	..	..	..	..
Bangladesh[3,4]	7.1	7.3	7.9	7.0	6.8	6.8	..	..	..	..	..	..
Bhutan[3,4]	7.4	5.8	4.6	7.6	6.4	6.4	..	..	..	..	..	..
India[3,4]	7.1	6.7	7.3	7.5	7.5	7.5	5.6	6.3	7.0	7.7	8.2	7.1
Maldives	6.2	7.1	8.0	6.3	5.6	5.6	..	..	..	..	..	..
Nepal[3,4]	0.6	7.9	6.3	5.9	6.0	6.0	..	..	..	..	..	..
Pakistan[3,4]	4.6	5.4	5.8	3.7	4.2	4.8	..	..	..	..	..	..
Sri Lanka	4.5	3.3	3.9	4.0	4.1	4.1	3.0	3.2	3.5	3.4	3.6	2.9
Sub-Saharan Africa	1.3	2.6	2.7	3.4	3.6	3.7	1.7	2.0	2.5	2.3	1.9	2.3
Angola	-2.6	-0.1	-1.8	2.9	2.6	2.8	..	..	..	..	..	..
Benin	4.0	5.8	6.0	6.2	6.5	6.6	..	..	..	..	..	..
Botswana[3]	4.3	2.4	4.4	3.9	4.1	4.1	1.0	3.5	6.3	4.5	5.1	4.2
Burkina Faso	5.9	6.3	6.0	6.0	6.0	6.0	..	..	..	..	..	..
Burundi	-0.6	0.5	1.9	2.3	2.5	2.8	..	..	..	..	..	..
Cabo Verde	4.7	4.0	4.5	4.7	4.9	4.9	..	..	..	..	..	..
Cameroon	4.6	3.5	3.8	4.2	4.5	4.5	..	..	..	..	..	..
Chad	-6.3	-3.0	3.1	4.6	6.1	4.9	..	..	..	..	..	..
Comoros	2.2	2.7	2.7	3.1	3.1	3.1	..	..	..	..	..	..
Congo, Dem. Rep.	2.4	3.4	4.1	4.6	5.5	5.9	..	..	..	..	..	..
Congo, Rep.	-2.8	-3.1	1.0	3.2	-0.1	-1.5	..	..	..	..	..	..
Côte d'Ivoire	8.0	7.7	7.5	7.3	7.4	6.8	..	..	..	..	..	..
Equatorial Guinea	-8.5	-4.9	-8.8	-2.1	-5.8	-5.8	..	..	..	..	..	..
Eswatini	3.2	1.9	-0.6	1.7	1.8	1.8	..	..	..	..	..	..
Ethiopia[3]	8.0	10.1	7.7	8.8	8.9	8.9	..	..	..	..	..	..
Gabon	2.1	0.5	2.0	3.0	3.7	3.7	..	..	..	..	..	..
Gambia, The	0.4	4.6	5.3	5.4	5.2	5.2	..	..	..	..	..	..
Ghana[6]	3.7	8.5	6.5	7.3	6.0	6.0	..	..	..	..	..	..
Guinea	10.5	8.2	5.8	5.9	6.0	6.0	..	..	..	..	..	..
Guinea-Bissau	5.8	5.9	3.9	4.2	4.4	4.5	..	..	..	..	..	..
Kenya	5.9	4.9	5.7	5.8	6.0	6.0	4.7	4.7	5.4	5.7	6.3	..
Lesotho	3.1	-1.7	1.2	1.2	0.2	1.8	..	..	..	..	..	..
Liberia	-1.6	2.5	3.0	4.5	4.8	4.8	..	..	..	..	..	..
Madagascar	4.2	4.2	5.2	5.4	5.3	5.3	..	..	..	..	..	..
Malawi	2.5	4.0	3.5	4.3	5.3	5.5	..	..	..	..	..	..
Mali	5.8	5.4	4.9	5.0	4.9	4.8	..	..	..	..	..	..
Mauritania	2.0	3.5	3.0	4.9	6.9	6.9	..	..	..	..	..	..
Mauritius	3.8	3.9	3.9	4.0	3.6	3.6	..	..	..	..	..	..
Mozambique	3.8	3.7	3.3	3.5	4.1	4.1	..	..	..	..	..	..
Namibia	0.6	-0.9	0.7	1.8	2.1	2.1	..	..	..	..	..	..
Niger	4.9	4.9	5.2	6.5	6.0	5.6	..	..	..	..	..	..
Nigeria	-1.6	0.8	1.9	2.2	2.4	2.4	0.7	1.2	2.0	2.1	1.5	1.8
Rwanda	6.0	6.1	7.2	7.8	8.0	8.0	..	..	..	..	..	..
Senegal	6.2	7.2	6.6	6.6	6.8	6.9	..	..	..	..	..	..
Seychelles	4.5	5.3	3.6	3.4	3.3	2.9	..	..	..	..	..	..

Real GDP growth *(continued)*

	Annual estimates and forecasts[1]						Quarterly growth[2]					
	2016	2017	2018e	2019f	2020f	2021f	17Q2	17Q3	17Q4	18Q1	18Q2	18Q3e
Sub-Saharan Africa (continued)												
Sierra Leone	6.3	3.7	3.7	5.1	6.3	6.3	..	..	..	..	..	..
South Africa	0.6	1.3	0.9	1.3	1.7	1.8	1.2	1.6	1.4	0.8	0.4	1.1
Sudan	4.7	4.3	3.1	3.6	3.8	3.8	..	..	..	..	..	..
Tanzania	7.0	7.1	6.6	6.8	7.0	7.0	7.8	6.8	8.4	..	..	..
Togo	5.1	4.4	4.5	4.8	5.1	5.1	..	..	..	..	..	..
Uganda[3]	4.8	3.9	6.1	6.0	6.4	6.5	6.4	7.0	6.1	6.2	5.0	..
Zambia	3.8	3.5	3.3	3.6	3.8	3.8	3.4	5.3	4.1	2.7	3.9	..
Zimbabwe	0.6	3.2	3.0	3.7	4.0	4.0	..	..	..	..	..	..

Source: World Bank and Haver Analytics.

Note: e = estimate; f = forecast.

1. Aggregate growth rates calculated using constant 2010 U.S. dollars GDP weights.

2. Year-over-year quarterly growth of not-seasonally-adjusted real GDP, except for Ecuador, the Euro Area, Tunisia, and the United Kingdom.

Regional averages are calculated based on data from following countries.

East Asia and Pacific: China, Indonesia, Malaysia, Mongolia, Philippines, Thailand, and Vietnam.

Europe and Central Asia: Albania, Belarus, Bosnia and Herzegovina, Bulgaria, Croatia, Georgia, Hungary, Kazakhstan, FYR Macedonia, Poland, Romania, Russia, Serbia, Turkey, and Ukraine.

Latin America and the Caribbean: Argentina, Bolivia, Brazil, Chile, Colombia, Costa Rica, Dominican Republic, Ecuador, El Salvador, Guatemala, Honduras, Jamaica, Mexico, Nicaragua, Paraguay, Peru, and Uruguay.

Middle East and North Africa: Egypt, Iran, Kuwait, Qatar, Saudi Arabia, and Tunisia.

South Asia: India and Sri Lanka.

Sub-Saharan Africa: Botswana, Kenya, Nigeria, South Africa, Tanzania, Uganda, and Zambia.

3. Annual GDP is on fiscal year basis, as per reporting practice in the country.

4. GDP data for Pakistan are based on factor cost. For Bangladesh, Bhutan, Nepal, and Pakistan, the column labeled 2017 refers to FY2016/17. For India, the column labeled 2016 refers to FY2016/17.

5. Quarterly data are preliminary.

6. Growth rates reflect GDP data prior to recent rebasing.

7. Growth rates based on the production approach.

For additional information, please see www.worldbank.org/gep.

Data and Forecast Conventions

The macroeconomic forecasts presented in this report are prepared by staff of the Prospects Group of the Development Economics Vice-Presidency, in coordination with staff from the Macroeconomics, Trade, and Investment Global Practice and from regional and country offices, and with input from regional Chief Economist offices. They are the result of an iterative process that incorporates data, macroeconometric models, and judgment.

Data. Data used to prepare country forecasts come from a variety of sources. National Income Accounts (NIA), Balance of Payments (BOP), and fiscal data are from Haver Analytics; the World Development Indicators by the World Bank; the World Economic Outlook, Balance of Payments Statistics, and International Financial Statistics by the International Monetary Fund. Population data and forecasts are from the United Nations World Population Prospects. Country- and lending-group classifications are from the World Bank. DECPG databases include commodity prices, data on previous forecast vintages, and in-house country classifications. Other internal databases include high-frequency indicators such as industrial production, consumer price indexes, house prices, exchange rates, exports, imports, and stock market indexes, based on data from Bloomberg, Haver Analytics, OECD Analytical House Prices Indicators, IMF Balance of Payments Statistics, and IMF International Financial Statistics.

Aggregations. Aggregate growth for the world and all sub-groups of countries (such as regions and income groups) is calculated as GDP-weighted average (at 2010 prices) of country-specific growth rates. Income groups are defined as in the World Bank's classification of country groups.

Forecast Process. The process starts with initial assumptions about advanced-economy growth and commodity price forecasts. These are used as conditioning assumptions for the first set of growth forecasts for EMDEs, which are produced using macroeconometric models, accounting frameworks to ensure national account identities and global consistency, estimates of spillovers from major economies, and high-frequency indicators. These forecasts are then evaluated to ensure consistency of treatment across similar EMDEs. This is followed by extensive discussions with World Bank country teams, who conduct continuous macroeconomic monitoring and dialogue with country authorities. Throughout the forecasting process, staff use macroeconometric models that allow the combination of judgement and consistency with model-based insights.

Global Economic Prospects: Selected Topics, 2015-19

Growth and Business Cycles			
Informality			
		Growing in the shadow: Challenges of informality	January 2019, Chapter 3
		Linkages between formal and informal sectors	January 2019, Box 3.1
		Regional dimensions of informality: An overview	January 2019, Box 3.2
		Casting a shadow: Productivity in formal and informal firms	January 2019, Box 3.3
		Under the magnifying glass: How do policies affect informality?	January 2019, Box 3.4
		East Asia and Pacific	January 2019, Box 2.1.1
		Europe and Central Asia	January 2019, Box 2.2.1
		Latin America and the Caribbean	January 2019, Box 2.3.1
		Middle East and North Africa	January 2019, Box 2.4.1
		South Asia	January 2019, Box 2.5.1
		Sub-Saharan Africa	January 2019, Box 2.6.1
Inflation			
		The great disinflation	January 2019, Box 1.1
Growth prospects			
		Long-term growth prospects: Downgraded no more?	June 2018, Box 1.1
Global output gap			
		Is the global economy turning the corner?	January 2018, Box 1.1
Potential growth			
		Building solid foundations: How to promote potential growth	January 2018, Chapter 3
		What is potential growth?	January 2018, Box 3.1
		Understanding the recent productivity slowdown: Facts and explanations	January 2018, Box 3.2
		Moving together? Investment and potential output	January 2018, Box 3.3
		The long shadow of contractions over potential output	January 2018, Box 3.4
		Productivity and investment growth during reforms	January 2018, Box 3.5
		East Asia and Pacific	January 2018, Box 2.1.1
		Europe and Central Asia	January 2018, Box 2.2.1
		Latin America and the Caribbean	January 2018, Box 2.3.1
		Middle East and North Africa	January 2018, Box 2.4.1
		South Asia	January 2018, Box 2.5.1
		Sub-Saharan Africa	January 2018, Box 2.6.1
Investment slowdown			
		Weak investment in uncertain times: Causes, implications and policy responses	January 2017, Chapter 3
		Investment-less credit booms	January 2017, Box 3.1
		Implications of rising uncertainty for investment in EMDEs	January 2017, Box 3.2
		Investment slowdown in China	January 2017, Box 3.3
		Interactions between public and private investment	January 2017, Box 3.4

Global Economic Prospects: Selected Topics, 2015-19

Global Economic Prospects: Selected Topics, 2015-19

Commodity Markets

The role of the EM7 in commodity production	June 2018, SF1, Box SF1.1
Commodity consumption: Implications of government policies	June 2018, SF1, Box SF1.2
With the benefit of hindsight: The impact of the 2014–16 oil price collapse	January 2018, SF1
From commodity discovery to production: Vulnerabilities and policies in LICs	January 2016, Chapter 1
After the commodities boom: What next for low-income countries?	June 2015, Chapter 1, SF
Low oil prices in perspective	June 2015, Box 1.2
Understanding the plunge in oil prices: Sources and implications	January 2015, Chapter 4
What do we know about the impact of oil prices on output and inflation? A brief survey	January 2015, Box 4.1

Globalization of Trade and Financial Flows

Poverty impact of food price shocks and policies	January 2019, Chapter 4
Arm's-Length trade: A source of post-crisis trade weakness	June 2017, SF
The U.S. economy and the world	January 2017, SF
Regulatory convergence in mega-regional trade agreements	January 2016, Box 4.1.1
Can remittances help promote consumption stability?	January 2016, Chapter 4
Potential macroeconomic implications of the Trans-Pacific Partnership Agreement	January 2016, Chapter 4
Regulatory convergence in mega-regional trade agreements	January 2016, Box 4.1.1
China's integration in global supply chains: Review and implications	January 2015, Box 2.1
What lies behind the global trade slowdown?	January 2015, Chapter 4

Monetary and Exchange Rate Policies

The great disinflation	January 2019, Box 1.1
Corporate debt: Financial stability and investment implications	June 2018, SF2
Recent credit surge in historical context	June 2016, SF1
Peg and control? The links between exchange rate regimes and capital account policies	January 2016, Chapter 4
Negative interest rates in Europe: A glance at their causes and implications	June 2015, Box 1.1
Hoping for the best, preparing for the worst: Risks around U.S. rate liftoff and policy options	June 2015, SF1.1
Countercyclical monetary policy in emerging markets: Review and evidence	January 2015, Box 1.2

Fiscal Policies

Debt in low-income countries: Evolution, implications, and remedies	January 2019, Chapter 4
Debt dynamics in emerging market and developing economies: Time to act?	June 2017, SF
Having fiscal space and using it: Fiscal challenges in developing economies	January 2015, Chapter 3
Revenue mobilization in South Asia: Policy challenges and recommendations	January 2015, Box 2.3
Fiscal policy in low-income countries	January 2015, Box 3.1
What affects the size of fiscal multipliers?	January 2015, Box 3.2
Chile's fiscal rule—an example of success	January 2015, Box 3.3
Narrow fiscal space and the risk of a debt crisis	January 2015, Box 3.4

Development Economics Prospects Group (DECPG): Selected Other Publications on the Global Economy, 2015-19

Commodity Markets Outlook	
The implications of tariffs for commodity markets	October 2018, Box
The changing of the guard: Shifts in industrial commodity demand	October 2018, SF
Oil exporters: Policies and challenges	April, 2018, SF
Investment weakness in commodity exporters	January 2017, SF
OPEC in historical context: Commodity agreements and market fundamentals	October 2016, SF
Energy and food prices: Moving in tandem?	July 2016, SF
Resource development in an era of cheap commodities	April 2016, SF
Weak growth in emerging market economies: What does it imply for commodity markets?	January 2016, SF
Understanding El Niño: What does it mean for commodity markets?	October 2015, SF
How important are China and India in global commodity consumption	July 2015, SF
Anatomy of the last four oil price crashes	April 2015, SF
Putting the recent plunge in oil prices in perspective	January 2015, SF

Inflation in Emerging and Developing Economies	
Inflation: Concepts, evolution, and correlates	Chapter 1
Understanding global inflation synchronization	Chapter 2
Sources of inflation: Global and domestic drivers	Chapter 3
Inflation expectations: Review and evidence	Chapter 4
Inflation and exchange rate pass-through	Chapter 5
Inflation in low-income countries	Chapter 6
Poverty impact of food price shocks and policies	Chapter 7

High-Frequency Monitoring	
Global Monthly newsletter	
Global Weekly newsletter	

www.ingramcontent.com/pod-product-compliance
Lightning Source LLC
Chambersburg PA
CBHW041950220326
41599CB00004BA/90